An Architectural History
of Harford County, Maryland

An Architectural History

of Harford County, Maryland

Christopher Weeks

THE JOHNS HOPKINS UNIVERSITY PRESS   BALTIMORE AND LONDON

This book has been brought to publication with the generous assistance of the citizens of Harford County, Maryland.

05 04 03 02 01 00 99 98 97 96   5 4 3 2 1

The Johns Hopkins University Press
2715 North Charles Street
Baltimore, Maryland 21218-4319
The Johns Hopkins Press Ltd., London

Frontispiece: Harriet Shriver Howard Rogers, her two children, Frances and William, and an unidentified playmate, relaxing in the garden at Olney, c. 1936.

Library of Congress Cataloging-in-Publication Data will be found at the end of this book.

A catalog record for this book is available from the British Library.

ISBN 0-8018-4913-6

CONTENTS

PREFACE AND ACKNOWLEDGMENTS

James Whistler once explained that he was the ideal person to paint a particular portrait because he would bring "a lifetime of experience" to the job. At the risk of sounding pretentious, I might meekly suggest that perhaps I was not the worst choice to paint this "portrait" of Harford County's architecture since it has been my happy fate to have known most of the people, places, and things described herein virtually all of my life.

Yet such intimate familiarity brings with it some obvious problems—for a historian if not for a painter—most important, of course, a set of powerful and highly subjective feelings toward the subject. Memories and prejudices can, however, be checked and verified and I was fortunate indeed to have had access to every conceivable sort of primary source check—unpublished letters, deeds, maps and plats, marriage records, orphans' court papers, ancient photographs, eighteenth-century travel accounts, paintings and sketches, interviews with many of the principals involved, newspaper stories.

Very special thanks are due—and herewith given—to the citizens of Harford County and Harford County Government for making this book possible. Special recognition is given to County Executive Eileen Rehrmann, as well as her predecessor, Habern Freeman, and the county councils from 1989 to the present.

The two-legged checkers and contributors to this project have been without parallel, too, and it is my happy task to be able to recognize and thank them now. First, I take great pleasure in thanking Patricia Hathaway, Marlene Magness, Mabel Andrews, Duncan MacKenzie, and James Chrismer, and all other board members of the Historical Society of Harford County, the oldest county historical society in Maryland, for cheerfully cooperating with me at every step. "Of all the counties in Maryland," wrote Hulbert Footner in his 1942 *Maryland Main and the Eastern Shore,* "Harford possesses the most intense county-consciousness"; it also certainly must possess the most affable and hardworking archivists. In addition, Gregory Weidman and Jeff Goldman made my forays to the Maryland Historical Society pleasant and fruitful and I owe them a great debt for that.

On a somewhat more abstract level, I thank very much those who shaped my way of looking at historic buildings and gardens, who taught me to look not just at the *what* but at the who, where, why, and how as well: so deep thanks indeed to Mario di Valmarana and William B. O'Neal of the University of Virginia School of Architecture, as well as to Susan Fass Morton, the late Sally Westminster, and (locally) Charles L. Robbins. If I am able to look at buildings and builders, gardens and gardeners with even a modicum of impartiality it is because of their guidance and inspiration.

Preparing this book simply would not have been possible had I not received the generous cooperation of a wide array of private property owners and residents (past and present) throughout the county. Space prohibits listing them all, but I would like to single out a few for special recognition: Julia Duryea Sprigg Cameron, Lois B. Reed, Josephine and Hope Harlan Dallam, Mary Helen Cadwalader, the late Harriet Shriver Rogers, Brodnax and Mignon Cameron, Bill Shimek, the entire Montgomery Meigs Green family, Vlasta Schmidt, Laura Peaker Wallace, Roenna Fahrney, John Hegeman, Dorsey and Janet Crocker, Eleanor Tydings Ditzen, Jay VanDeusen, Nan and Paul Barchowsky, Grace Muller-Thym, William O. Carr, Albert and Emily Laisy, Pattie Penniman, James Dorsey, Michael and Pose Crocker, Catherine Mitchell, William Presberry, Jim and Theo Easter, the late Hunter Sutherland, Hayes and Susan Gardiner, Richard and Peggy Wilson, Susan Osborn, and Gene and Jeannie Graybeal; those responsible for maintaining the publicly accessible sites deserve equal thanks, particularly Martha Robbins, Jean McCausland, Alice Ober, Bunny Hathaway, and Lena Caron of the Ladew Topiary Gardens, Catherine Brown and Peggy Kelly of the Liriodendron Foundation, Harry Sanders at Jerusalem Mill, Jeff Smart, historian at the Edgewood Arsenal, Reed MacMillan, director of environmental review at the Aberdeen Proving Ground, and Ellsworth Shank of the Susquehanna Lock House Museum.

Nancy Essig, former regional books editor at the Johns Hopkins University Press (now director of the University Press of Virginia), and her successor, Robert J. Brugger, were involved with the very conception of this book and the result is, in many ways, as much theirs as it is mine. In addition, my own research simply would not have been possible had it not been for the years of long, thorough work of a series of architectural historians who have labored in Harford, namely Jean Ewing, Susan Deeny, Natalie Shivers, Janet Davis, and Marilynn M. Larew.

Thanks are also due to William G. Carroll, former director of Planning and Zoning. In addition, Linda Settles, former secretary *extraordinaire* at Planning and Zoning, managed, in some superhuman manner, to type several drafts of the manuscript all the while keeping the entire department running smoothly—please, Linda, hurry back from Ohio!; intern Edson Beall snapped most of the photographs used in the catalog section of the book; Brian Williams, Janet Gleisner, Andy Meyer, Dan Rooney, Katharine Adams, and Steve Headley of the county's planning department all helped in various ways; and James Wollon, AIA, and Marion Morton Carroll kindly reviewed several drafts of the text, offered innumerable stylistic improvements, and corrected scores of errors of fact or judgment, for all of which I will keep candles lit in their honor. I will also light candles for editor Therese D. Boyd, who was responsible for whipping what must have seemed to her a dauntingly long manuscript into publishable form.

Historic preservation has become a virtual growth industry throughout America in the past few years. While many "preservationists" err, perhaps, by letting their enthusiasm and rampant nostalgia for the past overpower their intellect, and by confusing "the world we have lost" with the "world we have escaped," such is not the case in Harford, where the members of the Historic Preservation Commission brilliantly combine devotion to the task, knowledge of the subject, and common sense. These past and/or present members include Katy Dallam, Eloise Wilson, Wilfred Hathaway, Christine Tolbert, Suellen Wideman, Marlene Magness, Jan Stinchcomb, Robert Marks, Jean Ewing, Paul Thompson, Keir Sterling, and John Brown.

This list of thanks is becoming a virtual catalog. I was afraid it would. So, before it gets entirely out of hand, I would like to acknowledge the contributions of a somewhat diverse group of individuals for helping me in equally diverse ways: first, of course, my parents, Maurice and June Weeks; second, my physician, friend, and favorite bridge partner, Samuel J. Westrick, who has got me this far, at least. In addition, thanks and gratitude flow to Susan and Rachel Tobin, Mr. and Mrs. George Constable, David W. Roszel, John Dorsey, Betty di Valmarana, Robert Armacost, Jim Hart, Michael Trostel, FAIA, the late Natalie Jewett Marbury, Joel Cohen, Mr. and Mrs. Benjamin Griswold III, Christian Surridge, Daniel Conway, John Eggen, the late Eleanor Pinkerton Stewart, Peter Lang, L. S. MacPhail IV, John Boogher, Bill and Connie Biems, Rick Scrabis, Nancy Miller Schamu, E. Beck Dorsey, Vance Becker, and Ron Andrews.

Finally, while a book of this nature must of course try to draw knowingly from the past, it should look hopefully to the future. Thus and by way of dedication, I thank the late Brodnax Cameron, wise and wonderful Harford countian of *temps perdu* and Benjamin and Seth Ranneberger, equally wonderful and—one hopes—wise countians of the twenty-first century.

Optimism personified: On August 31, 1925, Sion Hill's Capt. John Rodgers, USN, embarked on a flight that would, he hoped, set a world record for air travel over water.

A Narrative History of Harford County:
Builders and Their Buildings

PROLOGUE

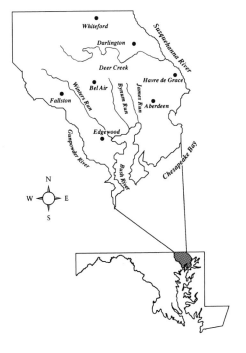

Perched at the point where the mighty Susquehanna flattens out to form the Chesapeake Bay, Harford County, Maryland, takes in 520-odd square miles of land and water. Roughly one-third of the county lies in the Tidewater, a flat, marshy mix of sand and water lazily washed by the tidal Bush and Gunpowder rivers. The rest of the county rolls away to the north and west into the increasingly hilly Piedmont. Although inland, this region is, like the Tidewater, well watered and the hills around present-day Darlington, Bel Air, and Fallston are pierced by dozens of fast-flowing streams: Deer Creek, the largest and best known, flows east into the Susquehanna; Winters Run, James Run, and Bynum Run flow more or less southerly into the bay.

Many regard the resulting landscape of hills and streams—steamy and mysterious in the summer, crisp and bracing in winter—as almost embarrassingly picturesque. It has certainly given rise to a good deal of purplish prose over many generations. "There is scarcely any other natural panorama in eastern America," one sightseer gushed,

> so much admired as the mouth of the Susquehanna River. . . . Southeastward the broad river merges majestically with the vast spread of the head waters of Chesapeake Bay, whose hazy lowlands rim the dimly visible horizon. . . . At that point, where sweet and briny waters meet and mingle, the rock-flecked surface of the river diminishes to a distant ribbon of silver and it vanishes in the lofty shadowy horizon where the banks roll up to heights of five hundred feet.[1]

Beautiful as Tidewater Harford is, the county's inland, upland stretches have proven no less seductive to those of romantic spirit. In the nineteenth century, for example, Dr. W. Stump Forwood rhapsodized in several newspaper articles over "the verdant hills and fertile valleys of the noble Deer Creek"; Forwood, gazing at the landscape around his native Darlington, even felt that a bit of Byron would not be amiss: "Oh, Christ!" he quoted,

> It is a goodly sight to see
> What Heaven hath done for this delicious land!
> What fruits of fragrance blush on every tree!
> What goodly prospect o'er the hills expand.[2]

If one goes further back, one finds men just as smitten by Harford's natural charms as Dr. Forwood was. George Alsop, who lived near what is now Havre de Grace around 1660, had nothing but praise for the county "dwelling pleasantly upon the Bay." He noted that "Nature doth . . . generously fructifie this piece of Earth" and wondered if there "is any place . . . that can parallel this fertile and pleasant piece of ground in . . . Nature's extravagancy of a superabounding plenty."[3]

Attentive readers will have noticed Alsop's frequent use of the word *pleasant;* this was no accident. The county has always been home to a famously easy-going, heterogeneous citizenry. Named for Henry Harford, illegitimate son of the last Lord Baltimore, the county is perhaps the only subdivision in America to eponymously honor a bastard. Countians have historically rejoiced in this distinction and have also showed themselves remarkably tolerant of human diversity. Larry MacPhail mixed pitches here and Harvey

1. Swepson Earle, *Chesapeake Bay Country* (Baltimore: Thomsen-Ellis, 1923), 230–31.

2. Dr. W. Stump Forwood, "Homes on Deer Creek," *Ægis,* March 19, 1880, in a series that ran from December 19, 1879, to May 28, 1880.

3. George Alsop, *A Character of the Province of Mary-Land* (Cleveland: Burrows Brothers, 1902), 36.

1

Ladew mixed martinis. John Rodgers of Havre de Grace invented the American navy, Edwin Booth of Fountain Green invented the American theater, and Howard Kelly of Bel Air invented women's medicine. If Robert Smith of Spesutia Island proved himself a good friend and faithful servant of Thomas Jefferson, four generations later Millard Tydings of Oakington proved himself an equally fierce (early) advocate of Franklin Roosevelt's New Deal. Finally, if Mary E. W. Risteau deserves praise for championing women's rights in the 1920s (and she does), she was in a sense merely filling her place in a continuum defined by countians Cupid Peaker, who had pioneered the rights of black men and women in the 1830s, and David Drake, playwright and champion of gay rights, whose *The Night Larry Kramer Kissed Me* won the prestigious Obie Award in 1992.

Crabbing on Bush River 1899: "A pleasant and bountiful land," wrote Calvin Dill Wilson of Harford County in the *New England Magazine*, "bordered by pleasant waters."

Before the *Ark* and the *Dove*

Susquehannock brave from John Smith's
c. 1608 map of the Chesapeake. The Susquehannocks, according to Smith, were "great and well
proportioned men" who wore "cassocks made
of Beares skins."

I t is important to bear in mind that Harford County had been home to a flourishing, pleasant civilization long before Larry MacPhail decided to retire to his Bel Air farm to escape the pressures of running a major league baseball club. Indeed, by the time the *Ark* and the *Dove* ventured up the Potomac in 1634, Harford had been the scene of a highly developed Native American civilization for centuries, and a surprisingly varied amount of material has endured to help historians understand this civilization and those who created it, the Susquehannocks. The happy consequence is that this evidence makes Harford's first residents full-bodied and real, not the evanescent wispy stuff of legends that Native Americans sometimes become in other locales. Everyone in Harford County knows who lived along the Susquehanna and Gunpowder before the Calverts founded St. Mary's City; everyone also knows what these people looked like, how they lived—even what they ate.

Sometimes modern historians get this information spoonfed through firsthand accounts of seventeenth-century English sojourners. Capt. John Smith, for one, sailed north from Jamestown and toured the Upper Chesapeake in July of 1608. Smith spent several weeks tacking and rowing in and out of the rivers and creeks that form the shorelines of modern Kent, Cecil, and Harford counties. Anyone who has sailed the bay in the summer must feel for Smith and his men,[1] but the captain tried to put a good face on it and after recording that "the sommer is hot as Spain" he added that "the coole breesas asswage the vehemency of the heat." (He was, however, silent on the subject of sea nettles.) Scudding and sweating in these uncharted waters, Smith mapped what he saw as he traveled from the tip of the Gunpowder Neck at what he called Powell's Island (modern

1. Today's experienced sailors burdened with weekend crews doubtless also empathize with Smith who complained that he had not a single "mariner nor any hand skill to trim the sayles but two saylers and myself, the rest being gentlemen or them as were ignorant of such toil and labor."

The Susquehannocks' Bald Friar petroglyphs, c. 1880. Although most of this "stone writing" has been destroyed, a few pieces are safely preserved at the Historical Society of Harford County.

Poole's Island, which Smith named to honor crewman Nathaniel Powell) northwards past Bush River (which he called "Willowbyes River in honor of the town our captaine was born in"), around Spesutia Island and past Oakington to the duck-filled Susquehanna Flats.

"At the end of the bay where it is 6 or 7 myles in breadth," Smith wrote, "it divides it-selfe into 4 branches, the best commeth northwest from among the mountains." This "best" branch is without doubt the Susquehanna (the others are probably, moving clock-wise, the North East, the Elk, and the Sassafras) and Smith decided to explore that route. Or at least he tried to, for its inviting appearance proved deceptive and he could only get a few miles upstream before his ship met "rockes" near present-day Lapidum. With his water-borne progress halted, the captain and his men put ashore and explored on foot, hacking their way northwards for about "a myle and a halfe" till they stumbled onto a spot where "runneth a creeke" that flowed from the west. Surely Smith and his party had stumbled onto Deer Creek, which indeed flows from the west about a half mile up the Susquehanna from the Lapidum rocks.

While Smith was gazing at Deer Creek, people on shore were gazing at him until even-tually, "60 . . . Sasquesahanocks . . . came to us." Although their impressions of the En-glish are lost, Smith's impressions of them have endured and, simply put, he liked what he saw. He liked their hospitality and generous good nature (they offered him presents of skins, bows, arrows, beads, and venison) and he liked their physiognomy. "Such great and well proportioned men are seldom seene," Smith swooned, before going on to deem the Susquehannocks "giants [compared] to the English. . . . The calfe [of one man] . . . was three quarters of a yard about, and all the rest of his limbs so answerable to that proportion that he seemed the goodliest man we had ever beheld." They *sounded* impressive, too, and Smith wrote that when the braves spoke, their deeply resonating words came "from them as a voyce in a vault."

These strapping men draped themselves in the strangest attire Smith had ever seen: "Some have cossacks made of beares heads and skins, that a man's head goes through the skinnes neck and the eares of the bear fastened to his shoulders the nose and teeth hanging down his breast, another beares face split behind him, and at the end of the nose hung a pawe. . . . One had the head of a wolfe hanging in a chaine for a jewell." The bejewelled man also had "a tobacco pipe three quarter of a yard long, prettily carved with a bird, a deare, or some such devise at . . . the end." In sum, the Susquehannocks so completely enraptured Smith that when he published his now-famous map of the Chesapeake region he used a sketch of one of the men to decorate the product.

Smith's mention of venison leads to the inference that the Susquehannocks, who lived in "pallisadoed . . . townes . . . brested about . . . very formally," managed to get their minimum daily requirement of red meat. They also fancied oysters (then safe and plentiful in the unpolluted Bush and Gunpowder) and the English colonists marveled at the immense piles of postprandial oyster shells the satiated Indians left behind, all white and gray and sparkling in the sun.[2] Finfish, too, abounded in the waters off Harford County, with runs of herring and shad "so thicke" that Smith's crew could lean out their boats and "catch them in frying pans." The Susquehannocks also evidently enjoyed these fish, for when they negotiated their seventeenth-century treaties with the English settlers, the tribe insisted the treaties guarantee that "the shores along the lower [Susquehanna] river were . . . to be retained forever . . . as fishing grounds."[3] The Susquehannocks balanced all this protein with grain, and archaeologists have unearthed several mortar-and-pestles; these findings have occurred throughout the county and the relics are of immense size, "sutuble" as Smith might have phrased it, to their users' "greatnesse."

Lest one dismiss Smith's praise of the Susquehannocks as the result of his having been out in the "sommer" sun too long, others echoed his impressions of the tribe.[4] For example, in 1666 George Alsop published his landmark *Character of the Province of Mary-Land* and this book more than corroborates Smith's opinions of the godlike Susquehannocks as "most noble and heroic . . . large . . . stately and majestic." Alsop, born in London in 1636,[5] sold himself into indentured service in exchange for passage to America and labored from 1658 to 1663 (or '64) on a farm near present-day Havre de Grace. A thorough creature of the bawdy Restoration era, Alsop also was reporter enough to recognize that minutiae give a work verisimilitude. Thus he concluded his account with

> one thing worthy your observation: For as our Grammar Rules have it, *Non decet quenquam mingere currentem aut mandatem:* It doth not become any man to piss running or eating. These Pagan men naturally observe the same Rule: for . . . like a Hare they squat to the ground as low as they can, while the Women stand bolt upright . . . performing the same action, in so confident and obscene a posture, as if they had taken their Degrees of Entrance at *Venice,* and commence Bawds of Art at *Legorne.*[6]

Alsop developed what he called "a deep interest" in the Susquehannocks and he devoted about one-fourth of his book to "the Wild and Naked Indians (or Susquehanokes) of Mary-Land." The *Character* also provides a fabulous (and surprisingly little-quoted) firsthand account of that mighty tribe for, as the author pointed out, he wrote with the benefit of having "convers'd" with the Susquehannocks and of having enjoyed "occular . . . view of . . . their Customs."[7]

Like Captain Smith, Alsop liked what he saw. The men, who stood "for the most part

2. Eighteenth-century countians used these mounds as surveying landmarks, much as they used streams or other natural phenomena (e.g., in deed JLG J/99 the description begins "at a remarkable bank or banks of oyster shells"). As recently as the early twentieth century scholars could count twenty-nine extant shell heaps in Harford and Kent counties, including one at the tip of Gunpowder Neck "more than a foot thick . . . and extending along the shore for considerable distances." William B. Marye, "Indian Shell Heaps," in Warren King Moorehead, *A Report of the Susquehanna River Expedition* (Andover, Mass.: Andover Press, 1938), 111.

3. Samuel Mason, *Historical Sketches of Harford County* (Darlington: privately printed, 1935), 76.

4. Moreover, Smith observed that Harford's mightly tribesmen differed from people he saw at other points around the bay, such as the "Wichcomoco" men whom he dismissed as "of little stature . . . and very rude."

5. J. A. Leo Lemay, *Men of Letters in Colonial Maryland* (Knoxville: University of Tennessee Press, 1972), 48.

6. Alsop, *Character,* 85–86.

7. Lemay, *Men of Letters,* 4, 5; Alsop, *Character,* 76.

seven foot high," towered above the English colonists while "their gate" was "strait, stately, and majestick." No wonder, then, that the "Christian inhabitants . . . [and] the rest of the Indians" viewed the Susquehannocks "as the most Noble and Heroick Nation of *Indians* that dwell upon the confines of *America.*"

"Their bodies," he related, "are cloth'd with no other Armour to defend them from the nipping frosts of a benumbing Winter, or the penetrating and scortching influence of the Sun in a hot Summer, then what Nature gave them. . . . The hair of their head is black, long and harsh" and well cared for; elsewhere on their bodies "they divert it (by an ancient custom) from its growth, by pulling it up hair by hair by the root." Like many a modern parent, Alsop regretted that the braves disfigured evidently perfect skin by tattooing "divers impressions on their breasts and armes," and by painting "their faces one stroke of red, another of green, another of white, and another of black, so that" they resembled "Representatives of the Furies." Alsop could merely shake his head and sigh that if they "did . . . not alter their bodies by their dyings, paintings, and cutting themselves, marring these Excellencies that Nature bestowed upon them . . . , there would be as amiable beauties amongst them as any *Alexandria* could afford, when *Mark Anthony* and *Cleopatra* dwelt there together."[8]

Most of the year these "amiable beauties" lived "at the head of a River that runs into the Bay of *Choesapike,* called by their own name *The Susquehannock River*" in "low and long [houses] . . . built with the Bark of Trees Arch-wise, standing thick and confusedly together" in walled towns. But "about *November* the best Hunters draw off to several remote places of the Woods, where they know the Deer, Bear, and Elke" roam. There "they build several Cottages which they call Winter-quarters" and there they "remain for the space of three months, untill they have killed up a sufficiency of Provisions to supply their Families with in the Summer." The Susquehannocks kept the roles of the sexes as cleanly cut as the braves' chests: the males are hunters who "kill the several Beasts which they meet withall in the Woods" while "the Women are the pack horses to fetch it" and later "skin the slain animals." The women also act as "the Butchers, Cooks and Tillers of the ground," because "the Men think it below the honour of a Masculine to stoop."[9]

Alsop tried to fathom the Susquehannocks' politics but gave up ("Their Government is wrapt up in so various and intricate a Laborynth, that the speculativ'st Artists in the whole World, with his artificial and natural Opticks, cannot see into the rule"); he did, however, discern an inherently democratic philosophy in the tribe whereby "he that is the most . . . Valorous is accounted the most Noble." In place of a hereditary English aristocracy (wherein "the ignorant believe they are lineally descended from the . . . Conquests") Alsop admired the simple beauty of the Susquehannock system—"he that fights best carries it here."

Although long-gone from the upper bay, the noble and heroic Susquehannocks still speak to twentieth-century Harford countians. And one can hear their words directly, without seventeenth-century interpreters like Smith and Alsop, for they left, on the rocks and small islands that jutted from the Susquehanna shoals, some of the most remarkable of all prehistoric American artifacts, the celebrated petroglyphs of Bald Friar. Curiously, however, no one quite knows why the Susquehannocks created these unique "stone-writings." While scholars have discerned fifty-three differentiable figures, each deeply ground into the stones "with sand as an abrasive . . . [and] a wooden stick,"[10] they have also spawned fifty-three differentiable theories as to the figures' ultimate meaning.

Darlington farmer and historian Samuel Mason, for example, has suggested that Harford's Indians placed great stock in the Evil Spirit, a creature in serpent form who lived underwater ("which was," suggested Mason, "an excellent place for him to remain") and who required "constant propitiation, either in the form of tobacco scattered on the water . . . or possibly serpent representations on rocks near his abode." Mason states "quite positively" that the spirit dwelt in the deepest reaches of the Susquehanna and "made his headquarters in the . . . part of the channel locally known as 'Job's Hole' at Conowingo,"

8. Alsop, *Character,* 77. See also George W. Archer, "History of Harford County," unpublished typescript in the archives of the Historical Society of Harford County, Bel Air (hereafter HSHC), p. 13.

9. It was not a good thing to be a Susquehannock prisoner of war. Alsop reports that the warriors eventually killed their captives, with the operative word being *eventually.* "The common and usual deaths they put their Prisoners to, is to bind them to stakes . . . then one or another of them, whose Genius delights in the art of Paganish dissection, with a sharp knife . . . cuts the . . . outermost skin of the brow so deep, untill their nails, or rather Talons, can fasten themselves firm . . . then (with a most rigid jerk) disrobeth the head of skin." They then "immediately apply to the skull . . . hot Embers. . . . While they are thus acting this cruelty, . . . several others are preparing pieces of Iron . . . which they make red hot, to sear each part and lineament of their [prisoners'] bodies. . . . And while they are thus in the midst of their torments . . . others . . . are cutting their flesh off, and eating it before their eyes raw." Alsop, *Character,* 84.

10. Paul Cresthull, "A Catalog of Maryland Petroglyphs," in *Maryland Archaeology* 9 (March–September 1973).

A NARRATIVE HISTORY OF HARFORD COUNTY

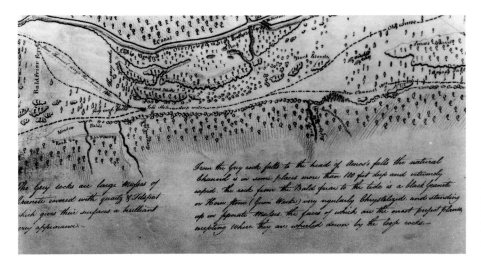

Most of the petroglyphs were carved onto rocks near "Job's Hole"; as architect Benjamin Henry Latrobe wrote on his c. 1810 map of the Susquehanna, the waters near Job's Hole were "more than 100 feet deep and extremely rapid."

a stretch of river that "runs swift and deep, with gliding whirlpools forming and disappearing as you watch them."[11] Researchers have determined that "Indians living thereabouts" regarded these swift, mysterious waters "with awe," making it easy to speculate that the Susquehannocks regarded the rocks in this swirling stretch as the perfect easels on which to incise images to propitiate the Evil Spirit.[12]

William B. Mayre, who describes the petroglyphs in his 1938 *Report of the Susquehanna River Expedition,* seconds Mason's suggestion that the drawings were to intended to pacify the serpentine Evil Spirit in the bottomless Job's Hole. Others suggest that the designs should be viewed purely as works of art; still others see a connection between the fish-shapes of some carvings and the immeasurable runs of shad that once filled the river. The late Paul Cresthull, dean of Harford archaeologists, wrote two papers on the petroglyphs and sounded a sensibly conciliatory note. Cresthull advised modern viewers against imposing modern aesthetics and meanings on the carving, warning "one can go astray by having a preconceived idea of what the figure should be." Everyone, however, who saw the petroglyphs *in situ* admired, in their "blending of human and animal features," just the sort of "rigid discipline"[13] one might expect of that mighty tribe—a discipline tempered, however, by the Susquehannocks' strongly developed aesthetic nature as evinced by the "prettily-carved" deer and bird images Capt. John Smith so admired in 1608.

Whatever their artistic or practical origins, the petroglyphs attracted the attention of scientists and historians in the 1860s; one T. C. Porter presented a paper on them to the annual meeting of the American Philosophical Society in 1868. Interest in the rock-writing quickened in this century and in 1916–17 joint teams from the Maryland Historical Society and the Maryland Academy of Sciences examined the carvings. "Considerable journalistic publicity" then ensued, beginning with Baltimore *Sun* reporter Felix Miles's 1923 story on "Hunting Ancient Relics Along the Susquehanna."[14] Miles, who visited the islands, opined that the "ancient rock carvings, unlike any other known in the United States," were fully equal to any of the world's archaeological treasures and hoped that they could be preserved with care "when considered in light of the vast expense . . . expended upon similar relics in Egypt, Mexico and Peru."

11. Mason, *Sketches,* 30, 32; William B. Marye, "Petroglyphs Near Bald Friar," in Moorehead, *A Report of the Susquehanna River Expedition,* 104.

12. Marye, "Petroglyphs Near Bald Friar," 103.

13. Cresthull, "Petroglyphs."

14. Marye, "Petroglyphs Near Bald Friar," 98; Felix Miles, "Hunting Ancient Relics along the Susquehanna," *Baltimore Sunday Sun Magazine,* September 30, 1923.

Before the *Ark* and the *Dove*　　　　7

Capt. John Smith found the head of the bay "6 or 7 myles in breadth"; present-day Lapidum (near "Smyths Falls"), Bush River ("Willowbyes"), and Pooles Island ("Powels") are all discernible in this detail of his 1608 map.

But it was not to be, for by the 1920s tourists and souvenir-seekers had begun to threaten the petroglyphs' very existence. Actually, destruction had been going on for years, at least as far back as 1881 when "some thirty-eight feet" of one island "had been blasted away by persons interested in obtaining rock for a shad-fishery."[15] The end came in the 1920s when the Philadelphia Electric Company, by damming the river at Conowingo, made Job's Hole deeper than it had ever been before and inundated the becarved islands. This could have been a dramatic and impressive end to the story; unfortunately, the truth is more squalid. Even as workmen completed the dam, scavengers slithered in to chip away at the stones. Concern grew in the scientific and academic worlds until, in desperation, Dr. Francis C. Nicholas of the Maryland Academy of Sciences removed some of the carvings for safekeeping and reassembled them in Baltimore. City bureaucrats shuttled the stones around town for decades, moving them from one inappropriate location to another until complete dispersal and anonymous private ownership seemed inevitable. Then, in the mid-1970s, a few historically minded Harford countians, sparked by the bicentennial, decided to track down the carvings and move them back to the county. The few they found are now quietly on display in the lobby of the Historical Society of Harford County's headquarters building.

In addition to creating the somewhat esoteric petroglyphs, the Susquehannocks also busied themselves in more practical tasks. When they weren't carving propitiating snakes, they were (it seems) fashioning bowls and cups, making a sort of "found art" (or craft) of utilitarian objects. A thick vein of soapstone underpins vast stretches of northern Harford County; while it generally rests far beneath the surface of the soil, here and there it breaks through to lie exposed to the air. The Susquehannocks knew all about these outcroppings and when members of the tribe felt the need for a particular stone vessel they simply walked to the closest site, took stock of the exposed boulders, and selected rocks that approximated the size of the desired object: a large piece for a great bowl, a smaller one for a cup, and so on. Archaeologists have identified one such outcropping near Broad Creek and have determined it "vital" to our knowledge of Susquehannock culture.[16]

Sadly, that culture could not last indefinitely. Indeed, when Alsop penned his portrait of the Susquehannocks the tribe was nearing the end of its power. In May 1661, encour-

15. Marye, "Petroglyphs Near Bald Friar," 101.
16. Wayne E. Clark, "Broad Creek Soapstone Quarries," nomination to the National Register of Historic Places; copy in the Harford County Department of Planning and Zoning, Bel Air.

aged by Alsop's employer, Thomas Stockett, they signed a one-sided treaty of peace with Maryland governor Philip Calvert, giving the English the right to establish settlements in the county. (A representative provision: "if any Englishman in the future finds an Indian killing cattle or hogs it shall be lawful for the Englishman to kill the Indian.") But perhaps the treaty was merely a clever Susquehannock tactic to buy peace on their southern flank, because in that same year the tribe began a war with the Iroquois Five Nations to the north.[17] The war, however, soon proved a minor problem, for "those gyant-like people" were suddenly beset by a scourge worse that Englishmen or Iroquois—disease, as smallpox ripped through the Susquehannock settlements. The warriors' well-muscled limbs proved no match for microbes and "by 1673 they could count fewer than half the warriors of the previous decade." Then, "after fleeing their customary haunts by the Head of the Bay, the pitiful remnants of this once-mighty tribe submitted to the Five Nations . . . [and] dwindled away in number."[18]

But before their ignominious end, and before Lord Baltimore's little band reached St. Mary's, the Susquehannocks bore witness to one other settler at the head of the bay. His name was Edward Palmer. Fortunately, and as was the case with the Susquehannocks, this pre-*Ark* English settler also left tangible records of his presence in the county. A native of Gloucestershire, Palmer has been called "an educated eccentric," "a wealthy art collector," and "an intellectual."[19] Although few biographical details exist, Palmer must have been odd indeed, for "his associates chose the word 'curious' to describe him."[20] Said to have been a member of the Virginia Company drawn here from Virginia "by [John Smith's] glowing description" of the fertile land, fish-filled waters, and attractive inhabitants Palmer established a trading post on what he called Palmer's Island around 1616.[21] The island, located at the mouth of the Susquehanna, its south flanks lapped by the bay, offers easy access up and down the Chesapeake. Palmer and the 200 men and women who followed him to the island did a brisk business buying pelts from the Susquehannocks and then reselling them to English colonists in Virginia. But something soured and the trading post failed. Palmer complained that "he had been 'betrayed' by dishonest agents," and he watched helplessly as his followers drifted away. While "it is not known how long Palmer and his friends remained on the island," it could not have been long because Palmer died in London in 1624.[22]

Palmer had not forgotten the land at the head of the bay, however, and he left the bulk of his estate "for the foundinge and maintenance of a universitie" to "be called Academia Virginiensis et Oxoniensis" and to be built on the site of that failed trading post. Thus Harford became the intended home of the first university in North America. One infers that Palmer was an Oxford man because he proposed, in his last will and testament, that the buildings at his Academia be laid out in Oxonian quadrangles placed on "severall streets or Alleyes of Twenty foot broade." While Palmer assumed that the young scholars who attended his school would take the usual courses in history, science, and language he also believed that the fine arts might prove a good method "for avoydinge of idlenesse"[23] and he left funds to hire "two paynters the one for oyle Coullers and the other for water coullers" so "said schollars shall or may learn the arts of payntinge."

One does wonder a bit just whom Palmer hoped to attract to his university since no English settler lived within 150 miles of Palmer's Island in the 1620s; perhaps he envisioned Susquehannock youths pacing the quadrangles, naked except for their mortarboards. Not surprisingly, nothing came of the wonderful, quixotic notion, and Palmer's university—"the impracticable dream of a visionary"—vanished without a trace except for "a few books found there when Lord Baltimore took over the island in 1637."[24] Where are those books now? What, at least, were a few of the titles—were there first editions of Shakespeare and Marlowe and Donne in Harford County in the 1620s? One also (venally) wonders what happened to the money: did Palmer's reputedly sizable estate simply get eaten up in lawyers' fees?

Less than a decade after Palmer died, the *Ark* and the *Dove* set sail for Lord Baltimore's

17. As Samuel Mason pithily explained, "The Iroquois and Susquehannocks could not agree on polity; the obvious remedy was for each if possible to exterminate the other." Mason, *Sketches*, 39.

18. Marilynn M. Larew, *Bel Air: The Town through Its Buildings* (Bel Air: Town of Bel Air, 1981), 5.

19. C. Milton Wright, *Our Harford Heritage* (Bel Air: privately printed, 1967), 17; Mason, *Sketches*, 15.

20. "The Idea of a University," paper presented by the University of Maryland McKeldin Library, College Park.

21. George W. Archer notes in the Hughes Collection, Manuscript No. 1675, Maryland Historical Society (hereafter MHS), Baltimore; "Idea of a University." The island was later named to honor a Mr. Watson, but no one knows anything about him. Since 1885 it has been called Garrett Island after John Work Garrett of the B&O Railroad.

22. "Idea of a University"; Wright, *Harford*, 18.

23. Will registered PCC 114 Bryde, London Public Records Office, Somerset House, London. Copy obtained by Eldon S. Scott, March 1991.

24. Archer notes, Hughes Collection, MHS; Wright, *Harford*, 17.

newly granted colony, Maryland. It is amusing to imagine a connection. One likes to think that the Calverts had heard glowing reports of Palmer's planned university. And— to continue the fantasy—since the lords Baltimore wanted to establish a colony based on religious freedom, if Edward Palmer thought Chesapeake air could make people look favorably on a venture as outré as art classes, surely, then, the same air might make citizens free-thinking enough to tolerate Catholics. Moreover, by the 1630s John Smith's glowing words had reached England and were widely read in court circles: everyone knew about the fresh "breesas" that cooled the land even in July and August; everyone had heard mouth-watering tales of waters brimming with shad; and everyone had read about the "great and well proportioned men" who lived along "Willowbye's River," hunting, fishing, and fashioning "prettily carved" tobacco pipes and who greeted alien visitors not with war whoops but with plates of venison. It must have sounded heaven on earth and in 1634 the Calverts set up permanent shop in this terrestrial paradise. Although those first colonists made their initial settlement on the shores of the Potomac, not the Susquehanna, they eventually corrected that foolish oversight and by the 1650s were claiming land and building homes and creating new lives for themselves on the Gunpowder Neck, on Spesutia Island, and at various other sites around the head of the bay.

The Dallam sisters at Broom's Bloom, c. 1890: Harford County "folk" life at its finest with a Chesapeake Bay retriever in the foreground and a spinning wheel just visible in a second-story window.

Just Plain Folk

[2]

It took twenty-four years after the *Ark* and the *Dove* had disgorged their passengers at St. Mary's City for anyone to summon the courage to sail north and claim land at the head of the bay. This delay was not entirely due to timidity, however, for the English Civil War and subsequent regicide had thrown the American colonies into legal chaos: the king had granted Maryland to the lords Baltimore, so if there was no king, who owned the colony? This confusion finally ended in 1657, when Philip Calvert (brother of the second Lord Baltimore) arrived in St. Mary's as chancellor of the colony and "established laws and procedures for the inheritance of property" and in general "brought a sense of stability and reliability to government,"[1] which encouraged further settlement.

Thus, beginning in 1658 a few souls ventured north from St. Mary's and secured the first land grants in what is now Harford (always excepting Edward Palmer's eccentric activities) by staking claim to such tracts as Woodpecker (200 acres in 1658 to George Gould-smith), Oakington (800 acres, 1658, Nathaniel Utie), Harmer's Town (200 acres, 1658, Godfrey Harmer, but sold in 1659 to Thomas Stockett), Eightrupp (500 acres, 1665, Thomas Griffith), and Land of Promise (Thomas Taylor, 1684). The land accounted for in these patents and deeds all hugged the shoreline. As a consequence the low-lying flanks of the Gunpowder and Bush as well as much of the lower Deer Creek Valley had been taken up well before the new century dawned. Most of these patentees viewed their holdings as speculative ventures, as today one might regard stock in, say, a Tibetan gold mine. And although Griffith, for example, is thought to have sailed up from his base in St. Mary's City to look at his newly acquired Eightrupp (which covers the site of modern Lapidum) he soon "lost" the property "as he failed to settle" on it.[2]

1. Edward C. Papenfuse, state archivist, quoted in Frank D. Roylance, "Meeting Philip Calvert," in the *Baltimore Sunday Sun*, November 22, 1992. Calvert died in St. Mary's in 1682 and it is thought that his lead coffin was one of three discovered and opened in 1992.

2. A. P. Silver, "History of Lapidum," talk given to the HSHC in 1888; manuscript in HSHC archives, p. 2. Even as late as 1700 one William Lofton owned 250 acres of Eightrupp, "but he did not reside upon it," according to Silver in "Lapidum," 3.

Eventually a trickle of brave—or desperate—men and women did make their way up the Chesapeake and actually lived in what was called Baltimore County, an enormous jurisdiction that took in all of northeastern Maryland from the Patapsco to the Sassafras and inland to present-day Westminster. Extrapolating from such sketchy evidence as exists, scholars estimate that the county contained "between 300 and 400" people by 1660 and perhaps twice that number a decade later, most of whom were single men who had arrived as indentured servants.[3] Territory east of the Susquehanna was separated to form Cecil County in 1674, but even so the number of residents in a much-reduced Baltimore County burgeoned to 1,740 by 1701.[4] (For simplicity's sake, this narrative will continue to refer to "Harford County" when dealing with the prerevolutionary era, even though the county wasn't officially separated from Baltimore until 1773.)

Words such as *crude* and *harsh* best describe Chesapeake society in the seventeenth century, and the county's 1,700 citizens lived lives devoid of any but the most basic of material goods: at least one-third of them never saw a knife or fork, for instance, and "bowls and spoons and fingers . . . prevailed" at the dining table—if there *was* a dining table.[5] More specifically, when Richard Perkins, who owned land along the well-named Mosquito Creek near Spesutia Island, died in 1705, taxmen made a list of everything he owned. It wasn't much, just a few head of cattle, a half-dozen horses, "2 old feather beds, . . . 2 old guns, . . . 3 iron tools, . . . [and] 1 brass still about 17 gallons" for a total gross worth of £67.14.6.[6] Recent archaeological digs in Calvert County have provided further "grim snapshots of life" in seventeenth-century Maryland, "of shoulders strained in lifting and hauling . . . of bones made brittle by disease, of malnutrition and early death."[7]

George Alsop's *Character* of Harford County

Among those hard-working citizens of the upper bay one finds George Alsop, whose 1666 book, *A Character of the Province of Mary-Land*, drew brief mention in chapter 1.[8] In 1658 the 22-year-old Alsop, "an outspoken Royalist . . . indentured himself to four years' service as a bondservant in Maryland . . . because of his disgust for" Oliver Cromwell's Puritan government in Britain. (Earlier that same year Alsop had published a piece likening the Puritans to "Theeves and Robbers" who had made England a "Sacreligious . . . Brothel-house," so one might view his decision to live clandestinely in Maryland as a sensible career move.) Thomas Stockett, recent purchaser of the tract Harmer's Town, paid Alsop's passage across the Atlantic and the youth spent his entire American sojourn in Stockett's employ "near the head of the Chesapeake, south of the Susquehanna River, by the present town of Havre de Grace."[9]

Alsop could hardly have done better by way of employers than Stockett (?–1671), a good, solid sort who served as a "captain in the militia" and as the Calverts' agent in dealing with the Susquehannocks. The two men certainly agreed on their politics, for Stockett has been called a "staunch supporter of King Charles II . . . [who] followed him into exile in 1651."[10] By the time Alsop gained his freedom in 1663 or 1664, England's government had changed for the better, at least to Alsop's mind. Cromwell was dead, his followers had dithered away their power, and Charles II had been returned to the throne of his father. So, with his term of service in the colonies up, Alsop sailed home to prosper in Restoration Britain as an ordained minister. He even gained a modicum of fame as an author, thanks to a few fugitive verses and (especially) to his *Character*.

And what a book it is! A bawdy, effervescing mix of classical allusions and puns, of the erudite and the scatological, it embodies the age of Nell Gwynn and Rochester and ranks as a Restoration-era literary masterpiece of the first order and as an irreplaceable work of reportage.[11] The wonderful wordsmith began by describing Maryland as "a Province situated upon the large extending bowels of *America*" and if "bowels" seems the perfect noun, his verbs, as will be seen, would have done Dryden proud. According to Alsop, all conceivable "Vegetables, as well as Flowers . . . Herbs, and Roots" flourish along the "multitude of Navigable Rivers and Creeks" here;[12] the province also abounded in

3. Robert J. Brugger, *Maryland, A Middle Temperament* (Baltimore: Johns Hopkins University Press, 1988), 24.

4. Arthur E. Karinen, "Maryland Population: 1631–1730," in *Maryland Historical Magazine* 54 (1959): 390.

5. Richard L. Bushman, *The Refinement of America* (New York: Knopf, 1992) 77.

6. See, for example, those of Thomas Griffith (1666) and Daniel Johnson (1715), on file, as is Perkins's, at the Maryland Hall of Records, Annapolis.

7. Douglas Birch, "Boxes Tell of Harsh Maryland Life in 1600s," *Baltimore Sun*, June 25, 1993.

8. See also Brugger, *Middle Temperament*, 26–27, who quotes sections of what he calls Alsop's "homely pamphlet"; Brugger states that Lord Baltimore "aided . . . George Alsop in publishing" the book.

9. Lemay, *Men of Letters*, 48–50. For the somewhat cloudy history of the tract, see Ellsworth Shank, "The Early Days," in Peter A. Jay, ed., *Havre de Grace: An Informal History* (Havre de Grace: Susquehanna Publishing, 1986), 2–3, and Wright, *Harford*, 311.

10. Brugger, *Middle Temperament*, 24; Lemay, *Men of Letters*, 50; Edward C. Papenfuse et al., *A Biographical Dictionary of the Maryland Legislature, 1635–1789* (Baltimore: Johns Hopkins University Press, 1985), 780.

11. One modern critic has called it "an extraordinary delight," "one of the most witty and scurrilous books of colonial America," and "the earliest in a long line of distinguished Southern works in baroque prose," thus linking Harford County to Faulkner's Yoknapatawpha, no less! See Lemay, *Men of Letters*, 69, 48, and 69.

12. Alsop, *Character*, 32–33.

Detail of the map in George Alsop's 1666 *Character of the Province of Mary-Land;* Alsop lived on a farm near the site of present-day Havre de Grace and placed the Western Shore rivers accurately (Susquehanna, Patapsco, and so forth); he was clearly less familiar with the rivers of the Eastern Shore

deer and venison, accordingly, was a dietary staple. "The Gentleman whom I served . . . had at one time in his house four-score Venisons . . . so that before . . . [they finished the meat] it so nauseated our appetites and stomachs that plain bread was rather courted and desired than it." Generations of Susquehanna Flats and Gunpowder Neck gunners can corroborate Alsop's claim that "fowls of all sourts . . . dwell . . . here," and many of the turkeys, partridges, pheasants, swans, geese, and ducks that "derogate in this point . . . in the millionous multitudes . . . about the middle of *September*" and "beleaguer . . . the shoar" found themselves "upon a Spit" by October. Fish teemed in every river and creek in "a providential greatness" of numbers and "all sorts of Grains as Wheat, Rye, Barley, Oates, Pease . . . increase and thrive here," thanks to "the natural richness of the earth."

Alsop reported that "Wolves, Bears, and Panthers" prowled about the county "in great multitudes," as did packs of raccoons, beavers, and otters, valuable "for their Hydes and Furs" (37–38). Many seventeenth-century Marylanders earned a shilling or two in the fur trade, including Alsop's employer, Stockett, who bought pelts from the Susquehannocks and resold them in Virginia. "Tobacco is the current Coyn of *Mary-Land,*" wrote the observant Alsop, and trading ships "arrive in *Mary-Land* about *September,* being most of them Ketches and Barkes, and such small Vessals" as may navigate "into several small Creeks to sell and dispose of their Commodities," particularly "*Medera*-Wines, Sugars, Salt, Wickar-Chairs, and Tin Candlesticks" (71).

As to the colonists themselves, Alsop described those "of the Masculine sex" as "generally confident, reservedly subtle, quick in apprehending but slow in resolving" while "the women . . . are extremely bashful at the first view, but after a continuance of time . . . they become . . . much more talkative than men" (51). Regarding colonial government, once a year "an Assembly [is] called," and voters in each county select "a number of men, and to them is deliver'd up the Grievances of the Country; and they maturely debate the matters, and . . . make Laws for the general good of the people." Alsop described the legislators as "for the most part good ordinary Householders . . . plain and honest": he knew of what he spoke, for Baltimore countians elected Stockett to the legislature from 1661 to 1664.[13]

The good-natured Alsop, who noted that he wrote his book not "to seduce or delude

13. See Papenfuse et al., *Biographical Dictionary,* 780; Alsop, *Character,* 36–38, 51, 71.

any, or to draw them from their native soyle, but out of a love to my Countrymen,"[14] encouraged his readers to join those reserved men and talkative women in Maryland even if it meant a few years of servitude, for in Maryland, he wrote, "in a small computation of years, by an industrious endeavor, [servants] may become Masters and Mistresses of Families. . . . And let this be spoke . . . that the four years I served there were not to me so slavish, as a two years Servitude . . . was here in *London*." Indeed,

the Servants here . . . of all Colonies . . . have the least cause to complain, either for strictness of Servitude, want of Provisions, or need of Apparel: Five dayes and a halfe in the Summer weeks is the alotted time that they work . . . and for two months, when the Sun predominates . . . they can claim an ancient and customary Priviledge, to repose themselves three hours a day within the house. . . . In the Winter time, which lasteth three months . . . they do little or no work . . . save cutting of wood . . . unless their ingenuity will prompt them to hunt the Deer . . . or recreate Themselves in Fowling. . . . For every Servant has a Gun . . . allowed to him to sport . . . if he be capable of using it or be willing to learn.[15]

Social advancement did not depend entirely on success in working the soil, for Alsop had seen enough to predict that if any of his more comely countrymen (or those endowed with what he calls "natural preferment") entered Maryland "in Servitude" they will soon "ryvet themselves . . . into the private . . . favour of their Mistress, if Age speak their Master deficient." (Indeed, several of Maryland's most respected families owe their start to such a "favored" young man.) Advancement was even easier for women who, Alsop stated, "are no sooner on shoar but . . . are courted into a Copulative Matrimony"—even those loose-living wenches who "let . . . [themselves] out" for "rent . . . untill the Gallows or Hospital called them away."[16]

George Alsop from his *Character of the Province of Mary-land;* "Those that read" Alsop's account of the colony, the engraver observed, "must fall in Love with it."

14. Alsop, *Character,* 55.
15. Ibid., 56.
16. Ibid., 60–61.
17. Howard C. Rice Jr. and Anne S. K. Brown, trans. and eds., *The American Campaigns of Rochambeau's Army,* 1780, 1781, 1782, 1783 (Princeton: Princeton University Press, 1972), 1:53.
18. See Raphel Semmes, *Baltimore as Seen by Visitors,* 1783–1860 (Baltimore: MHS, 1953), 30; also Wright, *Harford,* 118.
19. Lillian B. Miller, ed., *The Selected Papers of Charles Willson Peale and His Family,* vol. 1 (New Haven: Yale University Press, 1983), 35.
20. Semmes, *Visitors,* 30; and see Lillian Bayly Marks, "Tavern and Ordinary Licenses in Baltimore County, Maryland, 1755–1763," *Maryland Historical Magazine* 78 (1983): 326–30.

Life along the Post Road

Although Alsop touched on nearly every conceivable topic—from agronomy to natural science to sex—he omitted the two subjects perhaps most crucial to this narrative, that is, construction of the great post road through Harford County and architecture. The post road, envisioned in the 1660s as a land-link between Virginia and New England, was the great "infrastructure" project of Stockett's generation of Americans. Its initial route through Harford, completed c. 1670, carried it across the Little Gunpowder near the future site of Joppa, down the Gunpowder Neck to the Bush River, thence via ferry to Old Baltimore and up through what is now the Aberdeen Proving Ground to the ferry at the Susquehanna, that is, to Stockett's farm. That circuitous route was shortened and straightened a bit around 1687 when a "new" post road was laid out a few miles to the north; known as the "King's Road," this thoroughfare, which generally followed the same path as modern Route 7, played host to 150 years' worth of American and foreign luminaries, nearly all of whom commented on the execrable condition of the highway. Tree stumps dotted the upland sections of the roadbed while the low-lying stretches, laid out through streams and marshes, were routinely rendered impassable by rain and snow. During the Revolution Lafayette's soldiers couldn't believe how "frightful" and "abominable" the road was: "virtually impassable," grumbled one officer, "the horses risked breaking their legs."[17] A few years earlier, but still a full century after the road was "finished," George Washington complained that he'd had to abandon many a coach after travel through Maryland had "rendered [them] incapable of any further service."[18] The going proved just as rough for pedestrians; Charles Willson Peale's journals, for example, relate how he frequently found himself wading through streams with "mud and mire" over "the tops of my boots" while traveling the post road through Harford County.[19]

Inns and taverns soon sprouted up along the road "at intervals of ten or twelve miles between Baltimore and Philadelphia"[20] and in 1662 and 1735 the colonial legislature passed acts that set standards for these "victualling houses." Conditions, however, re-

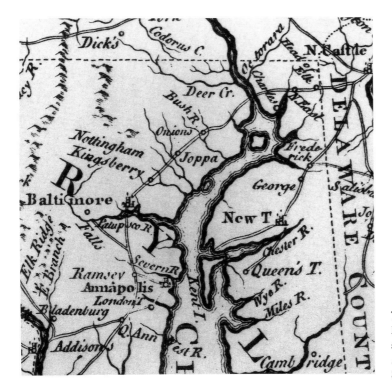

The post road shows up clearly in this "Map of Maryland" (detail) published in the August 1757 issue of the *London Magazine or Gentleman's Monthly Intelligencer.* ("Onion's," by the way, refers to Stephen Onion's iron furnace.)

mained a bit primitive, as the account of Dr. Alexander Hamilton's northerly 1744 sojourn on the road reveals.[21] After leaving the Patapsco Ferry, where he met "a certain captain of a tobacco ship . . . [who] talked inveterately against the clergy . . . [having] been lately cheated by one of our parsons," Dr. Hamilton arrived in "Joppa, a village pleasantly situated and lying close upon the river. There I called att . . . a good tavern in a large brick house." Then it was off to Bush, where

> I put up att one Tradaway's [Treadway's] about 10 miles from Joppa. . . . As I dismounted . . . I found a drunken club dismissing. Most of them had got upon their horses and were seated in an oblique situation, deviating much from a perpendicular to the horizontal plane. . . . Their discourse was as oblique as their position; the only thing intelligible in it was oaths and God dammes; the rest was an inarticulate sound like Rabelais' frozen words a thawing, interleaced with hickupings and belchings. I was uneasy till they were gone, and my landlord, seeing me stare, made that trite apology—that . . . these were . . . his neighbors and it was not prudent to dissoblige them.

The only other person at Bush Dr. Hamilton deemed "worth noting" was a "greasy thum'b fellow who . . . professed . . . surgery. In the drawing of teeth, he practices upon the house maid, a dirty piece of lumber, who made such screaming and squalling as made me imagine there was murder going forwards in the house. However, the artist got the tooth out . . . with a great clumsy pair of black-smith's forceps." Next morning, the doctor breakfasted "upon some dirty choclate" and left Bush. A few hours later he arrived at the Susquehanna, where he found another tavern, this one

> kept by a little old man whom I found att vittles with his wife and family upon a homely dish of fish without any kind of sauce . . . in a dirty, deep, wooden dish which they evacuated with their hands, cramming down skins scales, and all. They used neither knife, fork, spoon, plate or napkin because, I suppose, they had none to use.

The couple "desired me to eat, but I told them I had no stomach." Once he crossed over to the Cecil shore, he pressed on to the Elk where the chatty ferryman, "a young fellow

21. Carl Bridenbaugh, ed., *Alexander Hamilton, Gentleman's Progress* (Chapel Hill: University of North Carolina Press, 1948), xi.

[who] plyd his tongue much faster than his oar," bragged of his intimacy with "some of the chief dwellers in the neighborhood . . . for whom he had the honor to stand as pimp in their amours."[22]

So much for the post road. As for architecture, common sense dictates that Alsop and Stockett lived in some sort of shelter, and recall that Alsop referred to summer siestas "within the house"; one wishes one knew what sort of "house" it was. Unfortunately, no one can provide much information, largely because no buildings remain from that period: the Susquehannocks left more tangible traces of their presence in the county than Stockett and Alsop did. To make a bad situation worse, not only is Harford void of any seventeenth-century buildings, it is also void of any detailed secondhand information from that period, so the historian is left more or less dancing in the dark. But Harford's historians aren't alone in this terpsichore. Years of dogged sleuthing have produced only two churches and three houses in the entire Chesapeake area that can securely be dated to the seventeenth century.[23] This dearth of surviving buildings particularly astonishes because the region stood as the richest and most populous of England's American colonies and must have boasted a suitable collection of buildings. Yet New England, with fewer people and less money than Virginia and Maryland, retains over 200 seventeenth-century structures.

One of the reasons "they" have 200 and "we" have but 5 is climate: evidence suggests that the first colonists generally built frame houses with timbers placed directly in the ground. The wood simply rotted away in the course of 300 steamy Chesapeake summers. Moreover, termites thrive in hot, humid weather and those insects, which increased and became as "innumerable" as Alsop's hogs, made a feast of Maryland's early buildings. Finally, Stockett and Harford's other seventeenth-century pioneers, who placed themselves at the remotest rim of the civilized world, did not overly worry themselves with architecture. They "had a more lively concern with animal husbandry and the law than with any of the arts; the land-surveyor and the lawyer were more vital [to them] . . . than the highly skilled artificer in wood, stone, or brick."[24] But, after a generation or so, settlers in Virginia and Maryland, having successfully made themselves a civilization in what had been (in their eyes) a wilderness, began to abandon their ancestors' hastily fashioned "improvised expedients" in favor of a "more substantial dwelling."[25]

These later structures, generally called replacement houses, have been further classified as "folk" or "vernacular," distinctions based on real (if sometimes hard to detect) differences. Basically one might call a *folk* building "traditional." It was the sort of building erected simply because the builder "knew no other way" and represents the settlers' attempts to replicate "the 'fayre houses' that many yeomen and even husbandmen were used to from England."[26] But faced with a different climate, different building materials, and a different economy, most settlers quickly modified their folk traditions to create a new architecture to suit their new needs, now called *vernacular,* "a term invented by archaeologists to describe buildings that are built according to local custom to meet the personal requirements of the individuals for whom they are intended."[27] These two categories—folk and vernacular—dominated construction in Harford County (indeed in America) until well into the eighteenth century.

Readers should use these distinctions to help understand and appreciate Harford's built heritage. Too often people dismiss a rare surviving example of folk architecture simply because "it doesn't look like much"; too often people swoon over anything big, regardless of whether or not it is really important. One hoped-for byproduct of publications like this one is understanding: perhaps in the future public officials and public servants might assess the merits of, say, a house that sits in the path of a proposed road with more sensitivity than they have generally shown to date. Perhaps the county's historic preservation lobby might realize that not *everything* need be preserved and start to function in a manner that doesn't reduce every situation to a life-and-death pitched battle.

22. Ibid.

23. The churches are St. Luke's Episcopal near Smithfield, Virginia (c. 1680) and the Third Haven Friends Meetinghouse in Talbot County (1685); the residences are Holly Hill in Anne Arundel County (c. 1690) and, across the Potomac, Bacon's Castle in Surry County (1665) and the Adam Thoroughgood House in Virginia Beach (c. 1660).

24. John Summerson, *Architecture in Britain, 1530–1830* (Baltimore: Penguin Books, 1970), 23.

25. Cary Carson et al., "Impermanent Architecture in the Southern American Colonies," in *Winterthur Portfolio* 16 (1981): 139, 140.

26. Henry Glassie, *Pattern in the Material Folk Culture of the Eastern United States* (Philadelphia: University of Pennsylvania Press, 1968), 7 (hereafter Glassie, *Folk Culture*); Carson et al., "Impermanent," 140.

27. Carson et al., "Impermanent," 140.

The fireplace wall in the parlor of the Maxwell-Day House, photographed c. 1910, displays the closeted stair/closet/fireplace/closet sequence characteristic of Harford County's c. 1740 folk houses.

Despite the lack of existing firsthand evidence (to resume the narrative), one can make an educated guess about what *home* meant to the 1,700 men and women who lived in the county at the dawn of the eighteenth century by looking to see what similar people were doing in similar areas at about the same time. In 1974 historian Cary Carson, working for the St. Mary's City Commission, argued that what he termed the Virginia House was one "universally acceptable" answer "to planters' requirements on both sides of the Potomac."[28] It was certainly acceptable in Harford, for evidence proves that the county did in fact have a few Virginia Houses. Carson's Virginia House was a one- or one and one-half story frame dwelling covered with unpainted riven clapboards and punctuated by exterior gable-end chimneys; within, one found two rooms on the ground floor "embellished" by exposed, unchamfered beams, whitewashed ceilings, and lath-and-plaster walls; casement windows—that is, windows that swung open like doors—prevailed. In Harford, these houses were located along the shorelines of the Bush and Gunpowder (the areas first colonized), which brings up a somewhat idiosyncratic reason why the county is totally lacking in c. 1700 buildings: the U.S. Army condemned virtually all Harford's bay frontage in 1917 and turned productive tomato patches and peach orchards into weapons-testing sites.[29]

Yet one example, the Maxwell-Day House on the Gunpowder Neck, managed to linger on into the age of photography and it seems to fit all Carson's criteria. The house presided over a tract called Maxwell's Conclusion, 1,600-plus acres laid out in 1683 for one Mary Stansby and acquired by James Maxwell (about whom more later) in the early eighteenth century. Maxwell had the land resurveyed in 1731 and in 1742 gave 514 acres of it to his daughter Phillipa when she married John Day.[30] While it is possible that the house was standing before 1742, two factors argue that the couple built their Virginia House shortly after their wedding: first, father Maxwell made his base on land that grew into the town of Joppa and probably did not need a "country house" on the Neck; moreover, the house's interior woodwork is strikingly similar to woodwork found in the few Harford houses securely dated to the 1740s (discussed below).

When John Day died in 1801 (with personal property valued at just over £975) he left instructions for his executors to transfer over 300 acres, including "that part whereon my mansion House stands," to son James Maxwell Day, who in 1814 paid tax on 325 acres and

28. Ibid., 186.

29. John Hammond provided one much-quoted description in his *Tour in Several of the American Colonies,* 1679–80: "The dwellings are so wretchedly constructed that if you are not so close to the fire as almost to burn yourself, you cannot keep warm, for the wind blows through them everywhere." Quoted in Brugger, *Middle Temperament,* 25. And there's this: "Few Maryland colonists before 1725 could command the great skill, time and money to erect fine buildings of brick or timber frame. In 1678 it was reported that houses in Maryland were built 'very mean and Little and Generally after the manner of the meanest frame houses in England.'" See Mills Lane, *Architecture of the Old South, Maryland* (New York: Abbeville Press, 1991), 14.

30. Wright, *Harford,* 25.

Right: The Maxwell-Day House on the Gunpowder Neck in 1942—a 1740s "Virginia House" in Maryland. The Maxwell-Day House stood for 200 years but didn't survive the Army's experimental firebombing (below) during World War II.

"1 dwelling house wood 1 story 18 × 25." In 1848 Josiah Lee, covert agent for Gen. George Cadwalader, bought all of Maxwell's Conclusion that had "descended to James Maxwell Day by his father, John Day." A few years later the general insured the "frame dwelling . . . formerly owned by Mrs. Day" for $250. Yet if the ancient house (recognized as the "oldest dwelling in Harford County" in the 1930s) survived termites and rot and changes in ownership it could not survive World War II and its dramatic end came, thanks to an experimental firebomb, around 1943.[31]

You Can't Fight City Hall—Even If You Can Find It

When the Days and Maxwells, the Stocketts and Alsops wanted to record a deed or transact other legal business they made their way to the courthouse at the county seat, or rather *seats,* for a bewildering number of hamlets sequentially held that title in prerevolutionary times: Old Baltimore (from 1669 to 1691), Gunpowder (1691 to 1709), Joppa (1709 to 1768), and Dr. Hamilton's beloved Bush (1773 to 1782). That long litany leads to several questions. First, "Why on earth did the county's seat of government move so often?" The most obvious answer is that the unsettled state of something as important as the location of the county courthouse simply reflects the unsettled state of settlement in the upper Chesapeake: an organized society will not find its citizens wondering where to go to record their deeds and bring harassing legal actions against their neighbors. Still, Cambridge, Chestertown, Centreville, Leonardtown, Annapolis, Princess Anne, and Easton had all been settled centers of jurisprudence for decades, while the happy-go-lucky citizens of Baltimore County seemed content to hold court "at one place or another as convenience or occasion required."[32] Another possible explanation—there weren't enough people here to bother establishing anything permanent—does not completely satisfy either, since, as has been pointed out, the county had been home to a respectable number of citizens since the late seventeenth century and its 1730 population of 8,770 placed it "fourth in population among Maryland's counties."[33]

The issue has fascinated researchers for years; indeed, in the lead story in volume 1, number 1 of the Maryland Historical Society's quarterly magazine, Albert C. Ritchie discussed "Early County Seats and Court Houses of Baltimore County." But after a good

31. Deed HDG 34/195; Gen. George Cadwalader Papers, Historical Society of Pennsylvania, Philadelphia; H. Chandlee Forman, *Early Manor and Plantation Houses* (Baltimore: Bodine and Associates, 1982), 122.

32. Albert C. Ritchie, "The Early County Seats and Court Houses of Baltimore County," *Maryland Historical Magazine* 1 (March 1906): 5.

33. Karinen, "Maryland Population," 393.

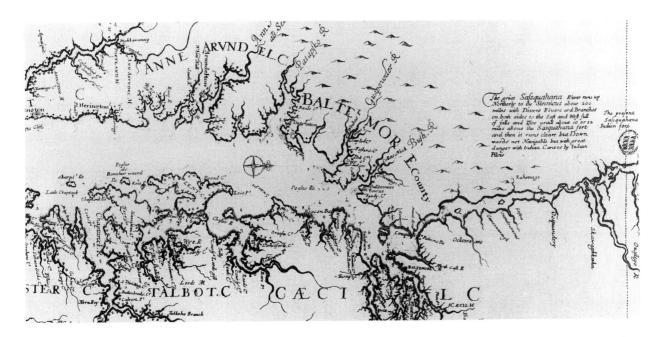

This detail of Augustine Herrman's 1670 map of Maryland clearly shows Harford's three main north-south rivers (Susquehanna, Bush, and Gunpowder) as well as Palmer's (now Garrett) Island and the first "Baltimore Towne."

deal of hemming and hawing, Ritchie simply threw up his hands and sighed, "While we know with tolerable accuracy the year of the erection of this county, we do not know from any documentary evidence . . . [the] location of its first County Seat, nor just when, within a certain period of eight years, the first Court house was built."[34]

The first mention of a Baltimore courthouse occurred in 1683 when Miles Gibson, "High Sheriff of this County," received authorization to hire two carpenters "for repairing the Court house and likewise to take care for the setting up of the pillory and stocks" (4). Two years later Gibson paid some other "carpenter" 1,500 pounds of tobacco "for pulling down the dormant windows of the court house and coursing the same well with good boards and the sap drawn out and for nailes" (103). Presumably, if the courthouse needed repairs in 1683 it had already existed for at least a few years. On the other hand, perhaps the first courthouse was as sloppily built as the county's first residences were, if the carpenters had to be reminded to use seasoned boards with the "sap drawn out." Gibson's courthouse was in Old Baltimore, a hamlet on the east bank of Bush River, near Chilbury Point in what is now the Aberdeen Proving Ground. Everything about Old Baltimore suggests the frontier: the primitive courthouse; those "pillory and stocks"; and the perceived threat of the Susquehannocks, a false threat but nonetheless a troubling one to the citizens who, according to historian Mendes Cohen, spent hours worrying about "the manner for giving and answering the alarm upon the approach of Indians" (100).

Actually, no one seems to have been enchanted with Old Baltimore, and as early as 1686 countians began petitioning to relocate the county seat.[35] One problem with Old Baltimore, a complaint spelled out in that petition, was the town's too-remote location ("in winter people cannot come for frost").[36] Another complaint—and this was not spelled out—may have been Old Baltimore's rollicking and, frankly, amoral nature: bribery was so rampant that one deed allowed a colonist to transfer land only on the stated condition that the clerk of the court would "receive on the 10th of each September during his life 300 gallons of good Syder [cider]" (101), and in 1676 countians' behavior had caused the Reverend John Yeo, rector of St. George's, Spesutia, to write to the archbishop of Canterbury to complain about "the deplorable condition" in the province. "The Lord's Day is profaned," he wailed. "Religion is despised, . . . all notorious vices are

34. Ritchie, "County Seats," 4.
35. Archives of Maryland, 5:473.
36. Ritchie, "County Seats," 105.

committed," and Baltimore County was little more than "a Sodom of uncleanness and a pesthouse of iniquity."[37]

Apparently, the county's center of jurisprudence did find a second home in the early 1690s, but the exact location is not at all clear. Ritchie, after complaining about "the lack of precision in the early surveys,"[38] used seventeenth-century deeds and Augustine Herrman's 1670 map to place the town at Sim's Point, near the evocatively named Wolves Harbor. Wherever it was, that second seat proved just as boisterous as Old Baltimore. The court's first order of business was to grant Michael Judd a license so he could keep a tavern for the "entertainment of Your worships" (110). Then, in 1693, the justices granted a similar license to Robert Benger and took pains to spell out that the tavern had to be "neare the court house" (105). Two years later, in February 1695, Moses Groome petitioned the court to pardon him "for vending and selling liquors by retail to his Majesty's Justices of this said County Court" at Groome's "dwelling plantation." The justices decided not to punish him for selling them booze. They didn't even admonish him—they simply granted him a license so "that he might freely and legally continue to sell his liquors to his Majesty's justices."[39]

On April Fool's Day of 1700 that bibulous group bought two acres from the aforesaid Michael Judd for 3,000 pounds of tobacco: the deed describes the land as being "whereon the courthouse of the said county now standeth," an interesting clause implying that the justices had built the courthouse without having bought the land.[40] Yet no sooner had the justices recorded the deed than they decided it was time to move again. In 1706 the colonial government legislated forty-two new towns into existence, including one at Taylor's Choice, across the Little Gunpowder from that mysterious second seat. In 1709 James Maxwell, one of the justices, received authority to build a courthouse and jail there, and that was the start of Joppa. A few semicomical complications later (Queen Anne, for instance, initially refused to sign that new-town law) things settled themselves and by 1712 Joppa had become the official county seat, complete with what was called a "new court house."[41]

Justice, as dispensed in that courthouse, came swift and severe. The problem of adultery proved particularly rankling or, rather, not adultery per se but the inevitable result, illegitimate children.[42] Numerous bastardy laws had been written into the Maryland lawbooks "as far back as 1658 with one goal: to make certain that bastards would not become a burden on the community" and after "1715 . . . unwed mothers . . . were subject to whipping, up to 39 lashes."[43] Faced with this, many women chose the only safe option, infanticide, and three separate reports of child murder appear in a single (1761) issue of the *Maryland Gazette,* including the news that

> Last Week a Woman . . . near Deer-Creek, was committed to Prison at Joppa, for the Murder of a Bastard Child. She was often tax'd with being with Child but always denied it; and at the Time of her Travail, went to the Creek Side, and was delivered of herself, and flung the Child in. A few Days after, the dead Child being found by the Children of the House, and she being charg'd, confess'd the Fact.[44]

Joppa's career as the center of Baltimore County proved brief. Even as the town was getting itself organized, its ultimate doom was being sealed. In 1729 Gov. Benedict Leonard Calvert authorized the founding of a new Baltimore on the Patapsco. In 1750, many of that new town's 200 or so residents watched eagerly as John Stevenson sent a shipment of flour to Europe from the deep, long harbor at Fells Point; Joppa's citizens, however, ignored the fact that their harbor was filling with silt. Baltimore's mid-century entrepreneurs built new wharves and cut deals to tempt others to ship their flour from the Patapsco; Joppa's residents, however, focused their attention on the complaint "of a certain Sarah Elliot that her husband John Elliot unlawfully cohabitates with a certain Ann Elliot wife of a Geo. Elliot." In July 1762 visitor Benjamin Mifflin wrote that Baltimore had about 150 houses and that the number "seems to Encrease very Fast."[45] At the

37. Quoted in Wright, *Harford,* 193; Ritchie, "County Seats," 101.

38. Ritchie, "County Seats," 12.

39. Ibid., 8. See also James H. Bready, "Maryland Rye," in *Maryland Historical Magazine* 85 (Winter 1990): 345–78.

40. Besides keeping a tavern and acting as a building contractor, Judd was also a shipwright and an attorney, although there is no record of Judd's legal career except that he was hauled in one to appear before the grand jury for behaving in "a scandalous manner." Ritchie, "County Seats," 108–9.

41. Larew, *Bel Air,* 6; June court proceedings, p. 313, Maryland Hall of Records, Annapolis.

42. Mary Helen Cadwalader, *A Short History of St. John's Episcopal Church* (Kingsville, Md.: privately printed, 1967), 16–17.

43. See also Peter F. Stevens, "A Jury of Her Peers," in *Maryland Magazine* (Autumn 1991): 32; Stevens discusses the case of Judith Catchpole, who sailed from England in 1655, settled as an indentured servant in Maryland, and was charged with infanticide in 1656; the colonial magistrates summoned an all-woman jury, who acquitted her.

44. *Maryland Gazette,* February 19, 1761.

45. Quoted in Edward C. Papenfuse et al., *A New Guide to the Old Line State* (Baltimore: Johns Hopkins University Press, 1976), 353.

same time a visitor to Joppa noticed that residents there concerned themselves with horse-racing, cock-fighting, and taverns and commented that the townsfolk "game high, spend free, and dress exceedingly gay." The inevitable came in 1768 when Baltimore, with over 3,000 inhabitants, was made county seat, thus sealing "the decline and eventual demise of Joppa."[46]

Today, nothing whatever remains of early Joppa. The jail and courthouse vanished long ago; so, too, did the brick St. John's Church—no great loss, for even 200 years ago parishioners grumbled that the church "was not built very well."[47] Now Joppa's only religious relics consist of a few vitriolic letters written by St. John's rector, the Reverend James Jones Wilmer. This worthy cleric had married a certain Letitia but lived to regret it, for he sizzled with complaints about "the vile Letitia . . . and her base conduct": since "the lying filthy Jezebel . . . boasts much of her property," he sneered, she wouldn't receive any more cash for clothes from *him,* although he charitably added that he might cough up a couple of pounds so "the aforesaid Jezebel" might be able "to purchase . . . a set of grinders and nostrums to sweeten her stinking breath and rotten carcass."[48] As for the town's residences, the only possible eighteenth-century survivor is what is known as the Rumsey Mansion, and although many date the gambrel-roofed brick house to the 1720s, it seems far likelier that Benjamin Rumsey built the extant 55-by-51-foot structure around 1768, on the occasion of his marriage that year to another of James Maxwell's heiress daughters.

Countians Move Inland

But if Joppa's buildings have all crumbled away from disuse and if firebombs and termites have wiped out all the county's late seventeenth-/early eighteenth-century folk houses, a few *mid*-eighteenth-century folk dwellings have somehow survived virtually intact. There assuredly aren't many of them and one recites their names—Prospect, Cranberry, Broom's Bloom, Joshua's Meadows—reverently, as if one were handling rosary beads, but there may be enough of them to allow a reasonably clear picture of what life was like among Harford's prosperous elite in the thirty or so years before the Revolution. Folk historians have noted that these and similar structures, all built by the last generation of English colonists in America, seem "very like the houses found in northern and western Ireland and Wales, and similar to some found in Scotland and England," and they therefore have dubbed them "British Cabins." Constructed "of stone, frame or log, with rectangular floor plans" and gable-end chimneys, these "cabins," generally one and one-half or two stories high, also represent an early form of modular building since they were composed of essentially independent units (or modules), each equipped with its own outside door, fireplace, and enclosed winder stair.[49] Some families made do with one module; others simply fused two or more modules together. The only real distinction among the buildings is size: Prospect contains one module, Broom's Bloom and Cranberry have two, and Joshua's Meadows, most ambitious of all, boasts three. But this is a distinction without a difference because in essence and in concept all four houses read the same.

The Norris family erected several such British Cabins throughout the Winters Run Valley in the mid-eighteenth century. While many have been remodeled (such as the house known as Woodview), one, Prospect, has endured more or less as built. In 1716 John Norris, a son of the Benjamin Norris who "settled in Harford County about 1690," bought 243 acres of Prospect from the speculative firm Bond & Hamilton.[50] He sold 116 of those acres in 1725 but retained the balance, which he willed to his son Joseph.[51] (When Joseph Norris sold that remainder in 1753 he explained in his deed that this represented the "dwelling plantation" he had inherited from his father, John.)[52] And certainly one of those early Norrises, either John or Joseph, built the one-and-one-half-story, one-room, 21-by-18-foot, rubblestone British Cabin that still presides over the tract. The single room on the main floor contains a large fireplace centered on the south wall between original

The courthouse at Joppa—conjectural sketch by James Wollon, AIA, and Jack Riggin using the original 1709 specifications: it was to be a brick building 24 by 35 feet with a roof ridge 14 feet about the second-story joists; shuttered casement windows were specified, as were two attic dormers. The courtroom filled the main story and two jury rooms were above.

46. Quoted in C. B. Holden Rogers, "A History of St. John's Church," pamphlet in files of Harford County Department of Planning and Zoning, Bel Air.

47. Ibid.

48. Cadwalader, *St. John's,* 26.

49. Glassie, *Folk Culture,* 48–49, 52–53.

50. Walter Preston, *History of Harford County* (Baltimore: Sun Book Office, 1901), 210.

51. Deed IS #H, p. 38.

52. Deed TR #D, p. 546.

The Norris family's c. 1740 21-by-18-foot rubble-stone, single-module "British Cabin" at Prospect; to safeguard a supply of fresh water, the Norrises carefully sited the house over a spring, which still bubbles forth in the half-exposed cellar.

The paneled parlor wall in the c. 1745 Bull House near Bel Air; photographed c. 1935. Every known pre-1750 folk house in Harford County displays a variation on this rhythm of closeted stair/closet/fireplace/closet.

A NARRATIVE HISTORY OF HARFORD COUNTY

The upper reaches of the Bush River; most of these tidewater acres became the property of John Hall I in the 1680s.

built-in cupboards and an enclosed winder stair, and that rhythm of closeted stair–fire-place–cupboard is a defining characteristic of virtually every known prerevolutionary house in Harford County, including the Maxwell-Day House.

Yet Norris (either father or son) evidently yearned for something beyond the Virginia House's normally utilitarian, unfinished interior, because someone enriched the main room with exposed beaded ceiling joists. Moreover, since the fireplace wall forms the functional heart of the module—the fireplace itself provided heat and a place for cooking food while the wall contained the closet stair upstairs and the built-in storage cupboards—and since (then as now) functional importance demands architectural decoration, Norris enriched the spaces between hearth and the various doors with beaded vertical board paneling, while leaving the three less important walls bare.

Cranberry, seat of the prominent Hall family, may be taken as representative of the multimodule cabins, partially because it is the least changed of its peers, despite its present location on the edge of rapidly expanding Aberdeen. While the first Halls to arrive in Maryland were Roman Catholics who settled St. Mary's County in the 1630s and '40s, "some of the later generations became members of the Church of England and removed [themselves] from St. Mary's,"[53] including Capt. John Hall I (born c. 1658), who had moved north to the Bush River area by 1682.

Hall prospered there and "became a leading figure in Baltimore County."[54] In 1694

53. William White Wiltbank et al., *Descendants of Colonel Thomas White of Maryland* (Philadelphia: privately printed, 1878), 127.

54. Papenfuse et al., *Biographical Dictionary*, 386.

he had his several tracts resurveyed under the name Cranberry and found that they totaled 1,539 acres. Perhaps he did this because he had married the year before—and he had married well. His heiress wife, née Martha Beadle (born 1667), was the wealthy widow of George Gouldsmith, who had died in 1692; she was also an heiress in her own right.[55] A Victorian-era descendant described Hall as "a personage of extensive possessions, and of high position in the province,"[56] and while such phrases, redolent of lavender and lemon verbena, usually set one's suspicions on guard, in this case they relate the simple truth. Hall's vast acreage meets virtually anyone's definition of "extensive possessions" and his elected and appointed offices (lower house in the legislature continuously from 1696 to 1704 and the upper house on and off from 1709 until his death) represent the highest positions a colonial could reasonably hope to reach.

When the Halls died (he in 1737, she in 1720) they willed son Edward (born 1697) "the tract of land whereon I [John] live known as Cranberry Hall." Other children and grandchildren inherited other lands, over 4,000 acres in all scattered throughout the county from the Chesapeake to Deer Creek. Edward Hall I's tenure at Cranberry was brief, for he died in 1742. He evidently had not even resided there, for he instructed his executors to "sell the place where I now live called Hall's Park" to pay his several debts and left Cranberry to his only son, John Hall III (born 1719). Still, if it is unclear *where* Edward Hall lived, it is clear *how* he lived: he had married Avarilla Carvil in 1717 and the couple furnished their house (using his estate inventory as a guide) with four beds (two of which were four-posters), six "Russian Leather chairs" worth £3, "9 prints in frame" worth a shilling apiece, and silver valued at £10. The Halls even had a library of sorts (a two-volume set of Rapin's *History* worth £2 and a miscellaneous "parcel old books" worth 10 shillings), which suggests that they were literate in a time and place where few others could make that claim. In all, Hall's assets (including £72 10s in "current money" and 8,435 pounds of "good tobacco" worth £63) totaled an impressive £1,013, a figure that may explain why his contemporaries referred to him as "Colonel Edward Hall, Gentleman," a respectful appellation that had not been granted his pioneering father.

Edward's son, John Hall III, who inherited the Cranberry tract, probably built the frame, gambrel-roofed dwelling that still stands there and that was known in the eighteenth century as the Halls' "mansion house." While Cranberry may seem small to 1990s eyes, 250 years ago it would have seemed grand indeed. Recall that "home" in prerevolutionary Harford didn't mean a 2,500-square-foot brick ranch house; it meant, by and large, a 300-square-foot, one-story wooden shack. The first comprehensive listing of the county's building stock dates to 1798, when the federal government sent tax assessors out to scour the new nation and write down what structures were standing, what they were made out of, how tall they were, what their dimensions were, their owners' names, the farm's acreage, and the number of slaves and outbuildings. The result is a wonderful document, full of information, capable of endless analysis.

The assessors found that Harford County contained about 657 taxable houses; of this number 534 (81%) were one story high, 7 were one and one-half stories, and 116 were two stories. They also broke the county down into fourteen regions called Hundreds (a medieval term brought from England) and placed Cranberry in Harford Lower Hundred, which took in all the land drained by Romney Creek, Bush River, and Cranberry Run. There were forty-nine other houses in that hundred in 1798 and since thirty-nine were only one story tall, Cranberry's one and one-half–story height gave it distinction, as did its 39-by-20-foot dimensions. For instance, one of the Halls' wealthier neighbors, Jonas Stevenson, lived in a "15 × 15 1-story wood house." One may rest assured that Stevenson's house contained a single room; that it was flimsily built; and that if it had windows at all they were unglazed holes in the walls.

And if the county's white landowners lived simply, the slaves lived under conditions impossible to imagine. Harford's surviving eighteenth-century slave dwellings are rare indeed, and are perhaps limited to a 10-by-12-foot brick and stone building at Joshua's

Cranberry, the c. 1742 "mansion house" of the Halls in the 1930s. The large sash windows are almost certainly late eighteenth-century replacements of the original casement openings.

55. Martha's father was Edward Beadle/Beedle/Bidwell. Among his land purchases was 500 acres of Oakington from Nathaniel Utie in 1668. Edward's only son predeceased him and his heirs were Martha (born 1667) and her sister, Mary. Mary's first husband is unknown but her second was George Utie, Nathaniel's brother; she eventually inherited Spesutia Island.

56. Wiltbank et al., *Descendants of White*, 29.

A NARRATIVE HISTORY OF HARFORD COUNTY

Left: The winder stair in the parlor at Cranberry creates a distinctly medieval feeling. Right: Parlor fireplace wall at Cranberry (closeted stair/closet/fireplace/closet), where the folk paneling is "dramatically out of level."

Meadows (where Buckler Bond kept his six slaves) and a stone building of similar dimensions at the Preston family's farm, The Vineyard, but documentary evidence has endured. For example, another of the Halls' neighbors, Clark Hollis, owned a 176-acre farm and nine slaves; among the farm's outbuildings one finds a "quarter 14 × 18 log" as well as a "stable 18 × 12 wood," and a "henhouse 13 × 11 wood." In other words, while the slaves' building—that quarter—was larger than the henhouse, Hollis treated the hens to planed lumber walls but felt the slaves could make do with unfinished logs. Moreover, since that 14-by-18 building was the only dwelling mentioned for the slaves, it means that nine people lived in a 14-by-18-foot one-story log cabin—*that's* what home meant to one-quarter of the county's population, since the 1790 census showed 3,417 slaves among the 14,976 people then in Harford County. These grim images—a 15-foot-square frame house for the typical white family, a 14-by-18 log cabin for as many as nine slaves—helps put Prospect, Cranberry, Broom's Bloom, and Joshua's Meadows into perspective.

Before discussing the Halls' grand house in more detail, it might be wise to discuss Cranberry's gambrel roof, particularly since a good deal of misinformation has innocently been written about it, such as the anonymous article in the September 1976 *Aberdeen Enterprise* that states, categorically, that "the gambrel roof is more characteristic of the Dutch colonial houses in New England." No, no, *no!* Gambrel roofs were common in late seventeenth-century Maryland and Virginia and remained popular in both places until the middle of the eighteenth century; both Dr. Charles Carroll and Charles Carroll of Annapolis ("probably the two wealthiest residents at that period")[57] and John Brice II all built gambrel-roofed houses in Maryland's capital in the 1740s and '50s, while John Moale's 1752 sketch of embryonic Baltimore shows that of the thirty buildings in town larger than sheds, no fewer than five had gambrel roofs. Harford contained its share of such structures, too, and at least a dozen of them survived into the twentieth century.[58]

The Halls' Cranberry, gambrel roof and all, crowns a hillock overlooking the upper reaches of a silted-in Cranberry Run, while tractor-trailers belch their gaseous ways along nearby routes 40 and 7. (In 1938 the intrepid researcher Alexis Shriver wrote that while he was certain Cranberry was "near Spesutia Church along Cranberry Run" the neighborhood had changed so much that "I have never been able to find" the house.)[59] Braced

57. Michael F. Trostel, FAIA, "The Annapolis Plan in Maryland," in Mario di Valmarana, ed., *Building by the Book* 2 (Charlottesville: University Press of Virginia, 1986), 3.

58. See also Henry Glassie's *Folk Culture* in which he discusses gambrel-roofed houses throughout the mid-Atlantic region; especially note 66–67 and 152–53.

59. Material in Hughes Collection, MHS.

The eighteenth-century Onion House on Toll-gate Road—near the present Winters Run Golf Course—as it appeared c. 1935. In 1798 Thomas Bond Onion paid taxes on 429 acres of land here improved by a "45 × 18 1-story hipped roof house." The massing and roof of the house bear obvious similarities to the Halls' Cranberry.

by its four-by-four framing, the house, according to a modern tape-measure, measures approximately 38 feet by 18 feet 6 inches, awfully close to the 39-by-20-foot dimensions cited in 1798. Its clapboard-covered walls, filled with mud for insulation, are lathed and plastered over on the interior, an unusual touch of elegance for the time. Within, Cranberry displays many features suggesting the folk/vernacular—one might say medieval—sensibilities of its builders and its two-room plan, typical of pre-Georgian architecture, contains two "Prospect modules." The southern or larger room was called the hall, a reference to the Great Hall of the medieval English manor house. This, the main living space, was where family members cooked (a massive fireplace originally filled half of Cranberry's south wall), ate, and spent most of their time. The Halls reserved the smaller, adjacent room, called the parlor, for formal gatherings; this space "had no direct counterpart in the medieval house. It was rather a product of the changing pattern of social behavior peculiar to the British middle-class," the segment of society that would have included successful colonials such as the Halls.[60]

As was the case at Prospect, Cranberry's builders reserved architectural enrichment for the main room's fireplace wall, which, significantly, contains the requisite center fireplace and flanking cupboard (behind its six-panel door) and enclosed stair (behind *its* six-panel door). This enrichment consists of squared wooden panels of seemingly random placement. Although a prominent architect has recently observed, with raised eyebrows, that "the upper rails of the paneling [at Cranberry] are dramatically out-of-level . . . and they apparently were built to that condition,"[61] one can only agree that they probably were since it isn't until *about* 1770 that paneling in the county begins to reflect a grasp of the classical orders. Cranberry's original windows, too, would have heightened the pre-Renaissance feel of the house; it is a near certainty that Cranberry's first windows were outward-opening casements,[62] similar to those found on virtually every surviving English folk house from Massachusetts to South Carolina. The house's present sash windows are doubtless postrevolutionary replacements added by Halls who had no use for an earlier generation's medieval imagery.

That imagery becomes, perhaps, most poignant in Cranberry's winder staircase. Think of the stairs in a medieval castle or manor house—tiny, narrow spaces that spiral

60. William H. Pierson Jr., *American Buildings and Their Architects: The Colonial and Neoclassical Style* (New York: Anchor Books, 1976), 27–28.

61. Cranberry nomination to the National Register of Historic Places, copy on file in Harford County Department of Planning and Zoning, Bel Air; see also Wiltbank et al., *Descendants of White*, 32.

62. Pierson, *Buildings, Colonial*, 26.

around a central newel post[63]—that was the inspiration for Harford's folk-houses' closeted winder stairs. Open staircases did not appear in England until the early seventeenth century, and then only at palaces built by men and women at the pinnacle of English life; it took generations before such radical notions gained acceptance in remote, colonial Maryland, as is discussed in the following chapter. All in all, Cranberry is quite remarkable. Despite being built in the eighteenth century, in many ways it seems nearer the War of the Roses than the War for Independence.[64]

John Hall III, who styled himself "John Hall of Cranberry," died in 1779 with material goods worth just over £1,561, a figure that represents a 50 percent net increase over his father's wealth thirty-seven years earlier and a figure that placed him firmly among the county's elite. (James Rigbie Jr., scion of one of north Harford's wealthiest families [see chapter 3], died the same year with goods valued at only £104.) Hall's estate inventory shows that he filled Cranberry with such elegant items as a "Japanned case with 2 doz. knives & forks," 33 ounces of silver (worth £13 15s), "1 large looking glass" (worth £2), a cherry dining table (£1 10s), six wine glasses (and one "horn cup"), a "backgammon table & dice box," and, his single most valuable piece of furniture, a cherry desk and bookcase worth £8. One also gathers that the squire was a bit deaf, for he owned "1 tin speaking trumpet." Hall had made Cranberry a profitable and diverse agricultural concern and he (and his 25 slaves) had seen to it that the farm's forty-eight sheep and scores of cattle and hogs had produced 84 pounds of wool (Hall kept a pair of "weaving looms"), 2,000 pounds of pork (£30), and 150 pounds of beef (£1 17s) while the earth had given forth 7½ bushels of rye (18s), 49 bushels of oats (£4 18s), and 200 bushels of wheat (£50).

Hall left the house and "all that part" of the farm that lay south and southeast of "the Great Road leading from Bush Town to Susquehanna Lower Ferry" to his eldest son, Edward Hall II, while his second son, John Beadle Hall, received the land north and west of the road. Edward also inherited his father's "Mill with twenty acres of land" provided he paid a third son, Josias, "Six Hundred Pounds Sterling, money of Great Britain."[65] Edward Hall II, like his grandfather Edward I, did not preside long at Cranberry; he died in 1788, at age 40. He willed the house, the farm (which now yielded hundreds of gallons of cider and "27 bushels apples" annually while its "1 hive of bees" filled "a 5 Gallon jug with honey"), the mill, the choicest pieces of furniture, nine enumerated slaves (of his nineteen), certain livestock (including "one horse called Yorick" and another named Scipio) to brother John Beadle. One can sense the importance of that stump-filled post road, even a century after its completion, for Edward's will stipulates that John would receive his inheritance only if he pledged to keep the road "from Harford Town to Susquehanna Lower Ferry" from being rerouted away from the house.

After some complications, ownership of Cranberry eventually vested in the wonderfully named Josias Carvil Cranberry Hall, a son of Josias Hall and a nephew to Edward and John.[66] When J.C.C. Hall died unmarried in 1855 he devoted many of the seventeen pages of his will to the matter of releasing the family's slaves from their bondage—some were to be freed after a specified time, others after they had reached a certain age. He also instructed his heirs to turn several ancestral acres into building lots (and houses) for the former bondsmen. They were to build ex-slave "Charles," for instance, a "comfortable dwelling 16 by 20, 1½ stories high" where he could live for free unless he used it to hold "disorderly . . . negro meetings to the annoyance of the neighborhood"; if he did, he would have to pay rent. J.C.C. Hall also left word that "my old arm chair, which has been in possession of my several forefathers for many years," and the "Hall family coat of arms" should descend together "forever"; this, coupled with his benevolent attitude toward "Charles," suggests that Hall felt imbued with a touch of *noblesse oblige*. Well, why not? By the mid-nineteenth century the Halls were no longer pioneers in an unchartered wilderness. Honorable members of the county's elite for a century and a half, they had evolved into benign aristocrats looking after their heirlooms and "their people."

Mention of Hall's inferred sense of social responsibility might serve as a reminder that

The interior of the Onion House, c. 1935:closeted stair, closet, fireplace.

63. Olive Cook, *The English House through Seven Centuries* (London: Thomas Nelson, 1968), 64, 65.

64. In plan and overall form, Cranberry resembles Eltonhead Manor, a gambrel-roofed house that formerly stood in Calvert County. Destroyed in the 1920s, Eltonhead Manor was much photographed in its time; its hall was saved and has been moved to the American Wing of the Baltimore Museum of Art. See William Voss Elder III, *Maryland Period Rooms at the Baltimore Museum of Art* (Baltimore: Baltimore Museum of Art, 1990), 9.

65. See will book SR 2, p. 306.

66. Not to be outdone, J. C. C. Hall's brother was called George Josias Ontario Hall.

Webster's Forest: the original, gambrel-roof section is in the foreground (or right); the c. 1820 addition rises beyond.

Broom's Bloom, c. 1935, showing the original 1740s "I House" (left) and the 1850s rear service wing. Much of the garden in the foreground now lies in the expanded right-of-way of Fountain Green Road.

67. *A Portrait and Biographical Record of Cecil and Harford Counties* (New York: Chapman Publishing, 1897), 182. DD 5/213; PL 2/11, Maryland Hall of Records, Annapolis.

68. Samuel had married Elizabeth Dallam in 1726, the beginning of several generations of Webster-Dallam weddings.

69. Patent BT & BY 3/334; deed HD K/147.

when analyzing houses such as Cranberry—or any house, for that matter—one needs to address many co-equal variables and when trying to determine *when* one must also give equal weight to *who* and *where*. While certain "who's" have always taken pains to keep themselves stylistically up-to-date, other "who's" seem to work hard to achieve the opposite result. Which leads the narrative to Broom's Bloom, a frame and stone dwelling near Creswell in the James Run Valley. John Webster (1667–1753), progenitor of what one historian has called "the oldest and most honored" of local families, patented a tract called Webster's Forest in 1704.[67] Webster and his wife, née Hannah Butterworth, had five children, including sons Samuel I (1710–86) and Isaac I (?–1759), and daughter, Hannah, who married Jacob Giles. This marriage is of more than genealogical interest, for Giles, one of the county's first important industrialists and land speculators, made a fortune in partnership with his brother-in-law Isaac Webster I. The two men (and John Hall of Cranberry) founded the Bush River Iron Works in 1746 and also bought and subdivided the vast Arabia Petrea tract, which sprawled across 5,000 acres in the Darlington/Dublin area.

All this obviously made Isaac Webster a rich man. When his father died, he inherited the 265 acres of the Creswell lands that lay on the west side of Bynum Run. Brother Samuel, then a tobacco inspector in Joppa, inherited the land on the east bank, including Webster's Forest.[68] Actually, Isaac had been trying to clarify the boundaries of that Bynum Run property since 1747, when he convinced Lord Baltimore to repatent those 265 acres in his, Isaac's, name. (To relieve any doubts, in 1788 Webster's son Samuel mortgaged the "land west of the small branch . . . [which was] given to the said Samuel by his father . . . whereon Samuel and his father lived.")[69]

Although it is not certain, it seems likely that Isaac began building Broom's Bloom around 1747, the time he began fussing about his farm's property lines. He certainly could have afforded it and it was, with its mid-county location, convenient to his recently acquired iron works. The house, still owned by his direct descendants and still discernible among its nineteenth- and twentieth-century additions, faces almost due south to catch the warming rays of the winter sun; its frame walls measure 36 by 20 feet and sit firmly on a fully excavated stone cellar. (Cranberry, too, boasts masonry foundations, which probably explains why these two houses have endured while their contemporary frame

At Joshua's Meadows the 2½-story stuccoed brick main block and rear 1½-story kitchen (between the two chimney stacks) date to the 1740s and formed a three-module "British Cabin." Originally detached, they were connected c. 1820. The porch of the 1930s kitchen wing is just discernible to the left as is the eighteenth-century slaves' quarters to the right.

peers, built with timbers directly in the ground, have rotted away.) Inside, Broom's Bloom displays the hierarchy of rooms seen at Cranberry—the more important hall received the more important woodwork (central fireplace flanked by a built-in cupboard and enclosed winder stair all placed in a sea of distinctly preclassical fielded paneling), while the less important parlor was more simply finished; upstairs, the bedrooms were simpler still.

While the house's two-room, hall-and-parlor plan fits snugly within the British Cabin canon, its massing suggests that countians were being influenced by yet another architectural folk form, the two-story, one-room-deep "I House." This species of building, which derives its name from its resemblance to an uppercase *I,* was popular throughout colonial tidewater Maryland, where it had an "almost exclusive association with economic success in an agricultural" society.[70] "Patterned closely after English originals," the I House remained an important house form of choice well into the nineteenth century "from Baltimore down the coast to North Carolina's Albemarle Sound and . . . inland to the foot of the Blue Ridge in Virginia."[71]

Located a few miles northwest of Broom's Bloom, Joshua's Meadows, built on a gentle hill overlooking Winters Run, also dates to the 1740s, the same decade that saw Broom's Bloom and Cranberry and Prospect rise from Harford farmland. Yet Joshua's Meadows presents a phenomenon altogether different from its contemporaries and is one of the few buildings in the county that can truly be called transitional. As was the case with Cranberry and the Halls and Broom's Bloom and the Websters, the history of Joshua's Meadows goes back to an ambitious young man's late seventeenth-century arrival into Harford County. In this case it was Peter Bond. He began acquiring land around 1660, and by the time he died in 1705 he owned tracts from present-day Bel Air southward to Bush and westward to the banks of the Patapsco at Gwynn's Falls.

Peter Bond II, as eldest son, inherited the bulk of these properties, which left his younger brothers, Thomas, William, and John, to fend for themselves. Thomas, at least, did so. He had settled in Harford before his father's death, had patented the tract Knave's Misfortune near Emmorton in 1703, and had lived there with his wife (née Anne Robertson) in a "substantial brick house which stood until about 1880."[72] Thomas kept busy patenting more and more piedmont lands, including Bond's Forest (3,100 acres in 1714

70. Fred Kniffen, "Folk Housing: Key to Diffusion," in *Annals of the Association of American Geographers* (December 1965): 8.

71. Glassie, *Folk Culture,* 64–67.

72. Preston, *History,* 206. Preston says that Thomas's house was "used as a smallpox hospital about the time of the Revolution" but gives no source for that story: perhaps he felt it was too well known to warrant a footnote.

Closeted stair, closet, and fireplace at Joshua's
Meadows: compare to the Maxwell-Day House,
the Onion House, and the Bull House.

near Benson), Poplar Neck (1,000 acres on both sides of Winters Run near Bel Air in
1726), and Bond's Manor (5,000 acres on the west bank of the Susquehanna in 1705),[73]
and he improved his Poplar Neck tract with the gristmill that appears on Dennis Griffith's 1794 map of the state. And if economics and agriculture interested Thomas, so did
religion. In 1749 he gave a small part of Bond's Forest, including "a house now built
intended for a meeting house," to "the people called Quakers to worship God in, . . .
also a schoolhouse already built."[74] This marks the beginning of Fallston's Little Falls
Meeting.

Thomas also built Joshua's Meadows. By the time he died in 1755, he had "settled each
of his sons in comfortable houses on 'plantations.'" He began deeding land along Winters Run to son Joshua around 1747 (Joshua supplemented his patrimony with a patent
or two of his own, one of which uses the name Joshua's Meadows), and in 1752 he split
his Poplar Neck tract, giving half to Joshua, "where the said Joshua's dwelling is," and
half—with no mention of a dwelling—to another son, Jacob. Thus while no one knows
exactly when the Bonds built the house, it seems reasonable to assume that it dates to the
1747–52 period.[75] Among the most imposing dwellings of its time in the county, the main
part of Joshua's Meadows measures 20 by 40 feet and rises two and one-half stories beneath a gable roof with a freestanding, one and one-half–story brick kitchen perpendicular to the south. It is also among the most solidly built structures ever put up in Harford, for all the walls—interior and exterior—are brick. In plan Joshua's Meadows
represents a simple doubling of the Norris house at Prospect, for there are two rooms per
floor in the main section, each with its own gable-end fireplace, built-in cupboards,
and enclosed winder stairs. And unlike Broom's Bloom and Cranberry, where only the
more formal hall has a stair, Joshua's Meadows is a true modular building: all rooms can
function independently; all have their own heat, staircase, and outside door. Actually,
Joshua's Meadows boasts three such modules, since the detached kitchen has a large walk-
in fireplace on the south wall and an enclosed winder stair on the north.

Joshua's Meadows most assuredly is *transitional*. While the house's somewhat conservative British Cabin form hearkens back to medieval times, other features suggest that
the Bonds were looking ahead to the high-style Georgian age; note the house's Flemish
bond brick walls, balanced, three-bay façade (suggestive of a center hall plan) and sash
windows. Where did the Bonds get these ideas? from travels? from books? They certainly didn't get the idea for the balanced façade from their neighbors, because there simply
weren't any center-hall buildings in Harford County in the 1740s. Thus if the Halls' Cranberry stands as a last link with the medieval, theocentric world, Joshua's Meadows arguably heralds the coming of Renaissance-based humanism to Maryland. Certainly in
one respect Joshua and his siblings emerge as a good deal worldlier than their father and
grandfather. Whereas Peter and Thomas Bond "were devout Quakers . . . four of
Thomas's sons, Jacob, James, Joshua, and Thomas Jr., were disciplined by the meeting
for fighting, for playing the fiddle and for 'marrying out.' Later disagreement over par-
ticipation in military activities would cause these four to leave the Society of Friends or
be disowned."[76]

When Joshua died, he left the house and land to his older son, James; in 1790 James
sold it to *his* younger brother, Buckler, for the hefty price of £2,500,[77] and Buckler's
name appears in the 1798 federal tax rolls as owner of 534 acres, six slaves, and a "40 × 20
2-story brick house" with a "20 × 16 kitchen." Buckler's deed also includes "5 Lottes in
Belle Air," showing that by then the Bonds of Joshua's Meadows had forged permanent
links to Bel Air, Harford's first (and only) postcolonial county seat: land taken from Poplar
Neck and Joshua's Meadows makes up most of the town and the family is memorialized
in Bond Street, one of the municipality's two principal north-south thoroughfares.

In every respect, then, Joshua's Meadows fittingly closes the county's 100-year folk period. And if it (or Cranberry or Broom's Bloom or Prospect) might seem but "a small
provincial English dwelling, of no greater significance than the many small houses in Eng-

73. In 1739 Bond sold part of Bond's Manor to
Thomas Cresap, Lord Baltimore's bulwark against
William Penn throughout the decades of border
wars with Pennsylvania; Cresap was a direct ances-
tor of Joshua's Meadows's present owner, Julia
Cameron, whose father was named James Cresap
Sprigg.

74. Preston, *History*, 207.

75. Ibid.; patent book BT & BY 3, p. 146; deed
TR, book D, pp. 463, 465. Preston, in his *History*,
32, suggests that the house Joshua's Meadows dates
to 1732. Jacob was perhaps the most prominent of
his generation of Bonds. He died in 1780 but by
that time he had already gone to Annapolis in 1774
to attend the convention called to protest the tea
tax; he represented Harford County in the 1776
convention to prepare the state's first constitution;
and he captained Company Eleven of the Harford
militia in the Revolution; one of his sons-in-law was
Bernard Preston, who built the large stone house
known as The Vineyard.

76. Hunter Sutherland, "The Bush River Friends
Meeting," *Maryland Historical Magazine* 82 (Winter 1987): 366.

77. JLG 1/045

land to which it is so closely related," it is important to note that these houses were not built in England; they were built in America. They should be valued as "reminders . . . of the slow but inexorable triumph of civilization. . . . Simple and awkward . . . they are tinged with their own poetry, a poetry of legend and folklore, rich, warm, and provocative. But it is the poetry of men and events rather than architecture." Viewed independently, the Websters, Norrises, Halls, and Bonds were nothing more than successful colonial entrepreneurs who wouldn't have even been noticed in England. Viewed as a group, however, these "restless men, driven on by whatever motive, [who] dared to cross the ocean and seek a new life in the unknown" form a small but vital cog in the worldwide expansion of European civilization. "It is as symbols of this quest" that Harford's folk houses gain meaning and importance.[78]

78. Pierson, *Buildings, Colonial,* 27–29.

Constance Hall Proctor descends the stair at her ancestors' 1768 Sophia's Dairy in 1962. A revolution in architectural taste had come to Harford County: compare this exceptional, almost regal, stair to the stairs at the nearby Cranberry (c. 1740 and also built by the Hall family).

Liberté, Egalité, Fraternité in Harford County [3]

Something began to twitch in Harford County's architectural psyche around 1760 just as something began to twitch in the county's politics. The Susquehanna no longer marked the remotest rim of the world. By the mid-eighteenth century families such as the Halls, Norrises, Websters, and Dallams were no longer pioneers taming the wilderness, they were leaders in a settled society with three generations of wealth and prominence behind them. And they knew they needed an ordered manner of building to reflect their ordered state of life. Countians had been on the verge of this change for some time. Recall that the Bonds who built Joshua's Meadows in the 1740s seemed to be yearning to escape their folk ethos—the only problem was, they didn't know what they wanted to escape to. But within the space of a single decade they and their neighbors found the answer and, at least among the architecturally aware, folk was suddenly out; classicism was in.

Or perhaps one should say *neo*classicism was in. Just as one might view folk houses like the Halls' Cranberry as the last gasp of medievalism, so might one view the Georgian and federal houses described in this chapter as the last flowering of the Renaissance, that rational, human-oriented approach to life and art. It took centuries, but from their native Tuscany, Renaissance principles filtered into mens' minds throughout the Western world. Pediments and pilasters had replaced gargoyles in Rome and Venice and other Italian cities by 1500; these building elements (and the broader, neoclassical principles they represent) traveled thence to Spain, to France, to Holland; they reached England by 1600 and "virtually all of the gentry [in Britain] . . . were housed in some version of a Renaissance house by 1740."[1] Finally, they trickled across the Atlantic and, under the general

1. Bushman, *Refinement of America*, 102.

The first known open stair in Harford County was at the Dallam family's c. 1750 house Fanny's Inheritance. The Dallams kept the twisty folk shape intact but took it out of its closet and embellished it with neoclassical trim. (The house was destroyed c. 1940; the stair is now in the Baltimore Museum of Art.)

heading of "Georgian design," gained a foothold in Britain's American colonies by the middle of the eighteenth century.

Georgian. The very word gives architectural historians the willies; its helpmate *federal* isn't much better. But despite their being notoriously vague, enemies to precision, and open to many interpretations, here they are again. And they will appear and reappear in this narrative simply because they have acquired, by force of being constantly (mis)used, a certain art-historical validity; that is, when one hears or reads of a Georgian or federal building (or painting or chair) a set of very real images comes to mind. Speaking in broadest terms, a "Georgian house" has come to suggest a structure with a symmetrical entrance façade instead of the somewhat helter-skelter window arrangements common to folk houses, double-hung sash windows instead of casements, and a gable roof; Flemish bond brick often enters the picture, as do rubbed-brick window arches, corner quoins, and a pedimented, wooden door surround. The interiors of these houses almost invariably contain a broad stairhall placed in the center (if the house is five bays wide) or to the side (if three), and classically inspired chairrails, cornices, and fireplaces. Speak of a "federal house" and the image becomes lighter and more curvaceous, with attenuated proportions, more delicate trim, round-arched windows (or window recesses), a fanlight (instead of a pediment) over the door, oval rooms, and so on. Those, at least, are the clichés.

And one thing people often forget about truisms is that, at least in Harford County, they are true. Mention a "Georgian" or "federal" house here and, to paraphrase comedian Flip Wilson, what you expect is what you get.

Rational and sensible, Harford's Georgian architecture brought an end to the complex dialectics of the Middle Ages. Nowhere is this better expressed than in the way countians decided to build stairs: no longer closeted in location and tortuous in form, after the mid-eighteenth century staircases were out in the open, expansive, and embellished with rare woods, intricately turned balusters, scrolled step-end trim, paneled undersides, shadow rails—nothing, suddenly, was too good for the stair.[2] The first known stair in the county to reflect these changes was built by the Dallam family at their c. 1750 house Fanny's Inheritance. The Dallams kept the staircase's basic folk shape intact (note the narrow steps and cramped configuration) but they took it out of its closet and gave it classically inspired trim such as squared, fluted columns for newel posts and metopes and dentils for step-end decorations.

Eventually this change in the stair's location affected all aspects of house design. Floor plans, for instance, became symmetrical around a central axial stairhall with equal-sized rooms to each side; this change in design led to a change in function, too, for it improved circulation (no longer was one forced to wander through one room to get to another—one simply and *rationally* used the stairhall) and this led to the development of specialized rooms. Prior to c. 1750, Harford's men, women, and children did not distinguish among the spaces in which they ate, slept, made love, and stored crops. Existing estate inventories show that until mid-century it was not at all uncommon to find a room furnished with a bed, a table, some farm equipment, and fifty barrels of corn. After mid-century, however, rooms were designed for a particular use, a change some have equated with a greater respect for individualism[3] and to a greater sense of self-worth as well. When the Dallams built Fanny's Inheritance, they (and some of their neighbors) did not think it appropriate to enter a room by popping out of a closet; they were important individuals and they wanted to be seen as such: thus they expected to descend from one story to another gracefully, grandly, ceremoniously.

This suggests that political changes were in the wind as well, and while it may seem extreme to state that everyone who could distinguish among Doric, Ionic, and Corinthian believed in life, liberty, and the pursuit of happiness, in Harford, at least, by and large the educated, liberal countians who led the fight for a new nation were the same men and women who effectively led the county to a new architecture. Late eighteenth-century Harford blazed as a "hot-bed of radical politics. Its populace had shown overwhelming support for the Revolution";[4] after the war, its leaders, such as Dr. John Archer (discussed in more detail below), always voted the straight Jeffersonian ticket.

Mention of Dr. Archer—to say nothing of Jefferson himself—accurately implies that these aesthetic and political revolutionaries formed the elite of the new nation. They could read and write when most of their neighbors could not, and they possessed large private libraries as well. And books, it cannot be overstressed, formed the foundation for Georgian architecture. John Harris, among the leading international architectural historians of the post–World War II era, has deemed architectural books "crucial to the development" of this new style. Georgian building, wrote Harris, did not come about "by immaculate conception! It was conceived by a form of what we would today call system building . . . [and] the frequent repetition of motifs in Bristol, Dublin, and Philadelphia was most likely due to the availability of the same pattern books."[5] Throughout the English-speaking world, where eager builders were numerous but architects few, design for high-style buildings was largely drawn from such tomes as *A Book of Architecture* and *Rules for Drawing the Several Parts of Architecture* (both by James Gibbs, 1728 and 1732) and *Rural Architecture* (Robert Morris, 1750). These publications—and hundreds of others—were filled with clearly engraved plates that made it easy for a patron to select and a work-

2. One scholar frets about the impracticality of such stairs, noting that "ease of ascent . . . was more than counterbalanced by the additional space they occupied." Ibid., 118; suffice it to say in response, economic determinism does not always hold true in the arts.

3. Mark Girouard, in his *Life in the English Country House* (New Haven: Yale University Press, 1979), notes that around 1650 "the problem of how to fit the main staircase into a symmetrical plan was solved by putting it in the great hall. This made the hall an unsuitable room for meals . . . [and] the hall became a superb room of entry and a proud means of ascent or introduction to the parlor and great chamber" (123).

4. William O. Carr, "Gabriel Christie: Harford's Jeffersonian Congressman," *Harford Historical Bulletin* (Spring 1992): 54.

5. John Harris, "The Pattern Book Phenomenon," in di Valmarana, ed., *Building by the Book* 2, 101.

man to copy *X* door surround or *Y* fireplace or *Z* cornice. And as Gibbs wrote in the preface to his *Book of Architecture,* these engravings proved especially valuable "in the remote parts of the Country, where little or no assistance for Designers can be procured."

Mount Pleasant and Sophia's Dairy Herald the New Age

A new era had dawned in American architecture just as surely as a new day had dawned in American politics. And if the blaring horns of the *Eroica* symphony would soon sound the triumphant beginning of a new era in Western music, so did the open stair and center hall boldly and proudly proclaim a new direction in Western architecture. Jacob Giles, perhaps the first in Harford to respond to the stirring notes, arrived in the county around 1730 with a sharp business sense and hazy antecedents. His full story appears in chapter 4; here it is enough to state that after making a bundle in the risky worlds of land speculation and iron smelting he used that money to build Mount Pleasant, a c. 1760 five-bay Georgian mansion situated in a 1,300-acre park outside what is now Havre de Grace. According to the 1798 federal tax assessors, the house (which was destroyed around 1905) had "4 rooms and a passage on each floor" and "hath been built near 40 years." That passage, a wide hall that "ran through the center of the house," contained "the main feature at the mansion . . . the stairway," and the stair, with its walnut handrail, "broad tread [and] easy rise . . . really was a fine work of art."[6] Mount Pleasant also may have introduced two other pivotal elements of Georgian design to Maryland; c. 1900 photographs of the stairhall show a magnificent Chinese Chippendale stair railing and, in the second-floor hall, a Palladian window. These elements would soon become reduced to Georgian-era clichés, but in 1760 they epitomized all the new, the bold, the *revolutionary.*

In the first movement of *Eroica,* the stirring notes of the strings are quickly picked up by the rest of the orchestra. In Harford County the hammering of the workmen on Mount Pleasant's stair had barely quieted when new pounding began to fill the air. These hammering sounds came from the venerable Hall family's tract of land known as Sophia's Dairy; more specifically, they came from "five redemptioners, two of whom were masons, two carpenters, and one a laborer," who were at work on a new house. Like George Alsop a century earlier, these redemptioners were Englishmen who had indentured themselves to an American master for a specific period of time in return for passage across the Atlantic. By fulfilling their contract they *redeemed* themselves of their debt and gained their freedom. Alsop plowed fields and traded furs to work off his time; the anonymous crew at Sophia's Dairy designed and erected a mansion and "when the building was finished, received their freedom for their reward."[7]

They certainly earned it. Sophia's Dairy is an artistic landmark by any standard and has been recognized as such virtually since it was completed in 1768. In 1984 faculty from the University of Maryland studied the house and peppered their account of it with the respectful adjectives "extraordinary" and "remarkable" and "elegant"; sixty years earlier Swepson Earle deemed the house "remarkably fine" in his *Chesapeake Bay Country,* and those precise words were used to describe the house even fifty years before *that.* Travel back two more generations to the Revolution. Sophia's Dairy is brand-new and its builders, Aquila and Sophia Hall, have just moved in. Sophia's sister has just married Robert Morris, the "Financier of the Revolution," who is sometimes in Philadelphia playing host ("George Washington," Morris wrote to a daughter, "is now our guest") and is sometimes in Maryland where he is a guest at "the mansion of Mr. Hall."[8]

The Halls built their "extraordinary" "elegant" house on land Sophia had inherited from her father, Thomas White, a London-born lawyer who had come to Maryland in 1720 in the retinue of Charles Calvert, governor of the colony (18). White quickly amassed some 7,772½ acres in what is now Harford County and, having made his fortune in Maryland, he abandoned the Chesapeake and moved to Philadelphia in 1745. Daughter Sophia (born 1731), however, remained a Marylander and when she chose to marry her Harford County first cousin, Aquila Hall (born 1727), she brought "more than 3,200

Jacob Giles's c. 1760 Mount Pleasant, shown here c. 1890, marks the coming of the neoclassical revolution to Harford County. (The house was demolished in the early twentieth century.)

6. *Harford County Directory* (1953), 320.

7. Earle, *Chesapeake Bay Country,* 241.

8. Ibid.; Wiltbank et al., *Descendants of White,* 29–30, 62, 63.

acres" to the marriage as part of her dowry and the couple built their new house on a part of that land.[9]

And that house, measuring 64 by 45 feet, effectively marks how thoroughly the Halls had embraced the new architecture. Simply compare it to the family's earlier seat, Cranberry. True, Cranberry's story and a half height made it large in its day, but Sophia and Aquila would have been the first to point out that that day had passed. Nor would Aquila and Sophia have wished to be reminded of those rough-and-tumble times. When Cranberry was new the county courts were filled with cases such as one involving "lame John Howard" who "killed a rattlesnake in the branches of Deer Creek and took out its heart and swallowed it." Shortly after that occurrence, an election was held in the county but the voting had to be postponed because one candidate "made many of the local voters drunk, not capable of giving their vote with prudence." The makeup election proved even worse, for it was characterized by "street fights in which two persons were killed."[10] Aquila and Sophia Hall would have had no patience with such carryings-on. "Swallowed its heart," one can almost see Sophia White Hall shuddering in genteel horror; "too drunk to vote," one can see Aquila's disgust at such foolishness—those people didn't have self-government and didn't deserve to.

And self-government was important to Sophia and Aquila Hall. Indeed, no countians were more actively and intimately involved in the patriot cause than they. One of seven men selected to govern Harford when the county was formed in 1773, Aquila owned the brick tavern in Bush that served as the new county's first courthouse. In 1774 he chaired a meeting held in the tavern when countians voted to support the recent revolutionary actions taken in Boston. As treasurer of the County War Committee (charged to gather funds "for the relief of . . . Boston or for the purchase of arms and ammunition for the defense of our Lives, Liberties, and Properties"), Aquila later chaired another meeting in his tavern when thirty-four Harford men signed the Bush Declaration, that cry for self-government that anticipated Jefferson's more famous document by some fourteen months. And when the Revolution finally exploded, Aquila "organized a militia company and was elected [its] captain [in] 1775." Promoted to colonel in 1776, White, upon hearing of Washington's struggles at Valley Forge, led a caravan of wheat-laden horses to

The original Chinese Chippendale stair at Mount Pleasant as photographed c. 1890 (left); much of the eighteenth-century woodwork was saved and reused at the "new" Mount Pleasant (right).

9. Papenfuse et al., *Biographical Dictionary,* 380. This has given rise to the often repeated tale, amusing if apocryphal, that the land was originally called Sophia's Dowry and that Harford's citizens, unfamiliar with such elegant terms, changed the name to something they understood, hence Sophia's Dairy. If so, the change antedated the Sophia White/Aquila Hall marriage since John Hall's will, probated in 1737, refers to Sophia's Dairy.

10. Wright, *Harford,* 54, 55.

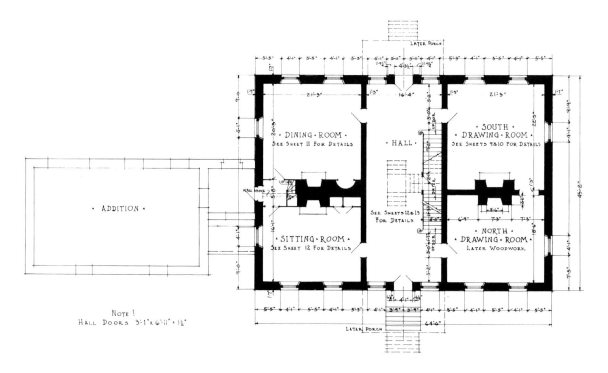

NOTE !
HALL DOORS 3'-1" x 6'-11" x 1½"

When completed in 1768, Sophia's Dairy, measuring roughly 65 feet by 45 feet, was easily the largest dwelling in this part of the state. Of note, too, are the house's regular, balanced plan and—especially—the grand through stairhall.

11. Papenfuse et al., *Biographical Dictionary,* 380; Sarah Wright, "Sophia's Dairy Awaits the Annual Pilgrimage," *Baltimore Evening Sun,* May 1, 1962.

12. Papenfuse et al., *Biographical Dictionary,* 380.

13. Wiltbank et al., *Descendants of White,* 34.

14. *Webster's New International Dictionary of the English Language,* W. T. Harris, editor-in-chief, (Springfield, Mass.: G. and C. Merriam Company, 1910), 227.

15. White, on being reminded that "the Bible called women the weaker vessel," responded, "Yes, as Sèvres is weaker than common crockery." Thomas White file, HSHC.

that encampment to ease the troops' distress. When he returned to Maryland some of his neighbors asked him why he wasn't given payment for the grain; he quietly answered, "I didn't ask for it."[11]

Sophia White Hall, pursuant to the standards of behavior of the times, confined her revolutionary activities to her family—but what a family! Her sister Mary (died 1827), recall, married Robert Morris, financier of the American Revolution, member of the Continental Congress, signer of the Declaration of Independence, and member of the U.S. Senate.[12] The sisters' half-brother William (born 1747) spent a bouncy, high jinx–filled youth (in 1765, for example, he and "Benjamin Franklin . . . assisted Miss Betty Shewell to elope . . . in order to marry Benjamin West"), but he eventually settled on a career in the church and in 1770 sailed to England to complete his religious education. In London he also found time to make "a happy . . . and pleasant circle of friends" and numbered Samuel Johnson and Oliver Goldsmith among his cronies.[13] On his return to Philadelphia he took up the pulpit at Christ Church until members of the Continental Congress asked him to serve as their chaplain; he accepted and retained that post throughout the war. After America had won its independence, White helped organize the Protestant Episcopal Church in the United States of America and in 1782 was selected as that new sect's first bishop, an office that "according to the episcopalian theory is held in direct succession from the apostles."[14] Perhaps. But if White did credit to his miter, he also retained much of his boyish enthusiasm. A posthumous account describes him as being "fond of society . . . [and] dancing" with an eye for the ladies and a weakness for good port and strong cigars. "He deeply deplored the evils of [religious] extremism" and continuously worked to stamp out any form of intolerance. When this beloved bon vivant died in Philadelphia in 1836, "there was a general suspension of business. . . . This was the first time . . . the flags of the city and of the shipping were placed at half-mast for a private citizen."[15]

Not for this generation the primitive, repressive politics of colonists; not for this generation the backward-looking folk architecture of their ancestors. Aquila and Sophia demanded something different from the gambrel-roofed Cranberry. And they got it with Sophia's Dairy. Gone is Cranberry's folk paneling. In its place Aquila and Sophia Hall

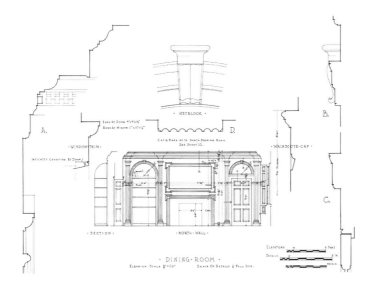

Compare the highly correct 1768 neoclassical paneling of the Hall family's Sophia's Dairy (shown in this c. 1935 drawing) with the decidedly folk c. 1740s paneling at same family's Cranberry.

crowned all rooms with the cornices thick in profile and bold with dentils; they gave the main rooms such elaborate pilastered fireplaces and such deep, crossetted window seats that these openings visually jump from the walls. Gone, too, is Cranberry's unbalanced, two-room plan. Sophia's Dairy spreads its four rooms per floor evenly and symmetrically around a center stairhall that, at 16 feet wide and 45 feet deep, ranks as one of the grandest such spaces in eighteenth-century America. Grand? Of course, it's grand: the Halls were grand—why shouldn't their hallway be, too? Emphatically gone is Cranberry's closeted winder staircase. To take its place Sophia and Aquila created what may be the spectacular house's finest feature, its unique and much-lauded hanging double stair. "Imperial in concept," exclaimed the University of Maryland professors, "two ranges of stairs converge from either end of the hall, a second short flight crosses the hall space, and then the stairs again diverge, running parallel to the main flight until they reach the upper floor."[16]

All this—the plan, the pilasters, the cornices, the stair—combines to create an interior able to hold its own with anything mid-eighteenth-century America can offer. To illustrate how up to date the Halls were, they completed Sophia's Dairy in 1768, when Annapolis glittered as Maryland's capital. The Upton Scott House, "the first great house of the city's [Annapolis's] golden age,"[17] dates to the 1760s. Three future signers of the Declaration of Independence were also building themselves neoclassic Annapolis residences in that decade (William Paca finished his in 1765, Samuel Chase began his in 1769, and Charles Carroll of Carrollton completed his in 1770) and work began on the new state house (and postrevolutionary national capitol) in 1772. When the Halls built Sophia's Dairy, Washington, D.C., didn't exist because the United States didn't exist and Baltimore was little more than a struggling village.

Eventually, Aquila's and Sophia's strenuous lives caught up with them: he died in 1779, she followed in 1785. Of their nine children the eldest, Thomas (born 1750), inherited Sophia's Dairy.[18] He was living there in 1798 when taxmen made their rounds through the county and noticed his "60 × 47 2-story brick house," his 1,149 acres, and his thirty-nine slaves. (To keep things in perspective, all thirty-nine slaves huddled in two buildings, each "19 × 16 wood.") In 1862 the Citizen's Bank of Baltimore, charged

16. Mary A. Dean, William Voss Elder III, John W. Hill, and David P. Fogle, *Three Hundred and Fifty Years of Art and Architecture in Maryland* (College Park: University of Maryland, 1984), 110.

17. Trostel, "Annapolis Plan," 8.

18. Will ALJ2/280, filed in the Orphans' Court of Harford County, Bel Air.

with selling Sophia's Dairy, printed a two-page circular describing the "large and handsome BRICK MANSION long known on the Records of Harford County, Maryland as the DAIRY . . . , [a] PARADISE . . . of such peculiar beauty that it needs but to be seen to be appreciated." This estate, older than the nation its builders helped bring into being, proudly and with *Eroica*-like clarity summoned Harford countians to leave their colonial folk houses and join in the Georgian revolution.

The "Generic Georgian" Aesthetic

No one has found a design source for Sophia's Dairy; no one knows what inspired the Halls (or those redemptionists). The building's Maryland peers, such as Annapolis's Brice House, have been noted and visual evidence suggests links between Sophia's Dairy's woodwork and that at certain houses in Virginia, notably Shirley (whose interior dates from the 1770s) and Wilton (completed in 1753). Had the Halls seen these places and copied them? Did all the builders use the same pattern book? Those questions cannot be answered with certainty. For now, the safest thing to say is that the owners of Sophia's Dairy, Wilton, and Shirley shared what might be called a "generic Georgian" aesthetic. And as suggested, the reason for this communality of thought can be given in a single word: *books*. If people like Aquila and Sophia Hall fueled America's political revolution, books fueled the simultaneous architectural revolution.

It is easy enough to see Harford County examples of this shared, book-based design sense. One need only glance down the post road from Sophia's Dairy to the house Benjamin Rumsey built in Joppa. Although Rumsey's house cannot be as securely dated as Sophia's Dairy (the Halls placed a datestone high in their house's west gable and Rumsey didn't), historian Albert C. Ritchie has offered one plausible construction scenario. He noted that members of the Maxwell family built an early house on the site and that an ambitious Benjamin Rumsey married a Maxwell heiress in 1768, thereby acquiring the Joppa house. All that is fact. Ritchie then surmised that Rumsey marked this happy turn in his life by enlarging the earlier humble dwelling. Ritchie's theory seems arguable: building a big house is certainly a time-honored way men celebrate their union with heiresses. Moreover, certain physical details of the Joppa building suggest the 1760s and specifically suggest the Halls' mansion. For example, both structures have center-hall plans (rare in the county at the time) and both display similar and locally unusual construction methods and ornament motifs. Taking this hypothesis a step further, one wonders if perhaps the two structures were built by the same workmen using the same pattern books.[19]

Unfortunately, specific proof for any of this is lacking. While it is known that both Rumsey and the Halls owned large libraries, there is no record of the specific titles on their shelves. For instance, in 1808, after Rumsey had died and his personal property was being valued, appraisers cited four bookcases in the Joppa house and "a number of Miscellaneous Books, $20"; they also jotted down "Library, $100," a disconcerting throwaway line indeed, for in 1808 $100 represented *a lot* of books since one could buy a small house in the county for that sum. (In fact, the 1798 tax assessors valued one Peregrine Brown's frame house in Abingdon at precisely $100.50.)

Regardless of what their private libraries contained, both Rumsey and the Halls had easy access to several of the earliest and largest public and private libraries in America, nearly all of which kept a few architectural pattern books on their shelves. They also had access to some of American's earliest documented booksellers as well, most notably the firm of Wallace, Davidson and Johnson, who opened for business in Annapolis in 1771, who are known to have encouraged their clients to buy one of the many available translations of the writings of Andrea Palladio (the eighteenth century's favorite Italian Renaissance architect), and who numbered among these c. 1770 clients Nathaniel Ramsay of Cecil and Harford counties. (Ramsay's daughter Sophia established Monmouth Farm near Emmorton in the 1830s and named the estate to commemorate her father's great Revolutionary War moment, the Battle of Monmouth.) In addition, many countians

19. Historian John Scharff has in fact written that "one workman made the details [at both houses] with the same tools." John Scharff, notes on Rumsey House at the Historic American Buildings Survey, Library of Congress.

A NARRATIVE HISTORY OF HARFORD COUNTY

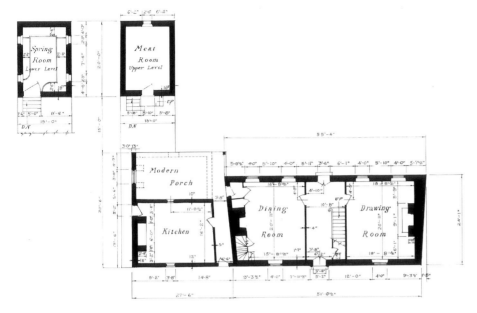

Rumsey House, Joppa: it is likely that Benjamin Rumsey incorporated the original dwelling here (marked "dining room" on this c. 1935 drawing) into his 1768 mansion—note especially how the rhythm of winder corner stair/closet/fireplace/ closet evokes folk houses such as Cranberry. Rumsey remodeled and expanded the old house to achieve a balanced plan, such as Sophia's Dairy's.

availed themselves of the "Philadelphia book-market" and "evidence of the close contact with Philadelphia is the fact that many . . . [Marylanders] subscribed to the *Pennsylvania Gazette*"; not only that, but when Benjamin Franklin scoured Maryland in 1754 to find two "agents to collect the annual subscriptions" to that paper, one of the pair chosen was William Young of Joppa.[20]

Those more interested in borrowing books than buying them were not left out. Maryland had been home to several circulating libraries at least as early as 1762, when William Rind of Annapolis established "a circulating library for the whole colony," perhaps the first such venture in America. (New York's circulating library dates to 1763, Boston's to 1765 [115].) Baltimoreans started their own public library in 1773 "and by 1790 at least three had been established" in that city (129). Libraries spread out to the hinterland, too, and the July 28, 1763, issue of the *Maryland Gazette* makes reference to "the Bohemia Library" in "Caecil County." Something along those lines may have existed in Harford as well, for Rumsey's estate papers make provocative reference to "1 Share in the Havre de Grace Library."

Rumsey's actions in Joppa—enlarging an earlier dwelling with (or without) the aid of one of the era's popular builder's guides—set the pattern for many other Georgian revolutionaries throughout the county, from the headwaters of the Bush River, where another Aquila Hall (not Sophia's husband) remodeled the house Poplar Hill around 1800, to the hills north of Deer Creek, where one finds two of the best-known remade revolutionary residences, the Rigbie House and Deer Park.

James Rigbie III (1720–90) inherited his house and land in 1752 on the death of his father, Nathaniel (born 1695). Nathaniel had moved to the Deer Creek Valley from Anne Arundel County around 1732 and his rolling, fertile fields (tended by his twenty-two slaves) yielded bountiful crops of tobacco, which he sent to London in his own ships from his own wharves at Lapidum. He also ran a store, and that trading post grew into Darlington. He and the Halls were the richest, most influential citizens of prerevolutionary Harford County; the lords Baltimore recognized them as such and showered both families with appointed offices. (They took turns, for example, serving as sheriff of the county, "which office carried with it dignity and importance second to none.")[21] The families

20. Joseph Towne Wheeler, "Booksellers and Circulating Libraries in Colonial Maryland," *Maryland Historical Magazine* 34 (June 1939): 111, 133–37.
21. Mason, *Sketches*, 48.

It seems likely that when James Rigbie inherited his father, Nathaniel's, dwelling in 1752 he replaced the original closeted stair with the grand one shown here and added the well-proportioned paneling.

The Rigbie House near Darlington, photographed c. 1935. Like the Rumsey House, it probably combines an early eighteenth-century dwelling and a late eighteenth-century remodeling.

22. His estate inventory is filed in the Maryland Hall of Records and among the more interesting items listed therein is "1 old backgammon table without men, boxes, or dice," valued at 4 shillings.

23. See Barbara W. Tuchman, *The First Salute* (New York: Ballantine Books, 1988), 269.

24. Preston, *History,* 141.

also entered into various business enterprises together, such as Cumberland Forge on Deer Creek, established in a three-way partnership of John Hall, Rigbie, and Mount Pleasant's Jacob Giles. All this gave Nathaniel a net worth of about £7,000, an eyebrow-raising figure for that rough-and-tumble time in Maryland.[22] He used some of these funds to construct the building now known as the Rigbie House.

But structural evidence suggests that James completely remodeled his father's house after he succeeded his father as de facto lord of the manor on the old man's death in 1752. Nathaniel's house probably had a folk form, with a single large room dominated by a massive fireplace and set off by a closet, an enclosed stair, and paneled walls—in other words, it probably looked very much like the houses discussed in chapter 2, the Halls' Cranberry, the Websters' Broom's Bloom, the Norrises' Prospect. This didn't appeal to James, who thus began building. For example, he added more paneling to the main room and the panels he added display distinct classical inspiration. He also gave the stair and the fireplace complete Georgian makeovers: while he did not change the location of the fireplace, he did make its opening smaller and its design more elegant. (Heavy masonry supports in the cellar show just how much larger the original fireplace was.) He also removed the original cupboard and winder stair and put double-hung sash windows in their place: the closet disappeared altogether while James placed his new, enlarged stair out in the open so that all could see and admire its walnut rail, carved step ends, turned balusters, and well-proportioned paneling.

It was James's house that played host in April 1781 to one of the county's more momentous events. Washington had ordered Lafayette to take a detachment of troops south to join General Green in Virginia. In his memoirs, Lafayette described how his men had to make "a diabolic crossing"[23] across the rocky, bitter-cold Susquehanna near Bald Friar. On gaining the Harford shore, they pitched camp in the fields around Rigbie's house. Wet and exhausted, ill-clad, ill-fed, shoeless, and unpaid, many troops threatened to desert; others threatened outright mutiny. Lafayette and his officers held a council of war in James Rigbie's house, and the resulting proclamations quelled the incipient uprising.[24] (Coincidentally at the same time Lafayette issued his proclamation, a local miller, accused of selling flour to the British, was hanged; it would be futile to try and determine whether actions or words—the hanging or the speech—spoke more loudly that April morning.) In any event, the mutiny was over and another Harford County building earned its niche in history.

Deer Park and the "Mass House"

Yet of all these Harford countians, neither Hall at Poplar Hill nor Rumsey in Joppa nor Rigbie in Darlington participated in the Georgian revolutions more vigorously than Ignatius Wheeler II (c. 1744–93) of Deer Park. And for complex reasons, none of these men benefited more from the era's political revolutions than Wheeler, either. Wheeler's library could not compare to Rumsey's (inventoried on his death, it contained "the Bible in 3 Volumes," one old Bible, "1 Family Dispentory" [Dispensery?], and "1 Dictionary"). While that collection might seem scanty today, it was a typical planter's library in Georgian-era Maryland, when "three-quarters of" such collections held "less than ten volumes."[25] Actually, that Wheeler owned any books at all is somewhat remarkable for he was probably illiterate and signed his legal documents with an "X."

Even so, Wheeler had family connections from the Potomac to the Susquehanna which placed him, if possible, on an even more exalted level of American society than the Halls. His grandfather Benjamin Wheeler settled near Hickory around 1715 on a tract he patented and called Wheeler's and Clark's Contrivance.[26] He then contrived to acquire more and more land until, at the time of his death in 1741, he owned 2,215 acres. This fiefdom passed in succession to his son and grandson, Ignatius I and II. Either Benjamin or Ignatius I began the house called Deer Park (their work forms the eastern two rooms in the present dwelling), but it was left to Ignatius II to expand that first house into the present mansion, among the oldest surviving frame examples of full-blown Georgian design in the South. Deer Park contains a virtual catalog of period architectural thinking: a balanced plan with two rooms to each side of a broad center stairhall, a magnificent open stair with turned balusters and scrolled step ends, and rooms trimmed with modillioned cornices, arched corner cupboards with pilasters and keystones, and classically proportioned paneled wainscoting.

In sum, Deer Park's ties to Georgian architecture seem self-evident. What is less easy to see, but no less important, is Ignatius's deep involvement in the political issues of the day, specifically with the revolutionary concept of freedom of religion. The Wheelers were staunch Roman Catholics who, according tradition, held church services in Deer Park's parlor because English law forbade the celebration of mass except in private houses.[27] This codified second-class status became intolerable to Ignatius II, who consequently became one of Harford's leading revolutionary patriots. In 1774 he subscribed to the Association of Freemen of Maryland and, in 1775, represented Harford in the convention convened in Annapolis to create a new government. During the war he volunteered for duty and was commissioned a lieutenant in the army.[28]

The Treaty of Paris officially ended the war with England in 1783 and county Catholics did not drag their feet in exercising the religious freedom they had just won. In 1786 they established St. Ignatius Church near Hickory, the oldest church in the archdiocese of Baltimore and "Colonel Ignatius Wheeler . . . was largely responsible for its founding."[29] Wheeler hired the stonemason for the new church (one Jack Reardon) and purportedly agreed to pay all the construction costs. He died before the church was finished (which led to some fiscal fireworks between his heirs and Bishop John Carroll), but he is remembered in the new building's name; it was christened "in honor of Col. Ignatius Wheeler's patron saint."[30] Wheeler and his wife, Henrietta Maria, are buried at St. Ignatius and Wheeler tombstones abound in the church's graveyard. (The most eye-catching of all may belong to Benjamin Wheeler, Ignatius's brother; carved by the Italian sculptor Capellano in the shape of a truncated obelisk, it is embellished with a number of symbols chiseled on the side.)[31]

The English anti-Catholicism that forced the Wheelers to celebrate the mass in Deer

The Wheeler family's Deer Park, c. 1930. Like the Rumsey House in Joppa, this symmetrical mid-eighteenth-century dwelling probably incorporates an older folk structure. Many feel that the notable exterior chimney stacks, which resemble those seen at houses in Charles and St. Mary's counties, suggest the family's southern Maryland origins.

25. Joseph Towne Wheeler, "Reading Interests of Maryland Planters and Merchants," *Maryland Historical Magazine* 37 (March 1942): 26.

26. Wheeler's patent describes the land as being "in the Woods, east of a branch called Green Spring Creek, which descends . . . eventually into the Susquehanna River." Patent EE 6/323.

27. The only cash bequest in Benjamin Wheeler's last will and testament was £5 "unto the clergy that Buries me, being a Roman Catholic." Will 22/436, Maryland Hall of Records.

28. Papenfuse et al., *New Guide,* 81.

29. Wright, *Harford,* 224.

30. *Portrait and Biographical Record,* 324. Wheeler also profited materially from the war by purchasing roughly 900 acres of land confiscated from British loyalists. When he died in 1793 he owned 3,020 acres, divided into three tracts, Home Place, Belle Farm, and Garden Spot.

31. Untitled clipping from the *Baltimore Sun,* February 6, 1952; in files of Harford County Department of Planning and Zoning.

Highly correct paneling at Deer Park: compare these pilasters, well-proportioned wainscotting, and modillion cornice to folk paneling at Cranberry.

32. Alsop, *Character,* 43–44.

33. John McGrain, "Priest Neale, His Mass House and His Successors," *Maryland Historical Magazine* (September 1967): 255.

34. Maryland's Catholics understandably felt a sense of betrayal, not to say entrapment. Charles Carroll, father of Charles Carroll of Carrollton, actually began negotiating with the French court with a view of securing a grant of land in French-held Louisiana; he wrote his son, the future Signer, who was then at school in Europe, "From what I have said, I leave you to judge whether Maryland be a tolerable residence for a Roman Catholic. Were I younger, I would certainly quit it" and move to France or Spain. See Charles H. Metzger, S.J., *Catholics and the American Revolution* (Chicago: Loyola University Press, 1962), 77–78.

35. Baltimore County deed TB No. C/465.

36. He even had charge, it seems, of the Carrolls' chapel at Doughoregan when the family couldn't find or keep a regular chaplain; McGrain, "Priest Neale," 260.

37. Quoted in Metzger, *Catholics,* 146.

38. Maggie Bunson, *Founding of Faith* (Boston: The Daughters of St. Paul, 1977), 185.

39. John Shea, *The Catholic Church in Colonial Days* (New York: privately printed, 1886), 18.

40. Metzger, *Catholics,* 97; Joseph J. Kelly Jr., *Life and Times in Colonial Philadelphia* (Harrisburg, Pa.: Stackpole Books, 1973), 146.

Park's parlor and that moved Ignatius II to political revolution also produced what may be the most historically important building in Harford County, the one-story, c. 1743, stuccoed-stone structure known as Priest Neale's Mass House. The little building, stalwartly poised atop a hillock overlooking Deer Creek near Priest's Ford, is as firmly rooted in the Georgian era as it is to its hill, since it is entirely a product of the society and the laws of the time. Yet it shares none of the "communal aesthetic" mentioned above; in fact, the Mass House shares nothing with any house anywhere and is thought to be unique in America: not rare, not unusual—unique.

Maryland, of course, had been settled in the 1630s by the Catholic Calvert family as a multidenominational haven; the experiment enjoyed early success and drew praise even from staunch seventeenth-century Anglicans, such as George Alsop, who wrote, "Here the *Roman Catholick,* and the *Protestant Episcopal,* . . . concur in an unanimous parallel of friendship and inseparable love."[32] But that paradise ended when William and Mary were swept to power in the Glorious Revolution of 1688–89. Their Parliament promulgated a series of laws that discriminated against Roman Catholics in virtually every possible way: Catholics were prohibited from holding office, from serving in the army, from being educated in their faith, and so on. Dancing to these Parliament-piped tunes, the "Maryland General Assembly in October 1704, passed a law to 'prevent the growth of popery within the province,' imposing a £50 fine on any popish priests, bishops, or Jesuits exercising their function or making converts."[33] When Queen Anne succeeded William and Mary, she modified her predecessors' legislated intolerance somewhat and decreed that priests could celebrate mass—but only in private houses. Exceptionally wealthy Catholics, including the Howard family in England and the Carroll family in Maryland, built actual chapels as part of their dwellings. Most worshipers, however, depended on circuit-riding missionaries.[34]

One such circuit dates to March 14, 1743, when John Digges, a Maryland-born, European-trained Jesuit, bought a tract of land on the south bank of Deer Creek and established the Mission of Saint Joseph on Paradice Plantation.[35] Digges used this land as a base from which he could set forth to attend to his flock.[36] He also remodeled the pre-existing house so it might better serve its unusual ecclesiastical role. Thus he gave it an unusually wide central hall, twin, 11-foot-square chambers to the west, and a single reception room to the east. The small cells and the reception room had fireplaces and Digges and his fellow priests used these heated spaces as bedrooms and living room, respectively, and held services in the large, unheated hall.

Nothing like this building exists anywhere else in America because the condition of Maryland Catholics was not duplicated anywhere else. Of all the colonies, only Maryland and Pennsylvania had any detectable Catholic population. There were few Catholics in the northeast; John Adams boasted that a New Englander "who cannot read or write is as rare an appearance as a Jacobite or a Roman Catholic, that is, as rare as . . . an earthquake,"[37] and John Jay proposed that the flag for New York State bear "the simple legend: 'No Popery!'"[38] Fewer still lived in Virginia and the South, where they were "degraded below the Negro slave, for though the Negro . . . could not be a witness against a white person, a Catholic could not be put on the stand as a witness against a white man or black" in Virginia.[39] Yet of the two colonies with any sizable Catholic population, only the Quakers in Pennsylvania practiced any tolerance toward Catholics. Ironically, in the eighteenth century it was better to be a Catholic in the colony of the Quaker Penns than in the colony of the Catholic Calverts: "While Catholics were less numerous than in Maryland, their lot was much happier," partially because "Pennsylvania ignored the edict of William III prohibiting the public celebration of the Mass, as it was inclined to ignore most royal proclamations."[40]

Digges's Deer Creek tenure ended when he died "'in Baltimore' in 1746 at the age of 34." He willed all his estate, real and personal, "to my well-beloved friend, Mr. Bennett Neale," born in 1709 and scion of one of Maryland's most influential families. Bennett's

Priest Neale's Mass House in 1888, a missionary outpost built by eighteenth-century Roman Catholic priests. The original hipped roof and overall proportions of this c. 1743 stuccoed stone dwelling have led many to believe that the priests (John Digges and Bennett Neale) drew inspiration for this building from structures they had known in their schooldays in rural France. It certainly doesn't look like any other known 1740s house in Harford County.

grandfather James Neale divided his time between America and Spain, where he represented Britain's royal family in "different capacities"; his aunt was, by family tradition, a goddaughter and namesake of Charles I's wife, Queen Henrietta Maria, and Henrietta Maria Neale "probably vies with . . . Margaret Brent for the distinction of being the most famous woman of early Maryland."[41]

Young Bennett had been sent abroad for his education, as was the custom among America's well-to-do Catholic families, and in 1728 he entered St. Omer's, a Jesuit school in Flanders. He "went on to study philosophy at Louvain, and theology at Liege,"[42] as had Digges, and several historians have seen in the Mass House's original hipped roof and stuccoed walls a more than passing resemblance to the sort of French farmhouses the young men knew from those schooldays abroad.[43]

When Neale got to Deer Creek he proved to be a bit of an entrepreneur. In 1750 he bought a long, narrow, eighteen-acre strip of land that meanders easterly along the shores of the creek. Here the young priest built a gristmill and millrace and his account book shows that his mill—perhaps "the first mill in the region"[44]—quickly became a booming operation, grinding grain for farmers throughout the valley. Neale used his profits to fund his religious endeavors. (Or some of these profits; often he was paid in kind, not in cash, e.g., "May 1765. Sent Hicks 20 bu sprouted wheat and 10 bu rye for which he paid me my share of whiskey, about 27 gallons.")[45] Neale kept up his missionary work at the Mass House for nearly twenty years, a quiet, satisfying existence punctuated by an occasional crisis or two. One such came in 1756, during the French and Indian War, when Neale and his neighbor Ignatius Wheeler II were arrested as "persons ill affected to His Majesty's Person and Government" and brought to Annapolis for trial. Under pressure and under oath, their accuser, one William Johnson, confessed that he had made the whole thing up—even a wonderful bit of verisimilitude about Neale passing secrets on to a one-eyed French spy—because he thought the authorities "would be pleased with my making some information against the Catholics."

Although Neale retired from his Deer Creek duties in 1773, priests continued operations at the Mass House until 1814 when Archbishop John Carroll sold the property to Dr. James Glasgow of Baltimore for $4,200.[46] By then America had broken with England,

41. McGrain, "Priest Neale," 260; J. Donnell Tilghman, "Wye House," unpublished typescript in MHS library, Baltimore, p. 93.

42. McGrain, "Priest Neale," 263–64.

43. See, for example, Charles V. Joerndt, *St. Ignatius, Hickory, and Its Mission* (Baltimore: Baltimore Publications Press, 1962), 36.

44. John McGrain, "The Molinography of Harford County," unpublished manuscript on file at the Harford County Department of Planning and Zoning, Bel Air.

45. Joerndt, *St. Ignatius,* 47.

46. Deed HD Z/255.

the Bill of Rights had been enacted, St. Ignatius Church had been established, and missions like Priest Neale's had been rendered obsolete. The memory and influence of these revolutionary Georgian-era Catholics, however, lingers on in north Harford: some of the Wheeler farms remained in the hands of Ignatius's descendants for several generations through intermarriages with the Jenkins and Rutledge families, while St. Omer's, the name of Digges's and Neale's Flemish school, is recalled in the name of a small stream that still flows north from Hickory to join Deer Creek near Sandy Hook.

From a Georgian Revolution to a Federal Republic

Harford's Georgian innovators gave the county an entirely new approach to domestic architecture—balanced floor plans, regular window arrangements, and open stairs. Moreover, this new architecture, of clean line and ordered arrangement, symbolizes the new rational, liberal, and reasonable spirit that affected virtually all other aspects of American life. And as the eighteenth century yielded to the nineteenth, the torch—as well as the drafting table, plumb line, and spackling can—passed to a new generation of Harfordians, and similar architectural dramas began to be played out during this, the county's *federal* era.

In politics, men and women of the 1780s shaped a collection of colonies to a loose confederation and, when that system of government proved unsatisfactory, kept the basic liberties intact but tweaked the rules to produce a tightly unified, constitutional federal republic. Similarly, federal-era builders kept their parents' design standards in place, but modified them. While they did not want to make as clean a break with the past as the 1760s builders had done, they did want to make enough of a break to ensure that they left their mark on the world. Put as simply as possible, they made their buildings more curvaceous and attenuated. They kept the door in the center of the façade, but replaced the earlier squared transom with a delicate fanlight. Double-hung sash windows still regularly punctuated the façades, but grew taller and more slender; sometimes rectangular openings were abandoned altogether in favor of semicircles. In plan, homeowners still favored symmetrically placed rooms, but the rooms themselves often sported rounded shapes while the trim, which continued to draw inspiration from the classical age, grew taller and thinner and blossomed with wooden and plaster garlands. A few especially ambitious builders painted wooden mantels to look like marble and grained pine doors to look like mahogany. Yet if federal-era builders added elegance and "movement" to what Georgian-era builders had kept solid and foursquare, in at least one respect they simplified what had been elaborate. In the Georgian era, stair balusters were turned and gouged to an almost contrapuntal complexity, as was seen at Sophia's Dairy; twenty years later they were reduced to slender squared posts.

Harford's most swashbuckling federal-era villas stride across the hills and islands around Havre de Grace, the county's most intensely federal-era city (see chapter 4) while the city itself boasts the county's best surviving federal-era urban dwelling, the Rodgers House at 226 North Washington Street. Dating to the 1780s and probably built either by ferry-line magnate John Rodgers or by his wife, Elizabeth, the house, with its Flemish bond brick walls, keystoned lintels, and classical window treatment (i.e., sixteen-over-sixteen panes on the ground floor; twelve-over-twelve above), is everything a federal-era townhouse ought to be and makes it the equal of "the better known houses of the eighteenth century towns along the Eastern seaboard."[47]

Yet the county's federal buildings are not restricted to that boomtown by the bay. Harford's inland regions spawned a quartet of rural residences that make all the necessary points, although they make them in a quieter way than the Havre de Grace villas do. Indeed, the gentle foursome—Col. John Streett's house near Rocks, Dr. John Archer's Medical Hall and the Reverend William Finney's Oak Farm (both near Churchville), and Dr. Joshua Wilson's Woodside near Emmorton—probably proved more influential than Havre de Grace's swaggering masterpieces such as Sion Hill, since they they were built in

The arched doorway and keystoned window lintels of the Rodgers' house (and probable tavern) at 226 North Washington Street, Havre de Grace, are hallmarks of federal-era American neoclassicism. The structure was owned by Commodore Rodgers's mother, Elizabeth; he himself lived nearby at Sion Hill.

47. James Wollon, AIA, "The Rodgers House," *Harford Historical Bulletin* (Spring 1985): 16.

a manner too elaborate and expensive for countians to emulate. The homes of Streett, Finney, Archer, and Wilson, on the other hand, were—are—of a scale countians deemed reasonable, just as the mens' occupations—a soldier, a minister, and two doctors—struck deeper, more sympathetic chords among their neighbors than those sounded by Havre de Grace's high-flying international entrepreneurs.

John Streett (1762–1836) was a son of Thomas Streett (?–1823), an Englishman who emigrated to Maryland in the early eighteenth century, moved to the wilderness north of Deer Creek, and amassed roughly 1,500 contiguous acres in the Rocks area. John continued his father's occupations of farming and land acquisition and by the time of the 1798 tax, the younger man owned 1,320 acres in his own name. These landholdings thrust him willy-nilly into a leadership role. He was regularly called on throughout the 1790s to sit on the county grand jury (more of an honor then than it sounds now) and in 1799 he was elected to what would be the first of twelve continuous terms in the Maryland legislature. No stranger to pro bono work, Streett served on the Bel Air Academy's first board of trustees, where he saw to it that the academy, incorporated in 1811 and the county's first preparatory school, had a "soundly classical curriculum."[48] When the War of 1812 broke out, Streett, "commissioned as Lieutenant Colonel of the 7th Regiment of Cavalry,"[49] left the legislature for the army. His grand moment came in 1814 when the British, having burned Havre de Grace and Washington, D.C., moved on Baltimore. To save the city, "a call was made for troops from the surrounding counties. Colonel Streett marched with his cavalry from Harford," and, "joining with Howard's troop from Baltimore County," stopped the British advance at the Battle of North Point. Maj. Gen. Samuel Smith, overall commander at the battle, commended Colonel Streett "for his bravery and efficiency in action."[50]

In the midst of this busy life Streett bought a tract of unimproved land just north of Rocks in 1801 and built himself the large, brick, federal-style dwelling now known simply as the John Streett House. The place must have been finished by 1814, because when federal tax assessors came through the county that year, they noted Streett's two-story "42 × 21" brick house; these dimensions line up nicely with those of the extant dwelling. Yet while technically accurate, the assessors' terse description does not do the place justice. Simply put, Streett created a mini-masterpiece of federal design. Note the house's crisply laid Flemish bond brick walls, corbeled brick cornices, elongated windows set off by slender muntins and rubbed brick arches, and delicately beaded mortar joints. That last feature deserves special mention since very few county house-builders (clients or masons) took the trouble to give a beaded profile to the mortar—the best-known other example occurs at Stafford, the c. 1800 stone house built by Harford's richest citizen, John Stump of Stafford and discussed in chapter 5.

The Streett house's exterior is at once just like and entirely different from the exterior of Sophia's Dairy, just as the interior, with its balanced plan and center stairhall, while of Georgian origin, is in every other respect very much of his time. Colonel Streett gave his rooms ten-foot ceilings, which combine with those tall windows to create airy spaces flooded with light, a sensation crucial to high-style federal design; moreover, the spaces themselves abound in excellent period details such as delicate chairrails, simple balusters, and a graceful, open-string stair. Finally, there is the house's *pièce de resistance,* its grained doors and marbleized mantels. Many houses once known for similar faux details have lost them (perhaps most famously Monticello—how much more federal can one get?).[51] That Streett's dark brown doors and blue-gray mantels have survived is one of Harford's happier architectural happenstances.

For nearly two centuries everyone who has examined Streett's house has remarked on its "sophisticated details,"[52] but no one has discovered what inspired Streett to create them. Some have suggested that he modeled his house on buildings he'd seen during his days as a legislator "in the fashionable city of Annapolis."[53] Perhaps. It is, however, just as easy to assume that he drew inspiration closer to home and that he was reinterpreting,

48. Larew, *Bel Air,* 28–29.

49. Wright, *Harford,* 421; see also Frederick Lee Cobourn and Brodnax Cameron Sr., *A Short Biography of Those Whose Portraits Adorn the Walls of the Court House, Bel Air* (Bel Air: privately printed, 1942), 51.

50. Preston, *History,* 226; Cobourn and Cameron, *Short Biography,* 51; Wright, *Harford,* 421. The commendation reads, in part, "Fatiguing as were the duties imposed on the United States Cavalry under Lieutenant Street[t], they were performed with alacrity and promptness highly honorable to officers and men."

51. It is documented that in March 1805 Jefferson hired one Richard Barry to come to Monticello to grain the six-panel doors there. Barry worked on the project for a year and a half and his doors were renowned throughout Virginia. Fashions change and in 1890 Monticello's then-owner had the graining painted over. Restoration is now (in 1994) underway.

52. James Wollon, AIA, notes on the Streett House, Harford County Department of Planning and Zoning.

53. Natalie Shivers, Streett House Historic Sites Survey Form, Harford County Department of Planning and Zoning.

Original marbleized mantel (detail) in the c. 1801 Col. John Streett House.

54. For that matter, Streett may have drawn inspiration for his house's massing from the Hall house called Rumney. That house has long been destroyed, but it formerly stood near Rumney (Romney) Creek on land now part of the Aberdeen Proving Ground. James Wollon described the two-part Flemish bond brick house as dating to "early in the first quarter of the nineteenth century." See *Harford Historical Bulletin* (Fall 1983): 12.

55. See George Webb Constable, "Constable," Appendix 1, unpublished manuscript in the library at George Webb Constable home, Monkton.

on a slightly smaller scale, motifs present on those newly built mansions outside Havre de Grace. Streett certainly knew those houses and anyone who had served with such distinction in America's armed services would have had easier entry to, say, Sion Hill (the villa of Streett's comrade-in-arms Commo. John Rodgers) than to the Annapolis residence of, say, Edward Lloyd V, the old-*old* monied aristocrat who presided over the state as governor while Streett sat in the legislature. But whither the inspiration doesn't really matter. What matters is that Streett created a gem.[54]

One countian who probably could have gained access to Lloyd's lair (if he'd wanted to) was Dr. John Archer. In fact, it is hard to imagine any house in America that wouldn't have been honored to receive Archer, a man who achieved more distinction in more fields than anyone who has ever lived in Harford County. He was born on the 250-acre family farm near Churchville in May 1741; his parents, Thomas and Elizabeth Stevenson Archer, sent him to the Nottingham Academy in Cecil County, where he not only received his basic education but also began a lifelong friendship with classmate Benjamin Rush. Both lads eventually went off to Princeton, where Rush received his diploma in 1760 and Archer in 1763 and where both decided to become doctors. Since America did not have a medical school in 1760, Rush sailed off to Edinburgh and was graduated with his medical degree in 1768. However, by the time Archer had left Princeton (and spent a few years dabbling at the Presbyterian ministry), a medical school had been established at the College of Philadelphia (now the University of Pennsylvania). Archer enrolled in that new school, a member of its first class. He and his classmates were graduated in 1769 and, because diplomas were awarded alphabetically, Archer received his first—the first diploma granted by an American school of medicine.

Archer returned to Harford in 1769 to begin a life "of ceaseless activity and usefulness." Since he was the only physician for miles around, Archer's professional services were in constant demand throughout northeastern Maryland. But, like his friend and colleague Rush, Archer refused to restrict himself to one field of endeavor. Since politics formed an almost visceral part of all thinking men and women in the eighteenth century, Archer and Rush immersed themselves in the revolutionary issues of their time. The latter cofounded America's first antislavery society (in 1771) and signed the Declaration of Independence; the former signed the Bush Resolution (1774) and the Bush Declaration (1775), helped write Maryland's first constitution (1776), fought in battle and attained the rank of captain, and, as noted above, was elected to the U.S. Congress, where he championed the policies of his idol, Thomas Jefferson. In the midst of all this Archer found time to take up the pen and his "prolific contributions to the medical literature of his day" (142) earned him the respect of his peers. And if all that wasn't enough, he established on the grounds of the family farm a well-regarded medical school where he trained fifty-one young men to become doctors. (That number includes all but one of his own six sons; the holdout, Stevenson, had evidently seen enough of stethoscopes and became an attorney.) Yet if Dr. Archer sounds a paragon, a man too good to be real, it is refreshing to report a few humanizing flaws: his "mind was of the combative order" and "his sarcasm, when roused, . . . [was] withering" (65).[55]

Archer not only ran his school at Medical Hall, he lived there as well, and started his healing career in one of the property's two original two-story houses. (The 1798 tax men described one of stone measuring 17 by 19 feet, and one of frame, 22 by 19.) Archer eventually decided to expand one of those early houses into a made-over federal mansion, much as James Rigbie had done to *his* father's house a bit earlier. In creating the extant stuccoed-stone structure, Archer stuck close to the design dicta of the time, for he gave the "new" Medical Hall regular massing, a center-hall plan, and an elaborate entrance with sidelights and transom, although that last Georgian-style detail seems a bit *retardataire* for one as sophisticated as Archer.

Dr. Archer died in 1810 after a long bout with rheumatism. Appraisers came through Medical Hall that June, prodding, peering, assessing. One wishes they had gone about

A NARRATIVE HISTORY OF HARFORD COUNTY

Medical Hall. Dr. John Archer (or his son) expanded an original house on the property into this grand, stuccoed stone, federal-era dwelling.

their business in an orderly fashion and had listed their findings room by room; instead, they jumbled everything together, making it impossible to get an exact sense of what the house looked like when the great man lived there. Still, it is clear he lived well, for included in the inventory are such items as a "spice mortar" and a "coffee mill," both decidedly rare in Harford County at the time, as well as the more common "1 copper still" valued at $50. (He also died owning "36 gallons Brandy, $68.") Because one didn't go into medicine to get rich in Dr. Archer's day, most federal-era physicians had to supplement their professional fees (if they could collect them) with other sources of income. Archer supplemented his with farming and his appraisers took note of "30 barrels corn," "16 bushels of buckwheat," "60 bushels of potatoes," and "28 bushels plaster of Paris" (an early fertilizer). Nevertheless, references to "medical books, $60," "1 lot of surgical instruments, $20.50," and "1 skeleton and case, $1" make his true calling clear. The doctor's last will and testament also makes his Jeffersonian love of humanity clear, for he instructed his executors to free all seven of his slaves; he also asked his heirs to go easy on those patients who still owed him money—and quite a few did, for delinquent fees amounted to a whopping £7,949, well over $500,000 in 1990s currency.

Stevenson Archer, the attorney son, eventually acquired Medical Hall. He also evidently inherited his father's flair for architecture and politics. He was elected to the state legislature (1809–11) and U.S. Congress (1811–17), and he marked Lafayette's triumphal 1824 return to America—and perhaps commemorated his father's own revolutionary activities—by decking Medical Hall out with French scenic wallpaper, replete with vignettes of the storming of the Bastille. Such papers were then wildly fashionable among America's upper crust and their "large scale, vivid color, and lively motifs . . . transformed the aspect of many early . . . interiors."[56] Scenic wallpapers like Medical Hall's regained their chic in the early 1960s when Jacqueline Kennedy installed roll after roll of similar coverings in the White House.

Only one other county house could match Medical Hall's scenic paper (Mount Pleasant; see chapter 4), just as it seems only one could match the Streett house's marbleizing. That house is Woodside, Dr. Joshua Wilson's 1823 residence near Emmorton. Wilson's great-grandfather William Wilson assembled several hundred acres in the area; he died

56. Elisabeth Donaghy Garrett, *At Home* (New York: Harry N. Abrams, 1990), 34.

Dr. John Archer's son Stevenson added this dramatic French-made scenic wallpaper to the hall of his father's Medical Hall to mark the Lafayette's 1824 return to America. Comparing this photograph, which dates to the 1930s, to the stairs at Sophia's Dairy shows how just how much federal-era builders simplified the design of stair balusters.

in 1753. Around 1770 either his son William Wilson II (1720–80) or grandson William Wilson III (1745–1819) built the Georgian-style Flemish bond brick house Gibson's Park on part of that land. This is where Joshua Wilson was born in 1797. Gibson's Park, off Wheel Road, is relevant to this history because when Joshua built Woodside, off Singer Road, he retained so many of his birthplace's essential features, such as the sidehall/double parlor plan. But if Dr. Wilson—he earned his medical degree from the University of Maryland in 1818—felt comfortable in a house with a Georgian shell, he also felt moved to embellish that shell with touches from his own time. He gave Woodside a more svelte massing than that of Gibson's Park, and in place of the turned balusters of his parents' house he chose simple, federal, squared balusters for Woodside's staircase. Similar simplifications can be seen in the new house's delicate mantles, thin chairrails, elongated beveled windows, and other trim. In all, Wilson made Woodside one of the ultimate expressions of federal design in the county.

Two important questions remain about Woodside, neither of which will probably ever be answered. First, one wonders whom Wilson employed to actually build the house, for its stone walls are laid with extraordinary finesse. (One wonders if Wilson borrowed stonemason David Hopkins, then working on houses for the Stump clan along Deer Creek, as is discussed in chapter 5.) Second, one wonders, did the scientific Dr. Wilson design Woodside himself? Or did he entrust the house to his (unknown) artisan? While most of the books that made up Wilson's extensive library remained in Woodside until 1994, their subject matter tended to be medical, not architectural. Still, the fine arts provided a highly suitable avocation for any educated gentleman of the period and it is known that Wilson took more than passing interest in the building art, for he intimately involved himself in creating St. Mary's Church, succinctly described as "the finest rural church in the diocese of Maryland"[57] (see chapter 6).

Countians did not confine their Georgian and federal-era building to houses, and several superb local churches date to the 1770–1820 period. It is interesting to see how the same aesthetic controlled the houses Harford's citizens built for themselves in this secular, rational age and the houses they built for their God. All one has to do is glance at the oldest places of worship in the county (the so-called Old Brick Baptist Church south of

57. Phoebe B. Stanton, *The Gothic Revival and American Church Architecture* (Baltimore: Johns Hopkins University Press, 1968), 289.

Jarrettsville, St. Ignatius near Hickory, St. John's in Havre de Grace, Calvary near Creswell, the Thomas Run Meetinghouse, and the Presbury Methodist Meetinghouse on the Gunpowder Neck) to see that any member of this foursquare group could easily pass for a private residence.

The oldest section of the Churchville Presbyterian Church belongs in that list of the county's federal-era churches just as its rector, the Reverend William Finney, belongs in any discussion of the county's federal-era builders. The local progenitor of one of the few families Harford countians can (and do) point to with unalloyed pride, Finney was actually a Pennsylvanian, born in Chester County in 1788.[58] He was graduated from Princeton in 1809[59] and then returned to his native soil to take up the Presbyterian ministry. While his innate talents made him a virtual overnight success above the Mason-Dixon Line in Chester County, his greatest and longest-lasting success came below the line in Harford County.

Harford's first Presbyterian congregation organized the Deer Creek Parish in 1738 and worshiped in a log structure near the creek, an odd location, indeed, since most parishioners lived near the bay. They corrected this "mistake" in 1759 when they built a new church in a more central site, near the hamlet called Herbert's Crossroads, present-day Churchville. This relocation improved matters briefly, but by the early nineteenth century things again looked bleak: the church had lost its minister and most of its communicants as well. So in 1812 two elders heard of a hot, young minister named Finney, traveled to Pennsylvania to "audition" this sensation, liked what they saw and heard, and invited him to come down to Harford and preach a trial service. He was a hit, was asked to stay, and moved south in November of 1813.

Finney immediately reversed the depressing state of things at Herbert's Crossroads by "building up a strong congregation and erecting a substantial brick church edifice," according to Dr. John M. T. Finney, who continues his ancestor's saga:

Tradition states that my grandfather . . . on his way to take charge of the church, arrived in Maryland on a very hot day. He stopped to eat his lunch under the shade of a beautiful spreading oak tree not far distant from his destination. While resting there, he was so pleased by the

58. The Finneys had been comfortably established in Chester County since Robert Finney emigrated there from Belfast in 1720, according to Dr. John M. T. Finney's memoirs, *A Surgeon's Life* (New York: Putnam's, 1940), 3, 4.

59. Finneys have flocked to Nassau Hall ever since; if there isn't a Finney undergraduate somewhere on the campus whenever this is being read, it is a fluke.

beauty of the surrounding country that he decided then and there to settle down and build a house on that spot. This he did after purchasing a large tract of land. The stone house erected by him still stands [known as Oak Farm].[60]

With its sidehall/double parlor plan and overall massing, the 2½-story, two-part Oak Farm joins the dwellings of Colonel Streett and Dr. Wilson as the finest of Harford's low-key federal residences.

Oak Farm certainly suggests that Finney had taken in what he'd seen while traveling around Philadelphia (then the largest, most sophisticated city in the country), for what he built in the fields near Herbert's Crossroads has details that are without peer in Harford County. Simply note the house's projecting stone beltcourse (built in a time and place when brick beltcourses were virtually unknown) and main door with its round-arched wooden frame, delicate, tapered pilasters, and fanlight. (That is the sort of door one would have expected to see at Medical Hall.) Yet as extraordinary as the beltcourse and door are, the house's true tour de force are the round-arched windows Finney placed on the west (road) façade. These "windows" are, in fact, false: the rector built them solely for their decorative effect, a high-style touch unique in Harford County.

What on earth inspired Finney to build Oak Farm? Houses he knew from Chester County? From Princeton? Certainly not the homes of his Herbert's Crossroads neighbors, who lived in buildings uniformly notable for their avoidance of any known architectural style. Perhaps the minister, a published author famous for "his fugitive pieces in poetry and prose,"[61] drew inspiration from a picture in a book he'd seen. One obituary noted that Finney "was a fine scholar, a man of learning and rare accomplishments, acquainted with the best English authors and classical writers."[62] And classical architects?

Finney certainly kept himself busy during the sixty years he lived in Harford County. His life as an intellectual parson bears striking similarity to the life of Jane Austen's (nearly) contemporary father.[63] The Marylander, one may now call him that, established a chapel of ease (Deer Creek Harmony Presbyterian Church) for north county Presbyterians and he reared a batch of brilliant descendants; he also entered fully into local issues for "the great pioneer of Presbyterianism in Harford County . . . encouraged all improvements, did much to advance Harford County in agriculture and the useful arts, and to elevate the tastes and habits of the people."[64] He certainly did much, through example and patronage, to "elevate the tastes" of his fellow countians in the useful art of architecture and his Oak Farm—along with the residences of Dr. Wilson, Dr. Archer, and Colonel Streett—did much to make federal design accessible to his less worldly neighbors.

The great rector retired in October of 1854. He died in 1873 and the congregation he had done so much to revive immediately set out to erect a monument to his life. Funds poured in and the parish commissioned a sculptor to fashion a memorial obelisk, which they placed directly in front of the church. When the monument was dedicated in 1874, the then-minister observed that his predecessor had been

> known and loved by fathers and sons, mothers and daughters during 60 years. Mr. Finney belongs to Harford County. . . . His memory is a trust confided to her people. . . . Mr. Finney lived for Harford County, for his people here, for the welfare of this community in temporal, moral, spiritual, and intellectual concerns.[65]

Francophilia in Harford County

Finney and Archer and Sophia Hall represent, in idealized form, the sort of people one learned in grammar school to regard as "typical" federal-era Harford countians, that is, white, educated Anglo-Saxons. But, in fact, they are not typical at all, for the county was then, as it is now, decidedly heterogeneous in its makeup. Recently, historians have begun to shed light on the county's numerous black population, both free and slave; some of these findings are discussed in chapter 5. More recently still, other historians are dis-

60. Finney, *Surgeon's Life,* 8.

61. *Portrait and Biographical Record,* 484.

62. *The Biographical Cyclopedia of Representative Men of Maryland and the District of Columbia* (Baltimore: National Biographical Publishing, 1879), 564.

63. Finney's life at Churchville is also suggestive of lives described by Kenneth Powell in the "Notes" column for the July 19, 1990, issue of the magazine *Country Life* (102–3), specifically "of George Herbert's Bemerton Rectory . . . , of Tennyson's birthplace at Somersby . . . and, of course, of the Brontes at Haworth. The Rev. Sydney Smith, appointed to the living of Foston, Yorkshire in 1806 is said to have designed a new rectory for the village."

64. *Biographical Cyclopedia,* 563.

65. Records of the Churchville Presbyterian Church, Churchville.

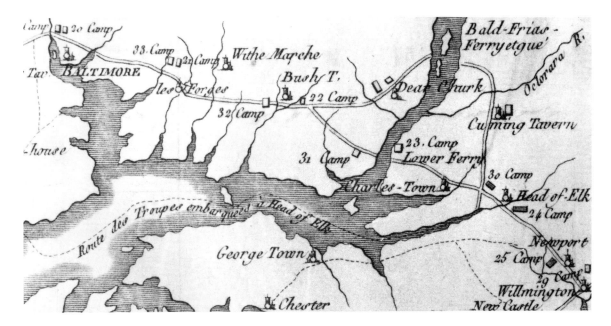

covering that the Anglo-Americans and African-Americans and Irish-Americans and Native Americans had in their midst a sizable number of Franco-Americans, most of whom moved here as a result of their own several political uprisings. First came the French Revolution, which flung an amazing and varied number of *ancien régime* types to these shores, including Louis Phillipe (a future king of France), the duc du Talleyrand, Chauteaubriand, and the duc de Rouchefoucauld. Then when the French colony of Santo Domingo (*Saint-Domingue*) erupted in slave rebellion in 1790, "several thousand" refugees fled to the "port cities of the United States. . . . By 1795, further insurrections on Saint-Domingue swelled these numbers," particularly in the southern ports of Savannah and Charleston. Baltimore gathered its share of Caribbean refugees, too, and, as one late eighteenth-century traveler noted, "since the war [American Revolution], a great many French have arrived [in Baltimore] both from France and from the West India islands."[66]

These refugees generally found a warm welcome in Maryland, where many influential citizens, including the brothers Robert and Samuel Smith, had been closet Francophiles for years. (They came running out of their closets—or *armoirs*—when Samuel Smith's niece Betsy Patterson married Napoleon's brother Jerome in 1803. Smith even named his country house Montebello to honor one of Napoleon's victories over Austria.)[67] After a few years in Baltimore to learn the difficult language and strange social customs of the new nation, a few émigrés ventured forth to the hinterland in search of homes and jobs. The city of Frederick, for example, "became a Mecca for Creole dancing masters."[68] A few brave refugees even made it up to the head of the bay, such as Jean Baptiste Aveilhe, who bought five lots in Havre de Grace in 1801. Aveilhe's deed to the property refers to him as being "of Charleston, South Carolina," but it is likely that he, like so many others, came to Charleston from Santo Domingo, for the house he built in Havre de Grace, with its concave hipped roof, stuccoed walls, and scalloped frieze, certainly suggests a Caribbean sense of design.[69]

The stucco Aveilhe used to coat his Havre de Grace cottage brings up a further important cultural point, namely, the émigrés' uniform practice of sheathing their American houses in whitewashed stucco, as if to repudiate the red-brick architecture that had dominated Anglo-American building practices. Stuccoed walls, *the* consistent leitmotif

This detail of the map made by Rochambeau's troops show the routes the French soldiers took through Maryland while going to and from Yorktown in 1781: some men were ferried down the Chesapeake from Head of Elk (note: *"Route des Troupes embarquées à Head of Elk"*); some crossed the Susquehanna at Perryville; some marched north to cross the river at Bald Friar and then marched south, via the Deer Creek Meetinghouse ("Dear Churck") to meet their comrades along the post road near Whitemarsh (*"Withe Marche"*). Two of the last group, soldiers surnamed de Gimat and Grême, became enamored of the Deer Creek Valley at Trap; after the war the pair returned to build the house Maiden's Bower.

66. Roger G. Kennedy, *Orders from France* (New York: Knopf, 1989), 143; Isaac Weld, *Travels through the States of North America* (London: J. Stockdale, 1800), 45.

67. Across the Chesapeake in Talbot County Jacob Gibson, "a well known . . . eccentric, . . . named his various estates [Jena, Marengo, and Austerlitz] after victories won by Bonaparte." See Papenfuse et al., *New Guide*, 169.

68. Walter Charlton Hartridge, "The Refugees from the Island of St. Domingo in Maryland," *Maryland Historical Magazine* 38 (June 1943): 118.

69. Deed JLG P/488. Marion Morton (now Carroll) did most of the groundwork here when she studied the architecture of Havre de Grace in 1978.

Maiden's Bower, c. 1880. As originally built by messrs. Grême and de Gimat c. 1785, the house had a hipped roof resembling the roofs at Priest Neale's Mass House and Bon Air.

of Harford's buildings with French origins, are certainly present, for example, at Maiden's Bower, a mini-château on Deer Creek with a romantic history that is locally second to none.

In 1781 two French soldiers surnamed de Gimat and Grême, while marching south with Lafayette to Virginia, climbed the hill near Trap and gazed down at the creek. "So enamored of the view" were they that "they immediately determined to buy the property and settle there" after the war so they might "end their days in happiness."[70] The astonishing thing is that they did just that. After Yorktown they returned to Harford and with funds furnished by de Gimat, "the wealthy member of the pair,"[71] bought the same 800 acres they had gazed at longingly. They then proceeded to build a stuccoed stone house on the property, which they called Maiden's Bower. They had completed their work by 1798, for the two-story, 30-foot-square stone dwelling appears in that year's tax rolls under Grême's name. (Well, sort of—the appraisers couldn't cope with *Grême* and listed him as *Graham*.) Sadly, de Gimat, a career officer, was ordered back to France and thence "with the French army to Santo Domingo," where he "was killed" and buried.[72] His friend, however, remained in Harford on the land the pair had so loved. (Grême died in 1800 and was buried at Trap Church, where one can still see his lichen-encrusted tombstone inscribed, in part, "Captain in the French Army Under Lafayette.")

And if Maiden's Bower stands as perhaps the most romantic French house in Maryland, then the stuccoed stone Bon Air earns the award for best known. But just because it is so well known doesn't mean it or the legends that have swirled around it for 200 years are well documented. As Alexis Shriver wrote in 1937, most of the so-called facts about Bon Air are nothing more than "playing cards" that impressionable historians use to "build our little romance."[73] Still, a few facts do exist. First, it is documented that Claude François Frederick de la Porte was a French soldier stationed in the Caribbean and that he arrived "at the Isle of San Domingo November 26th," 1781.[74] It is also documented that two years later his regiment was ordered back to France. De la Porte, however, apparently decided he liked life among the tradewinds and stayed on in Santo Domingo.

His stay there, however, was cut short when the brilliant revolutionary Toussaint l'Overture led the island's slaves into rebellion in 1793, causing most of the local Euro-

70. Kennedy, *Orders from France,* 9; *Harford County Directory* (1953), 106; Alexis Shriver, *Lafayette in Harford County* (Bel Air: privately printed, 1931), 30–31.

71. *Harford County Directory* (1953), 75.

72. Wright, *Harford,* 365.

73. Clipping from the *Bel Air Times* in the HSHC archives; thanks are given Bon Air's new owners, Mr. and Mrs. Albert Laisy, for unmasking many of those legends.

74. Shriver, in ibid.

peans to flee, *probably* including de la Porte. In any event, it is known that the former officer bought 200 acres overlooking Laurel Brook on June 25, 1793, for "600 pounds current money."[75] He and his wife, née Betsy Herbert, then began building the stuccoed house they called Bon Air, possibly after the Caribbean island of the same name. When they finished a year later, they marked the happy event with a datestone inscribed FDLP 1794. The de la Portes' house is perhaps unique in Anglo-America because it is so unmistakably French, from the site plan (with buildings placed so as to create a small courtyard) to the main house's hip roof and general massing, and from the trim (including some uniquely profiled wooden mantles) to the construction details, joinery, and hardware.[76]

While Bon Air, Maiden's Bower, and the Aveilhe house represent the tangible remains of revolutionary-era French culture in the county, they don't tell the whole story. They don't even suggest just how many Frenchmen lived in Harford around 1800. There were, for instance, members of the Raphel family. Etienne Raphel (born in Marseilles but brought to Martinique as a child) and his wife, Jeanne Elizabeth Fressenjat (who was baptized on the Caribbean island of St. Lucia), arrived in Baltimore in 1792, that is, at the crest of the wave of French refugees from the West Indies. On August 28, 1799, the pair paid George Presbury of William £1,225 for 361 acres of the tract Quiet Lodge on the east side of the Gunpowder River and "ever since the Raphels settled there" that stretch of the Gunpowder "has been known as Frenchman's Bay or Frenchman's Hollow." Etienne Raphel died in 1811 (by then he called himself Stephen) and in his will asked to be buried "on my farm . . . called Quiet Lodge."[77]

Then there is Pierre Charles Varlet. This native of Languedoc was a trained engineer; he emigrated to Santo Domingo around 1790, fled to America in 1793, and in 1798 was made superintendent of the Susquehanna Canal Company. He also published maps of Maryland, Delaware, and Virginia, joined the American Philosophical Society, and became a bosom friend of architect Benjamin Henry Latrobe.[78]

Other French-bred countians are a bit more evanescent. Who, for instance, was Jean René Compagnon? or Augustine Ballazar Simmonet? Their names certainly sound French and they surely play some role in the county's architectural history, since Simmonet bought part of what is now Monmouth Farm in 1794 and sold it to Compagnon

Original drawing of Bon Air, Claude François Frederick de la Porte's 1794 *petit château* near Fallston: compare both sections' hipped roofs to the original roof at Priest Neale's Mass House.

75. Deed JLG M/123.

76. De la Porte's will is filed at AJ2/181.

77. Hartridge, "Refugees," 115; deed JLG O/493. Presbury had been willed the land by his grandfather George Presbury.

78. John C. Van Horne and Lee W. Formwalt, eds., *The Correspondence and Miscellaneous Papers of Benjamin Henry Latrobe* (New Haven: Yale University Press, 1984), 1:218 n. 5.

in 1802. Others are ghostlier still and Harford's 1798 tax rolls include several surnames that suggest French antecedents, although one cannot be sure. (Recall how the assessors turned Grême into Graham.) Still, Charles Bevard (in Deer Creek Lower Hundred), James Radican (in Deer Creek Middle Hundred), and Labadat De Arlac (in Spesutia Lower Hundred) sound as if they had non-English backgrounds. But there can be no doubt at all about two men who lived together in a one-story, 40-by-20-foot frame house in Bush River Lower Hundred, for the assessors simply referred to them as "Monsieur Francis Delmas" and "Monsieur Campion."

By the time Etienne Raphel died at Quiet Lodge in 1811, the American Revolution, led by people like Sophia and Aquila Hall and John Archer, was long over. Archer and the Halls had helped bring a new, democratic nation into being, a nation where, thanks to the likes of Ignatius Wheeler, religious toleration and other rational, humanistic ideals had been codified into law. Those self-same liberal principles also found expression in the architecture and houses such as Sophia's Dairy and Oak Farm triumphantly reflect in brick and stone Harford County's Georgian/federal revolution. Yet it is important to recall that not everyone in 1800 Harford County was of Anglo-American or African-American stock and M. et Mme. Raphel, M. et Mme. de la Porte, and *les amis* Grême and de Gimat all underscore that in the new nation in matters of architecture, "lifestyle," politics, and religion it was *chacun à son goût.*

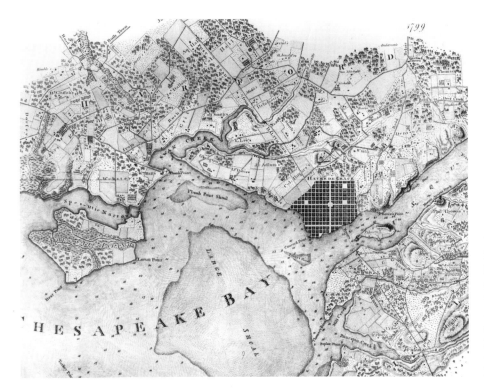

This detail of C. P. Hauducoeur's 1799 map of the Upper Chesapeake shows that the arc from Spesutia Island north to the Denison family's Sion Hill was already filling with villas: note, in addition to "Denison," Samuel Hughes's Mount Pleasant, the Smith family's Blenheim, Oakington, the farm marked "J. Adlum," which belonged to John Adlum, winemaking friend of Thomas Jefferson's, and the Rodgers family's ferryline across the Susquehanna.

"All the Advantage"
Havre de Grace's Federal Villas

[4]

In 1803 architect Benjamin Henry Latrobe took time off from commissions such as the U.S. Capitol to write Thomas Jefferson about the glorious future awaiting Havre de Grace: talk of canals filled the air and Latrobe forecast that the Harford town was destined to reap "all the advantage of the improved navigation of the Susquehanna," as well as "the advantage which the [Chesapeake and Delaware] Canal will produce." These infrastructure projects, when combined with Havre de Grace's long bay frontage ("as deep a harbor as Baltimore") guaranteed that the community would soon rival "Philadelphia as well as . . . Baltimore" as a commercial center. "One Million of Bricks were laid during the year 1801 in building stores and houses in Havre de Grace and double that number is expected this year" in happy anticipation of these inevitable riches.[1]

It was only natural that Latrobe would have written Jefferson about Havre de Grace, for Harford County blazed as a hotbed of Jeffersonianism. Both Havre de Grace resident Gabriel Christie and Dr. John Archer were elected to the U.S. Congress on a fiercely pro-Jefferson platform; agriculturist John Adlum (who in 1797 bought what is now called Swan Harbor Farm) worked with the Sage of Monticello to promote the nascent American winemaking industry;[2] and inns throughout the county contained virtual shrines to the third president. (Peregrine Nowland's tavern in Bush, for example, was dominated by a "picture of Jefferson in gilt frame.")[3] Moreover, it was Jefferson, a keen amateur architect who believed in a triangular interdependence among the beautiful, the morally good, and the politically virtuous, who more or less single-handedly introduced the concept that a neoclassical villa might make a highly suitable home to a liberal American humanist; thus it is not altogether surprising that it is the residences of Jefferson's principal

1. See Jay, ed., *Havre de Grace*, 5.

2. Deed JLG N/315, dated January 23, 1797. See Lucie T. Morton, *Winegrowing in Eastern America* (Ithaca, N.Y.: Cornell University Press, 1985), 24–25.

3. Estate Inventory of Peregrine Nowland, dated December 13, 1810; estate 1103, Harford County Register of Wills Office, Bel Air.

When Rochambeau's troops crossed the Susquehanna en route to Yorktown in 1781, all they saw on the Harford shore was the post road (*"Chemin de Bush Town"*) and the Rodgers family's tavern and ferry dock. (The large blocks on the Cecil shore represent troop encampments—not large buildings.)

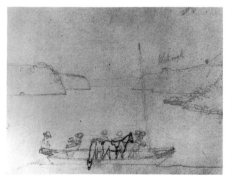

Benjamin Henry Latrobe's c. 1800 pencil sketch of horses being ferried across the Susquehanna.

4. See, for example, Jay, ed., *Havre de Grace,* 14.

Harford allies—Commodore Rodgers's Sion Hill, Mark Pringle's Bloomsbury, Paca Smith's Blenheim, and Robert Smith's Spesutia Island—that define the villa era in Havre de Grace.

The town's unrivaled site—that point at which the Susquehanna River widens to form the Chesapeake Bay—was patented as long ago as 1658, but the community owes its existence not to natural beauty but to travel and trade. In 1666 the colonial assembly passed "an Act for making high wayes" that resulted in the post road. Travelers along that "high waye" nonchalantly rode over ruts and through streams, but crossing the Susquehanna required a boat, and, consequently, ferrylines appeared here by the late seventeenth century. And since the vagaries of weather and tide rendered sailings unpredictable, most passengers perforce spent one pre- or post-boarding night in taverns on the Harford or Cecil shore. These three institutions—the road, the ferryline, and the taverns—determined Havre de Grace's early history. The place was even called Susquehanna Lower Ferry for a century or more (partially to distinguish it from Susquehanna Upper Ferry upstream). When the French army marched through the county in 1781 and '83 (en route to and from Yorktown) the soldiers' sketches of their *Bivouac à Lower Ferry* show that the *"Chemin de Bush Town,"* the ferryline, and the tavern remained the principal features of the town.

Eyewitness accounts of life at Lower Ferry uniformly suggest conditions that might politely be called "folksy." George Washington filled his journals with teeth-clenched complaints about the irregular ferry service (he was held up once by "turbulent and squally" winds, once by "lowness of tides," and many times by ice and snow) and others wrote horrified accounts of the primitive conditions that prevailed at the riverfront taverns (see chapter 2).[4]

But such conditions would not survive the eighteenth century. Even as the Frenchmen were making their maps, John and Elizabeth Rodgers were laying the foundations of Havre de Grace's—and their—fortunes. Innkeepers on the Harford shore in the 1770s, the Rodgerses eventually secured the licenses to manage the tavern in Cecil County and to run the ferryline. This monopoly guaranteed prosperity for the Rodgerses and helped set the stage for boom-time at the ferry. The couple certainly whipped their old taverns into shape; George Washington's journal makes reference to thirty-one happy stops at one or both of their establishments (including this for September 20, 1787, "Dined at Havre d. Gras at . . . Rogers," which suggests that the city's idiosyncratic pronunciation goes back further than one might have thought).[5] Information on the inns' *plats du jour* remains sketchy but Elizabeth Rodgers's estate inventory contains items such as "1 Bird Roaster" and "3 Oyster Knives," leading to succulent thoughts of the sky-blackening flocks of canvasback duck that once fed in the waters off Havre de Grace and to mounds of just-shucked Chesapeake oysters. In any event, in 1794 one bon vivant deemed the family's Harford County tavern "the best inn . . . in America, neat, clean, and pleasantly situated," where a traveler could expect "a good and abundant breakfast . . . of tea, coffee, eggs, and cold meat. Here seemed to be another instance of that degree of improvement to which everything . . . was advancing."[6]

"C'est Le Havre!"

Thanks in part to the Rodgerses, the sleepy hamlet started to stir with life as a surprisingly diversified group of men and women appeared on the scene. They came virtually overnight and they filled the arc that extends from Spesutia Island to Palmer's Island with seven brick, stone, and frame villas that were as up-to-the-minute sophisticated as any buildings in any similar space in the nation. The people who built the villas were as sophisticated as their new homes. Robert Smith and John Rodgers established the U.S. Navy; their neighbor William Smith of Blenheim traced his ancestry to an English duchess (and his son Paca Smith traced his to a Maryland governor). Swansbury's Martha Griffith Smith hobnobbed with George and Martha Washington and had "tea with two members of Congress" at a party where her dress was rated "as handsome as . . . any in the Ballroom";[7] her first husband, Col. Alexander Lawson Smith, cofounded the Society of the Cincinnati and her second husband, Samuel Jay, was a great-nephew of John Jay, first Chief Justice of the U.S. Supreme Court. Two different lords of Mount Pleasant, Jacob Giles and Samuel Hughes, pioneered the American iron industry; Mark Pringle of Bloomsbury connived with Napoleon to corner the world silver market. Clearly it was time to put "Susquehanna Lower Ferry" to bed. Thus as if on cue, in 1784 no less than the Marquis de Lafayette, while being ferried across the Susquehanna, saw the Harford town and, "impressed by its beauty and its resemblance to Le Havre . . . in France . . . exclaimed, 'C'est Le Havre!' . . . and the beautiful name of Havre de Grace has designated the city since that day."[8] The next year the Maryland General Assembly granted Havre de Grace a charter and in 1789 the new town's fame had spread so widely that it "was seriously considered for Capital of the United States," losing the distinction by one vote, according to the late J. Alexis Shriver.

And in addition to making fortunes smelting iron and buying and selling silver, all of Havre de Grace's villa-builders maintained a keen interest in the fine arts.[9] Moreover, they all had classical educations—or wished to appear that they had ("assume a virtue if you have it not," said Hamlet). When Abingdon's William Paca enrolled in what is now the University of Pennsylvania, for instance, he spent most of his time "reading from the classics" and was "encouraged in 'private hours'" to immerse himself in books such as "Isaac Ware's translation of *The Four Books of Andrea Palladio's Architecture.*"[10] Paca's neoclassical studies were at least matched by those of Princetonians Mark Pringle and Robert Smith, and that pair, along with Dr. James Biays, father-in-law of Oakington's builder, John W. Stump, were mainstays at the renowned Library Company of Baltimore, whose shelves groaned with one of the new republic's most extensive collections of neoclassical architectural books. (Nor did countians have to travel to Baltimore or Princeton to gain a neoclassical education, for the trustees of Abingdon's Cokesbury College chose Dr. Jacob Hall as that institution's president in 1788 "on account of . . . his knowledge in Greek and Latin.")[11] And while some villa-builders founded lending libraries, others amassed sizable private book collections on the shores of the Susquehanna, perhaps most notably William Paca's nephew Paca Smith. When Smith died at Blenheim in 1830 the over 400

5. Shriver, Rodgers Collection, MHS. Similarly, in June 1788 Charles Willson Peale noted in his diary that he had been at "a party at Haver de gras." See Miller, ed., *Papers of Charles Willson Peale*, 1:508.

6. Thomas Twining, *Travels in America 100 Years Ago* (New York: Harper and Brothers, 1894), 77–78. Even the finicky French troops a decade earlier approved of the "excellent lunch" they'd eaten "at the house of the proprietor of the ferry." See Rice and Brown, trans. and eds., *Rochambeau*, 2:182.

7. They were also keenly interested in making money: in an era before women had many legal rights, the Griffith daughters took charge of their fortunes. Note an undated letter from Frances Griffith to Mrs. Smith extolling the virtues of "the Alexandria bank stock" as "the most advantageous" investment she knew of since "they do not divide all the profits."

8. Quoted in Wright, *Harford*, 312. Rochambeau's own journal for 1780–83 notes "Mr. Stock [all but certainly *Stokes*], to whom belongs the land around Lower Ferry . . . has conceived the idea of a new town he is going to call Havre de Grace." See Lawrence Lee, trans., *Rochambeau Father and Son* (New York: Henry Holt, 1952), 251.

9. Samuel Hughes of Mount Pleasant, Commodore Rodgers of Sion Hill, Mark Pringle of Bloomsbury, and the wife, father-in-law, and namesake nephew of Robert Smith of Spesutia Island all commissioned Charles Willson Peale to paint portraits of themselves. See Joanne Greenspun, ed., *Charles Willson Peale and His World* (New York: Harry N. Abrams, 1983), 61–213; Miller, ed., *Papers of Charles Willson Peale*, 1:535, and vol. 3 (1991), 642–643.

10. Gregory A. Stiverson and Phebe R. Jacobsen, *William Paca* (Baltimore: MHS, 1976), 33–34.

11. J. Hall Pleasants, M.D., "Jacob Hall, Surgeon and Educator, 1747–1812," *Maryland Historical Magazine* 8 (September 1913): 226.

volumes in his library comprised one of the most impressive groupings of books then seen in the state. (To put Smith's volumes in perspective, Richard Chase assembled the largest known pre-1770 library in Maryland; it consisted of 186 titles.)

All this certainly leads one to suspect that at least a few residents of federal-era Havre de Grace enjoyed a certain familiarity with ancient authors. This is an important point, for throughout America, as the eighteenth century ended, the writings of Horace and Virgil "became icons of the . . . image that the early nationalists were struggling to define. . . . As they set about establishing a new republic based on a classical model, early American landowners identified themselves as participants in a pastoral tradition." More specifically, while the painter Charles Willson Peale, who frequently passed through these parts to paint portraits of the Havre de Grace elite, "embraced a classical . . . imagery for his garden," John Rodgers and Robert Smith embraced the entire ancient villa tradition. "The basic program of the villa has remained unchanged for two thousand years," wrote historian James Ackerman.[12] "It fills a need that never alters," that is, the need of educated citizens to be able to escape the urban pressures of money-making and power-dealing by withdrawing to the peace of an idealized country life. Tusculum provided the model 2,000 years ago: there in the hill country near Rome one could find Lucullus, Cicero, Titus, and other writers and emperors (a seemingly odd combination in the 1990s) happily rusticating. This symbolic pairing of farming and philosophizing was revived during the Renaissance, first in Italy and eventually in England, where it gained a narrow but deep popularity partially through the writings of Alexander Pope and Joseph Addison. Pope even turned his writing into action and created his own neoclassical villa in the London suburb of Twickenham in 1718.[13]

In America, this concept of neoclassical country life reached its zenith in the person of Thomas Jefferson, who once proudly boasted that "ours are the only farmers in the world who can read Homer."[14] Harford and Cecil counties even boasted farmers who could hum Mozart; when the *Central Courant and Port Deposit Intelligencer* ran a story on the history of the development of the clarinet, the author of the piece casually reminded his readers that many "composers employ the chalumeau, or lower octave, with singular effect: Notice its accompaniment 'Protegg il giusto solo' in Don Giovanni."[15] *Don Giovanni* had its American premier (in New York) in 1826[16]—yet in 1833 the editor of the Port Deposit newspaper felt free to make casual reference to it, apparently confident that his readers in Cecil and Harford counties knew the score inside and out. And indeed, they might have: Mark Pringle studied the violin and the clarinet at Bloomsbury and when the Reverend John Ireland ran a boys' school at Sion Hill in 1790—before the house entered its illustrious Rodgers phase—he employed a "singing master" to round out his charges' educations.

Thus was 1800 Havre de Grace ripe for villa-building. The city was booming, fortunes were being made, high-stakes politics filled the air, and the citizens knew their classics. No wonder a 1793 voyager was able to admire "the Hills back of the Ferry . . . [that] are decorated with handsome country seats."[17] No wonder that in 1794 the Anglo-Indian tea magnate Thomas Twining, while crossing the Susquehanna from Perryville, "contemplated, with peculiar pleasure . . . the new-built town of Havre de Grace, whose white houses . . . had supplanted the wigwams of the Susquehanna tribes."

Perhaps Sion Hill and Robert Smith's Spesutia Island villa might stand as representative of these "handsome country seats." The former house, although begun by an educator (John Ireland), was brought to international fame by Commo. John Rodgers, the politically minded "Father of the American Navy." The latter was built by a Revolutionary War hero who made a fortune as an international maritime lawyer (with a client list that included a man who "was said to be among the lovers of Catherine the Great"),[18] and who, when he served in President Jefferson's cabinet for eight years as secretary of the Navy, guided the careers not only of Commodore Rodgers but also of Benjamin Henry

12. Therese O'Malley, "Belfield in American Garden History," in Lillian B. Miller and David C. Ward, eds., *New Perspectives on Charles Willson Peale* (Pittsburgh: University of Pittsburgh Press, 1991), 270; James S. Ackerman, *The Villa* (London: Thames and Hudson, 1990), 9.

13. Twickenham was a center of English villa–building; Daniel Defoe observed in his *Tour through England and Scotland* an "abundance of curious seats of the nobility" at "Twittenham [*sic*]"; this is quoted in Norman G. Brett-James, *Middlesex* (London: Robert Hale, 1951), 188. Extant or destroyed examples of these "seats" include York House (c. 1700), Marble Hill House (c. 1725), Orleans House (c. 1730), Strawberry Hill (begun 1748), Wrotham Hall (1754), and Sandycombe Lodge, a "symmetrical villa . . . with lower wings" (like Sion Hill) begun c. 1812. For all see Nicholas Pevsner, *Middlesex* (London: Penguin Books, 1951), 157–66.

14. William Howard Adams, ed., *The Eye of Jefferson* (Washington, D.C.: National Gallery of Art, 1976), xxxix.

15. *Central Courant and Port Deposit Intelligencer*, vol. 1, L. A. Wilmer, publisher, May 3, 1833. The article continues: "Who has not sailed down the Rhine and held his oar to listen to its joyous notes in the grove! . . . Encircled by mountains, the peasant has a rich delight in pouring forth the tones of his instrument."

16. See Louis Biancalli and Robert Bagan, *The Victor Book of Opera* (New York: Simon and Schuster, 1949), 104.

17. "A New Yorker in Maryland: 1793 and 1821," *Maryland Historical Magazine* 47 (June 1952): 138.

18. Henry D. Harlan, "The Names of the Great Lawyers on the Frieze of the Baltimore Supreme Bench Court House," *Maryland Historical Magazine* 37 (1942): 261; Dumas Malone, ed., *Dictionary of American Biography* (New York: Scribner's, 1932), 9:341 (hereafter cited as *DAB*).

Latrobe, when that architect was awarded plum commissions at the new Washington Navy Yard. It would only be a slight exaggeration to suggest that Rodgers and Smith apotheosize one of the finest and most enduring of classical motifs, namely the mutually beneficial relationship that can exist between a warrior/farmer and his sagacious political commander.

Sion Hill and the "Unconquerable Spirit of the American Navy"

In May of 1787 the Reverend and Mrs. John Ireland bought a 59¼-acre plot of ground called Levell's Addition about a mile north of the ferry dock. He was "an Englishman of scholarly attainments" and rector of St. George's Episcopal Church, Spesutia, and she, Joanna, was the heiress daughter of Mount Pleasant's Jacob Giles.[19] Their property formed the quintessential site of a (neo)classical villa. Clearly intended for intellectual or recreational pursuits (its suburban size made it too small for serious farming), it crowned a long, low hill that yielded ten-mile panoramic views of the Upper Bay, with Havre de Grace artistically placed in the middle distance. These views deserve mention because what one historian has termed "the choice of prospect" has motivated villa-builders since ancient Rome: one hundred generations have agreed that the ideal villa "is . . . one that looks back on a city from a high and distant promontory" and just as Horace placed his villa outside Rome on high ground "to gain a vast panorama of the countryside" so, 1,500 years later, did "Cosimo de' Medici built his Fiesole villa on a manmade terrace . . . [to] enjoy in leisure hours visual command of Florence,"[20] and so, 1,800 years later, did John Ireland establish Sion Hill on its hill overlooking Havre de Grace.

Ireland immigrated to America from England where, according to legend, he had served as a tutor in the household of the duke of Northumberland at Syon House. The etymological connection between the duke's Syon House and Ireland's Sion Hill seems obvious. But Colin Shrimpton, the Northumberlands' current librarian, searched the family archives and found "no one called Rev. Ireland who served the first Duke (died 1786)." Shrimpton does, however, offer a tantalizing lead: "Could I suggest that the name of the house Sion Hill would suggest a link with the family of the Duke of Marlbor-

Many of America's federal-era villa-builders, in seeking to re-create the elegant era of Augustan-age England, Medicean Florence, and Republican Rome, drew inspiration from the villa that poet Alexander Pope built in the London suburb Twickenham. This c. 1735 painting of Pope's creation shows the house's restrained neoclassical design as well as the poet's extensive gardens, with their domed and columned pavilions.

19. Wright, *Harford*, 231.

20. George W. Archer, "History of St. George's Parish," unpublished typescript in files of the MHS, p. 77; Ackerman, *Villa*, 27.

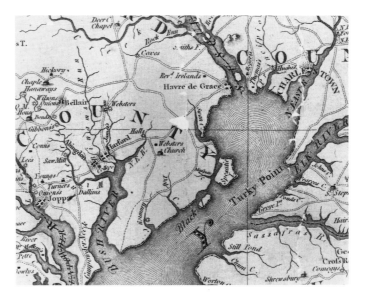

The Reverend John Ireland began the house Sion Hill in 1787; it shows up clearly on Dennis Griffith's 1794 map of Maryland, as do Samuel Hughes's Cecil County ironworks. (One wonders why Mount Pleasant and Blenheim do not appear.)

This view of the Chesapeake from Sion Hill shows the expansive vistas favored by (neo)classical villa-builders.

21. Colin Shrimpton to author, January 28, 1991.

22. See David Dallam, *The Dallam Family* (Philadelphia: George H. Buchanan, 1929), 20–23.

23. Note Plate 36 in Isaac Ware's *Complete Body of Architecture* (1756) and Plate 37 in Robert Morris's *Select Architecture* (1757).

ough. . . . There was a freehold property called Sion Hill [at Twickenham] . . . which served as a suburban villa for the Dukes of Marlborough in the eighteenth century."[21] All this is most interesting: Twickenham's importance in Anglo-American villa mythology has already been alluded to, and the estate that abuts Sion Hill to the south was named Blenheim in the early eighteenth century by a man who was a nephew of Sarah Jennings, duchess of Marlborough and mistress of Blenheim Palace.[22]

Havre de Grace's Sion Hill is a three-part, Flemish bond brick structure composed of a central 2½-story, gable-roofed main block and two-story, shed-roofed wings. (The wings' single-slope roofs sometimes cause surprise, but period architectural pattern books frequently illustrate buildings with similar one-pitch roofs.)[23] Visually, the house revolves around a central axis formed on the ground floor by an elaborate entrance, on the second floor by an exceptionally rich three-part window, and finally by a lunette attic window placed in a pedimented gable. Classical architects believed that a building's exterior ought to suggest what lies within and Sion Hill's certainly does. The main axis accurately implies the house's center-hall floor plan, just as the wings' small scale and lack of ornament reveals their utilitarian function. (Ireland placed the kitchen and pantry in the east wing and devoted the west wing to his Sion Hill Seminary.) One can even use the house's window treatment to gauge the rooms' hierarchy since windows in the important ground floor public rooms are taller than those of the less-important second-sto-

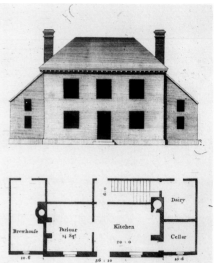

Left: Sion Hill. Begun by John Ireland, acquired by Gideon Denison, and completed by Denison's daughter, Minerva, and her husband, Commo. John Rodgers. Ireland ran a boy's school in the left wing; the other wing held—and holds—the kitchen. Also compare the keystone window lintels to those of the house completed by Commodore Rodgers's mother in Havre de Grace. Right: Designs for villas such as Sion Hill—where a two-story main block is flanked by sloping-roof wings—frequently appear in eighteenth-century English architectural books; American builders relied on such books for inspiration. This is Plate 36 in Isaac Ware's *Complete Body of Architecture* (1756).

ry bedrooms. Once inside, one discovers that the main block does indeed have the anticipated three-part plan focused on that broad hall: the two largest and most formal rooms (the equal-sized summer and winter dining rooms) open off the hall to the east while twin parlors and a stairway open off to the west. (Neo)classical architects loved to lace their buildings with intellectual games, ideally ones with mathematical bases, and it thus seems highly proper that Ireland playfully divided Sion Hill's plan into thirds with proportions of one (the hall), one-half (the dining rooms), and one-third (the parlors and stair).

Ireland's Sion Hill Seminary enjoyed a meteoric success and no less a figure than Dr. John Archer of Medical Hall enrolled a son in the institution; but, like a meteor, the glory was short-lived and in June 1795 the minister sold the house and its 59¼ acres to the New England merchant Gideon Denison.[24] Drawn south by the promise of profit, Denison moved from his native Connecticut to Philadelphia, the largest city in the country, and then to the boomtown by the bay, where he masterminded a far-flung commercial empire with agents throughout America, from Tennessee and Natchez to New York, Savannah, and Boston. Denison clearly had high hopes for Havre de Grace's future, for he proceeded to snap up over 1,800 acres around the town.

Although not much is known of Denison the man, it is possible to reconstruct a rather complete image of what life was like at Sion Hill during his tenure there, thanks to Christian P. Hauducoeur's 1799 map of the head of the Chesapeake Bay and Denison's own estate inventory, that is, the list of personal property he owned at the time of his death. After scanning that "Inventory of Goods and Chattels" (completed in January 1800) one may state with confidence that he lived well at Sion Hill—even though the 1798 tax assessors called the house "unfinished"—for he filled one of his two dining rooms with a pair of "dining tables with 2 end tables," a tea table, a sideboard, and a wine cooler (all of mahogany), and four pieces of "japan'd" furniture. He set off all that wood with a "pair large gilt looking glasses," "3 small oval gilt looking glasses," an "Epergne with cut glass," seven pairs of silver candelabra, and an array of miscellaneous silver *objets,* including four tureens, a "wine strainer," "4 doz. labels," urns for tea and coffee, baskets for fruit and sugar and bread, a "toast tray," and "2 goblets silver, gilt inside." After dinner, Denison

24. Ireland served as rector of St. Paul's in Baltimore until 1802 when he returned to Britain; back home he "attained some prominence" as the subject "of a highly complimentary poem . . . by Gifford . . . editor of the famous *London Quarterly Review,* a poet of considerable note—though his reputation in some respects, it must be owned, was none of the best." All from Archer, "St. George's," 78–81.

This c. 1940 photograph of Sion Hill suggests the house's mathematical plan: a wide, through center hall with twin spaces to the left (for two dining rooms) and three spaces to the right (for two parlors and an open stair alcove).

and his guests doubtless spent many amusing hours at his "back gammon table"—perhaps while dipping into the "10 gallons peach brandy," "27 gallons apple brandy," or "336 gallons cyder" that reposed in the cellars. When it was time to retire, Denison's inventory suggests that he, his family, and his guests would have all crawled into their own four-poster bed, because it includes five sets of matching bed and window curtains.

When Denison rode out to inspect his holdings, he did so in either his "single horse chair" or in his brass-trimmed "chariot," a stunning vehicle appraised at $120. That figure may not sound like much today; neither does $7,656.50, which is what the 1798 tax assessors figured Denison's house and land were worth. But 200 years ago they were immense sums, which leads to the tricky question of determining the relative values of 1790s and 1990s dollars. While it is unlikely that anyone will ever arrive at a precise rate of exchange, Roger Kennedy, former director of the Smithsonian Institution's Museum of American History, has recently suggested that the ratio 1:80 seems valid, except when discussing building construction; then, says Kennedy, 1:130 seems closer to the mark.[25] Viewed thus, the value of Denison's house and land approaches $1,000,000.

Several other period documents allow one an even clearer picture of Denison's Sion Hill. For instance, Hauducoeur's 1799 map shows that Denison's 1,800 acres spread out on both sides of the present Level Road, extending to the northeast as far as the banks of the Susquehanna. The map also shows that the squire had sculpted terraces around the house and had laid out boxwood gardens on the terraces, a formal sort of landscaping that would not have surprised Horace (or Jefferson). Almost miraculously, vestiges of the gardens remain today, discernible through stumps of ancient boxwood and in swaths of sloping lawns (see chapter 10). It is known that Denison kept quite a menagerie at Sion Hill and it is at least arguable that he did so to reinforce the conceit that he was living the life of a neoclassical farmer. His estate inventory includes 10 horses, 23 sheep, 3 pair of oxen, 15 cattle, and "2 breeding sows with 5 young pigs and 11 shoats." While some of those beasts doubtless served utilitarian functions, the pictorial value of sheep and cattle to neoclassicists cannot be denied—just think of the paintings of Claude Lorraine and John Constable.

25. Kennedy, *Orders from France,* 239–240.

Denison died in late 1799 and although his widow, Jerusha, lived on at Sion Hill, ownership eventually passed to their daughter, Minerva (1784–1877). Minerva married John Rodgers on October 21, 1806, and that event, which took place in the house's north parlor, marks the beginning of the Maryland villa's period of international significance. Of all the people who have ever lived in Harford County the careers of John Rodgers and his descendants come closest to paralleling the lives of classical heroes; if Ulysses and Achilles and Aeneas personify the glory of ancient Greece and Rome, so is "the story of . . . the Rodgers family . . . [the] history of the American navy."[26]

Rodgers was born in 1773, one of John and Elizabeth Rodgers's eight children.[27] Although his parents' innkeeping skills were already legendary, young John decided to play out his life on a larger stage than a hostelry—even a hostelry praised by George Washington—could provide. He had "read many books treating of sailors and seafaring life, which fired his imagination and aroused his curiosity" and in 1786 he apprenticed himself to Benjamin Folger, captain of the merchantman *Maryland*, based in Baltimore and owned by city financiers Samuel and John Smith. While Folger changed ships several times during the next few years, he always took his Harford County protégé with him; thus the teenage Rodgers made working cruises to France, the West Indies, and Holland. By 1793 Rodgers had so impressed the Smiths they gave him a vessel of his own—the 300-ton *Jane,* "twice as large as the average Baltimore ship of her day." Rodgers piloted her to ports throughout Europe and the Caribbean and returned to Baltimore with cargoes of "Brandy in pipes; choice Claret in tierces . . . Olives, Anchovies, and capers . . . ; Men and Women's . . . gloves."[28]

According to legend Rodgers was a remarkably strong and vigorous youth who had toughened his body by swimming in the icy Susquehanna to retrieve ducks shot from shore. Whether he had or not, the young man's physique was well documented: "remarkably strong and hardy," according to one admirer; "solid . . . [and] well-proportioned," according to another.[29] In 1811 Latrobe described his "most intimate friend" Rodgers as "the most powerful man in respect to bodily strength in the country" and Missouri senator Thomas Hart Benton's first glimpse of the commodore left the lawmaker breathless—although he recovered himself to write that the sailor's "very figure and face . . . combined in the perfect degree the idea of strength and endurance with the reality of manly comeliness."[30]

Throughout his lifetime, Rodgers had to rely on his muscled sinews to win the respect of his crews, especially at the start of his career, when his well-developed body was far more mature than his calendar age, a disparity that led to more than a few clashes between the pup captain and his crew of old seadogs. Perhaps the most memorable of these altercations occurred during a c. 1795 winter voyage to the frigid North Sea. On that journey "three of his crew . . . [had] frozen to death" and when Rodgers ordered a couple of sailors to climb up and secure the icy rigging, they refused and grumbled mutiny. Outraged, the young man "stripped off his jacket and shirt and, wearing only his trousers and shoes . . . went aloft, telling his crew he would show them what a man could do. Ashamed of their weakness, they soon followed and never afterwards showed a disposition to question his orders."[31]

Rodgers was clearly ready for something more challenging than importing capers and gloves to Baltimore. His chance came in 1798 when America found itself enmeshed in a mini–naval war with Napoleon and that March President Adams appointed Rodgers a second lieutenant on the 1,200-ton frigate *Constellation*. Rodgers and his frigate put an end to French harassment of America's Caribbean merchant fleet and as partial reward, on March 5, 1799, Adams promoted the Marylander to the rank of captain, "the first lieutenant in the navy under the Constitution to be advanced to this rank."[32] Adams also gave the new captain command of the sloop *Maryland,* and Rodgers used the ship to help suppress the West Indian slave trade (1800) and to deliver food and supplies to Santo

Commo. John Rodgers, whose "very figure and face," wrote Missouri senator Thomas Hart Benton, "combined in the perfect degree the idea of strength and endurance with the reality of manly comeliness."

26. Notes by J. Alexis Shriver, in Rodgers Collection, Manuscript 2612, MHS.

27. Charles Oscar Paullin, *Commodore John Rodgers* (Cleveland, Ohio: Arthur H. Clark, 1910), 30.

28. *Daily Intelligencer,* Baltimore, October 1794; microfilm at MHS.

29. *DAB* 8:76.

30. Paullin, *Rodgers,* 31.

31. Ibid., 32.

32. *DAB* 16:1676. Parenthetically, the *New York Times* was wrong in 1926 when it stated "there has been a John Rodgers in the Navy . . . ever since there was a Navy." Since the first John Rodgers joined the service in March of 1798, and since Adams didn't establish the Navy department until June of 1798, there was a John Rodgers in the Navy *before* there was a Navy.

Domingo in aid of the revolutionary Toussaint (1802). That latter adventure got him tossed into "a loathsome and pestiferous prison" by no less a figure than Napoleon's broth-er-in-law.[33] Released from jail in the spring of 1802 Rodgers returned to Havre de Grace to lick his wounds. He found himself quite the hometown hero, lionized, feted, and fussed over; he also found himself a bride.

While Rodgers's courtship of Minerva Denison may read like the worst sort of Bar-bara Cartland fiction—she, fresh from her Philadelphia finishing school, was described in an 1806 issue of the *Federal Gazette* as "a little girl with fair hair . . . so nice and sweet" who "sang remarkably well . . . and played the piano-forte with much skill," while he, quoting the same newspaper, was a "muscular, vigorous man, buoyantly alive, brave and modest," his "handsome face bronzed by sea winds and sunshine"—this is *not* a bodice-ripper romance. It is documented history, with much of the documentation coming from the heroine's own pen. According to Minerva's memoirs, in May of 1802 Mrs. Denison received a note from the chatelaine of a neighboring villa, Mrs. Samuel Hughes of Mount Pleasant, asking mother and daughter to drop in that evening to meet "Captain Rodgers [who] had been invited to dine." Atwitter with anticipation (Minerva wrote that she "had heard Captain Rodgers spoken of" and his adventures "had been much . . . published in the papers"), they arrived at Mount Pleasant just as dinner was breaking up and were shown into the parlor "where the ladies . . . were discussing Captain Rodgers. One maid-en lady . . . said, 'I think him very handsome. I think he resembles this picture'—hold-ing up a book . . . which I found to be Schiller's 'Robbers.'" At that point the men en-tered the room. One "came with [a] . . . quiet, steady step" and sat down near Minerva, hidden from her "by a large French clock. . . . I thought I would take a peep at the gen-tleman . . . [and] bent forward to do so and to my consternation I found a pair of pierc-ing black eyes fixed upon me. I withdrew my gaze hastily." Of course the piercing eyes belonged to Rodgers. Minerva somehow got through the evening and on their way back to Sion Hill she asked her mother's opinion of Rodgers, "who seemed to be the hero of the day. She replied that she did not like him at all," as the curtain falls on Act 1.

A few days later Minerva, quietly "sitting in my room with my book," was startled when her mother swooshed in to announce, "I have entirely changed my opinion of him." Consequently, the naval hero was allowed to call on Minerva "a day or two after that"; then "his visits became frequent and his attention . . . conspicuous." She didn't mind this one bit—but "Alas! Our love affair made no great progress" because the captain was sud-denly "ordered to sea." End of Act 2. When Rodgers returned to Havre de Grace in 1804 he found a bitter Minerva, "proof against all his ardor and devotion." But this was not a man to take defeat and he proceeded to "gain by siege what he had failed to conquer by direct attack. . . . We became engaged" and, after another hiatus, the two were married in one of the most celebrated weddings of the era. *Finis.*

Rodgers's courtship of Minerva took its sputtering, awkward course because of that generation's Middle East crisis, the wars with the Barbary Pirates. The pirates, who in-fested the 1,000 miles of Mediterranean shoreline between Morocco and Tunis, had grown rich, thanks to an economy based on blackmail, bondage, and harassment. Most nations, feebly attempting to buy peace for their merchant ships, paid the thugs protec-tion money and the budget of virtually every European nation contained what was, in ef-fect, a line item for pirate tribute. Even so, the corsairs periodically stormed out of their lairs, set upon defenseless sloops, seized the cargoes, and sold the crews into slavery. Pres-idents Washington and Adams, too, had routinely sent sacks of gold to North Africa. This state of affairs changed abruptly when Jefferson moved into the White House in 1801. Al-though viscerally fond of peace and thrift, the new president could not stomach the thought of blackmail. Believing "that the only effective language to employ against these brigands . . . was force," he ordered Rodgers to the Mediterranean and the American quickly and thoroughly routed the enemy all along "the shores of Tripoli." Rodgers then

33. Paullin, *Rodgers,* 80. See also Dumas Malone, *Jefferson the President: Second Term, 1805–1809* (Boston: Little, Brown, 1974), 38.

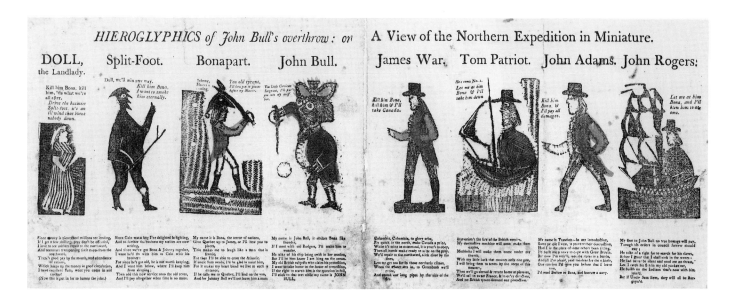

HIEROGLYPHICS of John Bull's overthrow: or A View of the Northern Expedition in Miniature.

sailed his fleet to Morocco where the emperor, "cowed by the sight of the American ships," sent the Harford countian "a present of cattle, sheep, and fowl" and agreed to sign a peace treaty "without . . . a cent for tribute." Jefferson, thrilled to the bone, immediately convened a special session of Congress so he could offer his "special approbation" to "the gallant Captain Rodgers."

No sooner had Rodgers sailed away, though, than the pirates resumed their outrages. By 1805 Jefferson had had enough and asked Rodgers to return to the Mediterranean and do whatever it took to ensure a final, lasting peace. Rodgers, masterfully in control of eighteen ships of the line, the largest gathering of American sea power to date and "the first extensive fleet activity by Americans outside the Western Hemisphere," "played a part exceeded in importance by that of no other naval officer." He freed 300 American prisoners; he destroyed the pirates' warships; and he "forced Tripoli to sign a treaty to end slavery of Christians." Rocked to international celebrity, Rodgers found himself "hailed and toasted as a popular" hero. Jefferson promoted him to the highest rank in the service (commodore) and offered him the most important job in the armed forces, command of the New York naval station.[34] Rodgers accepted the position and he and Jefferson then embarked on a remarkable series of innovative collaborations: they basically invented the concept of drydocking not-in-use vessels,[35] they established naval bases and other support installations up and down the Atlantic coast, and they revamped the makeup of the fleet, discarding large cumbersome ships in favor of smaller and cheaper gunboats. All the while Rodgers was living in style with his new bride (and growing family) at Sion Hill.

This peaceful, productive era ended with the War of 1812. Rodgers, chief commander of the entire American fleet, left his Harford County home and sailed off to best the Royal Navy in engagements fought throughout the Caribbean and North Atlantic. He even daringly entered British waters, intent on taking the war to the enemy, and launched several profitable raids of the coasts of Scotland where he captured thirty-five British ships without suffering a loss. (Rather endearingly, while he was thus engaged, Minerva Rodgers stayed quietly at Sion Hill, and sewed "extra-warm shirts to safeguard him against rheumatism.")[36] His heroics "caused an effusion of patriotic pride . . . through-

During the War of 1812 Commodore Rodgers—and Napoleon—sought what this period cartoon calls "John Bull's Overthrow." The doggerel below the image of "Rogers" [sic], at the far right, has the sailor saying, "My fleet to John Bull no true homage will pay. . . . He had better be silent and send me no threat / Lest I catch his fish in my old Yankee net."

34. Leonard F. Guttridge and Jay D. Smith, *The Commodores* (New York: Harper and Row, 1969), 105; Malone, *Jefferson, Second Term*, 38; *DAB* 16:76; *Who Was Who, Historical Volume* (Chicago: A. N. Marquis, 1943), 451.

35. Up to that time ships not in active use just sat in the water and rotted, a waste of equipment that horrified Rodgers and a waste of money that horrified Jefferson. See Dumas Malone, *Jefferson the President: First Term, 1801–1805* (Boston: Little, Brown, 1970), 102, 247–49. Jefferson brought Latrobe to Washington to supervise construction of this novelty and later made him surveyor of public buildings. Van Horne and Formwalt, eds., *Correspondence and Papers of Latrobe*, 1:208–11, 219.

36. Garrett, *At Home*, 122, 247–48.

Commodore Rodgers's raids of the British coast worked too well: in reprisal, British troops destroyed the commodore's hometown in May of 1813. One wonders if the plundered coach (object 6) was the elegant brass-trimmed "chariot" that belonged to Rodgers's father-in-law, Gideon Denison.

out the country,"[37] while he himself became the darling of the popular press, the leading man in the federal era's version of top-10 records, bar-room ballads, such as:

> And Rodgers with his gallant crew,
> O'er the wide ocean ride,
> To prove their loyal spirits true,
> And crush old Albion's pride.

Rodgers's successes proved too much for the country of Drake and Nelson and the editor of the London *Times* urged the Royal Navy to "Strike. Chastise the savages" (619). The navy happily complied. Perhaps not surprisingly, the sharpest blows fell in Commodore Rodgers's back yard, for in 1813 London ordered Adm. Sir George Cockburn to enter the Chesapeake and "destroy and lay waste" what he found there. With Rodgers still in the North Sea, the British sailed into the bay virtually unopposed, "plundering wherever they went." In April they seized the Smith family's Spesutia Island ("where Havre de Grace fishermen were busy setting nets for the spring run of shad") and slaughtered the cattle and sheep grazing there. Then, after a brief rampage through Cecil County (in which they burned Frenchtown and destroyed Samuel Hughes's Principio Iron Works), Cockburn turned his attention to Havre de Grace.[38]

On the morning of May 3 some 400 British troops landed and, despite the well-known heroics of John O'Neill,[39] managed to destroy the little town in just a few hours. The next day Latrobe wrote to Robert Fulton (of steamboat fame) to describe the horror.

> Not a house or shed is left standing, except an old church. . . . [The British] set fire to everything, threw over the stages into the river, killed the horses in the stables, and then methodically burnt every house and shed in the village. . . . The women and children fled to the woods. . . . It is supposed that the circumstances of Commodore Rodgers, being a native of Havre de Grace, this unmanly warfare is to be attributed.[40]

They stole what they did not destroy and Cockburn himself reputedly "coveted an elegant coach he saw and ordered it hauled aboard his vessel"—could it have been Denison's brass-studded chariot? Rodgers's wife, mother, and two sisters (Mrs. Howes Goldsbor-

37. Page Smith, *The Shaping of America* (New York: McGraw-Hill, 1980), 590.

38. Smith, *Shaping*, 619; Preston, *History*, 241; Jay, ed., *Havre de Grace*, 7.

39. O'Neill, an Irishman who presumably had his own grudges with the British, manned the battery on the ironically named Concord Point, and tried to hold off the invaders. For his heroism, in 1827 the grateful city (somewhat belatedly) awarded him the sinecure of lighthouse-keeper.

40. Quoted in Earle, *Chesapeake Bay Country*, 245–46. It is almost certain that the commodore's parents' tavern on North Washington Street, probably built in the 1780s, was also somehow spared.

A NARRATIVE HISTORY OF HARFORD COUNTY

ough and Mrs. William Pinckney) sought shelter in Mark Pringle's Bloomsbury. "When a detachment was sent up to burn that elegant building, Mrs. Goldsborough told the officer that she had an aged mother in it." The troops torched it anyway:

> She found it on fire, and met two men, one with a sheet, the other with a pillow-case crammed full [of plunder]. . . . An officer put his sword through a large elegant looking glass, attacked the windows and cut out several sashes. They cut hogs through the back, and some partly through, and then left them to run. Such wanton barbarity among civilized people I have never heard of.[41]

The following spring Cockburn destroyed the American army at the Battle of Bladensburg, burned Washington, and threatened Baltimore. Rodgers, finally ordered back to the Chesapeake, arrived in Baltimore that August to discover a "panic-stricken" town. But "the opportune arrival of the commodore . . . restored . . . confidence" and Rodgers immediately set to work planning the city's land and water defenses. (This was the sailor's first terrestrial tour of duty; he didn't miss the humor in it and wrote Minerva, with incredible *sang froid*, "if you were to see what a figure I cut with spurs on . . . on horseback, you'd split your sides laughing.")[42] Gen. Samuel Smith eventually assumed control of the ground forces, Rodgers went back to his boats, and the two men—and Fort McHenry—stopped the British, saved the city, and gave America a national anthem.

When peace came, Rodgers retired from active duty and, like that earlier model hero, Cincinnatus, resumed the life of a gentleman farmer. Applying the same dogged intelligence that he had used against the British fleet to issues such as crop rotation, Rodgers developed into a widely respected agronomist, a man known far and wide, in Latrobe's words, as "a good farmer" of "unimpeached and unimpeachable" standards. Ever the hero, Rodgers, again according to his friend Latrobe, became beloved in his hometown "for having at the risk of his life saved a family of negroes." One winter day the Susquehanna had seemingly frozen over and the family tried to walk across it. Without warning the ice started to break and the voyagers found themselves

> stranded on separate cakes . . . drifting into the Chesapeake Bay. The shore was lined with spectators—no one dared to go on to the ice—when Rodgers, taking up a parcel of boards went on to the river, laid bridges from cake to cake and . . . with great difficulty . . . saved all. . . . The strength of a giant was necessary to do all this, but few giants would have employed it thus.[43]

It is also thought that John and Minerva finally found time to complete Sion Hill in the early nineteenth century. (Recall that her father's 1798 tax assessment calls the house "unfinished.") They certainly proceeded to *furnish* the place splendidly. While they kept much of the Denisons' furniture they also added many pieces of their own—so many elegant things that when Mary Boardman Crowninshield learned that her husband, Jacob (scion of sophisticated and rich-rich New England merchants and, not incidentally, the then secretary of the Navy), was going to visit the Rodgerses at Havre de Grace, she ordered him flat out to examine the tables, chairs, looking glasses, and so on to find out "Is the furniture handsomer than ours?"[44]

But the Navy and Rodgers were not to part. In February 1815 Crowninshield and President Madison appointed the commodore head of the newly established Board of Naval Commissioners, which "ranked next to members of the cabinet in the administrative hierarchy of Washington."[45] Rodgers used this post to establish naval hospitals in Philadelphia, Norfolk, Boston, New York, and Pensacola, to organize the Depot of Charts and Instruments (which evolved into the Naval Observatory) and, possibly remembering his own on-the-job training, to pressure Congress to fund a professionally staffed naval academy at Annapolis. Rodgers's tenure at the board might truly be called epochal, for when he, whose days of glory had come in the age of sail, heard about Fulton's new steam engine, he recognized that therein lay the future, behaved accordingly, and guided the service into the age of steam. He died of cholera in 1837.[46]

41. Quoted in Preston, *History*, 243.

42. Quoted in Paullin, *Rodgers*, 85.

43. Quoted in Earle, *Chesapeake Bay Country*, 245–48.

44. Garrett, *At Home*, 122.

45. *DAB* 16:77.

46. While in Washington, Louisa Rodgers, one of John's and Minerva's daughters, met and married Gen. Montgomery Meigs, future Quartermaster General of the Union Army and builder of such well-known Washington landmarks as the Pension Building; it is from that marriage that the present owners of Sion Hill are descended.

Even though the commodore was gone, his descendants remained inextricably linked to the U.S. Navy—and to Sion Hill. From 1842 to 1860 son John Rodgers II was "in charge of vessels on surveying expeditions in the Mediterranean, North Pacific, and Arctic Ocean" and when the Civil War broke out, Lincoln personally gave him the single honor of hoisting "the first American flag on the rebellious soil of South Carolina." John II later commanded the Boston Navy Yard, the Mare Island Navy Yard in California, and the Naval Observatory in Washington. Nephew Christopher Rodgers served as superintendent of the Naval Academy and as commander in chief of the entire Pacific squadron.[47] Grandson John Augustus Rodgers, who gained the rank of rear admiral "for eminent conduct in battle" during the Spanish-American War, proved himself as visionary as the commodore had been; he took it upon himself to convince the Navy to adopt the newfangled wireless telegraph. And while the commodore's eldest son, Robert Smith Rodgers, was unaccountably an Army man, he, in effect, "married" the Navy; his bride was Sarah Perry, daughter of Cmdr. Matthew C. Perry, the man who "opened" Japan to Western trade. (Perry had served under John Rodgers during the wars with the Barbary Pirates where Rodgers, "a bluff disciplinarian," stamped "many of his qualities upon the young subaltern"; it can't have been mere chance that the frigate Matthew Perry sailed into Tokyo Bay in 1853 bore the name *Susquehanna*.)[48]

Just as the commodore took the Navy from the age of sail into the age of steam, it was left to his great-grandson, Capt. John Rodgers, to lead the service into the modern era of aircraft. After graduating from the Naval Academy in 1903 the youngest Rodgers heard about Wilbur and Orville Wright's experiments, packed his bags, left Sion Hill for Ohio, and moved in with the brothers to learn the secrets of aeronautics. He proved himself a good student: in 1911 he earned his pilot's license, single-handedly built and flew a biplane from Annapolis to Sion Hill (which caused no little stir in Havre de Grace), and, with cousin Calbraith Perry Rodgers, executed the first complete flight across America.

The following year Rodgers founded the San Diego Naval Air Station and in 1922 assumed command of the new base at Pearl Harbor. In 1925 he attempted to set a world record for nonstop flight over water by flying from San Francisco to Hawaii, a journey the *New York Times* trumpeted as "The Great Air Adventure Across the Pacific." Actually, it proved to be the great air adventure *into* the Pacific, for his plane crashed into the sea 400 miles short of his goal. But his enthusiasm for air travel remained undiminished. In 1926 he flew back east to urge congressional funding for a new seaplane he had tested in San Diego. This time his luck ran out; on August 27 he was killed when the plane he was piloting crashed into the Delaware River. Rodgers's death shocked the nation: Secretary of the Navy Curtis Wilbur bemoaned what he called a "great personal loss, . . . a loss to the United States Navy . . . , [and] a loss to the aeronautical world." The mayor of San Francisco wrote Rodgers's parents that their son was "a hero among heroes. . . . In his death San Francisco has lost a friend." The *Philadelphia Inquirer* ran an editorial about the "heroic figure" who was "held in honor in every household" in America. Even President Coolidge, "Silent Cal," found words enough to call the young man "an inspiration" when he telegraphed his condolences to Rodgers's parents at Sion Hill. Moreover, Rodgers's death ended an era; the aviator, who was unmarried, would become the last Sion Hill Rodgers to serve his country, the last of four generations of men to embody, according to the Baltimore *Sun*, "the unconquerable spirit of the American Navy."[49]

Robert Smith and the Jeffersonian Villa

The ties between Sion Hill and that other "representative" villa, Robert Smith's house on Spesutia Island, must be coming clear to inference-attuned readers. While Commodore Rodgers saw to it that America's frigates were kept shipshape, Smith, as Thomas Jefferson's secretary of the Navy, in effect handled the paperwork. The president freely admitted that naval matters "baffled" him, and he happily assigned to Smith "principle responsibility" for "the repair, construction, and . . . deployment of . . . [America's] small fleet."[50] (Dur-

Capt. John Rodgers, great-grandson of the commodore, pioneered naval aviation. He studied and lived with the Wright brothers and, as this photo shows, in 1911 he landed a "Wright Biplane" on the front field of his parents' Sion Hill.

47. *DAB* 14:78; Wright, *Harford*, 418; *DAB* 8:73.

48. For Perry, see *DAB* 14:78–488. An astonishing quantity of Perry memorabilia still overflows from Sion Hill's attic.

49. All quotes are from material in Rodgers Collection, MS 2612, MHS.

50. Guttridge and Smith, *Commodores*, 61. Smith occupied himself with "issues of personnel walfare" for the sailors and he "replaced the traditional issue of rum with whiskey . . . a more wholesome and economical drink." In the early nineteenth century the navy went through as estimated 45,000 gallons of rum per year; Smith hoped to replace this with 20,000 gallons of whiskey, "but it must be pure rye whiskey," he stipulated—Maryland rye? See Malone, *Jefferson, Second Term*, 321, 501.

ing the wars with the Barbary Pirates Rodgers bypassed the normal chain of command and sent his dispatches not to his direct superior, the secretary of war, but "to the Secretary of the Navy [Robert Smith]. This irritated [the] Secretary of War," but neither Smith nor Rodgers saw any reason to behave differently.)[51] Such affection developed between Sion Hill and Spesutia Island that Rodgers and Minerva even named their eldest surviving son Robert Smith Rodgers.

Moreover, both Smith and Rodgers were linked by their common devotion to Thomas Jefferson and, indeed, by Jefferson's fondness for both of them. While the commodore's loyalty to America's third president has been discussed, Smith's bonds to Jefferson are, if anything, even more remarkable. Smith (born 1757) was an "ambitious, industrious, courteous, and amiable" lawyer who was successively elected to the state senate, the House of Delegates, and the Baltimore city council as a "loyal . . . and ardent" Jeffersonian.[52] Indeed, Smith's whole family placed themselves in the Virginian's camp: older brother Samuel championed Jefferson's policies as U.S. senator, brother-in-law Wilson Cary Nicholas has been described as "an aristocratic Virginia planter [and] staunch Jeffersonian," and brother-in-law George Nicholas grew famous as a "Jeffersonian stalwart in Kentucky."[53] So well known was Smith family loyalty to the Virginian that when John Quincy Adams, no friend of Jefferson, ran for president he wrote off Maryland's electoral votes since, he said, "the moral, political, and commercial character of . . . Baltimore" was "formed, controlled, and modified almost entirely by" the Smith brothers, their "connections and dependents."[54]

Robert and Samuel were not only close to Jefferson professionally, they were also close to Jefferson the man. For example, in 1805 when the president was being reviled in the federal-era version of supermarket tabloids for alleged bigamy, he chose not to demean himself by answering the rumors in public, but instead to give his side of the story to only a few "particular friends," including Robert Smith.[55] Two years earlier Napoleon's brother Jerome Bonaparte had shocked the world by marrying Betsy Patterson of Baltimore.[56] Jefferson, who knew the emperor disapproved of the marriage, tried to calm Napoleon by explaining that Betsy's father, merchant William Patterson, had made a fortune in shipping and that riches "fix rank in a country where there are no hereditary titles." (When Jefferson gave an intimate "family" dinner party for Betsy and Jerome in the White House in 1804 he found room in the small guest list for Robert and Samuel Smith and their wives.)[57]

Smith and Jefferson's friendship lasted well beyond the men's Washington years. In fact, retirement only drew the two closer, for it gave them time to indulge in their shared passion for horticulture. On January 15, 1820, Smith and Jefferson were simultaneously inducted into the *Imperiale e Reale Accademia Economico Agraria* of Florence (the only Americans ever allowed to join that august group) and while it is not known how active either man was in the Italian organization, Smith eventually became president of the Maryland Agricultural Society (which he and Edward Lloyd V of Wye House had cofounded in 1818).[58] In that capacity he entertained Lafayette when the Frenchman made his celebrated return to America, or, as the November 25, 1824, issue of the *American Farmer* put it, "General LA FAYETTE, accompanied by the Honourable Robert Smith," toured the latter's Maryland farm "with its hundred cows, its extensive and well arranged dairy."

Now what on earth, one might well ask, does any of this have to do with Spesutia Island? Quite a bit. While most of the new nation's leaders dabbled in architecture, viewing it as an activity that formed a necessary part of any well-rounded gentleman, Jefferson's interest in the subject went far beyond mere dilettantism. He viewed the art of building seriously, as something that allowed him to give three-dimensionality to his other, more abstract interests. Just as he wrote the Declaration of Independence to set the nation's political course, so, by example and patronage, he encouraged a classical style of architecture to enhance the stature and solidity of the young United States in the eyes of

Around 1810 the French portraitist St. Memin depicted a somewhat jowly Secretary of the Navy Robert Smith.

51. See, for example, "Robert Smith and the Navy," *Maryland Historical Magazine* 14 (December 1919): 305–22.

52. *DAB* 9:340–341; Thomas W. Griffith, *Annals of Baltimore* (Baltimore: W. Wooddy, 1824), 71.

53. The two Nicholases were brothers. See John S. Pancake, *Samuel Smith and the Politics of Business* (University, Ala.: University of Alabama Press, 1972), 61.

54. Kennedy, *Orders from France*, 276.

55. Malone, *Jefferson, First Term*, 222.

56. The wedding itself caused quite a stir and "one shocked guest remarked that the bride's wedding dress was so scanty he could have put the whole thing in his pocketbook." Another dowager observed Mme. Bonaparte's visit to Washington and noted, "She has made a great noise here and mobs of boys have crowded around her splendid equipage to see what I hope will not often be seen in this country, an almost naked woman. An elegant and select party was given her by Mrs. Robert Smith. . . . Mrs. Smith and several other ladies sent her word that if she wished to meet them . . . she must promise to have more clothes on." Francis Beirne, *The Amiable Baltimoreans* (New York: E. P. Dutton, 1951), 107.

57. Malone, *Jefferson, First Term*, 383. To no avail: the emperor dissolved the marriage in 1807. See also Dumas Malone, *The Sage of Monticello* (Boston: Little, Brown, 1981), 30.

58. Brugger, *Middle Temperament*, 206.

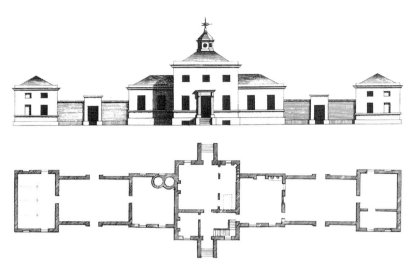

Robert Smith's great friend Thomas Jefferson hoped to fill America with neoclassical farmhouses; this was a favorite prototype—the "Roman Country House" shown in Robert Morris's book *Select Architecture* (1757). Jefferson knew that American builders didn't need—and probably couldn't afford—such an extensive house but he did encourage his peers to concentrate on the middle three sections.

Robert Smith's Spesutia Island villa in the 1950s. The original house contained three 18-by-18-foot rooms across the front on the ground floor and an 18-by-27-foot dining room to the rear. (The frame sections farther to the rear are additions.)

59. Quoted in John Dos Passos, *Prospects of a Golden Age* (Englewood Cliffs, N.J.: Prentice-Hall, 1959), 266.

the world. Jefferson, who believed that architecture was important "because it showed so much," worked hard to give the new republic buildings worthy of its role as the heir to Athenian democracy and Roman republicanism—"to embellish," in his words, "with Athenian taste the course of a nation looking far beyond the range of Athenian destinies."[59] To that end he designed a columned capitol building for Richmond, neoclassical courthouses for Buckingham and Botetourt counties in Virginia, and a Renaissance-style villa for the proposed White House in Washington. "Architecture is my delight," he once wrote. "But it is an enthusiasm of which I am not ashamed, as its object is to improve the taste of my countrymen, to increase their reputation, to reconcile them to the rest of the world, and procure them its praise."

Jefferson had thoughts on private buildings as well and he envisioned an America peopled by educated, humanistic farmers living in neoclassical villas, "which," he hoped, "would express the essence of the young republic" (253). "Buildings are often erected, by individuals, of considerable expense," he wrote in his *Notes on the State of Virginia* (1782). "To give these symmetry and taste, would not increase their cost. It would only change the arrangement of the materials, the form and combination of the members. This would often cost less than the burthen of barbarous ornaments with which these buildings are sometimes charged."

The bibliophile Jefferson found his earliest favorite prototype for an *un*barbarous building in Robert Morris's *Select Architecture* (1757): it was the "Roman Country House," a villa composed of a two-story, gable-fronted central section, intended to suggest a classical temple, and lower, symmetrical wings. Jefferson liked the concept so much, in fact, that his first plans for Monticello were nothing but a simplified version of that model. (Morris's original illustration contained seven parts, but Jefferson, who realized that such a dwelling was beyond the pocketbooks of most Americans—himself included—practically advocated three- and five-part compositions.) Morris's design appealed to Jefferson on three levels. First, in its modified form it was small enough to meet a citizen-farmer's budget. Second, its very name guaranteed passage of his neoclassical litmus test. Finally, he saw in its clean lines and sharp, symmetrical delineation definite reference to the works of the sixteenth-century Venetian architect Andrea Palladio. That last was no small point, for, simply put, Palladio was Jefferson's ideal. His "systematic and determinate arguments had a natural appeal to Jefferson's disciplined and orderly mind. Here was something, like a well-founded legal system, one could count on."[60] Jefferson kept several much-used copies of the Italian's magnum opus, *I Quattro Libri dell'Architettura,* at Monticello (he called the book the only true guide to "the noble architecture of antiquity"), and he was constantly recommending it to his Virginia friends. "Palladio is my bible," Jefferson famously wrote to his neighbor, Gen. John Hartwell Cocke. "You should get it and stick close to it." Recall that Jefferson's Maryland friends had easy access to Palladio, too, thanks to the Library Company of Baltimore, for its shelves contained Giacomo Leoni's 1742 translation of *I Quattro Libri;* recall also that the brothers Samuel and Robert Smith were founding members of that organization.

And while there isn't a shred of documentation to prove that Jefferson actually designed Smith's villa, there is more than enough visual and circumstantial evidence to suggest that he at least indirectly influenced its appearance. First, there is Jefferson's well-documented habit of designing neoclassical "residences, both for members of his family and for friends and neighbors."[61] When James Steptoe, "a life-long friend of Thomas Jefferson," set out to design a new Albemarle County house, for instance, "Jefferson's guiding architectural influence . . . led Steptoe to employ a Palladian-derived plan." Similarly, it was Jefferson's urging that prompted Benjamin Harris, also of Albemarle County, to abandon the usual Georgian massing at his proposed house in favor of "the more distinctive three-part plan." The list of Jefferson-influenced dwellings goes on and on, and includes Oak Lawn (1822), built in Charlottesville for a Virginia politician whose workmen had "learned the fundamentals of classicism while in the employ of Thomas Jefferson," Stono (1818), built in Lexington by John Jordan who was "associated with the construction work at Monticello," and Eppington, built near Richmond by Francis Eppes (a cousin of Jefferson's wife), a house whose three-part composition makes it "an early example of . . . Palladian massing . . . [in] Virginia."[62]

While Jefferson saw to it that three-part Roman houses dot the hills in and around central Virginia, that building form is not at all common in Maryland; in fact, the only known example was Robert Smith's Spesutia Island villa (which was abandoned and unforgivably allowed to crumble away in the mid-twentieth century). Smith acquired the 2,300-acre island when he "married a distant cousin, Margaret Smith."[63] Margaret Smith inherited the all-but-unimproved island shortly after her father purchased it in 1802,[64] and Robert and Margaret divided the island into three coequal parts and sold the villa and one-third of the island to their son Samuel in 1816. Based on the price the Smiths charged Samuel, one may infer that the couple had built something in the interval between 1802 and 1816, for they sold the two northern farms for $14,285.70 each but charged their son $21,428.60 for the part known to contain the villa.[65] Surely that extra $7,200 (or $900,000 in 1990s dollars) represents the cost of the brick building. And since Spesutia entered Robert Smith's life during the Marylander's most stridently Jeffersonian

60. Pierson, *Buildings, Colonial,* 290.

61. See Fiske Kimball, *Thomas Jefferson, Architect* (Boston: privately printed in an edition of 350 copies, 1916), which states that the first version of Monticello, drawn "probably before March 1771," was "derived from Robert Morris *Select Architecture*" and is "a house with a center block and flanking wings" which "became a favorite Virginia house plan," 3. Drawing 119.

62. Calder Loth, *The Virginia Landmarks Register* (Charlottesville: University Press of Virginia, 1986), 16, 90.

63. *DAB* 9:337.

64. See deed JLG P/659. The 1798 tax assessment only shows a "30 × 20" two-story frame house on the island.

65. See deeds HD Z/302, Z/358, and Z/363.

In 1816 Robert Smith established a private ferryline to link his Spesutia Island villa to the mainland. His descendants maintained the line (some are shown here enjoying the crossing breeze) until the family sold the villa in 1920.

66. James Wollon, AIA, "Smith House—Spesutia Island," in *Harford Historical Bulletin* (Summer 1974).

67. Garry Wills, *Inventing America* (New York: Vintage Books, 1979), 129.

68. See Rudolf Wittkower, "The Problem of Harmonic Proportion in Architecture," *Architectural Principles in the Age of Humanism* (New York: Norton, 1971), 101–54.

69. He wrote on page 34 that the pecan is an American native—"not described by Linnaeus, Millar, or Clayton"—and that it is found in the wild along the "Illinois, Wabash, Ohio, and Missippi" rivers. He described it "from memory" as "*Juglans alba, foliolis lanceolatis, acuminatis, serratis, tomentosis, fructu monore, ovato, compresso, vix insculpto, dulci, putamine tenerrimo.*" In the *Garden and Farm Book of Thomas Jefferson* (Golden, Colo.: Fulcrum, 1987), editor Robert C. Baron notes that in 1807 Jefferson wrote Anne Cary Randolph that he was sending her "a bag of paccan nuts for your papa for planting" (194); in 1794 he listed "paccans" among his "objects for the garden this year" (85); in 1794 he "planted 200 paccan nuts" at Monticello (86) and furthered this up with "a great number of Paccan nuts" in 1802 and with "allies of the Vineyards 25 Paccans" in 1812 (127).

70. Frederick D. Nichols and Ralph Griswold, *Thomas Jefferson, Landscape Architect* (Charlottesville: University Press of Virginia, 1978), 143–45.

71. George E. Davies, "Robert Smith and the American Navy," *Maryland Historical Magazine* (December 1919): 319.

72. See Smith papers, MS 766, MHS.

phase, no wonder, then, that this villa, with its temple-front central section and flanking one-story, hipped-roof wings, could be viewed as a textbook example of the master's favorite "Roman Country House."

Indeed, every element of the Spesutia building virtually screams for an Albemarle County connection. For instance, Smith took pains to place his new house's chimneys at the center of the roofs. This was important aesthetically (such placement stressed the villa's symmetry), but it raised some practical problems because it meant that the fireplace flues had to "rise diagonally . . . in order to pierce the roof at the central ridge." Architect James Wollon has explained that "although this is an extreme case, such tricks are not unusual . . . where a desired architectural effect overruled practicality"[66]—and in the America of 1800, no one cared more for a "desired architectural effect" than Thomas Jefferson. Similarly, in an article on the house in the Baltimore *Sunday Sun* of November 28, 1954, the reporter marveled that whoever designed the Smith house had hidden the stairs away "between the walls," thus clearly departing from the Harford County norm of flaunting the stairway (see chapter 3). But, of course, tiny tucked-away stairs are a hallmark of Jefferson design and visitors still gaze in astonishment at Monticello's narrow, twisty steps. Further, the dimensions of Smith's villa seem to have been based on the sort of mathematical relationships Jefferson so enjoyed (and might be taken as more advanced versions of the mathematical games evident in Sion Hill's floor plan). Smith's villa has a T-shape plan with three equal-sized rooms across the front and a dining room to the rear. In December 1990 the author measured the house's foundations and discovered that the front rooms were all 18-foot squares while the rear room, 18 feet wide, stretched back 27 feet. Thus if one assumes a 9-foot ceiling, one can reduce the villa's spaces to a series of $9' \times 9' \times 9'$ cubes and these were just that sort of proportional games that Jefferson delighted in. He "felt that . . . mathematical ratios . . . were as much a part of the natural order as the relation of a man's head to his torso,"[67] partially because similar issues had fascinated Palladio 200 years earlier. (He knew that Palladio opened "his celebrated system" by discussing proportions and by giving "the most beautiful ratios of width to length of rooms.")[68] While Jefferson played out similar games at Monticello, where the two rooms flanking the main entrance are $16'8''$ squares and where the dining room is an $18' \times 18' \times 18'$ cube, no other house in Harford County—and few at the time in America—approached the mathematical complexities of Smith's villa.

Finally, any reader still skeptical about a Spesutia-Monticello link is directed to George Archer's 1895 photograph of the Harford house, which shows a somewhat gawky pecan tree shading the dwelling. That tree has bothered writers for years (e.g., the 1954 reporter for the *Sun* puzzled at the Smith Island pecan, "one of a few of the species to grow in this latitude"). Robert Smith planted the pecan "on the day the Secretary's [grand]son, Robert Hall Smith, was born" and, again, all roads lead back to Monticello. Jefferson fervently admired the pecan. It is the only tree he described in detail in his *Notes on the State of Virginia*,[69] he himself spaded-in several saplings around Monticello, and "he . . . was constantly dispensing them to friends both here and abroad. . . . Many a Virginia garden and lawn is now shaded by pecan trees as a result of this pioneer plant distributor's interest."[70] Many a Virginia lawn—and possibly one lawn on Spesutia Island.

With his idol out of office, Smith quickly fell out with the Washington establishment; by 1811 he even called for Madison's impeachment.[71] Disillusioned with national politics, Secretary Smith refocused his interests on the Chesapeake. He helped establish the Baltimore Exchange in 1815 (and hired that other Jefferson favorite, Latrobe, to design a suitable home for it). In Harford he invested heavily in the new Havre de Grace Bank (Mark Pringle of Bloomsbury, president), in the Havre de Grace Ferry Company, and in the Baltimore and Havre de Grace Turnpike Company.[72] And because cross-currents and shallow shoals made sailing to Spesutia Island from mainland Harford County tricky (sailing to it up the bay from Baltimore or Washington was relatively simple), in 1816 Smith paid $1,500 for thirty acres at Woodpecker Point and constructed a private cable-

John Wilson Stump's Oakington (c. 1817) around 1890.

The locally unique "porch room" at Swansbury makes the late eighteenth-century house among the most architecturally interesting buildings in Harford County. Below: Pilaster fluting and bead-metope-star trim at Swansbury represent the height of American federal-era chic.

ferry to guarantee easy access to his Roman Country House.[73] Smith's descendants maintained the line for another 100 years, just as they maintained the villa—Maryland's one touch of Jefferson design. But five years after the secretary's grandson, pecan-tree baby Robert H. Smith, died in 1915, his executors sold the estate out of the family and now, like most of Harford's bayfront, all of Spesutia Island belongs to the U.S. Army.

Iron Foundries, Swag and Star Trim, and Chinese Sofas

Unfortunately, space does not allow so full a retelling of the wonderful histories of the other villas—Mount Pleasant, Bloomsbury, Swansbury, Blenheim, and Oakington—but this is not to suggest that any of these buildings is one whit less important than Sion Hill or Smith's Spesutia Roman Country House. Indeed, Oakington is probably among the best known houses in Maryland (thanks to the estate's mid-twentieth-century owners, Sen. and Mrs. Millard Tydings) and many would aver that Swansbury—with its acanthus-emblazoned mantel, exquisite swag-and-star trim, and unusual "porch room"—is the most architecturally interesting house in Harford County. Actually, because all seven estates are so interconnected through ties of ownership, architectural style, politics, and business, it may truly be said, in paraphrase of Spiro Agnew, that to know one villa is to know them all. The career of iron mogul Samuel Hughes serves as a case in point, for it was Hughes who sold Spesutia to Robert Smith's father-in-law, it was Hughes who

73. Deed HD Z/360.

eventually purchased Mount Pleasant, it was Hughes's cannon factories the British sought out in 1813 (and which supplied many of John Rodgers's warships), and it was Hughes, in partnership with Bloomsbury's Mark Pringle, who acted as ward of the infant Paca Smith, future owner of Blenheim, when the child's parents died in the 1790s.

Hughes had purchased Spesutia, described as an "Island . . . near the Head of the Bay," in 1779, but as of 1798 he hadn't done much with it, for that year's tax list notes that the property's principle residence was a "31 × 24 2-story wood house." Hughes bought the island so he could live there while overseeing operations at Cecil County's Principio Iron Works. In point of fact, Hughes, born around 1741, had an almost hereditary interest in heavy industry: his father, Barnabas, born in Donegal, Ireland, was a co-owner of the famous Mount Etna Ironworks in nearby Hagerstown and Samuel and "his brothers . . . gained control of the Antietam and other ironworks in the Antietam Valley . . . prior to the outbreak of the American Revolution."[74]

After the war Samuel decided to set out on his own. He "terminated his Washington County . . . operations" and reinvested his capital in "the iron-smelting and cannon-casting business" at Principio, which he renamed Cecil Furnace. This proved immensely profitable: Hughes "secured a contract with the government to produce cannon for new frigates," and Commodore Rodgers for one proved the reliability of Hughes's guns during the wars with the Barbary Pirates. Politically, Hughes served thirteen consecutive years in the Maryland legislature and, when Havre de Grace was incorporated in 1785, he was one of five men appointed to serve on the town's first board of commissioners. In 1785 and in 1795 he copetitioned the state legislature to let Havre de Grace expand its boundaries (a move that would coincidentally mean annexation of some of Hughes's land), and he lobbied "to improve the navigation of the river Susquehanna."[75] Hughes evidently thought it prudent to live closer to town so he sold Spesutia in 1802, and in 1803 bought 825 acres just outside Havre de Grace, "on which," according to the deed, "stands Mount Pleasant House."[76] Hughes continued to add to his mainland holdings and the 1814 tax rolls cite him with 1,400 acres associated with Mount Pleasant (valued at $16,800), 1,232 acres in other tracts near town ($9,856), and "200 Lotts in Havre de Grace" ($5,000). In all, his Harford real estate rang in at a hefty $43,882.

Mount Pleasant certainly lives up to its name. The brick house (described in 1798 as "2 stories, 45 × 33 with cellar"; "4 rooms and a passage on each floor"; "ceilings 10 feet high") was sited high on a manmade terrace facing southeast where, according to a rhapsodic 1952 account in the Baltimore *Sunpapers* "down goes the line of sight . . . , to be slowed by woodland at the bottom . . . and then bursting out in brilliant splendor at . . . the bay, Chesapeake Bay, fanning out in all its glory with the sunlight pouring down from a tumult of white clouds above."[77] Jacob Giles, who had actually built the house in the late 1750s (see chapter 3), called the place Mount Felix; while the meanings of the Latin *Felix* and the English *Pleasant* may be more or less the same, the former is certainly the more suggestive of classically educated owners.[78] And that sense of recreated Roman villa life remains strong even today at Mount Pleasant, where it is easy, if one squints a bit, to imagine Horace sitting in an Adirondack chair, sipping a gin and tonic, and forgetting for the moment his concerns over the fate of the republic or whether his latest sonnet scans. While there is, regrettably, little documented information about federal-era Mount Pleasant (although one post-facto writer has opined that Hughes "spared neither money nor labor in beautifying his plantation"), it does seem clear that the ironmaster had an interest in the fine arts; if nothing else, he hired Charles Willson Peale to paint his portrait. (The artist's journals reveal that he, a phonetic speller, more than once visited "pisusey Island" and he hopefully noted in his 1788 journal "I dined with . . . Mr. Hews near Susquehannah, who promised to give me a considerable job at painting next summer.")[79] Hughes also—apparently—beautified Mount Pleasant with "handsome wallpaper with its many colors, portraying Sir Walter Scott's poem, 'The Lady of the Lake,'" a rare touch indeed. Scenic papers, which represented the height of chic in the federal era, were all but

America's affluent federal-era builders frequently incorporated classical motifs such as acanthus leaves into their designs; Swansbury's stylized acanthus leaf (shown here) is the only such example in Harford County.

74. Deed JLG C/190; Papenfuse et al., *Biographical Dictionary,* 470.

75. Preston, *History,* 71.

76. Deed HD R/68.

77. Robert G. Breen, "Heaven Lies in Harford," *Baltimore Sunday Sun,* May 5, 1952.

78. By the time Hughes entered the picture, the house was called Mount Pleasant; today Mount Felix refers to a mid-nineteenth-century house between Mount Pleasant and Sion Hill.

79. *Harford County Directory* (1953), 320; Miller, ed., *Papers of Charles Willson Peale,* 1:526–535; if Peale completed the portrait no one seems to know its location; Peale *did* paint the island's William Smith (see chapter 10) and that portrait is at the Virginia Museum of Fine Arts, Richmond.

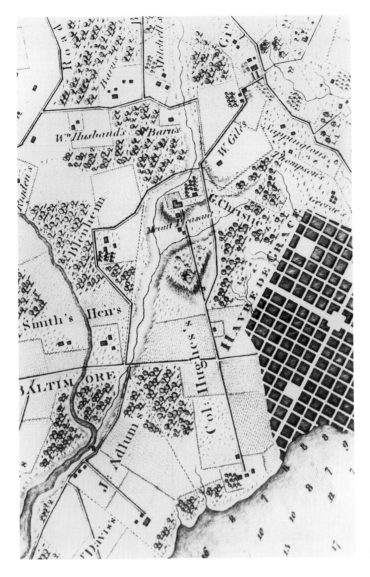

Samuel Hughes grew rich thanks to his iron forges at Principio in Cecil County. In the 1790s he used his wealth to buy the c. 1760 Mount Pleasant.

unknown in Harford, with the only other documented example in the hallway at the Archers' Medical Hall.

Hughes's later years at Mount Pleasant were sketchy in detail but inexorably grim in storyline. Latrobe reported that when the British burned Havre de Grace in 1813 they specifically "inquired for Colonel Hughes"; they evidently did not find him for they spared his house. But they did find his ironworks and Admiral Cockburn "burned . . . and destroyed" the cannon factory and all the other "buildings and facilities" there. After the war, "Hughes rebuilt, but it was a financial strain." He borrowed heavily from Baltimore merchant Robert Gilmor—and from Robert Smith—and was even reduced to mortgaging the "wood, coal, ore, and iron at said Furnace" to Gilmor and Smith. His last appearance in the county's land records comes in 1823 in a complex deed that begins by noting that there are judgments "levied against Samuel Hughes for a large sum of money." To settle these debts, Hughes had to sell Mount Pleasant and he and his wife, who "came to [Harford County] in a coach and four . . . left in a one-horse carriage." In 1834 Mount Pleasant passed to William B. Paca, a grandson of the great William Paca, who enjoyed the place as a summer retreat until 1851 when he inherited his grandfather's Wye Island estate in Queen Anne's County, moved to the Eastern Shore, and sold his Harford holdings to William Whitaker of Philadelphia for $6,500. The house was replaced by the present colonial revival mansion in the early twentieth century.[80]

80. Earle, *Chesapeake Bay Country,* 246; Papenfuse et al., *Biographical Dictionary,* 471; deeds HD 4/196 and HD 6/402; *Harford County Directory* (1953), 320.

If William B. Paca came to know Havre de Grace and its villas well, he was, in a sense, two generations late, for his famous grandfather had blood-ties to many of the villa owners, the Signer's sister Susanna having married William Smith of Blenheim. (To further the cat's-cradle of the villas' interlocking histories, Smith's first wife was Elizabeth Giles [and later the wife of Sion Hill's John Ireland], daughter of Mount Pleasant's Jacob Giles and Smith and his first father-in-law, as owners of the Cumberland Forge on Deer Creek, were business rivals of Samuel Hughes.) As mentioned above, William Smith, who lived in Maryland when it was a colony of Great Britain, had exalted antecedents few other colonials could claim; his grandfather, also named William, was a nephew of Sarah Jennings Churchill, the first duchess of Marlborough. Generations of Harford Smiths had used names such as Winston and Blenheim to mark their ducal connection, but by the late eighteenth century, the Smiths—like their Paca in-laws—were eager to end their ties to England. Thus while Paca signed Jefferson's Declaration of Independence in 1776, his brother-in-law Smith of Blenheim signed the equally revolutionary Bush Declaration in 1775. (He later captained a division of patriot troops in the war.)

When Smith of Blenheim died in 1795 he willed "my Dwelling Plantation commonly called . . . Blenheim . . . consisting of one hundred and eighty acres" to "my son Paca Smith," born in 1779. Hauducoeur's 1799 map shows the Blenheim tract and labels it "Smith's heirs." Because Paca Smith was a minor when his father died as, evidently, was his sister, Frances, their father placed them under the "care" of Samuel Hughes. Having Hughes on the scene generally meant that things became interesting, and they did. The ironmaster immediately ran up huge debts purportedly on the infants' behalf, including over £6,200 "current money" owed to the infants' famous uncle, William the Signer.[81] The three men who had allegedly witnessed Smith's will suddenly denied any knowledge of the document. One said he "never . . . heard [of] William Smith in his lifetime"; one claimed he had been "on Passage from England to America" when the alleged signing took place; and one said the whole thing "is so much out of his memory and recollection that he cannot" swear with any "certainty about it." Was someone indulging in a little funny business? The stakes were high; in addition to the deceased's landholdings (180 acres of Blenheim and some miscellaneous "Lotts in Havre de Grace"), Smith died with personal property worth a sizable £3,200, including fourteen *pounds* of silver and twenty-nine slaves.

But Paca Smith eventually came of age, threw the rascals out, and took charge of what remained of his patrimony. He also developed into one of the ablest lawyers of his time and place, and while his professional career forced him to deal with most of the area's key players he generally did so with his hand firmly on his wallet. For example, in 1809 the town council asked him to keep an eye on Hughes and ensure that that year's lottery profits were used "for the purpose of Erecting a Church in the Parish" instead of—well, one's mind reels.[82] Regrettably, it is not known what William and Paca Smith's Blenheim looked like; the house burned in the late nineteenth century and no images of it have surfaced. One intriguing clue exists deep in the undergrowth about two miles north of Route 40, where stands the ruins of a large, two-part stone structure. That building seems to have had a side stairhall/double parlor plan, a configuration that was highly fashionable in Harford during the federal era (recall the Reverend William Finney's Oak Farm and Dr. Joshua Wilson's Woodside discussed in chapter 3).

When Paca Smith died in 1830, as per his instructions he was buried in the walled-in, private graveyard "at my place called Blenheim." His horizontal tombstone is still there, near the ruins of the stone house, embowered in rampant honeysuckle and wild roses. His estate papers suggest that he shared a love of luxury with his fellow villa-owners, for he owned a gold watch worth $50, two "gilt frame looking glasses" worth $5 and $20, "15 Champaigne Glasses," and as much silver as the Denisons had at Sion Hill. He tempered this wealth, however, with a Jeffersonian love of liberty and learning. He used his will to

81. Deed JLG O/7.
82. Preston, *History,* 256.

free his slaves ("provided they leave Maryland"), he allocated "sufficient clothes to last them for six months after being discharged," and he also set up $30 annuities for "my two oldest negroes." In addition, he had covered Blenheim's walls with a dozen maps, more maps than have been found in any other Harford house of the period.

Significantly, the over 400 cited volumes in his library easily comprise the most significant private book collection in the county at the time.[83] Smith's library contained works by all the standard British authors (Pope and Dryden, Shakespeare and Dr. Johnson, Scott, Burns, and Stern), but because he was a good American he had a four-volume *Life of Washington,* two volumes of *Washington's Letters,* and ten volumes of *The Trials of Samuel Chase* (about which his uncle William could have talked for ten volumes more). The classical world was present and in force at Blenheim, with five volumes of Pope's landmark translations of Homer, a volume of Ovid, something called *Antiquities of Rome,* and a set of Gibbon. Smith also subscribed to a varied lot of periodicals, including the *Edinburgh Review,* a journal founded in 1802 "to provide a voice for liberal, Whig opinion" and whose editors "campaigned vigorously . . . against . . . slavery" while championing "Catholic emancipation, Church reform," and the works of the poet Keats.[84] In addition to his evident love of literature, Smith was also Jeffersonian enough to maintain an interest in the soil: there were miscellaneous volumes of the *Farmer's Magazine* at Blenheim and the "40 bushels of lime" noted in his inventory (one of the earlier such notations in Harford County) suggest that he was as progressive in agronomy as in politics. (He ground his harvest nearby. The appraisers included an "Inventory at Swansbury Mill, $442," including 80 barrels of "Superfine Flour, $360.")[85] Paca Smith had no children and in 1831 his nephew and heir, Gustavus Smith, sold the 180 acres of Blenheim to William Sappington for $2,000.[86]

Paca Smith acquired at least some of his magnificent library at the famous Bloomsbury auction of 1819. The records of that sale show that he paid the sizable sum of $307.20 for a collection of unnamed "Books and Maps." The auction was held on the death of one of the more fascinating of the villa-builders, Mark Pringle. Unlike Hughes, Robert Smith, and Commodore Rodgers, Pringle, born c. 1750, had no taste for military life: during the Revolution he carefully avoided guns and muskets and in May 1813, when Admiral Cockburn was rampaging around the upper Chesapeake, Latrobe reported that the British "went to Mr. Poingle's new house. . . . Mr. Poingle met them with a white cloth hung on a staff and begged them to spare the women and children who had sought shelter with him. They suffered the house to stand."

Instead of dedicating himself to the sword, Pringle dedicated himself to the task of getting rich, often in rather elaborate ways. For example, around 1806 he, Robert and Samuel Smith, and a few others concocted an involved—not to say bizarre—scheme with Napoleon to corner the Mexican gold and silver trade, an adventure "in which American bankers came to serve the hallowed roles of British pirates." Pringle balanced his portfolio by investing in other less-risky ventures, such as land in the newly laid out "Capital City" on the Potomac, as well as in the boomtown by the bay: the 1814 tax assessment shows him owning "438 lots in Havre de Grace, acreage not known."[87] He plunged into local affairs and served as a director of the Susquehanna Canal Company (Baltimore's Robert Gilmor, president) and as a member of the commission to investigate the practicality of improving Havre de Grace's harbor. Needless to say, whenever the town commissioners decided to raise money by holding a lottery, they routinely gave "full power and ample authority to Samuel Hughes and Mark Pringle, Esqrs." to concoct "any plan or scheme which may be lawfully done" to raise the required sums.[88]

Pringle also assembled a 600-acre estate he called Bloomsbury. It lay immediately west of town (indeed, more than 400 of those acres were within Havre de Grace's corporate limits), and he acquired most of the acreage from his sometime-business partner, Samuel Hughes. An estate needs an imposing house and in 1808 Pringle began work on

83. In 1771 Robert Skipwith, who married Thomas Jefferson's sister, asked his celebrated brother-in-law for a list of books for the library he was about to assemble. The bibliophile suggested that 148 titles might meet Skipwith's needs. See Edwin Wolf 2d, "The Library of Edward Lloyd IV of Wye House," *Winterthur Portfolio* 5 (Charlottesville: University Press of Virginia, 1969), 88.

84. Margaret Drabble, ed., *The Oxford Companion to English Literature,* 5th ed. (Oxford: Oxford University Press, 1985), 914.

85. According to mill historian John McGrain in his "Molinography of Harford County," Mark Pringle bought the seventeenth-century Swansbury Mill in 1807 and then replaced the old structure with a "brick [mill], four stories high, built in 1811 under the superintendence of that celebrated engineer, John Davis, Esq., without reference to cost."

86. Sappington practiced medicine as did his son John, who lived in Darlington. And if Paca Smith had no children, John Sappington may have tried to make up for him and is well remembered in the county as something of a roué. In 1832 "a deeply afflicted mother" circulated a printed warning throughout northeastern Maryland entitled "A Call Upon the Sympathies and Aid of an Enlightened Public"; the anonymous author called upon citizens to "rescue her daughter from the further treachery and villany of a MONSTER in human shape, known in Darlington, Harford County, by the name of Dr. John Sappington." Paca Smith clipping in the MHS library.

87. Sherry Olson, *Baltimore* (Baltimore: Johns Hopkins University Press, 1980), 46; Kennedy, *Orders from France,* 238. Pringle's total Harford assessment was $50,975, the third largest figure in the county after John Stump of Stafford ($118,600) and Spesutia Island's William Smith ($86,160); as noted, Pringle's neighbor Samuel Hughes placed fourth at $43,882.

88. Preston, *History,* 255.

89. Benson John Lossing, *Pictorial Field-Book of the War of* 1812 (New York: Harper and Bros., 1868), 674; Mark Pringle Letterbook, MS 680, MHS.

90. As was the wont of these adventurers, Thorowgood Smith "suffered severe financial losses" in 1799 "when several of his vessels were seized by the French. In February 1800 he declared himself bankrupt." But Smith bounced right back, recovered his fortune, and in 1804 was elected Baltimore's second mayor. William Voss Elder III, *Period Rooms in the Baltimore Museum of Art* (Baltimore: Baltimore Museum of Art, 1988), 22.

91. See Edith Rossiter Bevan, "Thomas Jefferson in Annapolis," *Maryland Historical Magazine* 41 (June 1946): 115–21. Jefferson's journal notes: "delv'd sd bill to Mark Pringle to sell for me in Baltimore" on November 28, 1783—the bill was from James Madison. Bevan, "Jefferson," 117.

92. Peter Kumpa, "Foray into High Culture: The Early Days of the Arts in Baltimore," *Baltimore Evening Sun*, December 10, 1990. In the same article Kumpa notes that many early nineteenth-century Americans suffered from a sense of cultural inferiority vis-à-vis Europe and England. Not so Betsy Patterson Bonaparte, who replied thus to one Englishman's taunts about her countrymen's alleged vulgarity: "If the Americans had been the descendants of the Indians or the Esquimaux there might have been some reason to be astonished. But as they are direct descendants of the English it is perfectly natural that they should be vulgarians."

93. Janice G. Schimmelman, *Architectural Treatises and Handbooks Available in American Libraries and Bookstores through* 1800 (Worcester, Mass.: American Antiquarian Society, 1986), 497. The Philadelphia Library boasted thirty-three architectural works and the New York Library Society fifteen, but those were the only public libraries with more building-oriented titles than Baltimore's.

94. On May 16, 1812, Pringle hired one Jared Sparks of Baltimore "as Tutor to my children." Pringle would pay Sparks $500 per year if Sparks lived on his own; Pringle would deduct "$200 for board" if Sparks lived at Bloomsbury. Pringle Letterbook, MHS.

a 2½-story, five-bay, brick dwelling that measured "58 × 48" according to the 1814 tax list. Pringle's letters reveal that he was finishing the house in the spring of 1812: on March 30 he wrote his builder, William Williams, to expect a shipment of "4 columns for portico" and "2 boxes window glass"; on April 8 he empowered Williams to contract "with the Carpenter who built 3 houses for Mr. Stump" to do work on Bloomsbury; and on May 4 he warned Williams that he hoped the work was over since "I expect my family will move up the latter end of next week. . . . You will be good enough to have the house . . . made tenantable." (Unfortunately the house was destroyed in the early twentieth century.) Bloomsbury was so elegant that in 1863 a reporter from *Harper's* magazine called it "the finest country residence in the state." The house's windows deserve particular mention, for each seems to have been placed within its own recessed, blind arch. This treatment—rare if not unique among the state's residential buildings at the time—suggests ties between Bloomsbury and such avant-garde works as Latrobe's Baltimore Cathedral (1806) and the Capitol building in Washington.[89]

While no specific design source has surfaced for Bloomsbury it is clear that Pringle had personal knowledge of the finest, most stylish local buildings: in 1797 the Reverend John Ireland, late of Sion Hill, married Pringle to Lucy Smith, daughter of merchant Thorowgood Smith, at her father's estate, Willow Brook, completed c. 1799 and described as "an elegant . . . villa built on a beautiful site overlooking . . . Baltimore and the Patapsco River."[90] Later, one of the Pringles' sons married a Miss Grundy of the equally elegant brick villa Bolton. Pringle augmented these blood-ties to Baltimore society and its architecture with commercial ventures, including frequent dealings with members of the Gilmor family, with a "Mr. Garrit" (possibly Robert Garrett, progenitor of the B&O clan), and even with Thomas Jefferson, the man who forms the leitmotif of this chapter.[91]

Finally, Pringle, of all the villa-builders discussed so far, was most intimately connected with that great center of neoclassical learning, the Library Company of Baltimore. He, his father-in-law, and a few other city merchants established the institution in 1795. Then, after some truly Lucullan working dinners (where they sipped "champagne and old madeira, then went to dine 'on venison, . . . pheasants, canvas back ducks, partridges and terrapin, with madeira, champagne, whiskey, punch and curacao'"),[92] they managed to publish the library's first catalog in 1797. That list included fourteen books on or relating to architecture, one of the largest such collections of its kind in America,[93] and all fourteen titles underscore the classical nature of the city's taste. One finds, simply by way of example, *The Ancient Buildings of Rome* by Desgodets (published in 1795) and two Palladian-related works, Leoni's 1742 landmark translation of *I Quattro Libri* and Pain's *British Palladio* (1786). (The company published another catalog in 1809; it contained no fewer than seventy-six such works in the "Architecture, Painting, Music &c" listing.)

Intriguingly, it seems possible that Pringle. upon moving to Harford County, tried to reincarnate Periclean Athens on the shores of the Susquehanna. Havre de Grace evidently boasted a library company of its own (Joppa's Benjamin Rumsey, for one, was a member)—had Pringle helped establish it? Moreover, ads in period newspapers make it clear that the area's federal-era citizenry could not get their fill of books: several issues of Bel Air's *Independent Citizen* urge readers to send off for volumes by mail from the "Select Circulating Library" of Philadelphia (which received "an early copy of every new book printed" in London and Edinburgh). Those who took the *Central Courant and Port Deposit Intelligencer,* the paper with those casual references to *Don Giovanni,* were tempted by titles offered by Carey's Library of Choice Literature. Finally, advertisers filled the pages of the *Susquehanna Advocate and Havre de Grace Intelligencer* with notices for journals treating subjects such as "Fine Arts" and "The Musical World." (Pringle valued education enough to employ a private tutor at Bloomsbury for his children and the tutor, it is said, went on to become president of Harvard College.)[94]

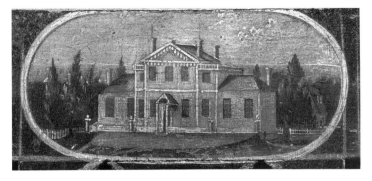

In 1797 Mark Pringle married Lucy Smith, whose father built the stylish villa Willow Brook near Baltimore. Willow Brook, destroyed but depicted on a c. 1800 armchair, certainly evokes Thomas Jefferson's "Roman Country House." Shortly after his marriage, Pringle built the house Bloomsbury near Havre de Grace.

Pringle survived the British invasion thanks to that white flag, but such stratagems could not shield him from his Baltimore enemies, who "lynched" him around 1819 in a "sinister mob action."[95] His lawyers then embarked on the Herculean task of straightening out his affairs (they did not finish until 1842). If one sifts through those mountains of probate papers, one will discover just how distantly Pringle had cast his many business nets. One finds (in addition to such expected local investments as 40 shares of Havre de Grace and Baltimore Turnpike stock, 50 shares "in Havre de Grace Bank," and 10 shares "in Ferry Company in Havre de Grace") references to "installments from the Treasury of the United States under the Neapolitan Treaty" (whatever that was) and monies from the "Treasury of the United States on account of Indemnity from France"—on which the lord of Bloomsbury had managed to secure a whopping "20% interest."

But if details about Pringle's business affairs are sketchy, his estate inventory (completed in February 1819) is most thorough. Not surprisingly, the value of the listed goods ($20,950.75) was the greatest of any estate up to that time in Harford County.[96] Bloomsbury's rooms burgeoned with "18 rush bottom painted chairs" (doubtless from Baltimore, then the American center of painted furniture), "1 Chinese Sopha," and a "Turkey Carpet" (the first known reference to an oriental rug in Harford County). The widowed Lucy Smith Pringle, however, was forced to sell these wondrous things to raise money; her late husband's sizable net assets of $27,000 paled before his debts of $157,000. She hired an auctioneer and the gavel began to pound on March 17, 1819. When it stopped, Lucy Pringle had realized $24,221.67, or 20 percent more than the chattels' appraised value. While several factors may account for the sums' discrepancy, the likeliest may be inferred from the auctioneer's note that bidders consumed 2½ dozen cases of beer, 12 demijohns of Madeira, a demijohn of whiskey, and six demijohns of "spirits" at the auction. Could those 95 gallons of spirits explain why John Dallam paid six times the estimate for the "Chinese Couch"—presumably the "Chinese sofa"? Regardless, one wishes one could have heard Mrs. Dallam's reaction when he returned that evening with his treasure.

Where is the Chinese sofa now? Where, indeed, are any of the splendors that originally filled the Havre de Grace villas? The Maryland Historical Society's intrepid Gregory Weidman has tracked down a few pieces of the splendid federal-era furniture that John Wilson Stump and his wife, née Sarah Biays, commissioned for their new house, Oakington, but most of the rest—Paca Smith's gilded mirrors, William Smith's pounds of eighteenth-century silver, the Peale portrait of Samuel Hughes, even Gideon Denison's beloved "chariot"—has vanished without a trace. The twentieth century, which has proven inimical to concepts such as neoclassical beauty, effectively brought an end to the phenomenon that was Havre de Grace's villa era. In the first years of the century Mount Pleasant, Blenheim, and Bloomsbury were all demolished; Oakington was altered beyond recognition; and the Spesutia Island villa, sold in 1915 and abandoned, entered a slow decline that eventually left it nothing but a pile of rubble. And even though Sion

95. Ellsworth Shank, conversation with author, December 18, 1990; Olson, *Baltimore*, 60.

96. His "Gig and harness" was valued at $200; his "carriage and harness" at $300—compare to Gideon Denison's "chariot" worth $120 in 1799.

Hill and Swansbury have (somehow) endured, their white elephant quality is inarguable and they seem odd relics of a distant era.

But 200 years ago it was a different story; 200 years ago, "there was no great citizen who had not built or was not in the process of building in the country a grand and rich estate . . . in the style of ancient Rome."[97] Well, actually that wasn't written about Havre de Grace; it was written about fourteenth-century Florence. Still, it must be clear by now how diligently Havre de Grace's classically educated federal-era men and women had worked to reestablish that sort of Medicean villa life on the hills of Harford County.

97. Giovanni Villani, *Chroniche storiche di Giovanni, Matteo e Fillipo Villani,* in Ackerman, *Villas,* 64, 167.

For over a century, Welsh miners such as these men and boys made the North Harford community of Cardiff a world center of the slate industry.

"They made Harford what it is" [5]

For reasons discussed in the previous two chapters, toward the close of the eighteenth century Aquila and Sophia Hall at Sophia's Dairy, Jacob Giles at Mount Pleasant, Martha Griffith Smith Jay at Swansbury, and several other Harford citizens found themselves—or placed themselves—in the forefront of an architectural revolution. In so doing they created houses that were as stylish and avant-garde as any citizen of Charleston, Newport, or Philadelphia could wish for. But fifty years of this evidently proved exhausting for most countians and by the early nineteenth century virtually all of Harford's builders gave up the new, the trendy, the fashionable, in favor of the comfortable, inconspicuous consumption that characterizes the county even today.

Of course, one might argue, Aquila and Sophia Hall could afford to indulge themselves in grand neoclassical creations because of their deep pockets. Yet money alone can not explain these very different approaches to building. Money enters into the equation, but so, too, does what Jeeves described to Bertie as "the psychology of the individual." Recall that as the Halls were throwing every stylish Georgian detail they could think of into Sophia's Dairy, a few miles north Ignatius Wheeler was embellishing his ancestral house, Deer Park, with some neoclassical touches of his own. The key word, though, is "touches," for Wheeler, unlike the Halls, simply added a new stairhall, some mantles, and a pilastered cupboard or two to his essentially astylar dwelling. It was not a question of mere money, for the 1798 tax assessors discovered that the owners of Deer Park and Sophia's Dairy had virtually identical fortunes. (The figures were $8,290.54 and $8,365.92, respectively.) Why did the Halls, not the Wheelers, choose to spend their riches on architecture?

Perhaps it would be easier to explain why the Wheelers chose not to. Put simply, architectural enthusiasms went against the grain of most countians, then and now a generally conservative group who favored incremental—not revolutionary—change. When historian Calvin Dill Wilson described Harford for the 1899 *New England Magazine,* for instance, he marveled at how "intensely" the "conservative and refined" countians basked in "satisfaction with their own ideals." He also cited "one prominent citizen of the locality [who] did not characterize himself alone when he declared that he never reads any book later than 'The Spectator.'"[1] And if nineteenth-century countians felt more comfortable with eighteenth-century essayists than with contemporary writers, some twentieth-century residents chose to look way back to the ancient world to find like-minded companions; one recalls Bradford Jacobs's observation that Brodnax Cameron Sr. of Joshua's Meadows "cultivated an old-shoe footing . . . with the ancient philosophers, especially the Greeks."[2]

Trickle-Down Design

Still, Cameron's fondness for the old—like Aquila and Sophia Hall's enthusiasm for the new—is extreme. By the early nineteenth century most countians accepted principles and motifs such as symmetry, sash windows, a center-hall plan, classically inspired woodwork, and an open stair. Perhaps this is because the classical motifs themselves had become relaxed as well. Simply compare the Davis house Belle Vue near Havre de Grace to the Halls' Sophia's Dairy: both are built on ancestral acres; both have walls laid in Flemish bond brick; both have a center stairhall. But Belle Vue is simpler and smaller than the grand Sophia's Dairy. It is one room deep, not two; the open stair rises in one flight, not several contrapuntal ones; and its woodwork is classically derived, but quietly so—no eight-foot carved pilasters for the Davises, just a few simple well-proportioned mantels and a bit of crisply planed paneling. Similarly, while the Halls depended on European-trained craftsmen for the actual construction of Sophia's Dairy and while Mark Pringle based his Havre de Grace villa, Bloomsbury, on designs he had seen in the latest tomes imported from London and Paris, when most nineteenth-century countians set out to design new houses and churches and courthouses, they placed their trust in locally trained artisans, not in foreign books. Neoclassicism, in effect, had trickled down into the consciousness of everyone of means in Harford County.[3]

The causes for these related phenomena remain a bit vague but a few possible explanations suggest themselves. First, in the early nineteenth century the county was nationally known as "a hotbed of radical politics" and Jeffersonian liberalism,[4] so perhaps the noblest way to view the countians' reliance on home-grown talent and reluctance to put on airs is that such actions manifest the countians' love of democracy. Moreover, this era saw the rise of privately funded schools throughout the county—and if the concept of an educated populace isn't central to Jeffersonian democracy, nothing is. On the other hand, many countians may have had more pragmatic reasons for their stylistic conservatism. Harford's late eighteenth-century elite had forged a many-level interdependence with their less affluent neighbors: they needed their neighbors' grain to run their mills; they needed their cash to keep their stores solvent; they needed their muscle to stoke their iron forges, to load their ships, to drive their mules, and to herd their cattle. Since tenant farmer, landowner, miller, and stevedore all worked together toward mutual gain, it behooved those on top to avoid too-lordly posturings.

Then again, perhaps it was a matter of demand meeting supply, for the county's self-taught artisans—black and white—proved to be a remarkably and diversely talented group and the unpretentious buildings they erected are at least as interesting as the grand piles that an earlier generation built using expensive books and imported workers. Happily, many of these artisans have not only left their handiwork in the county, they have also left their names. This, too, marks an enormous change from the eighteenth century, whose local masterpieces must be attributed to a tiresomely ubiquitous "Anonymous."

1. Calvin Dill Wilson, "Through an Old Southern County," *New England Magazine* (1899): 169.

2. Bradford Jacobs, "Brodnax Cameron: Harford Hero," *Baltimore Evening Sun,* June 2, 1980.

3. "Trickle-down classicism" is a new way to express an established, valid phenomenon; it is the aspect of validity that distinguishes it from "trickle-down economics."

4. See William O. Carr's analysis of Harford Jeffersonian congressman, Gabriel Christie, in the *Harford Historical Bulletin* (Spring 1992): 49–69, esp. 54–55.

Darlington farmer and historian Samuel Mason observed that it was black workers such as this couple, Mr. and Mrs. Maurice Dorsey of Berkley, photographed c. 1920, who "made Harford County what it is. They were the wheels that made our clock tick."

In the new century craftsmen came into their own; perhaps it was a result of democratization in America; perhaps it was by accident. Regardless of the cause, come into their own they did, and one is suddenly able to link specific artists and craftsman with occupations as varied as silversmithing, teaching, and stone masonry. This is also the era that the county's black citizens, too, came into their own, when real, documented faces—such as that of entrepreneur Cupid Peaker—begin to emerge from the county's sizable and heretofore dimly defined African-American population. Men and women like Peaker, Darlington farmer Sam Mason wrote in the 1930s, "made Harford County what it is. They were the wheels that made our clock tick"[5] and it is highly agreeable to be able to acknowledge them—and their work.

The Legacy of the Stumps

Harford County's fondness for low-key buildings comes through nowhere more clearly than in the architectural legacy left by the Stump family. Take, for example, the house built by William Stump (1764–1831). William's father, Henry Stump (1731–1814), settled in Harford around 1747 and married Rachel Perkins, daughter of the influential ferryman at Lapidum. The couple lived near the ferry dock (in a house long since destroyed) as Henry enterprisingly established a general store in town, bought several speculative tracts of land "in Deer Creek Forest," and organized "the first [commercial] fishery of which we have any account in this vicinity."[6] In 1794 William bought 144 acres of land from his father, decided to build a new house on the property ("fronting on the present highway from Darlington to Stafford"), and hired "David Hopkins . . . a celebrated stone mason of his day" for the job. This was a revolutionary development, for it marks the first time in Harford County that credit can be given to the actual designer and builder of a building.[7] According to William's grandson, Dr. William Stump Forwood, Hopkins "took unusual pains in the construction. . . . He selected his corners and frontings with extreme care; and arranged the stone in the front, so that each row whether wide or narrow, was continued exactly the same width entirely across from corner to corner, giving it a very handsome appearance." Nevertheless, when it came to matters such as massing and size, William Stump, so innovative in some ways, proved conservative.[8] His house,

5. Mason, *Sketches,* 148–49.

6. E.g., deed TR D/16, Hall of Records; Silver, "Lapidum," 5.

7. Martha Smith Jay hired one John Evans, "plasterer," to make additions and repairs to Swansbury around 1800, but the extent of his work remains unclear.

8. Forwood, "Homes on Deer Creek," December 19, 1879. A David Hopkins was a member of the Library Company of Baltimore in 1797 and thus had access to all the latest architectural books. Unfortunately there is no way to tell if that Hopkins and the Deer Creek Hopkins are the same man.

Francis Stokes, who bought and remodeled Wilson's Mill in 1931, is seen here inspecting the D.H. Springhouse, which mason David Hopkins built near Sandy Hook in 1816 for farmer James Smithson. The little building's highly geometrical finial, composed of a cube, a pyramid, and a sphere, is a true tour de force.

9. Notes for HSHC House Tour. Hopkins's initials have given the building its common name, the D.H. Springhouse.

five bays wide and two stories tall, with a gable roof, double-hung six-over-six windows, center stairhall plan, and cantilevered entrance hood (in place of a grander entrance portico), stands as a quintessential example of trickle-down Georgian design: it contains everything Sophia and Aquila Hall gave to Sophia's Dairy, but it comes forty years later and is much reduced in scale.

It seems safe to attribute William's house's conservatism to Stump himself, not to Hopkins, for another Deer Creek building shows what the artisan could do when allowed to work on his own. "David Hopkins left his *monument* in the construction of *Smithson's Spring House*," wrote Dr. Forwood. "Located up the Creek [from William Stump's property] . . . this is a beautiful piece of stone work, known far and near." Here Hopkins whimsically turned what could have been a boringly conventional building into something truly delightful. His springhouse is both functional and fun. The lower story contains stone shelves set underneath the cooling waters of the spring so farmer William Smithson, who commissioned the structure, could keep milk and other perishables fresh; Smithson used the second story as a private school, where neighborhood children attended to their lessons. Those functions, however, didn't need the classical and exotic forms Hopkins created.

Hopkins knew that the springhouse's main purpose was to shelter the cooling spring; he also knew that Smithson and his neighbors had to be able to enter and leave the building. Therefore, he reasoned, the important façades are those necessary to those uses, that is, the façade through which water flows from the dairy room and the façade that allows human access to the interior spaces. Accordingly (and as he had done at William Stump's), Hopkins proceeded to use masonry to symbolize the building's hierarchy of façades by laying the stones on the two important sides in coursed ashlar, and by using rough, uncoursed stones for the other two walls. Perhaps afraid that this was too subtle for countians, the mason further enriched the two important façades with carving: he chiseled an elegant arched opening over the door to the dairy room and gave the nearby window fanciful lintels with "curved shell or elephant-tusk forms" (as Dr. Forwood phrased it) and sills with a quarter-round profile, all carved in bas-relief. Finally, Hopkins crowned the building's water-oriented gable end with a three-part finial composed, perhaps in deference to that neoclassical era's fondness for mathematical games, of the three solid forms basic to geometry—cube, pyramid, and sphere—stacked on top of one another. Obviously pleased with his creation, Hopkins felt moved to sign the building and did so by placing a stone tablet beneath the finial, enframing it with Ionic pilasters, topping it off with a scrolled pediment, and curvaceously inscribing it with his initials "D.H." and the date "1816."[9]

Hopkins threw everything he had into the springhouse, doubtless hoping that such a tour de force would bring him new clients. Virtually no one, however, yielded to Hopkins's charms. William Stump had already done so, of course, and William Smithson would, for he hired Hopkins in 1819 to build a stone dwelling on a hillock overlooking the springhouse the mason had built a few years earlier. Regrettably, the house was destroyed in the middle of the nineteenth century and no photographs or descriptions of it have been unearthed: all that remains is a set of scrolled stone steps that once led to the front porch and a stone mounting block, inscribed with the date (1819) and those tell-tale initials (DH). The rest of the valley's early nineteenth-century residents proved resolutely immune to Hopkins's talents—indeed to any trace of high-style architecture in any form. What a loss! Imagine if the hills along the creek had been crowned with houses as imaginatively conceived and constructed as Smithson's springhouse.

This sense of missed opportunity must have been particularly poignant to Hopkins if the focus of the discussion is shifted from William Stump to his first cousin, John Stump of Stafford. The elder son of John Stump II and Hannah Husband Stump, Stump of Stafford (born 1752) began his career at age 12 clerking for his uncle Henry at the Lapidum store. By the time he was a teenager, though, John had wrested control of the store away

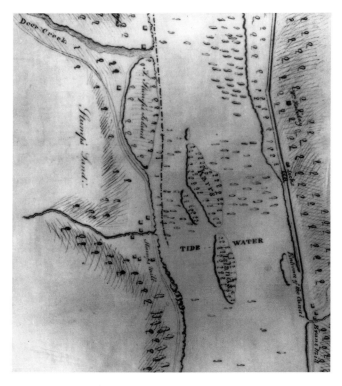

When architect Benjamin Henry Latrobe mapped the Susquehanna in the early nineteenth century, he made markings that suggest the vast landholdings of John Stump of Stafford: note here "Stump's Mill" (modern Rock Run), "Stump's Land," and "Stump's Island."

from Uncle Henry; he also substantially increased the store's business. Beginning in 1780 he invested his profits in Deer Creek Valley real estate, buying and patenting more and more land until his holdings extended westward from the Susquehanna along the north shore of the creek for five unbroken miles. Some of this land Stump farmed and some he timbered. But what really excited him—and what made him really rich—was the valley's potential for heavy industry.

He bought the forge called Stafford in 1782 and followed that up in 1794 by purchasing the Cumberland Forge and a gristmill on a tract then called Land of Promise. (Stump renamed the latter Rock Run.) When he added the Columbia Mill to his holdings in 1797 he found himself master of a series of contiguous industrial complexes and under his control they turned the Deer Creek Valley into a mini-Rhur. The cash rolled in faster and faster and, to diversify his skyrocketing wealth, Stump built warehouses, docks, and stores in Lapidum, a private community of his own at Stafford (complete with houses, stores, and post office), and "flour mills . . . at the Bush River, at Baltimore, and at Alexandria, Virginia"; he also purchased fleets of ships that allowed him to transport his iron and wheat directly to England without paying a middle man. He bought stock in several Baltimore banks and in such progressive ventures as the Baltimore and Frederick Turnpike and the Bush Town Road; he also owned three houses and seven other buildings in Baltimore, including "an old brick warehouse" on the east side of Charles Street with a lot "extending to the Tidal Basin"—the very heart of today's Inner Harbor. When he died in 1816 he had real estate, cash, and good securities worth $233,000, with another $109,000 in "debts due estate," phenomenal sums that made Stump "the richest man, in relative terms, who ever lived in Harford County."[10] Indeed, through hard work and luck Stump had climbed to the economic apex of Maryland, a lonely eminence he shared only with Edward Lloyd IV, Charles Carroll of Carrollton, Charles Ridgely, and a few Baltimore merchants such as William Gilmor and Robert Oliver.

Ridgely is well known today as the builder of Hampton Mansion (1790), the largest dwelling of its time in Maryland and with a "magnificence . . . and nobility . . . [that have been] universally admired"; Carroll turned his ancestors' Doughoregan Manor in Howard County into a 300-foot-long chateau; and Lloyd not only built the c. 1785 Wye

10. Wright, *Harford*, 175.

John Stump was the richest man who ever lived in Harford County. The heart of his empire was Stafford, the stone house and self-sufficient village he built around his Stafford mill and iron furnace on Deer Creek. Alexis Shriver of Olney snapped this photograph of the (decaying) village in 1894; Shriver's image shows an unidentified building in the foreground, the main house beyond (note the front porch), and the village at the foot of the hill along the creek.

House in Talbot County, a "Palladian . . . mansion" of "imposing . . . spaciousness and dignity" and perhaps the most baronial estate in Maryland, he also hired the renowned architect William Buckland to complete a massive, three-story brick townhouse in Annapolis, "one of the few three-story Georgian-Colonial townhouses south of New England" with a "rich, elegant . . . interior" evocative of "Lloyd's aristocratic background."[11]

And Stump? Despite Dr. Forwood's 1879 boast that his kinsman had made Stafford "the headquarters of wealth, refinement and of the best society,"[12] "refinement," at least in an architectural sense, was the last thing on Stump of Stafford's mind, for he was simply too busy making money to worry about spending it on a fancy residence. When the 1798 tax assessors examined Stump's 1,553-acre Stafford holdings, they found Harford County's Midas living in a "24 × 20, two-story wood house." He did own some stone buildings, of course. The Stafford property alone contained a meat house, a gristmill ("32 × 44"), and a storehouse ("28 × 30") all of stone; his Columbia Mill was described as "a stone structure 60 × 36";[13] and when he rebuilt the mill at Rock Run (1795) he erected a three-story stone structure that boasted keystoned window lintels, refinements that were then rare in the county's domestic architecture and unprecedented in its industrial structures. But the point is that Stump put up these sturdy structures to *make* money, not to eat it up.

Nevertheless, in his old age Stump began to mellow—a bit—and shortly after that 1798 tax assessment he and his wife moved out of their earlier frame residence and into the "Dwelling House, stone 45′ by 28′" cited in the 1814 tax rolls. Even so, to look at that new, improved Stafford, a near-twin of cousin William's house, one would never think that it was the residence of one of the half-dozen richest men in Maryland. Granted its masonry work is superb—the large, regularly shaped blocks of granite are set off by apex-pointing, that is, by mortar carefully troweled to a point between the stones (a rare bit of panache seen in the county also at Col. John Streett's remarkable brick house, discussed in chapter 3). Granted also that the interior contains a fashionable center stairhall plan (symbolized on the exterior by a cantilevered entrance hood instead of a portico), and that Stump embellished the stair with scroll step ends, clustered newel posts, and unusually exuberant shadow rail, and gave the ground floor rooms rich cornices with

11. See Papenfuse et al., *New Guide*, 298, 43, 158, 338–39.

12. Forwood, "Homes on Deer Creek," December 19, 1879.

13. *Maryland Journal* (June 4, 1794), quoted in McGrain, "Molinography."

Wall of Troy dentils and elegant chairrails and window casings. The point, however, is not that Stafford has an elegant stair (one would expect that), but that one would expect a good deal *more* elegance at Stafford than one finds there. This is part of what makes Stafford the ultimate exemplar of Harford's "trickle-down" Georgianism. Breaking new stylistic ground did not interest Stump; building a comfortable house did. And while he could have afforded to put up anything—*anything*—on the shores of Deer Creek, he did not build a Wye or a Hampton or a Doughoregan; he built Stafford, a relatively modest, clean-lined, foursquare house trimmed with woodwork incorporating motifs that had been used in the county for forty years.

Stump was as frugal when he furnished the new house as he was when he constructed it. While he bought the requisite mahogany furniture (sideboard, dining tables, tea tables, card tables, writing desks) of the federal-era rich none of these pieces was too grand, none too exotic, none—God forbid!—too expensive. Where was the "Chinese sopha" Mark Pringle gave Bloomsbury? or the hundreds of books Paca Smith bought for Blenheim? Sophisticated Washingtonians made special trips to gaze with awe at the splendid furnishings John and Minerva Rodgers bought for Sion Hill—did anyone do the same at Stafford? Not likely. Still, to give Stump his due, he did spend money on some things: at his death his estate appraisers found 15 decanters, "15 gallons French brandy," and one jolly (and somewhat rare for Maryland at the time) "case champaign" in the house.[14] They also found "1 new 4 wheel carriage" worth an amazing $900. This was far more valuable, for instance, than the stunning brass-trimmed "chariot" Gideon Denison had at Sion Hill, worth a paltry $120 in 1799. To suggest modern equivalents for these vehicles, conservative Stump tooled around the county in a souped-up Lamborghini while the otherwise style-conscious Denison made do with a sedate Volvo.

For a century or more after John and William Stump completed their foursquare stone houses, seemingly everyone else along the Deer Creek built something similar. Just follow the architectural careers of Stump of Stafford's children and their spouses. The patriarch's death in 1816 and the ensuing break-up of his empire let loose a good deal of heretofore closely held capital. Stump instructed his executors to divide his holdings equally among his seven children, each of whom received real estate then valued at about $25,000. Thus each of the seven was, instantly, a millionaire, for $25,000 in 1816 represents about 1.5 million 1990s dollars. (And there was liquid capital as well: Stump's "Bank, Insurance and Turnpike Stocks" alone were valued at $61,105.) While a few of the seven spent their new riches freely (John Wilson Stump, born 1792 and builder of the highly stylish Oakington, comes to mind, although his profligacy has always been attributed to his Baltimore-born wife, Sarah Biays), most played it cautiously.

Daughter Ann, born 1786, and her husband, Dr. John Archer Jr., were in fact so reluctant to spend money, they didn't build anything at all. But they didn't have to; their share of her father's real estate consisted of the mill and 242 acres at Rock Run, a 202-acre island in the mouth of Deer Creek, and a rental property referred to as "the farm house of Skipwith Coal[e]." This suited the Archers just fine, for the mill's acreage included not only a guaranteed source of income, thanks to the mill itself, it also included a wonderful place to live, the superb 1804 stone house built by John Carter. This phantom-like figure purchased a half-interest in the Rock Run property from Stump in 1801;[15] he died in 1805 and his son, Samuel, sold the half-interest back to Stump in 1808.

Stump must have approved of the house's distinctly unflashy lines. In fact, one suspects that in the design of the house Carter was deferring to the aesthetics of his senior partner. The main section of the Rock Run dwelling house is a near twin to Stafford: two stories tall, five bays wide, with a cantilevered entrance hood, a center-hall plan, and restrained, classically derived interior woodwork. (It is a near-twin to William Stump's house, too, and Hopkins is sometimes given credit for it, as he is for Stafford, but no documents exist to link him to either building.) John Carter and his wife, Rebecca, "signed" their new house with an oval datestone inscribed "J R C 1804," making the building, as

14. In his landmark study of *Wines and Other Potables* (Baltimore: privately printed, 1988), Michael Trostel notes a few references to champagne among Stump's contemporaries: Edward Lloyd IV of Wye House died in 1796 and "Clouet Champaigne" is lumped in with "Sherry Lisbon port . . . Burgundy and Rhenish wine"; Gov. Charles Ridgely had five bottles of "champaign @ $1" when he died at Hampton in 1829; the cellar of William Gilmor, however, effervesced with five cases of champagne (worth $36 in all) at his death in 1825.

15. Carter was kin of sorts: his mother was Hannah Stump Carter, a daughter of Henry Stump.

Ann Stump Archer inherited the Rock Run mill (foreground) and house when her father, Stump of Stafford, died in 1816. Her husband, Dr. John Archer Jr. (eldest son of Medical Hall's Dr. John Archer), was a prime mover in building the Rock Run Toll Bridge across the Susquehanna; the bridge's frame tollhouse appears in the background of this late nineteenth-century photograph.

architect James Wollon has written, "of the utmost value" to historians partially because it can be so securely dated; partially because "it retains nearly every original detail and feature including its basic form, its masonry, woodwork, hardware and finishes," and can thus act as a benchmark "in the identification and dating of similar features in undated houses";[16] and partially because it, with Stafford and William Stump's house, so neatly sums up the old-fashioned architectural tastes of Harford County's early nineteenth-century upper crust.

If the Rock Run house, conservative when built in 1804, was old-fashioned when Mrs. Archer inherited it in 1816, neither she nor her physician husband seem to have had the slightest desire to enlarge it or make it more stylish. Indeed, the restrained lines of the building perfectly matched the couple's own low-key approach to life and business. Archer, the eldest son of Medical Hall's Dr. John Archer, for instance, found that managing his wife's property "furnished him such full and agreeable occupation that he had neither time nor inclination" to do much in the way of medicine or politics, two activities that had so dominated his father's life (although he did allow his neighbors to elect him a presidential elector in 1828, when he cast his vote for Andrew Jackson). This is not to say that the Archers were sticks-in-the-mud; they were, in fact, eager to invest in capitalistic ventures and in what are now called "infrastructure" improvements. Shortly after Ann Archer came into her patrimony, for instance, her husband cofounded the Port Deposit and Bridge Banking Company, and as company president oversaw the construction of a toll bridge across the Susquehanna from Rock Run. He also hosted a promotional dinner for the venture at which, according to the Baltimore *Federal Gazette,* 150 "respectable . . . ladies and gentlemen from Cecil and Harford counties" gathered on Mrs. Archer's 202-acre island on July 4, 1817, to gaze rapturously at "the piers and abutments of an elegant Bridge, nearly finished," and feast on "delicious viands . . . and . . . the choicest liquors," and, "in the utmost good humor" congratulate Archer for encouraging this "work of . . . vast magnitude and public utility."[17]

The Archers' cautious approach certainly paid off. Even though the couple died by mid-century (he in 1830, she in 1867) their descendants held onto the property until well into the twentieth century, just as descendants of Stump of Stafford lived on in their an-

16. James Wollon, AIA, notes for HSHC House Tour.

17. *Federal Gazette,* July 18, 1817.

cestral stone house until 1946. This contrasts sharply, for example, with the history of Oakington, where Ann Archer's brother spent freely to build an ultra-fashionable stone villa and then immediately found himself wandering in and out of bankruptcy court, enmeshed in several years-long bouts of litigation, until he "lost" Oakington altogether. But the sorry saga of Oakington is sadly in keeping with the histories of most of the other flashy Havre de Grace villas: the Gileses of Mount Pleasant and Samuel Hughes of Spesutia also went bankrupt; Mark Pringle of Bloomsbury was lynched. These dramas are, however, the exciting exceptions to Harford's generally conservative rule. No Stump was lynched; most of them lived their lives quietly and happily made do with a low-key approach to architecture and a low-key, prosperous approach to business.

For instance, Archer and Hanna Hays, another branch of the Stump-Archer tree, made their own conservative statement in the handsome, buff-colored stone house they built in 1808 on their Churchville farm. Hays (1755–1827) was a highly successful farmer and his house, now the centerpiece of Harford Community College, is a building of so many fine qualities that some include it in David Hopkins's *oeuvre*. And it does bear several Hopkins-type features, such as the masonry-rendered hierarchy of façades, the exceptionally ornate stone plaque inscribed "A & H H, 1808," and the mortar, which is carefully tooled to a ridge in crude replication of the apex pointing Hopkins gave William Stump's house. Nevertheless, a single, strong—if subjective—point argues against Hopkins: the quality of the workmanship simply lacks the panache seen at Hopkins's documented projects.

Still, as conservative as Hays was, he must have had a streak of whimsy. His estate inventory contains, along with the expected sheep and cattle and mahogany tables, "1 bird cage." Many other affluent Americans of Hays's time shared his fondness for caged songbirds, note the "salty old parrot" that lived with "a pair of maiden ladies" in c. 1820 Salem, Massachusetts, and that, according to contemporary accounts, "had always about him an air of having been out all night." Thomas Jefferson preferred gentle mockingbirds to dissolute parrots. During his White House years he frequently "opened the cage and let [a favorite mockingbird] fly around the room. . . . When he retired . . . it would hop up the stairs after him and while he took his siesta, would set on his couch and pour forth its melodious strains."[18] Judging from estate inventories no countian but Hays kept pet birds in the federal era although "squirrel cages" do turn up frequently.

The Pacas, Abingdon, and Higher Education

Having determined that many of the county's early nineteenth-century builders embraced trickle-down neoclassicism, it might be wise to discuss the "pipes" that allowed this trickling to occur, namely interlocking improvements in transportation, communication, and education. Because developments in all those fields tend to suggest the presence of towns, and since the presence of towns suggests schools and trained artisans, it is no coincidence that the federal era saw the rise of the county's first permanent urban areas, namely Bel Air, founded in 1782, Havre de Grace, chartered in 1786, and Abingdon, laid out in 1779 by John Paca.

While the first two towns' contributions to the county's architectural history are discussed elsewhere, Abingdon and the Pacas might be profitably discussed here, in this chapter devoted to the county's multitalented citizens and their fondness for low-key design. The Pacas' American family history begins in the mid-seventeenth century when Robert Paca (?–1681), John's grandfather, arrived in Anne Arundel County as an indentured servant to John Hall.[19] Robert's son Aquila (?–1721) drifted north to the Bush and Gunpowder necks where, thanks to a rich wife's dowry, he became one of Baltimore County's leading landowners. His son John (1712–85) bought 630 acres between the Bush River and the post road, named the tract Paca's Park, and built a rambling, gambrel-roofed brick and frame house (long vanished) on a hilltop site overlooking this acreage. Here John and his heiress wife (née Elizabeth Smith) brought up their seven children, includ-

18. Garrett, *At Home,* 73, 92; the diaries of Margaret Bayard Smith, quoted in Adams, ed., *Eye of Jefferson,* 315.

19. Stiverson and Jacobsen, *William Paca,* 26.

John Paca probably built the gambrel-roofed Paca's Park (later called Rose Hill and long ago demolished) near Abingdon around 1740. The house was later purchased by the Sewell family, who probably added the front gable-roofed section.

Abingdon's Cokesbury College, begun in 1784, was an enormous building, 108 feet long, 40 feet deep, and three full stories tall. It was important enough to appear on Dennis Griffith's 1794 map of Maryland, but it burned to the ground two years later.

20. *Harford County Directory* (1953), 337. John and Elizabeth Paca's total landholdings in the county amounted to 2,688 acres.

21. Quoted in Jean Hughes, "Sketches of Early History of Harford County," typescript in the HSHC library, Bel Air.

22. C. Clark Jones, "Methodism in Harford County," *Harford Historical Bulletin* (Winter 1991): 15; Pleasants, "Jacob Hall," 217, 224.

23. Jones, "Methodism in Harford County," 15.

ing William (1740–99), future governor of Maryland and signer of the Declaration of Independence.

John Paca also laid out two communities on his Paca's Park tract, Washington (on the Bush River at Otter Point) and Abingdon, on the post road. Washington never amounted to much, but Abingdon took off. Paca divided the town into sixty-six lots of about an acre apiece all ranged around seven streets: Prospect and Washington streets ran north-south while High, Market, Harford, Johnson, and Paca (which took in the post road) ran east-west. The main streets of Paca and Washington were sixty-six feet wide; the less important others thirty-three. Artisans and educators flocked to Abingdon and the new town quickly eclipsed the older Bush and Joppa. Joseph Toy, Isaac Nichols, and William Wilson made the hamlet a center of Maryland silversmithing; William Dorney operated a gunsmith shop in Abingdon "said to be unsurpassed anywhere in the colonies";[20] and the excellence of Charles Sewell's silk hats, made in his shop at the corner of Paca and Washington streets, drew customers from as far away as the West Indies. Three cabinetmakers, a potter, and an undertaker all found profitable employment in Abingdon and the town was able to support the first newspaper in the county, the *Abingdon Patriot,* established in 1805. Joseph Scott observed, in his 1799 *U.S. Gazetteer,* that Paca's thriving creation contained

> 51 dwellings and 240 inhabitants of which 66 are black. It is situated on a lofty Eminence . . . [and] has 8 stores filled with West India produce and the various manufactures of Europe . . . , and several shops in which all the useful and mechanical arts are carried on . . . [,] two schoolhouses and a Methodist Episcopal Church.[21]

In fact Abingdon was so well known that the compilers of the first (1790) U.S. census used it to mark "the center of the United States," insofar as an equal number of Americans were estimated to live north and south, east and west, of the town.

The *Gazetteer's* off-hand reference to the Methodist church hints at Abingdon's greatest institution, Cokesbury College, established by the Reverend Thomas Coke and Bishop Francis Asbury. Coke and Asbury decided America needed a sectarian college, modeled on Wesley's famous Kingswood School in England, and because the Baltimore area held "the greatest concentration of Methodists in the nation," they felt that Abingdon, near that city and on the direct stage line to Philadelphia (the largest city in America) might make a successful site for the new institution. Accordingly, they bought a large lot in town from John Paca on July 3, 1784, and, after raising the sizable sum of $40,000, laid the college's cornerstone on June 5, 1785.[22]

It is not known if the Methodists hired an architect, but whoever designed the brick college building made no little plans. Cokesbury, a name created by fusing *Coke* and *Asbury,* was huge—108 feet long, 40 feet wide, and three stories tall, far, far larger than anything else in the county. One contemporary boasted that it was in "dimensions and style of architecture fully equal if not superior to anything of the kind in the country."[23] Actually, despite its gargantuan size, its quirky Georgian provincialisms, such as the five-bay pedimented entrance pavilion and curious steeple, make it a trickle-down version of the few American academic buildings that have survived from the eighteenth century, such as Nassau Hall at Princeton (c. 1756). Closer to home Cokesbury was a near-twin to the original building at Chestertown's Washington College, built c. 1785 and destroyed by fire in 1827.

Still, and notwithstanding these hopeful beginnings, Cokesbury's career did not last very long: as early as 1788 its president was fired for his inefficiency in teaching Latin; debts mounted; and in December 1795 the building anticipated the fate of its Chestertown mate and burned to the ground, the victim of suspected arson. No one attempted to rebuild. Indeed, on January 5, 1796, Bishop Asbury wrote that "Cokesbury is consumed to ashes. . . . Its enemies may rejoice, and its friends need not mourn. Would

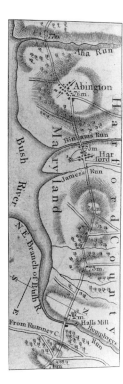

any man give me 10,000 pounds per year to do and suffer again what I have done for that house, I would not do it. The Lord called not . . . the Methodists to build colleges."[24]

During its brief existence Cokesbury College added immeasurably to the Harford scene: as one of the few institutions of higher learning in Maryland it certainly lent élan to the young town of Abingdon, largely thanks to its diverse, multitalented faculty. There was, for example, New Jersey–born Joseph Toy (1748–1826), who moved to Abingdon shortly after he married Frances Dallam in 1770 and whose "various occupations . . . underscore the fact that few eighteenth century [artisans] . . . made their living from their craft alone." In addition to silversmithing, Toy "concurrently held the position of professor of mathematics at . . . Cokesbury," and, after the college burned he added "bookseller and stationer" and "itinerant preacher" to his *curriculum vitae*.[25]

And there is Jacob Hall. Born near Philadelphia in 1747 (and no known relation to the noted Bush River family), Hall attended the Nottingham Academy with Harford's John Archer, "studied medicine under his cousin Benjamin Rush" at the University of Edinburgh, and spent a few years as a tutor in the household of Thomas Nelson, future governor of Virginia. During the Revolution, Hall enlisted in the American forces as a surgeon; after the war he "moved to Harford County . . . and began the practice of medicine near where Deer Creek enters the Susquehanna . . . at the house of Skipwith Coale, 'a Quaker of Whiggish principles,'" and a tenant of John Stump of Stafford. (Recall that Stump left Coale's house to Ann Archer.)

By 1788 Hall moved to Abingdon to practice medicine; he was elected president of Cokesbury College that year (to replace the man recently fired) because Coke saw in Hall "the Scholar, the Philosopher, and the Gentleman" the school needed. Others evidently agreed, for enrollment immediately picked up and there were "upwards of seventy students" studying there by 1792. But trouble loomed. In 1794 Hall wrote his friend Rush about several recent quarrels he had had with Coke and Asbury over money (the clergymen refused to establish "an ample and permanent [endowment] fund" or to have the in-

Abingdon grew because of its prime location of the post road, a thoroughfare shown meandering through Harford County on these maps from the 1800 *Traveller's Directory,* a sort of proto-AAA Trip Planner.

24. Quoted in B. F. Clarkson, "The Bell of Abingdon" (privately printed pamphlet, 1895), 22.

25. Jennifer Faulds Goldsborough, *Eighteenth- and Nineteenth-Century Maryland Silver in the Collection of the Baltimore Museum of Art* (Baltimore: Baltimore Museum of Art, 1975), 46–47.

stitution "cursed with public money"). They also disagreed over policy. When Cokesbury was founded, John Wesley wrote his protégés, "I pray you do not adopt any of the modern innovations"—and they didn't. "The boys were obliged to get up at 5 o'clock winter and summer" and college rules banned "anything which the world calls play."[26] Or, as Hall wrote to Rush, "the restraints laid upon the Youth" at the college were "so repugnant to human nature and the customs of the world"[27] that they discouraged potential students from attending the school. Disagreements grew heated and Hall resigned in 1794, although he continued to live in Abingdon until 1797.

That year, 1797, Hall's father-in-law, Richard Wilmot of Christopher's Camp, died and Hall and his wife, Mary, left the town for the central-county farm she had inherited. There Hall established a highly successful boys' boarding school. Evidently learning from Cokesbury's mistakes, he provided a well-rounded education for his charges, as opposed to the somewhat doctrinaire curriculum favored at Abingdon; his correspondence with Rush mentions courses in English, Latin, Greek, arithmetic, geography, navigation, agriculture, trigonometry, geometry, surveying, and natural philosophy. He also left ample time for exercise and what he called "play": each day "eight hours were to be devoted to study and four hours to recreation" (230–31). This regimen proved immensely popular and notwithstanding Hall's decision to limit the number of scholars to "a dozen Lads of genius and agreeable manners," he was beset by parental "requests that are constantly made to exceed that number," all of whom seemed willing to come up with the steep £60 annual fee. (That amount did, however, include "board, education, lodging, washing, mending, medicine, firewood, and candles.")

The Halls educated their own three sons at Christopher's Camp before the youths went off on to their own highly successful careers. Two, Richard Wilmot Hall, born 1785, and Thomas Parry Hall, born 1789, became doctors; Richard eventually held the chair of "professor of Obstetrics and Dean of the University of Maryland." William Wilmot Hall, born 1787, became a distinguished Baltimore attorney. More distantly based students included Benjamin Rush's two sons and William and George Pickering, whose father, Thomas Pickering, had been "Adjutant-General and Quartermaster under Washington and who later served successively as Postmaster General, Secretary of War, [and] Secretary of State" for the United States and as a senator from Massachusetts. Hall kept the school going until his health began to fail; he died at Christopher's Camp on May 7, 1812, and was buried on the farm.

Dr. Hall's career and his Christopher's Camp school synthesize the best qualities of that multifaceted age. That list of the school's subjects suggests the width and depth of the schoolmaster's own interests (he was the only teacher at Christopher's Camp) and his life suggests that he *knew* those subjects firsthand: not only did he practice medicine, he was also "a scientific farmer" who "devoted himself" to the land, "contributed . . . to the medical literature of his day" (his paper on "The effects of electricity on . . . the bilious duct" was "based upon experiments" he had made "upon himself"), and even found time to dabble in poetry. The variety of his interests is underscored by the diversity of books in his library, which range from the works of Ovid and Juvenal to *Rush's Essays* to *Electricity*. (Among his other goods, worth in toto $3,986.54½, Hall owned "1 electrical machine"; a similar entry—"1 electrical machine, £8 10s," appears in John Stump II's 1797 estate inventory. What *were* countians up to?) While it is not clear if Hall taught the principles of architecture at either Cokesbury or Christopher's Camp, he certainly could have. The doctor himself possessed an interest in the fine arts (he owned books such as *Antiquities of Athens* and *Antiquities of Rome*) and one modern historian has suggested that Abingdon, when Hall lived there, provided architects for booming Baltimore, whose "builders were generally trained by apprenticeship, from pattern books, or occasionally, at a school like Cokesbury College in Abingdon."[28]

Visible reminders of Abingdon's golden era today number precisely one, the Nelson-Reardon-Kennard House.[29] This highly important structure stands as another exhibit in

26. "A pool 6 feet square was provided for bathing. One pupil was permitted to bathe at a time and only for one minute with a master always being present. Bathing in Bush River was strictly prohibited." Wright, *Harford,* 237.

27. All from Pleasants, "Jacob Hall," 227–28.

28. Ibid., 232, 234; Natalie W. Shivers, *Those Old Placid Rows* (Baltimore: Maclay and Associates, 1981), 14.

29. Other houses may date from this period, but they are hidden beneath remodelings and layers of vinyl and asbestos.

The c. 1785 Nelson-Reardon-Kennard House, the most visible survivor of Abingdon's golden age, has a five-bay width and center-hall plan that suggest a "trickle down" version of the 1768 Sophia's Dairy.

support of the trickle-down Georgian theory. On May 9, 1785, Aquila Paca, eldest son of the founding John (who had died earlier that year), sold lot number 3 in Abingdon to John Reardon,[30] who built the present frame dwelling shortly thereafter. (He and his "2-story wood house" are listed in the 1798 tax list.) The building consists of two parts—a five-bay main portion, with a center stairhall flanked by a parlor and dining, and a rear service ell, reached from the dining room and containing the kitchen, pantry, and back stairs. Self-evidently sensible, this workable plan would reappear a generation later at William Finney's Greenwood (discussed below), from whence it came to dominate the county's architecture for a century. Moreover, Reardon's house secures another firm place in the county's architectural continuum as a middle-class frame interpretation of design principles that had grandly burst on the county a generation earlier. Reardon could not afford the Flemish bond brick the Halls used at Sophia's Dairy and had to settle for random-width weatherboards (still largely in place). Yet the controlling aesthetic is clear and, if one thinks about it, the house is really nothing but Sophia's *redux*.

A brace of father-and-son Harlan family houses might be used to illustrate not only the early nineteenth-century countians' fondness for trickle-down neoclassical design, but also the importance they gave to education. Jeremiah Harlan moved to Harford's Deer Creek Valley from his native Chester County, Pennsylvania, "in the last quarter of the eighteenth century,"[31] and the 1798 taxmen found him living in Deer Creek Lower Hundred in a "16 × 44 1-story wood house" owned by Stump of Stafford. In 1800 his material condition began to improve, for that year he married Esther Stump, a daughter of Henry Stump and a first cousin of Stump of Stafford. In 1812 Harlan paid his brother-in-law Reuben Stump $4,000 for 181 acres north of the creek, a truly splendid site, praised in 1897 as "most picturesque . . . situated high on the steep . . . precipitous hills [which are] covered with a dark olive cloak of cedar trees" and which yield vistas "of the bay far off shining in the sun."[32]

But these beauties appeal more to visitors today than they did to Harlan, for like his Stump in-laws when it came time to improve his acreage, farmer Harlan proved more a pragmatist than an aesthete. While willing to spend capital to erect a massive stone bank barn for the betterment of his agricultural ventures and a small two-story stone

30. Deed JLG G/41.

31. See Lower Deer Creek Valley Historic District, nomination to the National Register of Historic Places, HSHC, Bel Air.

32. *Portrait and Biographical Record*, 133.

"They made Harford what it is"

Jeremiah Harlan built this combination shop/schoolhouse around 1815; his son David was one of many distinguished countians to learn their lessons in the little building's second-floor schoolroom. The somewhat unusual cantilevered entrance hood suggests similarities to the house at Rock Run and William Stump's farmhouse on Stafford Road, both built by Jeremiah's inlaws.

shop/schoolhouse for the betterment of his children and their cousins (he hired one "Dr. Samuel Guile . . . [of] Harvard"[33] as tutor), when it came time to build a house for himself he was anything but free-spending and put up a decidedly unsplashy two-story, three-bay stone building that Dr. Forwood politely described as "comfortable" and built with "regard for the old style."[34] In contrast, Harlan gave the shop/school many locally avant-garde features, including a cantilevered entrance hood over the schoolroom door. That somewhat unusual detail closely resembles the entrance hood over the main door at William Stump's house: one wonders if Esther Stump Harlan borrowed mason David Hopkins from her brother William.

Jeremiah Harlan's decision to invest in the schoolhouse paid handsome dividends; the little building's list of alumni includes Maryland Chief Judge Henry D. Harlan and Circuit Court Judge John Price (a Stump cousin). It also includes Jeremiah's own son, David Harlan (1809–93), one of the few county natives who might legitimately be called "worldly." After being educated by tutors at home, David Harlan went off to study medicine first under Dr. Archer at Medical Hall and then at the Maryland Hospital in Baltimore, from which he was graduated in 1832. In 1835 he joined the navy as a ship's doctor and sailed off to see the world. His first trip, on the USS *Peacock,* lasted four years and he recorded seemingly every minute of it in his journal.

Because a son, Beatty Harlan, published excerpts from that journal in the 1897 *Portrait and Biographical Record of Cecil and Harford Counties,* modern readers can thrill with the young Harford County physician at "the glories of a phosphorescent sea in the tropics and the schools of flying fish." His adventures begin off Zanzibar, where Dr. Harlan and other members of the *Peacock's* crew fought off "a number of dhows filled with Bedouin Arab pirates." The Americans eventually limped into Muscat, on the southern edge of the Arabian peninsula, where they became favorites of the local sultan, who treated them to banquets of "boiled ant's eggs." After a few weeks the men had to depart that comfortable berth; Asia beckoned. At their first stop, Bombay, Dr. Harlan marveled at "the strange costumes of the females . . . [and] the absence of costume in the males; the variety of equipages; the Brahmin priests in yellow robes; naked devotees smeared all over with clay or dust." Even though Dr. Harlan liked India (he hired "four stalwart fellows

33. Lower Deer Creek Valley nomination.
34. *Portrait and Biographical Record,* 133.

to carry" him "all day on their shoulders in a silk-covered palanquin" and "a boy to run alongside to answer questions and wait on him"), he and his shipmates had to move on. In Ceylon, the Americans enjoyed "the courtesies of the English governor . . . and the officers of the garrison"; in Borneo they battled "head-hunting savages"; in Bangkok "his Magnificent Majesty, the King of Siam," feted the men at dinners where "the viands were served on gold and silver dishes" in palaces with "lizards and snakes . . . hiding in the walls." (Regrettably, "two of the crew died of dysentery.")

They then set out for Hawaii, where Harlan and his companions were befriended by the king of the islands, "whom they often met in the billiard rooms and bowling alleys[!]." "From Honolulu the *Peacock* made a quick voyage to Monterey, Upper California . . . [and] in this portion of the Pacific they constantly fell in with whalers." And with whales: once, in fact, "the boat rocked with the impulse of a wave and suddenly the whale reared his enormous head with open mouth. . . . One second later . . . and the whale would have come up directly under the boat and capsized it." Thence to Mexico and Peru, where the ship docked for six weeks, "which gave her officers a fine opportunity to become acquainted with the gay capital" and they "danced and sang, gambled and smoked" and attended their first bullfights. (Dr. Harlan didn't; he deemed those last spectacles "disgusting.")

Meanwhile, as Dr. Harlan was hobnobbing with the king of Siam and the sultan of Oman, his Stump relations were playing out their own sagas on the hills around Deer Creek. And if Dr. Harlan ever felt that the goings-on along the creek were less glamorous than, say, bowling a few frames with the king of Hawaii, nothing in his actions indicates this. For when his bachelor uncle Reuben Stump died in 1841 and left the Deer Creek farm he'd inherited from *his* father, Henry Stump, to David Harlan, the doctor did not hesitate a minute before deciding to chuck traveling around Bombay on a palanquin in favor of farming "at his home in Harford County."[35] Moreover, when the "old mansion burned . . . not long after the death of . . . Reuben Stump" and Dr. Harlan, world-traveler, had to replace it, did he replicate a Buddhist temple to remind himself of his adventures? No, he followed his ancestors' conservative design dicta and rebuilt "a new stone building . . . upon the foundations of the old."

Left: Dr. David Harlan, USN, favorite of the sultan of Muscat and bowling companion of the king of Hawaii. Right: Dr. Harlan moved back to his native Harford County when he inherited his uncle's Deer Creek farm in 1841. Five years later he married Margaret Herbert and the newlyweds moved into *her* ancestors' house, The Homelands, near Churchville. The house, shown here c. 1890, is still owned by David and Margaret Harlan's direct descendants.

35. See *Harford Historical Bulletin* (Winter 1992).

"They made Harford what it is" 97

Shortly after inheriting his Harford property, Dr. Harlan made the ultimate commitment toward a settled life: he married in 1846. His bride was Margaret Herbert and the couple moved to her family's farm, The Homelands, near Churchville. Dr. Harlan evidently found the main house there to his liking for neither he nor his descendants (who have continuously owned the property) felt compelled to make any substantial changes to it: they have added a porch here, a stained glass window there, but nothing to alter the house's conservative foursquare lines. Moreover, the Harlans' work (or lack thereof) at The Homelands curiously parallels (and precisely coincides with) the actions of their Churchville neighbor, the Reverend William Finney, whose substantial landholdings bordered The Homelands to the east.

Re-enter the Finneys

Recall that in 1821 the Reverend William Finney built Oak Farm, a massive stone house enriched with dazzlingly elegant details. But Oak Farm evidently proved too dazzling, for after living there twenty years Finney sold the place and built a decidedly simpler structure a bit nearer the village. He called his new five-bay, two-story, two-part frame dwelling Greenwood and the house's massing and plan closely resemble those seen at John Reardon's house in Abingdon and at Swansbury, one of the spectacular villas discussed in chapter 4. But don't look to Greenwood for Swansbury's superb Palladian window, or acanthus-studded mantel, or elegant bead-and-star trim. Finney had no use for any of that. Instead he built his new dwelling in a manner that makes it the frame equivalent of the Stumps' trickle-down stone houses.

Whatever Finney's motivation may have been at Greenwood the new building struck a deeply responsive chord in the county. It was this intentionally modest house—not the more upscale Oak Farm—that launched a thousand imitators. Indeed, to drive along Churchville Road today is to see literally scores of neo-Greenwoods: there is county sheriff William Carsins's five-bay, 2½-story, near-replica (built in 1853 on a hill overlooking the crossroads community then called Center Ville and now Carsins Run), blacksmith Christopher De Swann's c. 1866 slightly smaller version of the rector's house, the Carsins Run Store (which incorporates De Swann's smithy), the Bodt-Bowman House (c. 1875), the George Baker House (c. 1850), the old Churchville Presbyterian Church Rectory (1865), and the Chesney-Bodt House (1905); in addition to those neo-Greenwoods—which all front Churchville Road—one must also note the McGonnigal-Blackburn House (c. 1843) on Calvary Road and the Patterson-Sheridan House (c. 1860) and Hemlock Hall (c. 1870) on Creswell Road. *Everyone* in central Harford County, it seems, wanted a Greenwood of his own. Indeed, in 1884, John Finney Wakeland (named after the rector's doctor son) grew dissatisfied with the masonry house he had inherited on Grafton's Lane because it didn't look like Greenwood, so he added a Greenwood-esque frame wing perpendicular to the original structure.

The cumbersome word "Greenwood-esque" is no misprint. It is important to note that none of these houses is an exact copy of the rector's house. Some builders opted for three-bay dwellings, not five; some added an attic gable window on the main façade and/or a big bay window on any façade; some incorporated bracketed cornices and stained glass windows. But one must stress that all these details are just that, details, nothing more than early versions of what the automobile industry now calls "customizing." Still, customize county builders did, and for decades they added more and more accessories to Finney's 1841 trickle-down model. Perhaps it all culminated in John and Mary Cole's residence near Fountain Green. The Coles completed their house in 1897; that was also the year of Queen Victoria's Diamond Jubilee and the Harford couple, fittingly, lathered their new house with all the options so dear to Victorian-era builders—porches, oriel windows, dormers, stained glass—to create, in effect, a hot pink 1959 Cadillac convertible, with tail fins flashing and top down and with Jayne Mansfield, swathed in a leopard coat, blowing kisses and waving from the front seat. Still, one should not be misled by all

the Coles' spindles and stained glass; stripped of all its geegaws, their house doesn't evoke Jayne Mansfield at all; it evokes the Reverend Finney.

A virtually limitless number of other examples of the county elite's fondness for modest buildings suggest themselves: the Davis family's Belle Vue near Havre de Grace has been mentioned; there is also the Lees' Jerusalem (near the mill of the same name) and its near-twin neighbor, Olney; and back on Deer Creek is the Coale family's Wakefield. Moreover, having mastered the principles of trickle-down aesthetics, countians did not restrict themselves to designing trickle-down houses; they erected trickle-down public buildings, too, such as the "Old Brick" Baptist Church near Jarrettsville (begun in 1754 and altered somewhat in 1787), Calvary Methodist Church (1821), Watters Meeting House (c. 1840), Mount Carmel Church (1865)—even William Finney's own 1820 Churchville Presbyterian Church. In fact, when Finney set out to build his church, whose simple lines seem so appropriate to Protestant worship, he just contracted with one Daniel McNabb to dismantle the existing eighteenth-century church, "taking care and attention as to prevent the destruction or injury of any of the materials," store the "pews . . . in the graveyard [and] the sash . . . in W. James Herbert's house," clean "the brick and stone," and arrange with "Elijah Walton, undertaker" to erect a new, foursquare building "in a good, complete, and workmanlike manner," recycling as much of the old material as possible. That—combined with a very rough sketch—was how one built a church

The Reverend William Finney's c. 1845 Greenwood influenced two generations of builders in central Harford County; compare the rector's house (p. 313), for example, to these three structures: the De Swann-Lillie House (upper left), the Sequin House (shown below in two images, one taken c. 1900, the other c. 1914), and the Carsins Run Store (upper right, as photographed in the mid-1930s).

in Harford County in 1820. It was even how one built a courthouse, according to historian George W. Archer. In 1889, Archer discovered the "meager" plans architect J. Crawford Neilson had given to the builder and shook his head in amazement at how "comparatively trivial" his ancestors had viewed the task of putting up a "new temple of justice"—trivial, that is, compared to "the big job" of cleaning the "tobacco quids and squirtings that had by that time accumulated and been ground into the floors" of the court's temporary, rented quarters.[36]

Quarrymens' Cottages and the Home of a Mule Driver

To shift focus again, the house-builders mentioned in the above section—Carsins (the sheriff), Finney (the minister), and De Swann (the blacksmith)—were all members in good standing of the county's prosperous middle class. John Finney Wakeland earned his living as an ice cutter, which sounds unremunerative and esoteric today but which made him much in demand and guaranteed a steady, if not spectacular, income. What, one may well wonder, about the county's numerous blue-collar (or no-collar) population? It is clear that there were more of them than there were Stumps and Harlans. And it is probably safe to assume that they lived in houses less substantial than Sheriff Carsins's fine residence, which even boasted a dumbwaiter. But what exactly did those houses look like? Unfortunately, historians wobble onto shaky ground here partially because few such houses remain. Nor has much visual record of them endured. While tax rolls offer some help, they simply mark the existence of many small houses; they do not illustrate examples. The few places that have survived, therefore, should be valued and preserved—and recorded.

Based on existing evidence, it seems safe to say that the county's artisans were as fond of conservative, regular, trickle-down design as their middle-class—or upper-class—neighbors were. Note, for example, the stone cottage on Montgomery's Delight, a tract near the Cardiff slate quarries. John Montgomery patented the acreage in the late eighteenth century and, according to the 1798 tax rolls, lived in the "18 × 30, 1-story stone house" that probably forms the nucleus of the extant dwelling. Montgomery sold the house and 350 acres of his land to one James Hogstine in 1808, a small-scale farmer who died in 1822 with goods and chattels worth $578.37. (His most precious assets were "two beef steers" together worth $40, "20 acres of grain in ground" worth $45, two stills with a combined value of $40, and an "apple press and trough" worth $15.) Jeremiah Harlan and William Smithson built private schools for their children but Hogstine did not attend them—or any school. He died illiterate and had signed his will with an X, "his mark." Hogstine expanded Montgomery's original cottage and while he clearly did not have much surplus capital to spend on architectural niceties, what he had he spent well. He added a second story to the building and rearranged the ground floor to create a stylish side stairhall/parlor plan—conceptually, a small-scale version of Finney's Oak Farm. Hogstine's improvements extended to decorative elements, too. Not content with the gray stone walls of Montgomery's original dwelling, Hogstine embellished his additions with rocks that form a dazzling spectrum of color, from green to brown to yellow to pink; he even incorporated random pieces of dark slate as lintels and willy-nilly accents. The effect is, to say the least, memorable and may suggest some sort of intellectual tie-in with the Coles' Jayne Mansfield-esque house near Fountain Green.

It seems likely that Hogstine obtained his slate at the Cardiff quarries, as so many other county builders did. Indeed, historian and social activist Jean Ewing has written that Harford's "architecture owes its greatest single debt, perhaps, to the excellent slate roofs that protect and enhance many . . . houses, churches, schools, barns, and even minor farm buildings in the northern and central stretches of the county." The slate comes from a broad, deep vein that begins near Pylesville and then runs northeasterly for about twelve miles into Pennsylvania. Around 1725 two brothers, James and William Reese, arrived here from their native Wales and purchased a tract of land called York Barrens. While dig-

36. George W. Archer, "The Public Buildings of Harford County: The Court House," in the *Ægis,* March 22, 1889. Elijah Walton was called in to repair the original Bel Air courthouse in 1829 and 1832.

ging trenches for the foundations of their farm buildings the brothers discovered the slate bed, cut out some of the rock, and fashioned it into shingles, which they used to roof their new barn. This, the first known cut slate in America, quickly attracted immigrant Welsh miners to the county and by the early nineteenth century quarrymen with names like Jones and Davies and Williams had made Harford slate world famous. In 1850 Harford-quarried slate won first prize as the "World's Best" at the London Crystal Palace Exposition, and throughout the rest of the century architects and contractors specifically requested Peach Bottom slate for structures as varied as the Johns Hopkins Hospital and the buildings at both the Naval Academy in Annapolis and the Military Academy at West Point.[37]

The Welsh immigrants retained their mining secrets when they settled in Harford County (Ewing called them a "clannish group" who "never disclosed to an outsider, even if he owned the quarry, how they dressed the slate"). They also retained their native tongue; the Delta-Cardiff community supported five separate Welsh-language newspapers throughout the 1890s and "only in 1910 did the local Sunday School change . . . to English."[38] (The newspapers have folded but the language, with its perplexing combinations of consonants, endures in dozens of slate tombstones inscribed with bits of verse such as "Y guir Orud ef a gurai/Yr gywir, gyhoeddai.")

More pertinent to this narrative, the miners also brought the Welsh vernacular cottage with them to America. Folklorists have labeled such houses "Coulstown Cottages" after the nearby Pennsylvania hamlet of Coulstown, and have determined that they "resemble the slate quarrymen's cottages found in the Snowdonia region of northwest Wales. The . . . structures are simple, somewhat squat two-story rectangle[s] of moderate depth. The front and rear bays are aligned in two over three pattern with a central doorway."[39] But even though the miners' descendants kept the Welsh language alive for two or three generations, they quickly abandoned their ancestors' folk architecture in favor of mainstream, trickle-down, Harford neoclassicism and that quirky two-over-three bay alignment gave way to a more regular three-over-three pattern. And while "Welsh Cottages" continued to be built across the Mason-Dixon Line in Delta, where a few examples can still be found, they were abandoned as a viable style south of the Line and the nineteenth-century houses of Cardiff and Whiteford differ little, if at all, from houses built at the same time in such centers of trickle-downism as Darlington and Churchville.

While Hogstine and his cottage are documented, his occupation is not. He seems to have been a farmer but he could just as easily have cut slate in the Cardiff quarries. (Those two steers and stills may have merely represented what he needed for home consumption.) The county does contain, however, one laborer's cottage where owner and occupation are documented. In January 1886 William Jackson paid William Pyle $279.35 (and assumed a $710 mortgage) for twenty-nine acres of land on Ady Road and moved into the small, rubblestone house still on the property. Jackson's house, of straightforward design, two stories tall, three bays wide, two rooms per floor with wooden lintels above each window, and a plain box cornice, was probably abandoned shortly after he sold the property in 1930.[40] It has certainly been ignored since and is now in deplorable condition. But Jackson, in a sense, has outlived his house, for his reputation as the valued mule driver at the Husband Flint Mill has gained strength even as his house has decayed. The mill, established by some of the Stumps' in-laws, was located on Deer Creek, about three miles to the southeast from Jackson's cottage, and, as Ewing discovered in a series of interviews with long-time area residents, Jackson made the six-mile round trip every day on foot, until the operation closed around 1920.

The Remarkable Career and Heritage of Cupid Peaker

William Jackson was a black man and Samuel Mason was among the first in the county to acknowledge the debt Harford's white citizens owe their black neighbors. Most of these laborers "lived in small houses, often log cabins. . . . Each cabin had its garden-patch

Cardiff-quarried slate makes remarkably durable tombstones: the engraving of this stone for instance, dated 1876, is still crisp and easily legible—although its Welsh language text poses problems to most American readers.

37. Jean Ewing, Historic Sites Inventory Form for Slate Ridge Presbyterian Church, HA-941; Anne Cowie, "Cardiff, Where Slate Was King," *Maryland Magazine* 15 (Autumn 1982): 33. It wasn't only slate that came from the Cardiff quarries: beginning around 1910 the local green marble, known as Maryland Verde Antique, became popular; it now graces lobbies in structures such as the Empire State Building, Philadelphia's 30th Street Station, and the old House Office Building in Washington, D.C.

38. Ewing, Slate Ridge inventory; Cowie, "Cardiff," 33–35.

39. "Delta-Coulstown: An Architectural Walking Perspective" (York, Pa.: York County Planning Commission, 1981), 8–9.

40. Deeds ALJ 56/80 and SWC 213/555.

"They made Harford what it is"

and was usually located near a good spring of water."[41] Since Mason doesn't go into any more detail about the cabins, it is fortunate indeed that Jackson's stone cottage survived long enough to be photographed. Unfortunately, no court papers or other material on William Jackson has surfaced—no will, no estate inventory, no known daguerrotypes—so it is difficult to paint much of a picture of his life away from the mill. This wisp-like anonymity represents the norm for most of the county's numerous nineteenth-century free blacks and for virtually the entire slave population as well. According to the 1850 census, one-fourth of Harford's 19,356 residents were of African descent (2,777 free blacks and 2,166 slaves) and it reflects little credit on the county's white residents that so many of their fellow citizens have vanished virtually without a trace.

There are, however, a few exceptions. And proudly at the forefront of these exceptions stands Cupid Peaker, one of the most interesting mid-nineteenth-century countians of any color. His descendants spell their surname *Peaker* but he interchangeably called himself *Peaco* and *Paca* and that latter version suggests intriguing antecedents. On March 4, 1822, "Cupid Paca, freeman of color," paid $700 for fifty acres of land "on the main road leading from the Bald Friar Ferry to the [Darlington] Friends Meetinghouse."[42] Because there was no mortgage, one does wonder where all that cash came from. Perhaps Cupid had been a slave of Abingdon's white Paca family, since freed blacks customarily took the surname of their former owners. But while generations of white Pacas did own slaves in Harford County, none of the slaves, so far as can be determined, was named "Cupid." On the other hand, when Henry Stump freed five of his slaves shortly before his death in 1814, one of the lucky group included "Cupid, aged 35," which makes sense chronologically and geographically—but it doesn't explain why our man was not then known as Cupid Stump. It doesn't seem likely that Peaker's early history will ever be pinned down, but, ironically, much the same can be said of the white Pacas, for Robert, the immigrant, spelled his surname "in several ways . . . including Peaker, Pecker, Peaca, Peca, Paka, and Paca," and this "profusion of possible spellings" has frustrated generations of historians seeking "to trace Robert's origins."[43]

In any event, a free Cupid Peaker appeared in Darlington in 1822 with $700 in his pocket. His choice of residence shows good sense, for no other countians were as welcoming to blacks, free or otherwise, as residents of the Quaker village. (At least as far back as the 1790s black students regularly attended the Silver family's Green Spring School and learned their ABCs alongside young Silvers, Baylesses, and Stumps.)[44] Cupid Peaker bought his fifty acres from Cassandra Rigbie Corse, whose father, James Rigbie III, and grandfather Nathaniel Rigbie, with their thousands of acres and fleets of ships, are discussed in chapter 3. And in slave-states such as Maryland the welfare of free blacks depended on the kindness of sympathetic, powerful white families such as the Rigbie-Corses. While this suggestion of *noblesse oblige* may offend sensibilities in the 1990s, that is the way it was in Maryland 150 years ago.

Peaker "had married a woman who was a slave of Joseph Prigg, with whom he learned the trade of a shoemaker." The "thrifty Paca [Peaker] purchased his wife's freedom and that of an infant daughter" and he spent the rest of his prosperous life investing in real estate, farming, practicing cobbling and masonry (he and Moses Harris are remembered as "the principle builders of stone fences" around Darlington) and taking steps to ensure material comfort for the next generation. On March 20, 1844, he sold five of his fifty acres to his son Robert for $117 and ten days later he sold six acres to his daughter Ann and her husband, Alexander Berry.[45]

Peaker died in 1847 and left a doubly remarkable last will and testament. It is remarkable first that a Harford County black man left a will at all, since few of the county's white population bothered with such details. Second, it is a highly complex creation, with thirteen separate bequests and a variety of labyrinthine conditions. Basically, Peaker bequeathed son Joseph "the homestead property" (provided that an infant grandson could live there until he reached the age of 20), while son Cupid Jr. received "the woods

41. Mason, *Sketches*, 148–49.

42. Deed HD 5/438.

43. Stiverson and Jacobsen, *William Paca*, 26.

44. A. P. Silver quotes an old school ledger which lists the black students as "Negro Richard Husband," "Negro Benedict Stump," and "Negro Paris Jay," surnames that make sense in c. 1800 Glenville. Quoted in Benjamin Stump Silver, *Our Silver Heritage* (Gatesville, Tex.: Gatesville Publishing, 1976), 3201.

45. George Hensel, "Reminiscences," in *Harford Historical Bulletin* (Summer 1988): 79–80; deeds HD 29/322 and HD 29/320.

lot upon which he has lately erected a dwelling house" and son Jacob and daughter Margaret (wife of Samuel Scott) received other lands. The Berrys and son Robert were freed of the mortgages Cupid had held on their five- and six-acre parcels, several friends and relatives were left various sums of cash, and son Joseph was to receive "the farm utensils" and "1 bureau and a walnut table." A walnut table is certainly a genteel touch, and Peaker's estate inventory reveals many other solidly middle-class items, including "½ doz. breakfast plates," four "large silver spoons," a coffee mill, and an umbrella. His total estate, exclusive of land, was reckoned to be worth $527.32, less than most of the estates opened in 1847 but not by any means at the bottom of the orphan's court pile.

What is important, and what cannot be overstressed, is that a black man amassed that much capital when and where he did. It is little short of amazing because Peaker, while technically free, had to cope with restrictions—written and "customary"—of mind-boggling complexity. In the early nineteenth century, "black people had to contend themselves, by and large, with a menial position in the developing landscape of Maryland. Few obtained land of their own at all." Even those few, like Peaker, who did had no reason to feel secure for "there were evidently doubts as to whether real estate could be legally held by blacks."[46] Clearly "free" didn't mean to Cupid Peaker what "free" means to Marylanders today. "In 1807 the legislature passed a bill stating that 'no free black coming in . . . could stay over two weeks.'"[47] (If resident free blacks spent longer than two weeks out of Maryland they legally returned to slave status.) Laws controlled even the most minute acts of men like Peaker. As far back as 1805, responding to a "petition from the residents of Harford County," the general assembly passed a bill "allowing a free black man to keep one dog only." "In February 1860, a free black man was arrested in Harford County 'for possessing forbidden literature': the incendiary document in this case was . . . the *New York Tribune*." In 1831 the legislature made it illegal to "purchase from any colored person any bacon, pork, beef, mutton, corn, tobacco, rye, or oats" unless the seller could produce "a permit . . . from a justice or from three responsible persons in his neighborhood that he was believed to have acquired these goods honestly."[48] In other words, if Peaker wished to sell some of the crops he had been nurturing on his fifty acres (when he died, his estate inventory included entries for "Wheat in Sheaf" and a "lot of corn growing, . . . 5 acres"), he had to obtain a written statement saying that he had not stolen the produce.

Once the Civil War broke out, many African-Americans naturally viewed the conflict as a God-given opportunity to fight for their freedom. Politics, however, initially made enlisting in the armed forces difficult for blacks. During the first year or two after Fort Sumter, the Union government doggedly held the position that the fight was to stop secession, not to stop slavery. This stance led to confusion among the North's military leaders since no one would take a stand on how to deal with the thousands of runaway slaves who flocked to join the Army of the Potomac: should they be allowed to serve? should they be returned to their "owners"? Thus "as officials in Washington struggled to evade the question . . . , local commanders issued a steady stream of appeals for instructions regarding fugitives." One or two principled souls, however, showed no reluctance to take a position that supported abolition. Quartermaster General Montgomery Meigs, who had married Sion Hill's Louisa Rodgers, announced his independent policy as early as May 16, 1862, when he wrote that "negroes are, so far as the Army Officers are concerned, free. . . . The sooner they find employment," the better for the country. And if "employment" meant military service, so be it.[49]

But once Lincoln issued the Emancipation Proclamation in 1863, the Union army recruited black soldiers as a matter of course, and "by war's end, 179,000 black men—the vast majority former slaves—had served in the federal army."[50] Historians estimate that of these, some 8,700 were from Maryland. At least a few were Harford countians; recent research has revealed that in 1863 and '64 Jeremiah Presbury, James Collins, Jesse White, Lloyd Ramsay, Peter Moses, Abraham Turner, Santa Bowser, and Lewis Bowser—all former slaves from the Havre de Grace area—enlisted in the Union's armed forces. Although

At least eight former Harford County slaves enlisted in the Union army during the Civil War. Four of the eight (including Peter Moses, whose tombstone is shown here) are buried in the cemetery of St. James Church at Gravel Hill.

46. Barbara Jeanne Fields, *Slavery and Freedom on the Middle Ground* (New Haven: Yale University Press, 1985), 175, 194.

47. In Jeffrey R. Brackett, *The Negro in Maryland* (Baltimore: Johns Hopkins Press, 1889), 187.

48. Fields, *Slavery and Freedom*, 226, 212.

49. Ira Berlin, Steven F. Miller, Joseph P. Reidy, and Leslie S. Rowland, eds., *Freedom: A Documentary History of Emancipation, 1861–1867* (Cambridge: Cambridge University Press, 1993), 483, 499; see also Agnes Kane Cullum, *Colored Volunteers of Maryland* (Baltimore: Mullac Publishers, 1990).

50. Berlin et al., *Freedom*, 40.

more is known about Lewis Bowser than about the other veterans, material housed at the National Archives show that all eight soldiers served with distinction.

Bowser's war record is so thoroughly documented because he had to sue the government in 1905 to collect his military pension. (He won.) In his deposition in that legal action, he stated:

> [I] was born within one mile of Havre de Grace . . . , a slave of John Mitchell [presumably the builder of Mount Felix] and I remained his slave . . . until the war broke out. . . . I was married when a slave to Catherine Parker. . . . I had 12 children by her. . . . When I enlisted . . . I was about 25 or 26 years old. . . . I enlisted in Co. F. 43 U.S.C.I. [United States Colored Infantry] on April 7, 1864. . . . After my enlistment . . . we marched . . . to Washington, D.C., . . . and then into Virginia. . . . [At] Petersburg [I worked on] building forts . . . and our regiment was there when the mine was blown up. . . . After the surrender of Richmond I marched with my company into Richmond. We then . . . took a steamer to Texas. . . . We were in Texas until October '65.

Bowser and his comrades-in-arms Santa Bowser (no known relation), Peter Moses, and Abraham Turner are all buried in the cemetery of St. James African Methodist Episcopal Church at Gravel Hill, a fitting resting spot since Lewis Bowser and Turner had served as trustees of the church and since the church was an offshoot of Havre de Grace's Mount Zion, an institution brought into existence largely through the efforts of Cupid Peaker's son James. (The first worshipers met in James Peaker's Havre de Grace home, and, to honor him, the name of the church was changed from Mount Zion to St. James.)

James Peaker and his siblings, who all continued their father's struggle toward recognized equality, viewed education as the key to full citizenship. In so doing, they set themselves quite a task, for by mid-century the halcyon days of the integrated Green Spring School were a thing of the past. In 1858, for example, white citizens in liberal Frederick County petitioned the legislature to pass a law "to prohibit free blacks from holding schools."[51] The Peakers gained a powerful ally in 1864 when the federal government established the Freedmen's Bureau, with Gen. Lew Wallace, author of *Ben Hur,* as director. Under Wallace's leadership, the bureau established schools for free blacks and newly freed slaves; in Harford County alone, the bureau oversaw construction of two school buildings, one near Webster (which was burned in 1926, reputedly by the Ku Klux Klan) and the McComas Institute on Singer Road, which dates to September 10, 1867, when Charles Waters, Abraham Waters, Peter Bishop, Joseph Henry, and John H. Butler—all "persons of color"—bought an acre of land for $30 "in trust for the purpose of erecting or allowing to be erected thereon a schoolhouse for the use, benefit and Education of Colored People of Harford County."[52] The affluent George McComas, who lived nearby in his picturesque cottage, Linwood, acted as the group's local protector, much as the Rigbie-Corse family had done for Cupid Peaker, and the trustees gratefully named the school for their white friend.

Other Harford blacks, including Cupid Peaker's son Joseph, took matters into their own hands: they accepted lumber, nails, window glass, and other raw material from the bureau but then did the actual construction work themselves. On October 26, 1867, Joseph Peaker and other trustees of the Mount Zion African Methodist Episcopal Church arranged to build "a school for the colored people of Havre de Grace" on Stokes Street; then on January 8, 1868, Joseph sold a quarter-acre of "the homestead property" he had inherited from his father to five black men acting as trustees "for the purpose of a schoolhouse lot" there. The Havre de Grace building, called the Anderson Institute, is gone but that second creation, known as the Hosanna School, still stands, thanks to continuous and private maintenance by the Peakers, Presberrys,[53] Williamses, and other leading black families of the area.

The Freedmen's Bureau was disbanded in 1870. One modern historian has written that because of the bureau's work "sympathy and support began to take root and grow as

51. Fields, *Slavery and Freedom,* 30.

52. Deed WHD 19/267.

53. In the late nineteenth century "the Presberry boys (colored)" provided flint for industrialist Edward M. Allen's Stafford Flint Mill; "the flint came from the Castleton quarry" and, after the Presberrys dug it from the earth, it "was hauled by a mule team to the mill." Mason, *Sketches,* 68–69.

The Freedmen's Bureau, established in 1864, established schools throughout the South to educate former slaves. Of the two Freedmen's schools in Harford, only the McComas Institute on Singer Road remains.

it became more and more apparent that Negro schools . . . constituted no threat to the orderly ways of community life."[54] But if "sympathy and support" came to the Peakers, the process can only be called gradual. General Wallace told a colleague that despite the bureau's work "it is impossible to convey to you . . . any idea of the hundreds of abuses that have come to my knowledge" in Maryland. For example, in October 1867 a teacher walking home from the Anderson Institute was "struck, knocked down, and kicked from the sidewalk." She sued her assailant but the Harford County jury saw fit only to award her "damages of one cent."[55]

With the bureau gone, the Harford school board began to toy with the idea of helping out with the black schools. After years of dragging their collective feet, county officials finally decided "to ascertain the amount of tax paid by colored people for schools" and to then divide that sum "pro rata" among the county's school districts to fund "the colored schools" in each district. The year that plan went into effect, 1870, district 5, which contained Hosanna, received $55.36 of county funds and the school board set "the salary of the Colored Teachers of Harford County of the Colored Schools" at $70 per term.[56] While it is hard to establish precisely what $70 meant in 1871, for comparison purposes in 1873 the board set the secretary of the board's half-year salary at $500 and decided to spend $105 to build a privy at the whites-only Churchville grammar school.

If most late nineteenth-century Harford countians were a bit ambivalent toward their black neighbors (and they were), their feelings were even more confused a generation or two earlier. Not even all of Darlington's residents, generally the most tolerant people in the county in matters of race, shared the same benign attitudes of the Corses and Silvers. In the 1850s, for instance, merchant R. I. Jackson, who lived in a "beautiful stone house on the Stafford Road," reserved one room in that house as a dungeon where he locked up slaves behind "a door . . . barred with iron."[57] Many of the county's leading white citizens routinely bought and sold black men and women (until Maryland's 1864 constitution made that practice illegal), treating them as they would dogs or horses: note an 1838 announcement for a sale in Bel Air of "a negro Woman and 3 Children, also . . . Oak Shingles and . . . lumber."[58] Plantation owners in the Deep South provided a ready market for county slaves and local papers are replete with ads; a dealer named H. S. Slattery, for

54. Quoted in *Harford Historical Bulletin* (Winter 1988).

55. McComas Institute and Hosanna School nominations to the National Register of Historic Places.

56. All quotes from the Harford County Board of Education *Minutes* book, Bel Air.

57. Mason, *Sketches*, 71–72, 69–70; see also Wright, *Harford*, 152.

58. In the *Madisonian*, March 12, 1838; the sale was to settle the estate of Preston McComas.

"They made Harford what it is"

instance, advertised in the July 18, 1833, *Harford Republican* that he was "always buying and shipping [Maryland slaves] to New Orleans." So frequently did countians patronize one of Slattery's rivals, Baltimore slave-trader Austin Woolfolk, that "Woolfolk was the terrible name by which Negro mothers used to still their babes and to frighten their older children into obedience."[59] The county government even actively participated in this flesh-peddling, for if a slave owner went bankrupt the circuit court often empowered the sheriff to seize the slaves, sell them, and divide the proceeds among the insolvent's creditors.

Thomas Hays, the "Father of Bel Air," avoided the thorny issue of slavery when he made out his will by bequeathing freedom to four favored slaves ("provided they behave themselves") while keeping others in bondage. He did, however, prohibit his heirs from selling the slaves "beyond the limits of Harford County."[60] Others, including Dr. John Archer, did not bother with such complications and simply and unconditionally willed freedom to all their slaves. A few, including the de la Portes of Bon Air, even set aside some posthumous cash to help the newly freed men and women get started. (Recall J.C.C. Hall of Cranberry, whose last will and testament, probated in 1855, instructed his executors not only to free his slaves but to build houses for some of them: see chapter 2.) Still, freeing slaves in one's will was relatively painless since it did not cost the deceased a thing. A few countians, however, freed their slaves while still alive, an act that represented a considerable loss of money. Among this noble group one finds Isaac Webster of Broom's Bloom, who freed all five of his inherited slaves in 1785, writing that "the laws of God teach all men to do as they would be done unto," and Paca Smith of Blenheim, who "gave" the "little girl Polly to Isaac, her father" in 1802 and who freed "Negro Woman Rachel" in 1830 on condition that all four of her children be placed under the care of "the Trustees of the Deer Creek Friends Meeting until they reach legal age."

A few countians took an even more active role in the fight against slavery and bravely assisted in the famous Underground Railroad, that covert network of "free blacks . . . [and] members of radical Christian sects such as the Mennonites and Quakers" who fed, sheltered, and comforted runaway slaves fleeing to freedom in the Northern states or in Canada. The Railroad began around 1805 in southeastern Pennsylvania and slaves quickly "learned who their friends were in . . . the Free State, and it was as natural for those aspiring to liberty to move in that direction as for the waters of brooks to move toward higher streams." "However determined and courageous they were, slaves could not have escaped in any substantial numbers unless there had been . . . an intricate 'support system'" of "conductors" (both free blacks and liberal whites) who assisted them. Most of these conductors worked in secrecy, since Congress made aiding runaways a federal crime as far back as 1793. Blacks, if caught, were returned to slavery and faced "mutilation, including . . . the chopping off of a foot or the cropping of ears, noses, and fingers."[61] Whites who aided the attempted escape received fines and imprisonment. As a result, little firm documentation, in the usual sense of the word, exists about the Railroad and historians must rely on oral tradition and legend.

Harford, however, does boast one thoroughly documented "conductor," William Worthington, whose ancestors had been landowners in the Deer Creek area since the early eighteenth century.[62] In the 1930s historian and farmer Samuel Mason, whose "own grandfather was twice arrested for helping slaves," wrote that "in our part of Harford County, one of the [Underground Railroad's] routes across the river was at Worthington's Landing . . . and in the evening frequently one of his men would come to him and whisper, 'Uncle Billy, there's people on the hill,' thereupon Uncle Billy [Worthington] would order a sheep killed and cooked for the escaping slaves then hiding in the cornfields." Mason adds that "after dark a boat would be available at the landing to take them across the river. A colored man by the name of Had Harris undertook this service." While most of the fugitives who arrived at Worthington's had fled from the Deep South, a few, accord-

59. Quoted in *Harford Historical Bulletin* (Winter 1988): 22.

60. Will 7/752 probated August 5, 1861.

61. Smith, *Shaping of America*, 763, 764; Siebert, *Underground*, 121.

62. There is also the nearby farm Swallowfields, which contains an icehouse thought to have been a hideout for escaping slaves.

William Worthington operated his famous Underground Railroad station from his house overlooking the Susquehanna.

ing to Mason, had escaped local owners: "one slave, at least, escaped from the Hays property at Shuck's Corner and several others left the farm of Dr. Abraham Streett near the Rocks."[63]

Worthington died around 1850 and on February 4, 1854, his four children sold the six-acre Landing property to David Shure.[64] It eventually passed to Edward Shure, who owned it until the Philadelphia Electric Company condemned the land as part of its Conowingo Dam project. (In the 1930s Mason wrote that "William Worthington lived in the house recently owned by Edward Shure, since torn down.") The house at the Landing, as depicted in a nineteenth-century primitive painting owned by Worthington's direct descendant Jean Reed Graybeal, was a two-part vernacular cottage perched on a hilltop and embowered in flowering vines with the Susquehanna running beyond. In 1990 a group of historians trekked to the site and located the foundations of the house and detached kitchen. They also found bone knife handles, bits of pottery, and other relics from the era when "Uncle Billy" Worthington roasted sheep to feed slaves on their desperate flight for freedom on the Underground Railroad.[65]

Harford's Master Builders

Unfortunately it is not known if "Uncle Billy" Worthington designed and built his house himself, or if he relied on a local artisan, such as the multitalented Cupid Peaker—shoemaker, stonemason, farmer, and paterfamilias—for most of Peaker's fellow craftsmen are doomed to anonymity. No one, for example, knows precisely whom to credit for the exuberant sawn trim that graces the Mahan family's house, Woods Meadow, on Aldino Road or exactly which Mitchell blacksmith, carpenter, or wheelwright built which of the many family houses that still stand in the Carsins Run area. Still, historians throughout America are beginning—finally—to discover and venerate the names of local builders: in addition to David Hopkins and his work and Elijah Walton, who built William Finney's Churchville Presbyterian Church in 1820, Harford countians have long valued the free black man surnamed Rumsey (first name unknown) and his work in the Kalmia area (including 2802 Forge Hill Road and 3031 Lochary Road) and stonemason

63. Mason, *Sketches,* 118.

64. Deed ALJ 4/268.

65. The historians were Christine Tolbert, Jean Ewing, William Beims, and Christopher Weeks. Worthington's interest in freeing slaves took many forms. County deed HD 18/154 reveals that in 1831 he paid Cupid Peaker, then spelled *Paca,* $500 "conditioned that the said Cupid Paca's daughter Charlotte should depart the state of Maryland immediately never to return."

"They made Harford what it is"

Mid-nineteenth-century newspaper ads made it easy for countians to purchase mass-produced building parts as these enticements from the *Ægis* suggest.

66. See W. E. Silver and E. L. Shelling, *Deer Creek Harmony Presbyterian Church Centennial Celebration* (Darlington: privately printed, 1937).

67. See the *Ægis*, June 21, 1907, which reports that "Mr. Dennis J. Shannahan [*sic*] of Fallston" was "awarded the contract for the . . . fine house which Mr. Charles E. Bryan will build on his recent purchase near Havre de Grace.

68. See "Fallston's History in Its Homes," *Ægis*, September, 18, 1991. Violet Merryman and Margaret S. Bishop, two current directors of the HSHC, are researching a nineteenth-century artisan named Earle Baity, who worked in and around Jarrettsville.

69. Mary Wright Barnes, a Slee descendent, is quoted in the Historic Sites Survey Form for the house.

70. *Portrait and Biographical Record*, 562.

Joshua W. Stephens, responsible for such well-known structures as the Stephenson-Hopkins House near Lapidum, the first (or c. 1840) Rock Run Church,[66] and perhaps the Silver family's octagonal Prospect School (1837).

As the nineteenth century progressed—a verb beloved by all good Victorians—most of the trends discussed above progressed, too, that is, they remained valid in essence but changed in detail. For example, while county builders in the 1880s tended to use mass-produced window frames, doors, and porch spindles rather than the handcrafted elements available to David Hopkins or Cupid Peaker, the craftsmen used these mass-produced details to create buildings of great individuality. (Much the same might be said of the buildings designed by the county's first trained architects—J. Crawford Neilson, William Reasin, and George Archer—whose works form the core of chapter 6.) The career of Fallston builder Dennis J. Shanahan is a case in point. Born in Ireland, Shanahan emigrated to America and became a favorite contractor for Baltimore City architects, who entrusted him with such projects as St. Mark's Church (1887, Thomas Kennedy, architect), the new Mount Pleasant near Havre de Grace (c. 1907, Parker and Thomas),[67] and the Prince of Peace Chapel (1908–9, Laurence Hall Fowler). Not content with working for others, Shanahan also went out on his own and designed and built, on spec, the trio of houses now numbered 2410, 2412, and 2414 Watervale Road.[68] A few other individuals will live on, if sketchily, in the county's building histories, too. For instance, Cicero Slee, who owned Woodlawn Farm near Aberdeen in the 1880s and '90s, commissioned his son, John Bay Slee, to add a wonderful Gothic birdhouse/cupola/ventilator to a barn on the property and a Mount Vernon–esque portico to the main house. Yet while family tradition labels the young Slee "an architect," it is not clear if he was academically trained or if he learned his craft from a local builder or from a pattern book.[69]

Similar questions haunt the professional lives of the Dunnigan brothers, John and Andrew. Like their colleague Shanahan, the Dunnigans were born in Ireland;[70] they sailed to America around 1860 with their father and two siblings and somehow ended up on the rolling hills along the north bank of Deer Creek. Here John began buying land in small increments until he had amassed a fine farm of 153 acres. Dunnigan showed his neighbors that he not only wore many hats, he wore them well, in a manner reminiscent of Cupid Peaker. A skilled stonemason and carpenter, Dunnigan used these skills to distinctly, if esoterically, influence the county's architecture. Sometime around 1870 he and his wife (née Anna Clark) built the spirited dwelling still known as the John Dunnigan House. Put as pithily as possible, they took the basic, trickle-down Greenwood shell and went wild, adding an elaborate porch with chamfered posts and scroll brackets, sets of paired windows, some polygonal bay windows, a slew of large, rounded attic dormer windows, and, as a crowning touch, a squared-off projecting central tower: he obviously threw everything he knew into the house, hoping his self-evident mastery of many different styles and forms would win him commissions from awed passersby. This ancient form of advertising has been noted in Harford County as far back as David Hopkins's springhouse, discussed above.

While it is uncertain if Dunnigan's quite wonderful house secured him any paying carpentry work, it is tempting to credit him with the nearby and slightly later Ady-Laird House, for the two dwellings share similar idiosyncratic towered massing and other unusual details. It is also tempting to credit Dunnigan with the fantastic c. 1890 brackets on the McCann House on Forge Hill Road. Albert McCann bought an unremarkable three-bay frame house from William McCann in 1890 and then, for reasons known only to himself, decided to give the place the impress of his own personality: he relaid the roof slates in a decorative pattern, he added an overscale entrance hood to the existing porch, and then, in a moment of madness, he crafted (commissioned?) huge arts-and-crafts brackets embellished with duck heads to support the hood.

Dunnigan, like Peaker, was an outsider—one was an Irish immigrant, the other a black man whose wife was born into slavery—and these outsiders used their artisans' skills to fight the larger battle of assimilation into mainstream America. As Dunnigan's 1897 biography observes, "there are many of foreign birth, who have come to this country . . . [and] have succeeded in securing a good home and comfortable competence. . . . In Mr. Dunnigan we find a worth representative of this class."[71] Actually, John's brother Andrew meteorically outdid brother John in the assimilation process. Instead of assembling a farmstead incrementally, Andrew acquired one all-of-a-piece: and he did it the old-fashioned way—he married it. In the best Hollywood tradition Andrew Dunnigan, just off the boat, caught the eye of an heiress, Mary Forwood. Won over by Andrew's (presumed) good looks and Irish charm, Mary quickly married the lad. And while Andrew's contribution to the union consisted mainly of certain desirable, possibly hard to quantify, physical attributes, Mary's were easier to measure and consisted of a sizable piece of Deer Creek Valley real estate, including the ancient Forwood house she had inherited from her father, Dr. Parker Forwood, who died in 1866.

This discussion of the county's diversely talented nineteenth-century artisans might fittingly close with the careers of John Bailey of Level and Jacob Bull of Bel Air. Bailey, in fact, probably wins the prize for diversity of talents for he was a self-taught carpenter/cabinetmaker/undertaker/wheelwright/furniture-maker. (About the only thing he wasn't was a blacksmith, but Level then was home to E. H. Foard, one of the most celebrated blacksmiths in the county.) His best-known work is undoubtedly a frame house on Rock Run Road. Edward Wilkinson bought the property around 1880 and then hired Bailey to "open it up," according to the artisan's daughter, Mrs. Leonard Knight. Whether or not Bailey "opened" Wilkinson's house up, he certainly made it unique, for nothing else in the county resembles this thorough fantasy. Just note the corner turret, octagonal and shingled, with its floor-to-ceiling windows on the ground story, semi-enclosed sleeping porch above, and squatty, conical octagonal roof.

If a daughter's fondness for her father has immortalized Bailey's work for Wilkinson, familial devotion is also responsible for documenting the career of Jacob Bull, "Harford's Master Builder."[72] Although Bull was described in his lifetime as "the leading contractor in Harford County" he probably would have passed into an honorable oblivion had not his grandson J. Edmund Bull established that peerless repository of Harford's folk history, the Steppingstone Museum, and then donated his ancestor's papers to it. Jacob Bull was born near Bel Air, in a long-vanished community called Bull Town, in 1848. His father, Edmund, was a carpenter "known throughout the state as one of its most efficient . . . builders," which suggests that an innate sense of beauty, and hands dexterous enough to fashion that sensibility into three-dimensional reality, ran in the young man's blood. After "a common-school education supplemented by a brief attendance at the Bel Air Academy," Jacob set out to learn the builder's art. He initially apprenticed himself to his father but soon struck out on his own and secured his first solo job in 1872. His reputation spread and he quickly won commissions to erect "most of the fine buildings of Harford County," including the old Masonic Temple, "one of the most expensive and costly structures in northeastern Maryland" (and possibly actually designed by architect Jackson Gott), the 1886 Reckord House (built for mill-owner John H. Reckord) and the 1887 Doxen House (built for canning broker William Doxen). His end came suddenly in 1899, the result of an on-the-job accident: while inspecting the second story of a building the flooring gave way beneath him, and he plunged to his death. But his legacy lives on in the drawings at Steppingstone and in the "simple, comfortable houses that Bel Air and Harford County liked and understood."[73]

Although all three Bull buildings cited above were in Bel Air, his most ambitious project and crowning achievement, Blenheim, shifts the narrative to Aberdeen and to the 220 acres that canning magnate Henry Amos Osborn bought in 1875.[74] Along with the land, Osborn acquired the Smith family's federal-era villa discussed in chapter 4. While that older house may have been fine for its distant era, it was ill-suited to serve as principle seat of one of the leading farmers and canners in Harford County at a time when Har-

71. Ibid.
72. Larew, *Bel Air*, 66.
73. *Portrait and Biographical Record*, 151; James Wollon, AIA, conversation with author, May 26, 1992; Larew, *Bel Air*, 66.
74. Deed ALJ 33/63.

Around 1880 Edward Wilkinson of Level hired carpenter John Bailey to "open up" his house: Bailey complied and gave Wilkinson this truly idiosyncratic creation.

In the 1880s Jacob Bull, known as "Harford County's Master Builder," oversaw construction of the Masonic Temple in Bel Air (demolished in 1979 for the courthouse addition), which an awed viewer in 1897 described as "one of the most expensive and costly structures in northeastern Maryland."

75. Susan Osborn, daughter of Blenheim's present (1994) owner, reports that her cousin Inez Osborn (daughter of Blenheim's builder) always said Bull had designed the house; Susan Osborn, conversation with author, January 8, 1991.

ford was famous as the leading canning county in America. Accordingly, Osborn asked Bull to come up with something with a little more pizzazz.[75] And Bull did just that.

If nothing else, Bull gave Osborn a *big* house. Its wings and dormers and porches seem to ramble on forever, as does the interior, a complex maze of literally countless rooms. (The house's owner says there are seventeen of them; county tax appraisers feel there are twenty.) Nearly every room has a fireplace and every fireplace is a bravura performance. Each opening is bordered on three sides by ceramic tiles, and each set of tiles has its own theme, some playfully abstract, some shaped into recognizable forms such as miniature

sunbursts and wisteria vines. Around the tiles one finds the mantel shelf and supporting pilasters (stretching that last word to the limit of its possible meaning); above each shelf the woodwork explodes in a frenzy of mirrors and ledges and more shelves and who knows what else. Needless to say, no motif repeats. Ever.

Writers routinely use the adjective "exceptional" when they really mean "unusual." But Blenheim *is* exceptional. There is nothing remotely like it in Harford County. Moreover, it stands today as a multiple memorial. First, of course, it is a memorial to self-taught builder Jacob Bull, but it is also a memorial to the Osborn family and, more generally, to the land-based wealth that characterized Harford County in the mid- and late nineteenth century. Not every countian made a fortune from canning equal to Henry Osborn's and no one else hired Bull to build a Blenheim. For that matter, not everyone hired a carpenter like Bailey to create that smaller-scale fantasy near Level. Nor were all immigrants blessed with Andrew Dunnigan's capacity to woo and win heiresses. Nor did every free black man share Cupid Peaker's pluck. But, as has been pointed out, from Broad Creek to Swan Creek during the two generations on either side of the Civil War a lot of countians were doing a lot of building in a lot of vernacular styles.

Canning magnate Henry Amos Osborn began buying the ancient Blenheim tract between Aberdeen and Havre de Grace in 1875; he then hired Jacob Bull to design and build this sprawling mansion, a highly fitting residence for one of the county's most enterprising industrialists.

The Silver family's holdings south of Darlington—the heart of "that romantic and classical portion of our county through which courses the magnificent Deer Creek."

"The most tasty architecture"
Harford and the Picturesque

[6]

PIC NIC AT DARLINGTON

We were present by invitation at one of the most delightful pic nics of the season which came off on Tuesday last in the beautiful grove near the village of Darlington, that romantic and classical portion of our county through which courses the magnificent Deer Creek, whose banks are adorned by the most majestic scenery and dotted by specimens of the most tasty architecture.

Ægis and Intelligencer (August 14, 1858)

By the time the *Ægis* ran the story on the "pic nic at Darlington," America had been in the throes of a mania for picturesque architecture for twenty years, a mania few places were as viscerally susceptible to as Harford County. One suspects that the reason "picturesque" design found such a warm welcome here was because it so easily fit into the Harford scene. For instance, the adjectives applied to the style—rambling, informal, asymmetrical—are the very words that generations of visitors and natives alike applied to the county's almost aggressively picturesque scenery. In 1794 the Anglo-Indian nabob Thomas Twining, while riding the ferry from Perryville to Havre de Grace, "contemplated, with peculiar pleasure . . . the wild poetic cast of this enchanting spot."[1] In 1817, when Dr. John Archer Jr. and his wife (née Ann Stump) gave a party to mark the near-completion of their Rock Run Bridge to Cecil County, the newspaper reporter sent to cover the event lavished as much ink rhapsodizing over the "most romantic" site as over the bridge, just as a reporter for the Bel Air weekly the *Madisonian* relished a "truly sublime" February 1840 ice storm on the Susquehanna. When Dr. W. Stump Forwood dipped his pen into purple ink to produce his landmark 1879–80 *Ægis* series about "The Homes on

1. Twining, *Travels in America*, 76–79.

113

Deer Creek," virtually each line drips with the good doctor's painful pleasure in describing the valley's "delightful and beautiful" farmsteads and "wild and romantic" ruins. As if to reinforce the picturesque aura of Edgar Allan Poe, Forwood wrote that one of the ruins was "wrapped in mystery" and resembled a "mammoth death's head . . . so illustrative of the temporary character and comparative futility of man's works."[2] Then again, perhaps it is because the style fits in so well with countians' not-too-serious view of themselves and the world: after all, what other jurisdiction in America revels in being named for a bastard?

Moreover, generations of countians had had their picturesque spirits fed by a veritable flood of architectural books and magazines. Roughly 175 architectural books were published in the United States in the first half of the nineteenth century (93 in the 1850s alone); a number of these titles found their way to the shores of Deer Creek and Winters Run, and most of them promoted some form of picturesque design. Countians' spirits were also fed by trained architects, who made their first professional appearance in Harford in the 1840s and '50s. Significantly, this was a time when countians' pockets were deep enough to allow citizens to indulge in architectural experiments and other whimsies. R. S. Fisher's Maryland *Gazetteer* was pleased to note in 1852 that "few parts of the state are more varied . . . in the development of its resources" than Harford. "The roads are excellent"; "no district has greater commercial facilities"; in short, "progress has been rapid and substantial."[3] Indeed, it had, for the county's nonslave population shot up from 16,000 in 1820 to 20,000 in 1860.

Proper Churches and Grecian Perfection

As a result, and the general apathy of the Stumps and Harlans notwithstanding, a few mid-century countians actually began to take their architecture seriously. By the 1830s and '40s, many began to worry about the "purity" and "morality" of their buildings: one architect wrote that such issues excited him "almost to frenzy"; another said he was able to design only after he had been "morally awakened."[4] In sum, house and church design became impregnated with implications. If one built in a classical manner, which increasingly meant Greek, it showed a concern for the future of American, neo-Athenian democracy. If one chose Gothic—especially the right *kind* of Gothic—it showed concern for the salvation of one's soul. Egyptian structures became de rigeur for funerary architecture. And if one constructed a house or barn in what was loosely called a "picturesque" manner, it evinced a faith in American democracy and in the nation's "expanding middle class."[5]

Twentieth-century historians sometimes dismiss such concerns with a trivializing sniff about "the battle of styles" but, as one ought to glean from the rhetoric, period combatants were in earnest. For example, as early as 1815 the *Analectic Magazine* of Philadelphia editorialized about how "ponderous" and "cumbersome" any architecture seemed "when compared with the grandeur and the beauty of Grecian simplicity." In April 1835, a critic for the *American Monthly Magazine* ripped apart a plan to top the classical lines of the New York Custom House with a dome, "an excrescence, which, however elegant in itself, is utterly monstrous and barbarous when added to a model of Grecian" perfection.[6] Advocates of Gothic architecture, on the other hand, viewed pointed arches as "the only proper style." Anything else either evinced a "debased" personality on the part of the builder or, more generously, the "prejudices and parsimony of the age."[7]

Many of America's Victorian-era builders were not merely content with improving their own souls and backyards either; many, in a quasi-religious manner, sought the tasteful improvement of their neighbors as well. So while there was one architecture for hearth and home, one for state houses and capitols, and one for sacristies and sacraments, all three sought—in that obsessively Victorian way—*improvement*. In many eyes "good taste," in fact, according to a highly influential 1843 essay on the subject, became equated with "the Almighty. . . . Taste is God's legacy." "Every common man's house or cottage," the argument ran, should become "a little abode of tastefulness." Not only that,

2. *Federal Gazette,* July 18, 1817; "Susquehanna Frozen," *Madisonian,* February 14, 1840; Forwood, "Homes on Deer Creek," December 23, 1879. Dr. Forwood even began one installment with a quote from William Combe's *Tour of Dr. Syntax in Search of the Picturesque.*

3. R. S. Fisher, *Gazetteer of the State of Maryland* (New York: J. H. Colton Co., 1852), 74.

4. *Country Life,* December 13, 1990.

5. Ackerman, *Villa,* 229.

6. Talbot Hamlin, *Greek Revival Architecture in America* (New York: Dover Publications, 1964), 320–21, 324.

7. William H. Pierson Jr., *American Buildings and Their Architects, Technology and the Picturesque* (New York: Anchor Books, 1980), 173.

but the tasteful few were then morally obligated to "bring this . . . [enlightenment] to our countrymen" by erecting "tasteful" public buildings such as churches and schools and by performing other spiritually enriching acts.[8] Thus did the Silver family tastefully transform the countryside in and around Glenville in the 1840s and '50s; thus did the Jewetts, Kings, and Smiths transform Darlington a generation or so later.

The first of these exotic styles, at least nationally, was Greek revival. While countians had worn their classicism well but lightly for a generation or two (recall the polite, balanced façades of Rock Run and Woodside, the pilastered cupboards at Deer Park, and the acanthus-leafed mantel at Swansbury), around 1800 this unaggressive affinity for the ancient world began to be replaced as columns left the fireplaces and began to strut across entire fronts of buildings. The Greek revival was born. It had been in the womb, so to speak, since the 1780s and '90s when Thomas Jefferson chose to copy a Roman temple for the Virginia capitol in Richmond and when he and George Washington planned to use white marble columns to make the new "Capital City" on the Potomac shine as an outpost of Athenian civilization in the wilderness.

The infant finally cried aloud in 1818, when the directors of the Bank of the United States stipulated that their new building in Philadelphia be "a chaste imitation of Grecian architecture." Suddenly, wrote historian Talbot Hamlin, "it was as if man in America" had emerged "from the forest to sun-drenched, sea-bordered downs, all at once . . . conscious of bright sun and distance and freedom."[9] If anything, Hamlin was guilty of understatement, for throughout the new nation, from fishermen in Maine to cotton-planters in Mississippi, *everyone* had seen the sun; everyone was erecting Greek temples. Rows and rows of columns appeared not only on houses but on every conceivable type of building. James Fenimore Cooper was being only slightly satirical when he wrote in 1836 that "we build little besides temples for our churches, our banks, our taverns, our court houses, and our dwellings. A friend of mine has just built a brewery on the model of the Temple of the Four Winds."

Curiously, however, Harford's citizens remained unimpressed by all these evocations of Pirea—curious because when the Greek revival was reaching its zenith nationwide (from roughly 1820 to 1860) the county was expanding in both numbers and wealth, a combination that usually spells lots of new, stylish buildings. Yet nary a Temple of the Four Winds appeared from the Gunpowder to the Susquehanna. Perhaps it was due to countians' innate architectural conservatism (discussed in chapter 5). Perhaps it was because the citizens felt they did not need pediments to prove how settled they were; while marble columns rising from the Potomac slime may have been fine symbols for a new city intended to legitimize a new nation, few in long-settled Harford felt the need to be legitimized.

There is one templed exception, however, and it is a fine one: the 1852 First Presbyterian Church in Bel Air. (It is such a fine temple that some people are startled to remember that the building was created so that proper Presbyterians could meet to sing hymns, not so worshipers of Aphrodite could meet to perform their libidinous rites.) The church's most visible feature is its monumental Doric portico; even though it is *wooden,* not marble, it certainly creates the requisite image of solidarity and permanence. The main entrance's double doors, placed high above the ground behind the portico, open to a single large space. Reminiscent of the *naos* within a Greek temple, that space was originally flooded with light thanks to the tall, clear windows that ran along both long façades. (Later users shortened most of the windows—only the northernmost openings, those closest the street, remain unchanged—and replaced many of the clear panes with stained glass.) The Bel Air church must be regarded as the product of a single, highly intelligent aesthetic (nothing so crisp could come from a committee) and while no architect's name has surfaced, it seems safe to credit the Reverend Ebenezer Dickey Finney for the building's clean, powerful lines.

Finney (1825–1904) was one of six children born to Churchville's Rev. William

8. "Taste and Fashion," quoted in Bushman, *Refinement of America,* 330–31.

9. Hamlin, *Greek Revival Architecture,* 318.

Although Bel Air's First Presbyterian Church has been modified somewhat since it was completed in 1852 (note how most of the side windows have been shortened and filled with stained glass), it still suggests the power of Greek design.

Finney—"the great pioneer of Presbyterianism in Harford County." After prepping at Nottingham Academy, E. D. Finney continued his studies at Washington College (now Washington and Lee University) and at the Princeton Theological Seminary from which he was graduated in 1852. In July of that year he returned to Harford and "preached the first sermon" in the just-completed temple in Bel Air.[10] It seems likely that he had been involved with the congregation before that first sermon. It also seems possible that he lent a hand in designing the church's revolutionary temple-form, given the family's perennial interest in church-building. Later in 1852 Finney moved to Mississippi to accept the joint posts of pastor of the Greenwood Presbyterian Church in Natchez and principal of the affiliated boys' school. The Civil War dramatically ended the minister's Southern experience and shortly after Appomattox he returned to Harford County and moved into his father's new house, which they named Greenwood and which is discussed in chapter 5. Picking up where he had left off fifteen years earlier, Finney resumed his place in the pulpit in the Pennsylvania Avenue temple.

He also began ministering to Presbyterians in Fallston. "Since those were horse-and-buggy days," the rector's son, Dr. J.M.T. Finney, recalled, "[E. D. Finney] would drive old Fanny over on Sunday afternoons and hold service." Dr. Finney noted that "for some time these Sunday afternoon preaching services [in Fallston] were held in a house which had formerly been a saloon," but in 1873 E. D. Finney arranged to have a proper church built on the southern edge of the village.[11] What Finney assuredly built in Fallston makes an interesting mate to what he possibly built in Bel Air; it suggests that as the years had waned, so too had the rector's zealousness about the sanctity of Greek architecture. Bel Air's temple, worthy of Agamemnon and his warriors, is clean of line and pure of form; Fallston's, with its gingerbreadish modillions, rounded-arched windows (anathema to the Greeks and their flat-topped doors and windows), darkly stained glass windows, and bijou Ionic capitals in place of the more powerful Doric, seems more appropriate to Louisa May Alcott and her little women.

That brace of Finney churches constitutes Harford's entire body of Greek temples recast as Christian places of worship, an astonishingly small collection for so prosperous a county. As for temples recast as dwellings, if one looks hard one can find three, a low fig-

10. *Biographical Cyclopedia*, 563; Wright, *Harford*, 208.

11. Finney, *Surgeon's Life*, 32.

Compare the Reverend E. D. Finney's 1873 Presbyterian church building in Fallston to the temple in Bel Air—the windows' rounded tops, the stained glass, and the modillions add a non-Greek daintiness to the composition.

Leedom Moore's superb 1851 Greek revival house near Mill Green is clean of line, crisp of detail; note especially the second story's squared "Palladian window."

ure that suggests that countians had even more misgivings about Greek houses than they did about Greek churches. Interestingly, all three dwellings burst forth virtually simultaneously (1850, 1851, and 1852)—the same time Finney's Pennsylvania Avenue temple was rising.

The oldest of the group, Eli Turner's demi-temple just south of Norrisville, has a pure Greek pediment-front form, complete with portico (squared as the columns may be) and pilastered mantels in all main rooms. It also boasts properly flat window and door details—none of the Fallston church's curves here. A year or so after Turner began his wooden dwelling, Leedom Moore started work on a portico-less stone temple of his own near the thriving hamlet of Mill Green. Moore constructed a mini-masterpiece, for even without columns his house captures the essence of classicism as surely as Bel Air's Presbyterian church does: note the squared window and door openings, the overall proportions, and the fluted door trim within.

While Turner's and Moore's houses are essentially temples—as indeed are most American neo-Greek structures—in a marvelous bit of irony, what may be the county's greatest Greek house eschews that form altogether. In 1851 the maiden sisters Mary, Lydia, and Rebecca Titus paid $650 for a twenty-two-acre tract near Fallston and built Rochelle, one of the county's true domestic treasures.[12] Little is known of the Tituses except that they came from the New York suburb of New Rochelle (hence the name of the house) and that

12. Deed HDG 37/378.

In 1852 the sisters Mary, Lydia, and Rebecca Titus moved to Fallston from their native New York and built Rochelle; the house's tall pillars, hipped roof, and deep verandas suggest that the Quaker sisters were trying to fit in with their new Dixie neighbors.

they used their Maryland Rochelle as a retreat. They gave their house a perfectly square plan and enclosed the square in deep verandas. Dormer windows pierce the hipped roof, while a widow's walk tops it all.

Rochelle's form is unique in the county. The sisters must have brought the concept with them—they didn't copy something they had seen down the road, which is a simplified description of one way architectural styles spread. Marylanders today laugh when New Englanders suggest that the Deep South begins at the Mason-Dixon Line but evidently that myth dates back in the 1850s. The Quaker Tituses, after all, had come to a slave-owning state from New York; maybe they just wanted to fit in. That's certainly one explanation for the veranda, reached from within by floor-to-ceiling, triple-sash windows designed to capture every July breeze. (Because the windows also capture every February breeze, one winter at Rochelle would have convinced the sisters that Fallston and Mobile do not, in fact, lie in the same latitude.) When Lydia Titus died in 1862, her estate inventory showed that the house then was essentially identical to the present Rochelle; appraisers listed a parlor, hall, dining room, kitchen, kitchen chamber, pantry, and bathroom on the first story, four main bedrooms and a second story hall above, and a "garret" in the attic.

That clutch of buildings forms the entirety of Harford County's all-of-a-piece Greek revival structures. Since three houses and two churches wouldn't comprise the tiniest Peloponessian hamlet, it is safe to say that countians' enthusiasm for things Greek ran neither deep nor wide. But that does not mean that the Greek revival found no other allies in the county. Harford embraced the movement, but did so as it embraced most innovative architectural movements, piecemeal and diffidently, with a new mantle here and a molding there. One or two braver countians, however, did risk adding columns to their otherwise astylar dwellings, most notably the owners of the Jarrett-Cairnes House near Jarrettsville and John Adams Webster, hero of the War of 1812 and builder of the well-known Mount Adams near Creswell.

Webster (1789–1877) purchased 122 acres of his ancestral Broom's Bloom tract in 1817 and built the house he deferentially named for his mother, née Margaret Adams. That initial house certainly exemplifies countians' uneasiness regarding high-style architecture.

In the 1850s Capt. John Adams Webster used squared "Greek" columns to add a sense of unity to his added-to house, Mount Adams; even so, if one looks hard at the building's unusual door and window pattern, the building's casual history of growth can be discerned.

Webster gave Mount Adams a distinctly *retarditaire* plan with two rooms per floor, each with a gable-end chimney and an enclosed winder stair—a plan that virtually replicates Webster's birthplace, Broom's Bloom, which was built in the 1740s. When it came time to modify that house, Webster and his wife, née Rachel Biays, did so not because they had a burning urge to be fashionable but because they needed room for their fourteen children. Three of those children, on reaching adulthood (sons Dr. J. Biays Webster [born 1828] and William S. Webster [born 1838] and daughter Susan [born 1830]) chose to live at home with their parents. To accommodate these three, the senior Websters simply tacked a series of independent apartments onto the original section of the house, resulting in a somewhat bewildering configuration. At some point, and presumably to give the illusion of unity to the ramshackle composition, Webster strung a two-tier Greek revival wooden porch across the expanded house's main façade. Significantly, however, that portico, at first glance so monumental and classically correct, is actually anything but; its "columns" are simply squared posts that an anonymous artisan (possibly a family member) fashioned on the farm.

Yet if the Harford landscape proved inimical to columned buildings, thousands of temple-inspired structures did shoot up nationwide in the 1820s through the 1840s, so many temples in so many places for so many uses that an anti-Greek reaction began to set in. This movement was largely egged on by those with their own stylistic axes to grind, such as Arthur Gilman, an architect specializing in non-Greek buildings, who complained in the January 1843 issue of the *North American Review* that he had grown "weary of the eternal Grecian."[13] Others, such as sculptor Horatio Greenough, took a more moderate position and suggested that while Greek architecture had a place in America, it was a narrow place most properly restricted to structures such as government buildings. Other uses, Greenough wrote, called for other styles and he stated in no uncertain terms that churches demanded *"the Christian style"* (emphasis in original). So take away the pediments and bring on the gargoyles: the shadow of the Gothic revival was spreading across the land.

The Ecclesiologists, a no-nonsense, highly intellectual group of clerics and laymen, spearheaded the movement to make Gothic "the architecture of Christianity" (164). This

13. Quoted in Stanton, *The Gothic Revival and American Church Architecture*, 176.

was, in fact, but a "secondary plot in a much larger . . . drama" (xviii), for the Ecclesiologists set themselves the daunting task of purifying the Episcopal church of ungodly influences. The legacy of Cranmer and other Tudor-era heroes, they felt, was being degraded by a corrupt clergy and by intellectually lazy congregations. The outward and visible sign of this decay were the foursquare, neoclassical churches built by such worldly clerics as William White, chaplain to the Continental Congress and first bishop in the newly established Protestant Episcopal Church, who relished a good cigar and a glass of fish-house punch and who entered "with zest into the pleasures" life offered. Accordingly, the next generation's bluestockings automatically damned any building from his era as "worldly."[14] Maybe they were—consider St. John's in Havre de Grace (1809). While St. John's is highly appealing to most twentieth-century countians, to many Victorians that church's one foundation was shaky at best. The building was paid for with gambling profits and its round-arched windows, ornamental plaques, and Flemish bond brick walls all bear a suspiciously close similarity to Bloomsbury, the nearby mansion built by Havre de Grace's lottery czar Mark Pringle, a wheeler-dealer eventually lynched in Baltimore. Consider also the federal-era rector of St. John's, Joppa (mentioned in chapter 2), who wrote the vitriolic letters about his "lying, filthy Jezebel" of a wife.

Many tortured souls felt such goings-on left them no choice but to abandon the Episcopal church in favor of the new, more rigorous, nonconformist sects: Richard Webster of Webster's Forest, for example, became a Methodist. A few, made of sterner stuff, decided to remain in the church and to effect purifying reforms from within. The strictest of the reformers, the Ecclesiologists, actually promulgated rules for building new churches and issued numerous books and tracts on the subject. The Ecclesiologists abhorred clean-lined federal-era churches such as St. John's and urged a return to the mysteries and shadows of the Gothic era. *Until the present regular system of building both sides of a church exactly alike be broken up, no real good can be expected,* wrote—and italicized—Augustus Pugin, a leading (if not a particularly kindly) light of the movement. Because English Ecclesiologists had little need for large buildings (the great cathedrals of Salisbury, Canterbury, Durham, Lincoln, Wells were already there), they focused their considerable energies on designing small, rural churches; that fit cathedral-less American needs as snugly as a well-cut cassock.

Bishop White refused to be drawn into the debate. A product of the Enlightenment, he "deeply deplored the evils of extreme" and hoped that under his gentle leadership the church might retain a tolerant philosophy and "a broad, comprehensive" membership. "Free from narrow-mindedness himself," wrote one biographer, White "labored to make the church equally so."[15] Naturally such a Christian attitude rankled the early Victorian zealots and reformers. But White died in 1836. Suddenly there was a vacancy in the pulpit and first down the aisle, censers swinging to knock any opposition aside, trotted the Ecclesiologists.

Maryland's Episcopalians found themselves in the foreground of all this thanks largely to William Rollinson Whittingham, chosen bishop in 1840 "after a prolonged and difficult election." Once firmly ensconced under the baldachino, Whittingham, whose hobby was the study of "ecclesiastical architecture and its history," decreed his diocese to be "in dire need of new churches."[16] He set out to correct the situation following Ecclesiological guidelines and, in a virtual spate of building, erected dozens of small parish churches throughout the state. In 1840 he approved architect William Strickland's design for a gray and granite and spiky Christ Church in Easton; in 1845 he blessed Robert Cary Long Jr.'s designs for a trio of new churches in the Baltimore area, the only survivor of which is the granite Ascension in Westminster, a picture-perfect "English rural Gothic church."[17] In downtown Baltimore he gave the nod to Grace and St. Peter's, a masterpiece of lichen-encrusted stone and slate and marble, designed by architects Niernsee and Neilson in 1851; and he sanctioned Hillsboro Church in Talbot County and St. John's

The "worldly" clean lines of Havre de Grace's St. John's Church (1809 and shown here in an 1863 engraving for *Harper's* magazine) were exactly what upset mid-nineteenth-century Gothicists.

14 Pierson, *Buildings, Picturesque,* 151.

15. Ibid., 158; Wiltbank et al., *Descendants of White,* 37, 39.

16. Stanton, *Gothic Revival,* 216, 217.

17. Dean et al., *Three Hundred and Fifty Years,* 169.

Chapel near Cambridge (built 1851 and 1853, respectively), which show that the approved style could be successfully carried off in frame as well as in masonry.

Whittingham's influence spread into Harford County, too, when the bishop empowered the Reverend William Brand "to establish a parish, build a church, and collect a congregation at Emmorton." Brand, an ecclesiological true believer (and Whittingham's future biographer) was certainly the right man for the job.[18] Born in New Orleans in 1814, where his father had gained a certain fame as "a prominent architect and builder," Brand read law at the University of Virginia and returned to New Orleans where he was admitted to the bar. But suddenly the ministry called and he gave up his legal career for the priesthood. Fortuitously for Brand (and Whittingham) in 1842 the young clergyman married an heiress, Sophia Hall, a great-great-granddaughter of John Hall of Cranberry and a kinswoman to Bishop White. Brand convinced members of the Wilson family to donate land between their houses, Gibson's Park and Woodside, to the parish and then Mrs. Brand's "family . . . built for him a church, paying the entire expense with the exception of $35, which was donated by others."[19] The result, St. Mary's, is generally acknowledged to be "the finest rural church in the diocese of Maryland."[20] While tradition credits Brand with its design, a recently unearthed document at the Maryland Historical Society states that the church "was designed by" Niernsee and Neilson, "the well known Baltimore architects." Even so, the anonymous paper admits that St. Mary's "owes its existence to the activities . . . of the Rev. William F. Brand, who assumed control in 1849."[21]

Brand and Whittingham, in their quest to bring fourteenth-century Gloucestershire to nineteenth-century Harford, found themselves a fitting prototype in the "First Pointed Church" illustrated in the October 1849 issue of *New York Ecclesiologist*. The rector closely followed that illustration and the accompanying text, which bubbles with such helpful comments as place the south porch "no further east than the second bay from the west front"; make the nave's length twice its width; don't insist on a cruciform plan, but if the congregation demands transepts, be sure they are "fully developed, not ugly, ill-expressed extensions on the sides." In another issue the magazine opined that exposed roof timbers, as opposed to plastered ceilings, expressed "truth and reality," and Brand

Left: St. Mary's Episcopal Church—"the finest church in the diocese of Maryland," wrote Dr. Phoebe Stanton. Who would argue with her? This previously unpublished c. 1849 watercolor may have been a presentation proposal for the building by Baltimore architects J. Crawford Neilson and John Niernsee. When the Reverend William Brand actually set out to build St. Mary's, he chose to omit the rather feeble-looking steeple. Right: The Reverend William Brand (1814-1907) certainly looks calm enough here in old age; in his youth, however, his fiercely held beliefs about building design and theology set off still-felt changes in Harford County's church architecture.

18. Stanton, *Gothic Revival*, 289.

19. *Portrait and Biographical Record*, 26, which adds that the senior Brand was a great friend of Andrew Jackson, who "attended the christening of our subject [i.e., William]" and then went off to fight the Battle of New Orleans.

20. Stanton, *Gothic Revival*, 289.

21. "St. Mary's Chapel" paper accompanying watercolor of the church in the registrar's office of the MHS; accession number 1900.6.1.

Between 1851 and 1870 the Reverend William Brand bought fifteen English stained glass windows for St. Mary's. The windows, designed by the brilliant architect William Butterfield, depict the life of Christ (and always incorporate Mary, the church's namesake, somewhere in the design); they comprise the only complete set of matched Butterfield glass in America.

22. Oertel's distinguished career then took him to Washington, D.C., where he designed the ceiling for the House of Representatives chamber in 1857 and, later, worked on the embryonic National Cathedral. He returned to Harford County in the 1890s to design the original pulpit, lectern, credence table, and altar for Emmanuel Episcopal Church in Bel Air, as is described in Larew, *Bel Air,* III.

23. Rev. William Smith of St. Mary's, conversation with author, September 10, 1990.

24. Stanton, *Gothic Revival,* 289.

25. John Summerson, *Heavenly Mansions* (New York: Norton Library, 1969), 159, 160. Summerson's essay makes fascinating reading as does the entry on Butterfield in Roger Dixon and Stefan Mutheius's *Victorian Architecture* (New York: Oxford University Press, 1978), 204–9; Summerson describes Dickens and Butterfield with words such as *ruthless, brutal,* and *sadistic,* while Dixon and Mutheius pursue investigations into what they call "psychologically-motivated 'viciousness.'"

26. Summerson, *Heavenly Mansions,* 162.

27. Isaac Van Bibber's diary, in *Maryland Historical Magazine* 39 (September 1944): 254–55.

28. William Francis Brand, "Autobiography," *Maryland Historical Magazine* (1919): 120–21.

saw to it that St. Mary's true, real ceiling timbers were left bare. Once or twice, however, the rector designed a feature that ran counter to the published design. These modifications are important for they not only show Brand's developed sense of aesthetics (since every one of his changes improved on the original), they also make St. Mary's, consecrated in March 1851, an expressive work of art, not a slavishly copied piece from a pattern book.

Brand found most of the building material nearby, including granite from the quarries of Port Deposit and serpentine green marble from Cardiff. But he did not rely solely on local products and scoured Europe in search of the perfect finishing touches for his beloved church. Thus he imported Minton tiles from England for the floors and commissioned the German-born artist Johannes Oertel to paint frescoes for the church's chancel and sanctuary and to carve the lectern and pulpit.[22] (According to ancient rumor, Oertel gave the biblical worthies on the chancel walls faces of nineteenth-century Harford countians.[23] This delicious story, alas, may be apocryphal, for it simply sounds too frivolous for Brand.) Brand's quest for old-world artists also resulted in the church's most notable feature, the fifteen matched stained-glass windows that depict the life of Christ from the Annunciation to the Resurrection and Ascension. The windows, designed by the brilliant British architect/designer and fierce Ecclesiologist William Butterfield, "and purchased a few at a time, from 1851 to 1870,"[24] constitute the only complete set of matched Butterfield glass in America. This is no small point; the windows' designer, Butterfield was born in 1814, thus "within a year or two . . . of Dickens, Thackery, the Brontës, George Eliot, Anthony Trollope, and Robert Browning," writers who broke "the eighteenth-century rule of taste." If Dickens smashed the world of Jane Austen to pieces in prose, Butterfield, "that stern Anglican in steel-rimmed spectacles," did the same to polite Georgian church design.[25]

Upon reflection, one would be hard-pressed to find a better American personification of this revolution in taste than William Brand and St. Mary's, for Brand's church differs as sharply from St. John's in Havre de Grace as the Reverend Mr. Brand differs from Bishop White. The hail-fellow-well-met bishop, who hobnobbed with Benjamin Franklin, was valued by hostesses in Philadelphia and London as the effervescent life of many a dull party. Butterfield, on the other hand (and one feels certain Brand as well), was "the picture of a Victorian of the hardest, narrowest kind, unsoftened by any hint of humour."[26] While undeniably a man of the cloth, White took care that the cloth was a fine, well-tailored brocade. Brand, who "may without exaggeration, be called an oddity," paid attention to matters of style and decor, too: he designed his own picture frames and towel racks that were, according on one parishioner, "decidedly the ugliest things of the kind I had ever seen."[27] Moreover, the rector's autobiography (the bishop was too busy enjoying life to write one) is without doubt one of the most self-tortured such documents in existence. Every page oozes masochistic pleasure: in boarding school the young Brand had been "thrashed on my bare back by a window chord"; in law school he suffered under "a gross injustice on the part of a professor"; at seminary he subsisted on "crackers and cheese with an occasional egg and a quart of milk." While White delighted in the sophistication of Philadelphia, Brand bore the eternal shame of having grown up in New Orleans where his sensitive soul had been exposed to "*every* lascivious act that can be imagined but not spoken of."[28]

Patterns for *Rural Residences*

Despite Brand's earnest efforts, most countians remained unimpressed with strict Ecclesiology, although, as is discussed below, a few superb Gothic churches did, rather willy-nilly, appear on the local scene in the 1860s and '70s. But another post-federal manner of building, the *picturesque,* with its locally popular Italianate and Queen Anne offshoots, did find a great many Harford adherents. Alexander Jackson Davis (1803–92), who called himself an "architectural composer," led the American picturesque attack through his own writings and buildings and through the works of his followers.[29] However he accomplished it, Davis did nothing less than change the course of American architecture and his prose masterpiece, *Rural Residences,* remains among the most influential architectural books ever published in this country. He called it his "house pattern book" and he filled it with easily copied, hand-colored illustrations of cottages, farmhouses, villas, and village churches that stressed volume and plan. Volume and plan are important concepts, because until that time American architecture had been dominated by the Box, four walls and a floor, with a door in the long side, some regularly spaced sash windows, and a gable roof. To this, Davis added broken planes, dramatic, changing rooflines, "bay windows, oriels, turrets, and chimney shafts [to] give a pictorial effect to the elevations." Davis also tried to integrate house and landscape; he bemoaned buildings that displayed a "want of connection with site" and he encouraged architects to use porches to ease the transition from front parlor to front garden.

Davis also gave the word *villa* its popular modern meaning. Prior to this time a "villa" had been imbued with classical overtones and had been tied to an aristocratic—or at least a monied—way of life. The houses discussed in chapter 4, such as Sion Hill and Swansbury, were all part of a classical continuum that stretched back through the Medici to the Caesars. Davis "simply didn't know that tradition, or the classical architecture that went along with it."[30] He did not use the word *villa* to evoke Pliny and Horace debating philosophical niceties in columned splendor; he used it to mean "the country house of a person of competence or wealth sufficient to build and maintain it with some taste . . . a private house where beauty, taste, and moral culture are at home."

It was also a house where literature was at home, particularly the works of Sir Walter Scott. Davis set out to capture, on a domestic scale, some of the heroic drama inherent in Scott's novels and, as one critic has observed, his architecture proved ideal for "early nineteenth-century Americans who were already building their own legend of heroic deeds." The building did not have to be large—"the villa, indeed, may be as simple and chaste as a cottage"—but the concept was revolutionary and Davis's work marks "one of the most uniquely American developments of the nineteenth century."[31] As best-sellers are wont to do—and *Rural Residences* was a best-seller—Davis hatched a spate of imitators.

One of these spinoffs, William Ranlett's *The Architect,* even found its way to Harford County, when actor Junius Brutus Booth bought a copy in 1847 and duplicated the cottage shown in plates 44 and 45 near the banks of Bynum Run.[32] Booth, born in England in 1796, immigrated to America in 1821. Restlessly moving from Norfolk to Richmond to Baltimore, Booth eventually ended up to Harford County, where he acquired an interest in a 150-acre farm about four miles from Bel Air in 1824.[33] At first, Booth lived in a whitewashed log cabin (and encouraged his Harford neighbors to call him "Farmer Booth"),[34] but, after the cabin began to pall and with his copy of Ranlett in hand, he eventually built a more substantial, story-and-a-half, cross-plan, painted brick villa, complete with clustered chimneys, irregular profile, leaded windows, and balconies and porches placed seemingly at random. He called his new house Tudor Hall and one would have to travel far to find a better picturesque Gothic cottage.

Nor could Davis and Ranlett, who aimed their books at "men of imagination—men whose aspirations never leave them at rest—men whose ambition and energy will give them no peace within the mere bounds of rationality" (or so wrote one of Davis's disciples, A. J. Downing, in his *Architecture of Country Houses,* 1850) have created a better picturesque client than Junius Brutus Booth. "To find a really original man," Downing continued, "living in an original and characteristic house is as satisfactory as to find an eagle's nest built on the top of a mountain." Of course one problem with a life led beyond "the mere bounds of rationality" is that it too often disintegrates into chaos, bedeviled by irregularities. So it proved for Booth and Tudor Hall. The actor famously drank to excess, which often caused him to explode in fits of uncontrollable anger: more than once he

29. Dunlap, *History of the Arts of Design in the United States,* quoted in Pierson, *Buildings, Picturesque,* 271.

30. Ackerman, *Villa,* 229.

31. Pierson, *Buildings, Picturesque,* 290, 352–53, 306.

32. "Design No. XVII" for a "Parsonage in the Tudor style."

33. Deeds HD 7/407 and HD 8/261 dated 1824 and 1825. Booth was to pay annual rentals of "one cent" and "one peppercorn only if . . . lawfully demanded" respectively. In this, he comes across as a thorough Englishman. People in London who seem to own their own houses don't; they merely rent them from one of the great landed aristocrats such as the duke of Westminster or the earl of Cadogan. Thus while most American would have bought the property in Harford County, Booth merely took out a 1,000-year lease on it.

34. Howard Fox, owner of Tudor Hall, conversation with author, September 18, 1991.

Tudor Hall: compare this with the "Parsonage in the Tudor Style."

A "Parsonage in the Tudor Style," from architect William Ranlett's book, *The Architect*. This image guided actor Junius Brutus Booth in the design of his residence, Tudor Hall.

"attacked his manager with an andiron"; often "he hurled insults at his astonished audiences."[35] Although Booth married in 1815 (his bride gave birth five months later), the actor then fell bigamously in love with one Mary Ann Holmes, who accompanied him to America and lived with him in Harford. In 1851 Booth obtained a divorce from his first wife (who had remained in England) and married Holmes, with whom he had produced ten children, including the infamous John Wilkes. Suddenly the model of propriety, the actor then took pains to care for his new wife's financial future and subleased Tudor Hall for the "sole and separate use and benefit" of "Mary Ann Booth, formerly by her maiden name known as Mary Ann Holmes."[36] Booth died the following year, when a steamboat he was on blew up, and trustees for Holmes sold Tudor Hall out of the family in 1878.

Thus one finds a direct picturesque line from Davis through Ranlett to Booth and Harford County. Interestingly, if one looks hard, several other similar lines emerge between countians and leading proponents of this new building style. One of these leads to the Silver family and their villas along Deer Creek; another meanders south to tobacco-merchant George McComas and his cottage near Emmorton; a third encircles George Cadwalader and his 7,500-acre fiefdom on the Gunpowder Neck; yet another loops around J. Crawford Neilson, the leading architect in Maryland during the 1840s and '50s, and his farm at Priestford. Sometimes these lines cross each other; sometimes they pursue parallel paths. Their romantic irregularity makes them all more than a little confusing and a bit of background may help modern readers keep them clear.

In 1838 Davis received a fan letter from a young architect named Andrew Jackson Downing, then "busily engaged in preparing a work for press on Landscape Gardening and Rural Residences." The two men met, became personal friends, and "the direction that American domestic architecture would take between 1840 and 1875 was largely determined by" that meeting.[37] Downing (1815–52), with Davis's blessing, embarked on a publishing career of his own and produced in quick succession books with such titles as the *Theory and Practice of Landscape Gardening* (1841) and *Cottage Residences* (1842). Continuing his master's successful format, Downing filled these texts with all-of-a-piece creations complete with elevations, plans, building specifications, cost estimates, and gar-

35. Dorothy Fox, "Childhood Home of an American Arch-Villain," *Civil War Times* (March/April 1990): 16; Philip Van Doren Stern, *The Man Who Killed Lincoln* (New York: Random House, 1939), 238.

36. Deed HD 16/97.

37. Pierson, *Buildings, Picturesque*, 348.

den plans. It is probably worth an aside to point out that Downing marketed his books to affluent readers: although he stated, for instance, that "Design XI" in *Cottage Residences* was "so economical in construction" that it might serve "for the comfort and convenience of a *poor clergyman*" (emphasis in original), the design's $3,000 estimated cost represents about $390,000 today.

Downing's books brought him so much new work that he needed an assistant. In England in 1850, he met an architectural draftsman named Calvert Vaux (born 1824) whom he invited to America. Vaux came, the two became partners and immediately garnered the choicest work of the day, including an 1851 commission to landscape Washington D.C.'s "National Park," known today as The Mall. Downing died the following year (when the Hudson River steamboat *Henry Clay* exploded and sank with him aboard) but Vaux went on, enjoying a sort of *annus mirabilis* in 1857 when he published his only book, *Villas and Cottages,* and designed Central Park in New York.

Vaux's partner for Central Park was Frederick Law Olmsted Sr.; and since Vaux later worked with F. L. Olmsted Jr., his direct influence stretches from the presidency of Andrew Jackson to the New Deal. Geographically that influence stretches to Harford County, too, specifically to the banks of Deer Creek and to Benjamin Silver III's purchase of *Villas and Cottages.*[38] Silver paid two dollars for his copy, probably the most far-reaching two dollars ever spent in the county, at least in terms of architecture. Vaux wrote in his preface that "every young [man] . . . of means in America should aim to [have] excellent architecture . . . simply because it is *worth* having; on the same principle that every healthy man ought to enjoy dining daily."[39] That was just what Silver (1810–94), and his brothers John A. (1820–78), Jeremiah (1826–97), and Silas B. (1815–83) and their cousin, William Finney Silver (1820–89), had been waiting to hear. Between 1853 and 1859 these young men erected on the hills near Glenville a truly remarkable group of picturesque villas:[40] "taken altogether," wrote Dr. W. Stump Forwood in 1879–80, "perhaps there is no family in Maryland . . . [with] such a splendid set of buildings." Nor was there a family more imbued with Victorian public-spiritedness. The Silvers also built and underwrote schools and churches and lobbied for civic improvements such as mail service, all for the improvement of their Glenville neighbors.

The first of the family to settle in the region was the villa-builders' great-grandfather, Gershom (1725–75), who arrived in the Deer Creek Valley around 1763 and worked as a tenant farmer. He also saved his money and in 1770 was able to buy 200 acres of land on which he built a small, one-story stone cottage. Like most countians then, Silver raised or made nearly everything he needed himself; he did, however, shop occasionally at Henry Stump's store in Lapidum where, beginning in 1771, account books show him purchasing "2 lb. brown sugar @ 8c," "1 bolt narrow tape 1.0," "1 Gallon Rum 5.0," and other such necessities. When he died, appraisers valued his estate at £316.19.3, a respectable, if unspectacular, figure derived from goods and chattels that suggest simplicity and utility: horses, cattle, pigs, and sheep, axes, ploughs, hoes, and rope; the dining room (if his house had a dining room) contained thirteen pounds of "old pewter, £2 4s" and "2 pewter tea pots 2/6."

Benjamin Silver I (1753–1818), as eldest son, inherited the bulk of Gershom's property, including a 300-acre farm "near Deer Creek," valued at $1,236.37 in 1798 and $3,000 in 1814; the farm contained the old "dwelling house, stone, 1 story, 28 × 22," which added another $99 to his net worth. After he and his wife died, all 300 acres were divided equally among three of their sons, David, Amos, and James (since they hadn't done anything to "molest or trouble my wife during her natural life"), while three other sons, Benjamin II, William, and Gershom II, received cash bequests. Benjamin further stipulated that all six sons (and their heirs) should have equal access to the "Excellent stone quarry on one part of my plantation . . . for the purpose of building of houses or Barns," and that clause would stand generations of his descendants in good stead.

It was Benjamin Silver II (1782–1847), "a man of great energy and perseverance, hav-

38. Silver Houses nomination to the National Register of Historic Places.

39. Calvert Vaux, *Villas and Cottages* (New York: Harper and Bros., 1857), 40–42.

40. Another brother, James (1812–76), would build his frame house a bit farther west and would wait until 1870 to do so.

Commercial fishing on the Susquehanna, c. 1899: it was hauls such as this that financed the Silver family's superb stone villas in the 1840s and '50s.

ing a knack to manage and conduct a large amount of business," who amassed the family's first real fortune. Something of a visionary, he was among the first in Maryland to realize that fish could make one rich, and he revolutionized that industry by purchasing the rights to the innovative "Bailey Float," which was simply a log raft with a plank deck "sometimes as much as 300 feet square . . . equipped with shacks in which the itinerant fishermen stayed for the whole season." Before the float, commercial fishing had been carried on from the shore; with the float, fishermen could go out to the fish. Just one of Silver's float-made hauls produced 600 barrels of fish—"and even so many escaped." Silver invested his water-based riches in land, for he "possessed a peculiar desire for landed estate. . . . Whenever and wherever he could buy from those around him he did." He bought his first farm in 1812 (260 acres), adding to that modest beginning until, at the time of his death, he owned about 1,352 acres, stretching from Glenville eastward until stopped by the impenetrable Stump-Harlan holdings at Elbow Branch. A scientific farmer in an age when such thoughts were novel, Benjamin "used fish pickle from his own . . . fisheries" to improve "his lands while many around him neglected theirs."[41]

In good Victorian fashion, Silver not only improved his own condition in life, he also looked out for those less fortunate. In 1837 he helped establish the nearby Prospect School (he himself had attended the racially integrated Green Spring School near Glenville discussed in chapter 5) and while he "neither sought nor desired public office" he did agree to serve as state-appointed "commissioner to disburse [funds] for the education of poor children in his section of the county."[42] He gave splendid educations to those of his children so inclined (he sent son Benjamin III to Yale and son Silas first to Union College and then to the University of Pennsylvania's medical school) but he didn't insist on that route; sons John and Jeremiah moved happily from adolescence to an adulthood of farming and commercial fishing with apparently no thought of a collegiate stopover. Not obsessively interested in religion, nonetheless in 1837 Silver donated a lot on what is now the corner of Harmony Church Road and Route 161 and paid contractors to build a small, stone Presbyterian chapel of ease so his churchgoing kith would not have to trek to Churchville each Sunday. He got around to joining the congregation in 1846.

He died the following year owning $7,046.52 worth of personal property (including

41. Silver, *Our Silver Heritage*, 3204; Mason, *Sketches*, 76, 77.

42. Silver, *Our Silver Heritage*, 3205.

Dr. Silas Silver's villa, Silverton, c. 1890. Silas's brother Benjamin owned a copy of architect Calvert Vaux's *Villas and Cottages* (1857), which urged the home-builder to incorporate a deep front porch ("the most specifically American feature of a country house") into home design. Dr. Silver, who designed Silverton in 1858 with the help of architect William H. Reasin, evidently agreed.

roughly $2,500 of fishing-related goods), securities worth $374.80 (mostly bank stock and Tide Water Canal bonds), and safe, intrafamily IOUs of $5,911.53. Like his contemporary John Stump of Stafford (see chapter 5), Silver favored an unostentatious existence and spent more energy in capital accumulation than in worrying about the comforts such capital might provide, for he evidently continued to live in his father's and grandfather's one-story stone house (his estate inventory lacks key words like "stairs" that might imply a two-story dwelling), and his most valuable pieces of furniture were an eight-day clock and a sideboard, each valued at $20. After expenses, the net total weighed in at $13,125.64, or well over $1 million in modern currency. Dr. Forwood creates a superb period image of Benjamin's children restlessly cooped up in their "small . . . antique cottage in the vale." "Crammed and crowded for houseroom," the younger generation (Forwood fantasized) vowed that "they would, if the fates willed it, . . . build themselves large and commodious houses." The fates did will it and, armed with three generations of accumulated wealth, vast acreage, the family-owned stone quarry, and Benjamin III's copy of *Villas and Cottages,* four of Benjamin II's sons and a first cousin set forth to build their superb picturesque villas on the rolling hills around Harmony Church.

Virtually every feature of the Silvers' villas can be traced to Vaux. The cousins built the shells of their houses in stone ("a very agreeable and superior method for rural buildings," to quote *Villas and Cottages*) from their grandfather's quarry; they then enriched these shells with an array of Vauxian details such as Port Deposit granite quoins, steps, and window sills, elaborate wooden balconies, prominent dormer windows, Tuscan-columned porches, and heavy modillioned cornices. The Silvers did not build bell towers (a feature Downing, Davis, and Vaux encouraged) but elaborate dormers and fanciful brick chimneys add interest to the houses' skylines. They also crowned many of their outbuildings with cupolas and one need only flip the pages of *Villas and Cottages* to see Vaux's finely etched engravings of cupolas (or "Ventilators") and his pleas to employ these "useful" touches "for [their] convenience and artistic effect" to see how thoroughly the Marylanders had absorbed their picturesque lessons.[43]

Any number of other issues suggest the family's reliance on Vaux. For example, site was almost an obsession with Vaux, who wrote that "the great charm in the forms of nat-

43. Vaux, *Villas,* 107.

ural landscape . . . is the secret of success in every picturesque . . . country-house or cottage" (51). The Silvers, thanks to their ancestors' land-acquisitiveness, enjoyed house-sites of astonishing beauty, with panoramic views of "the verdant hills and fertile valleys of the noble Deer Creek . . . and the unfolding [of] Nature's grand panorama."[44] Moreover, they all graced their villas with deep porches that seem to reach out and join the house to this rolling landscape. Vaux liked porches, "perhaps the most specially American feature of a country house . . . nothing can compensate for its absence," but only if sparingly used; porches should not, for instance, extend all the way around a house since "most healthily-constituted persons like to have the opportunity to admit a stream of glorious, warm, congenial sunlight into their rooms."[45] The Silvers read and obeyed and gave their houses deep, one-story porches that shelter the front door but that leave most of the windows free to catch the sunlight.

Who could fail to be fascinated by the Silvers and their houses? Certainly not Dr. Forwood, who devotes page after glowing page to John Archer Silver and his house, Vignon, a twenty-room mansion "built of beautiful stone" that crowned "high ground and can be seen for many miles." (Silver began Vignon around 1844 and then doubled its size in 1870; the house burned to the ground in 1902.)[46] He was no less expansive regarding William Finney Silver's house,[47] an upwardly thrusting, Italianate stone cube begun c. 1857 and originally embellished with a pair of Vauxian porches that overflowed with wicker and houseplants. (Of all the family, William may have made best use of the Deer Creek hills for his estate inventory includes three sleighs and "1 Bob Sled, $10.") The doctor proved especially fond of the stone villas Jeremiah and Silas Silver built, respectively, in 1853[48] and 1858 to the designs of architect William H. Reasin—or *partially* to his designs: the architect provided drawings for the plan, elevations, "and front porches" for Jeremiah's dwelling, but Silas only asked "Mr. Reasin, the architect, to draw plans for house. B. Silver and I gave him the interior." The Silvers' hiring Reasin marks another local architectural revolution, since it is the first time anyone in Harford County used an architect for house design.

Reasin (pronounced "rasin") was born near Aberdeen "but when a youth went to Baltimore, where he studied architecture, and . . . became in time one of the leading architects" of that city. (He also maintained an office in Havre de Grace.) His large body of work, most of which perished in the 1904 Baltimore fire, showed "a preferential tendency" for the Italianate style, a popular picturesque manner of building characterized by prominent, bracketed cornices, square towers, and rounded, ornamented window hoods. Those elements certainly dominate what may be Reasin's best-known downtown project, his quirkish Engine House Number 6, a six-story Venetian Gothic campanile dating to 1853, the same year Reasin designed Jeremiah's villa.[49] The architect certainly did good work for the Silver clan. Dr. Forwood reckoned Jeremiah's villa "handsome" and deemed Silas's Silverton, bulging with porches and window hoods and ornamental chimney pots, "picturesque and beautiful."[50]

While the Silvers' diaries paint verbal portraits of all the family, no one, perhaps, emerges more vividly from those pages than the oldest of the brothers, Benjamin Silver III (1810–94). Educated at Yale "with the view of studying medicine" he changed his mind and returned to his native county to become the "most careful, pains-taking, and exact farmer" of the family. He was also master of an astonishing number of avocations: diarist, land surveyor, amateur architect, politician (he represented the county in the House of Delegates), "a good mechanic and machinist, a bee-keeper, [and unlike his father] a regular church attendee."[51] Far and away the most conservative of the family, Benjamin harumphed his way through life, battling one form of "progress" after another: in 1848 alone he circulated one "petition against railroad company bridging the river at Havre de Grace" and another "against further lottery grants." When the Civil War broke out, Benjamin, the sole slave-owning Silver, was also the family's only rebel.[52] Silas maintained an

44. Forwood, "Homes on Deer Creek," December 23, 1879.

45. Vaux, *Villas*, 82–89, 108.

46. Forwood, "Homes on Deer Creek," January 9, 1880; Silver, *Our Silver Heritage*, 3807.

47. Churchville's William Finney officiated at countless Silver weddings, baptisms, and burials; the rector was still living in his stone Oak Farm when the Silvers began building and it is likely that Oak Farm's locally innovative round-arched attic windows inspired similar details at Benjamin's and Jeremiah's houses.

48. According to Jeremiah's diary, one Henry Henmore began quarrying stone on January 5, 1853, and by that June "223 wagon loads of stone had been hauled to the house" from the family quarry while 38,562 feet of lumber had arrived "at Rock Run" in April.

49. *Portrait and Biographical Record*, 252–53; George A. Frederick, "Recollections on Baltimore Architecture," October 10, 1912, typescript in MHS. William Reasin also owned a copy of Vaux. Indeed, his 1867 estate inventory describes an immense architectural library of roughly sixty titles, including *Villas and Cottages* (valued at 1 dollar), as well as three books by Ruskin (*Seven Lamps of Architecture* [50 cents], *Modern Painters* [3 dollars], and *Stones of Venice* [5 dollars]), two by Pugin (*Gothic Architecture* [10 dollars] and *Gothic Ornament* [7 dollars]), and three by Downing (*Country Houses* [2 dollars], *Rural Essays* [50 cents], and *Landscape Gardening* [1 dollar])

John Dorsey and James Dilts, in their *Guide to Baltimore Architecture* (Cambridge, Md.: Tidewater Publishers, 1980), marvel at the firehouse's "eccentric use of Italian ideas" (xxvii) but Reasin's original plans, still preserved at the Peale Museum, are a good deal more peculiar than what was actually built.

50. Forwood, "Homes on Deer Creek," March 19, 1880; Silver Houses National Register; Vaux, *Villas*, 81.

51. Silver, *Our Silver Heritage*, 3401.

52. "Our Silver Heritage" reports that Benjamin would take his family "out on a hilltop . . . and sing the Long Meter Doxology in thanksgiving for Confederate victories," 3409.

uneasy neutrality; Jeremiah and John were firm Union men who spent the war nervously "on the lookout for the confederates."[53]

In a suitably iconoclastic manner, Benjamin, the Silver brother who bought Vaux's book, built the most conservative of the family's villas, eschewing most of the fashionable, picturesque architectural devices he had urged his brothers and cousin to employ. Yet if his conservatism controlled the design of his residence, his outbuildings—a frame bank barn, frame and hipped-roof servants' house, granite dairy, granite smokehouse, frame icehouse, frame corncrib, and a pair of frame carriage houses—suggest that he had a fanciful, even frivolous, soul beneath that gruff exterior. Those outbuildings also present a virtually unchanged testimony of the nineteenth-century picturesque movement at its best; he crowned the smokehouse and servants' house with decorative wooden finials and topped the icehouse and carriage houses with elaborate Vauxian cupolas.

The Silvers' active minds led them to all manner of other forms of picturesque self-expression. They not only built villas to live in and cupola-crowned cottages for their servants, they also laid out roads and constructed churches and even built a post office, all in a thoroughly Vauxian manner. Silas, appointed postmaster of Glenville in 1854, erected, at his expense, a wonderful, gingerbread-bedecked frame post office/store for the village; and on August 26 of that year, he wrote in his diary that "B. Silver is opening a public road from James F. Reasin to the road leading by Death's Ford to Churchville." (Blacksmith and wheelwright James Reasin was a brother of William and one suspects that the architect designed brother James's house, "a most beautiful frame dwelling in the most approved modern cottage style," wrote Dr. Forwood, "[with] ornamental porticos and handsome bay-windows resembling some of the most tasteful and picturesque villas.") That "new" road, Glenville Road, along with Harmony Church Road traverse Silver lands, were laid out under Silver guidance, and further underscore the family's reliance on Vaux, who told his readers that country roads should "wind in graceful curves . . . in accordance with the formation of the ground and the natural features. . . . [A] single existing tree ought . . . to be the all-sufficient reason for slightly diverting the line of a road, so as to take advantage of its shade, instead of cutting it down and grubbing up its roots."[54]

Harmony Church Road, of course, derives its name from Benjamin II's 1837 chapel of ease. After a generation or so of use that original 30-by-40-foot stone structure proved too small and, according to Dr. Forwood, "*too plain* for the present congregation." So in June 1868 the elders asked William F., John A., and Benjamin III to form a building committee; they also asked James Reasin, "a trustee . . . [who] gave about $1,000 towards the erection of the . . . [new] church" to join the committee to lend a nominal non-Silver voice.[55] Although church records credit architect John W. Hogg of Baltimore with the design of the new building, since William Reasin had been a member of the congregation since 1866, had served as church treasurer, had his brother on the building committee, and had so successfully completed work on the Silver villas, one suspects he volunteered an opinion or two. (One also suspects the Silvers, armed with Benjamin's well-worn copy of *Villas and Cottages,* lipped in freely as well.)

Vaux "earnestly" urged landowners like the Silvers to help "improve . . . [the appearance] of county churches" since "we are all compelled to look at [churches] . . . although we are perfectly free to attend or stay away from" them. He advised congregations to do this by building in stone, crowning the roofs with slate, and incorporating a "soaring, heaven-ward pointing spire, bold in outline and quiet in color" into the design.[56] Certainly the "new" Harmony church, completed in 1871 and in Forwood's words, "without doubt one of the handsomest churches to be found outside of the large cities," passes muster in every respect.[57]

Curiously, of all the picturesque touches the Silvers gave their houses—and church—none has more wide-ranging implications than the seemingly routine board-and-batten

Architect William H. Reasin, who assisted brothers Silas and Jeremiah Silver with the design of their stone villas near Darlington, did much work in Baltimore City. He had a predilection for Italianate motifs, clear from his best-known building, the quirkish Engine House No. 6 (1853) with its Venetian Gothic openings, shown here in 1926.

53. Jeremiah Silver diary, HSHC archives.
54. Vaux, *Villas,* 51–52.
55. *Portrait and Biographical Record,* 158.
56. Vaux, *Villas,* 116–18.
57. All quotes from Forwood, "Homes on Deer Creek," January 9, 1880.

siding Benjamin used to sheath his servants' quarters and smokehouse. While no one knows who invented board-and-batten, Davis and Downing did much to promote it: the former "was the first American to use and define it" and devoted several paragraphs of *Rural Residences* to the subject; the latter extolled it because it "better expresses the picturesque" than conventional clapboard and because of its "truthfulness." (Downing's conviction that the inherent qualities of materials should determine a building's design, "the material," he wrote "should *appear* to be what it is," anticipated the thinking of modern giants such as Gropius and Wright by a century.) Thanks to Davis and Downing, board-and-batten grew so popular that "by mid-century . . . [it] was used for the majority of wooden Gothic cottages in this country . . . [and] was, in fact, the most important mark of distinction which set American cottages apart from their equivalent in England."[58]

Board-and-batten proved popular in Harford County, too, not only among the Silvers, who used it for outbuildings, but also among homebuilders, who used it for cottages. The most intact of these dwellings shifts the scene from the rolling banks of Deer Creek to the flat fields of Emmorton, where George McComas purchased a 140-acre tract at the intersection of Singer and Clayton roads in 1855.[59] McComas worked quickly and his cottage, which he named Linwood, appears on the 1858 map of the county. Born in 1821, George was the second son of William McComas, a Harford-born housebuilder, and his wife, Ellen, a dressmaker. Just why George, who earned a comfortable living as a Baltimore tobacco merchant, decided to build a board-and-batten Gothic cottage in Harford County is not clear. One might, however, infer parental influences, since his mother often voiced her concern "about the evils of urban life,"[60] and his father, presumably, had a builder's guide or two lying around. A man of strong, philosophical conviction and a dedicated abolitionist, George McComas encouraged the Freedmen's Bureau to establish a church and school for ex-slaves on Singer Road near his new house; the bureau did so and named the school the McComas Institute after its local sponsor, as is discussed in chapter 5.

McComas's religious and political convictions are of more than academic interest; they bear directly on the design of his house, since Downing, among others, viewed board-and-batten Gothic cottages such as Linwood, with its sharp, pyramidal gables, in quasi-religious terms: "the worshipping principle . . . and the sentiment of Christian brotherhood," he wrote in *Cottage Residences,* is "expressed in the principle lines which are all vertical . . . the whole mass falling under . . . the pyramidal . . . form." Indeed, Linwood, with its sprawling, asymmetrical configuration, delicate and attenuated brackets, many porches, French doors, and varied window treatments, is so good it makes one wonder if a plate from a book could have been enough of a design guide for McComas. Had he used an architect?

Enter J. Crawford Neilson

The Silvers' hiring "Mr. Reasin" to design their Deer Creek villas marks the beginning of a new era in Harford's architecture, for it suggests that by the 1850s countians were at last willing to spend money on what might be called the finer things in life. Their timing in this was good, for throughout the 1840s and '50s, they suddenly had some topflight architects in their midst. There was not only William Reasin but also J. Crawford Neilson, whose firm "from the late '40s to the late '50s did the principle and best work in Baltimore."[61] Neilson's Baltimore commissions include the magnificent Camden Station (1851; the largest train station in the world when it opened and now incorporated into Oriole Park at Camden Yards), an Italianate makeover of Johns Hopkins's villa, Clifton (1852), the "flamboyantly Gothic" Greenmount Cemetery Chapel (1851–56),[62] and 1 West Mount Vernon Place (1849–51, one of the greatest period townhouses in America and now the home of the Walters Art Gallery's collection of Asian art).

Neilson, born in Baltimore in 1814, received his early schooling in England and Bel-

The theorist and architect A. J. Davis urged American builders to make use of board-and-batten construction since it "better expresses the picturesque" than conventional weatherboarding does. Shown here is Davis's suggested design for a picturesque board-and-batten cottage from his highly influential book, *Rural Residences.*

58. Pierson, *Buildings, Picturesque,* 406–7, 59, 57, 35–36, 432.

59. Deed ALJ 6/225.

60. Henry Clay McComas and Mary Winona McComas, "The McComas Saga, 1100 A.D.–1950," typescript in the Maryland Room, Enoch Pratt Free Library, Baltimore.

61. Frederick, "Recollections."

62. Dorsey and Dilts, *Guide to Baltimore Architecture,* 283.

Architect J. Crawford Neilson, who lived at his wife's Priestford farm and commuted to and from his office in Baltimore, and his partner, John Niernsee, designed the magnificent Camden Station for the B&O Railroad in 1851. The station (once the largest in the world and shown here decked out for the Democratic National Convention in 1912) suggests Neilson's fondness for Italianate motifs. Compare it to the Churchville Presbyterian Church's belltower or to Neilson's 1858 Harford County Courthouse.

gium but he returned to his hometown for good in 1831. Two years later he joined the Baltimore and Port Deposit Railroad as a draftsmen and surveyor and conducted a "survey for a Rail Road to the Susquehanna along the Valley of Deer Creek." Nothing came of the project except a map "made . . . in October 1835 . . . by J.C. Neilson." In 1842 he joined the B&O, for whom he drew maps and sketched profiles of roadbeds. In these sketches Neilson displays his concern for the architectonic problems of geometry and volume, even when dealing with a routine matter like pitching a tent. He also "designed a series of prefabricated iron roofs for freight houses, locomotive sheds, and stations which are the earliest known instances of composite iron roofs in this country."[63]

The thoroughly cosmopolitan Neilson, with his partner, the Austrian-born John R. Niernsee, brought the latest European trends to the Chesapeake; they were especially fond of the Italianate, and made use of that style at Clifton, Camden Yards, and One West. The date of Neilson's professional entry into Harford County is unclear but may have come as early as 1850, when he and Gen. George Cadwalader penned many letters to each other concerning new barns for the general's Gunpowder Neck estate. Neilson may or may not have designed barns for Cadwalader; he did, however, almost certainly design an overseer's cottage for him and that frame building (long since destroyed) had board-and-batten siding, steeply pitched roofs, pointed-arch windows, and sharp gables that made it a larger, earlier, and more sophisticated version of Linwood. (Cadwalader himself had a good eye for the latest trends in design. The Maryland Historical Society owns "a charming example of the popular Elizabethan/Cottage style turned chair," similar to one "illustrated in Downing" the general commissioned for his own Gunpowder Neck house.)[64]

The date of Neilson's personal entry into the county is, however, better documented. In 1840 he married Rosa Williams, a granddaughter of John Stump of Stafford (her mother was Stump's daughter Hannah); six years later Neilson bought his in-laws' family farm, Priestford, which Stump had willed to Mrs. Williams. This talented man lived at Priestford, with Rosa and their three children, the rest of his adult life and his meticulously kept *Priestford Notebook* records forty years of remodeling projects he carried out on the old Stump-Williams buildings.[65] In September 1858 he "began enlarging and altering

63. Ibid., 282.

64. Gregory R. Weidman, *Furniture in Maryland,* 1740–1940 (Baltimore; MHS, 1984), 227–28.

65. The children were Albert (the eldest, born 1841), Rosa, and Charles; two others died in infancy, James in 1845 and Virginia in 1848. The two deceased children were buried in a private cemetery at Priestford along with Neilson's Williams in-laws and "'Mammy Jane' Clarke—Slave—Nurse of Mrs. Rosa Neilson" who died in 1874.

In the 1850s Baltimore-born architect J. Crawford Neilson corresponded with Gen. George Cadwalader about the design of a barn for the latter's Gunpowder Neck estate. Neilson probably didn't get the barn job, but he probably did design this ultra-stylish overseer's (or, possibly, gardener's?) cottage for Cadwalader. (The general used the place for duck-hunting: note what appears to be the day's haul just to the right of the group of servant-women.)

J. Crawford Neilson and son, Albert, c. 1850.

66. Charles P. Dare, *Philadelphia, Wilmington & Baltimore Railroad Guide* (Philadelphia: Fitzgibbon and Van Ness, 1856), 50.

dwelling" and in 1860 he "added wing to dining room and chamber" to create a "two story frame dwelling 58 × 28 × 26 to square, irregular; front, back, and side porches." He also experimented with picturesque details, such as doors, porch trim, fireplace mantels, and, in one exotic moment, even a Venetian Gothic bookcase for his library. His work on the farm's outbuildings was also unceasing: "1849 Tenant's house . . . moved and enlarged"; "1857, old ice house and diary . . . moved and enlarged for servants; ice house enlarged . . . dairy built"; "1858 Beech Cottage built"; "Oct. 1866 finished removing schoolhouse and began shed"; "1867 finished smoke house and woodshed"; "1868 began to alter barn"; "1869 changed the old corn house into a carriage house . . . in August built ice house . . . commenced plant house," a reference to yet another of Neilson's interests, gardening. (See chapter 10.)

The *Notebook* also documents a generation's worth of Neilson's Harford County buildings, beginning in May 1851 when the vestry of St. George's Episcopal Church in Perryman asked "Messrs. Niernsee & Neilson . . . to furnish a plan for a new church." That July the architects completed "a plan of the Norman style of architecture"; church officials liked it and laid the cornerstone two months later, with the Reverend William Brand of St. Mary's in attendance. One suspects Brand really came to spy on things: What must he have thought? What invectives did he sputter to Mrs. Brand that evening over tea? For Neilson's St. George's, sensuously and beautifully picturesque, its brick walls sheathed in scored stucco and painted a gorgeous shade of taupe, with tall, clear-glass windows designed to allow every possible ray sunlight to stream in, stood diametrically opposite to everything the Ecclesiological Brand advocated in church design. More objective contemporaries, however, regarded St. George's a great success; the author of an 1856 passengers' guidebook for what is now the Amtrak mainline, for one, urged travelers entering Perryman to look sharp for "the neat Norman church . . . [a] chaste and beautiful edifice."[66]

In 1858 Neilson secured the most local important commission yet given an architect in the county, nothing less than a new courthouse in Bel Air. That year the state legislature appointed A. Lingan Jarrett, Stevenson Archer, Henry S. Harlan, James McCormick, and William H. Dallam "Commissioners to contract for and to superintend the build-

ing" of a new courthouse and in June the committee hired Neilson as "consulting architect" and Bel Air engineer and surveyor Frank Barr "superintendent architect" for the project. Neilson's talent, however, eventually won out and historian George W. Archer stated categorically in the March 22, 1889, *Ægis* that "J. Crawford Neilson . . . was the architect in the reconstruction."[67] Neilson concocted a thoroughly picturesque courthouse for his adopted county with "classical details wedded to the odd Italianate element, hard to classify but easy to look at."[68]

Neilson inferentially accepted these early Harford commissions on a pro bono basis since no mention of fees appears in St. George's or the courthouse's very complete records. It is certain he did so when he worked on a pair of later buildings closer to his Priestford home. In 1870 he met with the Reverend William Finney to discuss the pros and cons of remodeling (as opposed to replacing) the 1820 Presbyterian church in Churchville. These must have been the most agreeable meetings ever held between any architect and any client. An 1882 biography describes Neilson as "genial" (the Baltimore *Sun* reported that he "possessed . . . an engaging personality [and] quickly made friends"), while A. P. Silver remembered the rector as an "affable" man who "possessed a vein of genuine humor which was constantly bubbling forth in the apt remark and witty response."[69] Eventually the happy pair had to call in the congregation's elders to make the final decision and, according to church minutes, on August 9 "after considerable discussion," they accepted Neilson's suggestion to keep the old shell but reglaze the windows and add a restrained three-story Italianate belltower to the entrance façade. How different this comfortable, old-shoe plan sounds from the doctrinally correct St. Mary's—but how different the Reverend Mr. Finney sounds from the Reverend Dr. Brand, who described himself as "of an irascible impatient temper . . . moody and resentful."[70]

And if St. George's "Norman" design and Churchville's campanile set Brand's teeth on edge, which seems safe to assume, Neilson's work at Trap Church must have driven him to apoplexy. Begun as an Anglican chapel around 1760—purportedly so representatives from the established church could keep an eye on Roman Catholic goings-on at Priest Neale's Mass House—by the 1860s Trap, located about a half-mile north of Priestford, had become the virtual plaything of the local gentry, including Neilson and his

67. Archer also records that E. and J. Reynolds were the contractors, managed by Alonzo Reynolds; the cost was $14,600.

68. Larew, *Bel Air,* 4.

69. Clipping from the *Baltimore Sun,* October 12, 1954, on file at the Maryland Room, Pratt Library; A. P. Silver, *History of the Deer Creek Harmony Church of Glenville* (Glenville, Md.: privately printed, 1905), 12; Silver recalled once, when a friend asked for an autographed photograph, Finney complied, writing, "This is a pretty fair specimen of the ravages of time."

70. Brand, "Autobiography."

Stump wife, James Silver of Silvermount (a brother of Silas, Benjamin, and Jeremiah), and the Symingtons of Indian Spring Farm. In April of 1869 that first church burned beyond repair and Neilson designed a bijou-Gothic stone edifice to replace it. Work was slow—walls were only windowsill high in 1872—but, the architect wrote, on "June 24, 1875, the first service was held . . . the church being finished."

Neilson's new Trap Church, which one Symington descendant remembers as being "cute as a wink,"[71] really was not a church at all—it was a stage set, a toy created by the neighbors for their private amusement. God simply does not enter the picture. The amused, areligious nature at Trap crystallized in 1876 when "Mrs. Col. Symington" asked Neilson to design a "commemorative porch . . . as a memorial to her husband Mr. Col. Symington": Neilson did so and gave the solid, stub-ends of the granite railings, where one might expect to see an engraved cross or some other holy symbol, an engraved *S* for Symington. Since it was this sort of godless behavior that had so enraged the Ecclesiologists thirty years earlier, one should not be surprised at Brand's response to the new building—he simply tried to have it and its heathenish congregation removed from his flock. According to Neilson's *Notebook,* in May 1878 the parish "was divided . . . by a . . . line one mile . . . from Trap Church . . . principally by the efforts of Rev. W.F. Brand." (The next year, however, the bishop "rescinded" Brand's fit of pique.)

Fortunately for countians' blood pressure, other period church architects managed to strike a compromise between the strict Ecclesiology of Brand and the relaxed picturesqueness of Neilson. This is certainly the case with George Archer and his Holy Trinity in Churchville and Theophilus Chandler and his Grace Memorial in Darlington. Still, it remains a debatable point as to whether Archer and Chandler incorporated Gothic motifs into their design because of the motifs' decorative possibilities or because of their doctrinal implications.

Holy Trinity's history begins in 1866 when Dr. David Harlan of The Homelands "purchased six pleasant acres" near town where "he built a pretty little frame church of Gothic design, which was called the Church of the Holy Trinity."[72] To design the new house of worship, Harlan hired the Silvers' favorite architect, William Reasin, who devised a board-and-batten chapel that was completed in June of 1867. That frame building burned to the ground ten years later and in January 1878, Dr. Harlan called the vestry together to formulate plans for a cruciform-plan stone replacement, "with a belfry on the west gable" and "Gothic windows of ground glass,"[73] all to the design of architect George Archer.

Archer, a great-grandson of Dr. John Archer of Medical Hall, was born in 1848 at Allendale, a family farm just south of Deer Creek, where his father, Thomas, "one of the noted educators . . . of Harford County . . . conducted a private school."[74] George Archer was graduated from Princeton in 1870 and moved to Baltimore to work in the office of architect George Frederick, the young man (born 1842) who had designed the Baltimore City Hall in 1867. Archer opened his own design office in Maryland's metropolis in 1875 and embarked on a career that made him "one of the most successful architects in the city."[75] His many Harford County commissions include the remodeling of Christ Church, Rock Spring (1875), a new Presbyterian Church in Bel Air (1881) to replace Finney's temple, the house Windy Walls on Wheel Road (1894), and the Second National Bank in Bel Air (1900).

At about the same time Archer was working on the quite splendid Holy Trinity, Harford County received another of its finest churches—indeed, one of its finest buildings of any type—the 1876 Grace Memorial Church in Darlington, paid for by industrialist D. C. Wharton Smith as "a memorial to his father, Milton Smith."[76] Smith, a native Philadelphian, hired the young architect Theophilus P. Chandler (born 1845) to design the new church. Chandler was a Harvard-educated Bostonian who gained advanced training in Paris at the Atelier Vaudremer (not the usual background for nineteenth-century Darlington builders); he opened his office in Philadelphia in 1870 and promptly secured an impressively varied group of commissions including churches (such as the Swe-

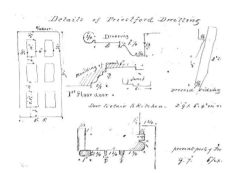

Throughout the last half of the nineteenth century, Neilson constantly tinkered with the design of his wife's Priestford house; here is one typical page of sketches from his *Priestford* notebook.

71. Mrs. Nicholas Penniman III (née Pattie Symington), conversation with author, June 10, 1991. Mrs. Penniman chose her words carefully, for she is a trained architect and knows what she's talking about.

72. *Portrait and Biographical Record,* 144.

73. Notes to and from Dr. Harlan and Archer, on file at the HSHC. Presented to the society by Katharine B. Harlan.

74. Wright, *Harford,* 404.

75. *Illustrated Baltimore.* Quoted in Irma Walker and James T. Wollon Jr., "George Archer's Life and Works," *Harford Historical Bulletin* (Spring 1993): 40.

76. *Harford Democrat,* undated clipping in files of HSHC.

denborgian Church at Chestnut and 22nd streets in Philadelphia, the First Presbyterian Church in Pittsburgh, and St. Thomas's Episcopal Church in Washington), townhouses (including one for merchant John Wanamaker in Philadelphia at 20th and Walnut and a mansion on Dupont Circle in Washington, D.C., for merchant-prince L. Z. Leiter), and country houses, such as Winterthur near Wilmington for the du Ponts.[77]

Smith and Chandler gave Darlington a pure, uncomplicated product of Gothic design and an eloquent expression of Christian faith. Moreover, everything about Grace Church echoes lines in the very first issue of the *New York Ecclesiologist,* namely that

> the great and true principle of Gothic architecture is . . . ornamenting construction and not constructing ornament. . . . No church should be pretty: it should be simple, or modest, or dignified, or rich or gorgeous; but there should never be anything puerile about it, to lower its tone or degrade its character.[78]

Chandler and Smith saw to it that Grace Church's walls were laid in carefully dressed Deer Creek soapstone, exposed inside and out, while slate shingles from nearby Cardiff cover the roof. Inside, the powerful roof trusses, designed to suggest medieval hammer-beams, spring directly from the exposed stone walls, their point of entry marked only by roughly carved, functional stone brackets; the simple furniture—oak pews, walnut altar, ungilded iron communion railing—continues the ecclesiological theme of purity. The windows do as well, for Chandler devised tall, narrow lances with the glass set directly into the stone walls without frames. Perhaps the most striking window in the church, the triple lancet in the south wall, contains a heroic St. Paul flanked by panels rich in color, bold in exuberance, and with a masculine spirit appropriate to that era's fondness for "muscular Christianity."

But to return to Neilson. While his many Harford County public works are thoroughly documented, the number of villas in the county that may be attributed to him is surprisingly small, "surprisingly" since he and Niernsee "produced scores of city and country residences."[79] It is tempting to think that he lent a neighborly hand to the Symingtons in the 1860s when they built a picturesque stone farmer's cottage at Indian Spring Farm and to James Silver when he, according to his brother Silas, "in the year 1870

Philadelphia architect Theophilus Chandler designed Grace Memorial Church in Darlington as a memorial to financier D. C. Wharton Smith's father in 1876. Left: A heroic St. Paul dominates the triple window of Grace Church's south façade. Right: The church's picturesque Deer Creek soapstone walls graced a page in the August 24, 1878, *American Architect and Building News.*

77. Born in Maryland, Leiter grew rich-rich as an early partner of Marshall Field; his daughter, Mary, married George Curzon and wound up Viceriene of India. That was the highest-ranking British title any American has ever secured, although Baltimore's Wallis Warfield certainly did her best. See Henry F. Withey and Elsie Rathburn Withey, *Biographical Dictionary of American Architects (Deceased)* (Los Angeles: New Age Publishing, 1956), 117–18.

78. *New York Ecclesiologist* 1 (October 1848): 11.

79. *Baltimore Sun,* October 12, 1954.

Harford and the Picturesque

. . . built . . . a very fine mansion" on land he had purchased from the Neilsons in 1847. Since both the Symington and Silver houses originally bristled with exceptionally complex and almost identical porch trim it seems safe to assume that the same hand designed both—the scrollwork is far more elaborate than anything known in the county—and if not the neighboring Neilson, then who?

No such speculation is necessary for what may be Neilson's local masterpiece; thanks to Dr. Forwood's "Homes on Deer Creek" series, it is clear that when Thomas King set out in the centennial year, 1876, to remodel the c. 1770 Husband-Jewett house, Lansdowne, "the architect, through whose professional talent and good judgment these improvements . . . have been accomplished, was Mr. J. Crawford Neilson of Priestford, this county." Joseph King, Thomas's father, had bought the acreage (and the 1770s stone house it contained) in 1843 from John and Susannah Judge Jewett, devout Quakers whose "upright lives and good works have established lasting memorials," according to historian Walter Preston. Preston particularly admired Mrs. Jewett, "a woman of strong mind and a powerful minister," who was clerk of the Baltimore Yearly Friends Meeting and "who often conducted services at the Deer Creek Friends Meeting House in Darlington."[80] (The Quaker spirit certainly ran in the family; John's abolitionist cousin John Punchard Jewett published *Uncle Tom's Cabin*.) When Joseph King died in 1865 he left the property to his two sons, Francis and Thomas. The latter, after spending "protracted periods"[81] in Europe, returned to America in 1875, decided to live in the Deer Creek Valley, bought out his brother's interest in the farm, and hired Neilson to enlarge the old house.

Neilson's and King's collaboration, completed in 1879, so moved Dr. Forwood that he devoted two entire 1880 *Ægis* articles to it. While the doctor's lengthy, purplish prose sometimes makes for rough going, readers are urged to stick with it for the narrative is as complete a period piece as the house. Because King's European years had left him with a "predilection for all that is beautiful in the antique," when he bought the ancient Husband house he made "a firm resolution to preserve as much of his old mansion as possible, instead of dismantling it and erecting a new dwelling, as he had previously thought of doing." But as Winston Churchill might have said, "Some preservation! Some additions!" When Neilson finished his work, one would have to look hard to see any of the original structure. He and King replaced "the old kitchen at the end" with "a very handsome addition . . . [containing] kitchen, pantry, and dining room," west of which "and extending on a line with the new addition" ran "a high wall, handsomely finished with fine stone and surmounted with a neat iron railing" designed "to conceal from view, in an artistic manner, the very convenient wood-house." Upstairs the service wing contained two servants' bedrooms and, reached from the master bedroom, "a large and first-class bathroom . . . finished in the highest style of bathroom art. . . . The bath-tub is of copper and the stop-cocks heavily plated with silver. . . . The casing of the tub is of walnut and maple." Windows in the service wing have "arching . . . red brick" tops in the "old English manner," a motif suggested, "we are informed, by Mr. Neilson," highly likely since round arched windows were one of Neilson's favorite details and he used them at all three of his other major Harford projects, the courthouse, St. George's, and the Churchville bell tower.

East of that wing, Neilson built a huge addition that contains a parlor, dining room, library, and stairhall on the ground story with bedrooms above; he crowned this new wing with an immense shingled roof that "projects well over the walls—two feet!—for their protection." He also gave the wing what Forwood called a "beautiful porch . . . forty-six feet in length and ten feet deep . . . [and] built in what is called the 'bracket style.' The novel beauty . . . of these porches is largely due to the good taste of the architect, Mr. Neilson." While the interiors of Neilson's other surviving Harford projects are rather simple, King gave him a free hand at Lansdowne and one can only agree with Dr. Forwood, who reckoned the rooms "beautiful and, we might almost say, *unique*," for the architect devised a winding main stair with "steps of walnut and risers of ash, the two colors of the

In 1884 railroad magnate Hugh Judge Jewett purchased the Lansdowne estate from the Kings (Jewett had been born in the property's original farmhouse in 1817) and hired Philadelphia architect Walter Cope to add a third wing to the house. The eighteenth-century stone house appears to the left in this c. 1899 photograph, as does the addition and porch architect J. C. Neilson built for Thomas King in 1875; curiously, Jewett's own new wing does not.

80. One of Mrs. Jewett's twentieth-century descendants, Natalie Jewett Marbury, suspects that Susanna Jewett was probably "a bit of a pill if you knew her." Mrs. William Marbury, conversation with author, October 17, 1990.

81. Forwood, "Homes on Deer Creek," May 21, 1880.

wood forming a very pretty contrast. Surmounted upon the massive newel-post stands a beautifully wrought figure of the anomalous *Griffin*—the mythological union of the lion and the eagle—carved in walnut. Gracefully poised upon the top of this singular figure, we find a highly ornamental brass globe lamp." Forwood also opined that "marble mantels, now so generally introduced in first-class houses, appear tame and commonplace beside" the "very large and high" wooden mantel Neilson gave Lansdowne's parlor, "one of the handsomest pieces of ornamental carving . . . we have ever seen. . . . The material is solid oak, and it is exquisitely carved into figures of fruits and flowers, beautifully interwoven and blended in numberless designs."

Not content with creating a picturesque house, King also laid out picturesque grounds and hired a blacksmith to cast iron deer and other animals and to sculpt a "very handsome fountain jet d'eau." King himself then placed "pots of many-hued blooming flowers" around the lawn "with admirable taste." In addition to this "manipulated" nature, King also left many of the "stately forest trees" he found on the property, valuing them for "the picturesqueness" they added to the carriage way as it wound "gracefully down the hill." Forwood concludes his description of the estate by crediting "the chief builder . . . Mr. A. M. Carroll of Baltimore, who was ably assisted by Messrs. Joseph Gorrell, Bannister and Harryman, of Harford County." Carroll's firm also built the Silvers' 1871 Harmony Church and one suspects that Joseph Gorrell was kin to Joshua Gorrell, the leading Darlington blacksmith of his day, for it would have taken a skilled blacksmith to execute the "exceptionally handsome Jappened iron" grates "of a pattern entirely new" that Neilson designed for Lansdowne's central heating system.

Wonderful as King's house must have been in its prime, it formed but a small component of his thoroughly mid-Victorian existence. There is, for instance, his charitable work. (Or, as Dr. Forwood put it, "besides possessing the graces and culture that adorn a gentleman . . . [King] exerts considerable influence through the judicious use of his ample means, towards alleviating the necessities of many suffering fellow-creatures.") A member of the Deer Creek Orthodox Friends Meeting, King was largely responsible ("through personal influence and pecuniary aid") for hiring Neilson to design the 1877 stone meetinghouse for the Friends; he also gave a magnificent greenstone baptismal font to Grace Memorial Episcopal Church, contributed heavily toward the Darlington Cemetery (paying blacksmith Gorrell to craft the wrought iron gates), and was a prime force behind the drives to build a public library and a town hall in the village. Moreover, when the great benefactor died in 1884 he left $5,000 in a perpetual fund "the interest to be applied to relief of the deserving poor, especially the sick poor, without regard to creed or color."[82] King was also "an excellent public speaker" with a "special talent" for reading aloud from "the writings of Charles Dickens. Indeed, it has been said that in . . . his ready talent for assuming the various voices in dialogue, he was a good imitator of the great master—Dickens—who read his own productions in public with such wonderful effect." Content with his gardening, his charity work, and his imitations of Little Nell, King never married (which Forwood fretted about in print, notwithstanding the doctor's own admission that "it would be obviously out of order and in violation of the rules of 'taste' to make any strictly personal remarks regarding" King).[83] Thus when King died, the 500-acre Deer Creek estate passed to his brother, Francis, who in 1886 sold the property to Hugh Judge Jewett, son of John and Susanna.

Hugh Jewett, who had been born in the old, pre-Neilson house in 1817, was just as representative of his own era as King was of his. After a traditional education Jewett grew restless and left his mother and father to trek west in search of his fortune. Since Ohio then represented "the west," Jewett settled there and became president of the Zanesville bank. But that was not enough and the young man was soon drawn into railroading, that era's cutting edge industry. "The people of Ohio . . . could form no conception of the results that awaited their State from the introduction of rails," wrote historian George Howard, but Jewett could and he "saw in them the agency which would revolutionize the

82. Letter from Hunter Sutherland to author, October 10, 1990.

83. Forwood also wrote, "Let us hope that the next great event which shall occur in the charming old Deer Creek Home will be another meeting of friends to . . . welcome and congratulate the advent of a hostess in the old homestead!"

Harford and the Picturesque

whole economy of things."[84] In fact, Jewett devoted his entire professional life to wheeling and dealing in rail lines, holding his own in bare-knuckle corporate brawls with the likes of Commodore Vanderbilt and Jay Gould. Beginning in 1857 he served as president or vice-president of at least five lines (often simultaneously) until 1874 when he was elected president of the Erie Railroad, whose directors proposed to pay him $40,000 a year, the highest salary paid to any railroad official to that time, on condition he give up his other interests and concentrate on the Erie for ten years. He agreed.

This was a particularly difficult time in the Erie's turbulent history, for the company, "thoroughly discredited and embarrassed" and known as "the Scarlet Woman of Wall Street," was owned by foreign investors who were manufacturing steady dividends for themselves by steadily borrowing against the company's assets. They were also about to launch "a wholesale plunder of the property" when Jewett "discovered their schemes . . . and promptly exposed them. Then came an open declaration of hostility, and nothing was left undone which would harass him personally." Jewett immediately declared the Erie bankrupt and had himself made receiver so he could reorganize and reform the old "Scarlett Woman."[85] He put "earnings back into the property rather than distributing them as dividends, he replaced the iron with steel rails, changed the gauge from six feet to standard, completed the double track from New York to Buffalo, improved the terminals, and extended the system in order to effect needed connections with the West."[86] (He also found time to dabble in politics and was elected to the Ohio senate and the U.S. Congress in 1873; he was even mentioned as a Democratic candidate for president in 1880, but nothing came of it.) His policy of reinvestment made him less than popular with many of those foreign stockholders, who, to retaliate against the reforming Jewett, encouraged "strikes and insubordination" among the Erie's workers, made "threats" to his life,[87] and, when his ten-year contract ended in 1884, had him purged from office. He must have been ready to retire anyway; he paid Francis King $14,500 for the old family estate, moved back to Harford County, and took up the life of a gentleman farmer.

Walter Cope and Picturesque Darlington

The Neilson/King mansion, Lansdowne, did not suit Jewett—or, according to family lore, did not suit his elegant wife—and he decided the place needed another enlargement. Curiously, though, instead of asking his neighbor Neilson to undertake the task, the railroad magnate went to Philadelphia and brought in the wet-behind-the-ears architect Walter Cope to add a large wing to the east. (Cope respectfully took care that the materials and massing of his work maintained the same picturesque quality the venerable Neilson had given his own additions a decade earlier.) Cope, born in Philadelphia in 1860, studied architecture under two of the city's leading practitioners, Theophilus Chandler and Frank Furness. He then spent fourteen months traveling and sketching in Europe before returning to Philadelphia in 1885 to arrange "an exhibit of sketches prepared during his tour."[88] That year he entered into partnership with the brothers John and Emlyn Stewardson to create "one of the leading architectural firms of the east." Known as perfectionists the men are perhaps best remembered for their collegiate work, including Bryn Mawr's Radnor Hall (1886, and regarded as the first important example of the American collegiate Gothic style), and a series of "epoch-making" commissions at Princeton, Haverford, and the University of Pennsylvania.[89] "Appointed chairman of a committee whose task was the restoration of Philadelphia's old Congress Hall [Independence Hall]," Cope developed a "deep interest in the preservation and restoration of old Colonial landmarks," and this fondness for history found expression in his other work, particularly in his "distinctive domestic architecture."[90]

Hugh Judge Jewett spent his remaining years in Cope-designed splendor (with winter forays to New York City and Augusta, Georgia) and he and the house grew so famous that the editors of the *New England Magazine* featured them in an 1899 issue: "Hugh Jewett . . . was at one time president of a great railroad," wrote author Calvin Dill Wilson.

84. George W. Howard, *The Monumental City* (Baltimore: M. Curlander, 1889), 656.

85. *Encyclopedia of American History,* 34; Howard, *Monumental City,* 658. See also "Erie" in *Encyclopaedia Britannica,* 15th ed.

86. *DAB* 10:68, for Jewett.

87. Howard, *Monumental City,* 658.

88. Withey and Withey, *Biographical Dictionary,* 139.

89. "Landmark Status Effort Seeks to Honor Pioneer," *New York Times,* April 28, 1991, sec. 2, p. 39. Their work at Princeton includes Blair Hall and flanking dormitories as well as the Ivy Club (1897), Stafford Little Hall (1899), and the gymnasium (1903).

90. Withey and Withey, *Biographical Dictionary,* 140.

But "when the farm on which he had been reared was put up for sale, he purchased it, re-fitted and rebuilt handsomely, and spent a great part of his later life among the scenes of his youth."[91] A good Quaker like his parents, in 1888 Jewett paid to restore the Deer Creek Friends Meetinghouse, that ancient stone building where his mother had held forth six-ty and more years earlier, and the February 16, 1889, issue of the *Friends Intelligencer* deemed his work there "both beautiful and neat and we do most assuredly appreciate his kindness."[92] (Not one for false modesty, Jewett placed a stone lintel over the meeting-house's side door and had it inscribed, "Founded 1737; Rebuilt 1784; Restored by Hugh J. Jewett 1888.") Jewett died in Augusta on March 6, 1898.

Cope's work at Lansdowne promptly brought him a wonderful series of commissions as Darlington-area plutocrats virtually fell all over themselves to secure his services for new houses, barns, and stables—that generation's "specimens of the most tasty architec-ture." First to line up at Cope's drafting board (in fact, he may have even nudged Jewett out of the way) was Daniel Clarke Wharton Smith, Philadelphia doctor and business-man, and patron of Grace Church. Smith had been enjoying the Darlington area as a place to escape the rigors of Broad Street since the 1850s. By the 1870s, however, he de-voted less and less time to the Quaker City and more and more time to the Quaker Vil-lage. In need of a place to live, on March 25, 1885, he bought a thirty-two-acre, hilltop tract at the southernmost tip of town and hired Cope to design a new house and out-buildings for him.[93] The result, Winstone, is a textbook example of Queen Anne con-struction, with a main house, guest house, windmill, and stable, all designed to form a picturesque mass of verandas, balconies, turrets, and towers executed in stone and frame with terracotta details.[94]

Winstone's plan, based on plasticity and volumetric expression, is very much a prod-uct of its time. Architects then were beginning to regard interiors as a series of open, flow-ing spaces. This aesthetic, in turn, was born of technology, for coal furnaces and hot-air ducts made it possible to shatter the crisp Georgian/federal concept of discreet rooms de-fined by closeable doors and heated by individual fireplaces. Porches were also becoming highly popular and architects valued these "semi-rooms" (Vaux's phrase) as transitional spaces between house and garden.

D. C. Wharton Smith hired Walter Cope to design a Darlington getaway, Winstone, around 1885. Shown here are the estate's guest house and stable with the base of the windmill beyond. Queen Anne in style, the house presents a picturesque mass of turrets, verandas, and mixed materials.

91. Wilson, "Southern County," 170–71.

92. HSHC archives.

93. Deed ALJ 53/421.

94. No one has ever explained why this style was called Queen Anne. It debuted in America in 1876 when Her Majesty's government constructed the British Building at Philadelphia's Centennial Expo-sition. Books such as *The American Builder* (1876) praised the style for being "simple, pure, and unso-phisticated." Antoinette F. Downing and Vincent Scully, *The Architectural Heritage of Newport, Rhode Island* (New York: Clarkson Potter, 1967), 156. Does it seem ironic that America was still influenced by trends in British art—and at an exposition intended to celebrate the 100th anniversary of the Revolu-tion? And that industrialists, having made their sooty pile, then sought to escape to a simpler, seem-ingly more innocent era? It may seem ironic to us today; it didn't to Americans in 1876.

Harford and the Picturesque

After his great success at Wharton Smith's Winstone, Walter Cope went on to design a series of picturesque houses in and around Darlington in the 1880s and '90s. Most of his clients were Philadelphia kin of his, including Jane C. Mason, shown here overseeing an unidentified gardener at Rosecrea around 1900.

Such changes were not greeted with universal applause, of course. Henry James, for one, stated his "emphatic reservation" about "this diffused vagueness of separation between . . . one room and another, between the one you are in and the one you are not in, between place of passage and place of privacy." James, whose art so depended on intimate, *private* conversation, was appalled at open plans, at the use "of voids for enclosing walls," and nostalgically longed for the houses of his youth, "for practicable doors, for controllable windows, for all the rest of the essence of room-character . . . [which allows] the play of social relation at any other pitch than the pitch of a shriek or a shout." Nor did James have any use for porches, whose appearance he viewed as a "conspiracy for nipping the interior in the bud, for denying its right to exist, for ignoring and defeating it in every possible way, . . . with all the ingenuity of young, fresh, frolicsome architecture aiding and abetting" these efforts.[95]

But few at the time agreed with James. Certainly few in Darlington did, where Cope-designed picturesque houses still give panache to the Deer Creek Valley. These commissions, including Red Gate and Rosecrea for the brothers Bernard Gilpin Smith and Joshua C. Smith, Grey Gables for Cope's own relatives Horace and Helen Stokes, a remodeling of Meadow Farm for the Samuel Mason/Hannah Evans clan, and Westacre for D. C. Wharton Smith's son, Courtauld W. Smith, form a unified body of work characterized by studied asymmetry, sweeping roofs, tall decorative chimneys, and varied wall coverings; within, the large, open rooms, with their varied paneling, expansive stairways, and elaborate chimney pieces, all rendered in native chestnut, pine, walnut, and oak, are, as a group, fully equal to anything of their kind in America.

Moreover, with their expansive façades and vast, continuous interiors that flow and pull, Cope's Darlington houses suggest the sense of primal energy that permeated all American art of the time. Historian Vincent Scully, writing of Winslow Homer's stormy sea scenes, marveled at their "embodiment of the power of the earth, that dark power [that] was shared by American architecture during those decades. It dealt with forms evoking nature and of a natural awesomeness."[96] Cope himself touched on this in his own eighteen-page "design testament" in which he contrasts classical architecture, "a creation in which the exterior controls," with picturesque buildings such as Winstone where

95. Henry James, *The American Scene* (New York: St. Martin's Press, 1987), 119.

96. Vincent Scully, *New World Visions of Household Gods and Sacred Places* (New York: Metropolitan Museum of Art, 1988), 130.

"the interior—that is to say, the life within, dictated the outward form. . . . It is one moment solemn—another playful. One moment it expresses power—ambition; another—contentment." As such, Cope wrote, the picturesque "has always, and will always appeal to us . . . as a style . . . which, like a tree, must either grow or die."[97]

Significantly, while Cope's Harford County clients all wielded the power he referred to in his "testament," they did so gently. Jewett ran railroads and was mentioned as a candidate for the White House; D.C.W. Smith and the brothers B. Gilpin and Joshua C. Smith owned the $3,000,000 Susquehanna Power and Paper Company, "the greatest industry in the county." But these plutocrats did not want to dominate the countryside, they wanted to fit in, just as their houses, elegant without ostentation, were built into the landscape, not onto it. Smith, for example, who "always called everybody by the first name and . . . would stop and talk to everyone, especially the children," not only underwrote Grace Church, he also built a new home for the Darlington Academy (1891); he was called "the Academy's best friend,"[98] and "often could be seen walking up to the home of A.F. Galbreath [the academy's headmaster] to play chess, a game of which they were both very fond."[99]

In addition, Smith cofounded the Darlington Cemetery Company (1881). Under his gentle leadership the cemetery's board purchased a grassy three-acre site overlooking the village and then turned that site into a veritable picturesque park, complete with winding, oyster-shell paths, informally clumped trees and shrubs, and a decorative octagonal frame sanctuary designed by local shopkeeper and board member Daniel F. Shure. Here, too, Darlington reflects larger trends for nineteenth-century American cemetery design "integrated various aspects of the ideal picturesque landscape: wild scenery, rolling or sharper terrain, and water. Roads and paths were serpentine." "Cemeteries here are all the rage," one nineteenth-century English tourist wrote back home from America. "People lounge in them and use them (as their tastes are inclined) for walking, making love, weeping, sentimentalizing, and every thing in short."[100] Smith, humanist that he was, also made certain that from the beginning the cemetery was open to all regardless of race, creed, or color.

Hymnist Harry Webb Farrington spent his orphaned youth in turn-of-the-century Darlington, a Darlington still dominated benignly by industrial titans such as Jewett and Smith. And while Cope and Neilson translated the area's picturesque landscape into architecture, Farrington captured those self-same qualities in his 1930 memoirs. "The flowers of Darlington were neither too well kept nor too wild," he wrote.

> The people were cultured enough to rise above that false kind of thrift that makes every clod and foot of earth to bring forth corn in order to raise hogs to sell in order to plant more corn to feed more hogs to sell. Darlington was natural enough to have her bramble bushes, briar patches, fence rows, and overgrown fields and thickets. . . . Had I to choose another home for another boyhood, I would still have it Darlington for . . . the beauty of the level fields and sloping meadows . . . left me without the provincial prejudice of either the plainsman or the mountaineer.[101]

Is it any wonder that throughout the mid- and late nineteenth century Darlington, where the shaggy hills were dotted with "specimens of the most tasty architecture," became a nationally known center of picturesque design?

97. In the Library of the American Institute of Architects, Washington, D.C.

98. Harry Webb Farrington, *Kilts to Togs* (New York: Macmillan, 1930), 268, 224, 228.

99. Fred C. Jones, "Darlington" (privately printed pamphlet, c. 1900), 5.

100. David Charles Sloane, *The Last Great Necessity* (Baltimore: Johns Hopkins University Press, 1991), 49, 94.

101. Farrington, *Kilts to Togs*, 145–48.

Seven of Dr. and Mrs. Howard Kelly's nine children relaxing around 1905 on the porch of Liriodendron, their parents' "small house in the country."

"A small house in the country"   [7]

"A small house in the country." That is how Baltimore physician Howard A. Kelly described his planned rural retreat in an 1895 letter to his mother. Kelly had married the German-born Laetitia Bredow in 1889, the same year he joined the staff of the newly founded Johns Hopkins Hospital. The young couple moved into a cavernous brownstone townhouse on Baltimore's Eutaw Place and immediately started looking for a suitable spot where they could slip away, relax, and teach their growing family (there were eventually nine children) how to swim, ride a horse, befriend a black snake, or tame an owl. "We have no summer plans yet," runs the complete sentence, "but Laetitia wants a small house in the country near by."[1]

The Kellys eventually built Liriodendron on the edge of Bel Air, and while that house is not exactly small (and no longer in the country), it symbolizes what might be called Harford's "Country Place Era," the years between the Civil War and World War I when dozens of families like the Kellys put up dozens of "small houses in the country" from Fallston to Darlington. The *Harford Democrat* suggested that the Kellys designed Liriodendron in "the English Renaissance style."[2] While that may not be technically correct, its spirit is right on the mark, for it is a romantically nostalgic sensibility coupled with an awareness that there was a life beyond the banks of the Gunpowder—all underwritten by a hefty bank balance—that made Liriodendron and other "small houses in the country" possible. From Stanford White's enlargements at Oakington for New Yorker James Breese to Ignatius Jenkins's Belle Farm, his Second Empire mansion near Whiteford, these "small houses" are all fashioned in exotic styles from distant lands and, as such, can be easily distinguished from creations more firmly rooted in the county's aesthetic soil.

1. All Kelly material, unless otherwise indicated, is taken from the uncatalogued Howard A. Kelly Collection of manuscripts and photographs at Liriodendron in Bel Air, Maryland; see also Christopher Weeks, "Liriodendron: Dr. Kelly's Summer Place," *Baltimore Sunday Sun Magazine,* April 26, 1981.

2. *Harford Democrat,* March 11, 1898.

Fallston's Worldly Quakers

This phenomenon of "small houses in the country" certainly preceded Dr. Kelly. In a sense, it began with émigré federal-era Frenchmen such as C.F.F. de la Porte and his chateau, Bon Air, near Fallston. In fact it is arguable that the entire Fallston community developed because of small houses in the country, for as two modern local historians have noted, "faster modes of transportation" such as the Ma and Pa Railroad ("the greatest contributing factor in the growth of population in this community") made it possible for scores of nineteenth-century Baltimore families to escape to "Fallston's beauty and its tranquility."[3]

But Fallston did not start out as a hub of the exotic. On the contrary, the community's beginnings go back to the quiet Quakerism of William Amos II (1718–1814). Born at Mount Soma, his parents' farm on Winters Run, Amos cut short his chosen military career in 1738 when he joined the Society of Friends and devoted the rest of his life to the cause of "meekness, resignation, piety, benevolence, and charity." He established the Little Falls Meeting in the wilderness that is now Fallston and the Friends who followed him there patterned their quiet, sober lives on his. "They were not only spiritually minded and able, but were persons who conscientiously approached their responsibilities with humility and compassion. Music, dancing, reading novels, gambling, attending plays and visiting taverns were to be avoided," as were "vain fashions and corrupting influences of the world."[4]

By mid-century, however, "small cracks were showing in the rigid armor which isolated Friends from the world at large." In 1838 Nathan Tyson, "a director of banks and corporations in Baltimore," retired to Fallston; other "Friends of prominence and wealth" soon followed and "brought to Little Falls cosmopolitan and progressive points of view."[5]

If Tyson started these changes, Benjamin P. Moore and his wife, Mary G. Moore, made them permanent parts of the Fallston scene. In 1842 Moore, a business partner of Johns Hopkins, decided that he had made enough money and retired from commerce; that same year he paid $1,250 for 125 acres on Laurel Brook Road and built Mosswood, a large, shingled house that still presides over its oak-shaded site. While the Quaker couple flourished in their new community—Mary Moore became a leading figure at Little Falls—they did so in a way that suggests that the meeting's simple days were over forever: "Never was there a more beautiful majestic person," one contemporary wrote of Mary Moore. "She had perfect features, full of dignity . . . with the greatest elegance of manners. What indignation there was when it was heard that a book agent had gone to her to sell a book on etiquette!"

The appearance of the couple's daughter-in-law, Estelle—"a musical genius"—clearly marked the end of an era. Gone were those eighteenth-century Friends who piously obeyed their *Book of Discipline* with its warning against "keeping company with such as would teach . . . vain fashions" and who condemned music, dancing, and gaming for their "tendency to alienate the mind from the council of divine wisdom." Estelle organized a vocal trio of Fallstonians with herself in the lead and when "an infection of the throat" forced her from the spotlight, she turned her talents to directing minstrel shows and arranging "evenings of dancing, oyster suppers, dramatic skits, and other entertainments."[6]

Other equally worldly Friends flocked to the Meeting, such as the James Watsons, who bought Bon Air in 1854 (she was "a perfect genius as a raconteur of Negro dialect and Irish brogue" who filled the house "with unforgettable Chippendale chairs" while he "used to give a great treat of fireworks to his neighbors every fourth of July") and the three maiden Titus sisters who moved to Fallston from their native New York and built Rochelle, the county's greatest Greek revival residence. And when the Amos Hollingsworth family—"always socially inclined"—bought Rochelle in 1869 and made it "the scene of many big social affairs in Fallston—teas, dances, etc., . . . [with] a series

3. Alva Mary Amoss and Alice Harlan Remsburg, "The Gateway," pamphlet prepared in 1976 by the Fallston–Upper Cross Roads Bicentennial Committee; copy in files of the Harford County Planning and Zoning Department, Bel Air.

4. Quotes from Hunter C. Sutherland, *The Little Falls Meeting of Friends* (Bel Air: HSHC, 1988), 9, 49, 27.

5. Ibid., 24, 29. Tyson's family had other interests: Isaac Tyson was known as the "Baltimore Chrome King" because from c. 1830 until his death in 1861 he held a virtual monopoly on the world's chrome supply; much of that mineral came from quarries in Harford County, hence "Chrome Hill Road."

6. Ibid., 15; Marian Curtiss, untitled memoirs, unpublished typescript in HSHC archives, p. 27; Amoss and Remsburg, "Gateway," 36.

Mr. and Mrs. James Watson bought Bon Air near Fallston in 1854; Mrs. Watson, "a perfect genius . . . at Irish brogue" (shown here, center), helped bring a sense of worldliness—and a menagerie of kittens, puppies, and goats—to the once-quiet Quaker community.

of Friday evenings all through the summer," Fallston's transformation from a simple Quaker village to a worldly Quaker village was complete.[7]

The once-solid Quaker community even took on a touch of ecumenicalism, thanks to Mr. and Mrs. Theodore Forbes of Baltimore's Bolton Hill, who, three months after buying what was grandly called Rochelle Farm in May of 1908, donated 1½ acres of the tract to the "Fallston Improvement Company . . . for the sole purpose of erecting . . . a Protestant Episcopal Church and Rectory." They then organized "jousting tournaments" and "musical comedy sketches" (the latter held "on the second floor of the feed and grain warehouse")[8] to raise building funds for the church, and, when they had sufficient cash in hand, they asked Baltimore architect Laurence Hall Fowler to prepare the necessary drawings for a church "in the California style."[9] They decided to call the new structure the Chapel of the Prince of Peace.

Fowler, born in Catonsville in 1876, studied at the Johns Hopkins University, Columbia, and the École des Beaux-Arts in Paris; he left the latter somewhat abruptly in 1904 and returned to Baltimore to open "his own architectural firm . . . at 347 North Charles Street." Although he secured several important institutional commissions (including buildings for St. Timothy's School [1913], Baltimore's War Memorial [1921], and the Hall of Records in Annapolis [1933]), Fowler is best remembered for his residential work. He built (or remodeled) townhouses for many of the Forbeses' Bolton Hill neighbors (e.g., Mrs. Lea Thom at 204 West Lanvale Street [1910] and D. K. Este Fisher at 1301 Park [1914]), and also constructed over sixty large houses in Guilford, Roland Park, and the Green Spring Valley for clients with such surnames as Garrett, Griswold, Jenkins, Deford, and Abell. These men and women, a veritable "Who's Who" of the city's financial/ social elite, favored well-mannered design and Fowler gave it to them. "Invention was not Fowler's forte," wrote one critic, "but synthesis was."[10] This is certainly true for his work at the Prince of Peace, an exquisite pastiche of motifs then popular among San Francisco–area architects, such as emphatically textured shingled walls, hinged windows, and an earth-bound massing.[11] And to strengthen his creation's artistic unity, Fowler also designed the pulpit, altar, and choir screen—even the lighting—for the little church, all in a studied informality.[12]

7. Curtiss memoirs, 26, 29.

8. C. B. Holden Rogers, manuscript history of the Prince of Peace chapel, in HSHC archives. Construction costs were estimated at $1,400.

9. Ibid.; the debit side of the ledger for these fund-raising events includes entries of "75c for Lemons," "$12.60 . . . Ice Cream for Tournament," and "$3 for servants."

10. Egon Verheyen, ed., *Laurence Hall Fowler, Architect* (Baltimore: Milton S. Eisenhower Library of the Johns Hopkins University, 1984), 3, 47.

11. Dennis J. Shanahan, a local builder discussed in chapter 5, oversaw construction; they had problems, evidently, with the locally unusual building, for on February 7, 1910, Shanahan had to write to explain how to correct "the west flue [which] smokes badly": he suggested putting "a top . . . on the present pipe." HSHC archives.

12. His signed drawings are preserved at Evergreen House, Baltimore; materials on the Prince of Peace are in folder 1908/08; he requested that the wood be "all of plain oak, stained, shellacked, and waxed." Alexis Shriver of Olney helped wire the building for electricity.

"A small house in the country"

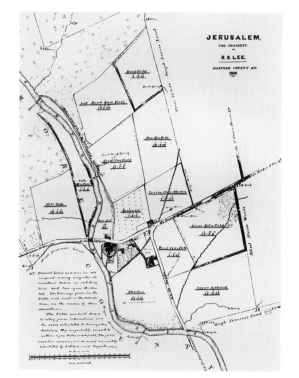

Educator George Graham Curtiss (1825-1900) not only established two schools near Fallston, he also platted the Lee family's Jerusalem Mill property (1860, and shown here) and planned the Bel Air quarter-mile racetrack. (The Lees used the various small fields for various purposes, e.g., they used the lime burned in the kiln on the "Lime Kiln Field" as fertilizer.)

George Curtiss's Oakland School (established 1865) brought coeducation to Harford County. The building, now destroyed, stood near the northwest corner of the intersection of Harford Road and Fallston Road.

13. Or 1850, *Harford Historical Bulletin* (Spring 1986): 42.

Many of the above anecdotes are taken from the memoirs of Miss Marian Curtiss (1867–1940), whose father, George Graham Curtiss (1825–1900), established the well-regarded Oakland Boarding School at the corner of Fallston and Harford roads. Mr. Curtiss, a Quaker and a Brown graduate (M.A., 1848), came to Harford County from his native Massachusetts in 1852 when Lloyd Norris of Olney, also a Quaker and cousin to the Tysons, asked him to open a private school in the Union Chapel at Wilna.[13] Curtiss, also a trained land surveyor who platted the village of Jerusalem, the buildings at Olney, and laid out the Bel Air fairgrounds and racetrack, agreed. Under his supervision, the school became a thriving institution until he mysteriously closed it around 1861 and went back to Massachusetts. (While research has not revealed his motives for returning north, politics must have played a part for he returned to the county in 1865.) Whatever the reason for his departure, whatever the reason for his return, Curtiss was now in Harford for good.

Instead of picking up where he had left off at Wilna, however, Curtiss bought a house nearer Fallston and proceeded to turn the building into the progressive, coed Oakland School. Until this time public schools simply did not exist in Harford County. And while a few prosperous individuals had established private schools for area youths, such as the Silver family and their Prospect School and the Reverend John Ireland's Sion Hill Academy, these institutions maintained a strict single-sex admissions policy. This did not sit well with Curtiss, who asked, in newspaper advertisements for his school, "How can we make our daughters useful [as well as our sons]?" Curtis then answered his own question. The only way "to fit them for the duties . . . demands and privileges of life," he said, "is to make them 'self-reliant' and the only way to do that is to educate them on equal footing with their brothers."[14]

Fluent in Greek, Latin, German, French, and Italian, and "recognized as a leader in cultural matters,"[15] Curtiss, aided by his wife and their six children, launched one of the first coeducational institutions in Maryland. He himself taught mathematics and the sciences (he even established a telescope-equipped weather station at Oakland); Mrs. Curtiss instructed the boys and girls in "painting in oil . . . and china painting"; daughter Marian, adept at "the piano, violin, and cello," and "skilled in athletic activities," taught instrumental music and physical education; daughter Ida was an instructor of Latin; and daughter Eva took care of "vocal music, elocution, and penmanship"; two other daughters, Dora and Ethel, looked after the business side of things while son Joseph "spent most of his time farming" and kept the larder well stocked with fresh produce. Curtiss set high standards for his students and any Oakland graduate could be automatically admitted to "the freshman class at Swarthmore on his certificate."[16]

Marian Curtiss also brought the glamour of distant lands to her father's school. She had lived for extended periods of time in both Spain and Italy and those years abroad "richly influenced her possessions and personality." Indeed they did for, sparked by her Mediterranean sojourns, she laid out a patio garden at the Oakland School complete with "trees and flat stones . . . brought in from the woods and a fountain placed in the center. She enjoyed eating her breakfast in this pleasant setting," and sometimes asked favored students to join her there for a caffe latte.[17]

Looking Beyond the Little Gunpowder

Breakfasting on a Spanish terrace garden; evenings spent scanning the heavens through a telescope: the Curtisses certainly helped Fallston's sons and daughters discover the large, fascinating world that lay beyond the Gunpowder. And, in a parallel development, growing numbers of Harford's adults began to realize that there was also more than one way to build a house. It did not have to have a gable roof; it did not have to be of British origin; it did not even have to have locally traceable precedents.

This loosening up affected all countians, even the most tradition-bound. For example, when Stevenson Archer Jr. (born 1828) set out to build a new house near Bel Air, he did not attempt to replicate his grandfather's Medical Hall or his aunt and uncle's Rock Run, but instead copied a c. 1810, French-influenced Mississippi Valley Creole cottage! Actually, he copied it for his wife, the former Jane C. Franklin of Sumner County, Tennessee. The two married in 1855 and settled in Bel Air, where he, in family tradition, embarked on a highly successful career in law and politics that included four terms in the U.S. House of Representatives.[18] Despite—or perhaps because of—her husband's triumphs, Jane Archer is said to have pined for the "colorful and gracious life" she had been born to in Tennessee. So "to dispel his wife's homesickness" Archer constructed a type of

14. Ad for Oakland School in the December 14, 1877, *Ægis and Intelligencer.*

15. Wright, *Harford,* 234.

16. Amoss and Remsburg, "Gateway," 31.

17. Ibid., 36; John Sherwood, "Memories Linger On in Abandoned School," *Baltimore Evening Sun,* February 10, 1961.

18. He also attended the Democratic national conventions of 1868 and 1876.

folk house built throughout the Lower Mississippi Valley by eighteenth-century French colonists, a one-story frame cottage on brick piers with fourteen-foot ceilings and a massive hipped roof that sweeps out over the walls to create deep verandas. The couple named the place Hazel Glen; it is now known as Hazel Dell. Whatever it is called, it is certainly, in the words of newspaperman Michael Chrismer, "one of the most distinctive homes in Maryland."[19]

Actually, Hazel Glen's aura of moonlight and magnolias was highly acceptable to that entire generation of Archers. Stevenson's father, after the requisite years at family-favored Princeton, served as a federal judge in the newly acquired and semi-organized Mississippi Territory; three siblings eventually moved to Gulf states; and five nephews served in the Confederate army. Perhaps the most notable of that latter group was Gen. James Archer (1817–64), a son of John and Ann Stump Archer of Rock Run, who fought alongside his friend Robert E. Lee in virtually every engagement in the Eastern theater until he was captured at Gettysburg and sent to the prison camp at Johnson's Island.

Needless to say, since Harford lies below the Mason-Dixon Line, Hazel Dell's builders weren't the county's only Southern sympathizers. Maj. William Stuart Symington of Indian Spring Farm, Joseph Shriver, who bought Olney in 1861 "to ride out the war," and William B. Duvall, who bought the Amos family's La Vista near Fallston in February of 1863 would all have been more likely to whistle "Dixie" than "The Battle Hymn of the Republic."[20]

Duvall's French Huguenot ancestors fled to America in the 1690s to escape persecution under Louis XIV and settled and prospered in Prince George's County, Maryland. One of the émigré's grandsons, Gabriel Duvall (born 1752), was a politically minded lawyer and a loyal follower of Jefferson who served as comptroller of the U.S. Treasury and as an associate justice of the Supreme Court.[21] And it was with the mansions of his native southern Maryland in mind that William Duvall added a monumental new 2½-story brick main wing, complete with classical entrance portico, Italian black-marble mantels, and splendid, three-story, spiral staircase to the Amoses' unpretentious farmhouse.

While Duvall was encasing La Vista in southern Maryland splendor, Baltimorean Thomas Symington was making over another old Harford house. He took the 1,000-acre tract Stump's Prospect and turned it into Indian Spring Farm, one of the best known estates in Maryland. Legends of high romance mistily swirl about the Symingtons, a clan of ancient Scots lineage. Whether or not all—or even most—of the tales are true is somewhat irrelevant since what they may lack in veracity they make up for in the color that seems to permeate all of the building projects featured in this chapter. Thomas's parents, James Symington and Margaret Fife, immigrated to America shortly after the Revolution; they landed in Philadelphia and were married in the home of Robert Morris— "Morris himself gave the bride away," wrote one descendant. The restless couple then incrementally moved south, first to the Brandywine Valley, where Thomas was born in 1792, and then to the growing city of Baltimore.[22] Around 1820 Thomas entered the marble business, a wise move in a city where, as great-grandson Missouri senator Stuart Symington noted, "home after home proudly displays short white marble steps at the front door."[23] Rip-roaringly successful, Thomas's quarries in Maryland, Vermont, and Tennessee not only gave Baltimore its famous white-marble steps, they also gave the raw material, the *Sun* proudly reported on September 14, 1850, "of which the National Monument is being constructed at Washington."[24]

Symington then invested some of his profits in city real estate, some in a chemical business, and some in a fertilizer concern, all of which produced still further gallons of black ink for his ledgers. Helping him in these lucrative endeavors was his wife, née Angeline Stuart, whom he married in 1825. (It was her father, William Stuart, who assumed command of Fort McHenry during the British attack purportedly when troops determined that the original commanding officer "was too drunk" for duty.) Her death in 1860

19. Pierson, *Buildings, Picturesque*, 456; Michael Chrismer, "Hazel Dell," *Ægis*, June 20, 1961; Glassie, *Folk Culture*, 117–18.

20. Mrs. C. B. Holden Rogers (Shriver's granddaughter), conversation with author, October 10, 1989; deed WG 14/17.

21. Duvall vowed to remain on the bench, despite increasing deafness and blindness, until another Marylander could be found to replace him: and one was, Roger Brooke Taney.

22. Charles J. Symington, *Skippin' the Details* (New York: privately printed, 1966), 4; Baby Thomas, it is said, was introduced to George Washington and Thomas's youngest son, John Fife, died at age 93 in 1962; thus two generations of the family spanned all American presidents from Washington to Kennedy.

23. Quoted in Symington, *Skippin' the Details*, 5.

24. Quoted in Charles J. Symington Jr., *Scotch and Soda* (Rochester, N.Y.: privately printed, 1984), 29.

crushed Symington, who sold his business interests in town, bought a 548-acre farm on Deer Creek, and retired there in 1862 to nurse his emotional wounds. The land was called Stump's Prospect and cost Symington $27,400.[25]

That sum was perhaps the most money paid for real estate in Harford up to that time. The sellers, heirs of John Stump of Stafford, were happy to get it since the family fortunes were, by then, distinctly on the decline. Stump of Stafford had acquired the property in 1805[26] and made it available to his son William (born 1781), who moved there with a friend. (The 1814 tax rolls show the 1,000-acre tract improved by an "old frame dwelling 20 × 30 where William Stump and Joseph Parker live.") When his father died in 1816, leaving substantial cash bequests to William and his siblings, William (and Parker?) tore down that modest frame house and replaced it with a more ambitious 2½-story, center-hall plan, stone dwelling, a "queer old house . . . romantic and exciting," a Symington granddaughter later recalled, "at the upper end of two long and winding lanes . . . hidden in a grove of very fine old beech, elm, walnut, hickory, and maple trees." William died childless in 1821 (with $117 worth of silver, "1 doz. wine glasses, $1.50," and an elaborate bookcase worth $50) and Stump's Prospect wound up in the hands of his brother John Wilson Stump and his heiress wife, Sarah Biays. (Parker's fate is unknown.) This extravagant duo had already "got through all . . . [the] other property" they had inherited, and to raise much-needed cash they tried to sell "500 acres of Deer Creek Land . . . called Stump's Prospect of which William Stump died seized," improved by "a MANSION HOUSE of modern style, built of stone . . . somewhat out of repair." But, wrote architect J. Crawford Neilson, "no one wanted the land" until the war "came and changed all values . . . [and] Mr. Symington, desiring such a country place . . . made an offer . . . of $50 an acre, about $28,000, which was taken."[27]

At first Thomas kept the Stump/Parker house intact, and, surrounded by his six children and numerous grandchildren, his life rolled uneventfully—if calorically—on: dinner was served "at three o'clock, and . . . the table was a sight" with "a roast turkey or goose, or saddle of mutton . . . at the upper end of the table" and "a hot, juicy country ham" at the other all accompanied by "five or six fresh vegetables from the garden . . . [and] mountains of delicious rolls, corn muffins, Sally Lunn, rice waffles and beaten bis-

When Thomas Symington bought the old Stump's Prospect tract in 1862 it came with William Stump's c. 1816 two-story stone dwelling (right). Thomas Symington, who renamed the place Indian Spring Farm, probably added a service wing (not shown) and a rear extension (left); his grandson Donald, who acquired the property in the 1920s, built a combination library/ballroom to the rear (far left with arched windows).

25. Symington, *Skippin' the Details,* 6; Symington, *Scotch and Soda,* 29; deed WG 13/322, dated November 25, 1862.

26. He bought three different tracts totaling 1,015 acres at a sheriff's sale (including 440 acres of the "confiscated lands of Josiah Lee" and land of the defunct Nottingham Forge) and repatented it all as Stump's Prospect.

27. Lelia Symington's unpublished memoirs, quoted in Symington, *Skippin' the Details,* 7; J. Crawford Neilson, *Priestford Notebook,* MS 613, MHS.

View from the main house to the farm buildings at Indian Spring, c. 1940.

cuits." That placid status quo changed dramatically in 1864 when Thomas, at age 71, married "Mary Archer Wilson, age 37, whom he had met at the Episcopal Church near 'Indian Spring' [i.e., Trap Church, discussed in chapter 6], where she was the organist."[28]

Encouraged by his young wife, Symington expanded the foursquare Stump/Parker house with vast extensions to the north and east to create, in the awed words of an 1870s observer, a veritable "Stone Manor House" with "all the modern improvements including hot and cold water, Bath Tubs, Water Closets, etc." He then jammed every inch of floor space with every conceivable sort of furnishing: how on earth, one wonders, did their cook manage to move about in the kitchen, filled as it was with "2 Ice Cream freezers," vast arrays of specialized table equipment including vegetable dishes, pickle dishes, crumb brushes, finger bowls, mustard spoons, a whole page of itemized silver, another whole page of linens—including "8 fruit napkins"—and a wonderful-sounding "1 Fly Brush, Peacock feathers, $1"? Beyond the main residence the newlyweds erected a "Gardener's House," a washhouse (which held "2 wash tubs, board & clothes horse, ironing board, clothes ringer, clothes boiler, clothes line"), and two frame tenant houses. And to keep the place going they built, in the words of an 1877 description, "a second and comparatively new STONE DWELLING," for Indian Spring's farmer. That rambling pile, now decaying, was complete with Gothicky attic gables, fancifully trimmed porches, intricate plaster ceiling medallions, and marble mantels.

Evidently either Thomas or his young wife enjoyed gardening (recall that "Gardener's House"); they created a "beautiful lawn" at Indian Spring and planted "50 varieties of evergreens and shade trees" around the house including a "great linden that over-shadows all the others." Symington also built a canning factory for the farm's corn and tomato crops and purchased a soapstone quarry and mill downstream at Stafford. No wonder that when Thomas gazed out on his revamped mini-kingdom, his new wife, and their two children (Mary, born in 1867 and J. Fife, born in 1869) he "burst with pride and joy."[29]

His death in 1875, however, put an end to that idyllic era. While he left substantial cash bequests to his wife and to each of his children (sums which his sizable estate could easily pay), no one knew quite what to do with Indian Spring. The adult children had all settled in Baltimore and their half-siblings were too young to manage the place.[30] How-

28. Lelia Symington, quoted in Symington, *Skippin' the Details,* 8–9; Symington, *Scotch and Soda,* 30.

29. Symington, *Skippin' the Details,* 9, 7. He entered the flint-mill business with his new brother-in-law, Edward M. Allen, who had married Mary Archer Wilson Symington's oldest sister.

30. Recall, from chapter 6, that Mrs. Symington used some of her inheritance to hire architect Neilson to design a stone porch at Trap Church in memory of "Mr. Col. Symington."

Thomas Symington built this impressive farmer's cottage at Indian Spring, "a second and comparatively new STONE DWELLING," according to an 1877 newspaper account. One wonders if his neighbor, architect J. Crawford Neilson (who lived across the road at Priestford), advised Symington on the porch trim and balconies.

ever, after a good deal of family squabbling, a daughter, Caroline, and her husband, Johns Hopkins Janney, agreed to buy the farm for $30,000 in 1878.[31] This did not end Indian Spring's troubles, though: The Janneys, according to the ever-watchful Neilson, proved slapdash agriculturists (they rented the fields "to a farmer who farmed [it] . . . with his own stock," animals inferentially inferior to the Symingtons' purebreds) and when Janney died massively in debt in 1897, his son Thomas Symington Janney sold the property's 549 acres to John Dawson "for the benefit of his wife, Mary Dawson," a "daughter of Thomas Symington, Sr.," by his second marriage. "It [had cost] her father," wrote Neilson disgustedly, "about $45,000 gold. Is now in bad condition and needs extensive repair."[32] Matters continued to deteriorate until 1926, when two of Thomas Symington's grandsons, Charles (born 1883) and Donald (born 1882), "horrified by the state of their ancestral home,"[33] pooled their considerable resources and purchased Indian Spring, determined to bring it back. Donald then bought out his brother. He also acquired 287 acres of the old James Silver property, Silvermount, as well as several hundred acres of Cool Spring Farm on the south shore of Deer Creek. These outlays represent substantial sums of money, sums that Donald Symington had made himself (or had acquired through his marriage to Elsie Jenkins of Baltimore). It was not money he had inherited from his parents, for his father, William Stuart Symington (born 1839), and mother (née Lelia Skipwith Wayles Powers, born 1844) were the victims of what a daughter called "financial difficulties."[34]

Still, what a couple they must have been! Compared to William Stuart Symington, Tyrone Power in his prime comes across as a milquetoastish accountant; compared to Lelia Powers, Scarlett O'Hara at her fieriest was but a sputtering ember. And while this dashing couple were only tangentially connected to Indian Spring, their high-spirited lives make them fit in perfectly with this chapter's other flamboyant creatures. Along with his kinsmen young Symington fiercely supported the secessionists and served the Confederacy first as a lieutenant in the infantry and then "until the close of the war" in the cavalry as "an aide to Gen. George E. Pickett." More than once he had his "horse . . . shot out from under" him; more than once his comrades had to "pick [him] up, wounded, from a ditch." Yet he "seemed to know no fear" and continuously "sought . . . danger."

31. Deed ALJ 37/272; see also Equity Case 2753.
32. Deed WSF 91/374, dated August 13, 1897; Neilson, *Priestford.*
33. Mrs. Nicholas Penniman III (née Pattie Symington, a daughter of Donald Symington), conversation with author, June 11, 1991.
34. Lelia Symington memoirs, quoted in Symington, *Skippin' the Details,* 19.

"A small house in the country"

Interior of Donald Symington's 1920s library/ballroom wing. Harford County has probably never contained a more comfortable-looking room.

To many eyes, Donald Symington's c. 1920 complex of barns and silos (built for his prize-winning Jersey cattle) resembles a village in Normandy.

In sum, "Maryland sent no more gallant soldier to fight for a forlorn hope than he." Nor did it send a better-looking one; Symington, gushed a reporter for the *Sun,* was "a true man" with piercing eyes, flowing dark hair, and a drooping moustache that made him "the handsomest man in the Confederate Army." But the swashbuckling major (whose "many admirers" had showered him with so many gifts "during his bachelor days" that it embarrassed the rest of the family) met his match when he encountered Lelia Powers during the siege of Petersburg. One day that "famous Southern belle" who "always was a daredevil sort," on a bet rode sidesaddle between the two armies, with "both Yankees and Confeds waving and cheering" her on. This, of course, "entirely captivated Major Symington" and although she liked what she saw when she looked at him, their courtship progressed slowly for they were delayed first by the war and then by the peace.[35]

After Appomattox the federal government required all former Confederates to take an oath of allegiance to the United States. This the insulted Symington refused to do, stating he preferred "expatriation to the oath." Thus he exiled himself to Germany and enrolled at the University of Heidelberg. But when "time . . . ameliorated the conditions at home" he returned to Baltimore where he and Lelia Powers were married in October 1866. Unlike most of the rest of the family, however, the major, a son pithily wrote, was a "very bad businessman" who preferred to devote his considerable energy not to the fertilizer factory but to sporting events, including a still-famous two-horse team race up

35. Symington, *Skippin' the Details,* 10–13, 19; Symington, *Scotch and Soda,* 35.

Charles Street with Michael Jenkins. He was also a renowned gourmand and his breakfasts of "steak or chops and broiled shad . . . broiled tomatoes . . . buckwheat cakes and sausage" remain firmly fixed in Baltimore lore. He took great pains to ensure that "there was . . . in season a barrel of live terrapins in the cellar," and went through innumerable cooks in a vain search for someone who knew how to roast a canvasback duck properly. (He said one must "leave the very hot oven door open and let the whole picked ducks fly through onto your plate and drink Madiera wine while eating.") Not one to take business seriously, he "refused to allow any of [his children] to air a single trouble or grievance. . . . He said . . . if not discussed at the table, the troubles would evaporate as the . . . day progressed." That his own didn't in no way diminishes the charm—or the gallantry—of the idea.[36]

Donald Symington, William and Lelia's eldest son, who had inherited some of his parents' flair (and more than a little of his grandfather's business savvy) spent lavishly to return Indian Spring to its glory: he added a library/ballroom to the rear of Thomas's extension, upgraded the kitchen, and built a spacious garage and servants' quarters. Turning his attention to the grounds, he built a ha-ha wall southwest of the house to keep his favorite "pets,"[37] a herd of prize-winning Jersey cattle, off the lawn and also gave the "pets" a state-of-the-art complex of barns and silos whose varied rooflines resemble, in the right light, a small village in Normandy.[38] Yet, as is discussed in chapter 10, Elsie Jenkins Symington outdid her husband's horticultural efforts; she became one of the most respected gardeners in the state and immortalized her work in her 1941 best-selling autobiography, *By Light of Sun*. "Rich in experience and mature in wisdom," wrote *House & Garden* editor Richardson Wright in a review, *By Light of Sun* "surely will bring greater understanding to that increasing number in the country who seek in cultivating their gardens a quickened spirit, dependable peace, and ever widening horizons."[39]

Mansard Roofs and Canned Corn

Most of the above houses, even Hazel Glen, have understandable American antecedents. Yet a few of Harford's "small houses" emphatically do not. Like Marian Curtiss's Spanish patio, they injected a decidedly foreign flavor into the county's once-solid Anglo-Saxon architectural psyche. This injection didn't only occur in Harford County, of course, for throughout America the creators of the nation's burgeoning post–Civil War industrial fortunes all developed seemingly insatiable cravings for buildings of genuine European design. The first of these stylistic imports to win nationwide popularity was the Second Empire, named in deference to Napoleon III's second French empire. (His uncle Napoleon had established the first.) During the 1850s and '60s Parisian architects revived the mansard roof and other French renaissance motifs in an attempt to create three-dimensional legitimacy for Napoleon III's only quasi-legitimate reign. The emperor's defeat by Bismarck in the 1870 Franco-Prussian War (and subsequent abdication) diminished some of the style's glamour in Europe, but not on this side of the Atlantic. Indeed, Second Empire building reached its American zenith during Grant's presidency (1869–77), although many here began to view it with suspicion, too, once Grant-era corruption became widely known.

Baltimore boasts one of the nation's earliest Second Empire statements, the new city hall, designed by architect George A. Frederick in 1867. Harford gained its Second Empire masterpiece shortly thereafter in the swaggering country house called Fair Meadows, which rose up near Creswell in 1868. The house was even commissioned by a Frenchman, Clement Dietrich, born in 1805 in Alsace-Lorraine, who made a fortune in the soap and candle business in Cincinnati. When the Civil War threatened to disrupt his life in Ohio, he simply sold his company to a new concern called Procter & Gamble and moved back to France. He returned to America in 1867 in style; that October he paid $70,000 cash for the 5,067-acre prime industrial property, Harford Furnace, and commissioned the fifteen-room mansion Fair Meadows.[40] Curiously, while all scholars agree that Dietrich

36. See Symington, *Skippin' the Details,* 15; Beirne, *Amiable Baltimoreans,* 346; Lelia Symington, quoted in Symington, *Skippin' the Details,* 14; William Symington obituary, *Baltimore Sun,* June 9, 1912.

37. Symington may not have been the first in the county to breed Jerseys; that honor may go to Joseph Hoopes, who kept a Jersey herd at his Woodside Farm on Hoopes Road in the 1880s.

38. Penniman, conversation with author.

39. Richardson Wright in Elsie Symington, *By Light of Sun* (New York: G. P. Putnam's, 1941), ix.

40. Deed WHD 19/187. Dietrich's doings provided much fodder for the local papers, of course; James Chrismer kindly pointed out a June 25, 1869, *Ægis* article in which the anonymous author discusses the "several large buildings" that "Mr. C. Dietrich" erected to make the furnace "the most extensive one of the kind in this country," including "a three-story chemical building of stone 192 × 25 feet . . . , a laboratory, . . . [a] Carbonization Building and . . . [a] Methylene Building" as well as "an exceedingly handsome smoke stack . . . [which] towers 85 feet in height," all "in addition to the original furnace buildings already erected. . . . It is expected that . . . here will be constantly employed about one hundred men."

Clement Dietrich's 1868 Fair Meadows, centerpiece of his 5,067-acre Harford Furnace holdings. Left: Mantle detail at Fair Meadows. Every inch of the house, which purportedly cost $93,000 to build, has something stuck into it or hung from it.

must have had an architect design the new house, no one knows who it was, although professional opinion has now narrowed the possibilities down to Jackson Gott, who designed the Masonic Temple in Bel Air (1886) and George Frederick, of Baltimore City Hall fame.[41]

Fair Meadows, rumored to have cost $93,000 in an era when laborers earned 15 cents an hour, instantly comes across as a rich man's house. (This would have embarrassed only a few Second Empire aficionados.) The mansion is five bays wide and two rooms deep. Its regularly laid ashlar walls and mansard roof create a virtual cube that is slathered with every decorative feature the canons of the style allowed—a cupola, dormers with round-arched windows and heavy hoods, patterned roofing slate, bulbous chimneys, a trio of thick cornices (one at the second story, a second at the crown of the roof, and the third at the cupola), rusticated trim around the windows and matching quoins . . . every inch has something stuck into it or hung from it or rising out of it. Nor did Dietrich skimp on the interior, for inlaid marble covers some floors, intricate parquets of imported woods cover others, and all main rooms have plaster ceilings and friezes sculpted into naturalistic or geometric patterns. Dietrich also turned his attention to landscaping and filled the estate grounds with decorative pools and statues; he even built a dozen or so outbuildings that echo, in reduced form, themes begun at the main house, including Harford's only stone, mansarded carriage house.

An 1897 biographer described Dietrich as having "a strong mind, a determined will, and a firm perseverance that knew no defeat. In some respects," the anonymous author continued, "he was a man of decided and inflexible traits of mind."[42] That determined man continued Harford Furnace's long-established iron works and flour mill and also tried to diversify operations by building a chemical plant to produce acetic acid, wood alcohol, and pyroligneous acid. Dietrich's conglomerate didn't last long, however, for he was bucking inexorable historical trends (so much for being "inflexible"). Between 1865 and 1885 changes in technology and labor forced entrepreneurs to abandon nineteen furnaces throughout Maryland; Dietrich's was one of those and the vast enterprise was divided up and sold at a sheriff's sale in 1876.

Second Empire houses, in their first, swaggering, Dietrich phase, present an energetic

41. Randy Chalfont, conversation with author, September 27, 1990; James T. Wollon Jr., AIA, "Fair Meadows," *Harford Historical Bulletin* (Summer 1992): 88–89.

42. *Portrait and Biographical Record*, 195.

kaleidoscope of wall surfaces, advancing and receding planes, and varied rooflines and window shapes, all appropriate, somehow, to the house-builders' own energetic personalities and varied business interests. In quiet Creswell, men like Dietrich and houses like Fair Meadows must have come as a jolt to conservative, agriculturally minded old-timers, such as the Websters, who in the 1860s still lived in their ancient family houses Broom's Bloom, Mount Adams, Best Endeavor, and Webster's Forest. Second Empire buildings continued to draw snickers and shudders in this century, too, thanks to Charles Addams who, in one well-known cartoon, depicts a Christmassy scene, with carolers grouped together in the snow, while the "family," high above on the mansard roof readies a cauldron of bubbling gawd-knows-what to pour onto the sweetly singing troupe. (The thought of Dietrich's vast chemical works adds a certain poignancy to the scene.)

As the nineteenth century wore on, however, toned-down Second Empire buildings became more and more acceptable parts of the Harford landscape. In 1870 Garrett Amos, a descendant of William Amos II, inherited Mount Soma and added a mansard roof to that venerable residence; Gabriel McComas built the c. 1880 mansard-roof dwelling Del Mar on the family farms he had inherited near Upper Crossroads; and when the Virginia-born Henry Reckord built himself a four-story flour mill on Rock Spring Avenue in Bel Air in 1886, he topped it with a mansard crown. Mary Dallam, widow of state's attorney William H. Dallam, then proceeded to lay out "Major Dallam's Addition" to Bel Air in the very shadow of the new mill. Amos, McComas, Dallam: here is proof-positive that the foreign-born style had gained respectability among Harford's old guard.

Speaking of respectable, no one has called any member of the Maryland Jenkins family "foreign-born" since the seventeenth century, when Thomas Jenkins settled in Charles County "under the patronage of Charles Calvert" and became the lord of the 1,300-acre St. Thomas Manor. Thomas and his descendants then set out on their varied—but always prosperous—careers, first in southern Maryland, then in the Long Green Valley of Baltimore County, and, eventually, in Baltimore City. (It was Thomas's great-great-great-grandson Michael Jenkins who competed with Major Symington in that famous horse race up Charles Street.) And when Ignatius Walter Jenkins, a great-great-grandson of the pioneering Thomas, set out to build himself a stone farmhouse near Pylesville, he gave it a mansard roof and nobody looked askance. He also gave the house, which he called Belle Farm, a volume virtually equal to Dietrich's Fair Meadows but he left off the flashy trim— no cupola, no thick window hoods, and comparatively restrained dormers. Perhaps that is why Jenkins's house is now and probably always has been a better-regarded neighbor. Or perhaps it is because of the two builders' different personalities. While Dietrich was "inflexible" and "determined," Jenkins was a "tall handsome . . . jovial man" who loved nothing better than taking his horse and buggy to Pylesville (which he called "the only finished city in the country for it ever remained the same size") to spend "a merry time with his cronies discussing the political news and poking fun at the politicians."[43]

Or perhaps it is due to the two builders' other interests; Dietrich put up acid factories on his acreage; Jenkins and his wife, née Ann Maria Brown, put up barns and smokehouses and churches on theirs. Indeed, a devout Roman Catholic spirit ran deep in both the Jenkins and Brown families. Her grandfather Ignatius Wheeler of Deer Park had founded St. Ignatius Church near Hickory in the 1780s, while his cousins Michael and Joseph Jenkins built, among other structures, the 1891 church Corpus Christi (correctly Jenkins Memorial) on Mount Royal Avenue in Baltimore. Henry Jenkins (Ignatius and Ann Maria's son) also built St. Mary's in Pylesville, a wonderful granite Gothic/ Romanesque hybrid, dedicated in 1895. People certainly did things right back then. Cardinal Gibbons, an old Jenkins family friend, came out from Baltimore for the dedication and arrived the day before by train in a "car . . . that had been reserved to be used for the first time on that occasion." A "guard of honor, consisting of sixty prominent citizens . . . mounted on fine horses and wearing cardinal sashes" met the distinguished guest, who, of course, spent the night at Belle Farm. The next day, "a special train of eight cars car-

Top: By 1886, when Henry Reckord built this mill in Bel Air (shown here c. 1920), Harford countians had begun to accept once-shocking architectural motifs such as mansard roofs. Bottom: Ignatius Walter Jenkins, builder of this Second Empire house near Pylesville, sits to the right in this family grouping. (He is holding grandson Michael Oswald Jenkins.)

43. Ibid., 523; and see Michael Oswald Jenkins, "Ancestry of Richard Hillen Jenkins," unpublished 1946 typescript in MHS library, pp. 103, 325–26.

"A small house in the country"   155

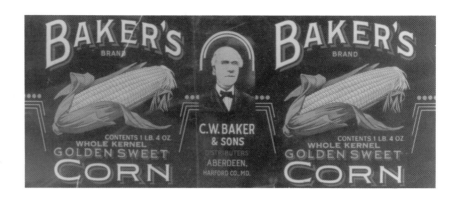

George Washington Baker (1815-88) of Aberdeen brought the canning industry to Harford County. The business made him rich, but it made his sons, George A., James, William, and Charles Winfield (whose label is shown here) even richer.

ried the [other] Baltimore visitors," including a choir from the cathedral to sing Haydn's Third Mass, while "hundreds drove from the country for twenty-five miles around" to witness the ceremony and attend a Jenkins-sponsored celebratory "concert in front of the priest's house."[44]

Jenkins, McComas, and Amos grew—or remained—wealthy thanks to Harford's booming agricultural economy. While the county's naturally fertile soils account for some of these families' prosperity, the real underpinnings of their wealth lay not only in the soils that produced Belle Farm's, Del Mar's, and Mount Soma's abundant crops, but in the canneries that preserved them. Entrepreneur Thomas Kensett gave birth to the modern canning industry when he began packing oysters in a shack at the foot of Baltimore's Federal Hill around 1840. (Kensett used tin-plated iron canisters instead of the customary glass ones and he shortened the phrase "tin-plated iron cannister" to "can.")[45] Almost overnight canneries sprung up throughout the state, providing the greatest single factor in the Maryland economy for the rest of the century. North of the Gunpowder, with over 100 commercial canneries in operation in the county (and several hundred private ones as well, for it seemed as if every nineteenth-century farm from Joppa to Whiteford had some sort of makeshift cannery), Harford grew famous as "the greatest canning county in America."[46]

According to often-repeated tradition, George Washington Baker (1815–88) brought the industry to Harford. As a young man he first tried to earn a living as a cabinetmaker. When that didn't pan out he tried the timber business. Nothing clicked until 1866 when he "decided to can for local market the blackberries, dewberries, and peaches from his own and neighboring farms," which netted him a profit. He reinvested the cash in his new enterprise and "from this humble beginning," wrote his 1890s biographer, Baker's empire grew until he owned "several large canning factories . . . in which were prepared for market the products of about three thousand acres planted to fruit and corn."[47] He then set up each of his sons in the business and they proved, if anything, "even more successful at it than their father as did . . . grandsons P. Tevis, Frank E., Lynn, Hollis, and Harold Baker."[48]

Booth Tarkington would have known the Bakers instantly. In fact, perhaps the most striking thing about the clan is its members' total predictability: they are all so thoroughly of and from late nineteenth-century, small-town America. And while not every Baker ran a cannery—Thomas (born 1871) became president of the Carnegie Institute of Technology, Nicholas H. (born 1851) and Charles H. (born 1879) were professional painters, and Howard W. (born c. 1870) won renown as a big league ballplayer—canning gave them their start, their money, and the security that made the comfortable exploration of other vocations possible.[49]

It also unleashed a remarkable burst of architectural energy as George Baker's sons and grandsons commissioned architect George Frederick to design a superb set of rambunctious frame mansions for them. As was briefly discussed above, Frederick (1842–1924) "laid his claim to fame with a youthful triumph, Baltimore City Hall

44. An undated but contemporary *Ægis* clipping said "thousands" attended. Clipping from the *Baltimore Sun,* September 16, 1895.

45. Margaret S. Bishop, "Canning in Harford County," *Harford Historical Bulletin* (Summer 1989): 76.

46. *Portrait and Biographical Record,* 363.

47. Ibid., 364; also George A. Baker, conversation with author, April 16, 1991.

48. Wright, *Harford,* 163.

49. Material on file at the Aberdeen Room, HSHC; J. Harlan Livezey, "The Baker Family of Aberdeen," *Harford Historical Bulletin* (Spring 1983): 5.

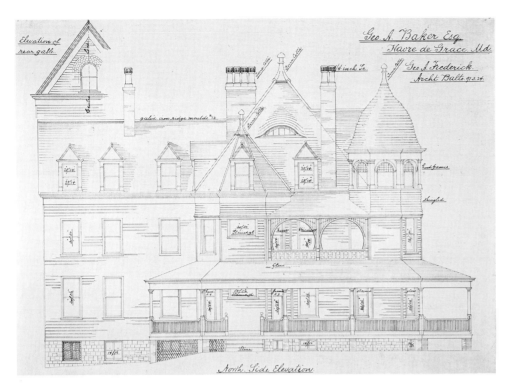

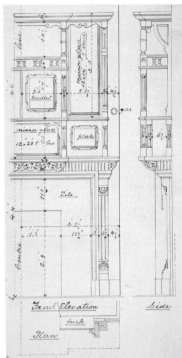

North Side Elevation

(1867–75)." But, wonderful as the city hall is, most scholars now feel that the architect "actually designed more winningly in his maturity,"[50] that is, when he produced the Second Empire mansion Cylburn for Baltimore industrialist Jesse Tyson (1889) and a collection of amusing pavilions and other whimsies for Druid Hill Park. In Harford, Frederick's work culminated in the Baker family's frame chateaux, specifically the turreted, dormered, and thoroughly be-porched twenty-one-room mansion he created for George A. Baker (1856–1909) in Havre de Grace in 1891 and the billowing, bulging 1893 extravaganza he designed for Charles Winfield Baker (1848–1918) on a vast lot at the corner of Bel Air and Paradise roads in Aberdeen. (Charles later landscaped that lot with "specimen and ornamental plants, shaped flower beds, curving carriage drives and walks,"[51] and built an elaborate cast-iron fence—with the monogram, in script, CWB, atop each gate—around the entire property.)

Those two commissions are thoroughly documented. But Frederick may well have been involved with other Baker family projects: some scholars feel that the architect also designed mansions for James Baker (1845–1912, Aberdeen postmaster under President Grant) and his brother William (1840–1911), founding president of the First National Bank of Aberdeen, member of Congress, and "the most influential of the Bakers on the growth . . . of Aberdeen."[52]

Their earthly rewards well in hand, the Bakers decided to turn their attention heavenward. Patriarch George W. established the Baker Cemetery, Inc., in 1887 on an acre of "the home farm" adjacent State Route 22. He died the following year, and his sons William, James, Charles, and George, who had acquired a controlling interest in the project, opened the cemetery's acreage to "friends in the community . . . seeking ground for burial purposes."[53] Many Aberdonians have so sought over the past century and the sloping property now bristles with non-Baker headstones. While the founding Baker's ten-foot-tall marble obelisk remains the most prominent memorial (prominent and apposite, enriched as it is with carved corncobs), the Baker surname may not be the best-known inscription in the three-acre cemetery today. A few hundred yards downhill from the corncob obelisk cluster a few modest stones simply—but resonantly—inscribed Ripken.

Left: In 1891 George Baker commissioned Baltimore architect George Frederick to design this twenty-one-room Havre de Grace mansion. The house was later home of the Harford Memorial Hospital and, still later, was demolished for the present hospital building. Right: Frederick enriched the billowing, bulging frame mansion he designed for Aberdeen canner Charles Winfield Baker with every conceivable detail. Here are his thoughts for a dining-room mantel—ash wood with embedded mirrors and ceramic plates.

50. Charles E. Brownell, Calder Loth, William M. S. Rasmussen, and Richard Guy Wilson, *The Making of Virginia Architecture* (Richmond: Virginia Museum of Fine Arts, 1992), 306.

51. James Wollon, AIA, "The Baker Houses," *Harford Historical Bulletin* (Spring 1983): 9.

52. *Portrait and Biographical Record,* 357; Livezey, "Baker Family," 4.

53. Deeds ALJ 61/171, ALJ 65/37.

"A small house in the country"

Some "Bad Old Boys" and an "Implacable Christian"

While the Ripken family has brought a good deal of national prestige to Harford County in the 1980s and 1990s, Oakington, a tract of land overlooking the bay near Havre de Grace, has been doing the same thing for more than 300 years: the name appears in deeds as far back as 1659, when Nathaniel Utie patented 800 acres he called Oakington[54] and, as Peter A. Jay has observed, "if you mention Oakington around Maryland today . . . you're likely to produce a respectful look: the name reeks of History." This respect, of course, derives primarily from the place's twentieth-century owners, Sen. and Mrs. Millard Tydings, who are discussed in more detail below. "Newspaper articles often identify it as 'the historic Tydings estate,'" Jay writes, and "it's implied . . . that there have been Tydingses at Oakington for generations, as there have been Churchills at Blenheim." This implication simply is not true; nor could it be true "in democratic America, [where] . . . families rise to prominence and fall again, all at a speed to make a European's head spin."[55] Yet the truth is far more fascinating than the fiction of an aristocratic succession of masters of Oakington could be, for the estate's heterogeneous owners touch virtually every aspect of American history—political, economic, architectural, horticultural, and philosophical—even sex scandals and murder.

John Stump of Stafford acquired Oakington from Utie's distant descendants in the 1790s. He died on Valentine's Day 1816 and left the 700 acres of "Oakington Farm, estimated at thirty thousand dollars"[56] to the profligate John Wilson Stump mentioned above and his Baltimore-born heiress wife, Sarah. The two immediately improved the tract with the elegant 2½-story, forty-foot-square stone villa discussed in chapter 4; they also, as architect J. C. Neilson wrote, ran through their inherited fortunes. To settle their debts, the "700 acres of [Oakington] with valuable dwellings and other improvements . . . where John W. Stump resides" had to be sold at a sheriff's sale in 1845. The estate briefly returned to the Stumps when John and Sarah's lawyer son, Herman (born 1835) bought it in December of 1862 for $25,000, but he turned around and sold it out of the family for good on May 2, 1866, for the phenomenal price of $62,500. He then bought Waverley, a house and 180 acres on Tollgate Road near Bel Air, whither he and his mother repaired. (Notwithstanding their substantial profit on the Oakington sale, Stump and his widowed mother carried on for years about how they had been "forced" from their ancestral acres.)[57]

Once his aged mother died, Herman, a 68-year-old bachelor, married the equally middle-aged Marie de Velasco, a redoubtable character who loved to discuss her (alleged) Spanish ducal forbears and who lived in great splendor thanks to her half-brother, Florida railroad magnate and land speculator Henry M. Flagler. The newlyweds' passion evidently did not match that of Abelard and Heloise; when Herman died he bequeathed Waverley and "all family portraits, silver . . . and household furniture which I brought from Oakington" to a nephew, Bertram Stump, leaving his bride with "whatever furniture there may be . . . not heretofore bequeathed." Still, she probably did not miss the Oakington treasures; she had several baubles of her own. (When she died in 1944, the list of her itemized jewelry includes thirty-eight pieces such as a "pearl necklace, 101 pearls," a "rose diamond and emerald bow," a "diamond crown," and a six-carat diamond solitaire ring.) Nor, evidently, did Mrs. Stump miss Herman overmuch, for she left Waverley to her strapping chauffeur as thanks for years of loyal service. (And also, as she explained in her will, because he was a veteran.)

Once Herman Stump and his mother had moved to Bel Air, Oakington grew notorious as a playground for rich Philadelphians and New Yorkers, climaxed, perhaps, in 1905 when the estate was purchased by James L. Breese, Wall Street wheeler-dealer and "a bad old boy of the first rank," to quote one of Oakington's later owners.[58] Breese used his stock-market killings to finance his real loves, namely amateur photography and what's now called life in the fast lane. He and Stanford White, his great friend and "kindred spir-

The Oakington conservatory, possibly designed by Stanford White for James Breese around 1905, resplendent in ferns, ivy, Tiffany lamps, and spittoons.

54. Maryland patent book 4, p. 453; Baltimore County land record book H, p. 331; transcripts in possession of Eleanor Davies Tydings Ditzen, Washington, D.C.; Mrs. Ditzen's second husband was Millard Tydings.

55. Peter A. Jay, editorial in the *Record,* June 18, 1986.

56. Will SR1/84.

57. Letter from Marie de Valasco Stump to Sen. Millard Tydings, September 20, 1935, in the archives of Mrs. Lowell Ditzen, Washington, D.C.

58. Ditzen, conversation with author.

it" (and one of the undeniable geniuses of American architecture) painted many towns several shades of red and devoted several rolls of film to photographs of shapely young things. Their escapades provided endless fodder for that era's tabloid publishers; Joseph Pulitzer, for one, rarely missed a chance to use his newspaper, the *World,* to editorialize against "bacchanalian revels in New York fashionable studios." Pulitzer, though, didn't begin to know the whole truth about those revels: when White was murdered apropos "the girl in the red velvet swing," his private secretary hurried to the architect's studio and secretly moved "some 160 books of erotica," flagellation, and sadism (e.g., *The Romance of Chastisement, Memoirs of Private Flagallation, The Pleasure of Cruelty*) from White's office to Breese's Long Island house, The Orchards.[59]

White and Breese collaborated on several architectural projects as well. At The Orchards, built in 1898, the architect gave the stockbroker an immense, porticoed mansion complete with a squash court, "a shooting tower for clay pigeon, a garage . . . where one Breese son later built the engine that powered the 'Spirit of St. Louis,'" and a "78-foot long high-ceilinged studio."[60] Breese also asked White to enlarge Oakington to make room for his favorite Ziegfeld Follies beauties. Deciding to work on a smaller scale than he had at The Orchard, White devised a pair of matching low frame wings to flank the Stumps' three-bay stone house; he also enriched the main entrance hall with a delicate, neoclassical marble mantel and an exquisite Adamesque plaster ceiling and (possibly) built a large, glassed-in conservatory overlooking the bay.[61] All these additions display the architect's talents at their best. He knew that these sorts of ceilings and mantels frequently graced stylish houses of the John W. Stump era and, he must have reasoned, if Oakington didn't originally have them, it *should* have.[62] The low frame wings show White's sensitivity to design in a different way: they instantly register "less important" and thus serve to accentuate the original stone structure.

After a few years Breese wearied of Oakington and in 1916 sold it to Commo. Leonard Richards of the New York Yacht Club.[63] Richards, who had made a fortune in the Atlas Powder Company, liked things big-scale. Worried that the Stump-Breese-White house was not sufficiently impressive, he replaced the north frame wing with a gargantuan stone pile that obviously gave the commodore more space (twenty-nine rooms, all told), but

Oakington c. 1920. The original three-bay Stump villa (behind the curved conservatory) is clear. Architect Stanford White flanked that building with two low frame wings around 1905 (one is visible to the left). Gunpowder tycoon Leonard Richards bought the property in 1916 and replaced one of White's wings with the large stone wing seen here; he also built the greenhouses and immense garage just visible to the far right.

59. Paul R. Baker, *Stanny: The Gilded Life of Stanford White* (New York: Free Press, 1989), 279, 284, 250–51, 375.

60. Mac Griswold and Eleanor Weller, *The Golden Age of American Gardens* (New York: Harry N. Abrams, Inc., 1991), 111; Baker, *Stanny,* 302; and see *Architectural Forum* 49 (September 1928): 305.

61. Ditzen, conversation with author.

62. Two such Baltimore ceilings are installed in the Baltimore Museum of Art: the ceiling from Willow Brook (1799, discussed in chapter 4) and the ceiling from a house in Waterloo Row (c. 1817). The Oakington ceiling is probably far better than any period Harford ceiling would have been; indeed no house left in the county has a ceiling that begins to approach Oakington's, although a house like Bloomsbury, now destroyed but still standing in 1906, might have.

63. Deed JAR 153/105.

"A small house in the country"   159

Leonard Richards designed Oakington's six-car garage himself shortly after purchasing the estate in 1916. The building also incorporated three separate ten-room servants' houses.

that, just as obviously, lacked the subtlety of White's almost demure wings. Richards also gave Oakington a cavernous stone garage that not only incorporated covered spaces for six cars but for three ten-room servants' houses as well. Notwithstanding the change at the top, life at Oakington maintained its high, gilded standards and Richards

> lived in royal splendor there until he died. . . . There was always an English valet and a French chef in the kitchen. He was always called Commodore and in the old days owned a 160′ steam brigantine. He had the Susquehanna dredged so he could moor it off Oakington. . . . The place was magnificent with splendid gardens, clipped hedges, a large greenhouse, boat dock, and even a private power plant.

The estate also maintained its standards for somewhat *outre* guests, too, for Richards allowed "torch singer Libby Holman, the mistress of Richard Reynolds, the tobacco heir" *and* his suspected murderer, to hide out at Oakington "until it was ruled that Reynolds' death was probably a suicide and she felt safe to reappear." But the Depression hit Richards hard. He "died broke"[64] and in 1933 his widow sold Oakington to Enoch Garey, a believer in progressive education, who established the Garey School in the house. Progressive, yes; Curtisslike, no, for Garey showed boys who were "eager and sensitive"—his phrase—how to trap and skin muskrats and sell the pelts (to teach the youths economic theory); he also took the students bear-hunting (to solve their emotional problems) and spelunking down coal mines (to learn "the value of endurance and stamina"). When the school failed to catch on, Garey was forced to sell the 550-acre property in 1935. The buyer, a corporation described as the "Oakington Company,"[65] was simply a front for the real purchaser, Millard Tydings (1890–1961), U.S. senator and the most successful and powerful politician the county has ever produced.

Well! Libby Holman and English valets certainly mark a change from William Amos and his Quaker prayers! Before things get too out of hand, it might be prudent to return to Dr. Kelly, who after all began this chapter, and to his "small house in the country," Liriodendron. Despite seemingly unbridgeable differences between Breese and the *Romance of Chastisement,* and Kelly, whose favorite reading was the Bible, the men's Harford houses do share one thing—personality. Just as the history of Oakington is completely

64. Quoted in Jay, ed., *Havre de Grace,* 159; Ditzen, conversation with author.

65. Deed SWC 237/471.

wrapped up in its very individualistic owners, so the history of Liriodendron is synonymous with the larger-than-life Dr. Kelly, one of the greatest surgeons of his day, author of over 600 books and articles, cornerstone of the newly founded Hopkins Hospital, renowned naturalist, disciple of Madame Curie, verbal sparring partner of H. L. Mencken, and, above all, a deeply religious human being. His unshaking faith made everything else possible for he believed—he would have said *he knew*—that we are put on earth to serve God and anything we do to that end is too little.

He was born in Camden, New Jersey, in 1858, the product of what he called "godly ancestors,"[66] for Quaker, Anglican, and Methodist ministers foliate his family tree. He also had economically astute ancestors; if the Bible provided the philosophical wherewithal for his life of good deeds, the family paper business relieved him from checkbook concerns. (Not that he would have had any. His Hopkins friend Dr. Bertram M. Bernheim described Kelly as "anything but materialistic. . . . Clubs and dinners and the social world . . . hadn't the slightest lure" for him. Moreover, between 1898 and 1912 Kelly earned $42,000 but gave $92,000 to charity.)[67] Kelly enrolled in the University of Pennsylvania, but collegiate life wore him out and his health broke. Thinking a year off might prove beneficial to him, his parents sent him to Colorado in 1881 to regain his strength working as a cowboy and for the next few months the pages of his diary crack with names and doings light-years removed from the antimacassars of Philadelphia: mining for gold at Grizzly Gulch; driving cattle around Pike's Peak; riding the Pony Express. He also found his faith in Colorado when, during an attack of snowblindness, he experienced "an overwhelming . . . great light" he took to be the presence of God, "leaving a realization and a conviction never afterwards to be questioned in all the vicissitudes of life, whatever they might be, a certainty above and beyond the process of human reasoning."[68]

Spiritually and physically enriched, Kelly returned to Penn and earned his medical degree in 1882. For his residency, he worked at the hospital in Kensington, a poor mill town in the Philadelphia area, where he specialized in treating women who had suffered the effect of working twelve-hour-day factory shifts. Based on these experiences, he developed a deep (and then unique in the medical world) interest in the problems of women's health. That interest guided him during the rest of his professional life; he established a women's hospital in Kensington in 1887 (only the sixth such clinic in America), moved on to head up Penn's gynecological department in 1888, and, in 1889, at the urging of Drs. Welch, Osler, and Halsted, came to Baltimore to take the obstetrics/gynecology chair at the new Johns Hopkins Hospital.

Kelly's reformist impulses found nonmedical outlets as well. He traveled throughout the East giving temperance lectures and teaching Bible classes, often in the company of the leading evangelist of the day, Billy Sunday. He ran for governor in 1920 as a Democrat, choosing that party because he deemed its members "the most corrupt" and he hoped to mend their ways. He didn't fare well with the voters, with his pro-prohibition and antiprostitution platform, but he was gracious in defeat. He also campaigned for pure food and drug laws and tried to reform the regulations governing child labor and women's rights. The same anti-alcohol bent that led to his defeat at the polls, coupled with his strict Christianity, also led to decades of friendly feuding with his fellow Baltimore giant, H. L. Mencken. Kelly, seeing chance for improvement in anyone, developed a habit of sending Mencken self-improvement tracts, which could not have helped matters; Mencken, clearly resigned to it all, usually referred to Kelly either as "Dr. Evangelical Extremus" or as "the most implacable Christian I have ever met." Curiously though, considering how unbelievable each must have seemed to the other, their outright clashes were few; perhaps each recognized the genius in the other and decided to make allowances. One can only shake one's head in wonder: surely any man whose circle of acquaintances included Mencken and Billy Sunday may truly be said to have lived a full life.

Kelly was also often accompanied on his crusades by his wife, the Prussian-born Laetitia Bredow, whom he met in his student days while traveling in Europe and whom he

66. Weeks, "Liriodendron."

67. Kelly once inherited $100,000 from a patient; his only thought was how to dispose of it all most equitably.

68. Quoted in Weeks, "Liriodendron."

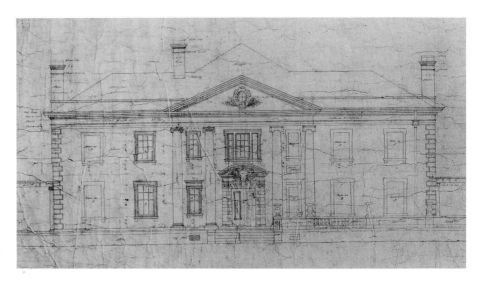

To ease the homesickness Laetitia Bredow Kelly felt for her native Prussia, her husband, Dr. Howard Kelly (1858-1943) built the splendid Liriodendron in 1897.

married in 1889. In Baltimore Kelly and his bride took up residence at 1406 Eutaw Place but, to escape the city's summer heat, they moved to the wilds of northern Ontario each June to camp, canoe, and fish. This regimen did not, however, enchant Mrs. Kelly, who longed for the settled, elegant life she had left behind in Europe. She did not want to spend her summers in a log cabin; she wanted to spend them in a Palladian villa. To meet that longing, the doctor began looking around Maryland for a suitable site. Nothing seemed right until Dr. John M. T. Finney, a Harford native and Kelly's colleague at the Hopkins, suggested the Bel Air/Fallston area, then so popular with the Symingtons, Tysons, and other affluent Baltimoreans. On October 19, 1897, the Kellys bought a 196-acre tract near the county seat, renamed their property to honor the many giant tulip poplars (*Liriodendron tulipifera*) they found there, and, to design the new summer house, engaged the Baltimore architectural firm of Wyatt & Nolting.

That was a wise choice indeed. J. B. Noel Wyatt and his various partners (William G. Nolting and Joseph Evans Sperry) produced a body of work that includes most what is basic in Baltimore: the city courthouse, the Keyser Building, the old Mercantile Building at Calvert and Redwood streets, the Hippodrome Theater, the Fifth Regiment Armory, and a dozen or so houses in Roland Park and Guilford. As that list suggests, the firm was not only prolific, it was versatile as well, a quality they maintained working in Harford County, where they gingerly style-hopped from the earthbound, Romanesque Emmanuel Episcopal Church in Bel Air one year (1896) to the neoclassical splendor of Liriodendron the next.

And Liriodendron is splendid. Architect Neilson, who watched developments from Priestford, wrote in his *Notebook* that "land near Bel Air sold to Dr. Kelly of Balto." who "improved [it] . . . *expensively*." Wyatt and Nolting gave Kelly a grand, T-plan, stuccoed villa whose exterior is dominated by a pedimented, Ionic central pavilion that, in turn, is enriched with vigorous terracotta trim. Yet while Liriodendron is obviously visually splendid, it made a practical house as well. The T plan simply and functionally creates airy axes to catch every breeze just as its large rooms and shady side porches hold every shadow. It also creates a hierarchical composition that gives a "true" picture of use: family rooms fill the elaborate front section; service rooms and servants' staircase are relegated to the more plainly finished stroke of the T. Beautiful to look at, comfortable to be in, intellectually and conceptually valid, Liriodendron stands as the very model of a modern summer house.

Henry James, who felt that the words "summer afternoon" formed the most beautiful phrase in the English language, probably never spent an August in Maryland. In Maryland "summer afternoon" means *hot*. When Liriodendron got too hot (one of the Kellys' daughters recalls that the Harford County place wasn't cool exactly, but "it *was* cooler than Eutaw Place"),[69] the family simply retired to the wisteria-shaded veranda that runs the length of the main façade. If that did not prove cooling enough, they would splash around in Liriodendron's two swimming pools or in the "10-foot hole on Winters Run at Lake Fanny," Friedrich H. "Fritz" Kelly recalled in 1976. Ball-playing on the sweeping lawns and horseback riding through the woods also helped blend the days together in idyllic bliss.

It was obviously too good to last. The century's increasing crassness struck a sharp contrast with the generous nature of men like Dr. Kelly. Fewer and fewer Americans automatically transferred 30 percent of their income to a special account for charity—but Kelly did and the doctor drew on this account to fund scholarships and subsidize lunches and shoes for inner-city children. He and Mrs. Kelly died just six hours apart in 1943.

There certainly can't be many "small houses in the country" built in America's wicked Gilded Age that have served the general public in so many ways for so many years as Liriodendron, now owned and maintained by the Harford County government as Heavenly Waters Park. More generally, those golden afternoons at Liriodendron, days filled with ponies and horses and swimming, recall Lelia Symington's nostalgic recollections of halcyon stays at Indian Spring, long, beautiful days spent hanging out with "a bunch of brothers, cousins and friends . . . [in] the jolliest times imaginable." While Oakington and Fair Meadows and the other "small houses" can never be created again, they and the lives they supported have endured: their colorful owners have been preserved in reminiscences and biographies and the buildings themselves still stand, eloquent testimony to a way of life far removed from ours in every way but time.

69. Mrs. Douglas Warner (née Margaret Kelly), conversation with author, October 10, 1980.

"Ain't we got fun!" indeed! Mr. and Mrs. Alexis Shriver dancing on the roof at Olney in 1926: they had just raised the transported marble columns for their new porch but had not yet roofed the porch or added the pediment.

"Ain't we got fun!" [8]

"Dad would be off in the Far East on his government projects for months at a time," Alexis Shriver's daughter, the late Harriet Rogers, once reminisced while walking through the barnyard at Olney, her family's farm on Old Joppa Road. During the 1910s Shriver served as a "special agent" for the Commerce Department and traveled throughout the world producing esoteric pamphlets with titles such as "Pineapple Canning Industry of the World." His wife and children remained at Olney and

> each month we'd get a new crate of porcelain and statuary—all sorts of surprises. It was wonderful. He was good about that but he was bad about remembering to leave any money with Mother. We had to live on what we raised and whatever credit shopkeepers would give us, all the while these gorgeous pieces of oriental art kept coming to us. It was just like that old song— how does it go?—"No money, but honey, Ain't we got fun!"[1]

During the first half of the twentieth century, Harford countians did indeed have fun huntin', shootin', and fishin'—to say nothing of buildin' and gardenin'. These diversions, of course, had long been staples of the local scene. The breeding of blooded horses dates back to the colonial era, and a national publication commented in the 1890s that "fox hunting . . . [is] almost universal" at the head of the bay. Generations of sportsmen lurked behind duck blinds along the soggy Gunpowder and Bush river necks, drawn by the canvasback that came in sky-blackening numbers to feed on the wild celery and other grasses that flourished in the shoals of the upper bay. (The *New England Magazine* spoke the simple truth in 1899 when it described Harford as "the most celebrated ducking point in our land.")[2] Countians had been wielding trowels and pruning shears at least as long as

1. Mrs. C. B. Holden Rogers, conversation with author, June 11, 1987.

2. Wilson, "Southern County," 167.

165

they had been shouldering Purdey shotguns, and Harford's formal pleasure grounds can be documented back to the mid-eighteenth century, as is discussed in chapter 10.

For a variety of reasons, however, all these trends intensified and coalesced at about the time Special Agent Shriver intrepidly set forth on his various tours of duty. During the interval between the two world wars, men and women from throughout America suddenly "discovered" the county's rich soils and picturesque countryside and began buying farms. Many of these farms had become, by the Jazz Age, more than a little run down, but that changed as folks in Harford County busied themselves with the chip-chip-chip of repointing. The principal players, all highly individualistic, had little more in common than a shared cheery attitude toward life: of varied origins, some hailed from New York, some from Virginia; a few, like Shriver, were indigenous to Harford County. Bankers and writers, lawyers and artists, sportsmen and scholars, these members of the lost generation truly found themselves when they wandered into the sleepy land between the Susquehanna Flats and the Gunpowder Falls.

They had, of course, been preceded in regarding Harford as a place to pursue pleasure. After all, Thomas Symington created Indian Spring Farm in the 1860s and, thanks to James Breese, Oakington had been a required out-of-town stop for Ziegfeld Follies girls since 1905. But the 1920s and '30s country houses differed from those of previous generations in several important respects, most important, perhaps, their builders' longing for simplicity. "There are no rooms not in every day use, there is no ornament . . . and the fundamental expression—for which even the parvenu learns to strive—is that of unpretentious decency and comfort," wrote Fiske Kimball, pioneering scholar on the architecture of Thomas Jefferson and director of the Philadelphia Museum of Art, in his landmark 1919 essay, "The American Country House."[3] Kimball also argued that "modern" country house architecture was a product of "the great wave of renewed love of out-of-door life" and from Bar Harbor to Marin County post–World War I country house architects aggressively demonstrated their clients' "fondness for out-of-door sports . . . [and] gardening."

Architects in Kimball's time also winced at their predecessors' wholesale and free-handed stylistic borrowing ("such . . . experiments as the Pompeian house at Saratoga") and, instead, began "the conscious revival or perpetuation of local traditions of style, materials, and workmanship." The very best architects, Kimball felt, studied a geographically small area, mastered its design characteristics, and then built totally within that local idiom.[4] "One theme emerged to dominate the 1920s country house: regionalism," wrote one modern critic, and discerning architects and clients alike agreed that each new country house should "fit its setting" and "reflect the best cultural traditions of its locality."[5]

Oakington, the New Deal, and Local History

In Harford all these themes crystallized dramatically in 1935 when Sen. and Mrs. Millard Tydings bought Oakington. The "tall, attractive, [and] sandy-haired" Tydings, a self-made man in the best American tradition, and his blue-blooded dynamo of a wife, née Eleanor Davies, blew into the county and brought with them a New Deal fresh breeze of gale-force strength.[6] They tossed out the spittoons and ferns and books on flagellation they found in the bayfront mansion (see chapter 7), brushed the ormoulued Sèvres off the entrance hall mantel, and banished generations' worth of Olde English furniture and Roman sarcophagi (all of doubtful authenticity) to storage sheds. In place of those dust-catchers came contemporary works of art (including a superb Russian constructivist painting Molotov presented to Eleanor Tydings), pastel portraits of Mrs. Tydings's two children, and authentic American antiques, including a grandfather's clock that had belonged to the senator's ancestor, War of 1812 hero John O'Neill.[7] "A tall, lean, muscular man" whose "favorite recreations are athletic,"[8] the vital senator simply had no interest in living in the pompous past: he and his Vassar-graduate wife much preferred to shape

3. Fiske Kimball, "The American Country House," *Architectural Record* 46 (October 1919): 397–99.

4. Among the most admired regionalists one finds William Lawrence Bottomley, a New York architect who arguably achieved his greatest country house triumphs in and around Richmond. He often deplored the earlier generation's houses that were "Italian, French, Japanese, anything! In this century, fortunately, we have come to realize the value—in fact the necessity—of a suitable artistic form for our American house." William Lawrence Bottomley, "The American Country House," *Architectural Record* (October 1920): 341.

5. Clive Aslet, *The American Country House* (New Haven: Yale University Press, 1990), 31; Bottomley, "American Country House," 344.

6. Jay, ed., *Havre de Grace*, 156.

7. Mrs. Tydings's father, diplomat Joseph Davies, was ambassador to the Soviet Union in the 1930s. Mrs. Tydings's first marriage, to the alcoholic Thomas Cheesborough, proved unhappy. She divorced him and married Senator Tydings, who adopted the two children she had had with Cheesborough. Caroline H. Keith, *"For Hell and a Brown Mule"* (New York: Madison Books, 1991), 280–81.

8. Anna Rothe, ed., *Current Biography, 1945* (New York: H. W. Wilson Co., 1945), 635.

When Sen. and Mrs. Millard Tydings bought Oakington in 1935, the energetic couple, who had no use for the previous generation's clutter, replaced the ornate bric-a-brac they found in the house with pastel portraits of Mrs. Tydings's children and with American antiques, such as the tallcase clock (shown here) that had belonged to the senator's ancestor, War of 1812 hero John O'Neill.

the exciting present and did so at the very highest levels. In the early 1930s, Tydings was FDR's man on Capitol Hill and was given the honor of making the seconding speech when Roosevelt was renominated in 1936. Once the campaign actually began, the new chatelaine of Oakington organized Harford County's first Democratic Women's Club, made a pro-Roosevelt rally at Oakington the club's principal order of business, and personally "rounded up every chair from every undertaker in Havre de Grace, Aberdeen, and Bel Air" to handle the 2,000 women (and smuggled-in men) who flocked to Oakington to attend the event held in a garden known thenceforth as "Democrat Grove."[9]

The Tydingses' work at Oakington accurately implies a booming interest in local history. This interest had, actually, surfaced as far back as 1885, when citizens established the Historical Society of Harford County, the first county historical society in the state and among the first in the nation. Society members set forth a virtual flood of still-valid articles and books on Harford's past, including Dr. W. Stump Forwood's *Ægis* series "Homes on Deer Creek" (1879–80), A. P. Silver's "History of Lapidum" (1888), the Reverend T. T. Wysong's pamphlet on "The Rocks of Deer Creek" (1880), and Judge Walter Preston's comprehensive *History of Harford County* (1901).

This interest grew after World War I. Local authors brought forth such important works as Samuel Mason's *Historical Sketches of Harford County* (1940) and Celia Mitchell's *Historical and Industrial Edition of the Ægis* (1930). Others, who took a somewhat broad-

9. For all quotes: Eleanor Davies Tydings Ditzen, conversation with author, December 10, 1991.

Encouraged by such local luminaries as Alexis Shriver and Gilman Paul, teams with the Historic American Buildings Survey (a WPA program begun in 1933) began photographing and drawing Harford's finest structures, including Deerfield (Wakefield) near Glenville, shown here in 1936. Thomas and Constance Hall Proctor, who bought the house the following year, restored it to its c. 1805 appearance.

er focus, produced a spate of books and articles on Chesapeake-area colonial architecture. Nevertheless, most of those larger-scale works do Harford's treasures proud: Swepson Earle's *Chesapeake Bay Country* (1923), for instance, includes descriptions and photographs of Sophia's Dairy, Spesutia Church, Sion Hill, and Cokesbury College, and the first of Chandlee Forman's many books, *Early Manor and Plantation Houses of Maryland* (1934), contains write-ups of Broom's Bloom, Sophia's Dairy, Deer Park, and Priest Neale's Mass House. And while it is hard to disentangle cause from effect, the advent of Maryland's first house museums, Annapolis's Hammond-Harwood House and Chase-Lloyd House, which opened their doors to a paying public during the 1920s and '30s, would seem more than coincidental, as would the Federated Garden Clubs of Maryland's first annual House and Garden Pilgrimage, which took place in 1930. Countians Gilman Paul and Harriet Shriver—Mrs. Alexis—served on the initial tour committees and saw to it that the 1930 itinerary included Olney, Box Hill, Mount Pleasant, and Sion Hill; in 1931 those stops were joined by Jerusalem Mill, Woodside, the Little Falls Meetinghouse, Tudor Hall, Monmouth Farm, Oakington, and the Rigbie House.

The museum world kept pace. Urged on by such Harford figures as Gilman Paul, the Baltimore Museum of Art acquired its first complete period room in 1925 and "when the new Museum building opened on Art Museum Drive in 1929, half the building's main floor was dedicated as 'The Maryland Wing.'"[10] Museum staff began saving elements from demolished buildings, too, including the c. 1750 stairway from the Dallam house Fanny's Inheritance, which arrived at the museum through the combined efforts of the J. Smith Michael family (who removed the stair when the federal government demolished the house) and Gilman Paul, who encouraged the Michaels to offer it and encouraged the museum to accept it.

Appreciation of the architecture of the past received federal sanction in 1933 when Tydings and his fellow senators voted to fund the Historic American Buildings Survey, or HABS. HABS-sponsored teams of architects and historians proceeded to comb the nation seeking and recording the finest houses, churches, and industrial buildings from the seventeenth, eighteenth, and nineteenth centuries. Harford proved a popular early destination for these scholars and, assisted by such local luminaries as historian George Van

10. Arnold Lehman, in William Voss Elder III and Jayne E. Stokes, *American Furniture, 1680–1880* (Baltimore: Baltimore Museum of Art, 1987), 7.

Bibber, Baltimore architects Laurence Hall Fowler and Lawrence Ewald, and the omnipresent Gilman Paul and Alexis Shriver, HABS teams immortalized dozens of county structures—1936 alone produced photographs and write-ups of Joshua's Meadows, Deerfield (Wakefield), Land of Promise, the Rigbie House, Bon Air, Sophia's Dairy, and the Rumsey House. In a parallel move, the American Institute of Architects established its own national historic buildings committee at about the same time, with Edward Donn, a close friend of Alexis Shriver, as vice-chairman.

While HABS, first staffed "by a handful of public servants in a burst of idealism and energy," seems a quintessential 1930s venture, it was not, by any means, the county's only New Deal project.[11] Churchville's Russell Lord, a founding staff writer with the *New Yorker* and author of such "proto-green" books as *The Agrarian Revival, The Wallaces of Iowa, Behold Our Land,* and *Men of Earth,* felt the lure of public service so compelling that he took a leave of absence from his typewriter and accepted appointment to the boards of a host of nascent New Deal projects, including the WPA Soil Conservation Service, the U.S. Forest Service, the Bureau of Agricultural Economics, the Commodity Credit Corporation, the Tennessee Valley Authority, and the Agriculture Extension Service. Lord caught the heady excitement of the times in his autobiography, *Forever the Land:*

> The early New Deal Days . . . were of somewhat fantastic excesses. . . . Many of the most intelligent, ardent, and amusing people that you used to know in New York . . . now popped up in Washington. The Capital City was suddenly full of eager-faced technicians and academicians with lean bodies and no bellies, running around hatless, acting rather breathlessly mysterious and important, calling one another and the President by their first names. . . . But permanent or transient, they were young men having a good time and acting as if they were having a good time while trying to serve their country.[12]

In 1933 Lord and his artist wife, Kate, paid $3,500 for "an honestly built old house . . . [with] good lines" and twenty-two acres of land adjacent Priest Ford Road. A bit derelict, the early nineteenth-century dwelling "responded readily, within and without, to the ministrations of native carpenters, plumbers, masons, and painters, men who respected sound work and performed it cheerfully, and were never in too great a hurry." The Lords named the place Thorn Meadow and decided to make it "a word farm. Words—and pictures—will be the one commercial crop. These worn fields will rest in sod while we strive to add to the word surplus" and eventually the place "yielded five books . . . and a sufficient miscellany of magazine pieces and pictures so that we didn't have to worry too much about money most of the time."[13]

Those zealous New Dealers, however, could not restrict themselves to their own ivory tower and introduced electricity and land-use reform to central Harford County. They urged their neighbors to "become, in a general way . . . [a] more diversified and meadowy farming country . . . [with] established rotations, [and] a decent respect for grass and cover crops." To further field-test his reformist theories, Lord helped Charles Bryan restore the wornout soil and revitalize the ailing apple orchards at Bryan's historic Havre de Grace estate, Mount Pleasant. "The land was washed and wasted," Lord wrote, and as a cure, he encouraged Bryan to construct a series of terraces on the hillside (to lessen erosion) and to cover the terraces with straw, lime, and "manure from the Havre de Grace race track" (to replenish the soil). Mount Pleasant responded buoyantly to these ministrations and by 1938 Bryan's trees were yielding "larger crops with a higher proportion of top-grade fruit . . . that in point of yield and profit outdo many modern commercial plantings in the Pacific Northwest."[14]

The Squire of Olney

Yet, notwithstanding the monumental actions of the Tydingses and Lords, the local epicenter of the "Ain't we got fun" era was undoubtedly Olney's Alexis Shriver (1872–1951),

Alexis Shriver, hired by the U.S. Department of Commerce as a "special agent" to observe farming in Asia and Europe, used his tours of duty in the Far East to collect a remarkable collection of *objets* which he shipped back to his wife and children at Olney. He also filled Olney with woodwork saved when his wife's family's eighteenth-century Fells Point house was torn down around 1905. Some of that woodwork and a few of Shriver's Asian treasures are shown above.

11. Charles E. Peterson, "The Historic American Buildings Survey: Its Beginnings," *Historic America* (Washington, D.C.: Library of Congress, 1983), 7.

12. Russell Lord and Kate Lord, *Forever the Land* (New York: Harper and Brothers, 1950), 12.

13. Ibid., 11, 12.

14. Russell Lord, *Behold Our Land* (Boston: Houghton Mifflin, 1938), 130, 135, 136–37.

"Harford's greatest historian" and one of the most interesting characters to ever live in Harford County.[15] Whoever wrote the *Sun*'s obituary of Mr. Shriver had the wit to take Shriver's remark that Olney represented "the combined desire for permanence with the irresistible one for change" and make it a paradigm for Shriver himself, a man whose "ancient Maryland" roots made him naturally interested in "the history of the State, in particular . . . of Harford County" but who also possessed a "desire for change." That last quality led to his collecting objects ranging from elephant's tusks to Haitian hex dolls; it also led to a lifelong interest in science and technology. In 1905 Shriver organized Harford County's first telephone system (a purely local, private concern to serve him and his immediate neighbors) and around 1910 he built the county's first two electrical plants, one near Olney at Wheel, the other about two miles away at Lake Fanny. How he ever billed his customers—*if* he ever billed his customers—remains unknown. He also lectured farmers throughout the East on the blessings of electricity and quixotically founded the Towson and Cockeysville Electric Railway Company, "which used a rare type of car powered by a storage battery," according to the Baltimore *Sun*.[16] ("You can just bet it was rare," commented his daughter.) The rail line never really succeeded, but Shriver, undeterred, talked it up for decades.

An agriculture major at Cornell, Shriver concocted his own milking machine, co-founded the Maryland Horticultural Society, and studied and documented the gardens not only at Olney but at historic houses throughout the Baltimore area. (His highly important work for the Garrett family at Montebello and Evergreen is discussed in chapter 10.) He also used his agronomist training to convince the U.S. Commerce Department to hire him as a special agent to travel around the world studying agriculture and canning. Notwithstanding the *Sun*'s cheeky suggestion that Shriver designed these trips more to satisfy his own "craving for collecting" than to make serious studies of "the market for canned goods" the special agent dutifully filed his reports and the department actually used them to produce (ostensibly) informative pamphlets for the public, who could, thanks to Shriver, read about "Restaurant Life in China" and "The Papaya and Its Uses."

Shriver satisfied his love of history in equally diverse ways. A prolific author, his published works include full-length biographies of Harfordians Thomas Cresap (1936) and Dr. John Archer (1932), the nationally acclaimed *Lafayette in Harford County* (1931), and a mammoth, three-volume study of the *Routes and Houses Visited by George Washington on His Trips through Maryland* (1932), which Shriver produced in his role as chairman of the Commission for the Celebration of the 200th Anniversary of the Birth of George Washington. Thanks to his efforts the State Roads Commission began erecting those now-familiar silver and black historical markers throughout Maryland. The *Sun* deemed those markers Shriver's "most ambitious contribution to State history" and noted that he "personally superintended most of the work."[17] Through his efforts there are over forty such markers in Harford County alone, with the first clutch appearing in 1930 along the Old Post Road and at the Jerusalem Mill.

He also organized the American Friends of Lafayette and served as Maryland's general advisor to the Historic American Buildings Survey, Corresponding Secretary of the Maryland Historical Society, and, to figure how to mark the 125th anniversary of the bombardment of Fort McHenry, as a vocal member of the 1939 Star Spangled Banner Committee. The individualistic Shriver did not, however, thrive at committee work. Shortly after Gov. Albert C. Ritchie appointed him general director of the Maryland Tercentenary Commission (and also asked him, "if it is not too demeaning," to head the committee to prepare a Maryland exhibit at the 1932 Chicago World's Fair)[18] Shriver and the governor had a falling out over finances and the Harford countian testily resigned from both projects.

Possibly to erase the horrors of committee meetings Shriver immersed himself in the history of Olney, the c. 1810 brick house and 264-acre farm he had inherited from his father in 1898. He also proceeded to transform it into a veritable museum of American art

15. Wright, *Harford,* 433.

16. He coined his own advertising phrase, "Lead the Electrical Life." Shriver obituary, *Baltimore Sun,* February 7, 1951.

17. *Baltimore Sun,* February 8, 1951; the same paper had earlier (January 14, 1934) pointed out that the system of highway markers was begun in 1932 by Shriver—"started chiefly by his energy and in numerous cases at his private expense."

18. All material in Alexis Shriver files in HSHC archives.

and architecture. Aided and abetted by architect Edward Donn, a boon companion since their undergraduate days together in Ithaca,[19] Shriver salvaged architectural bits from some of the region's finest buildings, hauled them to Harford, and incorporated them into the fabric of Olney. The first of these projects (which the *Sun* bemusedly called his "debonair decorative schemes")[20] involved treasures from a brace of old family houses in Baltimore City, that is, doors, chairrails, and other woodwork saved when the late eighteenth-century Van Bibber residence at 1621 Thames Street was demolished in 1904 (Shriver's wife was born Harriet Lewis Van Bibber), and huge built-in mahogany bookcases he removed when wrecking crews advanced on his own parents' townhouse at 518 Cathedral Street.

Emboldened by these initial successes, Shriver grew more ambitious. When Baltimore's Athenaeum Club closed around 1910 and another wrecking crew arrived on another scene, he was ready. The Athenaeum, a building of "the greatest taste and elegance" and located at the corner of Charles and Franklin streets, was built around 1830 to the design of William Small (1798–1832), "the first Baltimorean to be professionally trained as an architect."[21] All agreed that the Athenaeum's most striking feature was the building's monumental, four-column entrance portico. Shriver drove into Baltimore and had, as he phrased it, "a talk with a vandal who is destroying the building." This "brings forth the information that the marble portico [will] probably be broken into paving stones," but Shriver managed to convince the crew foreman to let him haul the columns to Olney.[22]

While it was one thing to secure ownership of four, thirty-foot-tall, marble Ionic columns, it was quite another to figure out how to transport them twenty-five miles to Olney. The columns had been sculpted at their Cockeysville quarry as eighteen-ton monoliths. In 1830 workmen loaded the first monolith onto a wagon for the trip into town. "Alas!" wrote Shriver, that "weighty shaft of beauty cut so deeply into the surface of the highways and made such frightful ruts and holes that a city ordinance was quickly passed prohibiting the repetition of such havoc." Accordingly, workmen cut the second column in half. But those nine-ton pieces simply "reopened the recently made ruts" and led to "a further protest by the City Fathers." Thus the third and fourth columns were cut in thirds and they then made the trip to Baltimore quietly and without further damage to the highways. History repeated itself when it became Shriver's turn to try to move "the monolith and its amputated sisters." The columns managed to arrive in Harford County without incident (thanks to two flatbed railroad cars), but when "twelve horses and a special wagon train" hauled them "from the country railroad station to their final destination" they once again sparked "the ire of the countryside by cutting in the country roads ruts as deep as those of 1830." Eventually, and "after various vicissitudes, heartburnings and delays," Shriver and Donn managed to raise the columns and incorporate them into Olney's garden façade.[23]

"Some people never learn, even by experience," Shriver wrote. "The rearrangement of doors, windows, [and] boxwood walks . . . to make place for the portico should have been sufficient to close the book" on his remodeling work at Olney. But in the early '20s, while in the midst of freelance historical research for the Philadelphia Electric Company (pursuant to the Conowingo Dam project), Shriver learned that "the original, carved marble doorhead made in 1795 for Robert Morris' Folly" in Philadelphia was available for the asking: this set his historian's antennae quivering and "all past difficulties were forgotten."[24] Here, in fact, was a real gem, for the doorhead had been designed by Pierre Charles L'Enfant in the midst of his main project, laying out the new city of Washington, D.C.

Morris, the Financier of the Revolution, one of the richest men in America, and in-law of the Sophia's Dairy Hall clan, asked L'Enfant to design "the finest private residence . . . in America"[25] and budgeted the immense sum of $60,000 for the project. L'Enfant, whose genius lay in designing cities, not buildings, gave the financier a block-long brick

19. Donn was the perfect choice, for as Shriver wrote, the architect had been responsible for "the rebuilding of Wakefield, the birthplace of George Washington, the restoration of Kenmore . . . at Fredericksburg, and . . . the Octagon House in Washington." Alexis Shriver, "The History of Old Olney" (Baltimore: Waverly Press, 1928), 7. Donn, something of a scholar himself, wrote the book *Monumental Work of the Georgian Period.*

20. *Baltimore Sun,* February 8, 1951.

21. During his brief career, Small produced such glories as the Archbishop's Residence (1829), the McKim Free School (1833), and Barnum's City Hotel (1825), a hostelry Frances Trollope (mother of Anthony) deemed "the most splendid in the Union." Raphael Semmes, *Baltimore as Seen by Visitors,* 1783–1860 (Baltimore: MHS, 1953), 98–99; Dorsey and Dilts, *Guide to Baltimore Architecture,* xxv; Frances Trollope, *Domestic Manners of the Americans* (1839; rpt., London: Century Publishing, 1984), 179.

22. Shriver, "History of Old Olney," 9.

23. Ibid., 8, 9.

24. Ibid.

25. One wonders if Shriver had seen Benjamin Latrobe's scathing attack on the Morris mansion. Note the April 26, 1798, entry in the great architect's *Virginia Journal:* "Among the buildings of Philadelphia, I did not mention the house of Robert Morris, because I knew not what to say about it in order to record the appearance of the monster in a few words. Indeed, I can scarcely at this moment believe in the existence of what I have seen many times, of its complicated, unintelligible mass. . . . Mr. L'enfans [*sic*], the architect never exhibited his drawings to any but Mr. Morris. . . . The external dimensions of the house are very large. I suppose the front must be at least 120 feet long, and I think the flank cannot be less than 60. . . . I went several times to the spot and gazed upon it with astonishment. . . . It is impossible to decide which of the two is the maddest, the architect or his employer." See Edward C. Carter II, ed., *The Virginia Journals of Benjamin Henry Latrobe,* vol. 2 (New Haven: Yale University Press, 1977), 376–78.

Around 1910 Baltimore's Athenaeum Club (1830) was torn down. Alexis Shriver saved the club's four marble columns, had them hauled to Olney, and re-erected them on Olney's garden façade. (Above, the garden façade, c. 1905; below in 1936 with Shriver's daughter, the late Harriet Shriver Howard Rogers, her two children, Frances and William, and an unidentified playmate.)

26. Shriver, "History of Old Olney," 11. The other doorhead was removed to Magnolia Gardens, near Charleston, S.C. Rogers, conversation with author.

box, with only a few well-positioned marble plaques to relieve the hulking bulk. By all accounts the finest of these plaques were two bas-relief allegorical doorheads on which cloud-born putti represent "Art and Literature" and "Music and Dancing." Work on the mansion progressed slowly and was halted altogether when Morris found himself tossed into debtor's prison. (One suspects that Shriver, a hit-or-miss bookkeeper himself, felt for Morris.) Creditors then sold the uncompleted shell to William Sansom, who demolished it and "proceeded to open a street named after himself through the middle of the property." The doorheads wound up in Conshohocken, a Philadelphia suburb, embedded in the wall of a house that was itself torn down in 1926. Thrilled to the bone, Shriver managed to salvage "Art and Literature" and used it to crown the door on Olney's newly columned garden façade.[26]

Renewed Stirrings in the Deer Creek Valley

Shriver and Tydings were native-born but the county's rollicking "Ain't we got fun" spirit also attracted a large group of men and women who had made (or inherited) their riches elsewhere and who flocked to Harford to kick their shoes off and relax. In a way this repeats the actions of D. C. Wharton Smith, Hugh Judge Jewett, and other rich-rich who moved to the Deer Creek Valley from Philadelphia, New York, and other centers of commerce in the 1870s and '80s. Significantly, and as is discussed in chapter 6, when those

Victorian-era plutocrats hired architect Walter Cope to design new houses in and around Darlington, they emphasized that their new buildings must fit into—not impose themselves onto—their adopted community. This marked the beginning of what architects now call "contextualism." And if Cope and his discerning clients were the first to stress regionalism in design, the trend was brought to maturity, according to Fiske Kimball, "in late years by Messers Mellor and Meigs," architects whose "comfortable . . . and liveable" houses were always designed with a concern for "close conformity with local precedent": just observe the firm's work for Philadelphians Francis and Lelia Stokes at Wilson's Mill on Deer Creek.[27]

The Stokeses and their architects bravely took on a job of paramount importance, for Wilson's Mill has, since the eighteenth century, formed the heart of the entire Deer Creek Valley: it has been owned by all the key players in the valley's history and in many ways synthesizes that history. Mellor & Meigs must have sensed this, because what they gave the Stokeses is nothing short of a masterpiece. But, then, the firm had been producing masterpieces for decades. Then, too, one must credit the Stokeses for selecting, perhaps, *the* American design firm best suited to the project: a 1916 story on the "Works of Mellor & Meigs" notes that the adjectives "informal, comfortable, well mannered, interesting, [and] sincere . . . epitomize" the architects, and those very adjectives have been used to describe the Deer Creek Valley for generations. Indeed, every one of the many articles and monographs on the firm has emphasized the same points: concern for local traditions, exquisite handling of local materials, in short, a desire to fit in. Or, as novelist Owen Wister and architect Paul Cret observe in their *Monograph of the Work of Mellor, Meigs, & Howe,* if one seeks an antidote to modern architecture ("a host of warts, large lumps, [and] long welts") one need only look to the buildings of Mellor & Meigs to see how "to keep the expiring spark of beauty alive and clothe our domestic moments with some form of grace."[28]

Meigs and Mellor altered and enlarged the mill property's c. 1856 main house and c. 1809 tenant house. They also converted the ancient gristmill to hydroelectricity (which generated current to power the farm), added a new four-car garage, a chicken coop, and a stone barn, and then, to tie it all together, created a seemingly simple system of courtyards and stone walls.[29] It seems safe to say that Mellor & Meigs's work at Wilson's Mill sums up the best of the era's revival thinking, whether Georgian revival, colonial revival, or, as at the mill, *vernacular* revival. The Wilson's Mill project isn't a recreation of any single existing structure, yet it embodies every important characteristic of Deer Creek Valley architecture. Nothing is a sham; nothing seems contrived; everything, instead, seems natural, even inevitable.

Dozens of other sophisticated rustics, some from within Harford County, some from without, quickly joined the Stokeses' campaign to buy and restore old houses in the valley. The William Silvers and the Harry Muller-Thyms spruced up dwellings in the hamlet of Glenville; the Edward C. Wilsons hired Baltimore architect Lawrence Ewald to remodel an old Coale house located between Glenville and the Stokes property; the mid-nineteenth-century stone Windmill Hill benefited from a sequence of restoration-minded owners including Mr. and Mrs. James Whitall and Mr. and Mrs. Peter Jay; and when diplomat J. Gilman D'Arcy Paul returned to America flush from a brilliant career with the State Department (first as a member of the American delegation at the Versailles conference that ended World War I and later at ambassadorial postings in Rio, Paris, and The Hague) the entire county benefited. Or, more accurately, the entire *state* benefited. As president of the board of trustees of the Baltimore Museum of Art (an office he held from 1942 to 1956), he did much to give that institution's American Wing its present nationwide reputation for excellence. As a vice-president of the Maryland Historical Society,[30] he contributed book reviews to the society's *Maryland Historical Magazine* on topics ranging from "Autographs: A Key to Collecting" to "Fifty Years in a Kitchen" to "Thomas Jefferson's Garden Book." Public-spirited always, toward the close of his life

Architects Mellor and Meigs doubled the size of the old house at Wilson's Mill for Francis and Lelia Stokes (the house is shown in the center with its new two-story porch), designed stables and garages for the property, and then tied the whole together with an ingenious system of paths and stone walls.

27. Kimball, "Country House," 338–40; Harold D. Eberlin, "Examples of the Work of Mellor & Meigs," *Architectural Record* (March 1916): 213.

28. Owen Wister, preface to *A Monograph of the Work of Mellor, Meigs & Howe* (New York: Architectural Book Publishing, 1923), 98.

29. Mellor and Meigs were good at this: in the 1920s they created a compound for Mrs. Arthur Meigs at Radnor, Pa., and found room for "a chicken yard, paddock, potager or formal vegetable garden, nursery, orchard, and various garden buildings" all on twenty-three acres. See Aslet, *American Country House,* 22.

30. Paul also served as a trustee of the Johns Hopkins University and on the board of the Peabody Institute.

In the 1950s retired diplomat Gilman Paul, assisted by Baltimore architect Laurence Hall Fowler, restored and remodeled the c. 1800 stone house Land of Promise near Rock Run. The property now contains the Steppingstone Museum.

31. James Wollon, AIA, notes on Rock Run for HSHC 1982 house tour.

32. Michael Chrismer, "Deerfield," *Ægis,* July 20, 1961.

33. Commissions 1928/11 and 1930/11. Fowler's *Journal II,* preserved at Evergreen House, notes that he received $175 in May 1937 from Paul for "sketches for Harford County House" and a further $506 in September 1940 for "remodeling house at Earlton" for Paul. (See also commissions 1937/05 and 1940/08.)

34. Eloise H. Wilson, conversation with author, September 8, 1993.

Paul convinced the state government to acquire and restore the important Rock Run complex and incorporate it into the proposed Susquehanna State Park.[31]

Paul also bought and restored two of Harford's greatest architectural treasures. In 1936 he purchased the 1807 house Deerfield near Glenville and, aghast at the house's many late nineteenth-century accretions, began removing the most outrageous of them, while safeguarding the building's fine, original features. (He even refused the Metropolitan Museum of Art when officials from that institution approached him about taking the house's main stairway to New York.)[32] Working with architect Laurence Hall Fowler, who also did much work at the diplomat's town residence, 16 Blythewood Road, Paul built himself a small stone guesthouse near the main dwelling[33] before somewhat inexplicably selling Deerfield in 1937 to Thomas H. and Constance Hall Proctor, who completed the house's restoration. Paul then resumed his own search for the Perfect Place and finally found it on a hilly site overlooking the Susquehanna: the tract, appropriately called Land of Promise, contained a decayed late eighteenth-century stone house (the 1783 tax rolls show the land unimproved but the 1814 assessment shows it with "1 dwelling house, stone, 40 × 18, 2 stories") that virtually called out to be restored.

Paul heeded the call and, again working with Fowler, preserved the original fabric, while adding such additions as were necessary to make the ancient dwelling suitable to mid-twentieth-century high life. So although he tacked a modern kitchen wing onto the old dwelling, he did so in a way that kept the building's original simple lines intact. Similarly, he preserved and restored the folk paneling he found in the parlor while adding paneled window insets and other woodwork stylistically appropriate to it.

The *bon viveur* also turned his attention to the grounds and remade the acreage around the house so it suited his highly particular way of life. He lived principally in Baltimore and thought of his Harford property as a place for parties: "When he decided to visit the house," one friend recalled, "he would have his cook prepare an elaborate picnic hamper; the chauffeur then loaded Mr. Paul and the hamper onto the back seat of a big black limousine and drove out."[34] Paul discovered that his new house had a truly magnificent hilltop site, which rises to 300 feet above sea level and then immediately plunges down to the Susquehanna in a 30 percent grade. Federal-era taxmen viewed that drop as a troublesome liability (in 1814 they wrote that "one half of this land [is] rendered unfit for cultivation by rocks and steep hills"), but to Gilman Paul it was a picturesque asset for it provided a place where he and his guests could—and did—sit out with a drink in one hand and an hors-d'oeuvre in another and gaze northwards to Pennsylvania or southwards to the broad Chesapeake. As if to underscore the relaxed picturesqueness of it all, Paul planted dozens of hybrid rhododendrons and other free-flowering shrubs in informal clumps around the property. No matter that the specific varieties used are, technically, all wrong since they were introduced to Maryland long after the federal era, when the house was built. The point is they are beautiful and it is hard to overstate the importance Paul and his friends placed on romantic, pictorial effects.[35]

Tally-ho!

Although Paul and Shriver were seemingly men of all-encompassing interests, they did draw the line at horses. While the former "liked to look at horses" and while Shriver "kept some ponies" for his children to ride, both mens' "real interests lay elsewhere."[36] Many of their contemporaries' and neighbors' interests, however, *did* lay with the Thoroughbred—so many, in fact, that in the '20s and '30s Harford became a nationally known equestrian center. One thinks immediately of the Cornelius Blisses, who purchased the old Thomas Stump farm at the corner of Noble's Mill and Harmony Church roads, and B. Vaughn Flannery, a professional artist and advertising executive who bought the old Ellis Tucker farm in 1931, built himself a freestanding stone studio there, and began "illustrating horses for owners such as Calumet Farms."[37] One also thinks of Bel Air native Anne McElderry (Mrs. Robert) Heighe, who established a stable at the 180-acre former Hays farm near Shuck's Corner in 1928. She renamed the place Prospect Hill and, with her mares and stallions, proceeded to "influence breeding throughout the State."[38]

Recognized as "Maryland's leading lady of the turf," Mrs. Heighe inherited most of her fabulous racing stock when her aunt, Mrs. Herman Duryea, died. Around 1910 Mrs. Duryea, an heiress in her own right, transplanted herself from her native New York to Normandy where she established a stud and training farm. Her horses proceeded to win races from Rome to Vienna to Dublin and the green and white Duryea colors became forces to be reckoned with throughout the Continent. Mrs. Duryea's greatest moment came at the last prewar Derby on May 30, 1914, when her prize stallion, Durbar II, won an upset victory over the favorite, a horse owned by King George V. Papers throughout the Empire spread the shocking news: the London *Times* headlined its story "Doleful Derby" while the *Daily Mirror* called the finish "the greatest racing upset of the season." Even the French press—which ought to have relished the defeat of an English horse by one Norman-bred, if American-owned—devoted columns of ink to the *fait remarquable* at *Le Derby Diabolique*.[39]

On her aunt's death, Anne Heighe brought over "the creme of mares at the Haras du Gazon and installed them in Maryland." She also hired "the capable Fritz Boniface" to manage her new farm and the horses the two bred and trained enjoyed such enormous success on scores of American tracks that several of their records still stand, including the "six-furlong at Pimlico . . . and the six-furlong . . . at Golden State Park."[40] They triumphed on the international circuit, too, for Mrs. Heighe shipped her stallions, including "Tourbillon, . . . France's leading sire in 1940, 1942, and 1945," and mares to four continents to service, and be serviced by, the best stock available. The Heighes developed a unique way of marking their foreign successes: the couple kept several flags at their Harford County home, a stone manorhouse the couple built on a picturesque, steeply sloping seventeen-acre site washed by Bynum Run and adjoining Moores Mill and Southampton roads. When one of their horses won a particularly important race "at, say Pimlico, up would go the American or French or British flag," depending on the victor's place of birth.[41]

The "leading lady of the turf" wasn't the first member of the international horsey

35. Consider Paul's foreword to the 1930 House and Garden Pilgrimage booklet, in which he waxes nostalgic over Maryland's ancient, "gently melancholy" dwellings, with "the echo of vanished music, of the laughter of dead youth in the hallways and garden paths" and the "green gardens" themselves with "the family graveyard often rising beyond the billowing masses of box."

36. Rogers, conversation with author.

37. See Jean S. Ewing, Historic Sites Survey Form for E. Tucker House.

38. "Prospect Hill Sold," *Maryland Horse* (November 1950): 9. See also D. Sterett Gittings, *Maryland and the Thoroughbred* (Baltimore: Maryland Horse Breeders Assoc., 1932), 71–76.

39. Clippings in possession of Bradford Jacobs, Stevenson, Md.; there are equally shocked German and Austrian accounts, too; see also "Prospect Hill," *Maryland Horse* (December 1936): 6.

40. Heighe obituary in the *American Racing Manual* (1953). The Bonifaces represent another Maryland racing dynasty: William and Mary Louise Boniface established Bonita Farm near Creswell and their son, William—or "Billy"—was the trainer of the 1983 Preakness winner, Deputed Testamony, a stallion his parents had bred at Bonita.

41. *Maryland Horse* (August 1947); Jacobs, conversation with author, March 12, 1991.

community to settle on Harford. Nor is she today the best known, although she probably held that distinction in her lifetime. Today it is safe to say that more people recognize the name Harvey Ladew than Anne Heighe. While his present fame rests on his gardening prowess it is likely that he would have described himself as a horse-man first and a gardener second; thus while his horticultural triumphs are recounted in chapter 10, his equestrian successes—and the story of his beloved Elkridge-Harford Hunt Club—belong to this chapter.

Ladew, "a bachelor and a real devotee of foxhunting," bought his My Lady's Manor property in 1929 generally because he was so smitten with the whole area—"What a natural wonderful country I found in Harford," he wrote. "There were many nice farmers, who for the most part sympathized with fox-hunting and enjoyed it themselves. . . . The fields . . . were fenced with some posts and rails, and . . . there were still many snake fences to be seen. There was not a strand of wire anywhere"—and specifically because its acres bordered the Harford Hunt Club.[42] Organized in 1915 through the efforts of John Rush Streett and his brother-in-law, Frank Bonsal, the club generally focused its activities on the fields around Streett's own big, ramshackle farmhouse on Jarrettsville Pike. (The club purchased the house and 411 acres in 1927.) In 1934 the Harford club merged with the Elkridge Hunt, a venerable institution that Frederick Shriver had helped organize back in 1878. (Frederick's brother, Alexis, who preferred a library to a paddock, nonetheless did what he could to help out and began writing what he called "a monumental work—as comprehensive as I can make it" on the history of foxhunting in America.)[43] The Elkridge's riders originally convened at the foot of the Washington Monument in downtown Baltimore but that location quickly proved impractical (if colorful) and the club moved farther and farther into the countryside, and deeper and deeper into Harford County. They first tried the coverts around Bel Air (as "members usually spent the night . . . at the Kenmore Inn," then sporting a new, Fowler-designed sign board and railing), but the farms around the county seat did not prove "particularly good hunting country" and members looked east

When Elkridge Hunt Club riders pursued their quarry in the fields and coverts around Bel Air, they spent the night in the rambling Kenmore Inn. Demolished in the 1960s, the inn stood across Main Street from the Van Bibber House. The façade fronting Route 1 is shown here about 1940.

> to the country around the village of Churchville. . . . A number of large farms such as Cool Spring and Indian Spring farms of the Symington family, the Umbarger farm, Jewett farm, Mrs. Vogel's Westwood Manor farm, the Blackwell farm and Silver farm made a contiguous area of land owned by farmers friendly to hunting.[44]

Riders assembled for the first Churchville hunt on October 27, 1927. That gathering was so successful it soon became "the custom to rent the Jewett farm [Lansdowne on Harmony Church Road] and quarter the hounds and horses there for the August and early September cubbing season each year." To accommodate the riders, the Jewetts built "a small kennel . . . and 30 box stalls" (54, 55). One huntsman found the hills and valleys along Deer Creek "ideal for fox hunting . . . , as fine as any in the U.S.A." and accounts of hunts there do sound idyllic even to nonriders:

> Last Thursday was one of those beautiful, crisp fall days that make your blood tingle. . . . The mist in the valley makes the surrounding countryside look as if it was dotted by a million lakes. . . . We started from the Jewett farm, at quarter to six, and after a short hack we drew the Silver covert. A fox broke out and carried the hounds at a fair pace down . . . to Elbow run, where he went to ground. Almost at once they found a second fox . . . and this bold customer carried the pack over . . . lovely open country. . . . After an almost continuous run of two hours and forty minutes we were then at Lapidum . . . and all agreed it was the run of the season.[45]

The first meet of the new Elkridge-Harford Hunt Club was held on April 26, 1935, with Harvey Ladew MFH. Ladew, who took his duties as Master seriously, suffered greatly when the clubhouse—the remodeled Streett farmhouse—caught fire one April night of 1938, and, despite the work of "firemen from Jarrettsville, Towson, and Bel Air," burned to the ground. But after a brief pause to catch his breath, Ladew, assisted by "Miss Edna Parlett and . . . architect James O'Connor of New York," who had helped Ladew trans-

42. J. Reiman McIntosh, *A History of the Elkridge Fox Hunting Club, the Elkridge Hounds, the Elkridge-Harford Hunt*, 1878–1978 (hereafter McIntosh, *Elkridge*) (Monkton, Md.: Elkridge-Harford Hunt, 1978), 70, 47; Harvey Ladew, "Random Recollections" (Monkton, Md.: Ladew Topiary Gardens Foundation, 1980), 18; Harvey Ladew, "Maryland in the Pink," *Town and Country* (November 1940): 54–55.

43. Shriver, letter to J. B. van Urk March 21, 1940, in Shriver files, HSHC. Shriver also wrote van Urk, "I think you can get a photograph of the original Elkridge Hunting Club (of which my brother, now deceased, was the organizer) from Mr. Alexander Brown, 'Mondawmin.' . . . He gave a copy of these photographs to the Maryland Club at my request and he evidently has the original films."

44. McIntosh, *Elkridge*, 54.

45. Ibid., 55–62. The splendors of hunting along Deer Creek even attracted a reporter from the *Wall Street Journal*, and that paper ran his somewhat bemused account of the experience on November 21, 1931.

Members of the Elkridge-Harford Hunt at Harvey Ladew's Pleasant Valley Farm in the 1930s. The club dates to 1935 when the Elkridge and Harford hunts merged. Ladew was the first MFH.

form the house on Pleasant Valley Farm, designed and built a new—and highly successful—Georgian revival clubhouse.[46]

While the Elkridge-Harford is a private club, many of Harford's other horsey activities were open to the public—sometimes *way* open, as was the case at the much-loved race tracks at Havre de Grace and Bel Air. The half-mile track at Bel Air (laid out by George Graham Curtiss of the Oakland School) was a somewhat folksy operation, but the Havre de Grace track, which opened on August 24, 1912, drew a serious clientele from throughout the East. (Both the B&O and Pennsylvania railroads ran special trains to the races from New York, Philadelphia, and Baltimore.) The caliber of horseflesh ran high, too, and "old horsemen who remember it say it was probably the best in the country." Man-O-War raced—and won—at Havre de Grace in 1920; Citation raced there three times, twice in his Triple Crown year, 1948; Sir Barton, another Triple Crown winner, won at Havre de Grace, as did War Admiral and Seabiscuit. Neither track is active today. The Bel Air track closed quietly in the early 1960s, to be replaced by the Harford Mall. The 1950 closing of the Havre de Grace course, on the other hand, was a highly colorful event involving financial flimflam and conflicts of interest "as naked as to appear, by the ethical standards generally demanded of public officials in the 1980s, quite extraordinary."[47]

When Citation ran in Havre de Grace in 1948, he lost once, to Saggy, a horse that was eventually put out to stud at "the oldest family-owned breeding farm in Maryland," Country Life Farm,[48] near Bel Air. Adolphe Pons, "a small, stocky man, always nattily presented, with a stylish mustache and a precise and colorful mode of expression," bought the rolling spread in 1933.[49] His eye for horseflesh and memory for bloodlines made him among the handful of top breeders in his day and in his pre–Country Life life he built New Yorker August Belmont's vast equestrian empire, engineered Belmont's purchase of Man-O-War, and also managed Thoroughbred operations for the likes of Averell Harriman, George Herbert Walker (grandfather of George Herbert Walker Bush), Fred Astaire, the Aga Kahn, Bing Crosby, and Paul Mellon. He also helped Alfred Gwynne Vanderbilt establish Sagamore Farm in Baltimore County's Worthington Valley.

Vanderbilt, who moved to Maryland at least partially due to the urging of Anne Heighe, injected enormous élan into the local scene, bringing in horses and people who

46. See ibid., 62, 73–74; *Harford County Directory* (1953), 305; *Baltimore Sun* of April 9, 1938, noted "within a few minutes after the sounding of the alarm, dozens of persons from surrounding estates were dragging furniture and valuable hunting prints . . . from the building."

47. Jay, ed., *Havre de Grace*, 89, 92, 93–95.

48. Ben Keenan, "Equestrian Enthusiasts Aren't Horsing Around," *Sunday Weekly*, August 26, 1990, 4. While at Country Life, Saggy sired (*inter alia*) Carry Back, a Kentucky Derby winner.

49. Josh Pons, *Country Life Diary* (Lexington, Ky.: Blood-Horse, 1992), ix; see also 360–61, 380, 415. Josh Pons is a grandson of Adolphe Pons.

"Ain't we got fun!"

changed forever the way Freestaters looked at racing. But one wonders if even he was prepared for the career one of his imports forged for himself in Maryland. In fact, even Vanderbilt's great-grandfather Cornelius, who bare-knuckled his way to mastership of the New York Central Railroad, might have given pause when, according to the *Evening Sun's* racing editor, William Boniface, "Alfred Gwynne Vanderbilt . . . encouraged Larry to get into the breeding game"—"Larry" being none other than Leland Stanford MacPhail.

It certainly must have seemed logical enough. Possibly even harmless. MacPhail was the boss of the Brooklyn Dodgers and "in the late thirties and early forties Vanderbilt was an ardent follower of the [team]. . . . Larry went to the races with Al in the afternoon and the latter returned the visit to the ball park in the evenings." Moreover, MacPhail had been publicly talking about rusticating at least as far back as 1941 when the *New Yorker* reported that "he is planning to give up baseball and retire to a soothing life in the country." (The magazine cited MacPhail's love of wrens as a contributing factor: "I'd like to go . . . sit on my front porch and listen to them chirp," he is alleged to have said. "Finest god-damn music on earth.") According to the *Evening Sun* MacPhail signed a contract renewal with the Dodgers in 1942 "and, with practically the same dip of ink, penned his name to a contract purchasing a run down farm in Maryland's fertile Harford County." While MacPhail actually bought the farm in 1941, the *Sun's* version does make a better story.[50]

And no one loved a good story—preferably one in which he held center stage—than Larry MacPhail, whom *Maryland Horse* publisher Snowden Carter described as always being "in the throes of one of life's most exciting chapters." MacPhail added a decade and a half to his biblically allotted three-score years and ten, but even eighty-five summers seems far, far too brief a time for anyone to accomplish all that he accomplished. Simply put, he single-handedly pushed professional baseball into the twentieth century, or as Red Barber phrased it, "MacPhail and Branch Rickey between them brought big-league baseball out of the horse-and-buggy days and into modern times. Take away the achievements of these two men and there wouldn't be any baseball as we know it."[51] MacPhail introduced the batting helmet, night games, and crowd-pleasing postgame hoopla, masterminded the first radio and TV game broadcasts, daringly pioneered air travel as a means of getting his team from game to game, instituted the nation's first baseball season-ticket plans, fought to integrate the sport, and anticipated the era of free-agency by buying and trading players in a "cost be damned" manner. He also sequentially piloted the Cincinnati Reds, Brooklyn Dodgers, and New York Yankees to champion seasons. He cut a wide swath away from the diamond, too; shortly after he took up horse breeding, his yearlings established world-record prices when they were sold at Saratoga in 1956 and, as the *New Yorker* noted, "It is probably safe to say that Larry MacPhail . . . is the only man in baseball who ever tried to kidnap a European monarch."[52]

MacPhail was born in Cass City, Michigan, in 1890, a grandson of Scots immigrants who (he said) before coming to America had lived next door to Robert Burns. But, "whereas the Burnses turned out to be dreamy, improvident souls who concerned themselves with daisies and field mice, the MacPhails had a knack for hardheaded finance" and MacPhail's father put together a midwestern banking empire. World War I broke out and, anticipating American involvement, MacPhail and a friend, U.S. senator "Colonel" Luke Lea of Tennessee, organized their own volunteer regiment and fought commendably on the Western front. They gained immortality, however, a few days after the Armistice when MacPhail and Lea decided the kaiser needed kidnapping. Accordingly, armed with several bottles of wine and a phony passport with Queen Wilhelmina's forged signature, on New Year's Day 1919 they and six enlisted men drove two cars into Holland, where Kaiser Wilhelm was staying in a château under a sort of house arrest. "Pausing frequently at roadside inns, they became increasingly certain of success," so when they arrived at the château, they nonchalantly strode inside. Reports of approaching Dutch troops nonplused the Americans, who ran back to their cars but "on the way out, MacPhail swept

The Bel Air racetrack about 1950; now the site of the Harford Mall.

50. Jacobs, conversation with author; William Boniface, "The MacPhail Story," *Baltimore Evening Sun*, September 24, 1956; Robert Lewis Taylor, "Borough Defender," *New Yorker*, July 12 and 19, 1941; deed GRG 267/435.

51. Snowden Carter, "Glenangus Mares," *Maryland Horse* (March 1948): 34; Red Barber, *The Broadcasters* (New York: Da Capo Press, 1970), 125.

52. The first night game was played on May 24, 1935; MacPhail's Reds beat the Phillies, 2-1. Taylor, "Borough Defender," July 19, 1941.

his trench coat over a table and scooped up an ornate ashtray with a bronze dog built into it." They leaped into the cars and sped off amid whistling bullets. Lea had the "passport" in his car, but MacPhail had MacPhail in his, so when that vehicle got to the border he "turned off [the] lights, got up a satisfactory speed, and carried a large barricade back into Belgium with him."[53]

After the war, MacPhail returned to the Midwest and dabbled in several ventures. Nothing really clicked until 1930, when he paid $100,000 for the AA baseball team in Columbus, Ohio. "It was when MacPhail became a baseball magnate that he really began to find himself. . . . Once free of the taint of law and commerce, his personality unfolded like a morning glory." He sold the team to Branch Rickey, moved himself to the Cincinnati Reds in 1933, and sportswriters uniformly credit him with "Cincinnati's subsequent climbing from bottom place to win the World Series."[54] At Cincinnati, he arranged for the first-ever live radio broadcast of a game (and brought in an unknown named Red Barber to do the play-by-play); he also oversaw the major league's first night game. Notwithstanding these successes, however, MacPhail didn't find his true, spiritual home, Ebbets Field, until he assumed control of the Brooklyn Dodgers in 1938.

He certainly had his work cut out for him: the Dodgers had finished the '37 season in last place, and the dispirited athletes routinely "threw the ball in the wrong direction, took naps in the outfield, and tried to pass each other while running bases." That, however, didn't last long, for now, as Red Barber recalled, "they had MacPhail. They had nothing else when he got there, but they had him, and he was the best."[55]

In his first year at the helm, MacPhail shook up the Dodger front office, bought and sold players with cagey abandon (once spending the shocking sum of $50,000 for a first baseman), purchased six minor-league teams, and hired Leo Durocher as manager.[56] The next season he arranged for the nation's first televised games (over the vehement protests of the Yankees and Giants) and brought Barber to New York from Cincinnati to do the broadcasting.[57] Fearing that TV and radio might cut into gate receipts, MacPhail organized postgame fireworks displays and other fan-pleasers such as a series of foot-races between Jesse Owens and various Dodger players to keep the turnstile busy. "An absolute genius in the art of public relations," during one spring training MacPhail unaccountably "became convinced that the Dodgers needed red meat to make them strong" and rather than buying the meat in Florida he "ordered four hundred sirloin steaks in New York and had them flown down in a plane. . . . Short of having [the players] roam the scrub with blowguns, he arranged for them to get [red meat] in the most spectacular way he could think of."[58] It all worked out well. Although MacPhail created "more havoc . . . than any man who was ever involved with baseball," he was also, as Barber observed, "the shrewdest executive in the history of the game," and his Dodgers climbed to third place in 1939, to second in 1940, and clinched the pennant in 1941, their first first-place finish since 1920.[59]

And although no one ever called MacPhail a flaming liberal, he did—rather tried to—integrate the game. In 1940 he declared he had "no use for the color line. I'd jump at the chance to sit down with anyone and see what could be worked out." Acting on his own, he met "with civic leaders, Negro and white, to discuss the matter" but then Pearl Harbor brought America into World War II, and MacPhail "went off to war" before anything could be resolved.[60] He turned the Dodgers over to Branch Rickey (who in 1947 did breach the "color line"), volunteered for duty, and, with the rank of colonel was made assistant to Robert Patterson, undersecretary of war, as "trouble shooter for miscellaneous generals."[61] In typical fashion, he popped up from Algiers, where he had to cope with de Gaulle (and vice-versa), to the Vatican, where he had to apologize to the pope because Allied bombs damaged some of His Holiness's buildings.[62]

In 1945 MacPhail reiterated his plans to retire from baseball and rusticate in Maryland. But then, as he explained to the *Sunpapers'* William Boniface, he "stumbled . . . upon an opportunity to purchase the Yankees for $3,000,000." That was too good to pass

53. See also John Dorsey, "The Lives of Larry MacPhail," *Baltimore Sunday Sun Magazine,* November 27, 1966. Taylor, "Borough Defender," July 19, 1941. The ashtray, and the story, stayed with MacPhail the rest of his life; the author, as a ten-year-old, frequently gazed on the former and listened, entranced, to the latter.

54. Taylor, "Borough Defender," July 12, 1941.

55. Ibid., July 19, 1941; Red Barber and Robert Creamer, *Rhubarb in the Catbird Seat* (Garden City, N.Y.: Doubleday, 1968), 25.

56. He ended up feuding with Durocher in 1946–47. "There had been a series of unpleasant stories involving, among other things, Durocher's reported friendships with people like George Raft and Bugsy Siegel. . . . Durocher was eventually suspended for the entire 1947 season." Bill James, *The Bill James Historical Abstract* (New York: Villard Books, 1986), 197.

57. MacPhail kept the broadcasts going because he himself so enjoyed them; in 1940 one game went into extra innings and "WOR telephoned to Ebbets Field that the broadcast would have to be cut off at six on account of a speech by Herbert Hoover. . . . MacPhail came roaring into the radio room. His face was flushed and . . . he started pulling plugs . . . and yelling something that sounded like 'The hell with Herbert Hoover!' . . . WOR was told that MacPhail refused to give way to Hoover and Barber completed the broadcast." See Taylor, "Borough Defender," July 12, 1941.

58. Barber and Creamer, *Catbird Seat,* 31; Taylor, "Borough Defender," July 12, 1941.

59. John Steadman, "The Laird of Glenangus," *Baltimore News American,* November 9, 1969; Barber and Creamer, *Catbird Seat,* 10.

60. See Rothe, ed., *Current Biography,* 377–78.

61. MacPhail had been ready to fight for some time and "when an officer of the America First Committee called him to ask about Ebbets Field for a rally, MacPhail's response "ran the gamut of known profanity." Taylor, "Borough Defender," July 19, 1941. Carter, "Glenangus Mares," 33.

62. MacPhail once bragged to Steadman that "the Pope told me he knew all about the Dodgers because he once visited Long Island when he was Papal Secretary of State." Steadman, "Laird of Glenangus."

"Ain't we got fun!"

Left: In 1941, when baseball genius Larry MacPhail bought the property and renamed it Glenangus Farms, it was a bit rundown. Right: Although MacPhail first planned to raise cattle on his Harford County farm, his pals Alfred Gwynne Vanderbilt and the Aly Kahn convinced him horses would be more fun. MacPhail (shown here c. 1950) began his Harford County breeding operations in the late '40s; in 1954 his yearlings fetched record-setting prices when he sold them at Saratoga.

63. Barber, *The Broadcasters,* 144; Carter, "Glenangus Mares," 34.

64. Boniface, "MacPhail Story"; M. H. Cadwalader, "Refugee from the Diamond Dust," *Baltimore Evening Sun,* July 12, 1942; "Glenangus Farms Yearling Sale" brochure, in files of Harford County Planning and Zoning Department, Bel Air.

up so he formed a consortium and bought the club. He, of course, ran things ("there is only one boss in a Larry MacPhail set up," wrote Barber) and in 1947 his Yankees won the World Series. So, again having accomplished precisely what he set out to do—and as Barber observed, "once Larry MacPhail has built something, he is no longer interested in it"—he sold his interest in the team and this time did retire to Harford County. "For good," he told the *Maryland Horse* in March 1948.[63]

When he arrived at Glenangus, he found he had bought himself yet another ruin. The property was "improved" by a dilapidated c. 1804 stone house and a host of falling-in outbuildings. Undeterred, and acting "as his own architect," he set about another massive restoration. "General renovation and a little adding-to are on the program for the house," reported the *Sun*'s M. H. Cadwalader in 1942. "The living room, hitherto, will become a library, and next to it on the south a new living room will be built. Long and spacious, with a glassed-in side, this will overlook most of MacPhail's lovely acres and [the] fat black grazing cattle" he "had shipped in from Scotland." Notwithstanding MacPhail's initial—if somewhat vague—plans to go into the cattle business, when his friend Vanderbilt gave him three broodmares he decided instead to become a horse breeder. He was completely ignorant about the subject—just as he had initially been ignorant about baseball—but his luck stayed with him and in 1950 Joe Palmer, turf editor of the New York *Herald Tribune,* made a trip to Harford County and left "convinced . . . that MacPhail knew what he was doing—whether he knew anything about it or not."[64]

Basically, he set out to have lightning strike twice and repeated the formula that had proven so successful with the Reds, Giants, and Yankees, that is, good stock + good nutrition = champions. First, he shopped around for the best horses he could buy and in 1949 paid $25,000 for a stallion he named General Staff, "a big bay, solidly made and rather flashy." He also bought several promising mares from another close friend, the Aly Kahn. Then he proceeded to make himself an expert on "which strains of grasses grow better in the Maryland climate, and which clovers cure better and easier. You would be none the better for having some of his theories repeated here," wrote one weary reporter after being subjected to several thousand of MacPhail's well-chosen words on the subject, "but . . . the farm has raised its production enormously, and the buildings and granaries are

Larry MacPhail's made-over Glenangus Farms, c. 1950: the main house and guest house are to the extreme right; stables, silos, cattle barns, and workers' cottages fill the foreground.

[in 1951] jammed to the roofs with superior feed of various sorts for various purposes." And history did, in fact, repeat itself, for even though the *Maryland Horse* had sniffed that "the evidence on General Staff isn't conclusive" when MacPhail bought the animal, a year later the stallion, filled with Harford-County oats, "became a top flight stake horse . . . [and] with purse earnings of $106,850, he paid for himself four times over before retiring to the new . . . barn at Glenangus." Thus in 1957 Boniface wrote, "Now that he has reached the peak as a horse trader and there's nowhere else to go in that branch of the game, Larry has announced his retirement from commercial breeding."[65]

Again, it was supposed to have been a retirement, but—and also again—it only lasted a few months. MacPhail suddenly decided to take a crack at the real estate game. He sold off some of the more distant reaches of the farm (at its peak, Glenangus took in about 1,000 acres) and created the Glenwood development; an avid golfer, he then laid out an eighteen-hole course for his own amusement and sold it ("at cost," he liked to point out) to the newly formed Maryland Golf and Country Club. And although MacPhail and the club had their ups and downs over the years, none could question his claim to being its founding father.[66]

Sadly, however, the once-charmed life began to sour. Marylanders who once laughed with him at his brawls grew tired of him and of them. He also began to stay away from Glenangus for longer and longer periods of time, restlessly moving between the Bahamas and Florida. It all came crashing down in June of 1975 when Glenangus, that former ruin he alone made a showplace, was auctioned off to satisfy his demanding creditors. He died a few months later, at the age of 85, in a Miami veterans' hospital. Still, he may have had the last, from-the-grave laugh. He had woven his financial threads into such an intricate web "that even bankers and one of the nation's top auction firms were unable to [untangle] . . . the complicated liens and mortgages."[67]

That is a too-squalid end to the MacPhail saga; he deserves better. There was far more to the man than baseball and horses, wheeling and dealing. M. H. Cadwalader picked up on this in her 1942 story. Although she described MacPhail's obvious public persona ("his cussing and gaudy colors"), she also saw through it all to a more hidden side: "At Glenangus the other half of his personality emerges," she wrote. "'Drop in any time,'" he once

65. "Glenangus Farms Yearling Sale" brochure; "Glenangus Farms," *Maryland Horse* (February 1951): 19; Boniface, "MacPhail Story"; William Boniface, "MacPhail to Retire," *Baltimore Evening Sun,* September 25, 1965.

66. He found a new toy in his later years, a battery-powered golf cart; the author speaks from first-hand experience in pointing out that the only thing the septuagenarian enjoyed more than riding himself around the farm on his golf cart was riding his younger daughter, Jeannie (born in 1950), and her playmates around in it.

67. "Glenangus Sold," *Ægis,* June 12, 1975.

told her "with a quiet neighborliness. 'I'm going to get down here oftener from now on. Going to live here permanently some day. Always have liked farms.'"[68] Even his 1941 *New Yorker* profile, written when he was at his colorful best, could not ignore that "other half." Though the writer gleefully recounted MacPhail's drinking and brawling, he ended the piece with the information that the Dodger skipper "plays the piano expertly and . . . when he sits down in his apartment, perhaps with a highball handy, and strikes the first chords of a Tchaikovsky scherzo, the signs of Ebbets Field leave his face and his mood mellows." But baseball is where MacPhail made his mark and baseball was where his heart, ultimately, lay. The last man to hire Babe Ruth ("I gave him a job coaching for the Dodgers when he was through as a player"), MacPhail not only knew a thing or two about the game, he also passed his genes on to his son Lee.[69] Surely the events of October 1966 should cause Marylanders to forgive the senior MacPhail any number of sins. It was, of course, son Lee who guided the Orioles to their first world championship, but, as Snowden Carter pointed out, the old colonel "had a hand in that one, too. . . . He sired Lee MacPhail, who made the trade for Frank Robinson. . . . And everybody knows that Frank Robinson is the man who made the beer cold."

Synthesis: Joshua's Meadows and the Camerons

Another "half-hidden" theme in the MacPhail saga—indeed in the sagas of all this chapter's leading players—is that despite their earnestness in saving farmland from cancerous erosion, or in piloting seemingly hapless Dodger teams to world championships, or in plotting the routes that Lafayette and Washington marched along, despite Depression-era worries about money, despite their having fought one war "to make the world safe for democracy" and another to halt the Fascists and the Nazis, and despite their uniform lawlessness (it's a safe bet that few people mentioned in this chapter were overly scrupulous about Prohibition)[70]—despite all that, they *did* have fun. Looking back from the 1990s, the generation of the '30s seems almost impossibly talented; they could and did do everything. And they did it all with such effortless panache.

Arguably, no place in Harford County crystallizes these thoughts quite the way the house called Joshua's Meadows does. When last touched on in chapter 2, Joshua's Meadows was owned by the Bond family, who built it in the 1740s. After the Bonds left in the 1820s the property passed to Thomas Hays, a man whose distinguished and busy career earned him the sobriquet "Father of Bel Air," and then to his brother, Nathaniel, who lived there long enough to build a stone peach-brandy distillery in a hollow below the house.

On Nathaniel's death in 1863, his heirs divided the farm's 300 acres into five parts which, over the years, they sold off piecemeal. Of the five, four have attracted developers of one stripe or another and now sprout housing developments, a bowling alley, a Montgomery Wards shopping center, used car lots, and other expressions of mid-twentieth-century vernacular building. But the house and 80 acres have survived. Since many a less vulnerable dwelling has been destroyed in the past 120 years, why has Joshua's Meadows, dangerously close to Route 1 and commercial development, been spared? The first six decades following the 1871 division offer no explanation for this phenomenon. They merely witnessed the house's steady deterioration as the structure's many roofs began to sag and leak; plaster fell from the walls; shutters dropped from their hinges; and window glass cracked and shattered as panes tinkled out of their beaded muntins. In October 1936 E. H. Pickering, a HABS photographer, hacked his way through the undergrowth that surrounded the unpainted ruin and snapped an image of what he found; looking at Pickering's photo today, one wonders how the walls withstood the vibrations the shutter's click set off. Then, just when the walls must have been ready to give a final shudder and collapse, Mr. and Mrs. Brodnax Cameron bought Joshua's Meadows and 78 acres in May 1937.[71] *That* is why the house has survived.

68. Cadwalader, "Diamond Dust."

69. And then to Andy, son of Lee, grandson of Larry, executive vice-president of the Minnesota Twins and the third generation of MacPhails to rise to prominence in the baseball world.

70. Alexis Shriver even installed a secret walk-in vault at Olney to safeguard his stash of bootleg Maryland rye.

71. Deed SWC 246/56.

Joshua's Meadows near Bel Air as it was in 1937 (above) when Mr. and Mrs. Brodnax Cameron bought it; as it looked (below) after they restored the two-part, eighteenth-century main house and, using foundation stones from ruined outbuildings, added a modern kitchen wing.

Upon graduation from the University of Virginia's law school in 1922, and armed with a degree in architecture from Princeton and a batch of battlefield decorations won in World War I, Cameron decided to launch his career in Baltimore. There he and his wife (née Julia Sprigg) moved and there they lived out the twenties as the twenties should have been lived—in a fizzy, heady mix of the frivolous and the intellectual with their friends and relations David Bruce, John Dos Passos, Marcia Davenport, and George Boas. The Depression and a growing family—the menagerie eventually included three sons, a nurse or two, a butler, and a pet goat—began to make that style of life increasingly less attractive, so the couple eventually settled, at the urging of Cameron's Gilman classmate and fellow lawyer, Frank Hays Jacobs, in Bel Air. The two men launched the law firm Jacobs and Cameron in a disreputable-looking building on Office Street and the Cameron clan ensconced themselves into rental quarters in that part of town called Dallam's Addition.

Then one day, while taking the Ma and Pa railroad into Baltimore, Julia Cameron serendipitously noticed an old house with an irregular roofline. She asked around for information and was given uniformly discouraging opinions, but she finally tracked it down. It was Joshua's Meadows and they bought it. If they had not yet earned the nickname (and one wonders), it quickly bubbled to the lips of all their friends who visited

"Ain't we got fun!"   183

Joshua's Meadows and left scratching their heads at this latest project of "the crazy Camerons." Oblivious to nay-sayers, the couple set to work.

The original house consisted of two detached sections. The Hayses had connected these sections and had built a new room along the flank of what had been the kitchen. When the Camerons decided to remove that "new" room's walls to create a porch, while leaving the Hayses' chairrail and built-in cupboards, they set off the first in a series of ironies that surrounds the "new" Joshua's Meadows. Countless unwary guests have wondered about a house that has a porch with a chairrail. Indeed, nothing at Joshua's Meadows was quite what it appeared, for the Camerons cloaked every detail in layered meanings. The couple reoriented the house so that the former main façade became unseen and unnecessary; they thus routed their guests not to the Bonds' front door but to the Camerons' front door—but the Camerons had *two* front doors. The Camerons also turned the old freestanding kitchen into a living room and then built a new, two-story stone kitchen off the main block, creating more ironies; architect Cameron designed the kitchen so well that many visitors conclude it is the original house and the eighteenth-century sections are the twentieth-century additions. How many guests have wondered about the set of winding, weathered-brick steps that lead from the chairrailed porch to the new garage? Enclosed winder stairs form so prominent a feature of the main house that many have asked, bewildered, if the Bonds built winder stairs outside, too. No, those stairs are Cameronian, as is the "picture window" he added to the dining room. It is, literally, a picture window, for it enframes unsurpassed vistas of rolling, gentle countryside. He often said he modeled it on a window in a shop on Baltimore's Gay Street that sold ladies' hats. Had he? He also said he put it where he did, to the right of his place at table, so he could amuse himself with the view when not amused by lunch guests. "If I'd meant it I wouldn't dare say it," was a frequent Cameron disclaimer. But again, one never knew.

And the furnishings! More than one visitor has suggested that Joshua's Meadows brings to mind Mrs. Gareth's eponymous house in Henry James's *The Spoils of Poynton,* where everything was contrived of-a-piece out of taste and talent, not merely tossed together and cemented with quantities of cash. "There were places much grander and richer," James wrote, "but there was no such complete work of art. . . . And . . . in selection . . . there was an element of creation, of personality . . . a fine arrogance, a sense of style which, however amused and amusing, never promised, nor stooped."[72]

Still, Joshua's Meadows *is* amusing. What *should* one make of the telescope? or the lithograph, "The Drunkard's Progress"? or Vaughn Flannery's painting of Lady Godiva?[73] or the portrait of Cameron in full laird's regalia, placed directly over the prie-dieu in the entrance hall? or the harp? That, at least, "was no joke to the extent that Brodnax Cameron knew how to play it and, when so moved, he did," wrote Bradford Jacobs, nephew to both Anne Heighe and Frank Hays Jacobs in his 1980 *Evening Sun* editorial-page obituary of the man he dubbed "Brodnax Cameron: Harford Hero." Jacobs, who had known the Camerons and Joshua's Meadows from childhood, observed that

> some men, at entry, freeze a roomful of people. Some men dazzle it, some make people uncomfortably snatch up their socks. Brodnax Cameron did none of these disturbing things. What he did was warm those around him with a personality of uncommon sunniness. He twinkled and, by his own twinkling, induced people to twinkle back; or, what's just as good and maybe better, led them to think that they did.

Jacobs also knew that music formed the core of life at Joshua's Meadows. If Brodnax Cameron made his harp sing out with "Nearer My God to Thee," Julia Cameron, whom Jacobs accurately labeled a "fountainhead of bubbling energy," was a skilled pianist who often slipped into a bit of Bach or Chopin. There was also that stereo system contrived and installed by youngest son George, its turntable discreetly hidden in a French Renaissance chest: sometimes the speakers filled the air with 78 RPM recordings of Lotte Lehmann's *Da geht er hin,* sometimes with the chorus of the peers from *Iolanthe,* some-

72. Both Camerons pretended to prefer Agatha Christie to James but the bookshelves at Joshua's Meadows sag with well-read copies of all of James's novels.

73. Part of the explanation is that Flannery and Cameron bumped into each other at a party. The latter said he really didn't like the former's painting. Why not? Well because as a Virginian he naturally preferred nudes to horses. "Someday," Flannery announced, "I'll paint something that'll please us both."

times—and God help the non-Caledonian—with the blare of four-score Highlanders piping "Scotland the Brave." And while hundreds of people have heard a good deal of music at Joshua's Meadows, no one heard either Cameron, at harp or piano, break into a chorus of "Ain't We Got Fun!" But, then, neither Cameron had to: it was all so wonderfully self-evident.

Housing developments shot up along Emmorton Road south of Bel Air in the 1950s and '60s. One can discern Wakefield Meadows (top between Emmorton Road and the "new" Route 24) with Colonial Acres, Fairmount, and Glenwood across the road and West Riding to the south.

L'Esprit Nouveau at the Head of the Bay [9]

Vue intérieure du Pavillion Batá: un beau cube bien proportionné et bien compartimenté. . . . Tout problème de standard soulève au décuple les difficultés.

    Le Corbuiser, *Oeuvre Complet*

The problems of starting a house were vast, few, and insoluble; the problems of getting one finished were small, multitudinous, and insoluble. . . . There was . . . the window hardware which would not work, and the one bathroom floor to which the linoleum would not adhere. . . . All the doors stuck except those that would not latch at all.

    Eric Hodgins, *Mr. Blandings Builds His Dream House*

In the 300 years since George Alsop wrote about William Stockett's farm, Harford's architecture, whether folk or high style, has stressed the single-family house. One finds notable exceptions here and there—St. Mary's Church comes to mind—but generally the county's architects and artisans have taken on one singular task: "to provide," in the elegant phrasing of Jaquelin T. Robertson, FAIA, the "resident culture with humane, practical, appropriate . . . accommodation in keeping with the requirements of purse, setting, and existing social convention."[1] What is important, and often overlooked, about these houses, whether they are determinedly fashionable (such as Sophia's Dairy, Tudor Hall, or Liriodendron), aggressively astylar (such as Greenwood) or, most often, somewhere comfortably in between, is that they grew out of an ethos of seemingly eternal stability. Agriculture and a few extractive industries formed a strikingly reliable economic base for a strikingly stable population—census takers enumerated 21,258 Har-

1. Jaquelin T. Robertson, foreword to William B. O'Neal and Christopher Weeks, *The Work of William Lawrence Bottomley in Richmond* (Charlottesville: University Press of Virginia, 1985), xvi.

fordians in 1810, 23,415 in 1860, and 27,965 in 1910. That last year any sane citizen, if asked to predict the population fifty years hence, might have thought a bit and then guessed maybe 30,000 or 35,000? But the 1960 population certainly was not 30,000; in fact, it had more than doubled, to 76,722. And it doubled again in the next thirty years, skyrocketing to 182,132 in 1990. What happened? Just as important, what did these immense and sudden increases—astonishing increases, really, since most people still view Harford as a rural county—mean for local architecture?

No simple, single explanation can account for either spurt: both involve complex sociological, economic, and technological forces unpredictable to even the most prescient McKinley-era observer. Yet varied as the causes and effects are, a common theme does wind through it all—increasingly efficient transportation. If one factor overrides all others in Harford's twentieth-century history, it is how railroads and highways have all but taken away the county's independence. In simplest terms, Harford is now little more than a bedroom community and its buildings (and builders) have lost most of their earlier individuality and provincial charm. This growth was not caused by railroads and highways alone, of course; it is hard to imagine how that first spurt could have occurred without the formation of the huge Army bases at Edgewood and Aberdeen in late 1917, just as it is impossible to imagine the 1950s boom without post–World War II federal housing initiatives such as the GI Bill. Still, transportation—particularly the automobile—holds the key to understanding the county's twentieth-century population explosion. Moreover, private cars and improved highways not only allowed for increased numbers of countians, they also more or less determined that those new residents would live in sprawling isolated subdivisions far removed from the residents' places of employment.

While some of these subdivisions still consist of artisan-built houses, as a rule, changes in technology have rendered carpenters and masons all but obsolete: fewer and fewer of the county's new houses are individually crafted; more and more are mass-produced in factories. In the 1910s and '20s a few countians, such as the sisters Sarah Helen and Florence Cronin of Aberdeen, happily bought houses by mail from Sears Roebuck & Company. In 1938 the Czechoslovakian Bata company filled its new town at Belcamp with small, inexpensive, interchangeable houses all built according to principles laid down by the Bata family's favorite architect, Le Corbusier, in his magazine, *l'Esprit Nouveau*. And in the late 1940s and early '50s, World War II veterans Frederick and Walter Ward and Melvin Bosely created the county's first self-contained "housing developments" by ordering prefab houses from the National Homes Corporation. "A new epoch has begun," Corbusier trumpeted in the first issue of *l'Esprit Nouveau;* indeed it had, and no one, c. 1890, could have predicted how thoroughly mass production would change every aspect of Harford County—of American—life.

Modern Homes and *Modern Homes*

Mass production is certainly not a twentieth-century phenomenon. Harfordians were happily using mass-produced bridges as long ago as 1883, when the county commissioners perused the Wrought Iron Bridge Company of Canton, Ohio's catalog, "Descriptive Pamphlet . . . of Bridges," found something they liked, ordered it, and, upon delivery, plopped it across Deer Creek adjacent Mr. Noble's mill. As was touched on in chapter 5, countians had been buying mass-produced house parts, such as doors, mantels, and window frames, since the Civil War. Thus the publication of Sears's first house-by-mail catalog in 1908 was but the next logical step in a long process: how easy, it must have seemed, to go from bridges-by-mail to houses-by-mail.[2]

That first catalog, a rather modest forty-four-page document called "Book of Modern Homes and Building Plans," offered potential customers twenty-two models to choose from, with prices from $650 to $2,500. All a homebuilder had to do was fill out

2. Everything could be bought mail-order: Thomas J. Schlereth in his recent book, *Victorian America,* relates how one order arrived at a turn-of-the-century Sears store: "Please send one wife Model 12-42 on page 112 as soon as possible"; one order from a Montgomery Wards customer, on the other hand, suggests that the honeymoon was, indeed, over: a woman requested embalming fluid and attached the query, "Must I pour it down [my husband's] throat just before he dies or rub it on after he is dead? Please rush!"

In 1883 the Harford County Commissioners ordered a new bridge for Deer Creek at Noble's Mill from the Wrought Iron Bridge Company of Canton Ohio's bridge-by-mail "Descriptive Pamphlet." (The company's metal plaque, just discernible, was stolen in the 1970s.)

and mail the order form and Sears would ship the average 30,000 separate house parts to the customer "for easy assembly on site." (Or so the company claimed.) Naturally, shipping depended on railroads, and throughout America "the largest concentrations of [Sears] houses were in . . . [areas] served by . . . rail lines." Notwithstanding certain embarrassing and much-publicized snafus (such as when a West Virginia couple discovered, upon "completing" their Sears bungalow, that "they had managed to assemble the house backward" and had to take it apart and start over again), Sears's house-by-mail business boomed. The company had to purchase its own lumber mill (1909) and millwork plant (1912), set up its own forty-acre lumberyards (1911 and 1925), and hire its own staff of architects (1919) to keep up with the demand. Business continued to grow all through the twenties but, like so many other forms of giddy, post–Great War euphoria (such as goldfish swallowing and flagpole sitting), house-buying by catalog could not survive the Depression. Sears scuttled its home-by-mail operations in 1940. Still, in *Modern Homes*'s three decades of existence Sears had become perhaps the single leading player in the nation's housing market. The compilers of the 1939 catalog estimated that the company had sold 100,000 house kits, providing shelter for 500,000 Americans.[3]

While those 100,000 houses represent approximately 450 different building models, two clear favorites emerged: the bungalow and what historians now call the "foursquare." The one-story bungalow, derived from a cottage form native to India (the word "bungalow" is a corruption of the Hindustani adjective *"bangla,"* meaning "of Bengal"), became immensely popular in the United States. "Within the means of all but actually poor . . . people," bungalows were viewed as "the all-American family house."[4] The style, with its prominent porches, proved especially well suited to Southern California, partially because that region's sunshine made bungalows a sensible design choice, and partially because "Los Angeles . . . was equated in the popular mind with . . . easy-going and slightly sensuous" subtropical places: "one can hardly look at these houses," one modern architect has observed, "and not remember Somerset Maugham's 'Rain.'"[5]

The foursquare, a building "two stories high, set on a raised basement with the first floor approached by steps, a verandah running the full width of the first story, capped by

3. Katherine Cole Stevenson and H. Ward Jandl, *Houses by Mail* (Washington, D.C.: Preservation Press, 1986), 29, 30, 19; quoted in Alan Gowans, *The Comfortable House* (Cambridge: MIT Press, 1987), 57–58.

4. See Herbert D. Croly, "The Country House in California," *Architectural Record* (December 1913): 482–519; Clifford Edward Clark Jr., *The American Family Home, 1800–1960* (Chapel Hill: University of North Carolina Press, 1986), 186, 183.

5. Dean et al., *Three Hundred and Fifty Years,* 209; Clark, *American Family Home,* 182.

"Every Customer Satisfied," trumpeted Sears Roebuck's *Modern Homes* catalog.

a low, pyramidal roof that usually contains at least one dormer," appealed to a slightly different audience. Its purchasers did not necessarily set out to emulate characters in *Rain* (such as Miss Sadie Thompson, a "tramp . . . [of] desperate earnestness"[6] who flounced around in off-shoulder blouses with a cigarette dangling from her pouty lips), but instead to achieve "a classical self-containment." The foursquare's origins certainly lack the exoticism of the Subcontinent. One historian has suggested that the form's "ancestor was the eighteenth-century Georgian mansion," which makes it locally the direct descendant of Sophia's Dairy, Stafford, and the other dwellings discussed in chapters 3 and 5. Whatever its antecedents, the foursquare's appeal was immediate and powerful. "Everybody knows the form," one scholar has observed. "Every American town built before 1930 has dozens . . . of them" and "every mail-order company offered variants of foursquares between 1908 and 1925."[7]

The first known example of a house-by-mail in Harford County dates to 1918, when two Aberdeen women "startled the community with their daring when they ordered a Sears house kit" and built their prefab house on a remote stretch of Paradise Road.[8] The "daring" ladies, two elementary schoolteachers, the Misses Florence and Sarah Helen Cronin, could not have been less like Sadie Thompson if they tried: while Maugham's character lured unwary sailors and soldiers of fortune into her home, the Cronin sisters made "little sandwiches and cakes for family reunions" in theirs.[9] Thus it is hardly surprising that the sisters avoided the prefab bungalow (and all it represented) and chose instead the prefab foursquare.

According to first cousin Elizabeth Cronin Prevas, the newly independent sisters (Sarah Helen, born 1890, and Florence, born 1887) were the first professional working women in their family and wanted to underline their independence by moving off the family farm and into a house of their own. Sears helped them make that dream a reality. The sisters quietly examined the 1918 issue of *Model Homes,* selected a design they liked, and sent off their order with a check for $2,600.[10]

A few days later B&O freight cars deposited everything "from the stone basement to the shingles on the roof" at the Aberdeen station. Horse and wagon teams then hauled the pieces the short distance to the Cronins' woodsy lot on Paradise Road.[11] The sisters' construction crew worked efficiently and the Cronins were able to move into their new, airy, nine-room, four-bedroom, two-story residence "more or less overnight." Not incidentally, just as the sisters chose a house-by-mail to assert their independence from their family, they also chose to assert their independence from Sears by adding extra touches that help disguise their foursquare's mass-produced origins: they embellished their house with wooden columns in the twin parlors and a set of French doors to close off the upstairs sitting room from the hallway; they added a powder room; they changed the location of the kitchen; and they enclosed the porch with jalousie windows. Even so, the basic Sears *Model Homes* shell remains intact and visible.

One would never know, to look at the sister's cozy prefab, that virtually next door Alexis Shriver, Gilman Paul, and the rest of the "Ain't we got fun" crowd discussed in chapter 8 were disporting themselves in their expensive, idiosyncratic creations. If a Sears cottage like the Cronins' represents "a house with which middle-class American could identify," the style left Paul and Shriver and the rest of the era's elite cold.[12] Of course Paul's and Shriver's hefty bank balances allowed them to ignore the era of the common man, an era companies like Sears celebrated and made possible. Similar elite/middle-class splits have, of course, always existed in the county and will exist in any community where wealth influences the arts. Still, there is no use asking which more typified its time, Shriver's incorporating thirty-foot, federal-era marble columns into the façade of Olney or the Cronins' purchasing a foursquare cottage from Sears, since each act accurately reflects a different—but equally valid—aspect of the period. One might instead ask who anticipated future building in the county, Shriver or the Cronins? The answer to that question is easy, for even as the Aberdeen sisters embraced traditional, Georgian-derived design,

6. Pauline Kael, *5001 Nights at the Movies* (New York: Holt, Rinehart and Winston, 1982), 483.

7. Gowans, *The Comfortable House,* 84.

8. Elizabeth Cronin Prevas, conversation with author, June 10, 1991; see also Karen Toussaint, "Old-fashioned House Shopping," *Ægis,* January 22, 1992.

9. Florence taught fourth grade in Havre de Grace Elementary School; Sarah Helen first grade in Aberdeen. Toussaint, "Old-fashioned House Shopping."

10. J. Harlan Livezey, "The Cronin Family," *Harford Historical Bulletin* (Fall 1992): 26. The sisters' original order form has disappeared but the house resembles several models offered in the 1916, 1917, 1918, and 1919 catalogs, e.g., "The Gladstone," "The Albion," "The Rockford," and "The Langford."

11. Toussaint, "Old-fashioned House Shopping."

12. Clark, *American Family Home,* 192.

In 1918 the Misses Sarah Helen and Florence Cronin of Aberdeen used a Sears kit to build themselves a new house on Paradise Road: it and one of the smiling sisters are shown here. Records don't indicate just which model the Cronins bought, but compare their house to the models shown in the previous figure.

they did so in a way that drew them into a worldwide revolution in mass-marketing, mass-production, and industrialism.

"An Ideal Machine Age Environment"

The German architect Walter Gropius, a leader of modernist design and theory, set out to challenge the West's architectural complacency when he established his Bauhaus school in Weimar in 1919—just one year after the Cronin sisters built their "modern" Sears house in Aberdeen. Gropius blasted the previous generation of builders, who had, he wrote, allowed architecture to "degenerate into a florid aestheticism, as weak as it was sentimental," who had hidden "the varieties of structure under a welter of heterogeneous ornament," and who had "lost touch with the rapid progress of technical developments." In place of the comfortable status quo, Gropius offered "a school in which fine arts, crafts, industrial design, and architecture were taught as parts of an all-embracing aesthetic discipline, bridging the gap between the artistic and industrial realms in pursuit of an ideal machine-age environment."[13] He replaced traditional closed-door floor plans with a "new conception of . . . free-flowing space . . . corresponding to the dynamic theory of our time."[14] He further urged architects not only to give new buildings open plans but to allow new, manmade materials to determine the shape those plans would take:

> Our fresh technical resources have furthered the disintegration of solid masses of masonry into slender piers. . . . New synthetic substances—steel, concrete, glass—are actively superseding the traditional raw materials of construction. . . . The role of the walls becomes restricted to that of mere screens stretched between the upright columns of the framework. . . . This, in turn, naturally leads to a progressively bolder [i.e., *wider*] opening up of the wall surfaces, . . . [and] glass is assuming an even greater . . . importance.[15]

Artists and architects from throughout Europe flocked to Gropius's new school, which he eventually moved from Weimar to the industrial city of Dessau, drawn by the prospect of hammering out "one universal style valid for all the arts and products of modern life."[16]

While Gropius was planning the Bauhaus curriculum, his contemporary, the pseudonymous Le Corbusier, was using his magazine, *l'Esprit Nouveau,* to give popular voice

13. Walter Gropius, *The New Architecture and the Bauhaus,* trans. P. Morton Shand from the German (Cambridge: MIT Press, 1965), 80–81; Marvin Trachtenberg and Isabelle Hyman, *Architecture* (New York: Harry Abrams, 1986), 523–24.

14. Walter Gropius, "The Role of the Architect in Modern Society," *Apollo in the Democracy* (New York: McGraw-Hill, 1968), 46–47.

15. Gropius, *New Architecture,* 25–29.

16. Trachtenberg and Hyman, *Architecture,* 524.

The Irwin Packard Company in Bel Air (shown here c. 1950; now Jackson's Television) displays an understanding of design tenets set down by Gropius, Le Corbusier, and other modernist masters. Note especially the horizontal emphasis, the flat roof, and the extensive use of glass.

to similar modernist principles and earned himself a place in Bartlett's for his phrase "a house is a machine to live in." A practicing architect as well as a theorist, Le Corbusier gave three-dimensional form to his philosophies in the series of small, inexpensive, simply designed, mass-producible dwellings he named his "Citrohan houses," a punning reference to mass-produced Citroen cars. Le Corbusier filled his Citrohan houses with innovative features that would eventually become modernist hallmarks, such as a raised ground floor, wide windows, roof terraces, open façades, and open plans; he also built the structures in a new, strong, and ductile material, reinforced concrete. His writings and buildings eventually won him a series of commissions from like-minded patrons throughout Europe, patrons who asked him to draw up plans for everything from individual houses to whole new cities. Among the latter are Pessac in France, where he "designed and built . . . fifty-one houses in the 1920s under the sponsorship of . . . industrialist Henry Frugès, who meant them to be a laboratory of new domestic, structural, and aesthetic ideas"[17] and Zlin in Czechoslovakia, completed in 1935 for the shoemaker Thomas Bata, at least partially so the enlightened industrialist could try out his radical reformist notion of giving "decent, common sense treatment" and a chance "for education and advancement" to his 22,000 employees. Thus, as Bata's son wrote, at a time "when social benefits, let alone a home of their own, were, for most individual workers, an impossible dream, Bata employees lived in low-rent modern houses, had free access to medical care, shopped in low-cost grocery stores and competed in company-owned sports facilities."[18]

Thomas Bata found a natural soulmate in Le Corbusier. Just as the industrialist brought the assembly line to the shoe business, the architect, who believed that each room is but a cog in a house and each house but a cog in a city, worked to prove that "the house can and ought to be made in the factory." Consequently, the Batas incorporated Corbusian principles in all the family's globe-spanning construction projects, from interchangeable shopfronts to a pavilion at the 1937 International Paris Exposition to factories in India and Venezuela to the new town they began at Belcamp, Harford County, Maryland: "Our factories all over the world are built from the same plans," said company president John Hoza in 1939. "That makes for efficiency."[19]

17. Ada Louise Huxtable, *Architecture, Anyone?* (Berkeley: University of California Press, 1986), 19, 13–15.

18. Thomas J. Bata, *Bata* (Toronto: Stoddart Publishing, 1990), 334, 4, 5.

19. Bata traveled to Lowell, Massachusetts, in 1904 and spent six months working on an assembly line there to learn "firsthand what American machinery and management techniques could do." Bata, *Bata,* 6; Le Corbusier and P. Jeanneret, *Oeuvre complet,* 26, 30, 33. Paul Berge, "Old Harford Face-to-Face with Industry," *Baltimore Sun,* June 18, 1939.

Le Corbusier designed the large new city of Zlin in Czechoslovakia for shoemaker Thomas Bata, whose descendants incorporated much of the architect's thinking when they laid out another new city—Belcamp, Harford County. The Belcamp factory buildings are in the foreground, workers' cottages are grouped in the middle right with the gymnasium on axis in the distance toward Bush River.

The gymnasium at Belcamp: its clean lines, flat roof, and glass walls were what the modernist 1930s International style was all about.

L'Esprit Nouveau at the Head of the Bay

The Batas arrived in Harford County in the early '30s when, as a hedge against an uncertain, Hitler-threatened Europe, they bought about 2,000 acres of tidewater farmland straddling the B&O railroad.[20] In 1938, with war all but certain, they began a massive relocation of capital and personnel to England, to Canada, and to Harford County, where they built a factory, a commercial center, an office tower, a hotel, and 70 workers' houses, all laid out in a cross-axial manner, and all incorporating Corbusier-sanctioned reinforced concrete, clean lines, and flat roofs. This is the Batas' Belcamp, "an American shoetown, a mirror-image of Zlin . . . on the shores of the Chesapeake Bay," an extremely rare American example of European modernist town-planning, and undoubtedly the most important work of twentieth-century architecture in Harford County.[21]

As the reformist Bata family, skeptical about the chances of "peace in our time," fled to America to escape the Nazis, so, too, did most of the Continent's forward-thinking architects. Gropius, forced to close the Bauhaus when stormtroopers ransacked it in 1932, wound up in Massachusetts, where he was appointed head of the faculty of Harvard's department of architecture in 1937; his fellow German Ludwig Mies van der Rohe, once an instructor at the Bauhaus, emigrated to Chicago to accept the post of director of the architectural department at the Armour Institute (now the Illinois Institute of Technology); and the Hungarian Marcel Breuer, who had also taught at the Bauhaus, followed Gropius to Massachusetts where he, too, joined the Harvard faculty. These men, along with such earlier émigrés as Louis Kahn from Estonia (who taught architecture at the University of Pennsylvania) and Richard Neutra from Austria (who practiced architecture in Southern California) then set out "to build and teach, . . . [and] transform the American landscape" along efficient, European modernist lines, to replace, in crude terms, bungalows, gable roofs, and defined rooms with glass walls, flat roofs, and open plans.[22]

Romance on the Road and "New Flexibility" at Home

Not everyone in America was ready to abandon the architectural romanticism (which the Cronins' prefab and Alexis Shriver's columns may be taken to represent) in favor of high-tech. Indeed, and somewhat ironically, one of American romanticism's last great flowerings occurred in buildings designed as a response to that most revolutionary of all twentieth-century innovations, the automobile, a contraption that E. B. White took to be "more than any other object, the expression of the nation's character and the nation's dream. In the free, billowing fender, in the blinding chromium grilles and the fluid control, in the ever widening front seat, we see the flowering of the America that we know." White, like so many who reached adulthood between the world wars, became entranced by the automobile. To many of that generation "driving was as magical as flying . . . , no wonder that . . . brand names arose like 'Sky Chief' and 'Superflight.'" Car designers, especially after World War II, paid homage to that spirit by infusing the terrestrial automobile with airplane motifs. In 1948 Harley Ford introduced tailfins onto Cadillacs to evoke the Lockheed P-38 Lightning "twin-engine fighter"; "1950 Fords and Studebakers [had] . . . grilles [that] suggested propellers"; and the Chrysler Corporation, "inspired by the jet and the rocket," embraced what its ad men called "the new shape of motion."[23]

When called on to produce automobile-related roadside structures, building designers responded to the romantic excitement of the age by shaping such seemingly utilitarian structures as garages and gas stations into "temples, miniature pagodas, lighthouses, windmills, and Renaissance villas," such as the terracotta tile–roofed, semi-Spanish, semi-beaux-arts service stations the Standard Oil Company built in Aberdeen on Route 40 and in Benson on Route 1. Impressively exotic as the gas stations were, when it came time to design buildings to service the drivers of the cars, architects proved, if anything, even more susceptible to new-age styling than designers of gas stations did, as Aberdeen's splendid Ideal Diner suggests. Manufactured in 1952 by the Jerry O'Mahony Company of New Jersey and transported to its Route 40 site in four sections, the Ideal Diner, its

20. Bata, *Bata,* 38.

21. The actual design was handled by company architects Vladimir Karfik and Joseph Polasek. Bata, *Bata,* 149. At the time it was rumored that Batas would relocate their entire "$350,000,000 complex to Maryland." Keith Wyatt, "New Shoes Pouring from Bata Plant," *Baltimore Sunday Sun Magazine,* November 17, 1939.

22. Ada Louise Huxtable, "The Future Grows Old," *Sunday New York Times,* May 18, 1975.

23. E. B. White, *One Man's Meat* (New York: Harper and Row, 1978), 164–67; Phil Patton, "The Great American Gas Station," *Diversions* (October 1990): 119–20; Thomas Hine, *Populuxe* (New York: Knopf, 1986), 87; Yates, "Detroit Iron," 60.

The Standard Oil Company's gas station on Route 40 at Aberdeen (replaced in the 1980s)—a curiously romantic structure for something as revolutionary as the automobile.

streamlined, aerodynamic lines sheathed in shiny stainless steel, creates a virtual apotheosis of America's romantic postwar optimism and suggests how widespread and acceptable the concept of mass-produced, factory-made architecture had become.

Thus, when an estimated 6 million young married couples set out to start building houses in 1945, they found themselves in the midst of a fierce architectural battle between the Bauhaus modernists and the romantic conservatives, personified by the decommissioned sergeant who told a reporter for *American Home* magazine that he was "against that drastic home blitzkrieg . . . tubular steel forms are great in a B-24 but in my own home I don't want that old easy chair sent off to the attic." It appeared to be a hopeless stand-off[24] until a conciliatory *dea ex machina* appeared in the person of Elizabeth Mock and her 1945 home-building show at the Museum of Modern Art, "Built in USA 1932–1944." To cleanse the word "modern" of its more extreme connotations, Mock took as her thesis the concept that "modern" didn't have to be all stainless steel and tubular frames. It was, she said, simply an *approach* to design, a way to achieve "a better, healthier way of life." Or, as she somewhat disingenuously wrote in *House & Garden* magazine (while taking a swipe at Le Corbusier), new buildings ought incorporate "convenience *and* pleasure, for the house which is merely convenient and efficient is not a house but a machine."[25]

Mock was, in fact, a modernist at heart and surreptitiously larded her exhibition (and follow-up interviews and articles) with several distinct selling points to win over the conservative home-building public. First, she pointed out how porches, patios, decks, interior courtyards, and open flexible plans—all elements in modernism's goal of fusing interior and exterior space—well fit the needs of America's young couples. She also explained how technology rendered modern design suitable to any local climate; for example, due to air conditioning and central heating, glass walls had become practical in both Vermont and Mississippi. Finally, and at the heart of it all, she argued that breakthrough materials such as lightweight alloys and stressed panels—the same elements that had helped America defeat Germany and Japan—could be and morally *should* be used to create prefabricated housing "suitable" (her word) to the needs of the triumphant GIs, their new brides, and their babies.[26]

24. Clark, *American Family Home,* 197; Sgt. Michael Pearman, "Dear American Home," *American Home* (September 1945): 32.

25. Harry Henderson, "The Mass-Produced Suburbs," *Harper's Magazine* (December 1953): 25–32; Elizabeth Mock, "Modern Houses: How to Look at Them," *House & Garden* (August 1945): 79.

26. Henderson, "Mass-Produced Suburbs," 32.

Others took up and amplified her points, including architect Arthur Stires, who wrote an article for *Architectural Record* about the benefits architecture's "new flexibility" would guarantee for the general public. Living patterns, he said, had become less formal—"we do our own cooking now and guests are a commonplace in the kitchen"—and it was thanks to modernism that architects were suddenly able to "bring the kitchen out of its ancient obscurity and make it a room—or a part of a room—with social standing equal to other rooms." A few dreamier sorts even viewed integrated floor plans as emblematic of an America that was, they hoped, heading toward full integration on every level of society; incorporating "the laundry room, sewing room, and play areas for children . . . into the kitchen" (so the argument ran) simply symbolized the larger fusion taking place throughout society as *Brown v. Board of Education* spelled the legal end of "separate but equal" schooling in 1954 and as Rosa Parks refused to get to the back of her Alabama bus in 1955.[27]

All these somewhat abstract—another key period word—thoughts came to tangible fruition in Harford County in the late 1940s when returning veterans Walter Ward and Melvin Bosely decided "to try their hands at housing." With the goal of creating well-designed, low-cost small homes appropriate to ex-servicemen, they incorporated themselves as Ward & Bosely, "bought Fritz Kelly's old tomato field" on the edge of Bel Air, and learned all they could about their new business. They had the land; they had helpful allies in Thomas Brookes, town planning director, and attorney Charles Reed; they even had a name for their on-paper development, Howard Park, to honor Dr. Howard Kelly since the land had been part of his Liriodendron property. Now all they needed were houses. To this end they purchased prefabricated structures from the new National Homes Corporation. According to Walter Ward's younger brother, Frederick, who soon joined the firm, "National Homes shipped the pieces to Bel Air and we glued them together" on lots along the new thoroughfares of Brookes Road, Reed Street, and Kelly Avenue. After laying out "miles of sidewalks" and planting "hundreds of flowering crabapples," Ward & Bosely opened their new community to buyers.[28]

The development immediately drew the scorn of the county. Fred Ward, who bought one of the prefab houses for his own family, recalled that "everyone said it'll be a slum in five years." It wasn't. Howard Park's prefab houses have worn well and have more than held their value. Now, nearly a half-century later, the trees have matured, the buildings have achieved a certain mellow patina, and the subdivision that once brought laughter has evolved into a comfortable, integral part of the town.

It also launched Ward & Bosely on its profitable way. In 1954 the company undertook a new and more ambitious venture, Wakefield Meadows, which they laid out on Emmorton Road about a half-mile south of Bel Air. This, according to Ward, was the "first planned subdivision in the area," that is, the first to be built independent of older towns and villages. At Howard Park, the developers had tied the new streets into a pre-existing pattern, but that was not possible at Wakefield Meadows, since "there wasn't anything to tie in to." So Ward & Bosely created a self-contained community with limited public access. Moreover, instead of imposing a grid pattern onto the land, they worked *with* the rolling topography and graded Wakefield Meadows's curving roadways and cul-de-sacs into the hills. They took pains to make sure that the development's 182 lots had irregular, naturalistic shapes, drawing inspiration from such "hot" period pieces as kidney-shaped coffee tables. They also gave their new neighborhood amenities aplenty—wide streets, building setbacks, curbing, as well as almost overly landscaped lots, with scores of pink-blooming crabapples interspersed with sycamore saplings, and a white pine and forsythia hedge to screen the new development, visibly and audibly, from Emmorton Road traffic.

Again, all they needed were buildings. And, since National Homes had provided the developers with a good prefab product in Howard Park, the two companies joined forces again in Wakefield Meadows. This time Ward & Bosely really backed a winner; Wake-

27. Clark, *American Family Home,* 204; Arthur McK. Stires, "Home Life and House Architecture," *Architectural Record* (April 1949): 103–8. See also Royal Barry Wills, "Space: Flexibility for the Small House," *Architectural Record* (May 1945): 76–84; Joseph Hudnut, "The Post-Modern Home," *Architectural Review* (May 1945): 70–75.

28. All quotes: Frederick Ward, conversation with author, June 3, 1991.

When developers Ward and Bosely laid out Wakefield Meadows in 1954 they gave their development curving roadways and irregularly shaped lots. They then filled those lots with prefab houses obtained from the new National Homes Corporation.

field Meadows's basic house, a model National Homes called "Fleetwood," proved more successful than anyone could have predicted. Architect Charles M. Goodman had designed the "Fleetwood" for National Homes, and while Ward & Bosely deserve credit for sensing the model's possibilities, Goodman certainly deserves a bit of applause for producing the design in the first place.

Born in New York City in 1906, Goodman studied architecture at Chicago's Armour Institute, future home to Mies van der Rohe. The New Deal then drew Goodman and his bride, Charlotte, to Washington where he got a job as a staff architect with the Treasury Department in 1934. He left the government and set up private practice in 1939 and his early projects, such as National Airport and pavilions at the 1939 New York World's Fair display glamorous—almost theatrical—art-deco influences. But Goodman quickly grew disenchanted with art deco's sometimes frivolous undertones and became an early champion of American modernism, rejecting the flashy Astaire-Rogers glitz and glamour in favor of "strong structural bay systems, hierarchical organization, and the relation of form to plan."[29]

After World War II Goodman, a decorated veteran, embarked on perhaps his two most important projects, designing the Hollin Hills subdivision in Fairfax County, Virginia, and designing prefabs for the National Homes Corporation. These proved to be dovetailing ventures and allowed Goodman to experiment with "prefabricated millwork, standardization, simplified carpentry . . . , and the use of modern technology and materials such as concrete slab floors [and] steel sash windows." Goodman once estimated that National Homes's conveyor belts turned out over 100,000 houses to his designs, a prodigious output that earned him the nickname "the Production House Architect." Significantly, nearly all 100,000 incorporate flat roofs, exterior walls that are either all-glass or solid three-foot sections of alloy siding, horizontal or transom windows, and fireplaces that Goodman "pulled out from the wall and treated as . . . abstract modern sculpture."[30]

Goodman, "Fleetwood," and Wakefield Meadows won a national design award in 1955, and the model was featured in a four-page spread in the March 1955 issue of *Woman's Home Companion*. One of the many glossy magazines that helped popularize the latest

29. See Brownell et al., *The Making of Virginia Architecture,* 394. This ambitious work covers 250 years of Virginia architectural drawings; Richard Wilson researched the sections on Charles Goodman.

30. Ibid., 394, 396.

The "Fleetwood" prefab from National Homes Corporation as shown in a 1955 issue of *Women's Home Companion*. Ward and Bosely favored this design-winning model for their new development, Wakefield Meadows.

trends in architecture, gardening, and furniture in the '50s,[31] *Woman's Home Companion* contained stories and bylines that distill the decade (that era Christopher Isherwood dubbed the time of "peaceprosperityexpandingeconomypermanentboom"):[32] if one flips through 1955's issues alone, one will be instructed by Grace Kelly on "How to Travel Light," might shed a happy tear as the Duchess of Windsor described "Our First Real Home," and will receive answers to the vexing problem of "What Should I Expect on my Honeymoon?" Each issue also featured a "Meal of the Month" such as "Swiss Steak Family Style" (that January) and "Skillet Meatloaf" (that September).

Elizabeth Matthews, the magazine's home decoration editor (and no stranger to the exclamation point), entitled her piece on Fleetwood "See How Good-Looking Prefabs Can Be!" She then proceeded to tell her readers about that distant "time . . . when factory-built houses reminded you of cracker-box toys laid in tight rows down the street. Now look at the change!" Now home-buyers have Fleetwood, a prefab that is both "simple and pleasing to the eye!"[33] Yet if one digs beneath Matthews's bubbly copy, one discovers that her prose addresses precisely the same points Elizabeth Mock made in her "Built in USA" Museum of Modern Art catalog. Just as Mock wanted postwar housing to use natural materials, especially wood, in an "honest" way, so Matthews devoted many column inches to Fleetwood's "wood grids . . . wood paneling, [and] folding bamboo storage doors." Just as Mock pointed out how modern heating and cooling systems and high-tech, corrosion-proof parts made modern design suitable to any American climate, Matthews gushed that owners of a Fleetwood house would be "comfortably at home in any part of the country," thanks to the model's "thoroughly insulated grooved plywood panels," sliding aluminum windows, warm-air heating system, air conditioning, and a floor plan that easily "adjusts to . . . exposures." And when Matthews exclaimed over Fleetwood's floor plan, with rooms designed to achieve "the greatest unity and feeling of space," she was merely repeating Mock's praise of open, flexible plans—just as Mock, in turn, had been merely echoing Gropius's Bauhaus lectures and Le Corbusier's designs for the Batas. But Matthews didn't invoke those highbrow Europeans. Instead, she argued that Fleetwood's "enclosed courtyards and gardens," its "close integration of indoor living with the out-

31. Ward, conversation with author. Other general-interest periodicals include *Better Homes and Gardens, Life, Look, Parents' Magazine, House Beautiful, House and Home, American Home, Sunset* (primarily Californian but with some affect nationally), and *Ladies' Home Journal.*

32. Quoted in David Fogle, Catherine Mahan, and Christopher Weeks, *Clues to American Gardens* (Washington, D.C.: Starrhill Press, 1987), 44.

33. Elizabeth Matthews, "See How Good-Looking Prefabs Can Be!" *Woman's Home Companion* (March 1955): 82–85.

In 1955 *Woman's Home Companion* praised the "Fleetwood" prefab for its "enclosed sunny patios" —perfect for all-American, post-World War II family living. Developers Ward and Bosely agreed and bought several "Fleetwoods" for their new Wakefield Meadows.

doors," and its "sunny patios" designed "to harmonize with the inside" made the prefab house the perfect vehicle to enable young couples to achieve a casual, all-American way of life.

There is nothing so encouraging as a few national awards (and booming sales), so with Fleetwood's praise ringing in their ears, Ward & Bosely embarked on other developments throughout Harford County, from Edgewood Meadows, a 700-unit project complete with its own shopping center, professional building, and seventeen-acre recreational area, to the more upscale Glenwood, built on land the developers purchased from Larry MacPhail. Other entrepreneurs smelled money in the air and joined Ward & Bosely in the subdivision business, so many, in fact, that the Baltimore *Sun,* in a May 3, 1959, piece on "The Building Boom in Harford County," related how "the sounds of power saws and of engines driving concrete mixers can be heard at many scattered points in Harford." One underlying implication of the article is that by 1959 open plans and prefab construction had become the name of the building-game in Harford; the *Sun* described projects then underway from north of Bel Air (Sutcliffe and Ward's Bel Forest, a community of "ranchers, split-level and two-story . . . factory manufactured houses") to Aberdeen (the McGrady Company's Paradise Heights and the Livezey Lumber Company's Northwood). And while none of these developers invoked Le Corbusier or Gropius by name, the line of descent from the Bauhaus to the Museum of Modern Art to Wakefield Meadows and *Woman's Home Companion* is not only clear, it also simply represents an updated version of the way architectural innovations have traditionally filtered through the county, that is, spreading out from an economic or cosmopolitan elite through books and other publications to general, middle-class acceptance.

It would, obviously, be overstating the case to suggest that *every* new house to appear in Harford County in the twentieth century was a prefab from a factory. In fact, even during Fleetwood's glory days in the early '50s, a few professional architects—both modernists and traditionalists—were able to eke out a living in the county. Alex Shaw, for example, continued along traditional paths to produce such highly appealing structures as the house he designed for industrialist H. P. White on Old Joppa Road, while

Architect Duryea Cameron designed a half-dozen superb small houses for young couples in Harford County in the late 1940s and early '50s, including this excellent "box-on-box" home for Charles and Lois Reed in Bel Air. Drawing inspiration for these designs from Frank Lloyd Wright's "Usonian Houses," Cameron set out to prove that modern architecture did not have to mean anonymous architecture.

Duryea Cameron, middle son of Brodnax and Julia Cameron, heartily embraced the modern masters who had taught him at Princeton and the Carnegie Institute of Technology.

Cameron, who adamantly maintains that "the individual house as a work of art is still alive,"[34] introduced Harford County to the thinking of Frank Lloyd Wright, specifically to Wright's dictum that the architect's greatest task was to reinterpret the small, private house and make it "suitable to life as life must be lived today."[35] To that end, Wright evolved what he called his "Usonian Houses." He hoped that these buildings would prove that it was possible to achieve an individualistic and "sane approach to prefabrication," to show that even in an industrial age the laws of human nature "require that all buildings do *not* resemble each other," and to achieve "average-income housing" that did not shy away from twentieth-century design. His 100 or so Usonian houses accomplished these ends largely through intelligent manipulation of plan and ceiling height: "the identity of this house lies," one Wright scholar has written,

> in its interior—in the "freedom of floor space" that lets the living room flow into the book place and fireplace, dining area and open areas toward the garden, and in the enclosure of its services and the privacy of its bedrooms.[36]

Moreover,

> the psychological effect of moving from a compressed space into an expanded one is that of release, giving a sense of repose and creating the illusion that the room is larger than it really is. The very small kitchen does not seem confined because it is high, while the extremely narrow and confined corridor has the effect of enhancing the apparent size of the small bedrooms. The glass walls create no visual barrier between inside and outside space, while solid walls create intimate, cozy interior nooks.[37]

Placing himself firmly in the Wright camp, Cameron designed a half-dozen Usonian houses for builders throughout Harford County, perhaps most successfully for Charles and Lois Reed in Bel Air.

34. Duryea Cameron, AIA, conversation with author, September 26, 1993.

35. Quoted by Edgar J. Kaufmann Jr., "The Usonian Pope-Leighey House," in *The Pope-Leighey House* (Washington, D.C.: National Trust for Historic Preservation, 1969), 119.

36. Ibid., 119–20.

37. H. Allen Brooks, "Frank Lloyd Wright," in *Pope-Leighey House,* 48.

Still, most postwar Harford countians, like most middle-class men and women nationwide, did not commission architect-designed houses. Instead, and again echoing nationwide trends, most had so thoroughly given in to the conformity of prefabs and "Swiss Steak Family Style" that by the 1950s the machine-made house had become, to paraphrase Le Corbusier, the home most countians built to live in.

Harvey Ladew, who "knew how to . . . perk up a drooping arrangement of tulips with a little gin," also knew how to have fun: he is shown here at his gardens around 1950.

Gardening in Harford County [10]

I t seems a virtual certainty that of all the works of art in Harford County only one—Harvey Ladew's garden—has achieved international recognition. And while Ladew is unquestionably Harford's best-known gardener, he was not the only countian who knew how to raise or lower a soil's pH, how to coddle a diffident camellia through Maryland's tricky winters, or how to muddy in a rose. Indeed, like their fellow Marylanders, Harford countians have been laying out gardens as long as they have been building houses. In fact, the histories of the two arts parallel each other, from hardscrabble folk beginnings to Revolutionary-era neoclassical elegance, from the divergent stylistic complexities of the mid-nineteenth century to post–World War II suburban simplicity.

Harford's—indeed, Maryland's—first colonists doubtless viewed their new surroundings with feelings that might charitably be called mixed. Here they were, 4,000 miles from whatever difficulties they had left the Old World to avoid, all set to begin new lives for themselves in a seemingly virgin and limitless wilderness. On the other hand, those first settlers were quickly made aware that they had also left behind their Old World weather and England's green and pleasant land became but a memory as they found themselves plopped down in a land that was green (in spring, anyway) but not by any stretch of the imagination climatically pleasant. What must they have thought of their first August—or February? Faced with such problems, most seventeenth-century colonists regarded gardening in primarily practical terms: cabbages and apples interested them, not delphiniums and hollyhocks. The Calverts gave each passenger on the *Ark* and the *Dove*, for example, preboarding instructions to bring "Seede Wheate, Rie, Barley and Oats" as well as "Kernalls . . . of Peares and Apples for making thereafter Cider" and "Seedes of all those fruite and roots and herbes which he desireth to have." The settlers evidently did just that, for a 1635 account of the colony reports bumper crops of "English Pease . . . also Muskmellons, Cowcumbers, . . . all sorts of garden Roots and Herbes . . . Carrots, Parsenips, Turnips, Cabbages, Radish, . . . Peares, Apples and several sorts of Plummes [and] Peaches." While one suspects that narrative was more a public relations tool than a slice-of-life description (the author brazenly claimed that "Orange and Limon Trees . . . thrive" in Maryland), one hard fact does emerge from all the puffery, namely the colonists' complete concentration on useful—as opposed to ornamental—gardening.[1]

Even so, up and down the East Coast nearly every early gardener seems to have wasted no time in augmenting productive rows of carrots and parsnips with plants grown purely for their decorative value: "Sweet Bryar, or Eglantine and English roses grow pleasantly" in seventeenth-century Massachusetts, according to John Josselyn's 1672 *New England Rarities Discovered;* Adrien van der Dock's 1650 *Description of New Netherland* indicates that colonists along the Hudson beautified their domestic landscapes with "peonies and hollyhocks . . . crown imperials, white lilies . . . violets, marigolds, etc.";[2] and Robert Beverly's 1705 *History and Present State of Virginia* notes that "the finest . . . Cardinal-flower, so much extoll'd for its Scarlett Colour" flourished in Old Dominion gardens as did "a Thousand others, not yet known to English herbalists. Almost all the Year round, the Levels and Vales are beautified with Flowers of one Kind or other." Beverly was also entranced by "the charming colours of the Humming Bird, which revels among the Flowers and licks off the Dew. . . . I have seen ten or a dozen of these Beautiful Creatures together, which sported about me so familiarly, that with their little Wings they often fanned my Face."[3]

Even though there are no accounts of seventeenth-century Bush River Neck gardeners being cooled by the beating of hummingbird wings, period documents make it clear that Harford's first colonists deeply appreciated the natural beauties they found here. For instance, George Alsop, whose 1650s tenure as an indentured servant at the head of the bay is discussed in chapter 2, lovingly described the "green, spreading, and delightful Woods" that covered the hills near the confluence of the Susquehanna and Chesapeake; he also suggested that anyone "who out of curiosity desires to see the Landskip of Creation drawn to life, or to read Natures universal Herbal without book, may . . . view *Mary-Land* drest in her green and fragrant Mantel of the Spring," a true "Terrestrial Paradice" of "vegetable plentiousness."[4]

In addition to residents, travelers of every description penned their praises of Harford's natural wonders throughout the colonial era. In 1745 Dr. Alexander Hamilton, an Annapolis physician, spent several hours hunting for wild ginseng, which "a virtuoso in botany . . . told me was to be found in the rich bottoms near Susquehanna."[5] In 1777 Ebenezer Hazard, asked to regularize mail service between the mobile American armies and the Continental Congress in Philadelphia, became distracted from his important task as he passed through Maryland in the spring, particularly after he left Cecil County—"a wild bleak Place"—and crossed into Harford, where the "beautifully decorated" countryside abounded in "Honey Suckles, a kind of blue Flower, yellow and white & red flowers, & a Kind, which from their appearance I take to be a species of Tulip." Edith Rossiter Bevan, Maryland's pioneering garden historian, provided helpful guesses as to what those flowers might be when she wrote that in mid-May

> you will find in the woods of Harford and Baltimore counties quantities of wild azalea (*Rhododendron nudiflorium*) a dwarf shrub with striking flowers of deep rose, pink, and white, . . . and called honeysuckle in New England. The blue flower was probably wild blue phlox (*Phlox divericata*), for it blooms at the same time and in the same kind of woods.

The other flowers she felt were "without doubt" wild columbine (*Aquilegia canadensis*), dog-tooth violet (*Erythonium americanum*), and bloodroot (*Sanguinaria canadensis*); it

1. Alice B. Lockwood, *Gardens of Colony and State* (New York: Garden Club of America, 1934), 115, 117–18.

2. See ibid., 116–18.

3. Anne Leighton, *American Gardens of the Eighteenth Century* (Amherst: University of Massachusetts Press, 1987), 18–26.

4. Alsop, *Character,* 32–34.

5. Bridenbaugh, ed., *Alexander Hamilton,* 5.

also seems likely that the white, tulip-like flowers Hazard admired were wild trillium, which beautifully blanket Harford's woods in the spring.[6]

Geometrical Parterres and Classical Terraces

Still, appreciating native plants is one thing; transforming the wilderness into a garden is quite another. For the earliest solid information about gardening in Harford County one must wait until the late eighteenth century. As was the case in architecture, the county's first documented gardeners were the local elite, specifically the men and women who built the elegant villas around Havre de Grace discussed in chapter 4. This seems reasonable enough since "from 1750 on, a garden was a requisite for every mansion"—a *formal* garden at that, for throughout the eighteenth and early nineteenth centuries "Marylanders . . . overwhelmingly designed their grounds" with "geometric parterres and classical terraces originally inspired by the Italian Renaissance" and used later at the royal gardens of Versailles.[7] A help-wanted advertisement in the February 28, 1824, *Baltimore American,* for instance, requested a gardener "acquainted with the French style" and in 1833 John Pendleton Kennedy, who delivered the opening address at the Maryland Horticultural Society's first flower show, "paid tribute to the useful and worthy French refugees from Santo Domingo . . . [who] had inherited the French traditions of fine gardens." These émigrés, said Kennedy, saw to it that federal-era Baltimore gardens consisted largely of "geometrically laid out beds of low growing annuals which resembled a floral rug spread on a lawn." While delivering his talk, Kennedy must have brushed a tear from his eye as he remembered "with a peculiar fondness, those days of infancy which were spent in playing through the labyrinths of the trimmed hedges of box . . . where the althea, the lilac and the hawthorn bounded the parterre."[8]

These "French rugs" certainly were spread as far as Havre de Grace; C. P. Hauducoeur's 1799 "Map of the Head of the Chesapeake Bay" clearly depicts the two-mile allee at Mount Pleasant that stretched down from the main house to the water's edge. It also shows that the land immediately around the house had been sculpted into manmade terraces with walks and crosswalks laid out perpendicular to the main allee. The estate's owners then planted the terraces lavishly, as if to heighten the orderliness of the composition: around 1802 one neighbor wrote how much she loved to visit Mount Pleasant and its "beautiful . . . green and terraced lawns where the first violets and primroses and early spring flowers were to be found" and the *Sun* reported that the estate's owners also "planted . . . lilacs and . . . daffodils" in clumps around the house.[9] Surprisingly, given the transitory nature of gardens, Mount Pleasant's leafy allee has lasted, in at least partial form, into the twentieth century. A 1907 map clearly shows the terraces and even labels the "row of trees" leading from the house toward the bay. And even though those trees have been largely replaced by boxwood, the formal "bones" of allee, terraced site, and cross axes remain intact.

Nor was Mount Pleasant Harford's only formal, Renaissance-inspired federal-era garden. War of 1812 hero Col. John Streett embellished the grounds of his superb c. 1805 house on Deer Creek with a highly formal garden. The "south front lawn, now a pasture," wrote architect James Wollon after investigating the site, "was shaped with a definite curving fall defining a terrace on which the house was built, with a set of stone steps down to the fall on axis with the house."[10] And although Mark Pringle's Bloomsbury garden was rambling and romantic, not crisp and classical (see below), he kept "3 sets of trees in pots" there, which certainly hints at standards or topiary specimens.

Moreover, just as the Hauducoeur map suggests the formal allee at Mount Pleasant, it also indicates equally formal gardens at Sion Hill, an estate whose acreage bordered Mount Pleasant to the north. The house at Sion Hill was begun around 1787 by the Reverend John Ireland, who, in all likelihood, started the gardens at the same time. The entire composition at Sion Hill resembled Mount Pleasant, since both estates contained a

6. See Fred Shelley, ed., "Ebenezer Hazard's Travels through Maryland," *Maryland Historical Magazine* 66 (1971): 47–48.

7. See Greenspun, ed., *Peale*, 225; Bushman, *Refinement of America,* 129–130; Barbara Wells Sarudy, "Eighteenth-Century Gardens of the Chesapeake," *Journal of Garden History* (July–September 1989): 104.

8. See Edith Rossiter Bevan, "Gardens and Gardening in Early Maryland," *Maryland Historical Magazine* (December 1950): 268-69; for Kennedy's complete text, see John P. Kennedy, "Address Delivered Before the Horticultural Society of Maryland" (Baltimore: John D. Toy, Printer, 1833).

9. See *Harford County Directory* (1953), 320.

10. James Wollon, AIA, notes on the Streett House, in Harford County Planning and Zoning Department, Bel Air.

In good Renaissance style, the eighteenth-century gardens at Mount Pleasant near Havre de Grace were focused on a tree-lined, two-mile allee that ran from the house to the Chesapeake. Most of the trees were replaced with boxwood in the early twentieth century (and the land near the city is no longer connected with the farm) but the formality of the design remains, as these two recent photographs suggest.

five-bay, 2½-story brick manor house placed on a cleared, raised terrace and set off by tightly regimented plantings—an allee and crosswalks at Mount Pleasant, boxwood parterres at Sion Hill. Parterres (etymologically akin to *parquet*) played a crucial role in the formal gardens of seventeenth-century France, Holland, and Britain and, also, as mentioned above, "overwhelmingly" characterized the late eighteenth-century gardens of Maryland.[11] Most of the Sion Hill boxwood disappeared long ago, the victim of blight and age, but a few stalwart bushes have endured, just where Hauducoeur drew them, as evergreen evidence of Sion Hill's original parterre gardens.

11. Sarudy, "Eighteenth-Century Gardens," 125.

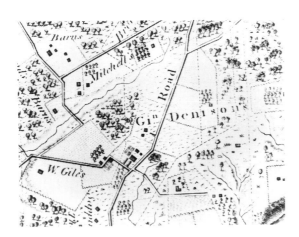

Hauducoeur's map also shows a rectangular, park-like swath of grass at Sion Hill just east of the house and boxwood. This, unlike the boxwood parterres, remains very much in its eighteenth-century state. Three of the flat grassy space's four sides are defined by specimen magnolia grandiflora, holly, beech, and osage orange trees, while the fourth, left open, faces south to afford expansive vistas of the Susquehanna River and Chesapeake Bay. While no known letters or other documents exist to shed light on this mini-park's original use, family tradition suggests it was a bowling green, highly possible since lawn bowling was a fashionable diversion in the late eighteenth century.

Lawn bowling; promenading; whatever the activity, federal-era Americans spent as much time as possible in their gardens. Many would have seconded Thomas Jefferson, who "wrote . . . in July 1793 that he never went to the house but at bedtime, preferring to breakfast, dine, write, read, and receive company under . . . plane-trees." When Jefferson and his Harford County counterparts settled themselves in their gardens, they sat on Windsor chairs, "strong yet portable and easily maintained, . . . [and] considered particularly adaptable to outdoor use." One New York cabinetmaker had advertised "Windsor chairs and settees 'fit for Piazza or Gardens'" as early as 1765,[12] and when Gideon Denison, who had purchased Sion Hill from Ireland in 1795, died in the house in 1800, his appraisers noted "14 Windsor chairs, $8.40," as well as "4 broken Windsor chairs, 50c"—broken, perhaps, from too much garden use? (They also found "5 painted glass flower pots, $1.")

The Jeffersonian Garden: "Abundant Room for Great Variety"

In addition to a shared interest in tilling the soil, Pringle, Denison, and their Havre de Grace neighbors shared a fierce devotion to Thomas Jefferson. They followed the Virginian's lead in politics, architecture, and gardening. And Jefferson's interest in gardening bordered on the fanatic. "By his own testimony Thomas Jefferson would have preferred to be a gardener than to have held any of the high posts that fell to his lot."[13] He wrote Charles Willson Peale in 1811, "If heaven had given me the choice of my position and calling, it would have been a rich spot of earth, well watered . . . for the productions of the garden. No occupation is so delightful to me as the cultivation of the earth, and no

Left: Merchant Gideon Denison bought the house Sion Hill near Havre de Grace in 1795. He also laid out formal boxwood parterres near the mansion. This detail of Hauducoeur's 1799 map of the area indicates such a planting just west of the house. Right: Elizabeth Chambers Rodgers (wife of Adm. John Rodgers) admires some Sion Hill boxwood around 1930. These immense bushes (now largely gone, victims of boxwood blight) stood just where the 1799 map suggests they did; planted in a highly formal pattern in the 1790s, they were left to grow "naturally" in the nineteenth century.

12. Garrett, *At Home*, 30–31.
13. Adams, ed., *Eye of Jefferson*, 315.

Charles Willson Peale's 1788 portrait of William Smith (and grandson Robert Smith Williams) includes a ripe peach, a pruning hook, and a book entitled *Gardening* to suggest the sitter's interest in gardening. The painter also placed the subjects in front of a fanciful classical building to suggest an interest in architectural design. William Smith's daughter, Margaret, married her distant cousin Robert Smith in 1790 and Robert Smith continued his father-in-law's neoclassical/horticultural traditions at Spesutia Island.

culture comparable to that of the garden." So, concluded the sexagenarian former president, "though an old man, I am but a young gardener."[14]

When John Adlum bought what is now called Swan Harbor Farm just outside the city in 1797, he turned its fields into one of Maryland's first documented vineyards. He sent a bottle of his wine to Jefferson in 1809. Jefferson tasted the gift, thanked his Harford County well-wisher for the "very fine wine, . . . so exactly resembling the red burgundy of Chambertin,"[15] and "ordered 165 cuttings of Adlum's grapes for planting at Monticello."[16] Adlum, too, was earnest about his horticultural pursuits. He kept a full-time gardener who lived in the "15 × 15, wood, house for the gardener" listed under Adlum's name in the 1798 tax list—the only gardener's house in the county, according to that very thorough document.

An even stronger Harford County/Albemarle County gardening connection exists in the person of Robert Smith of Spesutia Island. Smith served as secretary of the Navy during both of Jefferson's administrations and the Virginian regarded the Marylander as a member of his innermost circle of "particular friends." The two friends certainly shared an interest in horticulture. For instance, on March 23, 1802, the secretary, busy in Washington as part of the first Jeffersonian cabinet, nevertheless took time to write to tell his kinsman Campbell Smith in Baltimore that it was time to have his "Gardener a Negro man named Nat.," start "to work immediately in the garden."[17] Smith had his horticultural interests strengthened when he married his cousin Margaret Smith, for his bride came from a long line of gardeners. When Charles Willson Peale painted a portrait of her father, William Smith, in 1788, he included the subject's two-year-old grandson in the composition and "the little boy is shown holding a peach from Smith's farm." Peale also filled the canvas with "a peach tree branch, a pruning hook, and several books . . . [including an anonymous] *Gardening*," all to underscore how keenly his sitter pursued his chosen avocation.

Gardening connections between Robert Smith and Jefferson abound. Just as the former cofounded (with Edward Lloyd of Wye House) the Maryland Agricultural Society in 1818, so Jefferson cofounded the Albemarle Agricultural Society. So obsessed with horticulture were the two that on January 15, 1820, they simultaneously enrolled in the Flo-

14. Quoted in Malone, *Sage of Monticello,* 43.

15. See *American Wine Society Journal* (Spring 1989); see also Morton, *Winegrowing in Eastern America,* 24. Adlum eventually left Harford County and moved to Washington, D.C., where in 1823 he published what may have been the first serious American book on winemaking.

16. Bevan, "Gardening," 266.

17. In Robert Smith papers; MS 1427, MHS. Miller, ed., *Papers of Charles Willson Peale,* 1:535.

Henry Archer's c. 1895 photograph of Robert Smith's Jeffersonian villa on Spesutia Island suggests that Smith listened to his friend Jefferson and built a "Roman Country House" in Maryland. The pecan tree in the foreground, known to have been planted by Smith, suggests further Jefferson links for the Virginian greatly valued pecans and frequently gave saplings of the tree to friends throughout the Chesapeake region.

rentine *Imperiale e Reale Accademia Economico Agraria;* although there is no record of either man having gone to Italy to attend a meeting, it is worth mentioning that Smith and Jefferson were the only American members of the institution. Three-dimensional evidence of the pair's shared interest in gardening may be seen in the ancient pecan tree that stands watch over the ruins of Smith's c. 1810 Spesutia Island villa, discussed in chapter 4. According to the *Sunday Sun,* Smith planted the pecan the day his grandson, Robert Hall Smith, was born.[18] This almost certainly leads the narrative to Monticello. Jefferson was inordinately fond of this native American tree. He praised the pecan lavishly in his only published book, *Notes on the State of Virginia;* he nurtured several saplings in his own gardens; and he "was constantly dispensing them to friends both here and abroad. . . . Many a Virginia garden and lawn is now shaded by pecan trees as a result of this pioneer plant distributor's interest."[19] If Jeffersonian pecans do not shade many a Maryland garden, they do shade a few; Jefferson himself actually planted pecans at Marietta, the Prince George's County seat of his close friend Gabriel Duvall. And although there is no documentary evidence of Jeffersonian pecans in Harford County, it does not take much imagination to see how Jefferson could have sent his great friend and former Cabinet member a sapling of a favorite tree to mark the happy occasion of the birth of a first grandson.

Jefferson not only appreciated gardens for what might be called their intrinsic pleasures, he valued them for their more emblematic values as well. On a personal level, one May day, when he was nearing the age of 70, he wrote his eldest granddaughter to describe how "the flowers come forth like the belles of the day, have their short reign of beauty and splendor, and retire like them to the more interesting office of reproducing their kind. . . . The Irises are giving place to the Belladonas . . . as your Mama has done to you . . . and as I shall soon and cheerfully do to you all in wishing you a long, long good night."[20] He was also aware that the symbolic value of gardening could extend to politics.

Like other leaders of that time, Jefferson felt it was important to understand how a garden works, that is, how light, temperature, water, and wind affect the success (or failure) of plants. He "theorized that if you understand natural law, you could group and use

18. Katherine Scarborough, "'White Ghost Dog' Roams the Manor," *Baltimore Sunday Sun,* November 28, 1954.

19. Nichols and Griswold, *Thomas Jefferson, Landscape Architect,* 143–45.

20. Quoted in Malone, *Sage of Monticello,* 49.

the laws which governed society." And just as Jefferson helped effect a revolutionary change in American government, so did he help effect an equally radical change in American gardening. He condemned the earlier, formal style seen at Mount Pleasant and Sion Hill, "because of its association with European aristocratic" traditions.[21] To replace those sharply defined and hierarchical compositions, he advocated free and mixed plantings and gardens where sweeps of open lawn were "variegated with clumps of trees distributed with taste." Or, as his protégé, the architect Benjamin Henry Latrobe, wrote in his short "Essay on Landscape" (1798–99),

> The fault . . . [in old-style gardening] is formality, or want of ease. . . . It was the fashion all over Europe . . . to admire nature in every shape but her own . . . But *modern Philosophy*, . . . her innovating spirit in politics and religion . . . [led] to banishing that arrogance. . . . In America . . . till very lately we still loved straight unshaded Walks, and called them a Garden.[22]

Believing in action as well as words, Jefferson relandscaped the grounds of Monticello with "ornamental trees . . . chosen for the contrasting textures of their foliage" and redesigned the flowerbeds there as well.[23] The old "limited number of . . . beds will too much restrain the variety of flowers," he wrote, but a new, freer system of planting "would give us abundant room for great variety." Thus encouraged by Jefferson and Latrobe, "in the United States garden writers finally proclaimed their independence from Europe" and published such books as *The American Gardener* (1804) by Washington, D.C., resident David Hepburn and *The American Gardener's Calendar* (1806) by Bernard McMahon, a Philadelphia horticulturist whom "Jefferson entrusted with the seed collected from the Lewis and Clark expedition."[24]

All this may be seen in Harford County at Mark Pringle's Bloomsbury, mentioned above. Pringle was a keen gardener indeed. When he died in 1819 his gardening equipment included "1 new wheel barrow, $4," "5 spades, $2.50," some miscellaneous "garden tools, $3," and "2 [lawn] rollers, $2." (An early gardening "how-to" book, published, incidentally, in Baltimore, sternly stated that "to preserve tracts of lawn in a beautiful order, they must be frequently rolled. . . . The large stone or iron roller . . . must be used at all times, all the year, even in winter.")[25] Although Pringle's house and grounds were razed around 1910, an 1863 *Harper's* magazine engraving of the place reveals that Pringle had used his lawn rollers to give the grass around the house a billiard-table smoothness; it also shows that the gardens depended for their overall effect on a Jeffersonian contrast between that open lawn and a few specimen trees left to grow naturally.

Among the more notable of Pringle's trees, according to a 1905 description of Bloomsbury, were "primeval [white] oaks at the mansion, . . . and cedars . . . , likely the largest in the state." Both red and white cedar (*Juniperus virginiana* and *Chamaecyparis thyoides*) were highly popular among the new nation's "natural" federal-era gardeners,[26] including Jefferson, who sent some seeds of them and other favorite native trees to his friend Madame de Tessé in Paris in 1805. "Juniperus virgin," he called the plant in his accompanying note to her, adding, "I presume some method is known and practiced with you to make the seeds come up. I have never known but one person [to] succeed with them here. He crammed them down the throats of his poultry . . . and then sowed their dung." Keeping Jefferson's cedar seeds company in the box were seeds of *Quercus alba* (Pringle's white oak—"it is the finest of the whole family," Jefferson wrote de Tessé, and "may be called the Jupiter . . . of our groves")[27] and *Liriodendron tulipifera,* or tulip poplar. Significantly, in 1812 Pringle ordered "4 Tulip trees" from an unknown Baltimore nursery; his full order, in all its Jeffersonian variety, consisted of

6 silver Giliad Firs	12 Lombardy Poplars
4 China Arbor Vitae	4 Larch
4 Laburnums	2 double flowering peach
4 Athenian poplars	4 English Lady finger apples

21. Peter Martin, *The Pleasure Gardens of Virginia* (Princeton: Princeton University Press, 1991), 144; Mark Leone, "William Paca's Power Garden," *Maryland Humanities* (July/August 1994): 11; Therese O'Malley, "Appropriation and Adaption: Early Gardening Literature in America," *Huntington Library Quarterly* (Summer 1992): 423.

22. *The Virginia Journals of Benjamin Henry Latrobe,* ed. Carter, 2:499–500.

23. Peter J. Hatch, *The Gardens of Monticello* (Charlottesville: Thomas Jefferson Memorial Foundation, 1992), 34. Jefferson, in fact, planted "113 species of ornamental trees and sixty-five shrubs, over 100 species of herbaceous plants . . . , and 450 varieties of ninety-five species of fruits, vegetables, nuts, and herbs" at Monticello. Hatch, *Gardens of Monticello,* 15.

24. Quoted in Adams, *Eye of Jefferson,* 331–32; O'Malley, "Appropriation and Adaption," 425.

25. Fielding Lucas, *The Practical American Gardener* (Baltimore: Fielding Lucas, Jr., 1819), 269.

26. See Anne Leighton, "An Appendix of the Plants Most Frequently Cultivated in Eighteenth-Century Gardens," in her *American Gardens of the Eighteenth Century,* 404.

27. Quoted in Allen Lacy, ed., *The American Gardener* (New York: Farrar, Straus, Giroux, 1988), 169–70. Jefferson shipped the seeds from Baltimore in "a box 4 feet long and 1 foot wide and deep . . . to the care of William Patterson," Baltimore merchant and in 1805 "commercial agent of the U.S. at Nantes."

A NARRATIVE HISTORY OF HARFORD COUNTY

6 English Filiberts	6 New Town Pippins [Jefferson's
2 Silver Pines for Mr. Hughes [Samuel	favorite apple]
Hughes then of Mount Pleasant]	4 Tulip poplar trees

That March 20 Pringle wrote attorney Paca Smith, who managed his Harford affairs when he himself was detained elsewhere, that the Bloomsbury gardener, a slave named Pompey, should "plant 4 Catalpa trees according to the direction of Mr. Hughes"; ten days later he wrote attorney Howes Goldsborough, who had married a sister of Commo. John Rodgers, to keep an eye out for "4 [unnamed] trees, 1 Goose Berry Bush, and 2 Grape cuttings . . . to go to the House." Finally, on April 28, 1812, he wrote another agent to expect "a parcel of Fig Trees"; Pompey was to plant the figs "immediatly under the Bank where the Strawberries are planted but more to the eastward."[28]

Whether or not Pringle obtained his gardening ideas directly from Jefferson, the Harford countian did have access to all the latest in garden philosophies thanks to his membership in the Library Company of Baltimore. Chartered in 1795, the company owned more than forty books on horticultural subjects, including Thomas Butterfield Bayley's *Thoughts on Manure* (1775), Samuel Felton's *Miscellanies on Ancient and Modern Gardening* (1785), and Linneaus's highly important *The Families of Plants* (1787 edition). Indeed, Baltimore's bibliophiles "stepped into the [horticultural] limelight . . . early," for two of the nation's first garden books, Fielding Lucas's *The Practical American Gardener* (1819) and Joseph P. Casey's *Treatise on the Culture of Flower Roots and Greenhouse Plants* (1821) were published in the Monumental City.[29] Lucas, evidently a Jeffersonian himself, encouraged his readers to employ "greater variety" in their selection of plants than they had so far and told them that "a free interspersion of ornamental shrubs will afford variety and have an agreeable effect."[30]

In addition to the Smith/Jefferson connection, other real—or at least arguable—ties seem to exist between Harford's federal-era gardeners and the great thinkers and artists of the time. Take Pringle's friend, the aforementioned Samuel Hughes, who purchased Mount Pleasant in the 1790s. The 1798 federal tax rolls show that he built "2 small houses in the garden, 12 × 8, stone," almost certainly a pair of stone summerhouses or ornamental temples. (If they had been stone tenant-houses or slaves' quarters, they would have been so described.) Such structures represented the height of late eighteenth-century garden fashion. Strategically placed among the plantings and with sharp lines to counterbalance the foliage, neoclassical stone temples or follies made visual focal points for the garden's axes, provided shelters from sudden summer showers and noonday sun, made convenient locations for clandestine assignations,[31] and—perhaps most important—helped create "icons of the republican image that the early nationalists were striving to define. . . . As they set about establishing a new republic based on a classical model, early American landowners identified themselves as participants in a pastoral tradition" that stretched back to Pliny, Virgil, and the Roman republic. Jefferson himself designed several such temples for his own garden and placed them at "those spots on the walks most interesting."[32] He based one on Hadrian's Tomb since he believed that "Roman taste, genius, and magnificence excite ideas."

At virtually the same time Jefferson was building temples in the Monticello gardens, one of the early republic's favorite painters, Charles Willson Peale, was embellishing his garden, Belfield, near Philadelphia, with a neo-Egyptian masonry obelisk; Peale also "transformed a toolshed into a small triumphal arch."[33] Perhaps not coincidentally, Peale knew Robert Smith and Samuel Hughes, two of Harford County's greatest gardeners, well. The painter's journals show that he frequently stopped at Spesutia to see Robert Smith and to paint a portrait of Smith's wife. (Recall Peale also painted that symbol-laden portrait of Smith's father-in-law.)[34] Hughes went bankrupt around 1820 and his Peale portrait (completed in 1789) has disappeared. If, by some miracle, it should one day surface, one wonders if it will depict Hughes full-length with his stone garden-houses in the

This 1863 *Harper's* magazine illustration of Mark Pringle's Bloomsbury (near Havre de Grace) captures the estate's billiard-table smooth lawn (Pringle owned two lawn rollers) and contrasting dark-green cedar trees.

28. All correspondence from the Pringle Letterbook, MHS.

29. Bevan, "Gardening," 266; she adds that Baltimore was also "the first . . . home of *The American Farmer,* the first American magazine issued in the interest of agriculture with articles of horticultural interest as well."

30. Lucas, *Practical American Gardener,* 246.

31. An important period concern: think of the last act of *The Marriage of Figaro.*

32. Quoted in Martin, *Pleasure Gardens,* 158.

33. See Karl Lehmann, *Thomas Jefferson, American Humanist* (Charlottesville: University Press of Virginia, 1985), 175; Therese O'Malley, "Charles Willson Peale's Belfield," in Miller and Ward, eds., *New Perspectives on Charles Willson Peale,* 272.

34. See Miller, ed., *Papers of Charles Willson Peale.*

One wonders if Samuel Hughes's gardens outside Havre de Grace resembled William Paca's in Annapolis. It is known, for instance, that Hughes built "two stone houses" in his garden and they may have been similar to those shown in this detail of Peale's 1772 portrait of Paca; both gardens were terraced; and Paca and Hughes were well acquainted with each other.

background, much as Peale's 1772 portrait of Harford County native William Paca depicts *him* in his Annapolis garden with his stuccoed stone summerhouse prominent in the distance.

Actually, there are many similarities between Paca's garden in Annapolis and Hughes's near Havre de Grace: both had terraces, both had a broad central axis and crosswalks, and both had informal "wilderness" plantings. These similarities should not be altogether surprising, however, since Paca and Hughes were well known to each other: Hughes had been guardian of Paca Smith, mentioned above and William Paca's cousin, when that future gardener was an infant, and had borrowed vast sums of money purportedly on the child's behalf from the Annapolitan. Perhaps not coincidentally, from 1834 to 1851 Mount Pleasant was owned by Paca's grandson, William B. Paca.

Seed Merchants and Rosarians

Marylanders' burgeoning federal-era interest in gardening made local commercial nurseries economically feasible. Two of the earliest nurseries in the state, William Booth's and James Wilkes's, have probable ties to Harford County. Booth, "the most successful [of these] seed dealers, nursery owners, and gardeners in the late eighteenth century," had started operations by 1793. In April of that year he announced in Baltimore newspapers that "BOTANISTS, GARDENERS AND FLORISTS, and . . . all other gentlemen curious in ornamental, rare exotic or foreign plants and flowers" should be aware that he was growing and selling "garden seeds imported from London" and "tropical fruits and other rare and curious finely ornamental trees, shrubs and plants."[35] He sold these treasures from his rented quarters "at the home of Thorowgood Smith, Esq., in downtown Baltimore," a wonderful location, to be sure, for Smith's Baltimore estate, Willow Brook, was set off by "26 acres of . . . the choicest . . . trees, shrubs, flowers &c., collected from the best nurseries in America and Europe." To show what a cozy world it was, Thorowgood Smith's daughter, Lucy, married Mark Pringle in 1797 in a ceremony performed by the Reverend John Ireland, formerly of Sion Hill. Their son eventually married a daughter of George Grundy, who had laid out "elegant gardens" at his Baltimore estate, Bolton.[36]

Grundy hired the English gardener/seed-merchant James Wilkes to look after the

35. Sarudy, "Eighteenth-Century Gardens," 114.
36. *Federal Gazette,* April 18, 1800; genealogical clipping, MHS, Baltimore.

William Booth, who had worked as a gardener at Thorowgood Smith's estate Willow Brook in the 1790s, published the earliest remaining local seed/plant catalog in 1810. He also designed many Baltimore-area gardens including the parterres and terraces at Hampton, shown here. Did he design Mark Pringle's at Bloomsbury near Havre de Grace? No one knows, but Pringle, an avid gardener, married Thorowgood Smith's daughter, Lucy, in 1797.

place in 1800, but Wilkes left Grundy's employ in 1803 to set himself up in the nursery business "on the Philadelphia road about one mile from Baltimore," that is, on the road to Havre de Grace and Pringle's Bloomsbury. Wilkes tempted Baltimore-area gardeners with newspaper offerings of "FRUIT TREES, and all sorts of Shrubbery, Green House, Hot House Plants &c &c" and English garden seeds. After he died in 1818, "his widow, Margaret, . . . listed in the [Baltimore City] Directory as 'Vendor of garden seeds,' . . . continued the nursery and seed business" until about 1830.[37]

Like Wilkes, Booth, too, eventually quit working for Pringle in-laws and struck out on his own by opening a vast nursery and greenhouse in Baltimore. An enterprising entrepreneur, Booth propagated his own stock, rented out space in the greenhouse so "ladies" might "winter over tender potted plants," entered into joint ventures with seedsmen in New York and Philadelphia, and published "the earliest remaining Maryland seed and plant catalog" in 1810. He also "designed and planted some of Baltimore's most famous gardens including the extant terraced falls at Hampton." Booth created gardens for dozens of clients in Washington, Annapolis, and "busy Frederick town"—and, one wonders, in Havre de Grace, in the person of Mark Pringle, son-in-law of the man who gave him his start?[38]

Gardening continued to gain popularity as the century progressed, which "made it imperative that plants and seeds be much more readily and widely available. More peo-

37. Sarudy, "Eighteenth-Century Gardens," 114; Bevan, "Gardening," 263.

38. Sarudy, "Eighteenth-Century Gardens," 115, 114.

In the 1880s a Scandinavian diplomat wrote that there was only one other place in America "where roses grow to such perfection in the open air as Havre de Grace." The other place was *not* the Kelly family's Liriodendron; nonetheless, under the care of Mrs. Kelly (shown here c. 1910), the estate's roses flourished. Note also the wisteria-embowered metal arches over the terrace, and the pots and pots of tropical plants. The Kellys kept the latter happy in the winter in Liriodendron's four greenhouses.

ple than ever were laying out ornamental gardens and required flowers and decorative bushes and trees to embellish them." Demand appears to have been insatiable in Harford throughout the early nineteenth century, when virtually every local newspaper carried garden-related ads: on April 26, 1838, S. B. Richardson was "happy to inform his old customers" (i.e., readers of Bel Air's *Madisonian*) of his supply of "FRESH GARDEN SEED"; F. Irvine Hitchcock frequently notified countians throughout the 1830s, via the Bel Air–based *Independent Citizen,* of his "fruit and flower" plants and "Ornamental Trees, Shrubs, Plants, Vines, Roots &c" and "extensive assortment of books, periodicals on Agriculture, Horticulture, and Veterinary Subjects"; and "Prince's Linnaen Botanic Garden and Nursery" tempted readers in issue after issue of the *Harford Republican* with an "unrivaled . . . catalog of . . . *Ornamental Trees and Plants*" and "1,200 varieties of roses" throughout the antebellum decades.[39]

Twelve hundred varieties of rugosas, damasks, and centifolias sounds astonishingly high (and is, at least by sorry standards of nurseries today), but nineteenth-century Harford countians did love their roses. The German-born Mrs. Henry Ostheim had a garden in Fallston that was famously "full of roses." (Miss Marian Curtiss of the Oakland School, where generations of Fallstonians learned botany, said that Mrs. Ostheim had told her the secret for dealing with slugs: "'I dakes dem in me fingers, so, and smashes 'em, so.'") A Scandinavian diplomat reported that "roses . . . grow in great abundance" in Havre de Grace. "I know of only one other place in the United States, Cambridge, Md., where roses grow to such perfection in the open air as Havre de Grace," he wrote. And in Bel Air, Laetitia Kelly, who "took special trouble with the roses" at Liriodendron, is featured, with a daughter, in a c. 1910 photograph that depicts the two, long skirts rustling across the grass, slaving away to keep Liriodendron's 100-foot-long rosebed weed free.[40]

The Romantic Harford Garden

By the 1830s and '40s, particularly after 1844, the year Andrew Jackson Downing published his *Treatise on Landscape Gardening,* Thomas Jefferson's "natural" garden became,

39. Martin, *Pleasure Gardens,* 92. In the 1860s the *Bel Air National American* carried ads for "Eaton Farm Nursery 3 Miles north of Havre de Grace" (November 1, 1861), J. Tudor Cook's "Fruit and Ornamental Trees" at Cooksville (July 10, 1863), and A. H. Greenfield's "Shaker Garden Seeds" for sale "at Main Street and Port Deposit Avenue" in Bel Air (March 16, 1866). (The local papers hawked a variety of wares: did anyone give in to the December 16, 1859, *Bel Air National American* ad entitled "Manhood How Lost Restored"? Anyone who did was promised to be sent "in a sealed envelope" something that would "effectually remove . . . the awful consequences of self abuse.")

40. Louis Bagger, Vice Consul for Denmark, Sweden, and Norway, in the *Havre de Grace Republican,* May 20, 1887; Margaret Kelly Warner, conversation with author, October 10, 1980.

as it were, even more "natural" than Jefferson could have hoped for, thanks to the nationwide mania for "the picturesque" (discussed in chapter 6). Downing, who wrote that gardens ought to produce "a certain spiritual irregularity," advocated the use of dark-foliaged conifers to create "thickets, glades, and underwood, as in nature," all set off by trees with interestingly colored foliage such as purple and copper beeches. This was all very Jeffersonian. But Downing and his followers, influenced by the romantic spirit that affected every early Victorian artist, took Jefferson's thoughts about the "informal" landscape beyond anything at Monticello. Throughout America winding walks became *more* winding, meandering streams became *more* meandering. Rustic, cast-iron benches replaced neoclassical stone temples as the favored garden ornament. Accordingly, in 1854 when Harford County farmer Joshua Green set out to plant a garden at his Hidden Valley Farm, a rolling 256-acre spread near the upper reaches of the Little Gunpowder Falls, he gave the hilly site a "natural" garden in the best Downing tradition. And even though the passing decades have simplified Green's gardens somewhat, enough remains to make it easy to grasp the essence of his landscaping thoughts. Just as Downing had urged his readers to make their driveways "gently serpentine . . . [around] some groups of trees," so Green, whose herds of Jersey cattle made him "one of the richest farmers in the district," designed a teardrop-shaped driveway with mysterious dark-green spruce trees clumped seemingly at random along its loopy path.[41]

Splendid as Green's Hidden Valley garden is, he was not the first in the county to create a picturesque landscape. That honor goes to Mary Norris, whose husband, John, had inherited the tract Prospect, near Wilna, in 1803. The farm had belonged to Norris's ancestors since the mid-eighteenth century, but neither John nor Mary was enchanted with the house—or garden—they found there. To transform their inheritance, they built a grand brick house on the property and Mary Norris laid out a romantically informal garden around the new house. Mrs. Norris drew inspiration for her work—indeed for her romantic view of rural life—from her favorite poet, William Cowper (1731–1800), who spent his life happily pursuing "carpentry, gardening, horse exercising, walking, and the simple pleasures" of country life. Cowper is said to have anticipated Wordsworth in drawing "poetry back to the simple truths of . . . the English countryside" in lines such as these:

> For I have loved the rural walk through lanes
> Of grassy swarth, close cropped by nibbling sheep
> And skirted thick with intertexture firm
> Of thorny boughs; have loved the rural walk
> O'er hills, through valleys, and by rivers' brink.[42]

Inspired by Cowper, Mrs. Norris "between 1810 and 1840 laid out and planted a box-wood garden at the back of the new house. The original forest in front remained to shelter from the northwest winds; but the new types of evergreens, Norway and native spruce, were planted" in a romantically informal manner. She also had her husband change the name of the farm from Prospect to Olney, to honor Cowper's "Olney Hymns." Alexis Shriver, who owned Olney during the first half of the twentieth century, evidently became caught up in the spirit of it all, for he wrote that "on windy days [the evergreens] softly croon their sad realization that they, like the [owners], are not permanent."[43] Shriver was not alone in admiring Mrs. Norris's garden; whoever prepared the deed to Olney in 1850, when the family sold the farm, carefully sketched those crooning conifers onto the property plat.

Shriver, a leading force in the Maryland State Horticultural Society, not only documented the history of the Olney gardens, but also added some wonderful touches of his own, including the wisteria that still rambles across the house's north and west façades. The Olney wisteria is a "child" of an ancient vine that once embowered the c. 1800 house Montebello in Baltimore. When Montebello's early twentieth-century owners threatened

41. Leighton, *American Gardens of the Nineteenth Century*, 130; *Portrait and Biographical Record*, 202.
42. *Cambridge History of English Literature* (Cambridge: Cambridge University Press, 1982), 85, 77.
43. Shriver, "History of Old Olney," 5, 7.

Mary Norris helped bring the romantic movement to Harford County: she had her husband, John, change the name of their farm from Prospect to Olney to honor the "Olney Hymns" of her favorite poet, William Cowper, and she filled the garden around the brick house with lavish plantings of exotic evergreens. Alexis Shriver, whose father bought Olney in 1861, was a founding member of the Maryland Horticultural Society. He was also evidently something of a romantic gardener himself. Around 1910 he took a cutting from a wisteria vine at the Baltimore estate Montebello and planted it at Olney. It can be seen in this c. 1915 photograph rambling across Olney's south porch.

to demolish and pave over the place, Shriver raced onto the scene, clippers sharpened, and took a cutting of the vine, which he and his descendants have nurtured into the present house-engulfing monster. He also made cuttings from his cutting and presented them to his many gardening friends. Mr. and Mrs. John Work Garrett of Evergreen House in Baltimore received two such cuttings: "I can give you plenty of roots," Shriver assured the Garretts, "which your gardener . . . can probably train over your tea house."[44]

The Olney plantings must have been wonderful in their prime; one only wishes there was more of a record of them. In fact, because of the sketchy nature of early garden documentation in general, generations of local historians have given silent prayers of thanks to Darlington physician Dr. W. Stump Forwood and his wonderfully detailed descriptions of Deer Creek houses and gardens, and of byways made shaggy by "short-leaved laurel . . . mosses, ferns, and the trailing arbutus."[45] Here, for example, is the doctor's report on the Jewett-King estate, Lansdowne, whose gardens, he wrote, lay "sweetly embowered in the bosom of a beautiful vale" near Glenville:

From the public road which passes in front [of Lansdowne] we look down the charming vista and catch interesting glimpses of this historic mansion through many stately forest trees about the house, and many of the more ornamental varieties that, in their beauty, are evergreen. . . . The grounds between the entrance-gate at the highway and dwelling, extending several hundred yards in each direction, constitute a magnificent lawn, which comprises several acres within its bounds, and affords one of the chief attractions in interest and beauty outside of, or apart from the residence itself, that can be connected with a country home.

The carriage-way leading to the house, with a rustic, old style gate across it some distance from the entrance, and adding to the picturesqueness of the view, winds gracefully down the hill, and, at its base, crosses a rustic bridge which spans a small stream that meanders through the lawn. . . . After crossing the bridge, there is quite an eminence to be ascended before reaching the house; the roadway winds its serpentine course to the left, the carriages passing either entirely around the house, in the direction of the barn, or across the grounds to the front door of the dwelling. Many of the trees standing around, upon all sides, are natives of the American forest, as before intimated, and some of them are venerable and grand with age. . . .

44. Shriver file. Things must have worked out since Mr. Garrett wrote back two years later (in a "Dear Alexis" / "Fondly, John" vein) that "the wisteria is magnificent."

45. Forwood, "Homes on Deer Creek," March 19, 1880.

On the brow of the high ground to the right, looking from the public road, and immediately in front of the house, near a little rustic and cozy arbor, stands life-size and life-like the molded form (in iron) of a deer, with its numerous branching antlers. At a short distance to the left sits, in like enduring form, the faithful and 'honest watch-dog,' both appearing in semblance of form and in positions so natural and life-like, as at first glance to deceive the beholder with belief in their reality and vitality.

Between these representatives of the wild and of domestic life, rather nearer to the house, and opposite the front entrance door, is located a very handsome fountain jet d'eau—the spray from which, besides its beauty in sunshine, is delightfully refreshing during the long and hot days of summer. Around this fountain, to be bedewed by its spray, in the summer season, the proprietor, with admirable taste . . . arranges pots of many-hued blooming flowers, much to the delight and pleasure of his numerous . . . visitors, as well as to his own gratification.

When this fountain is in full play, and surrounded by the gay flowers and beautiful green trees, the many singing birds that annually build their nests and rear their young, secure from harm, in and upon the waving branches of the trees, and undisturbed sing their joyful songs, the scene is one that the busy business man of city life, whose hard fate it is to tramp day after day over the dry, hot pavements to and from his never-ending treadmill duties, might yearningly long for, and look upon as the realization of the Elysium of his enchanting dreams.[46]

The gardens at Lansdowne near Glenville: "The carriage-way," wrote Dr. W. Stump Forwood in 1880, "winds gracefully down the hill." The grounds around "this historic mansion," Forwood continued, are filled "with many stately forest trees . . . and many . . . in their beauty are evergreen."

Deep in the midst of Dr. Forwood's prose, a prose made dense with Cowperesque, thorny-bowed adjectives, one finds mention of an essential feature of Victorian-era gardens, namely cast-iron "furniture" such as Lansdowne's "faithful and 'honest watch-dog.'" Thanks to mass production, American factories turned out thousands of cast-iron urns, deer, hitching posts, planters, fences, and benches, beginning around 1870,[47] such as the "Rustic Bench in Yard" taxmen found when Ramsay McHenry of Monmouth Farm died in 1878.

Dr. Forwood's accounts of the Silver family's Glenville villas are not as long—or as turgid—as his description of Lansdowne, but they are no less important to this study of period horticulture. (For both Lansdowne and the Silver villas, see also chapter 6.) He begins his series with Dr. Silas Silver's Silverton (c. 1856), where

a splendid and spacious lawn, consisting of six or eight acres, slopes grandly down to the public road in front, like a charming landscape painted by the hand of a master. Beautiful evergreen trees, in endless variety, planted singly, and in groups, dot the lawn with their unfading verdure; while near the dwelling are many bright beds of flowers, which, in the spring, summer and autumn, delight the eyes of all beholders with their profusion of rare and sweetest blossoms.[48]

Three of Silas Silver's brothers and a first cousin joined the doctor in building stone villas on hills just south of Deer Creek; four of these houses survive and combine to create a nationally significant impression of high Victoriana. Moreover, the family's ventures into landscape design evidently proved catching since, following their example, blacksmith J. Frank Reasin "laid out a very pretty lawn about his house [in Glenville], and . . . planted a number of evergreen trees, together with shrubbery and flowers."[49]

All five Silvers were deeply interested in matters of design. In fact, Silas's oldest brother, Benjamin Silver III, owned a copy of Calvert Vaux's 1857 book, *Villas and Cottages,* perhaps the most influential publication of its time regarding architecture and gardening, and Benjamin and his kinsmen regularly consulted that tome when they designed houses and churches, laid out roads, and planned and planted their gardens. For example, Vaux urged his readers to construct "a plant cabinet or small conservatory" in the form of a large bay window at "the end of a dining room" with "glass doors of communication" to shut it off and trap the heat—*clear* glass doors to allow "a good view of the flowers, etc., when the sliding doors are closed." And a hexagonal plant cabinet complete with sliding doors—the only known Vauxian "plant cabinet" in Harford County—still

46. Ibid.

47. Patricia M. Tice, "Industry in the Garden," talk presented and transcribed in the 1988 seminar "Victorian Landscape in America," sponsored by the Philadelphia's Morris Arboretum, 27.

48. Forwood, "Homes on Deer Creek," March 19, 1880.

49. Ibid.; Reasin's brother, William, was an architect who helped design at least two of the Silver villas, as is discussed in chapter 6.

Dr. Silas Silver built his stone villa, Silverton, near Glenville in 1858. His brother Benjamin owned a copy of Calvert Vaux's highly influential book, *Villas and Cottages* (1857). Vaux urged homebuilders to include "a plant cabinet or small conservatory" in the form of a large bay window in their design; this is the plant cabinet at Silverton.

50. Vaux, *Villas,* 81. Old photographs suggest that Silas's cousin, William Finney Silver, built a plant cabinet at his villa, too; if he did, it was removed in later remodelings.

51. *The Garden* (London: Victoria and Albert Museum, 1979), 96; Americans were no strangers to plant importing either and our first minister to Mexico, Charlestonian Joel Poinsett, while on duty collected that red-"flowered" plant now known as poinsettia.

52. Cadwalader hired a "Scots" gardener in 1850 who evidently didn't work out, for in 1853 his foreman wrote to let him know he had hired another one, "highly recommended for pruning trees and everything." (He added, "I can't visit you in New Porte. I have to watch the guano market so closs that I must not leave.") In 1856 Cadwalader insured his "Gardener's House, frame" with the Harford Mutual Insurance Company for $250. Unless otherwise stated, all Cadwalader material is from the Cadwalader Collection, Historical Society of Pennsylvania.

graces the dining room at Silverton.[50] The Silvers were also caught up in the nationwide fascination with exotic plants. Throughout the middle of the century, botanists swarmed across the globe in such numbers that "it seemed . . . [as if] there were almost more plant collectors . . . than plants."[51] This was fine with the Silvers. Benjamin Silver III's detailed *Cash Book* notes that on March 21, 1860, he "pd. Walton, nursery man, Fallston, 50 cts. for Pawlonia, Japan, 50 cts. for European Larch, [and] 50 cts. for European Mountain Ash."

George Cadwalader and Maxwell's Point

Yet as remarkable as Silver's imported trees are, they pale when compared to the immense arboretum of exotics Maj. Gen. George Cadwalader created at Maxwell's Point on the Gunpowder Neck. And those gardens were—emphatically—*his* gardens; even though Cadwalader employed a series of full-time professionals to look after the plantings (and commissioned architect J. Crawford Neilson to design a gardener's cottage for them to live in),[52] his own detailed records show that he knew an amaryllis from an aspidistra. One 1865 memorandum of things to be done, for instance, contains reminders to check "the holly hedge around the garden [which] has been neglected," to look after the "pears neglected," and to prune his "Lady Banks running rose."

Cadwalader, a Philadelphian who lived "in more luxury & style than any man in town" ("several travelled persons said that they saw nothing handsomer in Europe" than the general's residence, 1519 Locust Street)[53] brought those selfsame characteristics with him when he dug his spade into Maxwell's Point's sandy soil. A noted sportsman with an especial weakness for duck-hunting, Cadwalader (born 1806) built himself a shooting lodge at Maxwell's and began buying up land on the Neck in the early 1840s. By the time he died in 1879, he owned virtually the entire peninsula bordered by the Gunpowder and Bush rivers and what is now the Amtrak main line, that is, over 7,500 acres washed by 28 miles of shoreline.

The general began his Maryland gardening on a practical note when he ordered 1,000 peach trees from Lloyd Rogers's nursery at Druid Hill in 1841. His annotated copy of the "Druid Hill Catalogue of . . . Very Choice . . . Peach Trees" suggests that he carefully chose varieties to ensure a summer-long supply, from "Early Anne," whose fruit ripened from "July 20th to 25th," to "Last of the Mohicans, Oct. 5th to 15th." Cadwalader added 200 apple trees to his Gunpowder orchard in 1842 and, over the years, scores of grapevines. Those plantings would stand him in good stead during the Civil War: when other Union officers had to make do with hardtack, Gen. Cadwalader feasted off boxes of fresh fruit (as well as turkeys, chickens, eggs, and in one notable instance, a "bottle of mushroom ketchup") from Maxwell's Point. Aware that the Gunpowder Neck's soggy flanks required an enormous expenditure of labor and money to make them fit for growing anything more ambitious than cattails, Cadwalader constantly requested his workmen to build and repair dikes and drainage canals; he also had them fertilize the sandy soil, ordering, for example, 1,500 bushels of ashes in September 1844 and 13,492 pounds of guano in September of 1849. Thanks to such feedings, the Neck supported a dozen prosperous tenant farms as well as the exotic gardens Cadwalader developed around his own house at "The Point."

The general, described in 1858 as "wholly worldly & earthy, a man of action and pleasure, . . . coarse & profligate . . . determined to enjoy life & fortune in his own way," a man who "keeps a mistress openly, without pretence at concealment . . . at his place in Maryland,"[54] also concerned himself with issues of garden design. A sketch drawn and labeled in his unmistakable hand, shows an elaborate moustache-shaped "Pattern for flower beds," and this suggests that he was, like many of his contemporaries, an enthusiastic bedder-out. Thus did gardeners of that era revive the parterre, which had been banished from stylish gardens for about a generation, but with a twist. Nineteenth-century gardeners of Cadwalader's time, bored at the thought of Sion Hill's uniformly green parterres, crammed their sinuous-shaped beds with a succession of flowers of a single species in a single color: monochromatic tulips in the spring; monochromatic dahlias and cannas in summer.

When it came time to fill those beds, Cadwalader, who demanded—and usually got—the best, dealt with one Mme. Ramel, a member "of the Horticulture Society of Paris," who imported her bulbs and roots directly from France and then distributed them among her customers from her shop at 147 Chestnut Street. The general spent freely with Mme. Ramel, too; one order alone consisted of five plants of the white camellia "Calypso," and twenty tree peonies.[55] The general patronized local nurseries as well, and bought "6 persian Iris," "12 Roses assorted," as well as lilacs, flowering almonds, wisteria, and an oak-leaf hydrangea from the Philadelphian "B. Duke" in April 1842.

While Mme. Ramel's Parisian roses and camellias may sound exotic to gardeners today, Cadwalader, in effect, took his trowel to even more distant shores in search of botanical rarities and imported saplings of *Paulownia tomentosa*, *Crytomeria*, *Acer japonicum atropurpuriem*, and *Ginkgo biloba* from Asia in the 1840s and '50s (America did not "open" Japan to Western trade until 1853), as well as chestnut trees from Spain, yews from Ireland, and cuttings of redwoods (*Sequoia sempervirens*) from that exotic place called California, which the United States had snatched from Mexico as recently as 1848. Wondrous as all those must have been, "pride of place," at Maxwell's, wrote the general's great-grand-

53. Quoted in Nicholas Wainwright, *Colonial Grandeur in Philadelphia* (Philadelphia: Historical Society of Pennsylvania, 1964), 132; see also Wainwright's edited edition of Sidney George Fisher's 1834–71 diaries, *A Philadelphia Perspective* (Philadelphia: Historical Society of Pennsylvania, 1967), 44. In 1839 Fisher wrote, after attending "a small but very beautiful recherché party at Mrs. George Cadwalader's," that while his host and hostess surround themselves with "sumptuous elegance . . . they have been accustomed to this thing all their lives and do it with ease, . . . very different from the gaudy show, crowded glitter and loaded tables of certain vulgar people here, who by mere force of money have got into a society to which they are not entitled by birth, education, or manners."

54. Fisher, *Philadelphia*, 311.

55. He placed the order in March 1842. Dumas *fils*'s *La Dame aux camelias* was published in 1848 and it would be wonderfully romantic to think that there may have been a connection between Cadwalader's mistress, one Miss Lavinia, and her white camellias and Marguerite and hers.

Throughout the 1840s and '50s George Cadwalader shipped exotic trees from all over the world to beautify his Gunpowder Neck estate. Despite hundreds of competitors (and what must have been the most elaborate greenhouse ever built in Harford County) "pride of place," wrote the general's great-grand-nephew, Capt. John Cadwalader, went to "the great Cedar of Lebanon," shown here c. 1900.

nephew John Cadwalader, went to the "great Cedar of Lebanon which stood at the corner of the house near stone steps leading down to the water."

Not wishing to restrict his hobby to Cedar of Lebanon–size exotics, though, in 1856 Cadwalader signed a contract with handyman Thomas Willis "for the purpose of building a Green House . . . at Maxwell's Point, 19′ × 50′, height 8′ in front by 19′ in the back" and the following year bought "1 coffee tree $3," "12 citrus $50," and various other tender plants for it. Modern greenhouse gardeners often find that theirs is an expensive and expanding recreation; so it was with the general who in 1865 had to order seventy-three new specially designed pots "for the green house" (with "handles to be made in the shape of a hook so they can be carried about with hand spikes") to meet the needs of his flourishing collection.

In the minds of high Victorians like Cadwalader, exotic animals and birds made a "natural" complement to exotic plantings, which may explain why the general ordered a menagerie of "German & Belgian Long Breed Canary Birds, Nightingales, Whistling Bulfinches, Larks, Pigeons" from Charles Rose's New York City aviary and partridges and golden pheasants from the firm of S.C. & C.N. Baker, No. 3 Half Moon Passage in London (and "the Pheasantry, Beaufort St., Chelsea"), "By Special Appointment to the Queen and H.R.H. Prince Albert Dealers in useful & Ornamental Poultry." (Something unpleasant, though, must have occurred, because in May 1855 one of the Bakers had to write the general, "we cannot account for the Golden Pheasants not travelling. They are hardy birds compared to Partridges and should have thought you would have got nearly all alive to America.") Cadwalader also embellished his estate with a deer park, which proved something of a mixed blessing. While he and his guests were doubtless kept amused watching the animals gambolling through the pine woods, the park also brought tragedy: "One of the deer died," his overseer wrote him in 1862. "The thing was well and played about the yard at 3 p.m. and at 6 o'clock I found it lying dead."

For a variety of reasons, Maxwell's Point entered a long decline in the 1870s. The general stayed away from his Maryland estate for years at a stretch, and when he did come down it was usually to cope with threatened sheriff's sales when his lackadaisical agents forgot to pay the property taxes or when arson-minded discharged employees sought revenge. Nevertheless he continuously maintained his interest in the Maxwell's Point gardens, and often fretted his concern that the exotic plants would not survive another winter in the increasingly neglected greenhouse: in October 1874 one overseer agreed to "cheerfully load them" on a boat and "ship them to Newport" (where Cadwalader had a splendid "cottage"), while in March 1878 Edward Lynch, the last of the general's gardeners, wrote to tell his employer to rest easy because "Mr. Shriver" had just removed the "tubs and 3 drinking fountains which was used hear by the pheasants" to Olney for safekeeping.

Cadwalader died childless the following February and Maxwell's Point passed to a nephew, John Cadwalader, who lovingly maintained the estate until October 1917 when the federal government condemned the property and turned it into a weapons-testing site. Most of the general's boxwood was transplanted to the Army Medical Center, Walter Reed Hospital; other shrubs small enough to survive being moved found new rootruns around officers' houses throughout the new base. But most of the imported trees, by then too large to move, were left to fend for themselves. It proved a losing struggle. When a Cadwalader contingent visited Maxwell's Point in the early 1980s, all they found was "a tangle of weeds and vines . . . [and] near the top of the stone steps, . . . a great prostrate tree trunk whose resinous wood showed it to be what was left of the Cedar of Lebanon. . . . There was nothing else."[56]

Harford's Other Late Victorian Gardeners: Hothouses and Cemeteries

Impressive as Cadwalader's 19-by-50-foot hothouse must have been, the general was by no means the only mid-Victorian countian to indulge in greenhouses and tender plants. Throughout the 1870s and '80s, issue after issue of the *Havre de Grace Republican*, for example, tempted county gardeners with ads for nurseryman E. D. Sturtevant's collection of "Rare Water Lilies . . . , Nymphaeas, Victoria Regina, The Sacred Lotus, [and] General Collection of Greenhouse Plants." It is also known that Otho Scott constructed some sort of greenhouse at his residence, Scott's Old Fields, on the northern outskirts of Bel Air. When he died in 1864, his estate appraisers found $2 worth of "Earthen Flower Pots in Hot House" and $3 worth of "Wooden Flower Boxes in Hot House." The Philadelphia banker D. C. Wharton Smith maintained a greenhouse ("presided over by . . . George Windolph")[57] at his 1885 picturesque country retreat, Winstone, in Darlington. J. Crawford Neilson built a "flowerhouse" on his Priestford farm near Deer Creek in 1862 (and replaced it with a "plant house" in 1884). Dr. Howard Kelly, a world-renowned naturalist, constructed an elaborate complex of four greenhouses at Liriodendron around 1900. Finally, when Aberdeen canning magnate James Baker died in 1912, his estate appraisers made mention of "contents of greenhouse, $75" as well as "flowers and plants outside Greenhouse, $10."[58]

Otho Scott's horticultural implements (to return to him for a moment) also included a "lawn roller" worth $15, "2 Watering Pots, 50c," and "2 Garden Scalpers, 50c." That last item probably refers to lawnmowers. Common enough by Scott's time, when machines "for cropping or shearing the vegetable surface of lawns, grass-plots, etc.," first hit the markets in the 1830s, they were real conversation pieces. Advertisements routinely observed that a "Country Gentleman may find in using the [mowing] machine themselves, an amusing, useful and healthy exercise." Locally, mid-Victorian era lawnmowers appear in the estate inventories of Dr. Silas Silver's brother John, who died in 1878, and first-cousin William Finney Silver, who died in 1898. William also owned a pair of "pruning shears, $1."[59]

In addition to puttering around his greenhouse and "scalping" his lawn, Otho Scott dabbled in bee-keeping and turned the grounds around his Bel Air house into a small-scale apiary; his estate inventory cites "2 Hives Bees, $4." Nineteenth-century countians could have seen more enthusiasm for honey and hives if they had rambled down to

By the 1870s American manufacturers were mass-producing lawnmowers; note this c. 1880 ad from the *Ægis*.

56. John Cadwalader, USN, "End of an Era," *Chesapeake* (Fall 1983): 49.

57. Jones, "Darlington," 20. Jones later comments that Windolph's brother, the town veterinarian, was also a gardener of note and his house at 2103 Shuresville Road was "trellised with grapevines," 30.

58. James Baker's brother Charles probably had a greenhouse on his Bel Air Avenue estate, too. He certainly spent much time and effort landscaping the property with "specimen and ornamental plants, shaped flower beds, [and] curving carriage drives and walks." See Wollon, "Baker Houses," 9.

59. *The Garden*, 112. English engineer Edwin Budding apparently invented the mechanical mower and "by the eighteen-sixties, horse-drawn mowers were in use at Kew Gardens. . . . In the same decade the gardener of an English insane asylum . . . found it easier not to bother with horses; he harnessed seven madmen to his machine. . . . Appropriately, the first power mower was conceived in Detroit . . . and in 1919 [Col. Edwin George] established a company [there] to make and sell his Moto-Mower." Katherine White, *Onward and Upward in the Garden* (New York: Farrar, Straus, and Giroux, 1979), 163.

Abingdon, where Howard Kennard kept thirty-five hives near his house at 3604 Philadelphia Road (when Kennard died in 1888, his bees were valued at $25), or to Darlington, where Benjamin Silver III, specifically referred to as a "bee-keeper" in the family's official history, *Our Silver Heritage*, tended six hives, worth $4. In fact, bee-keeping has been documented in America since the earliest times. Jefferson, in his *Notes on the State of Virginia*, comments that the bee had been unknown in America "until it was introduced by white settlers" in the 1620s, when hives and honeybees were shipped to Virginia "along with . . . pigeons and peacocks";[60] Benjamin Silver's paternal great-grandfather, Gershom, owned "2 swarms of bees, 10/0 each" when he died in 1775; and in the 1790s John Carter kept "a swarm of bees" worth $1 at Rock Run.

Most of the Scott's Old Fields gardens are now occupied by the Bel Air Memorial Gardens, highly fitting from a historical sense, since in the nineteenth century, when public gardens were rare in America, cemeteries served as "experimental gardens" to "foster . . . a taste for the pleasant, useful and refined art of Gardening."[61] Baltimore's Greenmount Cemetery, begun in 1838, was designed as a quasi-public park, as was its best-known Harford equivalent, the Darlington Cemetery, which came into being in 1883 when the company's directors (including garden-buffs Thomas King of Lansdowne and Dr. Forwood) purchased a grassy, south-facing knoll overlooking the village.[62] Dr. Forwood and his fellow directors then commissioned local artisans to design iron gates and railings for the cemetery (specifying that everything must "be a work of art and an ornament to the grounds") and spent days discussing such issues as the best design of hitching posts, the most attractive way of laying out roads and paths, and the relative merits of various trees and shrubs, all to ensure that their new "garden" would be "a monument to the good taste" of the age.

Most impressive about the Darlington cemetery is that the directors did it all themselves and never once called on their neighbor, architect Neilson, for advice. But well they might have, for Neilson, in addition to ranking as perhaps the leading mid-century designer of buildings in Maryland, was an intelligent, devoted gardener who, while at Priestford, continuously turned his restless intelligence to matters affecting the landscape. He also organized the Farmer's Club of Deer Creek in March 1873 and even devised his own "Insect Powder," concocted, he noted, "from the leaves of Pyrethrum Roseum" a plant that "when grown in California, [is] called 'Bushack'" and whose "flower looks like large single asters."

In the early 1840s, that is, shortly after he married Rosa Williams, who eventually inherited the Priestford farm from her Stump mother, Neilson sculpted a grassy hilltop terrace as a setting for his rambling dwelling: he "levelled up Croquet ground" in November 1866, and spent years fussing over the network of gravel and bark paths he laid out to criss-cross the property. In 1860 he "altered road to house . . . along orchard slope . . . and a new gravelled path from house east"; in 1861 he "made paths in garden and towards ice house . . . gravelled thinly"; and November 1869 planned another, "running SE from the Grove Walk to the main road . . . near flower bed." He also worked hard and long fashioning visual links through the woods from his own house to those of his immediate neighbors: on September 14, 1883, he "cut out view towards McGraw's and partial opening in direction of Glasgow's" (James Glasgow then owned Priest Neale's Mass House) and September 1886 he "re-opened Vista towards Glasgow's."

Showing himself the equal of General Cadwalader and Benjamin Silver (at least in spirit), Neilson filled Priestford's acres with a remarkable collection of imported trees, including Norway spruce, Norway pines, and exotic hollies. He arranged these evergreens to enframe his sight lines and constantly tinkered with the plants' positions, hoping for better effect: "October 21, 1873, Moved . . . Hemlock . . . from path to Point Look Out"; "replanted 25 evergreen this spring, 1873"; and "1877 moved arb. v. and N. pines to white gate . . . moved out to new path . . . a holly, have now over 50 . . . at path." He interest-

60. Silver, *Our Silver Heritage*, 3401; *Magnolia* (newsletter of the Southern Garden History Society) 7, no. 2 (Summer 1991): 6. Not all colonial encounters with bees were happy ones. North Carolina governor William Tryon, in his 1771 *Journal of the Expedition against the Insurgents* records how one evening camp was made at a site where "in an adjoining Garden were several Bee Hives [and] some Soldiers taking a Fancy for Honey overturned the Hives about Midnight the Bees being thus disturbed and enraged dispersed themselves among the Horses in the Pasture stinging them to such a degree that they broke in one confused Squadron over the fence, and Came on full Gallop & in full chorus of Bells up to the Camp."

61. David Charles Sloane, *The Last Great Necessity* (Baltimore: Johns Hopkins University Press, 1991), 65, 74.

62. The company's continuously kept minutes are in a leatherbound folio volume now in the possession of the Walter Jourdan family of Darlington, who graciously allowed the author to pore over the book.

A NARRATIVE HISTORY OF HARFORD COUNTY

The summerhouse and grotto at industrialist William E. Robinson's Rockdale.

ed himself in deciduous trees as well and his "Memoranda of Certain Trees Planted at Priestford" (in which he gave particular attention to those "planted by Mrs. Rosa Neilson with her own hands") includes "a maple . . . planted as a very small 6′ shoot about the time Burnside was attempting to get his forces by sea into North Carolina," "an oak . . . near the old Catalpa," "a Spanish chestnut . . . grown in a box from nut . . . beginning to bear about 1894 . . . very large but still . . . hardly fit to eat," and "a Beech planted about 1875 in a . . . tangle or 'Jungle' [beside] path down ravine."

One final place, canning broker and banker William E. Robinson's garden at Rockdale, must be discussed in this overview of mid-Victorian Harford horticulture, since it so neatly sums up the sometimes contradictory nature of that age. A fiercely competitive capitalist, Robinson also had a strong streak of social concern and willed $10,000 to a favorite grandson if the youth "refrained from the use of tobacco . . . [and] spiritous liquors" until the age of 21.[63] He also spent vast sums to help "americanize" his cannery's Polish-immigrant workforce: he established a school for them at Rockdale where "three college women . . . taught . . . English, religion, and various elementary subjects"; and he provided day care for workers' children, with a staff nurse and a cook who dished out "hot lunches for the 30 to 35 children at the nursery."[64]

Thus when Robinson, who foreclosed on his own brother's mortgage, bought Rockdale in 1887, he immediately transformed it in a way that reflects the divergent strains of his own vigorous personality. He built a conservatory off the main house, laid out terraced walkways from the south and southeast façades of the dwelling, dotted the ground with cast-iron gazebos and summerhouses, dug rosebeds, scattered thousands of bulbs throughout the grounds to produce "annual glorious bursts of who-knows-how-many varieties of daffodils," and established ferneries throughout the property.[65] A complex garden, Rockdale; a complicated man, Robinson.

63. Robinson's testamentary papers are in Estate 10, 095.

64. Larew, *Bel Air,* 70.

65. Mary Bristow, Maryland Historical Trust Historic Sites Survey form for Rockdale; on file at Harford County Department of Planning and Zoning, Bel Air.

Gardening in Harford County

Gardening in the Twentieth Century:
"America Will Soon Find Herself"

Throughout America, many of the men and women who came of age as the new century dawned, bored a bit by the previous generation's highly wrought gardens, began to simplify horticultural fashions. Or, as architect and scholar Fiske Kimball phrased it in his classic piece on "The American Country House,"

> such solecisms of our early attempts at formality . . . are now happily rare. . . . For this there are several causes . . . [the most important of which is] the strength and saneness of American traditions of informal landscape design, based not on artificial picturesqueness but on preservation and expression of the native and local color.[66]

Accordingly, garden design grew simpler and sinuous-shaped beds, such as General Cadwalader's, became increasingly rare; the choice of plants, too, became less complicated as exotic imports gave way to native shrubs and wildflowers. Finally, a new interest in American history encouraged garden designers to devise planting plans that would complement the architectural style called "colonial revival."

All these trends certainly found beautiful expression when newlyweds William and Eliza McCormick Finney began their remarkable gardens at Little Greenwood near Churchville in 1906. And it was a conscious "expression," too: Mrs. Finney is known to have followed the advice of garden writer Wilhelm Miller and her annotated copy of Miller's "how-to" book is still in the house. Miller told his readers to eschew exotic arboreta in favor of "our own American trees" (underplanted with "great quantities of wildflowers that will spread out of their own accord") because "the noblest lesson . . . gardens can teach us is this: *Let every country chiefly use its own native trees, shrubs, vines, and other permanent material.* . . . When we stop imitating and do this, America will soon find herself."[67] Miller also advised his readers to remove the randomly placed flowerbeds of the 1870s and, in their stead, to plant sweeping stretches of "unbroken lawn, which seems greater and richer than it really is, because its surface is not speckled with showy plants,"[68] and he suggested restricting beds of perennials to a few well-placed perimeter plantings of rich-textured material such as bergenia and hosta. Mrs. Finney read and obeyed; c. 1908 photos of Little Greenwood show the house embowered in hollyhocks and wisteria set in a vast, open lawn. To heighten the romantic charm of her new gardens, Mrs. Finney also laid out a "secret garden" a few yards south of the house, where she planted ninety-six boxwood in a rectangle with a single rose-arched opening for entry; the boxwood are still present, grown to enormous size, as is Mrs. Finney's arch-engulfing climbing rose, "Spanish Dancer."

Kimball observed that "new" American gardens of the Theodore Roosevelt era were intimately bound up in a healthy, nationwide "renewed love of out-of-door life . . . and of nature, . . . [and] the fondness for out-of-door sports." Similarly, Miller lectured his readers that "it is impossible to bring up children properly without a garden. We ought to live in our gardens a good part of the time and entertain our friends there." Both writers would have smiled at Little Greenwood, for the Finneys established an *al fresco* school on their house's front porch, where Finney children and cousins received the rudiments of spelling, math, geography, grammar, and botany from live-in tutors.[69] (Classes went on all year long thanks to the roll-down, bamboo shades and large glass panels that protected the children from summer sun and winter snows.) Elsewhere on the grounds the couple built a superb, open summerhouse, possibly because Miller advised homeowners to construct such structures because they "produce 'charm'" and provide the "coolness and shade . . . so essential in our hot climate." Finally, the energetic Finneys gave Little Greenwood "the first tennis court in Harford County."[70]

Mrs. Finney, Miller's book in hand, obviously acted as her own garden designer. Indeed, until this time all of Harford's gardens had been the loving products of their own-

66. Kimball, "Country House," 388.

67. Wilhelm Miller, *What England Can Teach Us about Gardening* (Garden City, N.Y.: Doubleday, 1908). "Great quantities of wildflowers" indeed: in 1984 Little Greenwood's present owners enumerated "176 species and varieties or subspecies" of native woody plants and 119 species of wildflowers found on the property. "List of Plant at Roedean [the Hathaways' name for the house]," in papers of Dr. and Mrs. Wilfred Hathaway, Churchville. If anything the present owners excel Mrs. Finney at horticulture; they maintain a greenhouse on the property, a refinement Mrs. Finney oddly missed.

68. Miller, *England*, 277.

69. Nancy Webster Barnes, conversation with author, May 21, 1991.

70. Miller, *England*, 31. Mrs. Brodnax Cameron Sr., conversation with author, January 11, 1989.

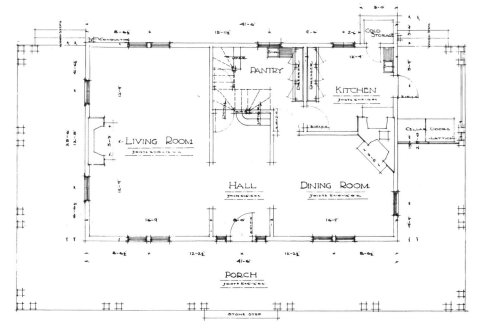

When Eliza McCormick Finney and her husband, William, laid out the gardens around their 1906 house, Little Greenwood, near Churchville she eschewed intricate flowerbeds in favor of sweeps of open lawn interspersed with a few native trees and shrubs. The Finneys sheltered three sides of their new home with a twelve-foot-deep porch, which housed an al fresco school for their children.

ers—possibly excepting any William Booth or James Wilkes may have designed for Mark Pringle two centuries ago. But that changed in the twentieth century as professional landscape architects entered the scene. Perhaps the first of these was Elwood Grier, who established his eponymous nursery on Grier Nursery Road in 1908 and then began designing gardens for clients throughout the county. While the exact extent of his work is unclear, Grier's son, George, has suggested that his father "landscaped most of the yards in Havre de Grace from about 1908 to 1935" as well as "the old Bayou Hotel [and] most of the Tydings Oakington Estate." That last may be regarded as the forgivable boasting of a loving son, since Mrs. Millard Tydings herself planned most of the Oakington grounds, and remains justifiably proud of her work there.[71]

Senator and Mrs. Tydings moved into Oakington in the mid-1930s, a time that saw several academically trained men and women join the self-taught Grier in the Harford landscape business. Among the most notable of these, by any standard, were the Philadelphia architectural firm Mellor & Meigs, whom Francis and Lelia Stokes brought in to make over the Wilson's Mill property in 1931, and Anna Merven Carrere. The Stokeses' choice of Mellor & Meigs was nothing less than brilliant, for the architects have long been lauded for their interest in uniting horticulture and architecture: the *Architectural Record* praised them in 1916 ("as in most ancient gardens there are traditions to be preserved. . . . The architects have done just enough and then stopped") and their knack for "building country pleasances" that respected the Philadelphia concept of shabby comfort has kept garden historians Mac Griswold and Eleanor Weller swooning into the 1990s. Showing themselves sensitive to the Harford landscape, the architects (well advised by Lelia Stokes herself)[72] cleared the property of brambles and trash-trees, added healthy new stands of dogwood, holly, and laurel, and underplanted it all with vast drifts of naturalized daffodils and bluebells. They then combed the county, buying old boxwood bushes, which work crews transplanted to the mill to create a sense of "instant history" that so perfectly sets off the new buildings the architects built at Wilson's Mill.[73]

Then there was Anna Merven Carrere. The daughter of the distinguished New York architect John Carrere,[74] Anna learned how to lay out a garden at the "most influential

71. Eleanor Tydings Ditzen, conversation with author, November 11, 1991. Horticulturist Nancy Webster Barnes, who did some work at Oakington for Mrs. Tydings, suggests that Grier may have "tossed out idea for a plant species or two."

72. Nancy Webster Barnes, for example, said that Mrs. Stokes "did everything exactly right; she knew when to stop; she didn't mess it all up with a lot of azaleas."

73. Eberlin, "Examples of the Works of Mellor and Meigs," 242. In 1923 the Olmsted brothers, in "one of the earliest successful instances of what was later to become almost a commonplace," had workmen transplant "huge box bushes, mostly from down-at-the-heel Virginia plantations" to Philadelphia; Mac Griswold and Eleanor Weller muse that "'ancient box,' as it seems invariably to have been called, became a strange estate garden fetish, conferring ancestry and dignity almost as certainly as family portraits." Griswold and Weller, *Gardens,* 129.

74. John Carrere and his partner Thomas Hastings enjoyed a "huge and prosperous practice" that ranged from resorts in Florida to country houses to the New York Public Library on Fifth Avenue. Adolf K. Placzek, ed., *Macmillan Encyclopedia of Architects* (New York: Macmillan, 1982), 387–88.

Searching for "instant history," Francis and Lelia Stokes combed the county in the 1930s for old boxwood to bring to their new garden at Wilson's Mill. They were often successful and this photograph illustrates workmen unloading some of the Stokeses' new/old treasures.

. . . Cambridge School of Architectural and Landscape Design." This pioneering institution—at the time the only landscape school in America to admit women—"began with one student studying the architectural orders of Vignola on a mahogany bridge table in her living room in 1915"; the curriculum soon expanded to include courses on "architectural design and construction" so that graduates might have "a better chance to create gardens entirely on their own—without a male architect to build the steps and balustrades while the women waited to fill the spaces with plants." The school closed in 1942, partially due to the exigencies of World War II; "that same year women were cautiously admitted to the Graduate School of Design at Harvard."[75]

Degree in hand, Carrere joined up with the noted Washington, D.C., landscape architect Rose Greeley; the two women remained in partnership for several decades and their work drew frequent praise from *House & Garden* and other national periodicals for the "singly successful" manner in which they applied "precise patterns to small gardens" in cities.[76]

Carrere also applied "precise patterns" to a few rural gardens in Harford County. In 1936, she decided to retire to the country and bought the old Bayless property on Harmony Church Road near Darlington, declaring, "I'd rather lose money farming in Harford County than playing the New York Stock Exchange."[77] Artist that she was, she soon learned she couldn't abandon her graph paper altogether and, to meet her innate need to create, laid out a series of stone walls and terraces around her new Harford house, details that obviously bespeak her Cambridge School training. She also helped a small circle of local friends design their gardens, offering advice about a particular species of magnolia here, suggesting a bit of pruning there.

In her "retirement," she undertook one substantial Harford gardening project—investment banker Lawrence Simmonds's estate, Box Hill, which took in the site of Aquila Hall's c. 1800 mansion, Lauretum. That venerable house burned around 1920, and to replace it Simmonds, working with a mysterious architect known today only as "Mr. Mackenzie," designed a five-part brick mansion that combined "Georgian formality in the symmetrical proportions of the main section . . . and Vernacular Tidewater architecture in the gambrel-roofed southern section."[78] Carrere's landscaping perfectly meshed

75. Griswold and Weller, *Gardens,* 199.

76. Nancy Webster Barnes, conversation with author. See, for example, *House & Garden* of October 1946, April 1940, and May 1941.

77. Cameron, conversation with author.

78. Francis Jencks, AIA, "Some Holiday Houses of Maryland, *Baltimore Sunday Sun Magazine,* April 19, 1931; Maryland Historical Trust Inventory form for Box Hill.

with Simmonds's building, for the formal, boxwood-lined terraces she designed for Simmonds beautifully evoke the formal gardens of such late eighteenth-century estates as Mount Pleasant and Sion Hill.[79] A reporter for the *Ægis* visited Box Hill in 1961 and was left virtually speechless over the "Gorgeous Garden" he saw there: oddly, he never credited Carrere but instead simply pointed out that "Mr. Simmonds has several terraced gardens, a herb garden and an oval garden featuring an original statue of Pauline Bonaparte as Venus by the Italian sculptor Canova."

Virtually all of Harford County experienced a impressive renewal of interest in the art and science of horticulture in the early twentieth century. The Garden Club of Harford County was founded in 1914, just a year after the Garden Club of America was established in Germantown, Pennsylvania. M. Lee Thomas, who as a youth assisted landscape architect Nancy Webster Barnes in projects throughout Harford and Baltimore counties, still maintains the "artistically landscaped boxwood . . . [and] flower gardens" his mother and father started in 1918 at Gate Hill Farm near Carsins Run.[80] Beginning around 1928 Anne McElderry Heighe, assisted by her gardener, the appropriately named Mr. Primrose, created a breathtakingly beautiful "natural" landscape around her new house on Moores Mill Road. Sometime-countian Gilman Paul worked with Alice G. B. Lockwood to create the monumental *Gardens of Colony and State,* published in 1934 for the Garden Club of America. Two generations of the Wilson family have made their ancestral home Woodside a showplace of boxwood, holly, rhododendron, and laurel. Jane Viele of Mount Friendship is well known in the gardening world for her work with azaleas and daffodils. Mary Woodward and Lois Reed in Bel Air and Harriet Tranberg in Joppa have separately shown what beautiful miracles can be wrought to potentially dreary quarter-acre plots. Elsie Jenkins Symington received national acclaim for the splendid gardens she established at Indian Spring Farm (and described her work there in her 1941 book, *By Light of Day*). Barbara Gallup, whose Czech émigré parents saved Sophia's Dairy from certain ruin, more or less single-handedly brought the art of topiary to national attention through her 1987 best-seller, *The Complete Book of Topiary,* just as Kurt Bluemel, who was also "driven from Czechoslovakia in World War II," bought a farm in Harford County and there began the now-nationwide craze for ornamental grasses.[81] In the 1930s

Landscape architect Anna Merven Carrere planned and planted formal gardens around her Glenville house in the 1930s. Little remains but her stone walls and terraces.

79. See Elizabeth Fisk Clapp, Charlton Merrick Gillet, and Romaine McI. Randall, *Maryland Houses and Gardens* (Baltimore: Federated Garden Clubs of Maryland, 1938).

80. Karen Toussaint, "Gardening," *Ægis,* October 16, 1991.

81. Kurt Lasher, "Czech Native Kurt Bluemel Pioneers Ornamental Grasses in U.S.," *Ægis* "Spring Home and Garden 1994" supplement, 6.

The gardens at Joshua's Meadows near Bel Air. Brodnax Cameron designed a highly formal series of axes for the garden and his wife, Julia, then softened that rigidity with lush plantings. Shown here are azalea and dogwood in full flower and (to the right) heavily budded peonies.

Brodnax and Julia Cameron (shown here c. 1975) hybridized daylilies in the Joshua's Meadows gardens.

and '40s, the classically minded Brodnax Cameron and his romantically minded wife, Julia, combined their different personalities in the wonderful gardens at Joshua's Meadows, where her lush plantings act as perfect foils to his tight geometry. Finally, it is important to note that twentieth-century gardening in the county has not been the exclusive domain of the wealthy, or even the middle class; when the Bata Shoe Company built its new village at Belcamp in the late '30s, its architects integrated small gardens for the workers into the elaborate whole.[82]

Still, without doubt *the* Harford County gardener is the transplanted New Yorker, the huntsman, raconteur, and bon vivant, the only man in the county who could "perk up a drooping arrangement of tulips with a little gin,"[83] Harvey Smith Ladew. Ladew, born into the fluid upper strata of New York society in 1887, purchased his 200-acre Pleasant Valley Farm in northwestern Harford County in 1929 and immediately began laying out twenty-two acres of formal gardens around the house. (A keen huntsman, Ladew fled his native Long Island because he felt it was becoming too suburban.) While there are several ways to view the Ladew Topiary Gardens (to use the present and official name), each of them merely reinforces the initial impression of how really *good* Ladew's work is.

First, of course, the garden is pretty and amusing. This is doubtless what most impresses most visitors—gorgeous flowerbeds and witty topiary—and that is a perfectly valid response. But the gardens work from a design-on-paper aspect, too, for Ladew created a well-defined system of axis and cross-axis. He laid out an 1,100-foot "spine" northerly from the house, crossed it with a secondary, east-west axis, and then fitted fifteen separate "garden rooms" within that tight framework. Mention of the garden rooms —discrete spaces, some of which are planted out with plants that flower in a single color, one of which contains a rose garden, one a Japanese garden, one a berry garden— brings up another way of looking at Ladew's creation, namely its place in the gardening continuum. The layout he devised has immense historical importance. Room-gardening (or compartment gardening) was a horticultural style developed by William Robinson, Gertrude Jekyll, William Morris, and other leaders of the English arts-and-crafts movement "as a reaction against the showy Italianate parterres that had been unrolled like car-

82. Corbusier and Jeanneret, *Oeuvres complet*, 24.
83. Griswold and Weller, *Gardens*, 149–50.

Harvey Smith Ladew, Harford County's preeminent gardener, trimming his topiary swans, c. 1950.

pets in front of the great Victorian country houses." (Or country houses built by great Victorians, such as General Cadwalader's Maxwell's Point.) In place of these strident geometrical swaths of color, room-gardeners wished to create a sense of "quiet and retirement, sheltered from the outside world by a yew hedge." They used paths, hedges, and walls to divide "the broad expanse of the garden . . . into separate, enclosed areas, each one of which is a private world." Clive Aslet, editor of the English magazine *Country Life,* has pointed out that in addition to offering philosophical solace to their makers, room gardens also "provided a way to cope with the immense range of styles" open to twentieth-century gardeners: "Because each compartment was secluded from the rest, it offered an opportunity for a different treatment, without threatening the unity of the whole."

Aslet further opined that the best English example of this style was Rodmarton Manor in Gloucestershire. Laid out around 1905 (and restored in the 1950s) Rodmarton has been called "the quintessential Arts and Crafts house and garden. . . . Peacocks and other fanciful finials adorn the tall hedges that section the . . . [garden] into intimate areas"; Rodmarton also contains separate areas for herbaceous borders, a summerhouse garden, and a "Leisure Garden, [a space] given over to a collection of topiary cakestands and cannonballs."[84] Room-gardening revolutionized horticulture world wide. Literally hundreds of garden rooms were created throughout Great Britain, perhaps most influentially by the American expatriate Lawrence Johnston, who began his garden at Hidcote Manor in Gloucestershire around 1910.[85] The poet/novelist V. Sackville-West and her husband, Harold Nicolson, helped ensure the style's success when they started their much-praised gardens at Sissinghurst Castle in Kent in 1930. Ladew, an Anglophile down to his wellies, knew those innovative and amusing gardens firsthand—and early on—thanks to his many prolonged visits to England, and the garden rooms he created in Harford County stand as among the very first American examples of this twentieth-century manner of landscape design. Actually, his single-color gardens may even predate Sackville-West's celebrated white garden at Sissinghurst, for the "very first suggestion . . . for a scheme of white flowers" there does not come until "December 1939" when Sackville-West wrote Nicholson of her "really lovely scheme . . . all white flowers, with some clumps

84. Clive Aslet, *The Last Country Houses* (New Haven: Yale University Press, 1982), 289, 297. Ethne Clark and George Wright, *English Topiary Gardens* (London: Weidenfeld and Nicolson, 1983), 37–38. Rodmarton's present owner describes her work there in Mary D. Biddulph, "Rodmarton Manor," in Alvilde Lees-Milne and Rosemary Verey, ed., *The Englishwoman's Garden* (London: Chatto & Windus, 1980), 31–34. V. Sackville-West, "Hidcote Manor," guidebook for the National Trust, p. 13.

85. See Jane Brown, *Vita's Other World* (New York: Viking, 1985), 106. Before Ladew planted anything in his new garden, "he first made an exact model of it in Plasticine to get the scale correct." "An Old Maryland House Recreated," *House & Garden* (March 1951): 108.

Gardening in Harford County

The almost baroque "Great Bowl" at Ladew's garden; he centered the bowl around his well-disguised swimming pool (shown in the foreground), built a series of terraces to join the bowl to his house, and lined it all with topiary hemlocks and yew. His is, according to the Garden Club of America, "the finest topiary garden in the country created without professional help."

86. In the National Trust guide to Hidcote, Sackville-West stated that "in a big garden . . . the area must . . . be broken up in such a way that each part shall be separate from the other yet all shall be disposed round the main lines of the garden in such a way as to give homogeneity to the whole. At Hidcote this has been achieved by the use of hedges" (4). Many feel that Hidcote may have influenced Ladew. But someone who would know, quoting Diana Binney of Kifsgate (who also would know), has stated emphatically that "Harvey didn't know Hidcote or Johnston." Mrs. Benjamin H. Griswold III, conversation with author, May 10, 1993.

87. Ladew's garden attracted much press coverage in the international press. Note, for example, *Town and Country* for May 1936, *Home & Garden* for May 1951, *Country Life* for April 3, 1986, *Maison & Jardin* for May 1986, and *Interview* for October 1987.

of pale pink. White clematis, white lavender, white agapanthus, white double primroses, white anemones, white camellias."[86]

Finally, however, as satisfying as it is to think that Ladew's experiments with color anticipated Sackville-West's, one must, when discussing Pleasant Valley Farm, return to clipped yews and hemlocks; just as "pride of place" at Maxwell's Point was the Cedar of Lebanon, pride of place at Pleasant Valley is topiary. Ladew embarked on his topiary career with his typical verve (and while still living on Long Island), when he sculpted a rooster atop a twenty-five-foot, four-tiered perch all in Japanese yew (*Taxus cuspidista* "Densiformis"). When he moved to Harford he brought his rooster with him and, pleased at the way it fit into the Maryland landscape, he took out his clippers in earnest. He enclosed his croquet court in clipped hemlock hedges punctuated with pyramidal hemlock finials and he created still other forms in hemlock—obelisks, walls draped with garlands and pierced by windows, exotic birds—on the terraces he laid out between the house and swimming pool. Serious about his craft, he built all his own frames and did his own pruning to create living forms few others would think of: a yew foxhunting scene, where a pair of life-size horse-and-riders and five hounds eternally pursue a pert fox (to remind himself of his favorite past-time), a seahorse (to remind himself of his favorite Florida winter retreat), a top hat and a hand raised in a V for Victory (to remind himself of his favorite politician), a heart pierced by an arrow (to remind himself of whom?), and many other shapes all in *T.* "Densiformis" or *T.* "Erecta Hilli."

Without doubt, Ladew's gardens have become far and away the most celebrated place in Harford County. Praised in magazines and newspapers throughout Europe and America, studied by university students of landscape architecture, analyzed at symposia, Ladew's creation grows in esteem with each passing year.[87] Of all these awards and honors, though, it is easy to know which must have best pleased him: in 1971 the Garden Club of America (GCA) presented him with a Distinguished Achievement Medal for "creating the most outstanding topiary garden in America without professional help." Shortly before he died in 1976, Ladew established a nonprofit foundation run by a hand-picked volunteer board of directors to manage his gardens. The board has succeeded beautifully and Elizabeth Constable, Barbara "Bunny" Hathaway, and Susan Russell, who have se-

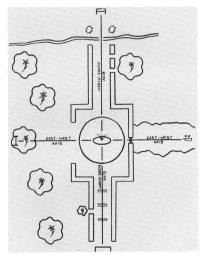

quentially chaired the garden committee at Ladew, have proven themselves at least his equal in their knowledge and love of plants. In recognition of the board's success, the GCA presented 1990's Achievement Award to Leith Griswold, prime mover in coaxing Ladew to establish the foundation in the first place. In making the award the club commended her and the board for ensuring that "Ladew Topiary Gardens is now an internationally known attraction and a tribute to the time-honored tradition of topiary art." In response, Mrs. Griswold thanked the GCA for "the thrill of a lifetime" and went on to acknowledge "Harvey Ladew's dedicated friends and neighbors," the "tireless labors . . . of the director [Lena Caron] and her staff," and the support of Ladew's nieces and nephews. "The Garden has now obtained worldwide recognition, visited and enjoyed by thousands of people from all walks of life and all parts of the globe. Please," Mrs. Griswold said, concluding with remarks that might fittingly end this chapter, "give us the opportunity to welcome each and every one of you to America's most renowned Topiary garden in the near future."[88]

Left: Ladew's garden relies on geometry to hold it together: this rough schematic suggests the garden's two axes and interspersed "garden rooms." Right: Ladew's famous topiary hunt scene served to remind its creator of his favorite sport.

88. Reprinted in the Ladew "Newsletter" (Summer 1990).

EPILOGUE

If, as was suggested in chapter 9, the 1950s marked the end of the age of the individual achievement in Harford home-building, the decade arguably did the same for the county's commercial and religious architecture. While the reasons for this sorry state of things are complex, underlying it all is the disturbing fact that most countians seem to have lost their provincial pride, their feisty sense of place. Alexis Shriver, Anne Carrere, Brodnax Cameron, and other wise members of the "Ain't we got fun" group recognized, as one writer put it, an "individuality" that "is easier to feel than to define. . . . There is a smarter, showier, and more opulent society in Baltimore County . . . whereas the . . . traditions of Harford are . . . bred in the bones."[1] Those same traditions also made most people value rising damp over knotty pine and shaggy fields of Queen Anne's lace over clipped azaleas. A generation earlier the *New England Magazine* commented on the citizens' habit, un-American but very Harford, of "caring little for the prestige of newly acquired riches." The magazine opined, because "the full tide of the modern spirit has not yet transformed the inherited customs and ideas or swept away many relics of things deemed quaint or unfashionable," Harford's "hills and valleys . . . at the headwaters of the great Chesapeake, make it a good part of the world . . . to abide within." Significantly, the county's black citizens shared this pride of place and, wrote the magazine, most of Lewis Bowser's and William Jackson's descendants, like their white neighbors, happily "find homes on the places where they were born."[2]

Who honestly believes that pride of place exists today? Who honestly would say that Harford is not now inundated by "the full tide of the modern spirit"? or that today's countians reject the smart, the showy, the opulent? The result, architecturally speaking, is a chaotic mess, an abandonment of the county's quite wonderful real past in favor of a false one and a simultaneous rejection of countians' historic interest in innovation in design and technology in favor of superficial glitz and glamour. One result is acre after acre of quarter-million-dollar houses laden with meretricious Williamsburg clichés; another is a succession of postmodern malls and "village centers," most of which resemble what the distinguished contemporary architect Warren Cox, FAIA, has mordantly dismissed as "comic book architecture."[3] And, indeed, it sometimes feels as if Batman and Wonder Woman—or guides from Disney World—play a more influential role in Harford County building than do the memories of John Rodgers or Cupid Peaker.

In chapter 9 mass production, per se, was deemed neither good nor bad; a prefabricated 1950s house—such as Wakefield Meadows's Fleetwood—had just as much chance of artistic success, according to its own lights, as a handcrafted 1850s cottage. But another product of twentieth-century elbow-tucking *is* bad, and its affects on the county have been unequivocally disastrous. This evil is *passivity*, a principle alien to Stump of Stafford, Dr. Kelly, and nearly every other countian of the past—but tragically present today. The simple truth is that countians have lost control of their fate. When the Silvers and Bakers built canneries in Aberdeen and Havre de Grace, when the Dallams laid out additions to Bel Air, and, yes, when Ward & Bosely ordered their prefab Fleetwood developments, the parties involved had a real stake in what the structures looked like when new, and in

1. Hulbert Footner, *Maryland Main and the Eastern Shore* (New York: Appleton-Century, 1942), 93–94.

2. Calvin Dill Wilson, "Through and Old Southern County," *New England Magazine* (1899): 174–76.

3. Warren J. Cox, FAIA, conversation with author, October 18, 1989.

what they would look like fifty years later. The reason was simple: the Silvers and Bakers and Dallams—and Ward & Bosely—themselves expected to be around fifty years later. On the other hand, most of the malls built in the county in the 1970s and '80s represent schemes funded in Chicago or Dallas and hatched by market survey–worshiping MBAs in New York or Los Angeles who do not care what goes up, or what happens to it, as long as the infamous bottom line checks out. Independent, locally run businessmen have become obsolete. Countians no longer feast on shoepeg corn or Susquehanna-spawned shad or canvasback duck, they buy bags of microwaveable chemicals. (Indeed, even when they read the "local" newspapers they submit to opinions written by transients employed by the Baltimore *Sun* which is, in turn, controlled by the Los Angeles Times-Mirror Corporation.) No wonder the county has had its heart ripped out. Of course, the county had always been influenced by men and women from outside its borders; but while countians had once been able to assimilate these outlanders—indeed it even "tamed" them, recall how architect J. Crawford Neilson developed a low-key manner of building just for Harford—now the county has been overwhelmed by them.[4]

Shriver and Cameron and Carrere, uniformed in wrinkled seersucker and moldy Harris tweeds, kept the Babbitts at bay as long as they could, but death has removed these guardians from the scene. In the 1960s Mary Helen Cadwalader picked up the mossback banner and still maintains the earnest battle against the world of air-conditioned malls and cable TV, but even she admits that it is a losing struggle, and at times veers depressingly close to being pathetic. "The little town where I worked as a young reporter has been devastated by a hurricane of ruthless demolitions and ugly improvements. A few forlorn relics survive here and there in the flood of shoddy little homes, advertising posters, neon lights, crummy supermarkets, and cement expressways," wrote one observer;[5] although he was describing a small town in upstate New York, one might well think the subject was Havre de Grace or Bel Air—which suggests that these gloomy thoughts have national application.

The point, though, goes far beyond simple negativism; the point is control. Two centuries ago most countians, for instance, *liked* new roads;[6] they embraced the technology that made these new arteries possible and they kept control of the pens that sketched in the rights of way. Abingdon silversmith William Toy, William Smith of Blenheim, John Hall of Cranberry, John Rutledge, David Lee, and John Stump of Stafford all eagerly set themselves up as eighteenth-century road czars;[7] Bel Air merchant Thomas Hays headed up the Bel Air and Harford Turnpike Company in 1816, which laid a crushed-stone toll highway from Baltimore City to Bel Air and Conowingo; Dr. John Archer Jr. and his coterie of friends and relations built themselves a pair of toll bridges across the Susquehanna around 1820; and when Churchville farmer William Woolsey died in 1888 he left his fortune to the county government on condition his wealth be used for "perfecting" (Woolsey's wording) the "public and county roads in said county by macadamizing."[8] The state of Harford County transportation today seems lackluster indeed. Where once the county boasted entrepreneurs like Archer and Hays and benefactors like Woolsey, colorful characters by any standard, now all it has is engineers. (About the only constant is a complaining, letter-writing public and any current issue of the *Ægis* will almost certainly contain the equivalent of Dr. Forwood's 1880s heartfelt attack on the county's highway department—"disgraceful," "shameful," and so on.)

Partly out of frustration, most architecturally minded countians now seem more concerned with *preservation* than with *creation*. They have certainly taken on quite a task. (One wishes them at least some of the success the resourceful and hardworking farmland preservationists have achieved. More than 7,000 productive acres are now under permanent easement.) Oakington now shelters recovering alcoholics, Liriodendron earns its keep as part museum, part dancehall, the few remaining petroglyphs are cared for by the county historical society, and the boards of the McComas Institute and Hosanna School have secured over $100,000 in state aid to help underwrite much-needed repairs. All this

4. "Taming" newcomers may have been something of a Baltimore-area speciality; historian Frank Beirne has written that historically whereas "new arrivals" to Baltimore "are full of ideas for making Baltimore over" the "native Baltimoreans . . . are thinking about . . . how much work they can get out of the newcomers before they, in their turn, succumb" fully to local traditions. See Beirne, *Amiable Baltimoreans,* 21.

5. Luigi Barzini, *O America* (New York: Harper and Row, 1977), 194. Columnist Ellen Goodman has recently written of "anti-chain legislation." It was, she contends, "introduced by people who wanted to protect more than small businesses. They unabashedly defended civic spirit, small-town democracy. . . . The resistance movement asks us to think of ourselves as citizens with a sense of place and an obligation to take care of that place." Ellen Goodman, "The Way We Live Now," *Baltimore Sun,* September 27, 1994.

6. They also liked new canals and lobbied strongly for such from Havre de Grace to Pennsylvania and, eventually, Baltimore; the *Baltimore Sun* editorialized that such canals would be "new and powerful incentives to cheer up Maryland." Reproduced in the April 26, 1838, *Madisonian.*

7. Wright, *Harford,* 104–5.

8. Woolsey's estate papers, Estate No. 4990.

is fine, but what about other white elephants? Will the building preservationists meet the challenge and devise ways to save and keep viable churches such as St. Ignatius and St. Mary's once the congregations have grown too large for the old, exquisite shells? Or commercial structures like Amos Mill and the Bata village at Belcamp, now that their markets have dried up? Or outbuildings on farms that don't pay for themselves? What will happen to Benjamin Silver III's carriage house, corn house, and smokehouse? What is to be done at Sion Hill, whose preservation ought to be a matter of national concern? How much longer will the descendants of Commo. John Rodgers be able to maintain their patrimony without outside help? How much longer should they be made to? Sion Hill and the Rodgers family are of undisputed, international significance, yet that hasn't kept state-roads gremlins from plotting highways and interchanges for the farm.

Harvey Ladew left instructions to the effect that the minute his gardens slip from the standard he himself set, they *must* be bulldozed. He could not stand the thought of his topiary being kept in a slip-shod manner; better an honorable death than a humiliating, semi sort of existence. With that in mind, while it is emotionally painful, it is intellectually possible to imagine that, should the historic-preservationists fail, one day soon everyone will simply shrug and say, "Bring on the bulldozers!"

Selected Historical Sites in Harford County

This section of the book contains a catalog of Harford's architecture, information on buildings and sites chosen from the county's historic sites inventory. There is certainly no need to apologize for that inventory, which, with its nearly 1,900 entries, is among the richest and most thorough such studies in Maryland. The sites selected for this catalog, however, may warrant an apology—or an *apologia*—because the selection was ultimately arbitrary. Nevertheless, it is hoped that the catalog will present a representative sampling of Harford's buildings, from mansions to smokehouses, from colonial-era churches to twentieth-century industrial complexes.

Copies of the complete inventory are on file at the Harford County Department of Planning and Zoning, the Historical Society of Harford County, and, in Crownsville, at the Maryland Historical Trust, and may be perused during normal business hours. Readers with corrections or comments on the following writeups are encouraged to contact any of those three agencies.

Entries have been arranged geographically; the six sections *loosely* correspond to the county's election districts. Within each section, there has been no attempt to create "tours" since most sites are privately owned and not open to the general public. This is also why there are no maps and why addresses are often (at the owners' requests) vague.

DISTRICT I

Abingdon, Joppa, and Edgewood

1-1. Rumsey House
Bridge Drive
c. 1720 (?); c. 1768; Private
National Register; Historic American
Buildings Survey   HA-1

One of the most recognized yet least understood houses in Harford County, this structure is generally acknowledged to be "all that remains of Old Joppa." *Something* existed on the site of what was to become Joppa back in the seventeenth century; John Taylor's 1661 patent Taylor's Choice was in this general area and the post road came through here the same year, as early maps indicate. But it is all rather vague. Queen Anne didn't help matters. In 1706 the Maryland assembly approved new town sites but the queen refused to approve the legislation. In 1709, the colonial legislature authorized Col. James Maxwell I (died c. 1727) to build a courthouse on Taylor's Choice (the site specified in 1706); he began work but again the queen said no. Things were finally settled by 1725 (Queen Anne had died) when the town was platted and lots were sold with the understanding that Colonel Maxwell's house—what we call the Rumsey House—was not to be interfered with.

Therein lies the question—just how much of the Rumsey House was standing in the 1720s? In 1768 Benjamin Rumsey married the widow of James Maxwell II and thus gained the Maxwell property; when Rumsey died in 1808 this house was essentially in place. What happened when? Historian Albert C. Ritchie (father of the governor) concluded that Rumsey acquired Maxwell Sr.'s one-story house and then expanded it to its present size and gave it its distinctive gambrel roof. In the 1930s, however, a historian with the Historic American Buildings Survey argued that Rumsey merely "modernized . . . by new interior finish" Maxwell's two-story dwelling. No one

will ever know for certain, but the smart money will go with Ritchie. If a house this size had existed in Maryland in the 1720s, it would have been so extraordinary as to have caused comment; since no known early description exists, one invokes Sherlock Holmes's dog that didn't bark. Moreover, construction details within and without closely resemble details seen at Sophia's Dairy, located nearby and firmly dated to 1768.

I-1

1-2. Sophia's Dairy
Route 40 at Belcamp
1768; Private
National Register; Harford County
Landmark; Historic American
Buildings Survey   HA-5

Generations of historians have continuously used such words as "elegant," "extraordinary," and "remarkable" when discussing Sophia's Dairy. And with good reason. The house is a truly remarkable survivor and it assuredly stands as *primus inter pares* among Harford's colonial-era dwellings. A brick in the west gable inscribed "AH 1768" offers succinct testimony that Aquila Hall (born 1727) built the house in 1768. Hall had married his first cousin Sophia White (born 1731) in 1750 and the house was built on land she brought to the wedding as her dowry. According to tradition, the Halls employed five redemptionists (two of whom were carpenters) to build the huge (64 feet by 54 feet) house. Simple to the point of severity on the exterior, the house's interior explodes in a glorious array of fashionably carved wood: Doric cornices, fluted pilasters, modillioned cornices, and crossetted window and door trim. Nothing else in Harford County can compare, although, perhaps, the original Mount Pleasant came close. But not even Mount Pleasant could equal Sophia's Dairy's famous double staircase: imperial in concept, flawless in execution, it remains

I-2

I-3

I-4

I-5

I-5

without peer in the state and makes one wish one knew who those redemptionist carpenters were. (This highly important building is more fully discussed in chapter 3.)

I-3. Presbury House
(Quiet Lodge)
Austin and Parrish Roads
Mid-eighteenth century; Private
National Register   HA-15

Its configurations (a 20-by-40-foot rectangle with a center through hall) and details (glazed Flemish bond brick and simple interior woodwork of native timber) link the Presbury House to dozens of similar structures throughout the Chesapeake region. From the James River to the Susquehanna Flats, during the mid-eighteenth century this is precisely what a prosperous planter/merchant would have built. But it is a rarity in Harford County in part because if there had been similar houses dotting the banks of the Gunpowder and Bush rivers, they were obliterated after the federal government took over Harford's bay frontage in 1917 for military use. (For a rare survivor, however, see the Davis farm, 6-4.) Deeds and other documents place the Presbury family in this area at an early date and suggest connections with this house. Moreover, a researcher for the Maryland Historical Society concluded that George Presbury, son of the immigrant James, built "the curious, little old 'mansion.'" When George Presbury of William sold this land (361 acres) on August 28, 1799, to Stephen Raphel for £1,225, the deed describes the land as being "all that left to George by his grandfather George" and grandfather George's will does bequeath to "my Grandson George Presbury son of William" the "lands lying on or near Gunpowder River." Several bricks in the house are inscribed with Presbury names and dates (e.g., "George Presbury born August 16, 1719," and "Gouldsmith Presbury born Sep 10, 1749"), but the markings' reliability is unclear. (Someone could have scratched the names in in 1935.) What is clear is that many Presburys were early converts to Methodism: they offered lodging here to itinerant ministers in the 1770s until the Gunpowder Neck Meetinghouse was built with Presbury help (see 1-14); Bishop Asbury's journal alone refers to fourteen separate visits to the Gunpowder Neck between 1772 and 1777. Incidentally, the name Quiet Lodge does not appear in Presbury deeds; its first, fleeting use is in Stephen Raphel's 1811 will,

but it then disappears, only to be revived c. 1900 as the name Mr. and Mrs. Thomas Francis Cadwalader gave their frame, 1½-story honeymoon cottage. (See also 1-16.) That cottage, much expanded, is now officer's housing and the Presbury house—also officer's housing—has willy-nilly acquired the moniker Quiet Lodge.

I-4. Morgan's Lott
900 Mountain Road
Eighteenth century; with additions;
Private   HA-155

This three-part house deserves to be better known than it is. The name is from the ancient patent Morgan's Lott, part of which was assigned to William Morgan in 1687. No one thinks this house is that old, however, since most land in the upper reaches of the Gunpowder, Bush, and Winters Run valleys was taken up purely on speculation during the late seventeenth century. Instead, it seems safer to ascribe the central portion of the present dwelling (and probably the north wing as well) to the affluent Bond family, one of whom, Thomas, acquired the land in 1729. It fits with other surviving Bond houses such as Joshua's Meadows since the center section has a two-room, end-fireplace, corner-stair plan typical of the time. The last Bond sold the tract to Robert Conn in 1774 and Dennis Griffith's 1794 map of the county shows something here labeled "Conn's." Other sections are harder to date, but it all must have come together by the mid-nineteenth century, for when the place was sold at a trustees sale in 1871 the Baltimore *Sun* ran a notice for "a substantial Stone Dwelling House containing on the first floor Hall, Parlor, Dining Room, Sitting Room, Pantry and Kitchen. In front and around the House is a Piazza [porch] 60 feet in length": those rooms are still here and that porch still rambles across the east façade.

I-5. St. Mary's Episcopal Church
St. Mary's Church Road
1849; Regular services
National Register; Harford County
Landmark   HA-168

"St. Mary's is the finest rural church in the diocese of Maryland," according to Phoebe Stanton. And Professor Stanton ought to know: she reigned for years as chairman of the Johns Hopkins University's Department of Art History and her 1968 book, *The Gothic*

Revival and American Church Architecture, remains the last word on the subject. St. Mary's important and excellent design may be directly attributed to its first rector, the Reverend Dr. William Francis Brand (1814–1907). Ordained in 1844 (after a brief flirtation with a legal career), Brand was an early convert to the Ecclesiological movement, whose adherents in England and America sought to reform the Anglican Church spiritually and intellectually. Believing that good Gothically designed churches were the outward and visible manifestations of a healthy congregation, they set about publishing builder's guides. St. Mary's, possibly designed by Baltimore architect J. Crawford Neilson, earns its niche in history for being among the first churches in America built according to Ecclesiologically sanctioned concepts: its Port Deposit granite walls are meant to suggest medieval English parish churches, as are the lancet-arched windows, the porch and chancel paved in Minton tiles, the green marble altar, and the intricately carved pulpit and lectern. Wonderful as the shell is—and it is—Brand's greatest triumph must be the complete set of Butterfield glass windows he purchased for St. Mary's. Designed by English architect William Butterfield, the fifteen windows form the only complete set of Butterfield glass in America; rich in color and pattern, the windows depict the life of Christ as witnessed by his mother, the church's namesake and patron saint, from the Annunciation to the Ascension.

1-6. Old St. Mary's Rectory
100 St. Mary's Church Road
Late nineteenth century; Private   HA-1772

The Reverend Dr. William Brand successfully dabbled in architecture for much of his adult life. Everyone gives him at least indirect credit for St. Mary's Church, where he took pains to keep the stone structure firmly within the accepted dicta of Anglican church design by following sanctioned pattern books, by directly ordering Butterfield glass from England (paid for by his heiress wife), and by overseeing the murals and other paintings within the church. Many local historians and parishioners also give him full credit for this rectory, whose dark brick walls and prominent gables evoke a medieval manor house in rural Kent or East Anglia. The brick is laid in Flemish bond on all four sides and the headers, also on all four sides, are often glazed; to Brand glazed headers evoked distant centuries, but to most modern

eyes they are simply fun as they cheerfully sparkle in the sun. The house is intact on the inside as well and its open rambling plan, front and back stairs, and marble mantels are very much what an educated late Victorian minister (with a rich wife) would have wanted. It is also what a twentieth-century educated socialite would have wanted, and by all accounts Edith Calvert Pierce, who with her husband bought the rectory from the church in 1938 after the new stone rectory was built, was very happy here. Calvert was the surname of the lords Baltimore and Mrs. Pierce was keenly aware of these connections. She often visited Kiplin Hall, the Calverts' manor house in Yorkshire; Kiplin's rambling brick configuration and gable-punctuated skyline (aided by a martini or two) are said to have reminded her of the old rectory.

1-7. Crouse-Kline House
400 Magnolia Road
1918; Private   HA-1606

Harford countians normally regard the years 1917–18 as years of destruction: the Aberdeen Proving Ground and Edgewood Arsenal came and the county's tidewater farms went. This house, therefore, is something of an exception since it was built, not destroyed, during those tumultuous times. Its prominent cross gables, wraparound porches, and a polygonal corner tower place it firmly in the Queen Anne style of design, but it is a late example of the style, since most similar structures date to the 1880–1900 period, as is discussed in chapter 6. One could also view the house as an example of rural site-planning, for the cross gables and tower suggest the nearby intersection of Magnolia and Trimble roads.

1-8. Middendorf-Hollingsworth House
Stockton Road
Mid-nineteenth century; Private   HA-299

Probably built by John Hollingsworth and his wife, Rebecca, this small frame house is one of several Hollingsworth-associated structures that still dot the banks of Winters Run. Devout Quakers all, the family lived prosperously in the valley for generations, thanks partly to farming (they marketed their produce in Baltimore), partly to milling, and partly to their wheel factory. John inherited roughly 108 acres from his father, Nathaniel, in 1834 (see 3-42); John died in 1874, leaving his estate

1-6

1-7

1-8

I-9

I-IO

I-II

I-I2

to Rebecca and their single daughters Margaret, Lydia, and Eliza, for life, thence to son Amos B.; John's last will and testament further gives Rebecca specific use of the "parlor, dining room, and kitchen and the room over the dining room." The irregularly placed windows of the four-bay, two-story dwelling suggest additions—if a house of this type had been built all-of-a-piece, the windows and doors would have been carefully aligned. Amos Hollingsworth died in 1905 and the house, called Montland, and 120 acres eventually ended up in the hands of Lydia and Eliza, who sold it ("adjoining the lands of the Hollingsworths Wheel Company") to the Middendorf family in 1906. The Middendorfs civilly agreed to let the maiden sisters live "in the house where they now reside" for two months "so as to enable them to convert part of their personal property into money and to move conveniently to Fallston."

I-9. Weaver-Hollingsworth House
Stockton Road
c. 1880; Private   HA-301

Interviews with family members suggest that Joel Hollingsworth and his wife, née Hannah Carter, built this "retirement" cottage after their children married and moved into their own quarters. To add interest to the otherwise standard three-bay, 1½-story frame configuration, the Hollingsworths gave the structure a variety of late Victorian picturesque devices, including a large peaked dormer over the front door and a clipped gable roof with round-arched windows in the attic. Hannah died in 1897 and Joel sold the property in 1907. The late Hunter Sutherland, historian and educator, edited the Hannah Hollingsworth diary; an excerpt, published in the Historical Society of Harford County's Autumn 1990 *Harford Historical Bulletin,* gives a fascinating picture of the family's life and times.

I-10. Spears-Hollingsworth House
Stockton Road
c. 1885; Private   HA-300

According to tradition, Barclay Hollingsworth remodeled this country Victorian cottage shortly after his marriage in 1885. Hollingsworth ran the prosperous wheel factory near here with his father, Joel, and brother, Harris. If he was a businessman, he was a thoroughly conservative one for he kept the classic L-plan shell of this house intact and unchanged from

what his counterpart built a generation earlier; details such as wide eaves, elaborate brick chimneys, and peaked dormers mark his only concessions to the generally flamboyant stylistic fashions of the late nineteenth century.

I-11. Leonard-Hollingsworth House
Stockton Road
1870; Private   HA-302

Situated at the edge of a wooded valley, this frame Hollingsworth house can be precisely dated to 1870, thanks to a bill of sale found during a 1970 remodeling. Two stories tall with an L-shaped plan, this quiet and traditional structure would not have raised anyone's late Victorian eyebrows. The younger generation of Hollingsworths were apparently more architecturally conservative than their parents. Harris Hollingsworth, who lived here, ran the nearby wheel factory, J. C. Hollingsworth & Sons, which manufactured wagon wheels for a half century; employing thirty-five men and capable of turning out twenty-five sets of wheels per day, the company played a crucial role in Harford's industrial history. (Fire destroyed the plant; the ruins are now at the bottom of Atkisson Reservoir but the enterprise lives on if only in name, thanks to Wheel Road.) Generations of Hollingsworths also maintained successful mills along Winters Run and the Little Gunpowder; in addition, a fine old barn on this property suggests that some family members used farming for additional income.

I-12. Robinson-McCourtney House
Singer and Winters Run Roads
Mid-nineteenth century; Private   HA-304

Sometimes called "the schoolhouse," this rambling frame structure exemplifies the sort of mixed-use career many county structures enjoyed in pre–zoning code days. The large, three-bay, two-story clapboard main dwelling once contained a hat shop; the one-story wing to the southeast, also clapboard and now a kitchen, once saw action as a neighborhood general store; the board-and-batten, gingerbreaded, two-bay, two-story wing to the southwest, so far as is known, has always been residential.

1-13. McComas Institute
Singer Road
1867; Private
National Register; Harford County
Landmark   HA-307

From a few feet south of Singer Road, this one-story frame building would be easy to glance at and dismiss. But to do so would be a mistake; despite its unprepossessing appearance the Institute is one of a figurative handful of Harford County structures with undeniable national importance, since it is Harford's only remaining visual evidence of the Freedmen's Bureau. (The well-known Hosanna School depended more on local free-black initiative than on the kindness of Washington-based strangers.) Maj. Gen. Lew Wallace (also remembered for writing *Ben Hur*) set up the Bureau of Refugees, Freedmen, and Abandoned Lands in 1864 to serve the many needs of the men and women freed by the Emancipation Proclamation. Under the bureau's sponsorship, a group of trustees bought an acre here in 1867 "in trust for the purpose of erecting or allowing to be erected thereon a schoolhouse for the use, benefit and Education of the Colored People of Harford County." Thus this structure marks, with the Hosanna School, the beginnings of a nationwide movement to correct 250 years of racial injustice.

Tobacco-merchant George McComas lived nearby at Linwood; an abolitionist before the Civil War and a life-long crusader on behalf of the downtrodden, McComas gained immortality when the new school was named after him.

1-14. Gunpowder Neck Meetinghouse
Magnolia Road
c. 1773 (?); Private   HA-357

Educator and historian C. Milton Wright wrote in *Our Harford Heritage* that he "believes [this] to be the oldest Methodist Meetinghouse still standing in America." Scholars from the United Methodist Historical Society in Baltimore have been investigating the issue and, while they have not proven Mr. Wright's thesis, neither have they disproved it. On the other hand, a strong body of knowledgeable opinion contends that the building is a c. 1850 replacement of an older log structure. (See the Spring 1990 issue of the *Harford Historical Bulletin*.) It is known that in 1773 Joseph Presbury, whose family owned Quiet Lodge and

several other farms in the Neck, deeded an acre of land here to a group "of the Wesleyans" and that deed refers to the "lately erected preaching house." Later deeds for land in the Neck refer to a meetinghouse on this site. In 1784, after Francis Asbury became bishop, he reported that six Methodist chapels already existed in the Baltimore circuit and one of the six was "Gunpowder Neck." There is little in the simple lines or straightforward construction of the 26-by-35-foot brick structure, with its oyster-shell mortar, to tip the scale to the eighteenth or the nineteenth century. (In fact it is maddening to see the now-blind semicircle in the south gable end; it was common practice to embellish such spaces with building dates and if a vandal hadn't stolen this stone the questions might be solved.) During the nineteenth century the Neck's white congregation abandoned the building and turned it over to a black group who used it for a church and for a school; since World War I the U.S. government has maintained it as part of Edgewood Arsenal.

1-15. Thomas Kell House
1810 Old Joppa Road
Late eighteenth century; with additions;
Private   HA-426

A 1970 report on this structure notes that the "stone and wooden house is hard to analyze." Amen. A few facts, however, are clear, and allow a few conclusions and suppositions. According to Walter Preston's 1901 *History of Harford County*, Thomas Kell of Fell's Point married Aliceanna Bond in 1767 and the couple "moved shortly afterwards to Kellville, Harford County, which was their home for the remainder of their lives." The intersection of Jerusalem and Old Joppa roads was for years known as Kellville and the county Orphan's Court papers show that "Capt." Thomas Kell died here in November 1790; material in the land records further suggests that he died in the three-bay, three-story uncoursed stone section of the present expanded dwelling. The Kells brought up their fifteen children here and at least one branch deserves further comment. Thomas Jr., born in 1772, swaggered as one of the foremost lawyers of his day: counsel for the far-flung enterprises of Samuel Jay & Co. (see 2-16) he eventually became the first Harford countian to serve as attorney general of Maryland; in 1835 his daughter, Elizabeth, married Augustus W. Bradford, the Bel Air native who suffered the strain of

1-13

1-14

1-15

1-16

1-17

being the Civil War governor of Maryland. Later owners of the property continued to build and Kell's original dwelling is now but one part of a rambling many-sectioned house. A bewildering array of outbuildings dots the grounds: the chickenhouse, garage, and root cellar were built by J. Edgar Gladden in the twentieth century, while the springhouse, barn, and corncrib probably date to the time of the Kells.

1-16. The Mound
2008 Old Joppa Road
1785; c. 1850; c. 1919; Private   HA-428

Is there such a thing as the quintessential Harford County house? To qualify, a building would have to have centuries-spanning connections with traditional county professions such as farming, milling, and the law; would have to have some association with Baltimore, a place that has played such an important role in shaping the county; would need a romantic legend or two; and, most important, would consist of several discernible, nonflashy sections. The Mound checks in all respects. Even the most myopic glance reveals the house's rambling growth pattern, but "rambling" doesn't mean haphazard, for each of the house's many sections can be explained.

The place sits on land called Groom's Chance, patented in 1687. George Mason, who came to the colonies from England in the mid-eighteenth century to run the iron foundries which then flourished in Maryland, acquired the land and, on his death, left it to his son John. John and his wife, Ann, then built the three-bay, 1½-story stone structure that forms the center (or dining room and study) of the extant house. (A datestone in the cellar of this section, inscribed "IMA 1785," marks *J*ohn and *A*nn *M*ason's completion of the house in that year [*J*s were often carved as *I*s].)

In 1839 John Carroll Walsh bought the farm; *his* father, Michael, had been contractor when the Baltimore Cathedral was built under the aegis of Archbishop John Carroll, which might explain young Walsh's name. J. C. Walsh married Sarah Amanda Lee, whose father owned the nearby Jerusalem Mill. Neither the Quaker Lees nor the Roman Catholic Walshes approved of the union and both planted cedar trees to block the view of the other's house. Walsh seems to have continuously attracted controversy: during the Civil War he aided Harry Gilmor when that Con-

federate made his dash through the county and consequently wound up cooling his Southern ardor in jail. Nevertheless, the couple prospered at The Mound and Walsh became president of the Harford Mutual Insurance Company. The old house evidently proved too small for this important executive and Walsh added the large, cubic, vaguely Italianate wing to the west.

In this century, Thomas F. Cadwalader, whose father, John, had inherited the vast family holdings on the Gunpowder Neck, planned to pursue a career in law while living on the Neck. To that end, he became the first male Cadwalader since Benjamin Franklin's time not to attend the University of Pennsylvania and chose, instead, to read law at the University of Maryland. But the Neck was summarily condemned by the federal government in 1917 and the displaced Cadwalader relocated to The Mound, which he bought in 1919. He and his descendants added the garage to the east and the modern kitchen to the south.

1-17. Jerusalem Mill
Jerusalem Road
1772; mid-nineteenth century; Public
National Register; Historic American
Buildings Survey   HA-433

In September 1769 millwright Isaiah Linton and miller David Lee entered into a partnership to build a mill on this low-lying, flat site on the Fall Line of the Gunpowder Falls. Their original building was completed in August 1772. Lee, born in 1740, had been a miller in Bucks County, Pennsylvania, but Baltimore City, with its rapidly growing port, swift streams, and fertile grain fields, lured him south. (It also lured Lee's cousins, the Ellicott brothers, who founded what became Ellicott City while Lee was settling here.) The mill provided the anchor for the little community of Jerusalem, which Lee had developed by 1814; Lee died in 1816 but his direct descendants owned the mill and village until the 1880s. Lee's creation forms an intact proto-company town dating to the time when entrepreneurs were first transforming America with the Industrial Revolution. The 1814 tax list suggests that the original Lee mill was built of stone and was two stories tall; what no one knows (despite much sleuthing) is which Lee added the present, impressive, superstructure—or when. Regardless, the extant structure is easily the most substantial survivor of the hundreds of mills that once flourished in Harford and Baltimore counties, and its double row of dormer windows, thought to be unique, gives added panache. Abandoned and neglected for years, the mill is now (1994) about to undergo a much-needed restoration, thanks to the Maryland Department of Natural Resources.

I-18. McCourtney's Store
2802 Jerusalem Road
c. 1844; Private
National Register   HA-429

By 1844 the village of Jerusalem had grown important enough to warrant its own post office; Washington agreed and established one that year and the Lee family erected this building to house it. Mail continued to be sorted here until the office was closed in 1923. In customary rural style, the post office shared space with the community store. (See also the Silver family's Glenville store and post office, 2-25.) Ralph Sackett Lee (1780–1862), who had inherited the Jerusalem property from his father, David, named his son-in-law John Carroll Walsh of The Mound postmaster while Lee himself operated the store. David Lee II (1808–86), who inherited the Jerusalem property from Ralph Sackett, leased the store to S. O. McCourtney in 1881; McCourtney bought the building outright from the Lees in 1921 and maintained the store here until he died in 1939.

I-19. Jerusalem House
2807 Jerusalem Road
c. 1800; c. 1840; c. 1869; Private
National Register   HA-431

Locally known as the Mansion House, this handsome 2½-story stuccoed stone and frame dwelling was built in three stages by three generations of Lees—David (1740–1816), his son Ralph S. (1780–1862), and *his* son David II (1808–86), all of whom lived here in semifeudal fashion running their Jerusalem mill and overseeing life in their surrounding village. The main (c. 1800) section stretches five bays long below a slate-covered gable roof; its general configuration and classic center through hall plan resemble Olney, a nearby brick house built about the same time by the Norris family, future in-laws of the Lees. A fire destroyed the interior of the Jerusalem house in the 1840s and R. S. Lee then re-outfitted the place with simple plastering and low-key woodwork

(such as paneling, doors, and mantles) typical of the time in Harford County. The Lees stayed on here until 1921 and, except for updated utilities and a two-story frame wing, the house has remained unchanged since R. S. Lee's era. In addition to the other described buildings in Jerusalem village, the Lees also built a stone springhouse in 1840 in a meadow across Jerusalem Road from "The Mansion" and a massive stone barn (now largely destroyed) south of the house. Both structures have datestones, a locally rare refinement for outbuildings and evidence of the high standards the Lees set for themselves.

I-20. Jerusalem Farm House
2805 Jerusalem Road
c. 1800; Private
National Register   HA-430

Ralph Sackett Lee hired educator and cartographer George Graham Curtiss to map Jerusalem Village in 1860 when the little community was at the height of its prosperity. Curtiss labeled the building on this site "Dwelling"; it is believed to have been the residence of one of the Lees' tenant farmers. The two-part house consists of two matching 2½-story modules, one shingle and frame, one rubblestone. Each module contains one room per floor. The west (stone) unit is older and shows up on David Lee's 1814 tax assessment; it has an interior brick chimney rising flush with the west wall to service a massive cooking fireplace in the basement and progressively smaller fireplaces in the main floor and attic; this module also contains the stairs, which rise in two parallel straight flights.

I-21. Cooper's Shop; Gun Factory
Behind 2811 Jerusalem Road
c. 1775; Public
National Register   HA-434

An eighteenth-century industrialist such as David Lee needed a skilled woodworker to turn out barrels, tubs, casks, and other vital material. It is generally believed that Lee hired such an artisan and set him up in this small, two-story rubblestone structure. (It is believed that workers here also made chair doors, porch trim, and balusters. One wonders how many area houses sport Jerusalem-made wooden details.) The little building, recently restored through the efforts of the Friends of Jerusalem Mill, suggests the same design sensibility seen at the Lees' farmer's house: both

I-18

I-19

I-20

I-21

1-22

1-23

1-24

1-25

1-25

originally had a plan of one room per floor with a side stair and minimal exterior adornment. Both also gained, at various times, a frame addition. During the Revolution Lee profited from the presence of his skilled hired hand. The Maryland legislature paid the Quaker miller £1,000 in gold and silver to make rifle stocks for the local militia. On his 1860 map of Jerusalem village, G. G. Curtiss labels this structure as "C. Shop," presumably cooper's shop, another enterprise necessary to the running of a flour mill.

1-22. Jerusalem Blacksmith Shop
Jerusalem Road
Early nineteenth century; Public
National Register   HA-425

An 1806 deed to David Lee refers to "a stone standing near David Lee's Blacksmith Shop," which suggests that Lee built this half-story stuccoed rubblestone structure as part of his self-sufficient Jerusalem industrial empire: his mill ground grain grown by his tenant farmers (and others, of course), which workers then packed in barrels made at his cooper shop and held together with barrel staves fashioned here. Ralph Sackett Lee's ledger—Ralph Sackett was David Lee's son—shows frequent purchases of bar iron. His 1862 estate inventory includes items such as "ole iron," a "Blacksmith vize," and "1 anville," all of which suggest that workers fashioned a good deal of wrought iron here: in addition to staves, likely products include mill gears, hardware for the village's houses, and farm implements.

1-23. Jericho Covered Bridge
Jericho Road at Gunpowder Falls
1865; Public
National Register; Historic American
Buildings Survey   HA-438

This well-known structure, a cooperative venture of Harford and Baltimore counties, is the only remaining covered bridge in either jurisdiction. Thomas Forsyth, a Baltimore City machinist, actually built the span and was paid $3,125 for his efforts; Hugh Simms, owner of the cotton duck factory in nearby Franklinville, supervised construction. Harford County government records document the bridge's construction in detail: the $2,000 "special appropriation"; the June 7, 1865, advertising for proposals ("80 feet span to be covered with shingles, and weatherboarded, with stone abutments, about fifteen feet high,

well cemented"); the selection of Simms and Forsyth; and Simms's final (December 1, 1865) report that "the bridge is finished according to the specifications . . . and reflects great credit upon Mr. Forsyth." The bridge crosses the Gunpowder 15 feet above water level; overhead clearance is 12 feet, 4 inches at the center of the roadway and 10 feet at the curb. Forsyth gave the bridge a Burr Truss, a support system named for Theodore Burr of Pennsylvania who designed and patented it in 1804.

1-24. Jerusalem Tenant House
2809 Jerusalem Road
c. 1850; Private
National Register   HA-487

The success of the Lees' milling enterprises grew throughout the nineteenth century and so, too, did the family's need for a guaranteed supply of grain; it was all right to act as intermediary for local farmers who paid to have their corn and wheat ground at the Jerusalem Mill, but it was far more desirable to be self-sufficient, to be able to control the entire process from sowing of seed to selling of flour. (It is all somewhat analogous to oil refining today.) To this end, David Lee built one tenant farmhouse around 1800; mill production and/or demand for flour continued to grow, and a half century later Lee's son Ralph Sackett Lee put up this frame building to house yet a second tenant farmer. The newer house, with two sections forming an L-shape plan, appears on the 1860 Curtiss map of Jerusalem Village—complete with L plan—and is marked "Farmer." A generation later, the Lees no longer had an interest in controlling grain and flour production: they sold the mill in 1886 and sold this house the same year. In all probability, the new owners gave the dwelling its fashionable mid-Victorian details, such as the wide-eaved roof, central attic peak dormer, and semicircular arched attic window.

1-25. Davidson House
Old Joppa Road
1841; Private   HA-440

On November 30, 1841, John S. Davidson bought 112 acres here (parts of two tracts, Turkey Hills and Archibald's Addition); he and his wife, Mary, must have immediately set about building, for a datestone in the south corner of the west wall of this rubblestone dwelling is inscribed "JMD 1841." (A rubblestone springhouse, southeast of the main dwelling, also dates to this time.) The David-sons built their residence into a bank so it stands 2½ stories tall on the warm south front but only 1½ stories on the north, an important consideration in the days before central heating and cooling. The cellar contained the kitchen and other services with more formal areas above, an arrangement replicated at the nearby Jerusalem Farm House. Although the Davidsons' house was completely remodeled on the interior in the 1940s, the exterior remains largely intact and holds an important place in the Jerusalem community, since it evinces how the Lees and their flourishing mill obviously caused others to start farms to take advantage of the rich soil and convenient gristmill.

1-26. Franklinville Bridge
(Harford County Bridge #1)
Franklinville Road at Gunpowder Falls
c. 1880; Public   HA-439

During the eighteenth and nineteenth centuries the Little Gunpowder Valley clattered and smoked as a sort of mini-Rhur with a flour mill, blacksmith shop, and cooper shop at Jerusalem, a spade factory, cotton mill, and wrought iron works at Franklinville, and another cotton mill at Jericho. Each plant spawned a cluster of subsidiary structures such as workers' houses, sheds, stores, dams, and so forth. Local entrepreneurs such as the Lees of Jerusalem must have viewed the Gunpowder as a mixed blessing: on one hand its waters powered the various industries but, on the other, the swift current certainly impeded wagon travel. So bridges became necessities. It is known that as early as 1832 Ralph Sackett Lee of Jerusalem pressured the Maryland legislature to build a covered bridge near his mill on Jerusalem Road. (The bridge washed away and was replaced by the present concrete span in 1929.) His son, David Lee II, overseer of the public road from Jerusalem Mill to Joppa, lobbied for a second covered bridge for the community and got it when the present Jericho bridge was completed in 1865. The Franklinville Road bridge, a 76-foot-long Pratt Truss span, should be viewed as an integral part of this complex system.

1-27. Woodside
400 Singer Road
1823; Private
National Register   HA-693

Crowning the crest of a hill with amiable dignity and overlooking a great sweep of lawn, Woodside—even at first glance—comes across as one of the truly important houses in Harford County. Dr. Joshua Wilson, born at nearby Gibson's Park and a son of William Wilson III, built Woodside to mark his marriage to Rebecca Lee (daughter of the owner of Jerusalem Mill); until 1994, the house was always owned by their direct descendants. The Wilsons gave their 2½-story stone dwelling a sidehall/double parlor plan, an urbane type of configuration not commonly seen in rural areas. The shell of the house deserves mention, too, for it boasts arguably the best stonework in this part of Maryland. Its lapidary walls are laid with a precision that would be remarkable anywhere, and the beautifully dressed monolith lintels, placed over each window and door, further attest to the skill of the mason and the fastidiousness of the owner. The same care may also be seen on the interior, where the delicate open-string stair, federal mantels, and marbleized baseboards have no local betters. Continuity of ownership doubtless helps explain Woodside's fine collection of outbuildings: a stone springhouse and log barn probably date to the doctor's era while later Wilsons have added structures such as woodsheds, a corncrib, and garages—even an early twentieth-century gas pump—as the need arose. Wilson received his medical degree from the University of Maryland Medical School in 1818; he was a civic-minded man who shared his wealth as he prospered (he donated land for St. Mary's Church, for example) and the dual traits of learning and *noblesse oblige* still characterize the family.

1-28. Glen Echo Farm
(Harford Glen)
Wheel Road
c. 1817; c. 1835; c. 1929; Public HA-699

The four stone sections of this rambling house are massed with a picturesqueness worthy of its romantic lakefront location. Thomas Hollingsworth, member of that enterprising clan who once owned most of the Winters Run Valley, bought 136 acres here from his father, Nathaniel, in 1817 and shortly thereafter built a two-part dwelling (see 3-42). The

1-26

1-27

1-27

1-28

1-29

1-30

house consisted of a two-section main unit with a lower, adjacent kitchen; both parts remain easily discernible. Thomas married in 1819, an event that may coincide with his architectural efforts. He died in 1820 and his sister Hannah bought the tract with her husband, Joel Carter, from Thomas's estate. (Joel and Hannah Carter are not to be confused with Joel and Hannah Hollingsworth, mentioned in 1-9; there was also a Joel Carter Hollingsworth.) In 1835 the Carters sold the place to Charlotte Ramsay of Baltimore City "for her daughter Charlotte Jane Hall, wife of Henry Hall."

The Halls almost certainly added the north wing, which contains the principal entrance leading to an ample stairhall and parlor. All details suggest the stylishness of the owners—woodwork and trim match examples in then-popular English pattern books and the English-made locks bear the monogram of King William IV, who reigned from 1830 to 1837. When Charlotte Jane Hall died in the spring of 1868, she left her daughter Charlotte Ramsay Hall the "farm on which I now reside commonly called Glen Echo." (Two sons, Henry and W.W.R. Hall, and another daughter, Sophia McHenry Brand [wife of the rector of St. Mary's church], were also taken care of.) The affluent Halls furnished Glen Echo comfortably: silver and mahogany throughout; books filled the library, from standard histories to *Paradise Lost* to collections of Cowper and Goldsmith; someone even enjoyed a backgammon set!

Charlotte sold the property out of the family on July 8, 1868. In 1929 Philadelphia financier Isaac Pennypacker bought the place and planned to use it as a summer retreat; he built the last addition (a large living room facing Winters Run), and carefully based his work on precedents set in the older sections of the house. The grounds, embowered in specimen trees, contain a highly important collection of nineteenth-century outbuildings (and ruins of outbuildings), including an icehouse, cornhouse, and stone dairy/meathouse all close to the dwelling and, farther afield, the pock-marked foundation walls of two of the county's best-known businesses, J. C. Hollingsworth & Sons wheel factory and Nathaniel Hollingsworth's gristmill. In 1942 the federal government condemned the property and built Atkisson Dam to ensure, by means of the resulting 75-acre lake, an adequate water supply for the military post at Edgewood.

1-29. Monmouth Farm
Wheel Road
c. 1770; c. 1845; c. 1950; Private   HA-703

The whole here far exceeds the sum of the parts. In spirit and in form, Monmouth Farm is, with Indian Spring Farm (5-57), perhaps Harford's greatest example of a late Victorian country estate. And even though the oldest building on the farm, the small gambrel-roofed center of the main house (still somewhat discernible), probably dates to the mid-eighteenth century (when the farm was owned by the Halls of Sophia's Dairy), the overriding sensibility here is "English Country House"–living from the Disraeli era. One Ramsay McHenry—whose family had a fort named for them—lived most of the year in Baltimore but owned Monmouth and used it as a summer retreat. He died in 1878 and his estate inventory reveals bedrooms replete with marble-topped furniture, a library with "Large Leather Cushioned Chairs," a smoking room, miscellaneous "glass decanters" and "bronze mantle ornaments" everywhere, and a garden complete with "flower pots" and "1 rustic bench." Mr. and Mrs. James McLean bought the farm in the 1940s and gloriously maintained McHenry's manner of living until they sold Monmouth in the 1970s. The extensive grounds contain a locally unsurpassed collection of outbuildings, including a brewery and an octagonal smokehouse.

1-30. Windy Walls
201 West Wheel Road
c. 1888; Private   HA-713

Col. Ramsay McHenry of Monmouth Farm died in 1878, and the next year his heirs sold 460 acres here (a small part of his holdings) to Baltimoreans Alexander and Margaret Bell. When Margaret died in 1882 she left the farm to her two sons, Alexander S. and William Boyd Bell, who drew up a deed of partition in 1888.

William acquired 200 of those acres and hired architect George Archer to design this house. Archer, a Harford native with offices in Baltimore, gave the county some of its most interesting buildings, including the First Presbyterian Church in Bel Air (designed in 1881 and his first local commission), the Harford National Bank (1882, destroyed for the courthouse addition), and the Second National Bank (on Office Street, 1900). The plans he drew up for Bell produced an irregularly massed stone and shingle pile, with a turreted tower, randomly sized gables, and massive chimneys bursting forth seemingly at will—in sum, one of Harford's most spirited exercises in the Queen Anne style. The "open" floor plan was locally revolutionary: here, thanks to central heating, living hall, parlor, and dining room all flowed into each other, marking a break with the era when lack of central heating demanded that all rooms had their own fireplace.

1-31. Emmorton Schoolhouse
West Wheel Road
1868; Private　　　　　　　　　　HA-715

Maryland's constitution of 1864—revised in 1867—required a statewide "thorough and efficient system of free public schools." Thus in 1868 the Harford County Board of School Commissioners bought a half-acre lot in Emmorton and built this one-story, one-room stone school. The building, of strictly utilitarian design, cost the commissioners $1,200, a high sum doubtless explained by the unusual choice of stone as a building material. (A 1916 survey of county schools revealed that ninety-four were frame, six were brick, and only two were stone.) In 1979, as part of an oral history program, interviewers talked to Margaret Robinson Gatchell, who taught grades 1 through 7 here during World War I. Mrs. Gatchell remembered that boys and girls sat on separate sides of the room with the teacher's desk in front on a dais; she also recalled a coal-fed pot belly stove, two children to a desk, one slate per child, and boys' and girls' outhouses in the woods. The school was closed in 1920 and the building has been adapted to residential use.

1-32. Park Farm/Gibson's Park
Wheel and Emmorton Roads
c. 1770; Private　　　　　　　　　HA-716

This stately brick house wears an air of dignity even in decay; exquisite examples of Georgian woodwork (stair and balusters, wainscotting, mantels, doors) grace the interior and Flemish bond brick walls convey a sense of solidity and permanence that vandals and scavengers have not diminished. William Wilson (?–1753) moved to the Emmorton area from southern Maryland in the early eighteenth century and purchased several hundred acres of Gibson's Park and other tracts; his descendants have been here ever since. Family legends and documentary sources all acknowledge that a later William Wilson built this superior Georgian house, but it is unclear whether credit goes to the first William's son William (1720–80) or grandson William (1745–1819). William Wilson II's last will and testament, however, suggests that he did *not* build the house, for he left his son Samuel 300 acres and "my Dwelling Plantation called Aquila's Inheritance," while 200 acres of Gibson's Park went to daughter Rachel and the remaining 400 went to William III. Rachel died in 1790 and left the land to her brothers; William bought Samuel's share in 1796. The 1798 tax assessment notes that "William Wilson, Esq." owned 600 acres, 18 slaves, and a 35-by-35-foot brick dwelling. (He also owned a "28 × 16 kitchen, 24 × 16 granary, 16 × 10 meathouse, 16 × 16 Negro quarters," and a stable.) The house's sidehall/double parlor floor plan proved influential: Dr. Joshua Wilson (1797–1885) was born here, a son of William Wilson III; Gibson's Park descended in the female line and Joshua built his own house, Woodside, in 1823 on the southern edge of these ancestral acres. When he did, he retained the Gibson's Park floor plan he knew from his youth.

1-33. Nelson-Reardon-Kennard House
3604 Philadelphia Road
c. 1785; c. 1888; Private
National Register; Harford County
Landmark　　　　　　　　　　HA-855

One of the half-dozen oldest frame buildings in Harford County, this excellent house stands as virtually all that remains of Old Abingdon, a town that flourished for a generation after its founding but which has slept soundly for the past 170 years or so. The Paca family laid out Abingdon in 1779; six years later Aquila Paca sold "Lot No. 3" to John Reardon for "5 shillings sterling." Reardon built the present structure (it is indicated in the 1798 Federal Direct Tax as a "2-story wood house") and it has remained intact ever since, with its one-room deep, center-stairhall plan and rear service wing. In the house's early days its Abingdon neighbors included Cokesbury College, the first Methodist college in the Western Hemisphere; there were also, according to Scott's 1799 *U.S. Gazetteer,* "51 dwellings . . . [and] 8 stores filled with West India produce and the various manufactures of Europe, a tanyard, and several shops in which all the

I-31

I-32

I-33

1-34

1-35

1-36

1-36

useful and mechanical arts are carried on." Times have changed.

1-34. Kintail Glebe
(The Glebe)
3019 Goat Hill Road
c. 1720 (?); c. 1790; Private
National Register   HA-871

In typical contradictory Harford County fashion, this, the original building associated with Harford Furnace, was not built as a part of Harford Furnace. The oldest section of this L-plan house is the four-bay north wing pictured here; most sources contend that it was built c. 1720 as a glebe house for Spesutia Church and if that date is correct, it makes this the oldest documented building in the county. In any event, it assumed its present L plan later in the century, after Daniel Robertson bought the place ("100 acres . . . called The Glebe") from the church in 1778. Robertson built a wing perpendicular to the old dwelling and the 1798 tax records show that his house had measurements virtually identical to those of the present structure. In 1800 Robertson sold his holdings to the Reverend John Allen, rector of Spesutia from 1795 to 1815, a crucial period when the Episcopal Church was perforce reorganizing itself after the Revolution. He abandoned the pulpit to teach mathematics at St. John's College, Annapolis (1815), and the University of Maryland (1821). The lot and house passed back to Spesutia Church in 1827, only to be sold in 1835 to three men who had just incorporated themselves as the Harford Furnace Company; for the next forty years the old house would serve as dormitory quarters for furnace workers.

1-35. Bush Hotel
4014 Old Philadelphia Road
c. 1800 (?); additions; Private
Harford County Landmark   HA-867

Standing two stories tall, with stuccoed brick walls measuring 20 feet by 42 feet, this seemingly straightforward building has proved an enigma to generations of historians. Despite years of research the basic question still hovers unanswered: Is this the Bush Hotel?

Bush became Harford's first seat when the new county was formed in 1773. Located on the main highway connecting the northern and southern colonies, Bush was popular among travelers in coach or on horseback as a place of lodging and refreshment; J. Alexis

Shriver of Olney discovered that George Washington himself records at least three stops in town in 1795: a breakfast on August 9, a dinner on September 10, and, on the night of October 17, actual lodging. But was it in this building? Architect James Wollon, AIA, conducted a thorough investigation of the structure in 1975 and concluded that it "probably dates from the late eighteenth or very early nineteenth century" and that, "original work includes the basic form . . . the chimneys, at least the roof shape, the basic plan, first floor joists, some window frames, a transom, some baseboard . . . and a door. All other surfaces were refinished in the renovations of ca. 1960 and all other remaining early details were removed at that time." For a more thorough discussion of Bush and the post road, see chapter 2.

1-36. Box Hill
(Lauretum)
3411 Emmorton Road
c. 1800; c. 1925; Private   HA-894

One of the most charming sites in Harford County, the Box Hill tract once belonged to Col. Thomas White of Philadelphia, father-in-law of Robert Morris, "Financier of the American Revolution." White gave the property, called Lauretum (after the laurel bushes that fill the surrounding woods), to another daughter, Sophia, and her husband, Aquila Hall; this couple would build Sophia's Dairy. Around 1800 one of their descendants built a large stone house here, placing it high on a hill overlooking the Chesapeake Bay and, in the distance, the Kent County shoreline. The Halls also laid out formal gardens around the house and some of their plantings—notably the boxwood and laurel—are thought to have survived to this day. The Halls also built a 1½-story stone schoolhouse north of the house, where their own and neighborhood children received a rudimentary education. In 1920 the Halls' great stone house burned. In 1925 investment banker and art patron Lawrence Simmonds bought the ruins and erected, possibly to his own design, the present brick colonial revival dwelling. (The Baltimore *Sun* of April 19, 1931, credited a "Mr. Mackenzie" with the design of the new house and praised him for the "rich, generous" ambiance of the place and for avoiding the "melodramatic quality which is so often associated" with colonial revival architecture.) Simmonds also remodeled the schoolhouse (which had escaped the blaze), and turned it into a guesthouse. The banker knew that any great house needs a great garden and to that end he hired landscape architect Anna Merven Carrere. Her formal system of allees and terraces perfectly set off the dwelling and instantly achieved the mellow aura of age.

1-37. Fair Meadows
Creswell Road
1868; Private
National Register   HA-1067

Set on a knoll shaded by beech, elm, and pine, Fair Meadows stands—almost swaggers—as a grand Second Empire mansion of the most splendid type. It looks as if it might have been built by a Frenchman, and it was. Clement Dietrich, builder of the house, was born in Alsace and emigrated to America in 1830. He moved to Cincinnati where he ran a soap and candle factory and became president of a railroad. He retired in 1862 (he sold the soap works to the company that grew into Procter and Gamble) and sat out the Civil War in Europe. When he returned to America in 1867 he settled in Harford County and purchased the 5,000-acre Harford Furnace complex. The next year he built the fifteen-room Fair Meadows at the extraordinary cost of $93,000 in an era when laborers got 15 cents an hour. Or perhaps the cost isn't so extraordinary—Dietrich embellished the house's imposing mansarded ashlar shell with floors of wood parquet and inlaid marble, with ceilings and friezes ornamented in geometric and naturalistic plaster designs, with crystal chandeliers, carved wooden screens, and elaborate marble mantels. Dietrich enriched the grounds with pools and statues and built a half-dozen outbuildings, including a mansard-roofed stone carriage house. Under his ownership, Harford Furnace produced iron, flour, and lumber; he also established a large chemical plant for pyroligneous acid, wood alcohol, and acetic acid. Glorious as it was, it didn't last long and Dietrich was forced to sell the property in 1876; he died in 1884. The furnace quickly disappeared but Fair Meadows was saved because Mary D. Walsh, one of Dietrich's daughters, bought the house and 121 acres and splendidly maintained the grand house and grounds until she died in 1936. Since 1958 it has been home to Eastern Christian College.

1-38. Bonita Farm
(Hemlock Hall)
Creswell Road
c. 1870; Private   HA-1068

This farm, with its fine Victorian frame house, rolling acres, and half-mile track, gained international fame in 1983 when Deputed Testamony, a horse trained by Bonita's then-owner, William Boniface, won the Preakness. Boniface, who moved to this farm in 1963, has since moved his operations northward to Darlington (see 2-40) but the Creswell farm has gone on. Amos Henry Strasbaugh purchased the roughly fifty-acre tract in 1870; nothing is shown on the 1858 Jennings and Herrick map of the county, but Strasbaugh and a house do appear on the 1878 Martenet map on this prime site, right across from the then-booming Harford Furnace. (A Strasbaugh in-law, William Pannell, owned Harford Furnace from 1861 till 1867.) A. H. Strasbaugh (executor of Pannell's estate) died in 1919 and left the farm to his grandson, William Pannell Strasbaugh. Viewed purely as architecture, the clapboarded main house, undoubtedly built by the Strasbaughs, would, with its center-hall, L-shape plan, wide eaves, and elaborate entrance porch, be notable even without its illustrious equine/industrial connections.

1-39. Harford Furnace Store
2605 Creswell Road
c. 1800; additions; Private
National Register   HA-1069

Old maps and deeds show that this two-story rubblestone structure was originally the general store for the Harford Furnace, an industrial complex that flourished hereabouts from the very early nineteenth century until 1876. The oldest section of the building comprises the southern three bays of the west (road) façade (to the right in the photograph); three bays were added (keeping the roofline the same) northwards in the middle of the nineteenth century, while a perpendicular rear section dates to the late nineteenth century. The interior has been altered to make it suitable for domestic use, but a c. 1870 photograph shows that the exterior looks substantially as it did when workers at the furnace's iron foundry, flour mill, lumber yard, chemical works, or many shops (cooper, blacksmith, wheelwright, and harness) gathered here to buy provisions.

1-37

1-38

1-39

1-40. Patterson-Sheridan House
2800 Creswell Road
c. 1860; Private   HA-1070

Nine-over-six ground floor window sashes, suggestive of the eighteenth century, belie the probable date of this two-story, cross-gable, clapboard farmhouse. William and Frances Patterson and John Patterson (relation unknown) paid $1,000 for eighty-eight acres here in 1858; the Jennings and Herrick Harford County map made that year shows nothing on this site but the 1878 Simon Martenet map has a dot here labeled "A. Patterson." Three years later John and Anna Patterson sold the same eighty-eight acres for $3,000. Except for the anachronistic window paning, the house, with its massing, center-hall plan, attic and porch gable, and simple interior trim, has several stylistic peers throughout the central Harford region; note, for example, the Churchville Presbyterian manse, the Carsins house, Bonita Farm, and, grandfather of them all, Greenwood.

1-41. Lilly-Cullum-Amberman House
3110 Nova Scotia Road
c. 1880; Private   HA-1072

During the eighteenth and nineteenth centuries industries dotted the James Run Valley: workers at Harford Furnace turned out iron products, lumber, and chemicals; millers at the valley's seemingly ubiquitous gristmills ground wheat and rye and corn for local farmers. About the time of the Civil War, John Lilly relocated his woolen mill here from the Rocks. Owned by Lilly (and, later, by members of the Cullum family) this little fieldstone house, now encased in twentieth-century additions, probably provided housing for the workers who toiled at one of these enterprises.

1-42. Cullum-Anderson Log House
Nova Scotia Road
c. 1850; Private   HA-1073

William Cullum, whose nineteenth-century family holdings in the central James Run Valley are commemorated in Cullum Road, bought the tract this log house sits on in 1850 and is shown living here in the 1878 Simon Martenet map of the county. Cullum's house is a rarity, for while dozens of county buildings are at least partially log, almost none has kept its logs exposed. Generally, owners

sheathed the log walls in clapboard or asbestos or some other more finished-looking siding. This was, in fact, the case here until the 1970s when the little cabin was encased in a larger frame addition.

1-43. Broom's Bloom
1616 South Fountain Green Road
c. 1747; c. 1848; 1992; Private
National Register; Historic American
Buildings Survey   HA-1075

When researchers for the Historic American Buildings Survey came through Harford County in the 1930s and photographed this house, they did not call it by its correct title, Broom's Bloom; they called it instead simply The Dallams. This, however, is excusable because here, as almost nowhere else in the county, the histories of owner and house have so intermingled and so developed a life of their own. Technically, however, the researchers should have called it The Webster-Dallams, since the house was a Webster seat originally and did not enter the Dallam family until Dr. William Dallam II (1822–89) and his wife (née Josephine Webster) bought the property ("where the late Samuel Webster died") in 1844. (Samuel, Josephine's father, had died in 1817; his son, John Adams Webster, was born here and went on to built Mount Adams.) Isaac Webster arrived in what is now Harford County at about the time of the English Civil War. His son, John (1667–1753), patented Webster's Forest and John's son, Isaac, received the Broom's Bloom tract in 1747 and began the present house. His initial dwelling was probably a "British Cabin," a form popular among the county's pre-revolutionary elite and discussed in chapter 2. Today that first house, with its end-wall fireplaces and corner winder stairs, remains in evidence and forms the eastern two-thirds of the front section of the present dwelling. Dr. and Mrs. Dallam added the slightly lower frame wing to the west and an attached kitchen to the north. The 1897 *Portrait and Biographical Record of Cecil and Harford Counties* observed that the Websters "were brave pioneers, developing the county that is now adorned with fine farms and busy towns. We who reap the harvest their hands have sown should honor them and hold their names in grateful remembrance." Indeed. A fire ripped through the house in the winter of 1990 but members of the Dallam family have beautifully restored their highly important inheritance.

1-40

1-41

1-42

1-43

I-44. Mount Adams/The Mount

1912 South Fountain Green Road
1817; with additions; Private
National Register; Historic American
Buildings Survey   HA-1076

John Adams Webster was born at his parents' farm, Broom's Bloom; he enlisted in the Navy, rose to the rank of captain, and more or less single-handedly won the Battle of Fort McHenry in the War of 1812. He then returned to his native county, bought the southern half of his parents' farm and began this charming house. Webster's original dwelling, two rooms on two full stories with an attic, grew to the west and north to keep pace with his growing family. The result was a rambling plan and irregular roofline, which Webster then attempted to camouflage with an imposing Greek revival front porch. (He was only partially successful.) The important Captain Webster and his equally important house are discussed more fully in chapter 5.

I-45. St. Francis de Salles Church

1450 Abingdon Road
1866; 1887; Regular services
Harford County Landmark   HA-1312

Roman Catholics had lived in the Abingdon area well before the town was founded in 1779, yet they had no church, and were forced to meet in private houses. But in 1865 William Pannell, the owner of Harford Furnace, donated four acres here ("on the west side of the road leading from Bel Air to Abingdon at the top of a hill") to the archdiocese and Rev. Patrick O'Connor broke ground for the new church on July 9, 1866. (One assumes that Pannell, a non-Catholic, was as motivated by the desire to keep his Irish and Eastern European millworkers happy as he was by more altruistic concerns.) The fieldstone, Romanesque, cruciform-plan structure was completed shortly thereafter, although it was not officially dedicated until 1887 when the bell tower was added. The resulting building is exceptionally picturesque and its pastoral hilltop setting, dark blond stone walls, and striking silhouette stand as landmarks throughout the area. To mark the church's centennial, His Eminence Lawrence Cardinal Shehan dedicated the arched shrine to St. Francis de Salles on September 25, 1966.

I-46. Bata Shoe Company

Route 40 at Belcamp
1939; Private   HA-1582

Easily the most significant twentieth-century architectural creation in Harford County, the Bata factory and community are possibly unique American examples of Bauhaus-influenced town planning. The Bata company was founded in Zlin in what is now Slovakia in the late nineteenth century. In the early twentieth century Thomas Bat'a (as the name was originally punctuated) visited Lowell, Massachusetts, and Detroit to study American factories. While in this country, he was impressed by Henry Ford's novel production line and returned to Europe determined to reorganize shoemaking (then largely a bench operation) along modern lines. His resulting expanded business quickly grew into one of the largest industries in Europe. Bat'a built the home plant at Zlin—a town of 50,000 people—to the designs of the great architect Le Corbusier, a leader in Modernist thinking, and the company built every other plant using Zlin as a model. (There were eventually plants throughout Europe and in Asia, Africa, and South America as well.) The company bought over 2,000 acres in Belcamp, near railroad lines and Route 40, in 1933 and, accelerated by the Nazi overrun of Europe, began work on a new community here in 1939. Although never as extensive as first planned, the new town, with its five-story factory, five-story hotel, gymnasium, and 70 workers' houses, is a clear reflection of the company's intent to create an efficient and clean fusion of living and working environments.

I-47. Lohr's Orchard

901 Lohr's Lane
Late eighteenth century; Private   HA-1601

Somewhat ironically, this late eighteenth-century house and its surrounding farm stand intact in the midst of one of the county's most heavily developed areas, virtually adjacent to the fringe of suburban Joppatown. The two-story, center hall–plan frame house (once owned by the Rumseys of the Rumsey House) still boasts most of its original details, including H and L hinges, heavy framing, mantels, and beaded siding. These touches and the building's overall massing and plan make the structure an interesting companion in time and location to the c. 1785 Nelson-Reardon-Kennard House in Abingdon. The Lohrs

I-44

I-45

I-46

I-47

1-48

1-49

1-50

1-51

bought the 200-acre tract in 1928, executed some slight modifications to the house (such as covering the parlor walls and ceiling with intricately stamped metal in 1932), and began their highly regarded (and recently discontinued) farming operations.

1-48. Margaret Demby House
Dembytown Road
c. 1920; Private   HA-1603

In one sweeping presidential proclamation in October 1917, the federal government snatched nearly all of Harford County's rich bay shoreline. The farms thus acquired had for generations produced bumper crops of tomatoes, corn, and peaches but would never do so again. The farm owners, the Cadwaladers, who held the Gunpowder Neck, and the Mitchells, Michaels, Bakers, and Taylors, who owned spreads around what had been called Michaelsville and Boothby Hill, received some payment from Washington for their lost acreages and many of them then purchased other farms elsewhere in the county and resumed their lives. The workers, generally black tenant farmers or sharecroppers, did not fare so well. They received nothing. Dembytown, started in 1917 when displaced members of the black Demby and Gilbert families bought land here from white farmer Joshua Hammond, is one of several similar communities to spring up in southern Harford County as a result of this World War I confusion. This one-story, two-room frame house, heretofore generally ignored, typifies the hastily erected shelters of that chaotic time.

1-49. Dembytown School
Dembytown Road
1920; Private   HA-1604

Vacant and deteriorated, this building represents one of Harford County's first efforts to comply with the state laws that required some form of public education for black—as well as for white—children. On December 1, 1918, the Gunpowder Station of the Methodist Episcopal Church passed a resolution to sell 7/10 of an acre "to be used as the site for a school for colored children" and the Harford County Board of Education actually bought the lot in 1919. (Dembytown was established in 1917 by former farm laborers displaced from the Gunpowder and Bush river necks.) The one-story, one-room frame school opened in 1920 and continued to function until 1951

when the new consolidated school for blacks opened in Hickory. During the past forty years this little building has been subdivided into two apartments and has had its German siding covered in asbestos; now abandoned altogether, it faces an uncertain future.

1-50. Maxwell's Point Ruins
Maxwell's Point
c. 1845; Public but inaccessible   HA-1716

For decades millions of canvasback ducks and Canadian geese gorged themselves on the grasses of the Gunpowder and Bush rivers and Susquehanna Flats; the birds, in turn, attracted generations of high-living sportsmen. This particular spot, a narrow marshy peninsula jutting out into the Gunpowder, played host to the hunting fraternity at least as long ago as 1819, when some Baltimoreans, "acting for and behalf of a society of gentlemen stiling themselves the Maxwell's Point Gunning Club" bought 180 acres here and built a lodge. Philadelphia bon vivant and future Mexican War hero Gen. George Cadwalader purchased "one share in Maxwell's Point" for $175 in 1838 and built a small wing for himself onto the existing clubhouse. Life here evidently pleased Cadwalader, for he began buying out other members of the club and became sole owner around 1850. His pleasure must have intensified, for he also began buying up farms throughout the Gunpowder Neck, eventually acquiring the entire 7,500-acre peninsula and its twenty-eight miles of shoreline. In the midst of all this, he remodeled the old, rambling, two-story frame clubhouse at Maxwell's Point into the family retreat shown here and embellished the grounds with exotic trees and shrubs, greenhouses and statuary, even a deer park. When General Cadwalader died in 1879 he left Maxwell's Point to his nephew John, whose family continued to enjoy and maintain the property, shooting and canoeing and riding and simply escaping the rigors of life in formal Philadelphia until 1917, when Maxwell's, and most of the county's bay frontage, was taken over by the federal government.

1-51. Linwood
3005 Clayton Road
c. 1856; Private   HA-306

Of immense importance, this board-and-batten Gothic cottage synthesizes an entire school of nineteenth-century thinking. Philosopher, landscape gardener, and architectural critic Andrew Jackson Downing (1815–52) tried, with no little success, to steer American architecture and gardening away from neoclassicism to the Gothic and the picturesque. To this end, Downing published best-selling books (such as *Cottage Residences,* 1842) which he amply illustrated with what he hoped would be appealing engravings of cottages with shady verandas, rhythmic sheathing, and varied window treatments. (See also the Proctor House.) Downing favored buildings with a vertical emphasis and couched his arguments in religious terms: "The worshipping principle, the loving reverence for that which is highest, and the sentiment of Christian brotherhood . . . expressed in the principal lines which are all vertical . . . the whole mass falling under . . . the pyramidal . . . form." He would certainly have been pleased with this cottage's board-and-batten siding and sharp, pendanted gables, all of which accent the vertical and suggest the pyramidal. Baltimorean George March McComas bought 140 acres of land here in 1855 (he added 38 acres the following year) and built this cottage as a summer retreat; he worked quickly for it appears on the 1858 county map. McComas, a social reformer with deeply felt beliefs, was honored when the government in Washington named the nearby Freedmen's school the McComas Institute for him.

1-52. Rose Hill (site)
Near Abingdon
Mid-eighteenth century;
Private   HA-859, 860, 861, 862

Was this the original Harford County homestead of the Pacas? One could certainly make a good case that it was, although the matter will probably never be fully and finally resolved. The Maryland progenitor of the family, Robert (?–1681), arrived in the colony around 1659 or '60 as an indentured servant to John Hall of Anne Arundel County. Hall died in 1660 leaving a wealthy widow, née Mary Parker, and infant son, John. By 1661 Paca had managed to marry the widow; the couple had one surviving son, Aquila (born c. 1675), who moved north to the Bush River area around 1690 with his half-brother, John Hall. Hall acquired vast lands around Cranberry Run and Paca, helped by a 1699 marriage to the heiress Martha Phillips, began buying land a bit farther west, around Otter Creek, at the northwest headwaters of Bush River. He prospered and served as county sheriff (1703–6) and del-

egate to the General Assembly (1708–11); he also converted to Quakerism and built, at his own expense, a meetinghouse for the Bush River Society of Friends around 1709.

Of Aquila and Martha's six children, two are of immediate interest: Priscilla (?–1742), who married Winston Smith of Blenheim, and John (1712–85), who married Winston's heiress sister Elizabeth in 1732. With the help of his wife's riches, John Paca continued the family's rise to prominence: he served on the vestry of St. John's Parish (Joppa) for thirteen years, captained a company of county militia, and, like his father, served in the general assembly. He was also the local tax collector and his 1763 account book, preserved at the Maryland Historical Society, shows that he paid tax on eleven tracts of land totaling 2,688 acres and ranging in value from Paca's Park (630 acres on which he paid a tax of £1.1. 2/2) to Chilberry Hall (10 acres; 2½ p.). Those figures certainly suggest that he lived at Paca's Park, his largest and costliest holding. In 1779 he laid out the village of Abingdon on part of Paca's Park; some of the village's original building lots are only a few hundred yards from the site of the house Rose Hill. John and Elizabeth had five daughters and two sons, all, according to Gregory Stiverson and Phebe Jacobsen's 1976 biography, *William Paca,* "born in the Paca house on the Bush River near the village of Abingdon." When John died in 1785, he left all the children lots in Abingdon, left cash bequests and slaves to the daughters, and left country property to his sons. Aquila (born 1738), the elder son, received, according to Stiverson and Jacobsen, "the bulk of the property . . . including his dwelling plantation." The younger—and more famous—son, William, born 1740, inherited "only a modest landed estate."

Aquila II, who died just two years after his father, evidently had no children, for he left the "moiety of a tract Paca's Park" to Parker Hall Lee, Samuel Lee, and James Lee Morgan in 1785; in 1812 these men sold the 525-acre Paca's Park to entrepreneur Charles Sewell, who renamed the property Rose Hill. Although the original house on the tract was destroyed in the mid-twentieth century (only a stuccoed-stone, hipped-roof outbuilding remains to give a suggestion of the Paca era), existing photographs and descriptions show a multipart structure consisting of a gambrel-roof, brick-and-frame core (measuring 36′6″ × 20′6″ with 8′2″ ceilings) with additions in front and behind. Does this mean that Rose

1-52

I-53

Hill was built by John Paca? Quite possibly: a near duplicate of the c. 1740 Hall home, Cranberry, it is exactly the sort of house a prosperous countian would have built in the 1730s and '40s. Paca was certainly well acquainted with his Hall kinsmen, and his marriage with the heiress Elizabeth Smith might well have prompted him to home-building. Whoever built the house's brick core, it seems a virtual certainty that it was Sewell (1779–1848) who added the frame wings. He was a prosperous, go-getting sort; he started the well-known Abingdon hat factory, maintained a private wharf at Otter Point for his fleet of commercial schooners, and served in the state legislature in the 1820s and '30s and as president of the board of trustees of the Abingdon Academy from 1829 until his death. When Sewell died, his estate inventory specifically called for a ten-room—plus "store room"—dwelling; and although Aquila Paca's inventory does not specify the number of rooms, it definitely suggests a smaller structure.

I-53. Bell's Shop
1700 Old Joppa Road
c. 1800; Private   HA-424

Only a few area residents remember when this 1½-story rubblestone structure held a blacksmith shop; almost everyone, however, enjoys speculating on its career as a stagecoach stop. Did innkeepers live in the eastern portion of the building and use the west wing to house carriages and travelers? The building's design encourages such thoughts, for its eastern section is made up of finished rooms (possibly living quarters) with beaded board doors and granite window lintels, while the more simply finished western section has large plank doors capable of admitting a horse and carriage; two (sleeping?) lofts are above. Author Mary H. Cadwalader wrote in one *Harford Historical Bulletin,* "One can easily envision a coach-and-four wheeling in the double doors, the hostlers scurrying to unhitch and stable the horses, and throwing down hay from the first loft before bedding down in the second." On July 10, 1864, Confederate Maj. Harry Gilmor and his raiders camped here before setting out the next day to burn the railroad bridge across the Gunpowder.

DISTRICT 2

Aberdeen, Perryman, and Glenville

2-1. Mount Friendship
Cooley Mill Road
c. 1776; 1821; Private
National Register   HA-8

One of the most advanced and sophisticated dwellings of its day in Harford County, Mount Friendship may be credited to Samuel Thomas, a prosperous Quaker. Thomas amassed roughly 700 acres here during the 1770s and then set about erecting this remarkable stone house, "remarkable" as a rare example of a building conceived of and created as a stylish Georgian mansion—as opposed to the Harford norm of houses that simply "grew." But there have been many changes. Thomas's house as built measured, according to the 1798 Federal Direct Tax, 47 feet by 33 feet and rose a full two stories tall with "1st story 12 feet; 2nd 11 ft"; there was also a "kitchen 30′ × 18′, 2 stories, stone." A fire, purportedly set by a deranged slave (Thomas owned twenty-nine slaves in 1798), destroyed the second story in the early nineteenth century. The 1814 tax list refers to "the dwelling house lately burnt." Amanda Jarrett (Thomas's granddaughter) and her husband, Abraham, gave Mount Friendship its present appearance in 1821, as a datestone attests. The Jarretts, who owned over 400 acres of land in the area, used a gable roof (the original was hipped) to cover the half-story attic level and reworked the floor plan. The exterior walls, however, with their carefully cut and matched blocks of granite embellished by smoothly polished lintels and quoins, date to the eighteenth century and still evince the architectural aspirations of the builder. Mount Friendship remained in the Thomas-Jarrett-Cooley family until 1939.

2-2. Cookville Tanbark Mill
Harmony Church Road
c. 1842; Private
National Register   HA-158

Constructed of partially stuccoed rubblestone and beautifully adapted to residential use, this peaceful-looking structure is a relic of Cookville's once-flourishing industrial past. Elisha Cook, an enterprising Quaker, bought several tracts of land along Deer Creek in 1816; he cleared some of the acreage and began farming. A man of ambition, Cook took note that many of his neighbors raised sheep and so he built a spinning and weaving mill to turn the fleeces to cloth. According to local historian Samuel Mason, that short-lived industry was forced to close "about 1850 . . . not being able to compete with modern spinning mills." The Cook family, under Elisha's son George, then diversified its operations and established a complex of buildings to tan cattle hides. This was the mill, wrote Mason, in which black oak bark, broken into small pieces, was "thrown into an iron hopper and a horse which was led onto the second floor . . . walked round and around grinding the bark to a powder" to tan the skins.

2-3. Cookville Tannery
Harmony Church Road, Darlington
1842; Private
National Register   HA-159

A century and a half ago, this and the nearby tanbark mill formed the core of the Cook family's elaborate industrial complex known as Cookville. Elisha Cook established the operations and built a small stone house for his son George along Harmony Church Road, intending a shopkeeping career for the young man. But George, who evidently was not content to deal in dry goods, built this tanbark mill and a house for its operator. (George

2-1

2-2

2-3

2-4

2-5

2-6

went on to study—and practice—medicine.) After black oak bark had been ground to a powder, it was steeped into a brew to tan cow hides. Darlington farmer and historian Samuel Mason wrote that Cook procured his hides from as far away as South America and they were then "run through a vat containing limewater . . . to remove the hair . . . then put down in the tan pits . . . and allowed to lie for nearly a year. . . . When the process was completed the hides were hung along the fences on both sides of the road to dry." It is hard to imagine all that going on at this idyllic site, let alone the stench.

2-4. Cookville School
3071 Harmony Church Road
c. 1842; Private
National Register   HA-160

Part of the Cook clan's once self-sufficient industrial fiefdom, this rubblestone structure has led a varied life. Local historian Samuel Mason wrote that Elisha Cook, progenitor of the family, built this "small stone house near the public road" in 1842 for George P. Cook, the son and heir. According to Mason, George's sister (unnamed) used the second story "as a private school . . . until 1862" when the whole building was turned into a public school. (Elisha, who died in 1858, had two daughters, his testamentary papers reveal; they were named Louisa and Sarah.) This simple building and its similar, utilitarian neighbors still manage to evoke a vigorous era that has long passed: no one in the Cooks' day had ever heard of venture capital, yet these busy individuals created and shaped an entire, functioning community using little but their determination and hard work.

2-5. Old George Cook House
3069 Harmony Church Road
c. 1842; Private
National Register   HA-161

Cookville, described by historian and farmer Samuel Mason as "one of the quaintest little settlements that could be found," has managed to retain its integrity surprisingly well during its 150-year existence. It is important to note that while one may agree with Mason's comments on the community's quaintness, one should remember that Cookville's enterprising Quaker founders would have neither understood nor appreciated that adjective. Even though the buildings' shells (now all qui-

etly domestic) generally look much as they originally did, their interiors were intended to bustle with industrial energy as cauldrons bubbled and mill wheels spun and freshly tanned steer hides flapped and dried in the wind. Architectural historian and civic activist Jean S. Ewing has researched all the Cookville structures and has determined that this particular two-story, rubblestone building was where Dr. George Cook lived (a son of the founding Elisha), thus making it a rarity in that it has always been used as a house and is not a converted bark mill. (Even the eastern frame wing is essentially original, although it was remodeled in the 1950s.) But past use cannot always be gleaned by present appearance, since all the structures in the community, with their simple lines and straightforward masonry construction, are the product of the same Quaker-based design aesthetic.

2-6. Griffith-Wright House
(Cranberry)
1120 Old Philadelphia Road
Mid-eighteenth century; Private
National Register; Harford County
Landmark   HA-163

Harford lost almost all of its rich tidewater farms in October 1917 when the Aberdeen and Edgewood Army installations were established by presidential proclamation. Luckily, this house escaped. Now undergoing a careful restoration, the building stands today as one of the county's few remaining examples of an eighteenth-century Chesapeake planter's mansion. Make no mistake about it: the gambrel-roof house may look small to us today, but to citizens of the colonial era, it would have been very grand indeed. John Hall III (1719–79) probably built the frame house on his 1500-acre Cranberry Hall tract; his heirs are cited in the 1798 tax list as owning a one-story wooden house measuring 39 feet by 20 feet with a piazza (porch) 7 feet deep and these dimensions neatly coincide with the 38- by 18½-foot (plus porch) dimensions of the present dwelling. Almost miraculously, the house's two-room plan and much of its interior trim, including one exceptional fully paneled wall, remain intact. (The meathouse, slaves' quarters, cornhouse, stable, and granary, all standing in 1798, vanished long ago.)

2-7. Poplar Hill
115 Poplar Hill Road
Mid-eighteenth century; Private
National Register   HA-164

Always maintained and never restored, Poplar Hill is one of the most important buildings in Harford County. Story-and-a-half structures such as this, of frame or of brick, were the bayfront house of choice for successful planters throughout the Chesapeake region in colonial Maryland and Virginia. Counties such as Talbot and St. Mary's still boast several examples but Poplar Hill and the Griffith-Wright House (or Cranberry) are the only two in Harford. Poplar Hill is exemplary: its unaltered massing wonderfully evokes its era and its interior trim, notably the parlor (north room) paneling can hold its own with any examples in more celebrated locales.

2-8. Deer Creek Harmony Presbyterian Church
Harmony Church Road
1871; Regular services
National Register; Harford County
Landmark   HA-165

In 1867, under the pastorate of Samuel Bayless, the Deer Creek Valley's Presbyterian parishioners resolved to build themselves a new church to replace their 1837 chapel of ease. The building committee of Benjamin Silver III, William F. Silver, John A. Silver, and James F. Reasin chose Baltimore architect John W. Hogg to design the church but one assumes that the Silver-dominated committee voiced opinions of their own (see chapter 6). Contractors Carroll and West of Port Deposit began work began in September 1870; by the following year they had the 50-by-39-foot stone church and its towering 91-foot spire ready for dedication. The wonderful restrained Gothic revival granite structure has been a local landmark ever since. Dr. W. Stump Forwood, first president of the Historical Society of Harford County, wrote in the January 9, 1880, *Ægis* that "this is without doubt one of the handsomest churches to be found outside of the large cities." Who today would argue with that assessment?

2-9. Rock Run Mill
Rock Run Road
1794; Public
National Register; Historic American
Buildings Survey   HA-191

Few buildings are as welcomingly familiar to Harford countians as the Rock Run Mill complex. John Stump of Stafford built the mill in 1794 to replace one erected by Nathaniel Giles around 1760 and, except for a brief period in this century, the rubblestone mill has been in operation ever since. Stump, easily the county's richest man at the time, had far-flung business interests including iron forges, tanyards, over 5,000 acres of valuable farmland, warehouses in Baltimore and Alexandria, and a shipping company with schooners to take Maryland produce such as tobacco, wheat, and corn to ports in the West Indies in exchange for molasses, sugar, and rum. No wonder, then, that Stump was able to give this utilitarian building high-style flourishes such as keystoned window arches! Water powers the mill's wheel, reached via an overshot pipe from the millrace across the road. (The wheel, which postdates Stump, dominates the south side of the building and bears a plaque reading "Fitz Water Wheel Company Hanover, Pa.") The mill's later history is thoroughly documented: the *Federal Gazette* observed in 1806 that the mill had two pair of six-foot burrs and a thirty-six-foot fall; at his death in 1816, Stump willed the mill to his daughter Ann Archer; the 1850 census records that the mill was capable of producing 2,000 barrels of flour (worth $12,000); in 1880 miller Kinsey Matthews reported that he turned out 6,000 bushels of wheat per year, worth $7,000—regarding "Rye, Barley, Buckwheat or Corn for Hominy [I] cannot state value of product but know I pay all expenses and have some money left"; and in 1970 the Baltimore *Evening Sun* headlined a story "Restored Rock Run Mill Is Historians' Delight," sentiments that remain true into the 1990s.

2-10. Rock Run Miller's House
Rock Run Road
c. 1800; Public
National Register   HA-197

Neglected for decades, this fine example of Harford County stone masonry was little more than a shell when the Maryland Department of Natural Resources acquired it in the 1960s as a part of the Susquehanna State Park.

2-7

2-8

2-9

2-10

2-11

2-11

2-12

Now rehabilitated and restored, the house, with its wood-shingle roof and prominent quoins, looks much as it did nearly two centuries ago when it was home to the men the Stumps and Carters and Archers hired to run the Rock Run Mill. Either John Stump of Stafford or John Carter (for a few years Stump's partner in the Rock Run venture) built the little dwelling; whichever man did, he was not oblivious to aesthetics, for he obviously attempted to give the house's rubble-stone walls a semblance of the defined courses seen also at Stump's elegant Rock Run Mill. Still, the minimalism here when compared with the elegance of the Carter-Archer mansion nearby offers a convenient comparison between employee and employer housing.

2-11. Carter-Archer House
Rock Run Road
1804; Public
National Register; Historic American
Buildings Survey   HA-192, 193, 194

An oval datestone enclosed by a ring of bricks and placed high in the west gable proudly announces "J R C 1804," that is, John and Rebecca (Harlan) Carter built this house in 1804. No wonder the Carters were proud, for this is one of the truly great houses of its time and place. It is also one of the most fascinating—it shows how one man resolved two usually hostile aspects of his own personality. Carter was the coequal partner of John Stump of Stafford in the Rock Run milling business, which made him a man of wealth; yet he was a devout Friend, which discouraged display. Thus while the superb stone masonry, interior details such as a shadow rail, and the very size of the house bespeak Carter's earthly riches, the simple massing and straightforward center-hall plan suggest his Quaker sensibilities. He could have built in the flashy manner of his economic co-equals such as Ridgely at Hampton in Baltimore County; he was educated enough to have known about the bookishly correct five-part villas the Pacas, Brices, Lloyds, and Teackles were building throughout the Chesapeake region. Yet he chose simplicity and in so doing arguably set the tone of inconspicuous consumption that county builders have favored ever since. Moreover, the house's details, almost entirely intact, as well as the barn, springhouse, and privy that still grace the grounds provide invaluable guides for dating other dwellings and dependencies. Carter died in 1805 and Stump

bought the house in 1808, leaving it, on his death in 1816, to his daughter Ann, wife of Dr. John Archer Jr. It stayed in the Archer family until the twentieth century.

2-12. Rock Run Bridge and Toll House
Stafford Road at the Susquehanna
1818; Public
National Register   HA-195, 196

Around 1815 the Maryland legislature authorized "a turnpike from Baltimore to Rock Run" (which would thence, presumably, continue on to Philadelphia). At about the same time a group of countians, led by Dr. John Archer Jr., incorporated themselves as the Rock Run Bridge and Banking Company and began building a toll bridge across the Susquehanna at the Stump-Archer family's bustling community of Rock Run. Completed in 1818, it was the first bridge in Maryland across the river. And did it have an eventful history! Beset by fires and floods and herds of galloping cattle (whose bounce and weight caused a large segment to collapse in 1854), the bridge was finally destroyed by an ice storm in the winter of 1856. Today nothing but a few granite piers remain to mark the span's presence. Although the bridge itself is gone, its frame tollhouse, which also dates to 1818, still stands in Rock Run Park. Saved thanks to the work of benefactors such as diplomat Gilman Paul and industrialist Donaldson Brown, the tollhouse and the entire Rock Run complex are now maintained by the Garden Club of Harford County. Led by the indomitable Vlasta Schmidt of Sophia's Dairy the women relandscaped this section of the park and their prowess with *hemerocalis* earned them a special commendation from Gov. Harry Hughes in 1983.

2-13. Gaughen House Site and Corn Crib
(Lower Farm site and Upper Farm corncrib)
Stafford Road
Mid-nineteenth century; Public
National Register   HA-198

The Lower Farm's three-part house had a three-bay, two-story stone central section and twin two-bay frame wings; a one-story porch shaded the east and south façades. As recently as 1970, one report noted that the prosperous farm, which "has great charm," was sited "on a plain below a long hill rising over the Susque-

2-13

hanna, with deer and other wildlife mingling with farm animals." Nonetheless, the Department of Natural Resources took over the property and demolished the house—as well as a hay barn, storage shed, and stable—in 1973. Somehow the Upper Farm's corncrib, representative of its type in form, survived. The structure, whose framing members appear to be all hand-hewn, mortised, tenoned, and pegged, is sheathed in vertical planks and topped by a standing seam tin gable roof. The functional, three-part plan allows for a central passage, wide enough to hold a wagon laden with corn, flanked by open slat storage racks.

2-14. Seaman-Smith House
718 Craig's Corner Road
1860; Private
National Register   HA-205

Thomas Smith (?–1791) is remembered for his ferry line across the Susquehanna and his patriotism during the Revolution; this land entered his family in 1813 and in 1860 a grandson, Charles Corman Smith, built the present dwelling. Its walls are laid in a local tan fieldstone which, with the exceptionally sandy mortar, dramatically contrasts with the gray granite quoins. Although altered several times, the interior still possesses many original features including several six-panel doors with their hardware and simple surrounds.

2-15. Stephenson-Archer House
(Hygeia Hall)
Wilkinson Road
c. 1824; Private   HA-207

Affluent twentieth-century countians maintain summer homes hundreds of miles away, in places like Nantucket and Maine. Five generations ago things were different: Dr. John Archer Jr. and his wife, Ann Stump Archer, for instance, lived most of the year at Rock Run, but when summer's heat became too unbearable, they traveled all of a mile or two to seek refuge in this 1½-story, vertical plank structure, which they built shortly after purchasing the land from the Reverend William Stephenson in 1824. The summerhouse rests on a high stone cellar that is fully above ground on the south (entrance) front. The massive exterior end stone chimneys are stepped, diminishing in size up to their brick caps. Stephenson deserves some mention: this worldly man of the cloth owned one slave in 1798 and actively promoted one of the earliest agricultural soci-

eties in America, "The Farmer's Society of Harford County," which he co-organized in 1804. In his capacity as that organization's treasurer, he bought an acre of land near Lapidum and erected a plaster mill to produce fertilizer. Stephenson also presided over the Rock Run Academy from 1813 until 1821.

2-16. Swansbury
Mount Royal Avenue
Mid-eighteenth century; c. 1800; Private
National Register   HA-240

This fascinating farm complex has been continuously owned by members of the Griffith-Smith-Jay family since the early eighteenth century. The house itself, one of the more intriguing structures in the county, began as a simple frame building but gained, in the federal era, a wealth of details and enlargements that are remarkable in concept and execution. Some of the details, such as the projecting second-story room, with its elaborate Palladian window, can be compared to such nationally known structures as the Carroll family's Mount Clare in Baltimore. Other features resemble Mount Vernon, and since Martha Griffith Smith Jay's first husband, Col. Alexander Lawson Smith, had been an intimate of General Washington's during the Revolution, it is not inconceivable that the connection between the two houses is more than coincidental. A dozen outbuildings form one of the richest such concentrations in Maryland and include a very early pegged and hand-hewn log slaves' quarters, a stone kitchen now somewhat in disrepair, as well as a meathouse, washhouse, chicken coop, and barn.

2-17. Spesutia Episcopal Church
(St. George's Parish)
Perryman and Spesutia Church Roads
1851; Private
Harford County Landmark; Historic
American Buildings Survey   HA-249

St. George's, established by 1671, is among the most venerable religious institutions in America. The ancient parish's first church is thought to have been at "Gravelly" near Michaelsville, now well within the Aberdeen Proving Ground and presumably obliterated. As settlement moved inland during the seventeenth and eighteenth centuries, the old building became increasingly inconvenient to its inland worshipers, and in 1718 the church hierarchy

2-14

2-15

2-16

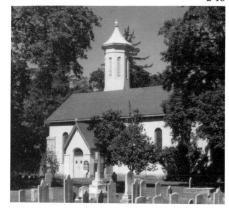

2-17

2-18

2-19

2-20

2-21

chose this more central two-acre site in Perryman for a new place of worship. That building, the second St. George's, was built c. 1718 but it deteriorated quickly. Thus another church was built on the Perryman site in 1758, but that structure, too, became obsolete. Then on May 12, 1851, the vestry asked the Baltimore architectural firm Niernsee and Neilson to design a new church "with two aisles and a gallery on one side . . . in the Norman style." That church, stuccoed brick with attenuated, round-arched windows, heavy buttresses, and octagonal belfry, has remained essentially unchanged ever since, with the exception of a few welcome modernisms, such as the glass in the three windows of the apse, designed by the distinguished artist Paul Barchowsky, a member of the congregation.

2-18. Spesutia Vestry House
Perryman Road
1766; Private
National Register; Harford County
Landmark; Historic American Buildings
Survey   HA-250

Colonial Maryland churches were more than places of worship; they were seats of government as well. Accordingly, vestry houses, built as places to conduct parish business, often functioned as courthouses, schoolhouses (clergymen could generally be trusted not to sow seditious ideas in young minds), and settings for other secular concerns. This particular vestry house dates to the era of the Reverend Andrew Lendrum, rector of St. George's from 1749 until 1770. The importance of the building doubtless explains the remarkably complete specifications present in the vestry records. The Flemish bond brick structure was to be 20 feet long and 16 feet wide with foundations "sunk eighteen inches in the ground" and with a roof of white oak joists and rafters covered in cypress shingles, "the Shingles to be Round'd"; the ceiling was to be plastered; and there were to be "Two Sash Windows on Each Side with Twelve Lights in Each Window the Glass to be Eight Inches by Ten Wide" and a "Corner Chimney well Support'd With a half inch & half Quarter Bar of Iron."

2-19. Woodlawn
3214 Harmony Church Road
Early nineteenth century; Private
National Register   HA-286

This intriguing—if ultimately maddening—house has managed to defy precise dating: in both plan and overall form it closely resembles the c. 1776 house Perry Point in Cecil County and the 1804 mansion at Rock Run. All three houses have associations with one very important man, John Stump of Stafford (1752–1816); his father built Perry Point, his business partner, John Carter, built Rock Run, and his mother's family, the Husbands, owned the land here. Yet Woodlawn remains a mystery. It does not appear in either the 1798 Federal Direct Tax list, or in the 1814 tax rolls, although that latter lists a "brick dwelling house and kitchen, 18' by 27'" which closely matches the present kitchen wing here. The property eventually passed to the notable Jewett family of Lansdowne who gave the building its present L plan. The main façade is four bays wide, laid in Flemish bond brick; the stroke is five bays laid in common bond with a further frame addition to the rear. Interior trim such as the chairrails, simply treated stair with its shadow rail, and pilastered mantel suggests an early date. In the twentieth century the Jewetts, actively involved in the Elkridge-Harford Hunt, built a large stable and kennel on the property in hopes that the club might make the farm its northern county base, as is discussed in chapter 8.

2-20. Gravity Flow
3226 Harmony Church Road
Late eighteenth century; Private
National Register   HA-287

One of several structures built on the once-vast landholdings of the Husband-Jewett family, this rubblestone house has been much altered over the years. Several local historians suggest that the building housed a tannery around 1800 and certainly the now-tranquil stretches of Harmony Church Road were once clanging and smoking with such industries. At one time the building was divided into two apartments, but a 1945 remodeling restored it to single-family use.

2-21. Lansdowne
(Kenton)
3300 Harmony Church Road
1770; c. 1876; c. 1886; Private
National Register   HA-288

Few houses anywhere can spin a tale as fascinating as the one centered on this sprawling, romantic pile. Lord Baltimore granted a 1,000-acre tract called Bachelor's Good Luck to one Enoch Spinks in 1703; shortly thereafter, the land passed into the Husband family.

Joseph Husband and his wife, Mary, are generally credited with building the first stone house here in 1770, for there is a datestone inscribed with that year and with the Husbands' initials. The land passed to the Jewetts (relations of the Husbands), but was sold in 1843 to the King family, the most notable of whom was Darlington's leading philanthropist, Thomas, who bought out his sibling's interest in 1876. Thomas King then hired the architect J. Crawford Neilson of Priestford to expand the old house, adding the central stone and frame section of the present mansion and seen to the right in this photograph. It was—*is*—a wonderful addition, too, described in 1880 as sporting "a beautiful porch" forty-six feet long and with ten deep, red brick window arches ("in the Old English style"), French doors, a massive walnut stair accented with ash risers and "surmounted on the massive newel post a beautifully wrought figure of the anomalous *Griffin*," and a variety of other touches to make this house "unlike any other in the vicinity." King died and the house was purchased back by the Jewetts in 1886, specifically by railroad magnate Hugh Judge Jewett. It was time for another addition, and Jewett brought the young architect Walter Cope down from Philadelphia to design a very formal third section to the east consisting of a morning room, music room, and drawing room.

2-22. Wakefield
(Deerfield)
Deth's Ford Road
1807; Private
National Register; Historic American
Buildings Survey   HA-289

Isaac and Rebecca Coale built the main section of this well-regarded stone house and then "signed it" with an oval datestone in the west gable end inscribed with their initials and with the year, 1807. Tradition, however, maintains that the 1½-story side wing is older and an earlier (1782) Coale will refers to the "dwelling house" here and leaves "Sarah and Ann [Coale] . . . the two back rooms . . . and one half of the garden . . . with the liberty of the kitchen to cook in." An 1880 account of the house in the *Ægis* noted that the house "is a large and commodious building, and Mr. [William T.] Easter has improved it very much since it came into his possession [in 1856]. He has re-pointed the walls, painted the woodwork, and erected a spacious piazza in front, very long and wide." (The piazza, or porch, was removed in a 1930s restoration; see chap-

ter 8.) The farm also boasts a notable nineteenth-century bank barn; its pine siding has two bored holes in the end of each plank because the trees used to make the planks were felled in Pennsylvania and the logs were then pegged together and rafted or "arked" down the Susquehanna during the spring floods to Rock Run or Port Deposit; the cargo was then sold and the arks were planed into boards and sold. (Similar planks may be seen at the William Silver Barn.) If all this weren't interesting enough, to the rear of the property traces of a millrace, mill pond, and a few scattered (but obviously quarried) stones suggest the presence of a tan- or gristmill and bear witness to the diversity of activity once common on county farms.

2-23. Glenville School
3502 Harmony Church Road
c. 1870; Private
National Register   HA-293

Adapted to residential use in the late 1930s, this one-story frame structure was built as an elementary school. New rooms have been created and modern plumbing has been installed, but the overall appearance—particularly the five tall windows on the northwest front—remains much as it did when generations of neighborhood youths attended to their lessons here.

2-24. Thymly
(Dr. Thomas C. Worthington House)
3510 Harmony Church Road
Eighteenth century; with additions; Private
National Register   HA-294

This charming dwelling has seen at least seven sections of growth from the eighteenth century through the 1930s. The oldest part seems to be a black walnut log house that boasts chestnut and oak flooring and beautiful (and locally unique) beaded pilasters; it also has a fireplace with a mantle similar to one in Wakefield. Dr. Thomas C. Worthington, who owned the house from 1818 until his death in 1855, enlarged the old two-room dwelling to suit his needs, probably adding the present library, main stair, and parlor. Dr. Worthington, a devout Quaker, was a son of John Worthington who died in 1803, leaving $1,000 "to educate my son Thomas . . . to practice Physick." (Thomas's brother William was a noted abolitionist and played an important part in the famous Underground Railroad, as is discussed in chapter 5). Dr. Worthington

2-22

2-23

2-24

2-25

2-26

2-27

2-28

gained some unintentional celebrity after his death when W. Stump Forwood cited him, in the 1879–80 *Ægis* series "Homes on Deer Creek," as an example of how poorly paid members of the medical profession were: "The same amount of education, industry and thrift devoted to any other honorable calling, will invariably yield a more abundant return," fumed Dr. Forwood. Silver family diaries reveal that after Worthington's death architect William Reasin occupied the house and probably made additions of his own.

2-25. Glenville Store and Post Office
Glenville and Harmony Church Roads
c. 1854; Private
National Register   HA-295

Abandoned in the 1930s, but saved and adapted to domestic use in the 1960s, this frame structure still looks much as it did when it served as the hub of Glenville, with villagers gathering to exchange news, purchase goods, and—thanks to Dr. Silas Silver of Silverton—collect their mail. Dr. Silver, who built the charming structure, lobbied to establish the Glenville post office and even served a stint as postmaster. Although the building has gained a wing to the north, Dr. Silver's post office is complete, even down to the machine-cut bargeboard trim that enlivens the eaves. At one time Harry Silver, member of that most prominent local clan, kept store here and posted a sign reading "Gentlemen will not and others should not spit on the counters."

2-26. Foard's Blacksmith Shop
Steppingstone Museum
c. 1882; Private
National Register   HA-312

Edson Foard bought a lot in Level in 1882 and built a smithy that quickly became the center of that farming community. The original frame structure, roughly 24 feet wide and 40 feet long, has been much added to, although its longitudinal plan is still clear. Large, eight-foot double doors open to the work area from the road; inside are two forges, a space for maneuvering, and an endless collection of tools and bits of iron. The waist-high forges measure roughly four feet square; built of stone, they are hollowed out to burn coal and are served by brick flues. Although covered in circular sawn boards, the building skeleton is an ancient post-beam and brace construction appropriate to such a venerable craft as black-

smithing. Threatened with demolition, the shop was moved to Steppingstone Museum in 1983.

2-27. Friendship
600 Craig's Corner Road
Before 1798; c. 1866; Private
National Register   HA-279

John Cooley (1755–1809) and his wife, née Sarah Anne Gilbert (1760–1832), owned and lived in the stone portion of this house in the late eighteenth century (with four slaves), according to the 1798 Federal Direct Tax. At that time, the house stood one story tall above a "good stone-walled cellar." That structure is still discernible today: in plan there is a side-hall to the west with two rooms (each with a corner fireplace) to the east; a closed string stair rises to the second floor from the northeast corner of the hall, with fully raised panels enclosing a closet beneath. Trim (such as hardware, doors, mantles, and plastered walls) seems to be original, as does the porch (although it was not cited in 1798) with a roof continuous with that of the main dwelling. In 1865 Stephen B. Hanna purchased the property and presumably soon thereafter added the two-story frame wing seen to the left. Eighteenth-century frame outbuildings (kitchen, cornhouse, and meathouse) have been replaced with a nineteenth-century cornhouse, smokehouse, and a particularly interesting stone springhouse.

2-28. Smith Ferry House
(Watts-Virdin House)
Lapidum and Stafford Roads
c. 1790 or earlier; with additions; Private
National Register   HA-378

Although of uncertain age, this house and its site are of crucial importance to the development of this part of Harford County. Albert P. Silver's 1888 history, "Lapidum," traces landownership here back to the seventeenth century. Several entrepreneurs piloted ferry boats and operated wharves and warehouses hereabouts. Operations eventually ended up in the hands of Thomas Smith in 1772. During the Revolution Smith ferried French troops across the river on their way to Yorktown and Silver cites the receipt: "To Thomas Smith . . . for his flat [boat] 8 days at 3 shillings a day." Silver also wrote that Smith "built part of the large stone house now occupied by Dr. . . . Virdin and lived there at the time of his death in 1791." The house passed through the Bell and Stump families (the line and the community, first known as Perkins Ferry, was variously called Smith's Ferry, then Bell's Ferry until Dr. Robert H. Archer named it Lapidum) before Dr. Virdin bought the "Ferry Property" in 1856; he is shown as living in this house in the 1878 Martenet map.

2-29. Spencer-Pugh House
Stafford Road
c. 1857; Private
National Register   HA-381

Obviously dating from the mid-nineteenth century, this two-story frame building may have briefly held a store. A. P. Silver's 1888 history of Lapidum notes that a store "was started in 1857 in . . . Spencer's new house" and members of the Spencer family owned the land here from 1810 until the early twentieth century. Fishing was for generations one of Lapidum's leading industries and Silver reported that J. W. Spencer, among the most skilled of the netmen (note Spencer's Island in the Susquehanna), "operated the first haul seine at Lapidum . . . and . . . later built the first float." In the nineteenth century a single haul of a seine sometimes yielded 600 barrels of shad or herring and Silver described one "haul . . . which employed forty men two nights and a day to clear the seine." The fish were then loaded into wagons by traders "not distinguished for their sobriety" and carted up to Pennsylvania. There is a spring to the rear of the property sheltered by a one-story stone springhouse that almost certainly antedates "Spencer's new house."

2-30. Lapidum Lock
Near Stafford Road
c. 1836; Public
National Register   HA-382

Work began on the Susquehanna and Tidewater Canal in 1836 and the water was let in in 1839. This was one of nine functioning locks in the canal's Harford County stretch: 150 feet long and 18 feet wide, constructed of granite blocks that were meticulously cut and fitted together, the lock was as much an engineering marvel as the canal itself. At other locks, similar magnificent stones have been carted away; that these have survived—even with a bit of gate and hardware intact—seems little short of miraculous. The lock is now (1994) being restored as a memorial to the late Charles

Hopkins Reed, attorney, scholar, musician, tennis buff, and for decades the beloved guiding light of the county's small liberal establishment.

2-31. Thomas Smith II House
4054 Wilkinson Road
c. 1840; with additions; Private
National Register   HA-383

Extensively remodeled, this house still retains some original features; foremost among these is the high stone cellar, exposed on the south, that served as the kitchen. The probable builder of the house, Thomas Smith II, was a grandson of the prominent ferryman Thomas Smith. The senior Smith died in 1791, leaving his widow, Hannah, with seven sons, five daughters, and several tracts of land, "most of which," wrote A. P. Silver in 1888, "descended to his three youngest sons, William, Nathaniel, and James, and some is still owned and occupied by their descendants." This is one such tract, remaining in Smith family ownership until the 1940s. In 1838 Nathaniel sold 160 acres to his son, Thomas II, who probably built this frame house shortly thereafter. (See also the Seaman-Smith House). West of the house and contemporary with it are two notable outbuildings, a small rubblestone springhouse, and a large frame barn whose hand-hewn interior beams are pegged together.

2-32. Jeremiah Silver House
(Lebanon)
337 Fox Road
1853; Private
National Register   HA-384

Jeremiah P. Silver (1826–97), a brother of Silas, John, James, and Benjamin, increased his substantial inherited funds through skillful dairy farming, at one point monitoring operations on five different farms. Like the rest of his family, he served as an elder in the Presbyterian church and took an active role in county and state government; unlike his relatives, and rather endearingly, he was a clock fancier. He married on New Year's Day 1852 and the following year began building this house. He also began his well-known *Diary* in 1853, in which he chronicled Lebanon's construction in detail: "5 January 1853. Walnut logs (492 feet) were cut. . . . Quarrying for stone for the house begun in earnest on 11 January." The architect was "Mr. Reasin [an Aberdeen native

2-29

2-30

2-31

2-32

2-34

2-35

trained in Baltimore] who agreed to furnish a plan for the house with front and side elevations and front porch for $25." By October 9 Silver could write "stone masons finished the house." Reasin gave Silver an exceptionally fine dwelling where details such as Tuscan columns, terracotta chimney pots, and varied gable treatments relieve the dignified massing from any hint of stolidness. Various outbuildings accompanied the residence (corn-, meat-, and carriage houses in 1856 and a springhouse in 1860), but only the two-story frame cornhouse still exists in anything like its original form. In 1866 Jeremiah ordered an "Egyptian stile" slate mantle, which is probably the mantle still in place in the living room.

2-33. John A. Silver House Site
(Vignon)
Darlington Road
c. 1845; c. 1870; Private
National Register   HA-385

Vignon was the earliest and largest of the structures in the Silver Houses Historic District. Its history begins with John Silver's marriage to Jane Pannell; to mark that occasion, the Silvers put up a ten-room stone house near the center of Gershom Silver's original (1770) land purchase. Mrs. Silver died in 1857 and John married Hannah Kennard in 1869. She seems to have been a woman of some determination. Under her rule, the residence grew from house to mansion: another ten rooms doubled its bulk; complete walnut paneling in all rooms added dignity; and trinkets picked up on a European honeymoon—tapestries, a suit of armor, bushels of silver—provided splashes of glamour. The second Mrs. Silver is also credited with giving the house its European name, Vignon, an intentional corruption of Avignon. (One of her schemes, however, may have gone too far. John is said to have balked at her request that he build a pergola from the house to Harmony Church so she could walk the quarter mile shaded from the sun.) It was all too grand to last and in June 1902 the house burned to the ground, an event one of John and Hannah's grandsons, Francis S. Silver, colorfully describes in *A Family Chronicle.* Although a huge board-and-batten bank barn, some wagon sheds, and a deteriorated tenant house still stand on the property, all that remains of the house are a few stone steps overgrown with weeds—the former entrance to the root cellar.

2-34. William F. Silver House
521 Darlington Road
c. 1857; Private
National Register   HA-389

Sporting definite Italianate flourishes such as emphatic cornice lines, a hipped roof, well-defined cornices and lintels, and an overall sense of compact verticality heightened by the tiny third-story windows, this may be the most "architectural" of all the Silver houses—at least on the outside. Within, the proportions are a bit awkward, particularly in the stairhall. But no matter, the *effect* works splendidly. No architect has ever been credited with the fine dwelling, although it seems likely that the family-favorite William Reasin lent a hand: he was working on Silas Silver's house at precisely the same time this house was under construction and he is known to have had a predelection for Italianate buildings, for example, his well-known Engine House Number 6 in Baltimore. William Finney Silver (1820–89), the builder of this house, was a cousin of John, Jeremiah, Silas, and Benjamin, and, like other members of the family, derived much of his evident wealth from fishing and farming. The farm passed from the Silver family in 1942; later owners include Jane Dewey, a scientist at Edgewood Arsenal and a daughter of the educator-philosopher John Dewey.

2-35. Benjamin Silver III House
3646 Harmony Church Road
1856; Private
National Register   HA-398

Perhaps the focus of the entire Silver Houses Historic District, this farm complex presents a remarkably complete picture of a prosperous agricultural life in mid-nineteenth-century Harford County. Silver (1810–94) attended Yale before taking up the life of a farmer, fishery owner, surveyor, and politician. Something of an amateur architect, he is known to have owned a copy of Calvert Vaux's seminal work, *Villas and Cottages,* and reliable family histories credit him with the design of this stone house and its many outbuildings (as well as with the interior of brother Silas's house, Silverton). The house's center-hall plan and solid massing are firmly conservative, and perhaps reflect Benjamin's personality: he was the only slave owner among the Silvers of his generation, and the only Confederate sympathizer. The notable outbuildings include a frame bank barn, frame and hipped-roof servants' quarters, granite dairy, granite smokehouse, frame icehouse, frame corncrib, a pair of frame carriage houses, and a calf pen and yard. These structures combine to present a virtually unchanged picture of nineteenth-century agriculture at its most complex and, perhaps, most perfectly evolved condition.

2-36. Silas B. Silver House

(Silverton)
3643 Harmony Church Road
1858; Private
National Register   HA-407

Historian Janet Davis has noted that in many ways Silverton "presages the twentieth century in its simplicity": the plan is direct without a side or rear wing, the kitchen is incorporated into the main block, the entire effect is at once commodious, compact, and efficient. At the same time, Silverton's wide, bracketed cornice, arched dormer windows, and attic window hood make it the most "decorated" of all the Silver Houses: in all it is a wonderful contradiction, that the simplest plan should be hidden beneath the most elaborate decoration. Silas B. Silver (1815–83) received his medical degree from the University of Pennsylvania in 1838, but never maintained a full-time practice; instead, he devoted his energies to consulting, to farming, and to sinecures (he was Glenville's first postmaster). *And* to writing, for this inveterate diarist documented every stage of Silverton's construction from April 1, 1858, when he "employed Mr. Reasin, the architect, to draw plans for house . . . charged $100" (Mr. Reasin only charged Silas's brother Jeremiah $25) through "22 April commenced to quarry stone," "21 June, began to erect the foundations" and so on until he was able to write a sentence all new homeowners will appreciate, "12 September [1859] we commenced to move into our new house and for the first time dined and slept there." Incidentally, Silas and his wife, née Susan Pannell, were the most enthusiastic of the Silvers in their datestones: a datestone at Jeremiah's house reads "1853 JPS" and one at Benjamin's reads "B S 1856," but Silverton boasts two; one is inscribed "1859" and the other "Dr. S & Mrs. S."

2-37. Wilson's Mill Tenant House

Stokes Road
c. 1800; Private
National Register   HA-392

An integral part of the highly important Wilson's Mill complex (most of which lies across Deer Creek), this two-story rubblestone structure overlooks the Deer Creek Valley. The building's small size and straightforward construction make it clear that this is simple worker's housing; yet it is equally clear that the house stands as evidence that *simple* housing need not necessarily mean *cheap* housing, a lesson many of today's developers and speculative builders ought to heed.

2-38. Isaac Coale House

2001 Glenville Road
c. 1878; with additions; Private
National Register   HA-396

In 1880 Dr. W. S. Forwood's "Homes on Deer Creek" *Ægis* series noted of this house, "Within the last two or three years Mr. [John W.] Coale has divided a portion of his farm . . . and gave it . . . to his son Isaac, upon the event of the latter's marriage. Mr. Isaac Coale has built a very neat and pretty stone house upon his portion of the farm, which adds considerably to the improvement of the neighborhood." Coale's two-story stone house is marked by quoins on the exterior and a center-hall plan within. Dr. Forwood observed that the stone for this house "came from a very fine quarry near by"; the quarry, mentioned in deeds at least as long ago as 1841, was actually on this property near Deer Creek, and presumably provided the stones for many of the area's buildings.

2-39. John W. Coale House

2000 Glenville Road
c. 1804; c. 1940; Private
National Register   HA-397

According to Dr. W. S. Forwood's 1879–80 series, "Homes on Deer Creek," this "old-style stone building, very comfortable and of good appearance externally . . . was erected [by John Coale] . . . in the year 1804 [but] the property has been in his family for a much longer time." Coale ownership hereabouts goes back well into the eighteenth century. To the rear of the present house, ruins of a stone chimney stack are all that remain of a log building that predated the present stone

2-36

2-37

2-38

2-39

2-40

2-41

2-42

house. The present owner, Edward C. Wilson Jr., whose ancestors left their beneficent mark on nearly every building in the Darlington area, hired the respected twentieth-century Baltimore architect Lawrence Ewald to design low-key frame extensions to the north.

2-40. William F. Bayless House
Harmony Church Road
1844; Private
National Register   HA-409

While not as elaborate or as stylish as some of the neighboring Silver houses, this two-story, three-part stone dwelling stands as a solid, straightforward example of Harford's prevailing nineteenth-century vernacular building traditions. The Baylesses acquired large land holdings in this area around 1770 and for generations the family played vital roles in many facets of Deer Creek Valley history, particularly in the formation of Harmony Church: Zephaniah Bayless, father of William F., helped organize the congregation in 1837 while the Reverend Samuel Bayless, another of Zephaniah's sons, was pastor when the present church was built. William and Samuel were, according to one church history, born "at the homestead near the church" in 1814 and 1810 respectively. The present house is not that aged, however, for a datestone placed high in the east gable end is inscribed "1844." William F. Bayless, the presumed builder and shown living here on the 1858 county map, died in 1873. His estate inventory notes (in the midst of a surprisingly large amount of silver) "14 yds. step carpeting," which certainly suggests a two-story building. In the 1930s and '40s this was home to Anna Merven Carrere, daughter of noted New York architect John Carrere and a distinguished landscape architect in her own right. Ms. Carrere is credited not only with the beautiful gardens here, but also with the more formal layout of the grounds at Box Hill (see chapter 10). Since 1984 it has been home to the equestrian operations of William Boniface, trainer of the 1983 Preakness winner, Deputed Testamony.

2-41. Prospect School
Darlington Road
c. 1850; Private
National Register; Historic American
Buildings Survey   HA-532

Located on a slope overlooking Darlington Road (Route 161) as that thoroughfare begins its descent down to Deer Creek, Prospect School is among Harford's better known architectural oddities. The county's school commissioners purchased the site in 1850 "for school use" and contracted with stonemason Joshua Stevens to build a new building to replace an 1837 log structure. Stevens, who purportedly gave the school a hexagonal shape on a dare, may have intended to use the building as an example of his masonry prowess. (See Rock Run Church and the Todd-Stephenson House for other Stevens projects.) An undated clipping from the *Baltimore American* reports that desks were "shaped to fit the building—tapering in height and length from the outside wall to the big wood stove in the center of the room," which makes the school sound like an early form of theater in the round. Students in grades 1 through 8 learned their lessons here until 1930, when the board of education sold the building.

2-42. Rock Run Church
Rock Run and Craig's Corner Roads
1843; Regular services
National Register   HA-565

As was often the case in the late eighteenth and early nineteenth centuries, this church owes its existence to the enthusiasm of one dedicated individual. Here it was William Stephenson, local landowner, planter, and early convert to Methodism. Stephenson, one of this country's first ordained Methodist ministers, founded the Rock Run congregation in 1785 at his nearby home, Belmont. The congregation built its first church on Stephenson's farm in 1813. The congregation continued to grow, making a new, larger building—the present church—necessary. In the 1840s James Stephenson, a nephew of William, donated land about a mile from the old church and the congregation hired local stonemason Joshua W. Stevens to construct this granite structure. Stevens must have been pleased with the result since he "signed" it by carving his initials in the west gable. Physically the simple rectangular building resembles the county's other period Methodist churches such as Watters and Calvary.

2-43. Fourteen Shillings
4125 Rock Run Road
c. 1800; c. 1836; c. 1930; Private
National Register   HA-566

Much altered in the twentieth century, the core of this frame house (the log center section) probably dates to Thomas family ownership. It passed to the Cooley clan in 1836, who enlarged it and owned it for most of the rest of the nineteenth century. Southeast of the house and somewhat downhill, a stone meathouse and, a bit farther on, a stone icehouse still suggest the Cooley era.

2-44. Todd-Stephenson House
(Stephenson-Hopkins House)
4223 Rock Run Road
c. 1840; Private
National Register   HA-569

The civic-minded William B. Stephenson, who founded the Lapidum Masonic Hall and whose ancestors were so intimately connected with Rock Run Church, lived here in the mid-nineteenth century; before his era the property had belonged to the Thomas family of Mount Friendship and to the Cooley family, who probably hired mason Joshua Stevens to construct the two-part, coursed granite dwelling. The house crowns a beautiful wooded knoll, with a notable barn and other outbuildings to the rear.

2-45. James Stephenson House
633 Craigs Corner Road
c. 1797; with additions; Private
National Register   HA-570

Of telescopic form and frame construction, this two-story house is a real local rarity. One usually associates telescope houses, so called because their diminishingly sized sections suggest they could be closed up like a telescope, with the Eastern Shore; Talbot and Dorchester counties, for instance, are filled with eighteenth-century examples of the breed. Whatever it is doing on the shores of the Susquehanna, the Stephenson house exemplifies the form; each of its three sections gives the appearance of being potentially independent. The center and east units are the older and retain many original features such as pegged ancient window frames and glass, and simple chairrails. Stephenson bought 162 acres here in 1797, and the 1798 tax list suggests that he immediately began building the house.

(While all this was going on, Stephenson's brother, William, occupied himself with founding the Rock Run Church, built on donated land that had been part of this farm.) Notable outbuildings include a stone meathouse east of the residence and a vertical-sheathed corncrib to the west. The complex remained in the Stephenson family until 1902.

2-46. Worthington-Minnick House
(Spencer House)
Craigs Corner Road
Mid-nineteenth century; Private   HA-572

Details *are* important. This two-part house was obviously built with economy in mind: note, merely for example, the walls are fieldstones, doubtless hauled here from surrounding pastures and laid with little or no thought to finishing them. Similarly, the stones are placed randomly—no one worried about coursing—and are held together with exceptionally large amounts of obviously inexpensive mortar. But it is emphatically not a crude house; the main door is well defined, and the porch brackets and brick arches over the windows add distinction to the otherwise simple structure.

2-47. "The Bird House"
Rock Run Road
c. 1800 (?); Public   HA-573

One of several stone houses making up the flourishing tri-village community of Lapidum–Rock Run–Stafford in the nineteenth century, this simple structure in the early and mid-twentieth century acquired its name when it was owned by the Maryland Ornithological Society. Essentially ageless in form and construction techniques, the house stands on a large tract owned by Samuel Gover in the late eighteenth century; this place is obviously not the 40-foot-square house sited under Gover's name in the 1798 tax list, but it may have been an outbuilding or tenant house. Its beaded door jambs and granite quoins and windowsills evince some sense of style. Gover's family was not without interest: his daughters Elizabeth, Margaret, Hannah, Susan, and Caroline ran a boarding school, the Gover Seminary, nearby until a fire in 1825 destroyed it. (Samuel Mason began a history of the seminary but did not delve too deeply, noting "a fascinating legend has lingered for many years about a small heap of stones on the hill overlooking Rock Run, but like a fra-

2-43

2-44

2-45

2-46

2-47

2-48

2-49

2-50

2-51

grant perfume, it vanishes when you attempt an analysis.") After the Gover era, the small, one-room-per-floor dwelling passed to the Archers of Rock Run, who certainly used it as a tenant house; it is now owned by the Department of Natural Resources.

2-48. Land of Promise
(Steppingstone Museum)
Quaker Bottom Road
Mid-eighteenth century (?); 1954; Public;
Regular hours
National Register; Historic American
Buildings Survey   HA-575

Does it seem curious that one of the best-known houses in Harford County is actually one of the *least* known, at least in terms of the historian's favorite questions, Who? and When? It is certain, for example, that vast tracts called Land of Promise passed back and forth among Jacob Giles (Sr. and Jr.), Nathaniel Giles, and John Stump of Stafford (all prominent industrialists and farmers) throughout the eighteenth century but, after generations of research, no one has established just who built this 1½-story multisectioned dwelling. Was it any of the Gileses? Stump? None of the above? Perhaps the air of mystery adds to the charm of the place. And this place has charm in abundance, mostly because of the house's more recent history. In 1954 J. Gilman D'Arcy Paul, diplomat, connoisseur, and bon vivant, bought the ruined house and restored it; he also brought back the surrounding and neglected farmland, laid out the site-enhancing gardens, and in general preserved one of the most beautiful tracts of land in the east. And perhaps the house's importance lies not in knowing which eighteenth-century entrepreneur built it on spec, but in knowing that in the twentieth century it was home to a gentleman of rare and cultivated taste. (See also chapter 8; incidentally, the building's plan is identical to the Botts-Worthington House.)

2-49. Eightrupp
445 Quaker Bottom Road
Late eighteenth century (?); c. 1935; Private
National Register   HA-579

Eightrupp is a three-part stone and stucco structure built into a terraced slope. The two-story main unit and the kitchen, placed slightly closer to the road, are probably contemporaries and may date to the 1700–1772 era when the Perkins family owned the tract Eightrupp,

ran a ferry line, and in general so controlled goings-on in Lapidum that the entire area was known as Perkins Ferry. A frame section connects the two once-separate buildings and probably dates to the early twentieth century when the house was owned by Benjamin Silver, whose skill at growing raspberries is still remembered by many. The interior of the main house remains in excellent condition and retains period wainscotting and pegged windows and door frames. East of the house stands a nineteenth-century corncrib with hand-hewn support beams joined together by a mortise-and-tenon pegging system; a nineteenth-century board-and-batten bank barn stands just southeast of the corncrib.

2-50. Botts-Worthington House
Quaker Bottom Road
c. 1780 (?); Private   HA-584

A marvelous spot—where else could one travel just a mile and a half from I-95 yet lose two centuries in time? Several local historians suggest that this puzzling, long-abandoned cottage and the house at Land of Promise are mirror images of each other. One feature the structures certainly have in common is their elusiveness, for neither can be dated with certainty. The main (stone) section here has a three-room plan. A large room occupies two bays (the door and window south of it); its paneled walls are now covered in plywood and its large end-wall fireplace once boasted a fine mantle. To the north, the rest of the space is divided into two small twin rooms, each with a corner fireplace that has somehow managed to retain its fine mantle. Documentary evidence for the house is vague and contradictory, but the 1798 tax list shows that John Hall Hughes owned land here improved by a 30-by-25-foot stone house and had "the widow Touchstone" for a tenant. Somewhat later (1831) land records for the property note that lawsuits had broken out among various Touchstones and Hugheses, which suggests that this is the house mentioned in 1798. It is inconclusive, but it is all there is.

2-51. Quaker Bottom Farm
Webster-Lapidum Road
c. 1868; Private
National Register   HA-585

In the late eighteenth century, the land here was part of the domain of Gideon Denison, Squire of Sion Hill. This house, of course, is not that old. It probably dates to the mid-nineteenth century: members of the Stillwell family bought a small portion of the tract in 1868 and Isaac Stillwell is shown as living here on the 1878 Harford County Martenet map. This is a good, solid, frame farmhouse given individuality by its unusual arched dormers, finely trimmed front porches, and curious peaked-roof rear wing. It is of more than passing interest that John M. Macklem bought the farm from Isaac Stillwell in 1881; Macklem, who lived here the rest of his life, was the penultimate Rock Run miller; he worked at the mill from 1904 until his death in the 1920s. The farm stayed in the Macklem family until the 1960s.

2-52. Amos Hughes House
Webster-Lapidum Road
1849; Private
National Register   HA-587

One of several old Hughes houses in the general area, this massive granite and rubblestone structure displays the skilled workmanship one associates with nineteenth-century Harford County masonry. It also displays something rare, something few of its mates can boast—a fixed date. Amos Hughes bought 100 acres of land here from his father, John, in 1848 and presumably began building this house, because someone carved "June 26th 1849" into a datestone in the western chimney, evidently a happy inscription to mark the completion of the dwelling. Moreover, "A. Hughes" is shown living here on the 1858 Jennings and Herrick county map. Since few vernacular structures in the county can be so securely dated, the Hughes house becomes something of a local benchmark: one can observe construction techniques here and then, based on this gathered visual evidence, *attribute* dates to nearby less-well-documented buildings. Hughes died in 1892 and his estate inventory cites a residence with four bedrooms, a parlor, a dining room, and a kitchen, rooms that match the existing spaces nicely; he also had $10 worth of "stuff" in his meathouse, 35 bushels of potatoes worth $12.50, and "100 tomato vines" worth a total of $2.

2-53. Golden Vein Farm
325 Lapidum Road
Late nineteenth century; Private
National Register   HA-588

This is one of many Hughes family houses that still dot the hills in the Webster-Lapidum area (the 1878 Martenet map of the county shows Evan T. Hughes living here). It was one of the most recent of the family houses to be built but, curiously, at the same time it is one of the oldest. This paradox is easily explained: the rear (kitchen) wing is often dated to c. 1800 while the five-bay main section is clearly a product of the late Victorian (or Evan Hughes) era. Anyone making a study of local craftsmen should note similarities between this house and the smaller—but obviously related—Quaker Bottom Farm; comparisons between the two structures' porches (note the side trim) could prove especially instructive.

2-54. Winsted
3844 West Chapel Road
c. 1800; Private
National Register; Historic American
Buildings Survey   HA-662

Brickmaker Christian Hoopman built this house for himself shortly after he purchased land here in 1797 and may have intended it to serve as a bit of self-promotion. Who could blame the craftsman? The eleven-room house stands as a monument to the masonry arts: the Flemish bond main façade is precisely laid, the bricks are of a beautiful color and uniform shape—even the thin mortar joints have grapevine striking, a locally rare refinement. A further wealth of original detail enlivens the interior: chairrails are found throughout the house and many rooms have wainscotting; cornices are elaborate; mantles sport pilasters; paneled doors still have their original hardware. The stair, which dominates the through center hall, is original down to its simple balusters and shadow rail. Hoopman, who immigrated to America from England with his brother Peter in 1775, was a stalwart member of the Methodist church: he donated land and, it is said, molded the bricks for the nearby Wesleyan chapel. "Mrs. Hoopman" (possibly a widowed daughter-in-law) is shown living here on the 1878 Martenet map of Harford County.

2-52

2-53

2-54

2-55

2-56

2-57

2-58

2-55. Chestnut Ridge
3850 West Chapel Road
c. 1750 (?); c. 1800; Private
National Register; Historic American
Buildings Survey   HA-664

The small frame section of this house was probably standing here when Christian Hoopman bought the Chestnut Ridge tract from William Wood in November 1797, since the 1798 tax assessment notes "Christian Hoofman" as owning 843 acres and a two-section house, part frame ("32′ × 16′") and part stone. What happened to the stone part is anybody's guess, but the extant frame wing's dimensions and many of its features (e.g., the two-room plan with centrally placed back-to-back fireplaces, the many pegged door and window frames, and the beaded beams) suggest an eighteenth-century date. Although the old wing has been somewhat altered, that so much of it remains is something of a miracle. Hoopman presumably built the large brick wing (but for whom?) since its center-stairhall plan and Flemish bond walls with scored mortar joints make it a small-scale version of Winsted, Hoopman's own grand house next door. Hoopman's brother Peter, a noted miller, established a mill on the Chestnut Ridge property and, not far from the house, one can still see the ruins of a mill.

2-56. Wesleyan Methodist Church
Chapel and Paradise Roads
1826; 1955; Regular services   HA-665

Jacob Walker, a grandson of Christian Hoopman, prepared a history of Wesleyan Church for the parish's centennial in 1926. Mr. Walker wrote that the two Hoopman brothers, Christian and Peter, came to America in the 1770s and prospered thanks to their skill at brickmaking and milling, respectively. "Coming now to the building of the chapel," wrote Walker, "so far as is known this was Christian's individual and personal enterprise." The brick magnate donated land for the building and its adjacent cemetery and then, according to Walker, "personally moulded the bricks . . . and physically built this splendid old building," notable for its fine jack arches and Flemish bonding. (Even allowing a loving grandson great leeway, one does wonder a bit about that last statement since Hoopman was 77 in 1826.) Hoopman died in 1837 and is buried in

the cemetery adjacent to the chapel that he worked so hard to bring into existence.

2-57. Westwood Tenant House
1108 Glenville Road
1796; c. 1870; Private
National Register   HA-668

A datestone in the middle of the west gable end of this two-part house proclaims that "W" and "R C" built the stone portion in 1796. Some researchers feel that WC stands for William Coale, who owned land in this neighborhood in the late eighteenth century, but an equally strong case could be made in favor of William Cox. Generations of the Cox family ran a mill a few yards from the house and that activity is suggested by the sheaf of wheat incised into the datestone. (Neither the 1798 nor the 1814 tax list is much help in this matter.) W and R C's house was later owned by the Davis family and by a Davis in-law, Dr. Roberts. The Davises' milling history is well documented: the 1850 census cites George Davis as owning a mill ("output 600 bbl meal and flour, $4000") and "G. Davis" is shown as living here, with his mill on nearby Mill Brook, on the 1858 Jennings and Herrick map of Harford County. The simple house, with its frame addition, became part of the Westwood Manor estate in this century.

2-58. Hopkins-Briney House
3403 Old Level Road
c. 1885; Private
National Register   HA-673

Visible for miles due to its hilltop location, and presiding over the roads that connect Churchville, Glenville, Darlington, and Level, this Second Empire house has been a true landmark in the county for generations. Actually, a building has been on the site at least since 1814. An 1831 newspaper ad for the property notes "a comfortable frame dwelling" as well as "a commodious STORE HOUSE, for many years occupied as such." If anything remains of that "frame dwelling," it is probably the rear wing of the present structure. Willmor Hopkins bought whatever was standing in 1846; when he died in 1880 his estate inventory suggests a small two-bedroom house. A mortgage made in 1886, however, certainly suggests that Hopkins's heirs built the present large residence, for the loan covered such items as "5 bedroom sets, 1 suit of parlor furniture, dining room furniture," etc. Five frame outbuildings complete the setting: three sheds, a gambrel-roof barn with flared eaves, and a two-story haymow/corncrib.

2-59. Windmill Hill
1530 Glenville Road
c. 1870; c. 1938; c. 1950; Private
National Register   HA-678

Well known in the racing world for the quality of the horses that hail from its fields, Windmill Hill Farm may truly be greater than the sum of its parts. The main residence began as a 2½-story rubblestone bank house five bays wide and one room deep; it has a center-hall plan with one roughly equal-sized room to each side. In this century the farm's fertile fields (a witness in an 1898 equity case involving the property noted the "good quality" land) attracted James and Mildred Whitall here in 1937; the Whitalls added amenities deemed necessary to a country estate such as a large modern kitchen, greenhouse, and servants' apartment. Roughly a decade later, Mr. and Mrs. Peter Jay bought the farm, rationalized the house, simplified the gardens, and established Windmill Hill firmly within Maryland's equestrian community. Regarding nomenclature, the farm's northern border is formed by a rise called Schoolhouse Hill but one wishes it had some other appellation, something more *cinquecento,* since the steep, craggy hill, dotted with randomly placed cedars, comes straight out of the background of every Italian Renaissance painting.

2-60. Westwood Manor
Glenville Road
1818; c. 1920; c. 1930; Private
National Register   HA-675

There can't be many Signer-associated houses left in private hands; nationwide, of the few still standing, most by now have been turned into museums *per gloriam majorum* of Rutledge or of Jay or of Hancock. So Westwood, built by a daughter of Samuel Chase, is a real rarity. In retrospect, Chase (1741–1811) comes across as the quintessential late-eighteenth-century self-made man: an ambitious lawyer, his career was marked with combinations of low lows (near-skirtings with bankruptcy court and prison) and high highs (appointment as associate justice on the Supreme Court and signer of the Declaration of Independence). His daughter Elizabeth began the house shortly after she married Harford

County native Skipwith Coale (c. 1788–c. 1832, and who received his medical degree from the University of Maryland in 1816), and Westwood stayed in the Coale family until the twentieth century. It is hard to assess just how much of that original house remains. Mr. and Mrs. Freeman Coale added a pair of three-story wings to their inheritance in the early 1920s before selling the place to Mr. and Mrs. Frederick Vogel in 1927. Mr. Vogel died shortly after purchasing Westwood, but Mrs. Vogel, according to a 1961 *Ægis* story by Michael Chrismer, set about "to reshape the old house to suit herself." She built a series of porches (some could properly be called porticoes), paneled the heretofore plastered interior walls, and embellished the windows and doors with elaborate cornices. So even though Westwood today is more evocative of 1930s madcap heiresses than Signers, it is a very, very fine example of its type. The grounds, entirely the work of Mrs. Vogel, deserve particular praise, especially the five-acre formal garden, with its 5,000 boxwood bushes and 100 species of blooming perennials.

2-61. Aquila's Inheritance
Hall-Richardson-Worthington Farm
3366 Aldino Road
Late eighteenth century; c. 1840;
c. 1940; Private   HA-591

This house's many clearly defined sections are entirely built of rubblestone, yet clarity and uniformity of construction do not necessarily make for clarity of history. Most authorities agree that the two oldest parts of the dwelling date to the eighteenth century and formed the seat of the 1,000-acre Hall tract known as Aquila's Inheritance. Exit the Halls, enter the Barneses—in 1840 one Hosea Barnes began buying land here and he (or his descendants) gave the house its present rambling configuration. (An 1850 insurance policy on the place, taken out with the Harford Mutual Insurance Company, suggests that even that far back the house consisted of many randomly added parts.) The Worthington family, who have owned the impressive (if low-key) structure for most of the twentieth century, have transformed the house and grounds into a true showplace.

2-59

2-60

2-61

2-62

2-63

2-64

2-65

2-66

2-62. Robin Hood Farm
222 Robin Hood Road
c. 1800 (?); c. 1870; Private   HA-728

Here is another Harford County house that "just grew." This frame structure began as a 1½-story dwelling with a two-room plan, back-to-back central fireplaces, and closeted winder stairs that clearly relate in plan and detail to other nearby eighteenth-century houses, such as the c. 1750 frame wing of Chestnut Ridge. Israel Maulsby probably built this original dwelling, since he owned the property until 1824; his son William P. Maulsby, who became circuit court judge in 1870, was born here. The large addition to the east, with its enthusiastic roofline and floor-to-ceiling windows, is not without its own charms.

2-63. Donnell Mitchell House
817 Paradise Road
c. 1880; Private   HA-742

Familiarity sometimes breeds anything but contempt. This conventional three-bay, two-section frame farmhouse is one of hundreds of similar structures built throughout Harford County during the mid- and late nineteenth century. Yet, a century later their presence offers a sense of reassuring continuity in a rapidly changing landscape. Two porches give this house individuality; the one on the entrance (west) façade is appropriately more elaborate since one of its functions is to draw the visitor to the front door.

2-64. Bowman-Taylor House
Level Road
c. 1800; with additions; Private   HA-920

Throughout its long history, this log and frame structure has helped define the word *evolutionary;* five distinct sections can be seen in the building. The oldest of these, the easternmost two rooms of the much-expanded dwelling, is said to have been an inn on the Baltimore-Philadelphia Road. The property is rich in local history, too; for example, a frame outbuilding that formerly stood toward the rear of the lot was once well known as the temporary digs of "Chic the Tomato Pic." According to an interview with one long-time resident, "every summer when the tomatoes were 'in' Chic would arrive. He picked tomatoes and he ate them along with the bread that was given him. The picker slept in the loft of

this outbuilding and when the tomatoes were gone, so was Chic."

2-65. Bowman-Stearns House
3707 Rock Run Road
c. 1850; with additions; Private   HA-921

This two-part frame house has grown and changed with its surrounding community, the village of Level. The older (east) section, clearly shown on the 1858 map of Harford County, is built of log with one room on each of two stories, a massive fireplace, and a corner winder stair. Slightly northeast of the house is a frame shed built to house a cabinetmaker's shop. (Note the July 9, 1859, ad from the *Harford Democrat* in which William S. Bowman announced that his "Cabinet Making and Undertaking Enterprise" "will manufacture to order bureaus, Beadsteads, wash stands, tables, cradles, etc. [as well as] coffins of all kinds, furnished to good order, walnut, mahogany, cherry, poplar, etc.") The property left the Bowman family in 1888. The late Annie Stearns, who owned the house for much of the twentieth century, was interviewed at length about Level; her descriptions of the community, preserved in the archives of the Historical Society of Harford County, are much valued by historians throughout the state.

2-66. Avondale Christian Church
Aldino and Stepney Roads
1878; with additions; Private   HA-930

In 1877 the Trustees of the Christian Church at Avondale (now Aldino) bought a half-acre lot and built this fine country Gothic structure. A surprising amount of that original building remains, too, including the overall massing, board-and-batten siding, and Gothic window arches and muntins. The word "surprising" was used because the building has not led an uneventful existence: from 1913 until 1943 it was owned by the seemingly oxymoronic "Aldino Country Club"; during World War II it served as the town hall (and as a theater for minstrel shows); and since 1976 merchants have sold farm machinery and antiques from here.

2-67. Knight's Stone House
844 Carsins Run Road
c. 1852; with additions; Private   HA-989

The extensive eighteenth-century land holdings of the Herbert-Greenland family were divided on the death of Mary Greenland in 1848. (The holdings had been large enough so that the original name for Churchville was Herbert's Crossroads.) Richard Hopkins bought 102 acres out of her estate in 1852 and probably built the original two-story rubble-stone section of this house shortly thereafter, since he is shown as living here on the 1858 map of Harford County. Hopkins gave his house granite window lintels, an elaborate entrance door with transom, cornice, and sidelights, and a classic center-hall plan. Interestingly, a virtual twin of the house was built on Carsins Run Road just north of Tower Road; numbered HA-987 in the county's inventory of historic sites, it is in near-ruinous condition.

2-68. Carsins House
3467 Churchville Road
1853; Private   HA-991

William Carsins (1822–94) built this substantial house on land his family had owned for decades. Set on top of a hill, the two-story, two-part frame structure impresses through scale and site. While close examination reveals basically another five-bay, center-hall farmhouse, several details set it apart from its apparent peers. On the outside the shuttered sash gable window and the central pediment on the front porch are somewhat unusual; inside, the cellar kitchen is known to have had a dumbwaiter and a windmill-powered cooling trough for butter and cream, all local rarities. Carsins's father, John, served as sheriff of Harford County and made William a deputy when the lad was but 16 years old; law enforcement proved a sympathetic calling and William ran for and was elected to the office of sheriff in his own right. During his years with the badge he proved, as his 1897 biographer noted, "a capable and efficient officer, fearless in the discharge of his duties, and [he] won the confidence and commendation of all." The biographer also observed that Carsins "took pride in keeping abreast with the progressive spirit of the age, and his place showed many evidences of the careful supervision of the owner"—how else should one view the dumbwaiter and that cooling contraption? Whether it was the important office two generations of Carsins held or the commanding site of this relatively elaborate house, something clicked in citizens' minds; the crossroads community here, originally called Center Ville, was renamed Carsins Run in the 1870s.

2-69. Old Presbyterian Manse
3008 Churchville Road
1865; Private   HA-994

The trustees of the venerable Churchville Presbyterian Church bought a fourteen-acre lot here in 1865 and shortly thereafter built this two-story, five-bay, two-part frame house as the residence for their minister. (The church's earlier rector, the Reverend William Finney, had, of course, built not one but three residences for himself, Oak Farm, Greenwood, and the Finney-Marks House.) At first glance the building seems typical of its time and place (see, for example, the Carsins House, 2-68) but examination reveals that the main section of the gable-roofed house extends a bit deeper than usual, presumably so it can accommodate a four-room, center-hall plan. The house served as a manse until the congregation retired it in 1952.

2-70. Calvary Methodist Church
Calvary Road
1821; Regular services   HA-997

Most of Harford's nineteenth-century churches owe their existence to the spirit of one or two determined individuals; in this case, Richard Webster of Webster's Forest, among the first people in America to embrace the doctrines of Methodism. (Although many men and women on this side of the Atlantic viewed the new denomination as a dangerous, radical sect, Harford countians rushed to join, and the national Methodist Conference has long recognized Bush Forest Chapel, nearby on the road from Stepney to Carsins Run, as the third Methodist meetinghouse in the country.) A man of action as well as conviction, Webster donated some of his ancestral acres so the church could build a new house of worship and even contributed funds to the new building's construction. The church's very complete records show that Webster hired Paul Andrew as mason (just to be sure of recognition, however, Andrew carved his initials in the datestone), Samuel Dever as blacksmith to make the nails and the shutter hardware, and a "Mr. Spear" as chief carpenter. The simple stone building, among the most intact of the county's early churches (windows, shutters, and interior balcony all appear to be original) is perhaps most visually notable for Mr. Andrew's masonry: he gave the granite walls nice, clear courses (the stones retain their

2-67

2-68

2-69

2-70

original pointing) and, as a visual contrast, dressed black basalt lintels and quoins.

2-71

2-71. Kral-Gilbert House
822 Aldino-Stepney Road
c. 1860; 1867; Private   HA-998

Immortality comes in odd ways: one Bennett Gilbert owned this stone house in the mid-nineteenth century and since his death in 1893 virtually every subsequent deed has referred to this property as the "Bennett Gilbert Home Place," although few people now seem sure just who Mr. Gilbert was—or what he did. One thing he certainly did was build this ambitious, two-part dwelling, beginning with the three-bay western section. Whether or not Gilbert was a Methodist, it is clear that he gave his house heavy stone lintels very similar to those of the 1821 Calvary Church.

2-72

2-72. Baker Homestead
(Rodman House)
Churchville Road
c. 1775; 1801; c. 1900; c. 1955; Private   HA-999

While many houses in Harford County have simply "grown" over the years, it would be hard to find a more evolutionary specimen than this multipart frame structure. Nicholas Baker II (1748–80) purchased land here at the time of the Revolution and lived on this farm until his death, when his son Nicholas III inherited the property; the younger Baker married Elizabeth Cole in 1801 and the couple then began building the main section of the present house, a five-bay 2½-story frame unit with a center-hall plan. Several notable members of the illustrious Baker family were born in this "new" house—a congressman, a college president and, perhaps most important of all, George W. Baker, the man who brought the canning industry to Harford County, as is discussed in chapter 7. The Bakers, most of whom had built (or were planning) elaborate palaces in Aberdeen and Havre de Grace, sold the old homestead in 1881 but the house's career had just begun. Charles Osborn, whose name also suggests canneries, acquired the farm at auction in 1900 and, it is thought, shortly thereafter remodeled the Bakers' house into a picturesque cottage by giving it cross gables, exposed eaves, a front porch, a bay window, and more and larger sash windows. Further changes were to come: Ellis Hardison and his wife, Evelyn, ran an inn and raised dogs here in the 1920s and '30s (Mr. Hardison

2-73

2-73

2-74

gained national attention when *Life* magazine ran an article on him and his career as a dog psychologist), and in 1948 Dr. and Mrs. Peter Rodman bought the ancient house and set about making alterations of their own.

2-73. Woodlawn Farm
4800 Old Philadelphia Road
c. 1790 (?); c. 1883; 1907; Private   HA-1088

When Cicero Slee bought the farm here in 1883 it was, wrote his son George, "completely surrounded by wood land, not bordering any road or highway." The house on the farm was "a large one . . . , nicely situated on high ground, . . . [the product of] three generations." Still, it is not known who built the original, 2½-story rubblestone section of the present seventeen-room house; members of the Perryman family owned land around here in the eighteenth century but the early tax rolls do not indicate a Perryman house of the right size or material. Historians reach firmer ground with the Slees. Prosperous farmers and canners, this family almost certainly built the present large frame wings and portico. Historian Mary Wright Barnes, herself a relative of the Slees, has written that architect John Bay Slee, a brother of George, oversaw a 1907 remodeling of the property. In addition, John Bay Slee should probably be credited with the farm's large, and quite splendid, frame barn.

2-74. Wood's Meadow
3507 Aldino Road
Mid-nineteenth century (?); Private   HA-1221

Although this property's list of owners is clear and straightforward back to the time of the Revolution (when the Mahan family owned the farm), the house's construction date is murky. Simple visual evidence suggests that the present two-part frame structure, with its exuberant trim, dates to the Victorian period but area residents contend that the building has much earlier beginnings. Perhaps the original house formed the two rooms (three bays) to the north; the larger of these rooms sports a large end-wall fireplace and adjacent closet, just the sort of arrangement that characterized so many of the county's larger eighteenth-century dwellings. (See, for example, Broom's Bloom and Cranberry.) This is, however, a bit academic, for whatever may have been built in the eighteenth century is swallowed up in nineteenth-century additions.

2-75. Gilbert's Pipe
740 Gilbert Road
c. 1860; with additions; Private

In the middle of the nineteenth century there were so many Gilbert farms in this neighborhood that the intersection of what are now called Aldino-Stepney and Gilbert roads was known as Gilbert Town. While of uncertain vintage, this particular fieldstone house has definite Gilbert associations, since the family owned the tract from the mid-eighteenth century until 1895. Which Gilbert built the place, however, is not known. Was it Charles (1723–98), a justice of the peace? or Michael (1754–96) an officer in the Revolution? or shoemaker Amos (1774–1836)? or Preston (1841–93), the first mayor of Bel Air?

2-76. Baker Cemetery
Churchville Road
1887 (established); Private   HA-1554

The 1897 *Portrait and Biographical Record of Cecil and Harford Counties* notes, in prose typical of the era, that "through the years of the century now drawing to a close, the Baker family has been identified with the history of Harford County, its members having borne an honorable part in many of its important enterprises." Thomas S. Baker gained distinction as an educator and eventually became president of the Carnegie Institute of Technology in Pittsburgh; William B. Baker, a U.S. congressman, was responsible for establishing the rural free delivery system. But the Bakers' greatest contribution to the Harford scene (and to their collective wallets) was their pioneer work in the canning business. George W. Baker, who started it all, set aside one acre here "for the purpose of a cemetery" and left it to his sons to manage the operation as a private family enterprise, although they could also admit "such persons as they may desire." (Since 1971 the cemetery has been under the care of Aberdeen's Grace Methodist Church, an institution with strong and venerable Baker connections.) Among the cemetery's scores of marble and granite memorials, certainly the most striking are the obelisks of the late nineteenth-century Bakers whose prepossessing stones—and plots—are outlined by concrete curbs. Of these, George W.'s may be the best: its square base has a frieze decorated with corn cobs, highly appropriate to one recognized as "the pioneer canning packer" in America. Among the names inscribed on the non-Baker

stones, doubtless the one most recognizable to 1990s Marylanders is Ripken.

2-77. Aberdeen Esso Station
Route 40 and Bel Air Avenue
c. 1930; Private   HA-1556

Before it was demolished around 1981, this one-story, roadside, concrete service station was one of the least altered such structures in the county. Indeed, it summed up an entire era, the generation between the world wars when the automobile stopped being a novelty and became an accepted—and welcome—fact of life. (It is still an accepted fact of life in the 1990s, of course, but its pleasing novelty has certainly worn a bit thin.) While such buildings were undeniably efficient and utilitarian (note the simple office, covered gas pumps, public restrooms, and convenient highway location), something else was going on in the minds of the Standard Oil brass when they instructed their architects to embellish the "service station" with decorative details far more elaborate than strict utility would demand. Note the concrete corbels, the columns, the "Spanish" tile roof, and the pressed tin ceiling.

2-78. James B. Baker House
452 West Bel Air Avenue
1896; Private
National Register   HA-1559

In the generation after the Civil War, the newly incorporated town of Aberdeen swaggered with an architectural braggadocio unparalleled in Harford County. Nearly every house billowed and bulged with gables or bay windows or patterned shingles or stained glass or bulbous chimney stacks, thanks to the piles of lovely new money the canning industry was bringing to town. And while the town as a whole rocked in architectural self-expression (and self-satisfaction), no family rocked more than the Bakers, a fitting state of things, after all, since George W. Baker pioneered the industry. Still, even though it was George who brought canning to Aberdeen, it was his sons who erected the most spectacular houses and of these let James B. Baker's house stand as a worthy representative. When the young man (he lived from 1845 to 1912) built his new residence, which still reads as a textbook example of the Queen Anne style, it commanded a landscaped site dotted with outbuildings; it even had its own greenhouse. The lot has been reduced, the greenhouse is gone, but the main

2-75

2-76

2-77

2-78

2-79

2-80

2-81

2-82

house, although deteriorated, is still intact; the interior deserves particular mention, especially the many fireplaces with their colorful glazed brick facings, elaborate mantels, and accompanying mirrors.

2-79. Edward Wilkinson Farm
3747 Rock Run Road
c. 1900 (remodeling); Private   HA-1569

Perhaps the most stylish house in Level, this frame fantasy is the work of John B. Bailey, a local carpenter-cabinetmaker-wheelwright-undertaker. Thoroughly of its period, the structure may be thought of as a unique cliché, for no other house in the county uses so many period motifs (such as turrets, decorated porches, and bay windows) so enthusiastically. (Bailey's furniture, much valued by those who own pieces, displays the same innate yet idiosyncratic design sense seen in the house.) Edward Wilkinson bought the property in 1880 and hired Bailey to remodel the simple frame house already on it; Bailey's daughter, Mrs. Leonard Knight, recalled that her father tried to "open up" the Wilkinson house so one "could see straight through it." The tenant house and barn, based on construction techniques, seem to date from c. 1900. Both have flourishes that link them to Bailey: the tenant house's porch and the barn's cupola and unique board-and-batten siding—the battens aren't simply squared, they were given an ovolo shape—are too elaborate to be explained away as accidental.

2-80. New Ideal Diner
104 South Philadelphia Blvd.
1952; Private   HA-1560

Virtually unaltered, the New Ideal Diner exemplifies the Eisenhower-era ideal of streamlined, fast-paced, and efficient automobile transportation. Interestingly, while reveling in the present and looking to the future, the diner took its form from the past since it is basically a reworked railroad dining car. But it is the reworking that is important: the interior, all pink formica and vinyl, retains period touches such as booths and stools, a satellite clock and jukeboxes, while the outside, sheathed in shiny stainless steel with green glass accents beneath a glowing red neon sign of stylized freestanding letters, could easily have lured the Ricardos and Mertzes in for a bite—of what? Salisbury steak? chicken pot pie?—during their 1954 drive to California.

2-81. Samuel Famous House
3710 Rock Run Road
c. 1884; Private   HA-1575

Typical of its time and place, this two-story front-gable frame house is one of several structures that define the village of Level. In 1883 Samuel Famous paid Edson and Emma Foard $50 for the unimproved lot here (the Foards owned the adjacent blacksmith property); Famous sold the property in 1885 for $500, and the difference in price strongly suggests that he had built the house in the interim.

2-82. Reasin-Silver House
1826 Glenville Road
c. 1875; Private   HA-1591

In an 1880 *Ægis* article Dr. W. Stump Forwood rhapsodized about this house, which blacksmith and inventor J. Frank Reasin had recently completed ("within the last four or five years"). Dr. Forwood called it "a most beautiful frame dwelling, in the most approved modern cottage style. It has a number of ornamental porticos and handsome bay-windows, resembling some of the most tasteful and picturesque villas often seen in the suburbs of the large cities. It is the most stylish building of the kind that we know in the neighborhood." But that's not all. According to Forwood (who noticed such things) Reasin also "laid out a very pretty lawn about his house, . . . [with] a number of evergreen trees, . . . shrubbery and flowers." Frank Reasin's brother, William, was a Baltimore architect who worked on some of the nearby Silver houses and it is reasonable to assume William might have fraternally helped out here. (William also rented the Dr. Worthington house after that physician died.) Considerably simplified on the exterior, the house's interior, with its tall ceilings and asymmetrical room arrangement, still suggests "the most approved modern cottage style."

2-83. U.S. Post Office
Perryman
428 Michaelsville Road
1914; Public   HA-1658

It may not look it, but this small, frame, hipped-roof structure was something of an innovation in its day. During the nineteenth century—and for much of the twentieth, as well—village post offices were located in general stores. Construction of this structure, built *as* a post office, thus marks a departure from the norm. The building is unusual in another respect: a century ago nearly every Harford County crossroad community had its own post office; nearly all have been abandoned in "cost-saving" movements (Federal Hill, Jerusalem Mill, Prospect, and Dublin come to mind), yet Perryman's has managed to survive. One wishes it well. Architecturally, the building's vaguely colonial revival lines harmonize nicely with the F. O. Mitchell headquarters across the street and the posts that support the roof aren't the usual turned "Victorian" porch posts but, with their chamfered edges and embryonic capitals and bases, suggest neoclassical aspirations.

2-83

2-84. F. O. Mitchell Brothers, Inc.
427 Michaelsville Road
c. 1900; Private   HA-1659

At first, one would not think that a quiet village like Perryman would be the place to go in search of cutting-edge architecture. Yet this office building and, to a lesser extent, the post office across the street are, if not *avant-garde,* at least up to date. This building headquartered the last large canning operation in Harford County: Parker Mitchell began the family concern and, according to an 1897 history of the firm, Parker's son Evan and grandsons John S. and E. Lewis all became wealthy as "extensive growers and canners of sweet corn." In so doing, they (along with the Bakers, Osborns, and a few others) helped Harford gain preeminence as the leading canning county in America. So, after all, perhaps Perryman, the center of the Mitchells' canning empire, *would* be a good place to look for stylish buildings. At least one historian, for instance, has argued that this structure, with "its dark shingles, tapered columns and exposed rafters . . . has a slight flavor of 'California Mission' about it."

2-84

2-85. Union Chapel M.E. Church
700 Post Road
1918; Regular services   HA-1616

This simple country chapel represents the triumph of humanity's spiritual life over seemingly overwhelming obstacles. For 200 years Harford's rich tidewater farms were home to hundreds of black men and women, some free, some slave. But even the "free" blacks weren't really free: when Michaelsville's black Methodists, for instance, attended church, free and slaves were all herded up into the bal-

cony of the whites-only Garrison Chapel M. E. Church. By 1849, black communicants decided that that state of affairs had gone on long enough and built a church of their own about two miles southeast of Perryman. This church eventually proved too small and the congregation erected a replacement in the 1880s; then, for the convenience of those worshipers living closer to Bush River, the congregation built a chapel of ease near High Timber in 1894. Both sites were taken over by the federal government when Washington condemned the entire Bush River Neck in October 1917 for the Aberdeen Proving Ground. Forced to relocate, the displaced congregations bought the present site in 1918, and, under the direction of William B. Tildon, started work on this church building. On the inside, the tongue-and-groove dado and pressed-tin ceiling appear to be original, but the pews, floor, communion rail, and lectern are relatively modern, and evince the congregation's continued dynamism and prosperity.

2-86. Stump-Harlan House
862 Craigs Corner Road
c. 1845; Private
National Register   HA-204

Facing east, this two-story, coursed-stone house commands wide views of Deer Creek with the Susquehanna rolling on in the background. Dr. W. S. Forwood commented on the site in an 1880 installment of his "Homes on Deer Creek" series, sighing wistfully that the creek, "so rough and rugged" only a few yards away, "presents a changed aspect" here: "The rocks, trees and bushes are absent for a short distance and the smiling fields of rich verdure extend down the gentle slope to the banks of the Creek." John Stump of Stafford sold 222 acres of Lines Tents to his uncle Henry Stump Sr. in 1793 for "500 pounds current money of Maryland"; the metes and bounds description in the deed follows "the meanders of Elbow branch" in minute detail. Henry must have been put out with some of his children; when he died in 1814 his will somewhat snippily stated "having heretofore given to my 3 sons John, Henry and William and to my daughter Mary all that I intend to give them" the "whole tract whereon I now reside . . . together with the dwelling house" was to go to son Reuben. (Reuben also received his father's fishery on the Susquehanna and Rock Island in the river.) Reuben, wrote Dr. Forwood, "dwelt here in peace and content to the end of

2-85

2-86

2-86

a long life. Dying [in 1841] without children, the property came into the hands of his nephew Dr. David Harlan, U.S.N., of Churchville." (Dr. Harlan had been brought up in what is called the Henry Harlan House, 5-7; his mother was Esther Stump.) Forwood helpfully explained that the "old mansion burned . . . not long after the death of . . . Reuben Stump. A new stone building was erected upon the foundations of the old one," presumably by David Harlan. In designing the new house, which he rented to tenant farmers, David Harlan clearly chose to follow closely the county's architectural traditions— just compare it to older Stump houses nearby, such as Stafford and the Stump-Holloway House. Dr. Harlan's eventful life is explored elsewhere (see chapter 5); suffice it to say that

after he retired from the Navy he spent his latter years managing his several farms. When he died in 1893 he left this farm to son W. Beatty Harlan, who sold it out of the family in 1920. That last deed reserves the right to go to and from the old Stump family graveyard, an ancient, walled-in site where are interred dozens of those who, wrote Dr. Forwood (a lover of the bittersweet), "in life wielded much influence and power" yet "here they lie and are forgotten and yet the world still moves on." Among those buried here are John Stump of Stafford, both Reuben and Henry Stump, and Dr. Forwood and his grandparents William and Duckett Stump.

Bel Air, Fallston, Forest Hill, and Churchville

3-1. Medical Hall
Medical Hall Road
Early nineteenth century; Private
National Register   HA-3

When Medical Hall was listed in the National Register of Historic Places in 1973, the preparer of the form came right to the point, stating that "the importance of the Medical Hall complex centers around its historical associations with John Archer (1741–1810)." Archer, the first person in America to get a medical degree (1768), also earned distinction as a revolutionary patriot (signer of the Bush Resolution in 1774 and the Bush Declaration in 1775 and captain in the colonial army) and statesman (elected as a Jeffersonian congressman in 1802 and 1804). When he died he was, according to Judge Walter Preston's 1901 county history, "honored and respected by all who knew him. . . . His house near Churchville was at times like a medical college, so numerous were the young men who sought his tuition." Archer himself attended medical school in Philadelphia, easily the most sophisticated spot in America at the time, and his "house near Churchville," Medical Hall, is a fine example of the late-Georgian/federal manner of building he could have seen in the city along the Schuylkill: note the regular massing, the elaborate entrance with sidelights and transom, and the center-hall plan. (The extant house replaced an earlier one on the property; Archer's 1798 tax assessment indicates a much smaller building and the doctor probably incorporated that older house into the new one.) The hallway boasts panels of French scenic wallpaper with images of the French Revolution one of Archer's sons installed to mark the return visit of Lafayette in 1824. (Some feel the son built the existing house.) The grounds contain a prime archaeological site—the ruins of Dr. Archer's own medical school where he taught five of his own six sons as well as forty-five other young men in the healing arts.

3-2. Bon Air
2501 Laurel Brook Road
1794; Private
National Register; Harford County
Landmark   HA-6

Legends and fancies swirl around Bon Air, easily among Maryland's most intriguing architectural sites; the legends are, as Alexis Shriver wrote in 1937, "playing cards," which historians have used to "build our fragile house of romance at 'Bon Air.'" According to tradition, Claude François Frederick de la Porte, a French count and colonel "en second" in Lafayette's "Veinnois" regiment, passed through Harford County en route to Yorktown; he then settled in Santo Domingo, a French colony, understandably preferring living as a mercantile shipper to dealing with tumbrels and guillotines. But events caught up with him; Santo Domingo exploded in a slave rebellion in 1793 and de la Porte fled to America where on June 25, 1793, he and his wife, née Betsy Herbert, paid "600 pounds current money" for roughly 200 acres overlooking Laurel Brook. They then built this stuccoed stone house, as the datestone inscribed "FDLP 1794" attests. Bon Air's present owners, in their thorough research, are beginning to question the military portion of the tale, but everything else checks. The "French connection" is certainly there for de la Porte's *maison* is perhaps unique in Anglo-America in that it is thoroughly French from its basic form (especially the hipped roof) to its site plan (the outbuildings are placed to create a courtyard) to its construction details (the carpentry, joinery, and metal work suggest that de la Porte may have brought workmen with him from Santo Domingo). When the count died in 1797 he left "Betsy Herbert de la Porte,

3-1

3-2

3-3

3-4

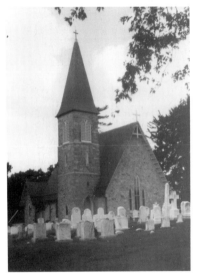

3-5

my faithful help mate and beloved wife" all his property for her life. She died in 1803 and everything passed to the builder's brother, Francis, and two sisters, Elizabeth and Joanna. The house and farm, expanded to over 330 acres, eventually ended up in the hands of a nephew, Pierre Lewis Auguste Marchand, who sold it for $3,000 in 1831. Bon Air, the recent beneficiary of a first-class restoration, stands today much as it must have two centuries ago, a bastion of *la civilisation français* in the American wilderness.

3-3. Walter's Mill
Walter's Mill Road
c. 1900; Private
National Register   HA-16

Where once there were dozens . . . For two centuries the Harford landscape was dominated by gristmills grinding grain grown by local farmers. At the end of the nineteenth century, however, technology—and the vast, flat fields of the Midwest—rendered the industry obsolete. A few former mills still stand, converted to domestic use (such as Whitaker's Mill and Noble's Mill) but still recognizable; still fewer remain in their original form (such as Rock Run Mill and Ivory Mill) but they are emasculated and do not, except for a few souvenir bags of flour ground for the tourist trade, actually function as they were intended. Walter's Mill, named for the family who has been running it since Charles S. Walter bought "the mill lot" from John Smith on November 22, 1911, is an exception in that it is a real, working mill. Milling has been carried on at this site since the mid-eighteenth century but the present two-story stone and frame structure was built to replace an earlier mill destroyed in a fire in 1900. Electricity now assists water as the power source but the wheels, blowers, dryers, and separators still turn out cornmeal and buckwheat flour under the undeniably true name of "Deer Creek's Best."

3-4. Spittle Craft
3023 Ady Road
1811; Private
National Register   HA-17

Traditionally associated with Walter's Mill across the road, this large brick and stone house suggests the economic success that grinders of corn and wheat once enjoyed (see also Jerusalem and the Carter-Archer House). The building is exceptionally well docu-

mented, thanks to letters written to and from various members of the Forwood family and now in the county historical society archives. Brothers John and Samuel Forwood built a mill on the Walter's Mill site shortly after they moved to Harford County from the Brandywine Valley at about the time of the Revolution. John sold his share to Samuel in 1790 and went on to excel in other endeavors: he farmed over 900 acres of land; he ran a stagecoach line between Baltimore and Chester County, Pennsylvania (and, not coincidentally, was president of the Conowingo Bridge Company, whose coffers were enriched by the stage line); he served as a justice of the peace at various times; and he represented the county in the House of Delegates from 1806 to 1820. He also had his slaves fire brick and build this center-hall house in 1811. John died in 1835 and his wonderfully thorough estate inventory makes it clear that his 2½-story house had a garret, a full second floor with several bedrooms, a hallway on the ground floor, a well-stocked library, outbuildings including a wagon house, granary, cornhouse, and meathouse, a main front and back cellar, and a kitchen front and back cellar. He left his son John C. and daughter Julian "the farm where they and I now live on the south side of Deer Creek" while other children (sons Parker, Jacob, and Amos) received other lands. (Evidently John and Julian did not get along; their father added a codicil describing a division line "to pass through the middle of the house . . . through the middle of the kitchen . . . to the lightning rod at the southwest part of the house." He even had to continue the line "through the water and meat house . . . then with a fence . . . to the eighth row of apple trees.") The house retains a vast amount of original material including its massing, brick cornices, and window arches, and, on the inside, stairway (with pegged rail and balusters) and simple mantels. In one of the letters mentioned above, the writer recalls the "bright red color" of the bricks, which disproves the current widely held belief that all nineteenth-century brick houses were painted.

3-5. Christ Episcopal Church
Rock Spring Road
1805; 1875; c. 1908; Regular services   HA-28

Organized in 1805, Christ Protestant Episcopal Church of Rock Spring Parish was originally served by the Reverend John Coleman from St. James, ten miles away on My Lady's

Manor. Mr. Coleman died in 1816 and is buried here. He is also memorialized by a marble tablet placed in the front wall of the building. That first structure was a plain, rectangular-plan edifice with clear glass windows and a low-pitch roof—a typical Harford County federal-era church (such as St. John's in Havre de Grace). In 1875 George Archer (1848–1920), a Churchville-born, Princeton-trained architect, gave the building a steeper (more "medieval") roof and in general reworked the church to bring it closer to the Gothic ideal, as James Wollon describes in the Spring 1993 *Harford Historical Bulletin.* The belltower was added in the twentieth century.

3-6. La Grange Furnace
204 Rocks Road
c. 1800; Private   HA-30

Despite its present pastoral appearance, for generations the area around the intersection of Rocks and St. Clair Bridge roads thrived as a center of iron industry. It all began around 1800 when Isaac Rogers migrated here from Chester County, Pennsylvania, bought about 2,000 acres of land, and, with his sons, Joseph, Ivan, and Stanley, began the La Grange community. It was a splendid site for the Rogerses' operations. Deer Creek provided water power. The forests could be burned for charcoal to turn the rich deposits of iron ore that underlay the land into bar iron others used to fashion the machinery that propelled America's Industrial Revolution. La Grange iron proved vital to the nation's interests and oral tradition maintains that iron from here was used to build the epochal ship *Monitor;* it proved vital to others as well, for it is documented that Baltimorean Ross Winans, under contract with Czar Nicholas I, relied on La Grange pig iron for the railroads he built from Moscow to St. Petersburg. The stuccoed stone house here, although somewhat altered, probably dates from the early Rogers era, as do various outbuildings including a stone warehouse, frame schoolhouse, stone privy, stone icehouse, and stone smokehouse. A two-story frame store may be somewhat later; its entrance (west) façade still faintly bears the shopkeeper's credo, ALL COUNTRY PRODUCE TAKEN IN EXCHANGE FOR MERCHANDISE. The foundry closed in 1886 but the store, run for a while by the Rutledge family, lingered on into this century.

3-7. St. Ignatius Church
533 East Jarrettsville Road
1792; with additions; Regular services
National Register   HA-41

The core of this rubblestone building (the three western bays) makes up the oldest Roman Catholic church in the archdiocese of Baltimore and one of the few known eighteenth-century Catholic churches in Anglo-America. In the colonial era English "anti-popery" laws curtailed the celebration of the mass; thus while Jesuit priests bought land here in 1779 it took Yorktown and the first amendment ("Congress shall make no law respecting the establishment of religion or prohibiting the free exercise thereof") to make it safe for them to erect churches. (The Jesuit order ran into financial difficulties in 1817 and the archbishop of Baltimore assumed control of the parish, a control exercised into the present day.) The south wing was added in 1822 as a priest's house; the church was lengthened to its present dimensions in 1848; the tower dates to 1865 and the sacristy to 1887. All these additions were carefully designed to blend in with the original church and the result reads as a single, uniform creation.

3-8. D.H. Springhouse
Sandy Hook Road
1816; Private
National Register; Harford County
Landmark   HA-44

Artisan David Hopkins built and signed (*D* and *H*) this amusing eccentricity, a building beloved of generations of county historians. In 1980, Hopkins's work prompted architect James Wollon to call the springhouse a "monument to the art of stonemasonry." A century earlier W. Stump Forwood, in his "Homes on Deer Creek" series, described Hopkins as "a celebrated stone mason of his day" and deemed the springhouse "a beautiful piece of stone work, known far and near." William Smithson, a nephew and namesake of Judge William Smithson who signed the Bush Declaration, hired Hopkins to construct this structure. The building was to have a utilitarian use, but instead of settling on a utilitarian form, Hopkins gave Smithson something that was both functional and fun: note the coursed ashlar walls, Ionic pilasters, arched entrance, shell-embellished lintels, and—most of all—pyramidal, ball-topped finial. The ground sto-

3-6

3-7

3-8

3-9

3-10

3-11

3-12

ry shelters the spring and also contains shelves so Smithson could keep perishable dairy products cool; the upper level contained a private, one-room school. Abandoned for years, the building was saved in the 1980s by Duncan MacKenzie, who bought it, restored it, and adapted into his stock brokerage office.

3-9. Gleeson House
2215 Allibone Road
c. 1860; Private
National Register   HA-43

Unprepossessing appearance and all, this two-section frame house plays an important role in the history of the county's architecture: during the nineteenth century most countians did not live in mansions like Fair Meadows; they lived in modest dwellings like this. Since most such places have disappeared (or have been altered beyond recognition), this rare survivor should be cherished and preserved. The rear wing in particular deserves protection as an example of log construction, a once-common manner of building with fewer and fewer extant samples. The front section is somewhat more "high style," with its sidehall entry and paneled porch posts. One "P. Gleeson" is shown living here on the county's 1878 Martenet map.

3-10. Preacher House
3031 Lochary Road
c. 1773; 1969; Private
National Register   HA-46

According to long-time Kalmia resident Annie Presbury, a free black stonemason surnamed Rumsey built this and five other similar houses in the area at the time of the Revolution. (Mrs. Presbury specifically dates this house to 1773; see also the Bussey House and the Preston Stone House.) This building serves as an instructive example of how an obviously skilled but presumably untrained artisan emulated more polished period structures: note particularly the difference between the clearly discernible quoining and the uncoursed rubblestone walls and how Rumsey used brick jack arches to add visual appeal and contrast. A modern frame addition extends to the west and south.

3-11. Preston Stone House
2802 Forge Hill Road
Early nineteenth century; Private
National Register   HA-47

While it is hard to assign a sure date to this modest vernacular stone house, it is clearly among the oldest standing structures in the community of Kalmia. It is also probably typical of the sort of house built by the workers at the nearby flint mill and forge that gave rise to the road's name and to the entire neighborhood. The 1878 Martenet map of the county shows "Jane Preston co'ld" living here; the 1858 county map indicates a building owned by "A. Greme," suggesting that it may have been a tenant (or slave) house for the (then-deceased) Angus Grême of Maiden's Bower. The one-room plan of the main section remains unchanged, adding to the house's historic importance, while the contrast between the simplicity of the rubblestone walls and the crude but still clear quoins and the brick jack arches suggests a well-defined aesthetic sense at work. Its simple form, use of local materials, and plain craftsmanship link it generally to other period vernacular dwellings, but it would be nice to determine what—if any—connections exist between the builder of this structure and the Preacher House, Archer-Hawkins House, and Bussey House.

3-12. Clark's Chapel M.E. Church
2001 Kalmia Road
1885; 1972; Regular services
National Register   HA-48

Black Methodists in the Kalmia area have been worshiping in a church on this site since before the Civil War but what the precursor(s) of this stuccoed stone building looked like is at present unknown. Northeast of the church is an ancient cemetery containing scores of ancient headstones, but with the exception of a few (one reads "Milky Gover, Died 1886, Age 77"), they are too weathered to be legible. The church was expanded in 1972; its old pointed-arch windows remain in place.

3-13. Thomas Run Church
(Watters Meetinghouse)
Thomas Run Road
c. 1840; Regular services
National Register; Harford County
Landmark   HA-49

One of the oldest Methodist-associated sites in America, the present simple stone church replaced a much older structure that probably dated to around 1780. County native William Watters (born 1751) converted to Methodism in 1771 and became one of the first itinerant preachers of the religion outside England. He also regularly conducted services at his brother Henry's house; Francis Asbury records attending a "powerful meeting at Henry Watters near Deer Creek" in 1772 and again in 1777. The first deed concerning a church here is dated 1782 and refers to "that lately erected house." The church's trustees, including silversmith Joseph Toy, Bernard Preston Sr. of The Vineyard, and William's brother Walter Watters, bought the land from Henry Watters and others for five shillings. No one knows what was then built or what happened to it, because the present church seems to date from the 1840s or '50s, although it follows early Methodist precepts in having simple lines and restrained details. Nonetheless, the building displays some awareness of current fashion in its Greek temple form (less portico) as well as in its Greek-influenced woodwork (exterior window and door trim, crown moldings, and, within, gallery and pulpit paneling). These Grecian overtones receive reinforcement from the building's setting, a serene and seemingly secluded hilltop with a view that has remained essentially unchanged for a century.

3-14. Archer-Hawkins House
2626 Thomas Run Road
c. 1850; 1866; Private
National Register   HA-51

Exemplifying Harford's larger-scale vernacular dwellings, the construction techniques apparent in this two-part stone house encourage comparison with several structures in the area both large (e.g., the Preacher House) and small (e.g., the Preston Stone House), sacred (the Watters Meetinghouse) and secular (the Bussey House). Mary Archer, wife of Dr. Robert H. Archer, bought 57½ acres here on July 1, 1846, and is shown owning a house on this site on the 1858 county map. Mrs. Archer probably built the three-bay, two-story house

still evident on the west façade of the expanded dwelling: its rubblestone walls peer out beneath a thinning coat of stucco and flat brick arches top the ground floor windows and door; chimney placement suggests a two-room, center-hall plan, each room warmed by an end-wall fireplace. On October 6, 1866, Mrs. Archer's heir, Hannah Archer, sold the same 57½ acres to William Hawkins for the very high price of $9,000. Hawkins is credited with adding a somewhat smaller section (also of rubblestone) to the north and, in a wooden door jamb at the entrance to this section, one can faintly make out some indecipherable initials and the date 1866.

3-15. Lochary Farm
1424 Thomas Run Road
Late eighteenth century (?); additions;
Private
National Register   HA-52

Several local sources believe that the center section of the present large frame house was standing at the time of the 1798 federal tax assessment. The land, a large tract called Leigh of Leighton, was investment property owned at various times by the prominent Morris family of Philadelphia, and, more locally, by members of the Presbury, Lee, and Archer clans. The Locharys took title in 1865 and remained here until 1961. They evidently added onto whatever older house was extant and, at various times, added onto their own additions; the north wing (c. 1930) is credited to county architect Alex Shaw, but other changes lack attribution. There is an attractive rubblestone and frame bank barn southwest of the house.

3-16. Bruggeman House
2390 Churchville Road
Late eighteenth century; Private   HA-116

Owned by various members of the Harlan family from 1849 until 1922, this gambrel-roofed frame house is thought to date to the 1798 tax assessment. It certainly has stylistic peers that old; note the Hays House in Bel Air and the Griffith-Wright House and Poplar Hill near Aberdeen. This house's corner chimneys, however, make it somewhat unusual. The gambrel roof was a very practical form: it gives almost as much second-floor headroom as a two-story house but is less costly to build; moreover, tax assessors generally noted a size difference and owners of 1½-story houses paid

3-13

3-14

3-15

3-16

3-17

3-18

3-19

less in taxes than owners of two-story houses did. The house, deteriorated seemingly beyond repair and swarming with termites, faces an uncertain future. If it is demolished, one hopes that the fine paneling on the east room's fireplace wall will be saved.

3-17. Tudor Hall
Tudor Lane
1847; Private
National Register; Historic American
Buildings Survey   HA-117

Tudor Hall is best known as the home of the Booth family but even without their fame (and infamy) the structure would be of national importance because of its architecture. It was one of the earliest Gothic revival cottages in Maryland and remains one of the finest examples of the style in America. Junius Brutus Booth (1796–1852), a noted Shakespearian actor, emigrated to Maryland from England in the 1820s and leased this tract of land in 1824. He had a log house moved here in which he and his family lived until 1847 when he began the present house. Booth had seen William Ranlett's book, *The Architect,* one of several "How to build your own Gothic fantasy" publications popular among sophisticated folk in the 1840s and '50s. Booth admired one design (No. XVII) and set to work copying it. The result, Tudor Hall, was all any romantic could have wished for: the painted brick cottage has a cross plan enlivened by a cluster of shaped chimneys, windows of varying sizes, balconies here, and porches there. For a fuller discussion of this most important structure, see chapter 6.

3-18. Hidden Brook
522 Thomas Run Road
c. 1785; Private   HA-130

Although much added on to over the years, the original 2½-story stone portion of this house is not only easily discernible, it is also one of the finest structures of its type and time in the county, comparable to Gibson's Park near Emmorton. Around 1680 the Irishman John Hays emigrated to Maryland, purportedly with his cousin John Archer; both men began families that proved of immeasurable importance to Harford and Cecil counties. Hays's son John (c. 1720–1802) built this side-hall/double parlor house on the tract, called Uncle's Good Will. The compilers of the 1783 Maryland tax list noted Hays as owning 361

acres here and the 1798 federal tax assessors credited him with a "30 feet by 24 feet two story stone" house (as well as a frame kitchen, stables, outhouse, and stone springhouse). The house's plan, granite windowsills and lintels, and some interior trim (notably the stairway) all almost certainly date to John Hays's ownership. Hays left "the stone part of the dwelling house" to his wife for her life; on her death it was to go to son John Jr. (Another son, Archer Hays [1755–1827], went off to build the Hays-Heighe House in 1808.) Thomas Archer Hays (born 1780) eventually acquired this property. His 1861 estate inventory suggests what the major rooms were and how they were furnished: parlor (with "7 Japanned waiters"), sitting room (with a virtual ton of mahogany), stair and passage ("carpet, rods, and matting"), large breakfast room (with a settee), breakfast room, and six "chambers" (one with a "Yankee clock"). The garret had "lot of old bedsteads" and the cellar had "old barrels." The property left the Hays family in 1895. North of the house, the huge barn (it covers 4,000 square feet) ranks as one of Harford's better known agrarian landmarks.

3-19. Cain-McGuirk House
Thomas Run Road
c. 1800; 1817; 1939; 1954; Private
National Register   HA-133

Thomas White, one of colonial Maryland's more successful entrepreneurs, owned over 7,000 acres of land in Harford County. His most famous tract today is Sophia's Dairy near the Bush River. His holdings sprawled into the upper reaches of the county, too, and included this large patent called Leigh of Leighton. White probably viewed these upland farms as speculative ventures, and it is doubtful if he built anything on this particular tract. James Cain bought 130 acres from White's daughter Mary in 1783 and almost certainly began the present dwelling. A frame Cain house is cited in the 1798 tax rolls; described as one story tall and measuring 25 by 20 feet, it probably forms part of the present southeastern wing. (If so, it was covered in stone and absorbed into that wing in the early nineteenth century.) While one of James's sons is memorialized in a stained glass window at St. Ignatius Church, this house is primarily valuable not for whatever ancient Cain associations may exist but for its more recent expansions. The first of these (the long middle section) dates to the 1930s and the tenure of Mr.

and Mrs. Robert H. Sayre III; the second may be credited to the present owners, Mr. and Mrs. William McGuirk. Both the Sayres' and the McGuirks' additions are splendid successes in that they provide comforts necessary to modern, large-scale family life but are stylistically compatible with the older dwelling.

3-20. Ruff's Chance

2330 Thomas Run Road
c. 1800; Private
National Register   HA-134

Ruffs have lived in this substantial, if restrained, Flemish bond brick house since about the time of Thomas Jefferson's presidency. That may sound impressive, but the family has continuously owned the land a good deal longer—in fact the Ruffs have been here since Richard Ruff patented 650 acres hereabouts in 1684. A generation later, in 1714, Lord Baltimore issued a confirmatory grant; two generations later, in 1798, "Henry Ruff's heirs" were assessed for two small tracts improved by four small frame buildings, while Richard Ruff owned 808 acres with a "28 × 18 frame house, kitchen 22 × 18 (stone)" and several outbuildings. Richard died in 1812, leaving his property to the children of his brother, Henry, and they probably built the federal-style house; the wing to the north was added a few years later. A stone springhouse on the property probably dates to the eighteenth century.

3-21. Maiden's Bower

(Grême House)
Cool Spring Road
c. 1793; Private
National Register   HA-136

Harford County is today generally known for its conservatism and the prideful provincialism of its residents. How surprised many current citizens would be by the international flavor of the air here two centuries ago, when Frenchmen routinely bought and sold land in the Bel Air area and built themselves houses. The saga of Bon Air is well known, but the history of Maiden's Bower loses nothing in comparison. Lafayette marched his troops though the county in the spring of 1781 en route to Yorktown; one of the young marquis's aides was Col. J. J. de Gimat; one of his captains was Angus Grême. (There must be a story behind the name Angus.) The two officers, great friends, both fell in love with the Deer Creek Valley and vowed to return after the

war. And, astonishingly, they did. Grême, reportedly funded by de Gimat, began buying land here in 1793—66 acres for £375 on September 27, and 300 acres for £487 on October 14; then on February 29, 1796, he paid "William Paca of Annapolis" 3,800 pounds (whether tobacco or currency is not clear) for 465 acres "on Deer Creek." Grême finished building the present stone house in time for the 1798 tax assessors, who show "Angus Graham" with 860 acres and a two-story, 30-foot-square stone house, which corresponds to the central section of the present dwelling. (Investigation of the roof rafters suggests that the original roof may have been hipped, a configuration certainly more French than the present gable covering.) Career soldier de Gimat returned to France and was killed on the field of battle, but Grême has remained along his beloved shores of Deer Creek: he died at Maiden's Bower in 1800 and is buried at the old Trap Church cemetery, where one can still see his aged tombstone, inscribed in part, "Captain in the French Army Under Lafayette." Whatever pleasant understanding existed between the two soldiers then exploded in massive and Gaelic legal complications between Grême's heirs here and de Gimat's in Bordeaux (including the wonderfully named James Calixtus Michael de Leyrits), but matters were finally settled in 1822 when Stevenson Archer of nearby Medical Hall bought the property. Grême's sword has been passed down among members of the Allen family and Grême's house remained in the Archer family until the present owners took title in 1968.

3-22. Parker Hall Lee House

(Cool Spring)
2505 Cool Spring Road
c. 1780; additions; Private
National Register   HA-137

In 1718 James Lee (died c. 1743) moved north from Anne Arundel County and acquired 300 or so acres of Friendship, a tract near Bush River. His numerous descendants include great-grandson Parker Hall Lee (1759–1829), a Revolutionary War hero who amassed vast holdings in the Cool Spring area and, according to tradition, began both this house and the house known as Jericho (now ruins). This house consists of two stuccoed stone sections, both 2½ stories tall, both with gable roofs, both with a sidehall plan, similarities that make it all but impossible to determine which section was built when. Lee's estate inventory

3-20

3-21

3-22

3-23

3-24

3-25

makes it clear that he lived in some style (note items such as looking glasses, eight-day clocks, an "old High-post Bedstead," five gallons of apple brandy, and a keg of a then-fashionable punch called Bounce) and conducted extensive farming operations. Outbuildings included a granary, barn, cornhouse, sawmill, and "barrick," with quantities of hay kept "above Sam's House" and "in Old House." Lees are shown living here on the 1858 and 1878 county maps, but the farm left the family in 1913. In the 1920s and '30s it formed a part of Donald Symington's vast Indian Spring holdings.

3-23. Homelands
Priestford Road
1806; with additions; Private   HA-139

Homelands, begun by John Herbert in 1806 and continuously owned by members of the Herbert-Harlan family, is by all accounts the manor house of Churchville. A case could be made to grant that distinction jointly to the Finney houses but they are off to the northeast hidden by trees, while Homelands, crowning the brow of its own hill, visually dominates the village. Herbert's original house, with a sidehall/double parlor plan, forms the western (or left) three bays of the present dwelling, a house that has evolved through succeeding generations. Dr. David Harlan (1809–93, who married Herbert's granddaughter in 1846) added the easterly two bays (another double parlor) and widow's walk around 1870, while the doctor's son William Beatty Harlan added the porch and leaded glass windows in the early years of this century. Dr. Harlan's career gained him national renown: he studied medicine under Dr. John Archer Jr. of Rock Run, then joined the Navy. He sailed around the world several times, the most memorable trip being his first, made in the 1830s when, as his extant diary reveals, he aided in obtaining treaties with such exotic potentates as the Sultan of Muscat and the King of Siam; in India four men "carried [him] about all day . . . in a silk-cushioned palanquin"; in Borneo he observed "head-hunting savages" and collected "water snakes of strange colors and shapes." He later saw service in the Mexican and Civil wars, was responsible for building Holy Trinity Church near his farm, and eventually retired to Churchville in 1871 with the rank of Medical Director of the Navy. The inventory made at Homelands after his death cites a "Library, Dining Room, Parlor," and five bedrooms in the house. The doctor rather sweetly

left each of his sons "a cabinet of shells and curiosities collected by me in my travels."

3-24. The Land
(Thorn Meadow)
317 Priestford Road
Essentially 1930s; Private   HA-140

Although the center section of the present dwelling probably dates to the nineteenth century when the farm was owned by generations of the George Smith family, the house gained its general appearance—and its most illustrious owners—after 1933 when Russell and Kate Lord bought the small farm. The Lords were among the leading ecologists (although they wouldn't have liked that cumbersome word) of their time: he edited *Land* magazine, was on the staff of the *New Yorker,* and wrote bestselling farm preservation books such as *Forever the Land,* while she illustrated his works with delicate yet evocative pen-and-ink drawings. The Lords more than doubled the size of the old house, built a variety of outbuildings, and gave the place the pleasing "twentieth-century country manor" feeling that, despite changes to structure and setting, it has managed to retain.

3-25. Waffle Hill Farm
3332 Cool Branch Road
c. 1840; additions; Private
National Register   HA-145

Although hard to pinpoint as to exact age, it seems likely that this handsome sidehall/double parlor house was built by a grandson of Samuel Chase, signer of the Declaration of Independence. Chase's daughter Eliza married Skipwith Coale and the couple lived at Westwood Manor. Coale died in 1832 and left the estate to his wife and, on her death, to their four children "in the rank of seniority"; the real estate consisted of two farms, Westwood ("the home farm") and this apparently unimproved tract called the Hartley Farm. Final division took place in 1856, when son Samuel Chase Coale received the northern portion of Hartley. Since his deed reads "which I now occupy," one assumes that the house was standing and that it was built between Skipwith's death and the final division. Samuel Chase Coale quickly ran into financial trouble and his brother Isaac W. Coale had to buy the house from him in 1858 for $3,000. Isaac Coale (1823–1904), educated in Baltimore, enjoyed success at farming and also served as chief judge of the Harford County Orphan's Court; his descendants continued to live here until 1960. In proportion and in detail, the Coale house ranks among the finest of its time in the county and its plan suggests an urbane, well-traveled mind, even though the question of *whose* mind remains unclear.

3-26. Cox-Davis-Barnes House
1000 Glenville Road
c. 1760 (?); Private
National Register   HA-147

In 1751 William Cox took out a writ of *ad quod damnum* on the stream that flows just east of this stone house and stone kitchen. Cox then built a mill, and both mill and miller gained enough local prominence to be used to help settle a boundary question in 1770 (one was a physical landmark, one provided testimony). But even though Cox certainly built the mill, no one knows if he built this house and kitchen. One could argue yes: he died in 1782, leaving one-third of his estate to his widow for life and two-thirds to their son, William Cox Jr.; the property in question consisted of "the houses . . . grist mill, malt house, brew house, saw mill, and houses contiguous thereto." (Regrettably, the usually helpful 1798 and 1814 tax rolls shed no light on whether any of *those* houses is *this* house.) Cox junior died in 1833 after a long illness. In 1835 his property was sold to settle the estate and a February 26, 1835, newspaper ad for the sale notes a "THREE STORY STONE MILL" and several subsidiary frame structures; it also notes "conveniently situated to the GRIST MILL, a comfortable STONE DWELLING HOUSE with a STONE KITCHEN in good repair . . . and as healthy a situation as any in the county." George C. Davis bought the property and the 1858 county map shows his mill on Cool Branch with two other buildings (presumably the house and kitchen) nearby across the stream. The stream, which meanders northerly from Churchville to Deer Creek, is still called Mill Brook to commemorate the Cox-Davis mill. In the 1960s and early '70s this was the home of Nancy Webster Barnes, a highly regarded landscape architect.

3-27. Oak Farm
517 Glenville Road
1821; Private
National Register   HA-149

Harford County, while generally quiet and low key, is nonetheless able to boast of a few

families who have gained national renown. The seafaring Rodgerses are certainly one, and the Finneys, famed in ecclesiastical and medical circles, are another. The local progenitor of this illustrious clan, William Finney (1788–1873), graduated from Princeton in 1809 and then took up the Presbyterian ministry. In 1813 he was asked to come to take charge of the languishing parish at what was called Herbert's Crossroads and he did so. He revived the congregation, built a new brick church, and gave the village the new name of Churchville. He also began buying land (eventually running to dozens of deeds for hundreds of acres) and built this superlative stone house, named, according to grandson Dr. John M. T. Finney in *A Surgeon's Life,* for the "beautiful spreading oak tree" under which the young minister ate a refreshing lunch "on a very hot day [while] on his way to take charge of the church." The 2½-story fieldstone house is replete with elegant and original flourishes rare in Harford at the time: interior and exterior woodwork (mantels, doors, cornices, and so on) has only a figurative handful of county peers while the stone beltcourse on the main façade and the blind windows (put in solely for their decorative effect) on the west wall may well be locally unique. Pride may be a deadly sin, and taking pride in men of the cloth may be doubly deadly, but Harford has for generations taken pride in the enduring accomplishments of the Finneys.

3-28. Hays-Heighe House
(Prospect Hill)
1808; Open business hours
Harford Community College;
National Register   HA-152

When John Hays died in 1802 he left his 1½-story stone house (now Hidden Brook) to his eldest son, John Jr., and left his other children to fend for themselves. One younger son, Archer Hays (1755–1827), seems to have done quite nicely indeed and his success at farming enabled him to build this handsome granite dwelling, a house larger than his father's. The names of Hays's masons are unknown but the men were clearly masters of their trade, for they expertly laid the buff-colored stone walls and carefully crafted the window and door openings. (Some scholars, but not the author, feel that the similarities between this building and the D.H. Springhouse suggest that the same artisan built both structures.) Hays had

3-26

3-27

3-28

3-29

3-30

3-31

five sons and left this house to the eldest, Thomas A. Hays (1780–1861), who lived here while he nearly single-handedly turned the struggling hamlet called Bel Air into a full-fledged village. In the 1920s and '30s, Anne McElderry Heighe, herself a Hays descendent, used the rich fields around the house to pasture her herd of magnificent Thoroughbreds, as discussed in chapter 8. In the 1960s the community college gently adapted the house's 4,000 square feet of floor space into offices, carefully preserving the old floors, staircase, woodwork, and hardware.

3-29. Norris-Stirling House
(Mount Pleasant)
Ring Factory Road
c. 1804; c. 1936; Private
National Register   HA-153

Two completely different manners of building are here fused together beautifully and smoothly. In 1803 Aquilla Norris sold 73 acres here to his son Rhesa, who then built the original section of the present house. By then the Norris family had been building stone houses in the Winters Run Valley for a century and young Norris seems to have been ready to experiment. While his ancestors favored "British Cabins," a vernacular building form typified by Prospect about a mile to the south, Rhesa Norris abandoned that ancient building's one-room plan and instead erected a house whose fieldstone shell may look as if it came from the 1740s but whose sidehall/parlor plan was very up to date. The woodwork, too, is stylish and the elegant open string stair, with halfpace landings and delicate balusters, deserves particular attention. The house remained in the family until 1892. In 1936 Amelia Prescott Stirling and her husband, Campbell Lloyd Stirling, purchased the house and 45 acres; they hired Baltimore architect Lawrence Ewald, a man thoroughly familiar with Harford's building traditions, to restore the old dwelling and to add touches such as a kitchen, bathroom, maid's room, two porches, and a garage necessary for twentieth-century living.

3-30. Olney
1001 Old Joppa Road
1810; 1850; c. 1914; Private
National Register   HA-154

Nothing at Olney is quite what one expects. Even the name may come as a surprise, for the tract, during much of its existence, wasn't called Olney at all; it was called Prospect. Edward Norris patented the farm under that name in 1705 and John Norris built the oldest house on the place around 1765. The Norrises were happy in that small stone cabin until 1810 when John Saurin Norris, "on whom by industry and marriage, greater fortune had smiled" (wrote historian J. Alexis Shriver), decided to build a 2½-story, five-bay, center-hall, federal-style brick house about 200 yards from the old dwelling. In 1850 both houses left the Norris family when Mr. and Mrs. Josiah Lee bought the farm; they ignored the stone cabin and added a rather ungainly formal parlor onto the brick house. Then in 1861 Joseph A. Shriver, looking for an investment that would help him safely ride out the vicissitudes of the Civil War, bought the farm and added the porch that still wraps around the west and north façades, a summer kitchen, and, to square off the Lees' parlor, a smoking room.

Olney's modern era began in 1890 when Joseph Shriver died and left the property to his son J. Alexis. Shriver, among the most interesting individuals (two key words when speaking of Olney) ever to live in Harford County, successfully turned his active mind to history, farming, scientific innovation, landscape gardening, and biography—and to architecture, for he gave Olney its well-known present appearance by adding columns from the demolished Baltimore Athenaeum to the house's garden façade.

3-31. Holy Trinity Episcopal Church
Level Road
1878; Regular services   HA-167

The Reverend Edward A. Colburn, rector here from 1867 to 1903, had the rare ecclesiastical treat of being able to build two churches for his parish. Actually, he even founded the parish. In all these ventures he was aided by Dr. David Harlan, USN (Harlan lived nearby at Homelands; when he deeded part of the farm to the church, he said he hoped it would be "a slight manifestation of profound gratitude to Almighty God for many great mercies vouchsafed to him during many years"). Harlan and Colburn persuaded the Episcopal diocese of Maryland to establish a Churchville parish in 1867; they also selected this site and hired local architect William Reasin to design the new building, which Dr. Harlan quietly paid for. Reasin's frame country Gothic church burned to the ground in December 1877. One month later, Dr. Harlan assembled a new building committee, which hired George Archer to design the present building. Archer, a Princeton-trained, Harford-born architect who practiced in Baltimore, evidently had had enough of fires and specified that the new church be built of stone. Regarding style, Archer, guided by Colburn and Colburn's great friend, the Reverend W. F. Brand of St. Mary's, kept the new building firmly within the Gothic guidelines approved by the Ecclesiological movement, as is discussed in chapter 6. The church's low, thick, buttressed walls and tall lancet-arched windows successfully achieve their builders' aims of suggesting a Perpendicular Gothic church in a rural English parish. Thanks to the generosity of the Harlans the parish's very complete records have been preserved in the Historical Society of Harford County.

3-32. Brooks End Farm
Harmony Church Road
1847; Private
National Register   HA-162

Blessed with a strikingly beautiful setting—with wide vistas north toward and across Deer Creek—this stone house has resolutely resisted the twentieth century. Credit for the house, and for most of the buildings along this "Cookville" stretch of Harmony Church Road, goes to Elisha Cook and his son George. The senior Cook purchased this forty-four-acre tract for $305 on May 7, 1847, and then, it is thought, hired local masons to construct the house. They were superb artisans; the stone work—carefully laid, precisely cut, and set off by notable quoins and lintels—is exemplary. When Cook died in 1859, he left this portion of his farm to son George; son Joel received an adjacent 96-acre tract, son Samuel an adjacent 92-acre tract. A good Quaker, Elisha took pains in his will to specify that the "volumes of 'The Friends Review' [would be] bound and distributed among my children." (Equally devout George, called on to appraise the personal property of Thomas Stump in 1859, took the list, which someone else prepared, saw that it included three slaves, and with bold strokes of his pen Xed out the slaves and wrote "I do not place value on slaves.") When George Cook died in 1873 he left his wife "half the dwelling house in which I now reside," and it clearly was a two-story house for there is mention of "stair carpet." He also divided the Cookville industrial property among his children. In this century, this

house was the home of Lloyd Weaver, a stonemason of considerable note and a celebrated landscape painter.

3-33. Graham-Crocker House
30 North Main Street
c. 1825; Private
National Register; Bel Air Landmark   HA-214

One of the oldest buildings still standing in Bel Air, this 2½-story frame house provides a sense of domesticity rare in the town's commercial center. One Henry Foy paid $57 for this lot in 1824; he sold off the western half of the lot and then, in 1831, sold the remaining half "where Foy now resides" for $300, which certainly suggests that the house was built in the interim. Foy's house had a sidehall/double parlor plan embellished by simple wooden trim within and without. At some point, an unknown owner added a shed wing to the side (south); this room became a kitchen and it was from here that, in the 1930s, the house's owners, sisters Clara Pue Graham and Berthenia Pue Crocker, operated their still-famous tea room, drawing clients from as far away as Philadelphia. In the 1980s attorneys John Clark and John Love successfully adapted the house to law office use.

3-34. Harford County Courthouse
Main Street
1858; 1904; c. 1980; Open business hours
National Register; Bel Air Landmark   HA-218

Occupying a block in the middle of Bel Air, this much-expanded building forms the heart of the entire county and, in a sense, symbolizes the history of the county as well. (Many would suggest it also symbolizes the steady deterioration in Harford's architecture.) The courthouse is easily the most important building in Bel Air; it is the reason for the town's existence and the cause of its continued prosperity. The first courthouse, built around 1790, burned in February 1858. The county's officialdom immediately set about rebuilding, organizing a committee consisting of Stevenson Archer, Henry S. Harlan, William H. Dallam, and others. The committee chose architect J. Crawford Neilson as "consulting architect" for the new work and Neilson produced a restrained Italianate structure of great dignity. Little of his work remains, however (although his 1858 courtroom is largely intact on the second story) because of twentieth-century remodelings. In 1904 J. A. Dempwolf of York,

3-32

3-33

3-34

3-35

3-36

3-37

Pennsylvania, designed remarkably sensitive neoclassical additions for the front and rear, resulting in an overall H-shaped plan. The result was a satisfying and coherent whole. The new wing (not shown here) was designed by the Baltimore firm of Meyer, Ayers, Saint, Stewart, Inc.

3-35. Van Bibber House
303 South Main Street
1789; with additions; Private
Bel Air Landmark   HA-224

Once, not so very long ago, each of the four corners of this busy intersection boasted a c. 1800 house. This venerable building, a rambling structure of considerable charm, is the sole survivor and has stalwartly stood its ground while its contemporaries and neighbors have succumbed to the wrecking ball. How venerable it is is a relative question, and on those terms the answer is "very" for it is the oldest structure in Bel Air on its original site. (The Hays House, its senior by just a few months, was moved.) The original house here, three bays wide, two stories tall, with Flemish bond brick walls and a sidehall/parlor plan, forms the northern (or left) section of the much-expanded structure. The slightly taller clapboard section to the south (containing a single room per floor) was up by 1800. The enlarged dwelling then embarked on its busy history: in the 1850s it housed Miss Davenport's (Female) Seminary; from 1883 until 1907 it was, in effect, the Presbyterian manse, for the Reverend Ebenezer Finney purchased the place in fee simple and lived here with his family; from 1907 until 1979 various members of the Van Bibber family owned it; and, in the late 1980s the old spaces were outfitted for their present commercial use.

3-36. Hays House
324 South Kenmore Avenue
c. 1788; with additions; 1960; Regularly open
National Register; Harford County
Landmark   HA-225

A building of several (if subtle) distinctions, this is both the oldest structure of any type in Bel Air and the possessor of the town's only gambrel roof. Current research suggests that one John Bull began the house after he bought the lots (numbers 39 and 41) on April 3, 1788. Bull sold the property on September 23, 1789, and the difference in price (£54 in 1788 and £150 a year later) suggests that he had im-

proved the land with the three-bay, 1½-story frame dwelling with a sidehall plan and one room per floor that forms the northern two-thirds of the present building. Thomas Hays, "father of Bel Air," bought the house in 1811 and added two bays to the left. Later in the century, members of the Hays and Jacobs family built a large, two-story stone wing, dwarfing the old house. In the late 1950s the property was purchased by the Safeway grocery store chain, which threatened to demolish the rambling residence; led by Paul Hicks, members of the Historical Society of Harford County moved the frame section to its present site, spruced it up, and opened it as a house museum. (The stone addition was then demolished for the store.)

3-37. McKinney-Graybeal House
West Gordon Street
c. 1830; Private
National Register   HA-229

Bel Air owes its existence to politics and to the handmaiden trades of newspaper publishing and innkeeping. Thus it is highly fitting that this house, one of the most distinguished in or near the town, was built by a man prominent in such circles. John McKinney bought 92 acres here in 1828 for the ridiculously low figure of $554. (He bought an additional 100+ acres in 1843.) McKinney managed the Union Tavern for town boss Thomas Hays, and served as postmaster in the 1820s and '30s; McKinney also edited the weekly paper, the *Independent Citizen,* which he cofounded in 1828 at least partly to boost the presidential candidacy of his hero, John Quincy Adams. The paper moved to Port Deposit in 1836, but McKinney stayed on here in his handsome brick house. It is a curious house, too, for it manages to be at once stylish and conservative. It is stylish in its detailing—America was in the throes of the Greek revival in the 1820s and McKinney gave his house such *au courant* Greek features as a pedimented entrance porch and temple-suggesting mantels—but conservative in overall massing. If it had been built in one of the real boom areas of its era, such as upstate New York, Mississippi, or Ohio, it would have been shaped like a temple, complete with massive columned portico. Is this a mark of McKinney's conservatism or the county's? McKinney moved to Washington, D.C., and sold the property in 1853. Since 1961 the house has been owned by members of the Eugene Graybeal family, who have restored and maintained this important, and telling, structure.

3-38. Liriodendron
West Gordon Street
1898; Regularly open
National Register   HA-230

The year 1889 was busy for Howard Atwood Kelly: fresh from the University of Pennsylvania's medical school, he accepted the chairmanship of the gynecology and obstetric department of the newly founded Johns Hopkins Hospital and, fresh from a bicontinental romance, he wed Olga Elizabeth Laetitia Bredow in the cathedral of her native Danzig. The Kellys then settled into a large brownstone on Eutaw Place in Baltimore with summer escapes, after 1891, to a rustic camp in Ontario. This regimen didn't wholly suit the cosmopolitan Mrs. Kelly, who longed for something to evoke the elegant summers of her European past. Liriodendron is the result. At the suggestion of Hopkins colleague Dr. John M. T. Finney, in 1897 the Kellys bought a 196-acre tract in Harford County and hired Baltimore architect J. B. Noel Wyatt to design this stucco and marble, terracotta and limestone neoclassical palace. They named the estate to honor the majestic tulip poplar trees (*Liriodendron tulipifera*) that still tower over the site and shade the house. Here Dr. and Mrs. Kelly brought up their nine children—happy, golden times recounted by son "Fritz" Kelly years later: "We all had ponies and carts, or horses, and in the mornings we would gather and decide what we were going to do. If we left in the morning, we might not return until time for the evening meal." Since 1980 Liriodendron has been owned by the county and open to the public: a photographic exhibit on Dr. Kelly fills the former library and music room while the rest of the house serves as a popular backdrop for weddings and other festivities that, as Dr. Kelly would have wished, celebrate life.

3-39. First Presbyterian Church
(Odd Fellows' Lodge)
21 Pennsylvania Avenue
1852; Private
National Register   HA-238

That this is a unique structure underscores Harford County's innate architectural conservatism. The county enjoyed rapid population growth and economic development between 1820 and 1860, years that saw the full-flowering of the Greek revival in America as the country effervesced with thoughts of Athenian democracy; towns were christened Troy or Syracuse or Athens; little temples dotted the landscape—temple-form houses, temple-form banks, temple-form churches, even temple-form privies, any use was all right for the inside as long as the outside suggested that Aristotle or Plato or Homer might suddenly appear. One would think that Harford County would boast its share of temples, yet this is the only one. But it is a good one: its Doric portico is well executed; the overall form is correct; the proportions are pleasing. That there was an architect involved, probably someone from Baltimore, seems obvious, but his name is not known. The original client is known and the little temple was built not to house sacrificial offerings to Zeus or celebratory rites to Aphrodite, but for the First Presbyterian Church. It must have been a moment of wild abandon for them but they had sufficiently recovered their propriety by 1881 when they hired county native George Archer to design a new, proper Gothic church for them on Main Street. The abandoned temple was then host to a variety of uses—it was even the scene of a professional prize fight—until the Odd Fellows leased the premises.

3-38

3-39

3-40

3-40. Proctor House
54 East Gordon Street
1865; 1884; Private
National Register; Bel Air Landmark HA-258

This board-and-batten cottage, along with Linwood, stands as Harford's frame contribution to what might be termed the "anti-classical" movement of the mid-nineteenth century. (Tudor Hall is the masonry contribution.) Andrew Jackson Downing led the crusade; indeed, his followers were possessed of an almost religious militancy. Downing (1815–52) was a landscape gardener and architectural critic who tried to woo Americans from Jeffersonian classicism and Greek revival temples locally typified by the First Presbyterian Church (now the Odd Fellow's Lodge) on Pennsylvania Avenue. Not an architect himself, Downing published the designs of others such as Richard Upjohn and A. J. Davis in best-selling books, including *Cottage Residences* (1842). The Proctor House's rhythmic siding, steeppitched gable roof, ornamented bargeboards and finials, and porch brackets were all elements of this nationwide campaign. It is

3-41

3-42

thought that Cassandra Gilbert built the original sections of the house, which stand to the right in this photograph; a generation or so later C. W. Proctor bought the little cottage and extended it to the west, carefully maintaining the trim, siding, and roofline. Inside, the painted slate mantel in the east room and the fat, faceted Gothic newel post merit attention. Proctor's descendants maintained this important building until the board of education bought it in 1965; it now houses offices.

3-41. Union Chapel
1012 Old Joppa Road
1900; Regular services   HA-265

Generations ago, Harford's citizens displayed an ecumenical, open-armed spirit worthy of Vatican II, a spirit that drove the early history of this church. In 1821, with the blessing of the Maryland General Assembly, a group of seven men incorporated themselves as the Union Chapel. Of these original trustees, two were Methodists (including Rhesa Norris), three were Episcopalians (John Norris of Olney, among them), and two (including Ralph Sackett Lee of Jerusalem) were Quakers. They then built a one-story gable-roofed structure in which all these sects (as well as members of the Christian Church) could and did worship freely. That little building, moved to the Smith Magness farm in 1948, was log covered in clapboard. One early description notes that the pulpit was inscribed with the words "How Amiable Are Thy Tabernacles, Oh, Lord of Hosts" and that there were wooden benches "so rigidly upright as to guarantee complete wakefulness." This amiable unity lasted until the congregations grew rich enough to be self-supporting, move away, and start their own separate churches. By 1834 the Episcopalians had withdrawn to Kingsville and Bel Air, the Quakers to Fallston, and the Christians to Franklinville, leaving the Methodists in sole possession of the little chapel. Plans for the present church building, largely underwritten by members of the Archer family, date to 1899 and call for pine sheathing and cypress shingles "sawed fancy"; Baltimore contractor James L. Norwood & Son built the church following the specifications of Harry M. Norwood; dedication services were held March 25, 1900.

3-42. Claggett's Forest
Hollingsworth Road
c. 1820; Private   HA-266

For generations the Winters Run Valley was Hollingsworth country. The family at one time owned roughly 1,000 acres here, which they filled with farms, gristmills, wheel factories, and other lucrative industries. They called their empire Claggett's Forest. According to family tradition Nathaniel Hollingsworth moved here from Chester County, Pennsylvania, in 1806, and built the small house nearby (3-43) while waiting for this larger residence to be constructed. (The house reflects the Hollingsworths' Chester County origins since it so firmly resembles houses there, particularly the four-bay, two-door front.) The 1814 tax rolls list Hollingsworth as owning several houses and other buildings all of wood and all generally described as "very sorry" or "old" so a new stone house may have appealed. Hollingsworth died in 1834 and his fascinating will suggests that the present house was finished. He left his wife, Abigail, a yearly stipend as well as free use of certain rooms "in the house which I now occupy," that is, "our lodging room and the room over it, the western division of the cellar and a free passage thereto . . . our front parlor, [and] kitchen," the last two rooms to be used "in common with [their son] Nathaniel." The large Claggett's Forest tract was then divided among the children (Nathaniel had a plat prepared in the 1820s for this eventuality): sons Eli, Nathaniel Jr., and John each received various 100+-acre parcels as did daughters Hannah (Carter) and Abigail, assuming the children provided stipulated services for their mother. (Eli was to give her "wheat flour"; milk, firewood, pork, and bacon were to come from Nathaniel; John was to "convey her to meeting.") He also left instructions for opening up a new road "from my dwelling house southwardly," and the children were instructed to "keep open" the road "leading from my dwelling towards the road which leads from the Union Chapel to Bel Air," in other words, Hollingsworth Road from Stockton Road to Old Joppa Road. Daughter Abigail apparently moved into the old house, which remained in the family until 1932 when the widowed Alice Hollingsworth sold it.

3-43. Windy Knoll
Hollingsworth Road
c. 1806; Private   HA-298

On July 1, 1806, Nathaniel Hollingsworth "of Chester County, Pennsylvania, Farmer," paid William Stewart "of George Town in the Territory of Columbia" the remarkably high figure of $8,000 "current money" for 1,307 acres of Claggett's Forest. (Stewart was acting as attorney for the Bordley and Dulany families, the original owners of the patent.) According to family tradition, Hollingsworth then built this small one-room-per-floor rubblestone cabin as temporary shelter until a larger house could be erected. That scenario certainly seems reasonable, judging from the architecture of the two houses: this building is a rather late but still convincing example of a "British Cabin," the sort of one-room dwelling traditionally associated with first-generation settlers in Harford County. (Fifty years or so earlier the Norrises built the one-room rubblestone Prospect, while the somewhat more prosperous Bonds built Joshua's Meadows and the Whitakers built Woodview, which are, respectively, three and two one-room "British Cabins" fused together.) Hollingsworth and his wife, Abigail, did not stay in the small house long, since the larger house is traditionally dated to around 1820. They were certainly living in it when he died in 1834, because his will and estate inventory together describe a house with more rooms than are—or would have been—seen here. Hollingsworth left his seven children subdivisions of Claggett's Forest; his maiden daughter, Abigail, received the 116 acres that included this house (provided she and her siblings kept their mother comfortable) and an 1859 plat prepared by G. G. Curtiss notes "Miss Abigail Hollingsworth" living here. She died in 1887, living in spartanly furnished rooms, but with $4,500 worth of Baltimore City stock; the house passed from the family in 1906.

3-44. Joshua's Meadows
Tollgate Road
c. 1747; 1823; 1937; Private
National Register; Historic American
Buildings Survey   HA-356

Credit is quickly given this house's twentieth-century owners, Mr. and Mrs. Brodnax Cameron Sr., for accomplishing the impossible: the Camerons, blessed with uncommonly sensitive eyes and unerring aesthetics, managed to create a house that clearly displays its three eras of growth—in effect synthesizing the best of two centuries of county architecture—even as it reads as a cogent and charming whole. In 1726 Thomas Bond purchased a 1,000-acre tract here, land that took in the hills that border Winters Run to the east. Thomas and his brothers lined that waterway (and other streams) with stone gristmills. In the 1740s Thomas began dividing his holdings among his children: he gave son Joshua land in this neighborhood, and a 1752 deed refers to land "where the said Joshua's dwelling now is." That dwelling comprises the main, 2½-story section and original separate kitchen of the extant Joshua's Meadows (to the left in this photograph). The main block of Joshua's house has the identical plan on its two main floors and attic, that is, two rooms per floor, each with an end-wall fireplace bordered by a corner winder stair. This plan fits the house firmly into the county's building history, as is discussed in chapter 2. (House and detached kitchen are clearly indicated in the 1798 and 1814 tax rolls.) Joshua's younger son, Buckler, inherited the property; in 1823 he sold it to Thomas Hays ("the dwelling house and the mill . . . part of Joshua's Meadows"), who passed it to *his* brother, Nathaniel. (The Hays brothers' father had built the Hays-Heighe House [or Prospect Hill]; their grandfather built the large stone house on Thomas Run Road, now known as Hidden Brook.) Either Thomas or Nathaniel connected the kitchen to the main block and added the mantels and other interior period trim still in evidence. Nathaniel Hays died in 1871 and the house gradually began a period of decline, which ended in 1937 when the building was seen, bought, and rescued by the Camerons. This energetic couple restored the Bonds' work, kept the best of the Hayses', and added flourishes of their own; the result caused Baltimore *Evening Sun* editor Bradford Jacobs, in Mr. Cameron's 1980 obituary, to praise "Joshua's Meadows [a] 200-year old house set on a woodsy knoll. . . . Its casualness was overriding but deceptive: in reality it was and remains a rare potpourri," a perpetual tribute to the "deep sensitivity and human perception" of both Camerons.

3-45. Aquila Scott House
Tollgate Road
c. 1780; Open business hours   HA-370

Sloughed off for years as "the old farmhouse by the Poor Farm," this two-story brick struc-

3-43

3-44

3-45

3-46

3-47

ture is now valued as the home of Aquila Scott, arguably the father of Bel Air. Aquila and his ancestors had owned the land now crossed by Bond and Main streets since the early eighteenth century. By the time of the Revolution, thanks to the primitive agricultural practices of the time, the soil was played out and the tract was known as "Scott's Old Fields." (This was even noted in the 1795 *U.S. Gazetteer:* "In the vicinity of the town . . . the soil . . . is extremely thin.") When in 1782 it was time to choose a site for the new county seat, Harford's voters selected Scott's Old Fields, Aquila Scott subdivided the land, and Bel Air was laid out. The exact date of this house is not known but the brick portion shows up in the 1798 tax list, which cites Aquila as owning 230 acres, six slaves, and a "36 × 22 2-story brick house." (There were also various outbuildings including a "shed," meathouse, and chicken house.) The exterior of the Scott house repeats certain elements seen down the road at Joshua's Meadows, including a three-bay façade, Flemish bond brick work, a beltcourse, and a low service wing. (While Joshua's Meadows remains intact within and without, the Scott house, largely original without, acquired a center-hall plan in the early nineteenth century.) Encouraged by architect James Wollon, AIA, in 1978 the county parks and recreation department rescued Scott's house from certain demolition and adapted its rooms into offices, carefully keeping most of the surviving doors, chairrails, mantels and other original trim.

3-46. Hazel Dell
Vale Road
1859; Private   HA-372

In one of the county's more romantic gestures, Stevenson Archer (the younger) built this locally unique house to ease the homesickness suffered by his new bride, Jane Franklin Archer, a true daughter of the Deep South. Structures similar to this can still be seen along the bayous and creeks of Louisiana and Mississippi, one-story frame structures perched high on piers, houses whose primary design aim was to catch the breezes and hold the shade. To these same ends, Hazel Dell (originally Hazel Glen and so named for the tall hazelnut trees that still shade the site) has fourteen-foot ceilings to trap cooling air as it billows through floor-length widows and a hipped-roof attic story to insulate the main living areas from the summer sun. The

Archers even designed the house's porches with the sun in mind; the porch roof is angled to keep out the rays when the sun is high in the summer sky but to welcome the lower, warming rays of winter. Victor and Adelaide Noyes bought the house and 39 acres in 1941: Mr. Noyes raised and trained prize-winning Thoroughbreds on the grounds while Mrs. Noyes, a well-known social reformer and antiwar activist, filled the house with her magnificent, inherited collection of American antiques.

3-47. The Vineyard
Conowingo Road
1804; with additions; Private   HA-417

The entrepreneurial James Preston patented several tracts (totaling 1,500 acres) in north-central Harford County between 1709 and 1761. One of these was for The Vineyard; acquired in 1741, the farm has been continuously owned by Preston's direct descendants ever since. James's grandson Bernard Preston began the present stone house, the third on the site, and placed the building on a knoll so it overlooks roughly 300 ancestral acres, much as a distinguished actor might dominate an amphitheater. Preston's original sidehall/double parlor house forms the western three bays of an expanded dwelling. Built of fieldstone, it clearly evinces its builder's familiarity with current design trends: the plan was up to date, and the stones are laid so as to create flat arches complete with keystones over the windows and door. (See also the Rock Run Mill.) In 1879 The Vineyard passed to John B. Wysong who added the two bays to the east, the front attic gable, and many of the farm's unsurpassed collection of stone outbuildings (which march along in a row just north of the house). Richard B. Wysong, who inherited The Vineyard in the 1920s, maintained a dairy farm here while simultaneously serving as president of the Chesapeake pilot boat captains' association. (Captain Wysong credited his cousin, Baltimore mayor James Preston, with instilling nautical interests in him.) The new kitchen to the east, completely sympathetic in design to the older wings, comes from the pen of Baltimore architect Walter Schamu, AIA.

3-48. Priest Neale's Mass House
(The Mission of St. Joseph on Paradice Plantation)
Cool Spring Road
c. 1745; with additions; Private
National Register   HA-138

One of the few buildings in the county of international importance, the "mass house" may truly be called unique. The complex reasons for the stuccoed-stone building's existence are discussed at length in chapter 3. Put as simply as possible, beginning in the late seventeenth century a wave of anti-Catholicism swept over England and its colonies; this led to, among other things, a series of "anti-popery" laws, including one that prohibited the celebration of mass except in private houses. A few Catholics (such as the Howards in England and the Carrolls in America) were wealthy enough to build private chapels onto their houses and hire their own priests. The vast majority, however, relied on circuit-riding clergy who rode from house to house to conduct services. One such circuit was based here, beginning in 1743 when John Digges, S.J., bought a tract of land on the south bank of Deer Creek and established this mission. Digges died in 1746 and left the property to his friend and fellow Jesuit Bennett Neale, S.J., who continued to live here while ministering to the faithful from Ellicott City to Frederick and from Cecil County to Hanover, Pennsylvania, until he retired in 1773. The new archdiocese of Maryland acquired the house and farm after the Revolution; with freedom of religion guaranteed by the Bill of Rights, the little building was "retired"; the church sold the property to Dr. Samuel Glasgow in 1814 and it has been a private residence ever since.

3-49. Churchville Presbyterian Church
Routes 22 and 136
1820; 1870; 1950; Regular services
National Register; Harford County
Landmark   HA-441

Since it was built in 1820, this handsome brick church has formed the heart of this part of Harford County. Indeed, it is said that the community of Churchville owes its very name to the church. (When the parish marked its 150th year, the Baltimore *Sun* noted "the influence of this church throughout the county has been marked, and it comes to its . . . anniversary with a consciousness that it has been a

blessing far and wide.") The congregation's history goes back much further, possibly to 1738 when members incorporated themselves as the Deer Creek Presbyterian Congregation, certainly to 1759 when they moved to this site and built themselves a new brick meetinghouse. But the congregation dwindled and the parish was about to disappear, only to be saved in the nick of time by the timely arrival of the Reverend William Finney in 1813. Thanks to Finney the congregation prospered, so much so they decided to build a new church in 1820. (The building committee consisted of Finney, Benjamin Silver II [a leading figure in fishing and farming circles], Reuben H. Davis [first or 1814 headmaster of the Bel Air Academy], and other luminaries.) Finney retired in 1854 and a series of short-term ministers followed until the Reverend John Paxton arrived in 1870. Paxton and Finney (as rector *ex officio*) persuaded Priestford's J. Crawford Neilson, of the firm Niernsee and Neilson, to volunteer "a plan for repairing the present building" and to design a restrained Italianate bell tower for the east end. Four years later Paxton built an obelisk to honor Finney (who died in 1873), a "marble shaft to simply testify to the love we bear his memory"; he also hired local cabinetmaker William Shuck to design and build new black walnut pews and other furniture.

3-50. Webster's Forest
500 Asbury Road
Early eighteenth century; c. 1825; 1966;
Private
National Register   HA-442

This sturdy stone house stands on a tract of land John Webster (1667–1753) patented in 1704, although the house probably is not quite that old. A man of varied interests, the Quaker Webster belonged to the Bush River Friends Meeting and served as a delegate to the Nottingham Monthly Meeting; late in his life (1740) he became embroiled in *the* major local political issue of the day when he testified, on Lord Baltimore's behalf, in the Maryland-Pennsylvania border dispute. In his spare time, he probably built the 1½-story, gambrel-roofed house that forms the eastern wing of the present dwelling. The house has a two-room plan with corner fireplaces, beaded ceiling joists, and a cellar kitchen. (Just how Webster got up- and downstairs is not clear: structural evidence indicates that the present side stairhall was built in at least two stages,

3-48

3-49

3-50

3-51

3-52

3-53

but its original configuration is not known; perhaps there was a small stair tower—or a ladder.) Webster left the property to his son Samuel (1710–86), who married Elizabeth Dallam; another son, Isaac, built Broom's Bloom (1-43), while daughter Hannah married Jacob Giles, builder of Mount Pleasant. Samuel and Elizabeth Webster left Webster's Forest to their son Richard (1741–1824), a prosperous farmer and miller and an early convert to Methodism. (He donated land for Calvary Church.) Richard, cited in the 1798 tax list as owning a "dwelling house 30 × 20 feet, stone," left Webster's Forest (the "main house where I now live") to son Henry (1793–1872). Henry added the three-story stone wing to the west and remodeled the stairhall to its present configuration. The house remained in the Webster family until the 1920s. A fire gutted the older wing in 1966 but the then-owner, John Joesting, undertook the building's careful restoration.

3-51. Webster-Fielder Tenant House
Calvary Road
c. 1780; Private   HA-533

Neglect often acts as the preservationist's best friend—just note the surprisingly large amount of original material still present in this obviously forgotten house. The rubblestone walls remain intact (even if the stucco doesn't) and the massing seems unchanged down to the rear shed–roofed kitchen wing. These features, combined with a wealth of interior beaded board trim, make the house a prime candidate for restoration. A member of the Webster family (see Webster's Forest, Best Endeavor, and Broom's Bloom) almost certainly built the cottage, perhaps for a tenant farmer, perhaps for a worker at the family's James Run gristmill and iron works, perhaps for a newly married son or daughter.

3-52. Sawyer-Kracke House
211 Patterson Mill Road
c. 1815; Private   HA-534

In 1814 one William Sawyer began buying land along what is now Patterson Mill Road (for example, 260 acres on April 22 and 113 acres on July 18), and then began building this two-story, stuccoed stone house. It is a dwelling of classic lines and details: its deep center-hall plan and balanced façade now seem traditional but, when the house was new, represented the height of fashion. The win-

dows' stone sills and beaded frames seem original, as do many interior elements, including the open stair, corner fireplaces, and plaster walls. Sawyer died in 1857 and it is clear that the house then standing had the same general configuration as the one now standing; it also boasted a "passage carpet," "40 yards parlour carpeting," and "2 parlour stoves."

3-53. Fallston Presbyterian Church
Route 152
c. 1873; Regular services   HA-607

What can it be about Harford's Presbyterians and Greek revival architecture? Countians generally eschewed that style, so popular elsewhere in America in the mid- nineteenth century, but Presbyterian congregations in both Bel Air and Fallston chose to build their houses of worship behind classical porticoes. The reason is simple and can be personified in one individual, the Reverend E. D. Finney (1825–1904), a son of the Reverend William Finney of Churchville. The younger Finney, after completing his studies at Princeton Theological Seminary in 1852, preached the first service in the new Bel Air temple and then moved to Natchez, Mississippi. After the Civil War he returned to Harford County, where he resumed his place in the Bel Air pulpit. In 1873 he arranged for the church in Fallston to be built (on land donated that year by J. K. Hamilton), and its columns make a small echo of the porticoes he knew from Bel Air and—most certainly—from Natchez. The two Harford County temples make an interesting comparison: the one in Bel Air, built when the Greek revival really ruled the land, is austere and powerful, clean of line, simple of form. Fallston's came a generation later and in the interval the power of classicism had weakened. The clapboard Fallston temple isn't austere or simple; in fact, it's almost cute, with gingerbreadish modillions, arched windows (anathema to Greeks), and diminutive Ionic capitals. Finney stayed on here (part-time) as rector until 1891 and the church prospered under his leadership: but one wonders if anything ever equaled his first service in the village, held in 1872 in a bar with (he wrote in his memoirs) a "good, large, and attentive" congregation.

3-54. Little Falls Meetinghouse
Old Fallston Road
1843; Regular services
National Register; Harford County
Landmark   HA-609

The Little Falls meeting was the fourth
Friends meeting established in what is now
Harford County; the first two were in the
tidewater region, and the third, Deer Creek,
was in Darlington. With the northern and
southern sections of the county thus covered,
around 1738 William Amos (1718–1814) of
Mount Soma decided to organize the meeting
at Little Falls, a location convenient to worshipers in the central stretches of the county.
Thomas Bond conveyed part of his Bond's
Forest tract to the group in 1749 and they built
a log meetinghouse; that original structure
was replaced by a stone one in 1773 which, in
turn, gave way to the present clean-lined edifice. Many Friends deserve at least partial
credit for the one-story stone building, serene
in its oak-shaded lot: the Tyson family of Baltimore contributed funds to the project and
amateur architect Benjamin Ferris, who had
purchased Bon Air in 1841, contributed the
design. Ferris's 40-by-50-foot stone building
typifies Maryland and Pennsylvania Quaker
meetinghouses: five bays wide and two long,
its windows have the customary paneled shutters, wooden sills, and brick arches; the double
doors (at the center bay of the main or west
façade) lead to twin rooms (one for men, one
for women) divided by a partition. Bond's
1749 deed to the Friends mentions "a schoolhouse already built." While this seems fully in
keeping with the traditional Quaker emphasis
on education, whatever was there in 1749 had
vanished by the nineteenth century and the
present frame school, covered in overlapping
hand-split boards, was erected in 1850. The
meetinghouse's large lot also contains an ancient cemetery, the very picture of shady tranquility, dotted with many mossy headstones;
among these is William Amos's. He died and
was buried at Mount Soma, but when that
house was sold out of the family in 1915 his
casket was disinterred and moved here, an appropriate resting place for that venerable
Quaker since, in the words of Hunter Sutherland's definitive history, "the Little Falls Meeting . . . owes its existence to the special conviction and personal magnetism of William
Amos."

3-55. Ostheim-Jameson House
Old Fallston Road
c. 1853; Private   HA-612

With its rambling frame sections and attractive oak-shaded lot, this house contributes
mightily to the charm of Fallston. It is, in fact,
precisely the sort of house one expects to see
in a late nineteenth-century village and if Fallston today suggests high-priced housing developments, structures such as the Ostheim-
Jameson House serve as important reminders
of what Fallston—and Jarrettsville and Forest
Hill and Edgewood—originally looked like.
The Henry Ostheims bought this unimproved
lot from Amos Hollingsworth in 1853 and presumably began their house shortly thereafter.
Miss Marian Curtiss, daughter of Oakland
School's George Graham Curtiss, wrote a
booklet of reminiscences about the community. In it she notes that the Ostheims were German immigrants; he was a well-regarded shoemaker and she was a keen gardener who kept
their "front yard . . . full of roses."

3-56. Church of the Prince of Peace
Old Fallston Road
1908; Regular services   HA-617

Commuting problems seem to have dominated Fallston's history; today's ex-urbanites worry about traffic as they drive to and from work
in Towson and Hunt Valley; earlier generations worried about the distance between their
village homes (such as 3-55) and their places of
worship. Doubting readers should recall that
commuting complaints led William Amos of
Mount Soma and other Quakers to establish
the Little Falls meeting in the 1730s, led the
Lynches, Shanahans, and other Catholics to
establish St. Mark's in the 1880s (they were
tired of traveling to St. John's in the Long
Green Valley), and led Episcopalians to establish the chapel of the Prince of Peace in 1908.
(*They* were tired of driving to Emmanuel
Church in Bel Air partially because of the distance and partially because "they were forbidden to leave their horses and carriages nearby.") On August 18, 1908, Mr. and Mrs.
Theodore Forbes of Rochelle donated one-
half acre here to the "Fallston Improvement
Company . . . for the sole purpose of erecting
and maintaining . . . a Protestant Episcopal
Church and Rectory." The cornerstone, visible at the southeast corner, was laid on August
29, 1908, and the first service was held on
April 18, 1909. The architect, Laurence Hall

3-54

3-55

3-56

3-57

3-58

Fowler of Baltimore, created a fascinating East Coast example of the sort of arts and crafts buildings then stylish in the San Francisco Bay area—all shingley with hinged windows and other pointedly informal touches. William Atwell of Laurel Brook Road furnished lumber for the cruciform-plan chapel including the chestnut shingles that still cover the sides and roof. Altar brass (six brass candlesticks and a crucifix) were cast at Thomas Fitchett's foundry (now Koppers Company) in Glen Arm.

3-57. Mosswood
Laurel Brook Road
c. 1850; with additions; Private   HA-688

Even the name here is relaxed. Mosswood, a rambling frame house whose many parts rest beneath umbrageous oaks and tulip poplars, seems the very model of an informal Victorian country house. Curiously, and while it doesn't look it, the house owes its beginnings to such pretentious-sounding events as mass migrations. Around 1840, according to Hunter Sutherland's 1988 history of the Little Falls Meeting, "a number of [Baltimore City] Friends of prominence and wealth moved their residence and membership to Little Falls"; this group included members of the Tyson and Ellicott families and "Benjamin P. Moore, who had been a partner with Johns Hopkins, retired from business . . . married Mary G. Jones . . . and purchased the estate, Mosswood, which had been assembled by her father, Amos Jones, a soldier in the American Revolution." Land records flesh out the picture. In April 1842 Moore paid the Jones heirs $1,250 for 127 acres "where Amos Jones lived at the time of his death." Miss Marian Curtiss of Oakland School fondly described Mosswood and its owners, such as Estelle Moore, a woman who "had a great influence for the good of Fallston. She was a musical genius and most generous with her gifts." Then there was Mary Moore, Estelle's mother-in-law "and a minister in the Friends' Meeting. Never was there a more beautiful majestic person. . . . She was always gracious with the greatest elegance of manners. What indignation there was in the village when it was heard that a book agent had gone to her to sell a book on etiquette!" Judge Walter Preston adds in his 1901 history of the county that Moore "with his cultivated wife, Mary, lived 'and died the death of the righteous' near Fallston where their home life of refinement, gracious hospi-

tality and piety have left a lasting impression." Benjamin Moore's 1875 estate papers suggest that the present house was then more or less in place; furniture was appraised in a sitting room, parlor, hall, two rooms "for hands," upstairs hall, and five bedrooms. The grounds contained a tenanthouse, cornhouse, and workshop, all kept in good shape thanks to Moore's goodly amount of Baltimore bank stock.

3-58. Rochelle
Rochelle Drive
c. 1851; 1908; Private   HA-690

In the middle of the nineteenth century, well-to-do Quakers fleeing the urban sources of their wealth helped put Fallston on the map. It is well known that merchants such as the Tysons and Moores sought to escape the rigors of life in Baltimore on the banks of the Little Gunpowder. It is less well known that Fallston's charms drew people from even farther away: on October 17, 1851, for example, the three maiden sisters Mary, Rebecca, and Lydia Titus bought a twenty-two-acre tract from Thomas Bond; they then built Rochelle, a house they named for their native New Rochelle, New York. Little is known of the Titus sisters, although stories abound, but they must have been an interesting group. They clearly brought with them a sense of architectural style, because Rochelle is easily Harford's greatest Greek revival residence. Its main two-story block has a basically square plan beneath a hipped roof, which is crowned by a widow's walk. A simple portico dominates the main (east) façade, and is reached from within by tall windows and French doors. It is clear the sisters had completed the house by 1862, because Lydia died that year and her estate inventory cites a parlor, hall, dining room, kitchen, kitchen chamber, pantry, bathroom, second-story hall, four main bedrooms, and garret. The two surviving sisters sold the house to Amos Hollingsworth in 1869 for $4,000; he had been buying up land in the area since 1857 and his family maintained Rochelle in high style until forced out in a 1905 equity suit (in which attorney S. A. Williams described Rochelle as "somewhat old timey").

In 1908 the Theodore Forbes family, noted equestrians and soon-to-be founders of the Prince of Peace Chapel, bought "Rochelle Farm" and spent summers here to escape the heat of Baltimore's Bolton Hill. The Forbeses reworked the second floor (adding bathrooms and rearranging the bedrooms), put a sleeping porch on the rear (west) façade and moved the kitchen from its original basement location to a new wing, connecting it to the main house by means of a butler's pantry.

3-59. Smithson-Webster House
2950 Sandy Hook Road
1819; c. 1850; Private
National Register   HA-870

On November 27, 1813, William Smithson paid $3,954 for 247 acres of a tract called Green's Disappointment. Smithson, a nephew and namesake of a signer of the Bush Declaration, was evidently blessed with a sense of architectural design, since he hired stonemason David Hopkins to build the unique and truly whimsical outbuilding now known as the D.H. Springhouse. In all likelihood Smithson also hired Hopkins to build a residence, and a wonderful house it must have been, judging by the springhouse and by Hopkins's other known work, such as the Stump-Holloway House. But nothing is known of it, for all that remains is the stone mounting block (inscribed with the date 1819 flanked by the telling initials D and H) and the front porch steps (the topmost of which sports carved scroll ends). Smithson died in 1836; his estate had to be settled through an equity case and the farm "on which he resided" was sold to Henry Webster on May 16, 1850, for $4,000. It seems clear from stylistic evidence that the present frame house's exterior dates to Henry Webster's ownership although certain interior details (such as the raised paneled wainscot) could date to the Smithson era. (Webster could have demolished the old house and saved the woodwork for his new residence.) Websters are shown here on the 1858 and 1878 county maps and in fact, the Websters' tenure lasted until Edwin H. Webster sold the farm to Harry Carver in 1920.

3-60. Prospect
(John Norris House)
Old Joppa Road
Early eighteenth century; Private
National Register; Historic American
Buildings Survey   HA-881

While much has been written about the large 1810 brick house on the Olney farm, this rubblestone structure, located down a hill and across a stream from the main dwelling, is at least as important as its more celebrated neighbor. In fact, it ranks among the most important structures in Harford County, because it is a nearly unaltered example of the sort of shelter put up by the first generation of settlers in this region. A speculative firm called Bond & Hamilton patented the land here, Prospect, in the late seventeenth century and in 1716 sold 243 acres of the tract to John Norris, who built the existing house. Since this was the frontier, where a guaranteed supply of fresh water was crucial to survival, Norris placed his house directly over a powerful spring, and the spring still bubbles forth in the single cellar room. Above, Norris built a true folk house of a form scholars now call a "British Cabin." Popular in Pennsylvania (from whence the Norrises came), this sort of house, wrote folk historian Henry Glassie, "of stone, frame or log, with rectangular floor plans and gable-end chimneys, [is] very like the houses found in northern and western Ireland and Wales, and similar to some found in Scotland and England." In other words, this was probably the sort of house the Norrises knew before they emigrated to America. Other general characteristics of the type—and all present here—include a corner, winder stair, a fireplace placed centrally on an exterior wall, and (if the family was affluent enough) a built-in cupboard. In addition, the Norris house boasts original exposed ceiling joists, beaded paneling on the fireplace wall, and original pine beams in the attic, scored with Roman numerals from I through VII. For a further discussion of this estimable building, see chapter 2.

3-61. Paca's Meadow
(Southampton)
1112 Moores Mill Road
c. 1790; Private   HA-933

"What happened to Moores Mill?" queried a 1987 issue of the *Harford Historical Bulletin.* Actually, it may surprise even long-time countians to learn that there ever was a Moores Mill. Well, there was; in fact, there were several. The first, a gristmill, was built around 1750 on Bynum Run and purchased by James Moores in 1773. A sawmill came with the deal and Moores, a tanner, used the sawmill to remove bark from oak trees and then used the bark to tan hides. Moores prospered and on November 28, 1787, he paid William Paca (yes, *the* William Paca) £132 "current money"

3-59

3-60

3-61

3-62

3-63

for twenty-two acres of land called Paca's Meadow, on which he built this two-story brick house. Moores's house, with its Flemish bond brick façade, four-row beltcourse, water table, and center-hall plan, is one of the better examples of "Country Georgian" architecture in the county. Much of the interior woodwork (mantels, paneled fireplace walls, and the superb stair) is original and notable. When Moores died in 1791, he left his widow "one half the Brick House and cellar, one half of the Garden yard and Barn . . . one third of the saw mill and one third of the grist mill" for her life, with the residue and remainder to their son Daniel. (Another son, John, went off to build the present Southampton Farm.) In 1793 Daniel sold his parents' old residence to Harry Dorsey Gough, cited in the 1798 tax rolls as owning this "47 × 24" brick house. Gough served in the War of 1812 and was later elected to two terms in the legislature in Annapolis. And while Gough flourished, so too did the tanyard and mill; the gristmill is shown on the 1858 county map and "J. and A.P. Moores tanners" were cited in the 1850 census as having $2,000 capital and two employees who turned out "700 skins and hides ($1,400) by horse and hand power." But whatever happened to Moores Mill? Mrs. Robert Heighe bought it in 1928 and replaced it with the handsome stone residence, still known as the Heighe House (3-113).

3-62. Christopher's Camp
1219 Fountain Green Road
1771; c. 1845; c. 1865; Private
Harford County Landmark   HA-937

Even though one Christopher Bayne patented 1,000 acres of Christopher's Camp as long ago as 1684, nothing much happened here until 1771 when Richard Wilmot built the oldest section of the now-familiar house and "signed" his work with a datestone, placed high in the west gable end, inscribed "R+M W June 1771." While regrettably little is known of Wilmot, he was clearly aware of the architectural fashions of his day; he gave his two-story, three-bay stone house (to the left in the photograph) decorative, keystoned arches above the windows. Such arches are usually structural; they help ease the pressure solid wall exerts on open spaces (see Sion Hill and the Elizabeth Rodgers House) but the arches at Christopher's Camp are purely decorative and consist of wooden boards cut in the proper shape (the keystones are a superb touch) and

affixed to the stone walls. When Wilmot died in 1797 he willed to his "relation Ruth Wilmot, daughter of John Wilmot, the two front rooms both in the first and second stories of the dwelling house where I now live" and left the residue of his estate to his daughter Mary Hall, wife of the noted surgeon, educator, and amateur poet, Dr. Jacob Hall. (The 1798 tax rolls list Hall owning 400 acres and a "33 × 27 2-story stone house" with assorted outbuildings.) Dr. Hall (1747–1812), a cousin of physician Benjamin Rush and briefly president of Abingdon's Cokesbury College, established a private school at Christopher's Camp, with a varied curriculum; his library included two volumes of *Greek Grammar,* something called *Christian Armour,* and a primer on *Electricity.* In 1844 the Reverend John Davis of Washington, D.C., bought the house from the trustees of Richard Hall, "insolvent debtor." Davis, too, ran a school here; moreover, he almost certainly added the two-bay stone section to give the house its present sixty-foot front. In 1865 James Warden of Baltimore bought the farm and added the frame wing to the rear.

3-63. St. Omer's Farm
2706 Sandy Hook Road
c. 1805 (earlier wing?); Private
National Register   HA-965

Five regularly spaced bays wide with a center-hall plan, the main section of this substantial stone house virtually screams "early nineteenth century." And, for once, documentary and visual evidence corroborate each other. Benjamin Wheeler owned this and several other tracts in the area. He died in 1802 and his executors sold this 352-acre parcel to Benjamin Green in 1803 who, in turn, sold the place to Augustus Greme in 1817 for $8,000, a high figure that suggests Green built the house. (One wonders if the buyer was a son of the French-born Angus Grême of Maiden's Bower.) But matters may not be quite so straightforward. Persistent, generations-long legends abound here. The tract was surveyed in 1727 for an earlier Benjamin Wheeler who, according to Clarence Joerndt's recent history of St. Ignatius, may have operated a Jesuit "mass house" along the lines of Priest Neale's Mass House and may have named the farm (and nearby stream) after the school at St. Omer's in Flanders, where American and English Jesuits, like Father Neale, received training. Support for this theory comes from the

Wheeler family's long, strong association with the Catholic Church (see St. Ignatius). On the other hand, nothing in the 1798 tax list suggests the right combination of Wheeler and house. Bennett Wheeler owned 730 acres and a "32 × 18 1-story wood house"; Joseph 1,582 acres with a "14 × 30 1-story wood house"; while Benjamin—surely the man who died in 1802—had 920 acres with a "36 × 18 1-story wood house." But even if the house's romantic Jesuit past does eventually prove chimerical, its coursed main façade, bold quoins, and emphatic lintels will always make it a fine example of federal-era masonry.

3-64. Edmund Hoopes House
2603 Hoopes Road
1855; Private   HA-966

Two stories tall and three bays wide, this dignified stone house gains local significance as the homestead of the Hoopes family, agriculturists and pillars of several Quaker meetings. Edmund Hoopes, like so many Friends before and after him, moved to Harford from Chester County, Pennsylvania. He married Phoebe Trimble, whose father, Joseph, owned three large farms called Sunnyside, Woodside, and the Michael Place along St. Omer's Branch. (Trimble had purchased the farms, which in aggregate totaled about 500 acres, in 1825.) Joseph Trimble gave the newlyweds Edmund and Phoebe the Woodside tract; the couple then built this center hall–plan house, commemorating their work with a datestone inscribed "E & P T H 1855." Edmund's estate inventory (1863) lists rooms identical to those seen today, that is, two "Garrett" rooms, four bedrooms "up stairs," a parlor, a sitting room, a kitchen, and a cellar. Several outbuildings here probably date to the Edmund-Phoebe era, including a board-and-batten carriage house (Edmund owned two carriages when he died), and a frame barn. Incidentally, Edmund's brothers, named Darlington and William, sensed that their sibling was on to something and followed suit: each married one of Phoebe's sisters and each acquired one of the Trimble farms. William and Darlington flourished in their new community: they built and ran Hoopes Mill (long gone but with a still-visible tailrace); Hunter Sutherland's 1988 history of the Little Falls Meeting notes that Darlington Hoopes served as minister there and gained esteem "for his ability to find respectful solutions to problems confronting individuals" and, according to Preston's *History*

of Harford County, for his "unspotted life." In 1875 the widowed Phoebe Trimble Hoopes sold Woodside to her nephew (Darlington's son) Joseph, remembered as a keen agriculturist: he was among the first in America to breed Jersey cattle (c. 1880) and, a Hoopes family history proudly observes, built the first silos in Maryland "when there were only three in the entire country."

3-64

3-65. Corbin Grafton House
909 Deer Creek Church Road
c. 1850; Private   HA-971

The invaluable 1897 *Portrait and Biographical Record of Cecil and Harford Counties* notes that Corbin Grafton, born in 1820, was "the fourth generation in descent from the founder of the family in this country." But since Corbin's carpenter father, James, led a respected but impecunious life Corbin "had few advantages [and] at an early age he was obliged to begin work for himself. For some time he worked in the employ of various farmers in the neighborhood. Meanwhile he saved his earnings until he was able, in 1840, to purchase a farm of his own . . . near Chestnut Hill where he has since resided." (Actually, he bought the farm on May 26, 1847.) The farm's current owners, still named Grafton, suggest that Corbin built the house around 1850, which seems reasonable. Corbin Grafton died in 1906 but the preparer of his entry in the 1897 *Portrait* had already composed the best possible epitaph: Mr. Grafton "accords to every man what he claims for himself, the right to his own opinion."

3-65

3-66. Smith Barn
1331 Deer Creek Church Road
c. 1870; Private
National Register   HA-976

Throughout late nineteenth-century America many farmers embellished their otherwise utilitarian buildings with flashes of style. Scroll-sawn bargeboards, cupolas, and brackets enlivened barns and wagonsheds from Maine to Oregon. Harford had its share of these fancies but, regrettably, very few remain. This wonderful barn, however, does and its Gothic-arched vents—covering openings made for the prosaic purpose of airing out the building, so the hay doesn't mold—still add a bit of stylish fun to the landscape.

3-66

3-67

3-68

3-69

3-67. E. F. Bussey House

Conowingo Road
1819; Private   HA-978

This rubblestone dwelling deserves a better end than the slow, steady deterioration it is apparently fated to receive. Deterioration has been public, too; the house sits exposed and open in a cornfield just east of busy U.S. Route 1. Edward F. Bussey, who owned several tracts "on" (according to some of his deeds) "the road from Hickory Tavern to the Conowingo Bridge" between 1817 and 1834, built this two-story house. He must have been pleased with his work, too (however ungrateful later generations appear to be), because he capped it off with a trapezoidal datestone in the southwest gable end inscribed "1819 E.F. Bussey." Evidently a man of some religious convictions (and why not, with the just-completed St. Ignatius across the road), Bussey further embellished the datestone with a cross that he had placed above both the date and his own name. (Some historians believe that masonry techniques evident here may link the house to several stone buildings in the Kalmia area, including the Preston Stone House and the Preacher House.)

3-68. Wakeland-Sequin House

2906 Grafton's Lane
c. 1855; c. 1901; Private   HA-1049

Built in two parts, this stone and frame farmhouse housed several generations of the Wakeland family from 1855 until 1956. William Wakeland, a shoemaker by trade, bought part of the large Stoney Ridge tract on December 28, 1855, and then built the stone (east) wing of the present L-plan dwelling. Sitting high on fieldstone foundations (to give light and air to the original basement kitchen [since replaced] and to contain, beyond the kitchen, a root cellar), that building is a well-mannered structure with a central door and a symmetrical placement of windows. The parlor and sitting room filled the main story and there were three bedrooms above. Wakeland also built a simple porch to shade the parlor and sitting room. When he died in 1884, he willed "the farm where I reside" to his son, John Finney Wakeland. The younger Wakeland, who cut and sold ice for a living, added the frame section to the old house early in this century, possibly in 1901 (when he took out a $400 mortgage), but certainly by November 1914, when he hired someone to shoot a photographic

postcard of the family proudly grouped in front of the new wing (and beneath the world's most elaborate birdhouse; see p. 99). Young Wakeland embellished his new section with a one-story porch and took pains to ensure it continued the original porch's lines.

3-69. Otho Scott House

(Scott's Old Fields)
Route 24 and Moores Mill Road
1825; with additions; Private   HA-1046

The Scott family's land holdings sprawled from what is now the Bel Air Memorial Gardens southerly to the present Harford County Equestrian Center on Tollgate Road. In the 1780s Aquila Scott took part of that tract and laid out Bel Air; in the 1820s Aquila's grandson Otho took another part and built this handsome, hipped-roof frame dwelling, whose cruciform plan was unique in the county. He sheathed his new house in clapboard and embellished its façade with a two-story porch; the porch gives way to a well-proportioned entrance hall containing the house's famous double stairway, a pine (with cherry handrail) creation Scott is said to have modeled on the imperial stair at Sophia's Dairy (1-2). All in all, it is a thoroughly elegant creation, eminently suitable to the grandson of Bel Air's founder. Otho Scott, not content to rest on inherited laurels, became one of the leading lawyers of his day: in 1860 he codified the *Laws of Maryland,* "condensing," Judge Preston's 1901 county history notes, "into two volumes all the varied and unskillfully framed laws passed in the State since its foundation. The Code of 1860 stands as a monument to his memory, . . . [and it is regarded as] the best code ever produced." Scott died in 1864 and his estate inventory suggests that he lived in a manner equal to his superb house: all the twenty rooms were well furnished; there was a "hot house" containing "earthen and wooden flower pots"; and his "Liquor Closet" was brimming over with a demijohn each of "port wine, Peach Brandy [two of these], Cordial, Blackberry Cordial, Scotch Whiskey, and Gin." (Otho's son Daniel built Heritage Hill.) Between 1870 and 1875 the house was home to Mr. Jeffries School for Girls. Mr. and Mrs. Harvey M. Chesney acquired the place in 1945 and set about restoring it to its Scott-era grandeur.

3-70. James-Moore-Jones House
3303 Churchville Road
c. 1856; Private   HA-1053

While elegant mansions such as Sophia's Dairy or houses with romantic histories such as Bon Air add spice to the soup that is Harford's architectural history, it is the county's many simple frame farmhouses that give the broth its body. One of the best extant groupings of these sturdy dwellings may be seen in the cluster of frame houses that form the Snake Lane–Churchville Road neighborhood, where utility reigns and the stylistic conceits of the great world receive only a passing nod. Jarvis and Deborah James bought 50 acres here in 1856 and probably then began this representative three-part dwelling. The house is composed of a series of two-story modules, all sheathed in clapboard, all with their own entrances, all with one-room plans. The Jameses lived here quietly but after a decade or so, for unknown reasons, sold the farm to Jarrett Moore on March 25, 1865, for $1,200. The county's 1897 *Portrait and Biographical Record* explains that Moore, born in Bel Air in 1837, began adulthood as a carpenter (thus following his father in choice of vocation) until, at age 29, he decided to become a farmer, whereupon he bought the old James place and spent the rest of his life raising grain and tomatoes. (He also built most of the extant outbuildings, including the board-and-batten smokehouse and the frame barn, where he [or someone] carved the date 1881 into an interior beam.) Moore's descendants still (1993) own the house, giving the property a comforting sense of stability impossible to duplicate.

3-71. Whitaker's Mill
1212 Whitaker Mill Road
1851; Private
National Register; Harford County
Landmark   HA-1117

For nearly two centuries gristmills, which crowded the banks of Harford's swift-flowing streams, were among the dominant features on the county's landscape. Sadly, of the 400 mills once present, only a few remain. This is one of the best. Franklin Whitaker and his wife (née Rebecca Pue; see Woodview) built the sturdy 40-by-60-foot, 2½-story stone structure on a site that had seen milling since the 1790s. In its prime, the undershot wheel (one of the "few in Harford County" according to C. Milton Wright) helped make the

Whitakers' enterprise the most productive of all the county's mills, in terms of value of goods produced. Whitaker's mill weathered changes in technology, economic crises, and even floods, but could not compete with the vast grain crops of the Midwest. After Whitaker died in 1895, his heirs abandoned milling operations here. The mill then fell into disrepair only to be saved c. 1960 when its new owners gently adapted it to residential use.

3-72. Miller's House
1214 Whitaker Mill Road
c. 1851 (or earlier?); Private
National Register; Harford County
Landmark   HA-1117

When Rebecca Pue Whitaker of Woodview inherited this Winters Run site from her deceased father, Caleb Pue, in the 1840s it included a gristmill that may have been built fifty years earlier. But seeking the newest and best, she and her husband, Franklin Whitaker, replaced that ancient structure with the present handsome mill. She probably also acquired this rubblestone, two-rooms-per-floor miller's house, in which the Whitakers housed their millers. (A few sources, however, suggest that the Whitakers built the miller's house from scratch.) In 1975 the present owners added a small frame wing to the west; designed by architect James Wollon, AIA, the new section—intentionally kept visually separate and linked to the original structure by an almost invisible frame and glass hyphen—nicely complements the old in shape and scale.

3-73. Whitaker-Magness House
1213 Whitaker Mill Road
c. 1800; 1851; Private
National Register   HA-1089

Built of log, the original section of this much-expanded house stands 1½ stories tall and two equal-sized rooms deep. That is the building Franklin and Rebecca Pue Whitaker acquired in the middle of the nineteenth century after her father, Caleb Pue, died. The Whitakers built a new (and highly profitable) mill across the road. They, of course, did not want to run the mill themselves (she, after all, was an heiress of notable lineage, and he had recently been elected a delegate to the general assembly), so they employed a miller who lived adjacent the mill to do the actual work and remodeled this old cabin into a suitable

3-70

3-71

3-72

3-73

3-74

3-75

3-76

residence for themselves. This they did by adding a large frame wing to the west: it is 2½ stories tall, three bays wide, with a side-hall/double parlor plan and replete with stylish Greek revival flourishes such as squared posts on the entrance porch (a restrained Greek touch) and parlor mantle with anthemion-embellished frieze (an elaborate Greek touch).

3-74. Harford County Bridge No. 51
Whitaker Mill Road
1878 (replaced 1991); Public
National Register   HA-1237

A report for the National Park Service observes that metal truss bridges, a quintessential part of the nineteenth century, "represent some of the finest achievements of American engineering. . . . [They were] uniquely indigenous to America; no other country experimented with the truss concept as we did during the nineteenth century." Moreover, "the more modest spans maintain a sense of scale with the rural landscape not duplicated in the concrete girders that replace them." Harford County's court records show that this single-span, bowstring truss bridge was crafted by workers at the Ramsay Bridge Company. The old span, 72 feet long and 13 feet wide, had an eventful history, including an 1885 flood which, according to an *Ægis* account, "lifted [it] up at one end but dropped [it] back." A valued part of the Harford scene, the old bridge, patched beyond repair over the years, has been removed but carefully replicated by the county public works department.

3-75. Best Endeavor
1612 Calvary Road
c. 1745(?); c. 1785; c. 1841; Private
National Register   HA-1056

The early history of this multisectioned stone house is bound up with the history of the Webster family. John Webster (1667–1753) patented Webster's Forest, whose acreage took in this site and John's son Samuel and grandson Richard continued to live in the old house while achieving steady prosperity through farming (tobacco, then grain), milling on James Run, and investing in the iron industry. When Richard died in 1824 he left Webster's Forest to his son Henry; he also left an interest in his gristmill to son Richard Jr. (1765–1855), who had been living here while running the mill. (The 1814 tax list assessed him for 250

acres "of land called Best Endeavor" as well as a two-story stone house measuring "40′ × 35′.") Some historians suggest that Richard Jr. found a c. 1745, two-room stone house on the Best Endeavor property (the western sections of the present dwelling) and then added the formal sidehall/double parlor stone wing to the east, toward the road and mill. (The house was remodeled in the 1950s but most surviving evidence, structural and stylistic, tends to corroborate this opinion.) In any event, in 1841 Richard deeded to his son Noah (1808–73) "all the land called Best Endeavor where the said Noah now lives," and the young man added the still-extant Greek revival interior woodwork. Noah continued farming until he died, when Best Endeavor passed to his son Richard E. Webster (1833–1908), whose biography notes that he (who "has known no other home but this") raised cattle on his ancestral acres and also "planted . . . fruit, for [he] is one of the many who have found the canning industry a profitable and pleasant business in which to engage." Although Best Endeavor left the Webster family with Richard E.'s death, the house's subsequent owners have carefully maintained this fascinating dwelling.

3-76. Deaver-Adams Farmhouse
1410 Calvary Road
1770; Private   HA-1055

According to tradition this is an old Deaver family farmstead and, indeed, a plaque placed high in the west end gable wall reads "1770 I:M:A:D Pit/Liberty." Even if the "D" is thus explained, it is unclear what the other letters mean. Do they refer to the John Deaver who was the mason for the 1758 Spesutia Church? Not likely, for that would have been a prohibitively long commute. Perhaps to the Richard Deaver who was a second lieutenant in the Revolution—but there's no "R" in the inscription. How about Aquila Deaver, a private in that war and who in 1781 (again according to tradition) carried Lafayette across the Susquehanna on his back after the Frenchman's scow sunk? Possibly, since the "A" and the date would be right; the political sentiments would be right, too, if one interprets the inscription as masonry, colonial (misspelled) support of the liberty-loving British prime minister William Pitt. In any event, this is clearly the house of an advanced-thinking man, not only for the Pitt reference (if that's what it is) but also because it has one of the earlier center-hall plans found in central Harford County.

The building's coursed stone walls and well-defined stone lintels further indicate that whoever built the house was (or employed) a knowledgeable artisan of no little skill. Although the interior has been remodeled, many original details have survived, such as box locks, the staircase, and a window with "BMD" scratched into its ancient glass.

3-77. Howard's Forest
615 Schuck's Road
c. 1810; c. 1900; c. 1961; Private   HA-1060

The prominent Hays family began this dwelling as a tenant house on land they owned from the 1780s until 1844. The oldest or Hays section forms the two-story coursed rubble-stone east wing of the present dwelling: probably dating to the early nineteenth century, this building abounds in original material, including walls, stone window lintels, chestnut log framing (visible in the cellar), oak flooring, beaded beams, enclosed stair, box locks, and (in places) chairrail. In 1898 one William Derickson bought the house and farm. While little else is known of Derickson, one important thing is: his tenure marks the first time the house was owner-occupied, and so it seems reasonable to credit him—proud owner—with the two-story frame wing to the west. This wing gave Derickson a formal entrance hallway and a large dining room. The Sydney Peverley family, who bought the farm in 1961, added yet another wing, this one to the south.

3-78. Livezey-Waterman House
Churchville Road
c. 1855; Private   HA-1062

In 1844 members of the Livezey and Waterman families moved to Harford County from Lower Dublin Township near Philadelphia, and that December Jacob Ott Livezey purchased this land (and other tracts) from the Hays family. In December 1855 Livezey and his wife, née Priscilla Waterman, sold this 104-acre parcel to her brother, Joseph. Family tradition holds that Joseph then proceeded to build this two-story, five-bay, center-hall, common bond brick house which he ran as an inn. If true, the house stands as a somewhat *retarditaire* example of the sort of house first seen in the county two or three generations earlier. (Note, as one example, the eighteenth-century Davis house near Havre de Grace, Belle Vue Farm.) Old-fashioned or not, Wa-

terman's house is certainly well executed and, just as important, it remains largely intact.

3-79. Churchmouse Meadows
Churchville Road
c. 1875; Private   HA-1063

Within, this frame house forms a virtual museum of mid-Victorian architectural features: high ceilings, shaped rooms opening off one another in a flowing pattern, elaborate paneling, a fantastic newel post (in which a Doric column festooned with flowers supports a statue of a Pilgrim holding an electric light). All these devices—and more—keep visitors on their aesthetic toes. (The exterior, said to have been equally exciting, had several dormer windows and yards and yards of gingerbread removed in the 1960s.) In the early nineteenth century, this tract was a small part of the Herbert family's vast holdings, and for "vast" read most of what is now Churchville. (Until c. 1850 the village was known as "Herbert's Crossroads.") The roughly ninety acres that go with the present house left the Herbert-Kennedy family in 1874. Jesse Burbank paid $1,312 for the land that year and probably built the house shortly thereafter; he is shown as living in a house on this site on the 1878 county map. (For an equally fantastic newel post—this one documented to 1876—see Lansdowne.)

3-80. Mount Carmel Methodist Church
Old Emmorton Road
1865; Regular services   HA-1065

According to Magness family history, Elijah Magness experienced "a religious awakening," which caused him to donate roughly two acres of land here to the "Trustees of the Mount Carmel Methodist Protestant Church" on November 11, 1865. The trustees then erected the present handsome, stone "country Greek revival" structure capping off their work with a datestone inscribed "1865." (Compare this building's simple straightforward lines with those of the old First Presbyterian Church in Bel Air.) The trustees obviously had access to a skilled mason, because the builder carefully coursed the church's stones; the lintels and quoins, too, display the hand of a superlative artisan. A period cemetery virtually surrounds the old church. Among the many notable plots, the Pieper family's deserves mention if

3-77

3-78

3-79

3-80

3-81

3-82

3-83

only for its elaborate iron fence, complete with mourning doves sadly marking the entrance gate. No longer a Methodist church (the congregation merged with Bel Air's in the 1950s) the old building has been gently adapted to the needs of its new Byzantine Catholic occupants.

3-81. Mount Repose
2030 Calvary Road
c. 1893 (remodeling); Private   HA-1066

In 1893 Frederick W. Smith paid $4,250 for this house and the surrounding 60 acres; well, *sort* of. He actually bought the land and a much simpler dwelling, one probably built by Thomas Hanway, who purchased the land (then totaling 212 acres) for $4,252 in 1847, began the house, and kept store in the building until he died in 1862. Hanway's testamentary papers indicate the presence of a two-story structure. Specified rooms included four chambers, a parlor, sitting room, dining room, two passages (one *"upstairs"* and one down), and kitchen. Yet while the bulk of the present dwelling dates to c. 1850, the low, slim, and elegant configuration of the present house almost certainly resulted from Smith's remodeling. These two distinct eras have produced a building full of fascinating visual juxtapositions. Note especially how the highly academic hipped roof, smooth stucco, and fret-work porch railing (Smith-built) contrast with the roughly textured exposed log ends (probably Hanway-built) that thrust themselves out of the southeast corner. Despite its busy beginnings, the house remains virtually unchanged from its 1920 appearance, exposed log ends and all. In that year it was featured in the *Ægis*'s commemorative county booklet in a half-page ad for "F.W. Smith & Sons Growers and Packers of 'Scotland Brand' CORN and TOMATOES" that includes photos of the house as well as the "Plant and Packing House."

3-82. Major's Choice (Poplar Grove)
Moores Mill Road
1787; Private   HA-1080

The *Ægis*'s 1920 Harford County souvenir booklet calls this house "Poplar Grove" and gives it the subhead, "The Ancestral Home of Men Who Have Loved Their Country and Were Lovers of Home." It might, therefore, be surprising to learn that the builder of the handsome stone house was a Scotsman. (Perhaps he loved *two* countries.) Shortly before

the Revolution, Phillip Henderson, who had earned a medical degree from the University of Edinburgh, married Rebecca Matthews, sister and heiress of James Maxwell Matthews. Rebecca had received the 600-acre tract Major's Choice from her brother, who, in turn, had received it from his uncle, James Maxwell of the Gunpowder Neck. Dr. Henderson served in the Maryland militia during the Revolution and, shortly after Yorktown, started work on this clean-lined stone dwelling. He finished it in 1787, according to a date-stone in the northwest wall, and in 1798 was taxed on 500 acres, twelve slaves, and a "33 × 30 2-story stone house." The doctor willed the property to his nephew, the presidentially named James Monroe McCormick, and it remained in the McCormick family (who remodeled the interior) until 1929.

3-83. The Grove
Smith Lane
c. 1780; Private   HA-1081

Tranquilly sited beneath ancient trees, this three-part stone house was associated with members of the Amos family for most of the nineteenth century. Its stone walls and conservative massing certainly suggest the Quaker aesthetic one associates with those prominent Friends. How surprising, therefore, to learn that the house was built—or at least begun—not by the Amoses at all but by Samuel Calwell (although Calwell's wife, Mary, *was* an Amos). Mr. Calwell, a county native and a blacksmith by trade, led a life Judge Walter Preston's 1901 county history describes as "quiet and uneventful . . . as few reminiscences have been handed down to his descendants." Nonetheless it is known that Calwell signed the 1775 Bush Declaration (a suggestion of prominence and interest in politics) and served in the American militia during the Revolution. Preston further notes that Calwell and his wife "lived for many years on a farm called The Grove, on Winters Run"; their house forms the southern two bays of the present dwelling. After the war Calwell ventured into land speculation; assessed for 111 acres of The Grove in the 1783 tax rolls (with "sorry" soil), in March 1797 he and William Amos received a further 695 acres of The Grove from Chancellor A. C. Hanson (acting on behalf of the State) which the pair subdivided. Calwell died in 1800 and his testamentary papers show that his house was elegantly furnished with items such as "silver cream jug," several mahogany tables, and "1 sword" (that last doubtless from his Revolutionary days). His widow continued to live here, but in 1830 an equity case among their children forced the sale of 119 acres of The Grove ("whereof Samuel Calwell died seized"). It passed back to the Amos family in 1854 and it is likely that they gave the house its present shape and size by adding the wings. And what of the Calwells? Preston notes that son William Calwell was a Bel Air merchant, son Thomas "removed to Baltimore and established large and successful flour mills there," and (somewhat surprisingly) son James "migrated to Virginia, and was the founder and owner of the Greenbrier, White Sulphur Springs, which he conducted for many years."

3-84. La Vista
Watervale Road
c. 1797; c. 1811; 1863; Private   HA-1082

James Amos of James probably began this L-plan house shortly after he acquired 193 acres here in May 1797 from his uncle William Amos of Mount Soma and from Samuel Calwell of The Grove. (The pair, in partnership, had received 695 acres here earlier that year.) James prospered as a farmer and died in 1811 owning twenty-five slaves and personal property worth an impressive $7,595. But little is left of his two-story, two-bay house (the stone northernmost section of the stem of the L): the interior has been remodeled and the stone walls covered over in brick. These alterations date to the ownership of James's son George R. Amos, who inherited this tract and then proceeded to buy ten adjacent parcels, eventually accumulating over 780 acres. (James also left George "my two stills and cider mill after his mother has finished with them.") George Amos doubled the size of his father's house with a new two-story brick wing to the south; he also built the stone meathouse and blacksmith shop that are still standing. But even in its expanded state, La Vista, similar to other several nearby houses, would not have caused anyone to look twice. That changed dramatically in 1863 when Amos sold his 780 acres ("La Vista where said George now resides") to the wealthy William B. Duvall for $39,014.75. Duvall, scion of a family long prominent in southern Maryland, completely altered the appearance of the old house by adding a monumental five-bay, 2½-story brick wing across the south and shown in this photograph. The "new" wing, with its jack arches over the windows, superb classic en-

trance portico, grand spiral staircase, marble mantels, and two-tier rear porch, certainly suggests Duvall's southern Maryland origins. The Duvall era here was brief, however: the family reportedly lost most of their money in the Civil War and in 1867 William divided his holdings and sold the house and 472 acres to William M. Edelin.

3-85. Keech-Reed House
Reckord Road
c. 1835; Private   HA-1086

It may be hard to find a transatlantic equivalent for the concept of an English bishop's palace; nothing in America seems quite able to evoke the majesty of Lambeth or the other dwellings of the major British clergy. Here, however, is Harford's version, a massive enough house (by local standards) but thankfully lacking in gargoyles. On December 4, 1835, the Reverend John R. Keech paid $258 for forty-three acres "on the new cut road laid out for the turnpike from Baltimore to Bel Air." Keech divided his ministering among Christ Church at Rock Spring, St. John's in Kingsville, and St. James on My Lady's Manor, and doubtless chose this as a more or less central location. He then started building and created a three-story mansion with rough stone walls stuccoed and scored to suggest more finely quarried and laid stone. (The house originally had a two-tier portico across the main or south façade but only vestiges of it remain.) Keech died in 1862, and his estate inventory shows that he ran a school here ("Schoolroom Furniture $68"). It also cites a dining room, parlor, passages no. 1 and 2, two servants' rooms, "passage and porch," pantry, kitchen, and eight other rooms of unspecified use. The grounds contained a springhouse and a washhouse. The rector owned two slaves, as well as a substantial amount of stocks and bonds, which doubtless explains the grandeur of his dwelling. The house stayed in the Keech family until 1901.

3-86. Southampton Farm
1101 Southampton Road
c. 1800; with additions; Private   HA-1092

When prominent miller and tanner James Moores died in 1791, he left the bulk of his estate (house, mill, tanyard) to his son Daniel, while son John received "the remaining part of my land" as well as the "tanning and currying utensils and one twelfth part of my estate . . .

3-84

3-85

3-86

3-87

3-88

except the land bequeathed to my son Daniel." (John was instructed to provide his mother with "firewood brought to the door or to pay her ten pounds per year"; in contrast, Moores wrote that "no charge be brought against my son Daniel.") So while Daniel stayed in his father's house, Paca's Meadow, John went off to fend for himself. In 1796 he paid Michael Denny £242 for 280 acres of land and began building the 2½-story stone section of this well-known dwelling. (Its largely intact interior boasts paneled walls, chair-rails, and dentiled cornices.) The civic-minded Moores served on several juries (a greater distinction then than it sounds now) and in 1812 was selected one of the original trustees of the Bel Air Academy, an institution Marilynn Larew described as "the focus of the intellectual life of the town." When he died in 1823 he was worth a respectable $7,683 (roughly the same amount as blacksmith and land speculator Samuel Calwell of The Grove was worth in 1800). His estate appraisal specifically refers to a dining room, a parlor, some "carpet upstairs," and a "passage carpet and staircase." Moores's descendants continued to live here, making alterations and additions in a relaxed manner, until John Moores II died in 1912.

3-87. Em's Delight
812 Moores Mill Road
c. 1840; Private   HA-1140

One of several houses in the immediate neighborhood associated with the Moores family, this classic sidehall/double parlor stone dwelling postdates the better-known Southampton and Paca's Meadow. When John Moores died in 1823, leaving no will but owning roughly 600 acres of land, his estate passed to his children, James, Samuel, Aquila, Parker, and Elizabeth; by 1842 James and Aquila began buying out their siblings and their deed from brother Samuel for his interest in the 600-acre patrimony notes it is the "land whereon Aquila and James now reside." Since James was living at Southampton, Aquila was probably living here. Stylistically the house certainly suggests the late federal era; its plan and overall massing (and, superficially, material) remind one of Dr. Joshua Wilson's Woodside. But it is a later and older Woodside: Dr. Wilson's house sparkles with youthful panache, its stones carefully laid, its interior woodwork elegant and very much up to the minute; the Moores house, built a generation later, simply lacks Woodside's verve. But it is a fine place

nonetheless and retains its original paneled doors (most with their box locks), stairway with pegged handrail, and poplar flooring. The house stayed in the Moores family until 1888, when Sallie B. Lee purchased it; it stayed in the Lee family for an even longer period, until John L. G. Lee sold it to Alan S. Weisheit in 1947.

3-88. Rockdale
1724 Carr's Mill Road
Late eighteenth century; c. 1900; Private
National Register   HA-1229

Rockdale may be best viewed as a polarized product of the very beginning and end of the nineteenth century: part comes from the genteel era of Washington and Jefferson, part from the rip-roaring age of William McKinley and Theodore Roosevelt. Isaac Bull took out a writ of *ad quod damnum* on "a Draught of water leading into Bush River called Winters Run" in 1761 and for a century or so thereafter members of the Bull family operated the Rockdale Mill. The miller William Bull and his wife, née Sarah Billingslea, lived on the property in the 1780s in a stone house that forms what is now called the "Old Kitchen"; in 1811 Billingslea Bull (surely William and Sarah's son) and others sold the land to Walter Bull who, according to the 1814 tax rolls, owned a one-story brick house ("30 × 21") and a stone house (no height but "20 × 16"). But precious little physical evidence remains from the Bulls' ownership, because self-made canning millionaire William E. Robinson (1860–1935) purchased the house and 171 acres in 1887 and completely remade the old building(s) in his own vigorous Victorian image: he thrust an ornate, two-story frame library wing onto the north façade (with a Tudor arch here, fluted columns there); he extended the front porch; and he made the south front bulge with a two-story conservatory. He also created an elaborate terraced garden that he ornamented with fountains (gone), a grotto (traces remain), and a pair of summerhouses (present; see chapter 10). Robinson died in 1935 and his wife soon followed; daughter Julia Robinson inherited Rockdale and lived here until she died in 1971; the former showplace then slowly slipped downhill, a decline the present owners are bravely trying to reverse.

3-89. Summit Manor
402 Summit Drive
c. 1855; Private   HA-I24I

With an exterior nobly austere and surprisingly intact, this grand stone house stands as a monument to mid-Victorian classicism. In 1855 Samuel Bowne began buying up land here (sixty-eight acres on February 24, seven more on April 9) and presumably started construction shortly thereafter. An 1865 deed refers to this property as the land "where Samuel Bowne now resides." Stylistically, everything about the house's shell suggests the strength of the mid-nineteenth century: note the cubic proportions, restrained cornice (restrained so as not to diminish the overall sense of power), simple stonework, and windows that are correctly taller on the ground story than they are on the second. The interior, on the other hand, is more eclectic and may represent various remodelings. The center-hall plan (with a double parlor to the east) and overscaled Greek revival woodwork probably dates to Bowne's day but other trim, more federally inspired, suggests a bookish 1920s colonial revival aesthetic, particularly the mantels and door and the monumental Doric portico, now so dominant but not present in a 1920 *Ægis* photograph of the house. (The very federal Woodside also gained a large wooden portico during the 1920s.)

3-90. Hoskins-Guidice House
1118 Baltimore Pike
Mid-nineteenth century; Private   HA-I259

This building's site—virtually smack in the southbound lane of U.S. Route 1—is at once its greatest blessing and its probably fatal curse: it is a blessing since it ensures that the long, stone structure is among the most visible buildings in the county, but it is a curse since demolition looms as an ever-present threat. Members of the Hoskins family owned the property at least as far back as 1840; they are shown here on the 1858 county map and they may have built the original (or northern), three-bay half of the building, a structure whose ground-story openings (reading window-arched door-window) strengthen the popular theory that it served as a stage stop. Windows in this section display interesting stone arches that suggest federal-era keystones, while windows in the newer half are less imaginatively detailed.

3-91. Mount Soma
1120 Bel Air Road
c. 1715 (?); with additions; Private   HA-I260

Impressive even in decay, this rambling stone house was the seat of the Amos family for six generations. For two centuries they lived here, making forays from the hilltop to play pivotal roles in the county's religious, political, and economic history, but always coming back to Mount Soma. The very name underscores the connection—the "Mount" obviously refers to the hillock while "Soma" is simply Amos spelled backwards. The first William Amos (1690–1759) came to Maryland from England; he was married in Joppa in 1713 and on March 3, 1715 ("in the first year of the Dominion of Lord baron of Baltimore," according to the deed) he paid "Thirty Pounds Sterling" for a 200-acre tract on Winters Run "in the Woods" and moved there with his bride. The tract had been called "Clarkson's Purchase," but it soon became Mount Soma. It is unclear if any of the present house survives from the first William's era (although parts certainly date to the eighteenth century), but when he died he left the farm "where I now live" to his son William (1718–1814).

William Amos II prospered as one of Harford's leading farmers and land speculators, but his exemplary life more than repaid his monetary riches. As a youth he fought with distinction in the 1730s border wars with Pennsylvania, but then he had a revelation, converted to Quakerism, returned to Mount Soma, and helped establish the Little Falls Meeting, where, the records show, he espoused "meekness, resignation, piety, benevolence, and charity." He was also one of the county's earliest abolitionists, "a jealous advocate in the cause of the oppressed descendants of the Africans," to quote his funeral eulogy. On his death Mount Soma passed to son James, who was assessed that year for two, two-story stone dwellings (one "22 × 18," one "22 × 18") with a 1½-story kitchen. When James died in 1845 he left his daughter, the widowed Mary Calwell of The Grove, $1,000 and instructed his executors to divide the rest of his estate between his sons, William Lee and Oliver. William L.'s son, Garrett, inherited Mount Soma in 1870 and almost certainly remodeled the house by giving it its present distinctive mansard roof. Then on January 1, 1918, came a truly epochal deed: on that day William L. Amos sold the farm for $12,717.90; and suddenly, 203 years after William Amos

3-89

3-90

3-91

3-92

3-93

3-94

3-95

first got that 200-acre grant "in the woods," Mount Soma was owned by someone not surnamed Amos. Recently gutted by a fire of mysterious origins, Mount Soma faced a bleak future, but restoration seems now assured.

3-92. Dibb House
1737 Churchville Road
1897; Private
National Register   HA-1261

Shaded by 150-year-old-trees, and flaunting a dizzying array of late Victorian motifs, the Dibb House has much to say about the architectural thoughts of Harford County's citizens. During the nineteenth century, prosperous and stylish Americans about to commence home-building could choose from a bewildering number of styles, all equally flamboyant, all equally acceptable. That is, this predicament faced home-builders nearly everywhere in America—but *not* in conservative Harford County, where the few frame or masonry fantasies that were built were (generally) built by people who had moved here from elsewhere (see Fair Meadows). Thus it is interesting to note that when county natives John and Mary Cole bought this fifteen-acre parcel in 1897, they chose to work within a traditional form. True, they covered this shell with porches, oriel windows, dormers, and stained glass double windows, that's all self-evident—but these stylish decorations are superficial; they are merely *applied* to a traditional L-plan form. Scrape all that away and the result is simply a center hall flanked by twin rooms with a rear service wing, in other words, the Reverend Finney's Greenwood.

3-93. Booth-Wagner Barn
Near Churchville Road
Mid-nineteenth century; Private   HA-1265

During the past twenty years or so, barns, once ubiquitous features in the Harford landscape (and near-flawless indicators of a farmer's wealth) have all but disappeared, the victims of macadam, changes in agriculture, and arson. This two-story stone and frame barn is a valuable and welcome survivor. A trio of horse stalls fill the masonry ground story, while the board-and-batten level above is given over to a corncrib (to the southeast) and hay storage. Moreover, the barn's hand-hewn log joists (many with bark still on them), tapered posts and rafters, and tenoned and nailed beams all stand as unchanged examples

of nineteenth-century building technology. In addition and from a historicist's point of view, the barn gains importance for its probable associations with the Booth family, who controlled the farm from 1824, when Junius Brutus Booth leased it, until 1878, when his widow, Mary Ann Booth, sold the family's interest.

3-94. Forest Hill Railroad Station
Jarrettsville Road
1914; Private   HA-1272

Trains on the much-lamented Ma and Pa first rumbled into Forest Hill in June 1883; passengers who wished to ride the line (Number 6) on its circuitous paths toward Baltimore or York used Tucker's General Store as a waiting room/ticket office. The store burned in 1914 and that ended the earlier, folksy arrangement. When it came time to rebuild, everyone agreed that the booming village needed a proper railroad station, hence this charming, one-story shingled structure, with its notable hipped roof, enormous flaring eaves, and oversized wooden brackets. (The Tuckers built themselves a new brick store at the same time.) The Ma and Pa stopped service in 1959 and the tracks were torn up; for a while it looked as if the station might go, too, but private owners (led by Mr. and Mrs. Ralph Klein) stepped in, bought the building, restored it, and have maintained it ever since. Today the old station may well be the single best preserved and most architecturally interesting remnant of the company that played such an important role in developing Harford County.

3-95. Little Greenwood
Glenville Road
1906; with additions; Private
National Register   HA-1277

Beginning in 1858 the Reverend William Finney began selling portions of his large landholdings to his youngest son, George (1830–1906) who, unlike his siblings, chose agriculture—not medicine or theology—as a career. And during the last year of *his* life, George Finney gave his son William and new daughter-in-law (née Eliza McCormick) a twenty-acre parcel on which the newlyweds built this superb two-story house which they called Little Greenwood, in deference to the rector's own home, Greenwood, across Glenville Road. The young couple hired the

Baltimore architectural firm of Parker and Thomas to design their new house. Parker and Thomas had already created some of the city's better-known landmarks (such as the Alex. Brown Building, 1900, the Belvedere Hotel, 1903, and the headquarters for the B&O Railroad, 1906); they certainly retained their standard of excellence here for they gave the Finneys precisely the sort of house this prosperous and sophisticated suburban couple deserved ("suburban" was then regarded as a complimentary adjective). Its soaring and flared hipped roof, deep porch with distinctive clustered posts, and distinctive window treatment add up to one of the best period buildings in this part of the state. Mrs. Finney, still famous for her horticultural skills, planted gardens that set off the house to perfection. The Finneys built two wings (1915 and 1935) to the north and the present owners have put a new (1980) music room to the southeast, but all these additions have been carefully designed to complement the original structure. This house and Mrs. Finney's green thumb are more fully discovered in chapter 10.

3-96. Finney-Marks House
426 Glenville Road
c. 1868; Private
National Register   HA-1278

During the 1860s the Reverend William Finney saw that his household was shrinking and decided to retrench to smaller quarters. (His wife died in 1865 and their children were setting themselves up in their chosen professions.) So in 1868 he and his bachelor son, John, built and moved into this 2½-story, hipped-roof, frame structure across the road from Oak Farm and Greenwood. The senior Finney died in 1873, but John, who had earned a medical degree at the University of Pennsylvania, continued on here and the house formed the base from which he conducted his extensive rural practice. Dr. Finney died here, according to the 1897 *Portrait and Biographical Record of Cecil and Harford Counties,* in "1896 after a long life spent in the interests of suffering humanity."

3-97. Greenwood
331 Glenville Road
1841; Private
National Register;   HA-1279

For unknown reasons, in 1841 the Reverend William Finney sold Oak Farm and 200 acres

to a friend and built this frame house to which he, his wife, and their six children moved. It is interesting to speculate on his motives. Perhaps he was slightly embarrassed by Oak Farm's stylishness; Greenwood is certainly less prepossessing, and perhaps he felt it more seemly that he, a man of the cloth, should practice the inconspicuous consumption that was (and to a degree still is) innate among Harford countians. Greenwood is a 2½-story, five-bay, two-section, L-plan house set on fieldstone foundations and sheathed in cream-colored clapboard. Its center-hall plan with rooms, windows, and doors regularly placed throughout superbly captures the downward worldly aspirations of its builder. Ironically, it proved to be a far more potent force on the county's architecture than the very grand Oak Farm and may have helped spawn two generations of imitators, as is discussed in chapter 5. But none of these imitators can boast anything like the two-story stone, combination spring- and smokehouse that stands just east of the service ell. With a barrel-vaulted spring cell on the ground floor and a room for hanging and curing meat on the second, the little building incorporates flagstones from St. George's Church (built in 1759 and demolished in 1851). Two barns to the north and informal grounds fittingly complete the attractive picture.

3-98. McGonnigal-Blackburn House
Calvary Road
c. 1843; Private   HA-1280

During the generation or so on either side of the Civil War, the area south of Churchville became thickly settled. Even today stretches of Calvary Road and the thoroughfares radiating from it (Snake Lane, Grafton's Lane) remain dotted with the homes of prosperous small-scale farming families and with those whose livelihoods depended on the success of those families. In 1843 and '44 one Daniel McGonnigal put together a respectable spread (he bought eighty acres one year, twenty-nine the next) and built this five-bay, 2½-story, cross-gable frame house, which is shown on the 1858 county map. While his house has scores of peers in the neighborhood it gets some individuality through its ample proportions and Gothic-arched attic window. In 1867 McGonnigal sold the property to Philadelphia attorney John Blackburn, who apparently—and hard as this is to believe in the litigious 1990s—needed to augment his income from

3-96

3-97

3-98

3-99

3-100

3-101

the law with profits from farming. When he died in 1887 his estate included, in addition to substantial amounts of Philadelphia real estate, "the farm . . . in or near Churchville" as well as the "canning house machinery and fixtures, kettles and cranes"; in his will Blackburn left his son Charles the farm, the livestock, and "the canning establishment" (together with all material necessary "for the purpose of canning and preserving fruits and vegetables"). With the exception of a brief interlude from 1888 to 1890, when it was part of the Baker family's canning empire, the farm remained in Charles's ownership until 1926.

3-99. Mitchell House
3006 Snake Lane
c. 1875; 1884; Private   HA-1286

Beginning in 1875 Robert Louis Mitchell (1847–c. 1880) began buying land in this neighborhood from his father, Robert, a collier and farmer. The younger Mitchell had a varied career, first as an apprentice carpenter, then as a wheelwright, and, eventually, as a farmer. (In 1897, his biographer observed that "it was not possible for him to spend much time in school, but the defects in his education have been remedied to a large extent by thoughtful reading and . . . close observation.") He married Alice Gorrell in 1874, an event that apparently caused him to begin this two-section house. Mitchell's four-bay first part, which appears on the 1878 county map, faces south and is covered in poplar weatherboarding; it has a two-room plan and both ground-floor rooms have their own front door, making the building a rather late example of a folk plan common in southeastern Pennsylvania and central Maryland in the eighteenth century. (Shortly after Mitchell "finished" the house, Snake Lane was laid out, partially through his farm, and he had to move his house out of the new road's path.) Mitchell, praised for his work on behalf of Calvary Church (particularly in the Sunday school where he was "instrumental in promoting the cause among the children of the vicinity") died childless around 1880 and left the property to his nephew Alonzo Mitchell, a blacksmith. In 1884 Alonzo and/or his father, Samuel, added the two-bay, one-room north section, complete with datestone. Interestingly, even though the two sections were built within a dozen years of each other they reveal real changes in building technology: the cellar of the 1870s unit, for example, displays primi-

tive joists (whole logs with bark still attached), but when the second wave of Mitchells built the newer room, they used sawn wood exclusively. The important, essentially unaltered, two-part house remains in the Mitchell family.

3-100. De Swann–Lillie House
Churchville Road
c. 1870; Private   HA-1294

While William Carsins was serving as county sheriff, he was also guaranteeing that the eponymous community of Carsins Run would prosper, for he subdivided his family's holdings there. He sold large lots to men and women of substance, who then built their own frame dwellings, generally using Carsins's own house as a model. Christopher De Swann may serve as a representative example of all this. In 1866 he paid Carsins $1,000 for eight acres of ground and then began work on the extant, two-story, three-bay frame house (completing work in time to have the house shown on Martenet's 1878 county map) and plain, visual evidence shows that De Swann created a smaller, simpler version of the Carsins house. Moreover, De Swann was a blacksmith, a trade then crucial to all rural communities, and he practiced his profession in a shop at the corner of Churchville and Carsins Run roads. (The compilers of that 1878 map called the blacksmith "Capt.," a probable honorific indicating how highly his contemporaries esteemed that trade.) De Swann gave this house to his daughter Mary E. Lillie in 1892.

3-101. George W. Baker House
3647 Churchville Road
c. 1850; with additions; Private   HA-1296

Despite its present deteriorated appearance, this frame house ranks among the more important structures in Harford County. Its importance flows chiefly from its builder, George Washington Baker, to whom the 1897 *Portrait and Biographical Record* grants "the distinction of being the pioneer canning packer of this county, which is now the banner canner in the world." Baker, born in 1815 in his father's house nearby, first turned his hand to cabinetmaking, then to the ship timber business; he was thus successfully employed in 1849 when he bought a fourteen-acre lot from his siblings and began building this house. (It is easy to date, thanks to a mortgage he took out in 1850; that instrument also includes a "steam engine . . . used for sawing and turning chairs . . . also 1 mill . . . for sawing chair tops.") In 1866 Baker abandoned chairs and began canning fruit, "on a very small scale, somewhat similar to the canning operations of thousands of housewives." But it didn't stay "small scale" for long and by the time he died in 1888 he owned 3,000 acres of farmland and several large canning factories. Baker used some of his substantial profits to cloak his initially simple dwelling with lavish Italianate ornament; most has been removed but the few touches that remain (note the brackets and dormer windows) tantalizingly suggest the place's former splendor. Yet notwithstanding his enormous wealth, Baker remained at heart a Harford County farmer, for the ornament was merely applied to a structure that is essentially yet another L-plan frame house, similar to scores of others throughout the Churchville/Aberdeen area. (To see what a difference a generation makes, compare this house, so firmly of its place, to the mansions Baker's sons built along Bel Air Avenue in Aberdeen.)

3-102. Chesney-Bodt House
2924 Churchville Road
1905; Private HA-1524

Charles Chesney, a blacksmith who also kept store with Winfield Hawkins, seems to have been cut from a more traditional cloth than his business partner. Whereas Hawkins experimented a bit with one of the county's most time-honored home-building forms (his house, HA-1522, has been demolished), Chesney stuck close to it and his five-bay, two-story, one-room-deep clapboard house is essentially timeless: it could have been built any time from roughly 1840 to 1920. It is, however, easy to date for Margaret Harlan of Homelands died in 1903 and her heirs then created a few lots out of her vast land-holdings. Chesney bought one and built his house on it. (He also carved the date 1905 into an interior door frame.) Chesney and his wife, Annie, sold the house and its acre and a half of land in 1915.

3-103. Coale-Zaleski House
3141 Churchville Road
c. 1870; Private HA-1530

Although its massing is simple and unremarkable, this house *is* remarkable for its material (stone, in an area where frame is nearly universal) and plan (two ground-floor rooms,

each with its own front door as opposed to the more symmetrical center-hall arrangement). In 1869 William S. Coale acquired thirty-eight acres of the Stoney Ridge tract; he took out two mortgages, one in 1869 for $400, one in 1872 for $750. He defaulted on the latter, and the property was sold in 1874 to Philip F. Coale (born in 1852 and a prominent canner of fruit and tomatoes) for $1,300 and "Philip Cole" is shown living here on the county's 1878 map. Whichever Coale built the solidly constructed house evidently had an eye for color, for the contrast between the dark rubblestone walls and the red brick of the chimneys and the window and door arches is striking. Four frame outbuildings still stand just east of the house (and appear to be contemporary with it), the most notable of which is undoubtedly a one-story shed-roofed structure with hand-hewn posts and rafters and pegged construction.

3-104. Bodt-Bowman House
3334 Churchville Road
c. 1875; Private HA-1532

In 1875 Frederika Bodt bought four acres of land here from Aquila Greenland for $275; the deed refers to Frederika as the "wife of Edward Bodt," but it also makes clear that this property was "for her sole and separate use." Had there been matrimonial troubles, or was the couple simply making shrewd, independent investments? Whatever, Frederika Bodt's house is very much of its time and place, although its ample proportions create a slight variation on the usual L-plan frame farmhouse theme that so dominated residential building in the area in the late nineteenth century. Frederika and Edward Bodt sold this house to Eva Catherine Kondries, "wife of Henry Kondries," in 1896 for $1,000, but this stretch of Churchville Road is still often called "Bodt Corner."

3-105. Greenland-Maloy Springhouse
3336 Churchville Road
Mid-nineteenth century; Private HA-1534

For much of the nineteenth century, the Greenland family owned most of the land between Churchville and Carsins Run. (What they didn't own, the Bodts and Mitchells did. Not inconsequently, Mary Greenland married Nicholas Baker IV in 1855, thus forging a truly impressive alliance.) Although the original

3-102

3-103

3-104

3-105

3-106

3-107

3-108

c. 1815 Greenland residence has been altered beyond recognition, its period rubblestone springhouse has endured. Elisha Greenland began buying land in the neighborhood in 1814 and his descendants continued to farm here until 1941.

3-106. Carsins Run Store
3478 Churchville Road
c. 1890 (and earlier?); Private   HA-1536

The whims of commercial fashion (what to sell and how to display it) have guaranteed this building's nearly nonstop series of remodelings. In 1855 William Carsins, sometime sheriff and full-time entrepreneur for "his" community of Carsins Run, bought a lot here from the Baker family and began this structure, labeled "shop" on the 1858 county map. He bought more land from the Bakers in 1866 (and the two small frame buildings behind the main structure could easily date to that 1850–60 period) but then turned around the same year and sold his commercial holdings to Christopher De Swann for $1,000. De Swann proved almost as important to this community's growth as Carsins himself, for he built a house nearby and established himself as the area's indispensable blacksmith. In 1892 De Swann sold two acres here with "a store building and shops" for $1,000; one wonders if one of the "shops" contained De Swann's smithy. In 1895 Levi Bechtel paid $3,500 for the same two acres, a change in price that suggests that the six-bay store had been built during the interval.

3-107. Durham-Billingslea-Kahoe House
333 Bynum Ridge Road
c. 1800; Private   HA-1537

Twentieth-century stucco and aluminum sheath the outside of this house belying the wealth of ancient architectural detail within. In the late eighteenth century, two Samuel Durhams, father and son, owned roughly 625 acres hereabouts and grew wealthy through the farming of tobacco. (When Samuel Sr. died in 1786 his estate inventory included ten slaves and such genteel touches as tablecloths, silver spoons, books, and a copper still.) William Billingslea then bought the farm in 1802. In 1814 tax assessors noted his 230 acres "near Bel Air" and his two-story, "20′ × 16′" stone house; those measurements align nearly perfectly with those of the stone rear wing of the extant dwelling. (The present kitchen, located in the rear wing, contains a massive fireplace and, in the ceiling, four wrought iron hooks said to have been used to support quilting frames.) Although his 1814 assessment was $1,840, a year later Billingslea sold the property for $3,307, which may suggest that he had completed the two-part house one sees today. And if the rear wing contains utilitarian touches, the five-bay, center-hall front section is replete with vast amounts of stylish original woodwork, including a parlor mantel embellished with columns and corner blocks, a dining-room mantel with pilasters, and upstairs bedrooms with architrave trim.

3-108. Woolsey Farm Outbuildings
706 Glenville Road
Various dates; Private   HA-1538

The house that went with the farm here is gone, but a remarkable array of outbuildings, dating from c. 1840 until the early twentieth century, remains. William Woolsey was the proprietor of it all for much of the time: he bought the farm in 1844 (308 acres at $11 per acre) and died here in 1888. Woolsey was a fascinating individual, a public-spirited man who single-handedly brought paved roads to Harford County. At the time of his death, all roads were gravel or dirt (except for a small stretch of road near Darlington); in his will the bachelor Woolsey established a trust fund with income to go to the county commissioners so they could "perfect" the "public and county roads in said county by macadamizing." He specified five roads to be "perfected," and all, not incidentally, radiated out from his native Churchville. In 1910 the farm was the subject of an equity suit which provided the following description: "The land is of strong quality. . . . Mr. William Woolsey . . . was an excellent farmer. . . . The present barn . . . is very large and substantially built. . . . There is also another tenant house on the place and all necessary outbuildings . . . including an implement house, barrack, dairy, ice house, cistern, etc." Also present (but not enumerated in 1910) are a blacksmith shop, dairy/meathouse, privy/washhouse, and carriage house.

3-109. Waverly
1003 Tollgate Road
c. 1870; Private   HA-1257

Members of the Norris family owned this tract from the Revolution until 1866 and at least portions of this multisectioned frame house date to their era(s). But Waverly is best known as the residence of Herman Stump, who also gave the house its present form. Stump, a grandson of John Stump of Stafford, was born at his father's house, Oakington, in 1837. Admitted to the Harford County Bar in 1856, Stump apparently enjoyed his youth; his *Ægis* obituary notes that for the next twenty years he "took a prominent part in [the county's] social life . . . as a host in his own home his genial hospitality ranked him as the peer of any American gentleman." He eventually entered politics and was elected to the state Senate in 1878 and the U.S. Congress in 1889 ("to the Colonel fell the honor of leaving the impress of his genius upon the legislature of his state and nation"). Stump had purchased 180 acres of the Waverly property from the William B. Norris family in May of 1866 for roughly $10,000; while the deed states that it is where the Norrises "now reside," it is clear that Stump made over the frame house, draping it with stylish sawn trim, adding stained glass to the attic dormers, and probably tacking on the porte-cochere to the east so guests—and this would be important during both Stump's social and political incarnations—could alight from their carriages in comfort regardless of the weather. President Cleveland named him the nation's first commissioner of immigration in 1892, a post he held until 1897 when he "gradually gave up active pursuits," and resumed the existence "of an easy-going gentleman." Late in life (1903) he married Marie de Velasco of New York, rich and well known in her own right and a half sister of financier Henry Flagler, the railroad magnate who, through his series of grand resort hotels, single-handedly put Florida on the map. Stump died in 1917, and his appraisers noted "a frame dwelling in good condition, four tenant houses, large bank barn, springhouse, corn house and wagon shed, carriage house and garage, shop, hog pen, hen house, ice house, meat house." He left Waverly as well as the "portraits, silver and furniture from Oakington" to his nephew Bertram Stump, who in 1922 sold it back to the widowed Marie de V. Stump. Mrs. Stump kept the place going in grand style until her death in 1944, when she willed it to her chauffeur.

3-110. Country Life Farm
Old Joppa Road
Early twentieth century; Private   HA-1718

This superb, relaxed Queen Anne house forms the centerpiece of one of the region's best-known Thoroughbred-breeding establishments, Country Life Farm. Adolphe Pons bought the land in 1933 (it was originally known as Rockland Farm) and, with other equestrians such as Anne Heighe and Harvey Ladew, set about earning Harford County a firm niche in the international horse community. Pons, still regarded as one of the century's premier experts on bloodlines, oversaw vast breeding operations throughout America, and his clients included Alfred Vanderbilt, Averell Harriman, George Herbert Walker (President Bush's namesake and grandfather), Paul Mellon, Bing Crosby, Fred Astaire, and the Aga Kahn. More locally, in 1948 the great Citation suffered an upset in a race at Havre de Grace when Saggy beat him; Saggy went on to stand at stud here at Country Life and one of his Harford-bred sons, Carry Back, later won the Kentucky Derby. Perhaps Pons's greatest moment came when he convinced client August Belmont to buy a promising yearling called Man-O-War. Pons's sons, Joseph and John, and numerous grandchildren still work to maintain Country Life's great traditions; grandson Josh captured much of the farm's special spirit in his wonderful book, *Country Life Diary* (1992).

3-111. Glenangus Farms
MacPhail Road
1804; c. 1948; Private   HA-1719

For over a quarter century, this was the lair of Col. L. S. "Larry" MacPhail. Baltimore sports columnist John Steadman observed in 1969, in an article entitled "The Laird of Glenangus," that "with an unbending determination, fed by the strongest will God ever put in a man, Leland Stanford MacPhail has made a lasting impression on the world around him." The colonel certainly made a lasting impression on Harford County where, beginning in 1941, he put together this model horse-breeding and cattle farm, an estate that at its peak totaled 1,000 acres. The main house had a distinguished history even before Colonel MacPhail blasted onto the scene. It was built as the showplace of a 460-acre farm assembled in the late eighteenth century by James Amos, a descendent of William Amos of Mount Soma, and it stayed in the Amos family until the

3-109

3-110

3-111

3-112

3-113

3-114

1870s. Life was grand indeed in the Amos era: when James died in 1840 (owning land and crops including "lot of corn near the meeting-house"), his household inventory included "2 High post bedsteads," massive amounts of mahogany, "a set of guilt [gilt] china," and other elegant items. The place gradually declined and as a 1941 article in *Sports Illustrated* observed, "it was fairly run down. . . . The main residence, though architecturally pleasant enough, had been neglected about a half a century too long and the farm buildings were only there because they had been built of enduring stone." But Colonel MacPhail, with the help of architect Lawrence Ewald, put things to right. No one could ever fully capture all the wonders of Colonel MacPhail, although scribes for publications as varied as the *Ægis* and the *New Yorker* have tried. As Snowden Carter, editor of the *Maryland Horse* wrote, with understatement, in 1966, "The 76-year-old red-haired dynamo . . . seems always to be in the throes of one of life's most exciting chapters." (See chapter 8.)

3-112. Heritage Hill
304 Vale Road
c. 1863; Private   HA-1720

Daniel Scott began the front section of this deep frame house shortly after he acquired the land in 1863. This was one of several Scott tracts in the Bel Air area and, indeed, the family is arguably responsible for the very existence of the town. Daniel's great-grandfather Aquila Scott deeded the community its land, Daniel's grandfather (confusingly named Daniel) surveyed that land so the courthouse could be built, and our Daniel's father, Otho, was regarded as Maryland's leading lawyer. Otho lived about a mile to the east, and it is thought that the younger Scott may have modeled his new house on his father's. Both are exceptionally formal dwellings: this one has a large, projecting entrance hall dominated by a grand double staircase; behind the stair lie the principal rooms (double parlor and dining room) with a service wing beyond. Interesting stone outbuildings of mysterious use (they have been called slave quarters, a jail, and a fortress) lie to the rear.

3-113. Heighe House
Southampton Road
1928; Private
National Register   HA-932

In 1928 Anne McElderry (Mrs. Robert) Heighe commissioned Washington architect John M. Donn to design a country seat here on the edge of Bel Air. Mrs. Heighe, a Harford County horse-breeder esteemed, in the words of the *Maryland Horse* as "the first lady of Maryland racing," centered her equestrian operations on the old ancestral house Prospect Hill but apparently wanted something newer to live in. She bought the site of the derelict Moores Mill and built, to Donn's designs, a 2½-story stone and frame house on the old mill's foundations; she also built, across the road, a 1½-story frame chauffeur's quarters and a 1½-story stone and frame guesthouse. All these structures are gently nestled in a romantic landscape, created at the same time the buildings were built: the garden's principal physical features are the remains of the ancient millrace and pond and the meandering Bynum Run, which courses through the site. Mrs. Heighe and her gardener, the appropriately named Mr. Primrose, laid out an elaborate system of streams and ponds and waterfalls, bark-covered paths and stepping stones, across the seventeen-acre site, all embowered in a hardwood forest underplanted in rhododendron and azalea spinneys and vast drifts of wildflowers.

3-114. Woodview (Gibson's Ridge)
1236 Somerville Road
c. 1744; c. 1820; Private
National Register   HA-1228

Built in two still-discernible sections, Woodview synthesizes 150 years of Harford County history. Its 500-acre patent, Gibson's Ridge, dates to the era of King Charles II (reigned 1660–80), a time when absentee land speculators kept themselves busy in what is now Harford County by buying up the wild woods and valleys along Winters and Bynum runs. By the middle of the eighteenth century, Harford's bayfront had been settled and people began to move inland. In 1744 Benjamin Norris, a prosperous miller and farmer, bought 270 acres of Gibson's Ridge and began building the present house; his work makes up the eastern portion of what one sees today. It originally consisted of two rooms per floor, each with an end-wall fireplace and a corner closet stair, a plan that resembles the plan of Joshua's Meadows, a contemporary house located about a mile up Winters Run. In 1771 Norris's grandson sold the house and 125 acres to Isaac Whitaker, member of another prominent milling and farming family. The property passed to Caleb Pue in 1817, whose descendants have owned it and lived here ever since. Pue led the life of a successful entrepreneur, buying and selling farms in Harford County as well as lots in downtown Baltimore. He also remodeled the old Norris house, adding an elegant parlor to the west (with windows clearly larger than those in the older section) and giving the entire structure up-to-date wood trim such as door surrounds and bookcases. About 150 yards south of the house is a still-functioning springhouse. Of uncertain date, its streamstone walls are laid to make a barrel-vaulted roof resembling a modern Quonset hut in design.

3-115

3-116

cious ham and bread . . . baked cakes of every character and gallons and gallons of . . . ice cream.") Business was obviously booming. In June of 1914 the old store burned but a new building—the present structure—was quickly erected and opened for business that October. The present brick structure is larger than the old one had been (50 by 100 feet versus 60 feet square); its street (west) façade has the requisite plate glass display windows on the ground floor while upper levels boast more varied window treatment (note the second-story semi-Palladian opening with its Gothic arch tracery). Placed prominently above everything, a marble plaque in the gable is inscribed "E. Tucker & Co., Inc., 1858–1914." In 1948 Mr. and Mrs. Maurice Klein, with their son, Ralph, bought the store. The Kleins made three additions to this old building (in 1955, 1963, and 1967) and have since expanded operations to other locations in the county.

3-115. Tucker's Store
Rock Spring Road
1914; Private   HA-1273

A 1979 *Ægis* article on this building noted that at the turn of the century "in every American town, the general store along with the community church served as the hub of activity. It was the general store where the staples of life were either bought or bartered, good and bad news was exchanged, political ideologies were argued, and livestock, farm equipment and crop sales were arranged." Merchants have kept store on this important site, at the intersection of two state roads and thus convenient to the area's prosperous farmers, since before the Civil War when Shununk & Roe opened up shop. That company, clearly shown on the 1858 map of the county, played a key role in the growth of Forest Hill: indeed, in its later incarnations (it evolved into Roe & Tucker and then, after 1910, simply the E. Tucker Company) the firm actually developed the town, trading in building lots as well as in dry goods and "notions." C. Milton Wright noted that "in the early 1900s, Eugene Tucker was head of the firm of E. Tucker and Company, and under his management it became one of the leading stores in Harford County," and the logical site of the Forest Hill post office and (in 1883) railroad station. (The Towson *Maryland Journal* reported that the station was officially opened October 5, 1883, when "Messrs. Roe and Tucker" put on quite a party with "huge platters of fried chicken . . . deli-

3-116. Hoskins-White House
601 Whitaker Mill Road
c. 1860; c. 1950; Private   HA-1552

A testament to the skill of architect Alex Shaw, this well-known house successfully combines two distinct building periods. Various members of the Hoskins family owned several tracts of land here in the early and mid-nineteenth century, so much land, in fact, that the intersection of Old Joppa and Whitaker Mill roads was called Hoskins Corner. In February 1848 Cheney Hoskins ("of Baltimore City") bought this particular tract from Joseph Hoskins and, while nothing is shown on the site on the 1858 county map, the 1878 mapmaker was able to draw a dot here and label it "Cheyney [*sic*] Hoskins." When Hoskins died in 1884, his estate appraisers noted that the house then contained a carpeted attic, a "small room," north, west, and south bedrooms, a parlor, a "south room downstairs," a carpeted sitting room (which also had an "oil cloth and rug"), a kitchen, and a cellar; outbuildings included a woodshed and a carriage house. The house remained intact and was passed down in the Hoskins family until 1939. In 1951 Henry Packard White and his wife, Nancy Allen White, bought the place and hired Shaw to adapt it to modern needs and fashions. Shaw solved these design and function issues by remodeling the original L-plan stone and frame house and by adding 1½-story wings to the east and west.

3-117

3-118

3-118

3-119

3-117. Wilson-Fristoe House
Grafton Shop Road
1770 (remodeled); Private   HA-276

A fireplace brick in this two-part house is inscribed "H. Wilson 1770," fueling the locally held belief that the house was built by Henry Wilson. The trouble is, there were two Henry Wilsons, father and son, active in Harford at that time. Walter Preston's 1901 history of the county notes that Wilson senior was "a Quaker of much influence who was noted for his patriotic zeal during the Revolution." As were his children, notably daughter, Cassandra, who married John Stump of Stafford in 1779, and son Henry Jr., who "was a member of the Committee of Observation of his native county and was conspicuous in collecting and forwarding supplies for the relief of the people of Boston during its blockade by the British squadron." In 1776 young Henry was chosen "a delegate to the first constitutional convention of the State." Wilson's house—assuming it is one of the Wilsons' house—is a stylish product of its time: the walls of the two-story section (the section that contains the fireplace that contains the inscribed brick) are laid in Flemish bond brick (since thickly whitewashed) with a watertable and a beltcourse. The house was built with a pent roof (since removed) across the main façade, a distinct touch of Pennsylvania perhaps explainable by the senior Wilson's Quaker background. Within, this section had a center-hall plan with an open spiral staircase in the hall; the stair—which must have been among the most notable in the county—was removed in the 1930s. The smaller section, to the west and of uncertain age, is stone.

3-118. Hall's Rich Neck
3230 Cool Branch Road
1860; Private   HA-143

In 1843 one Jeremiah McIlvain purchased part of the tract Hall's Rich Neck, a tract whose ownership is easily traced back through the Freeborn Brown family to Thomas Hall, who was assessed for 652 acres of Hall's Rich Neck in 1783. But this rubblestone and granite house is not that old: it was built—presumably by McIlvain—in 1860, according to a reliable-looking datestone in the west gable end. The one room–plan house is much altered: two fires have destroyed most of the interior (a few charred beams are visible in the attic) and frame additions have been placed adjacent the north and east walls. One thing that has not changed, however, is the ornate and intriguing cast-iron door between the first and second stories on the west façade. The present owner of the house believes that the door was involved with the original heating-ventilating system, since interior pipes once fed it and the door's central, floral motif was probably once adjustable to control the flow of air to the stove(s).

3-119. Jewens-Schreiber House
3509 Churchville Road
c. 1870; Private   HA-1293

Holding a firm place in Harford's architectural continuum, this well-maintained, L-plan frame house was built by William Jewens after he paid $1,500 for 20 acres here in November 1863. Jewens (1831–95) and his family lived in a log structure on the property until he was able to build the present house, modeling it, according to tradition, on the nearby Carsins House. And, indeed, the later building is clearly a scaled-down version of the earlier: Jewens's house is three bays wide, not five, and the ell is one room deep, not two; one researcher has described the Jewens porch as "less piquant" than Carsins's, but one glance reveals that, in general, exterior massing and detail are remarkably similar. The same is true on the interior: both had center-hall plans (the Jewens house has been remodeled) with a service stair in the ell—Jewens even copied the Carsins House's dumbwaiter! Jewens, shown as living here on the 1878 county map, left the house to his daughter, Belle Sheridan. His estate inventory makes it clear that he oversaw a flourishing, diversified farm (augmented with "$100 bank stock"): the appraisal was made in September and there were 100 bushels of wheat, 120 bushels of oats, twelve tons of hay, eight pigs, three cows, five horses, and "1 dog cart" (worth $5); the house had a parlor, dining room, and kitchen on one floor, and three bedrooms upstairs. (The stair had "carpet and rods.") Mr. Sheridan was a canner with a cannery nearby on Churchville Road; according to family legend, he summoned his workers to their jobs by crying, "All ye peelers!"

3-120. Nicholas Baker IV House
913 Stepney Road
c. 1861 (earlier wing?); Private   HA-1553

On the first of June, 1839, Nicholas Baker IV bought thirty-eight acres here from Francis Cloman for $304. Baker's parents lived nearby (see 2-72) and his brother George gained renown as the county's leading canner (see 3-101). Nicholas Baker (1810–96) had married Elizabeth Carsins in 1837 (her brother was William Carsins) and, it is thought, the couple lived here in what is the rear wing of the much-expanded house. Baker tried his hand at chairmaking (as had brother George) and ran a furniture factory with James Everett, but he later took up what was becoming a family obsession, the canning of fruits and vegetables. This made him truly prosperous and he displayed his new wealth in architecture by adding the large front section of the house. (Descendants suggest the wing was built "the year Fort Sumter was fired on"; it is also said that the original house faced Churchville Road but was turned around when the new wing was added.) And a very stylish creation it must have seemed, too, with its elaborate porch, attic gable and dormers, and (around the main entrance) etched glass transom and sidelights. Yet, and as is true at brother George's house, for all its Victorian ornament, the Baker house is at heart just another five-bay Harford County frame farmhouse along the lines of Greenwood. Elizabeth Baker died and Nicholas then married Mary Greenland; on Baker's death in 1896 the property passed to a son by the second marriage, Winfield L. Baker, who also continued his father's canning operations. The house is still owned by Baker descendants.

3-120

3-121

3-121. Jacob Livezey House
West Medical Hall Road
c. 1844 (earlier wing?); Private   HA-132

From earliest times, Harford County has benefited from the numerous Quaker families who have migrated here from southern Pennsylvania; in the nineteenth century these "new" arrivals included members of the Livezey and Waterman clans. Jacob Ott Livezey and his wife (née Priscilla Waterman) began acquiring several tracts of land in this part of central Harford shortly after they arrived here in 1844 from Philadelphia. They sold one parcel to Priscilla's brother, Joseph, in 1855 who built a family-run inn while the Livezeys apparently lived and farmed here. When the Livezeys bought the property, it may have come with a small stone house on it; the 1814 tax records note such a structure that (more or less) lines up with the two-bay, two-story southern section of the present dwelling. But it is clear that the Livezeys made whatever was here their own and within and without the extant house, with its five-bay stone section and large frame rear wing, certainly reads as a product of the mid-nineteenth century. Many county farmsteads contain notable outbuildings; that is the case here, for the two-story stone and frame smokehouse and the one-story stone privy certainly deserve mention.

DISTRICT 4

Norrisville, Pylesville, and Upper Cross Roads

4-1

4-2

4-3

4-1. Black Horse Tavern
Troyer Road and Route 23
1849; Private   HA-39

It may be hard to imagine, but there once real-ly was a thriving community called Black Horse, laid out on land Abraham Jarrett patented in 1771 as The Barrens. (Jarrett was either descriptive or trenchant for he named another patent Hills of Poverty.) The main colonial-era road between Baltimore and York ran through The Barrens and, it is said, a tav-ern was built on this site in the 1770s to serve that interstate traffic. (One account suggests that George Washington himself stayed here on June 5, 1773, while en route back to Mount Vernon from visiting his stepson, Jackie Custis, then studying at King's College [Co-lumbia] in New York.) In any event, in the early nineteenth century, Robert Henderson bought The Barrens and the property re-mained in that family for nearly a century. In 1849 Henderson's grandson, the Reverend Thomas Henderson, remodeled—some say tore down—the old tavern, and it is clear that the present five-bay frame structure in its pres-ent incarnation dates to his era. Thomas Hen-derson, according to C. Milton Wright, was "probably one of the best educated men in the county, a scholar of Latin, Greek, and other languages": he ran a school here, was a promi-nent land surveyor, and "published a book on algebra which was used extensively"—not the usual avocations one associates with innkeep-ing! In Henderson's day, Black Horse boasted (in addition to the inn) a Methodist church, a general store, a blacksmith shop, and (after 1883) a public school.

4-2. Amos Mill
Amos Mill Road
c. 1800; Private   HA-40

One of the most aggressively picturesque structures in Maryland, the Amos Mill (as photographed by Aubrey Bodine) has graced dozens of book jackets and magazine covers. The problem is, no one is quite certain when the mill was built. It is popularly dated to the eighteenth century (doubtless in part because it just "looks old") but it is not shown on any of the usual period documents, that is the 1783 and '98 tax lists and the 1795 Griffith map. The mill stands on a 110-acre tract that David Wiley inherited from his father, Matthew Wi-ley, in 1840; deeds in the 1840s often refer to "the road leading from David Wiley's Mill." (During the last century several other Wiley mills dotted North Harford's streambeds; see, for example, the Ivory Mill.) David Wiley died in 1857, leaving instructions that "my mill property . . . be sold," which it finally was, but not until the 1880s. Isaac Amos purchased the "20-acre Wiley Mill property" for $1,400 on February 19, 1891, and his descendants still own it. Amos's son, John (who died in 1972), had to repair (and replace) much of the anti-quated three-story building—for instance in 1926 he took out the rotted wooded water-wheel and put in a steel one—but he did so without lessening one whit the aura of age that so completely surrounds the place. Non-functioning for several years, the wonderful building awaits a new use.

4-3. My Lady's Manor
Manor, Hess, and Old York Roads
1713 (patent); Private and public
National Register   HA-57

In 1713, on the occasion of his fourth mar-riage, Charles Calvert, third Lord Baltimore, gave his new bride a 10,000-acre tract he called My Lady's Manor. Other lords Baltimore had also attempted to establish manors in their colony of Maryland: following long-established English tradition, these manors were large grants of land given to a landlord (or landlady) and then subdivided into smaller farms peopled with rent-paying tenants. The 1713 venture did not prove particularly successful. Lord Baltimore died in 1715, and Charlotte, his daughter and the wife of Thomas Brerewood, eventually inherited the largely vacant manor. Thomas's father came to America in 1731 to manage the estate and to establish the community of Charlottetown, on the Big Gunpowder, where he built structures to make the most of what he hoped would become a flourishing tobacco-based economy. When Brerewood died in 1746 William Dallam (the tobacco inspector in Joppa) became the Baltimores' agent for the manor. Matters deteriorated: questions of ownership arose and lawsuits ensued; tobacco never really took off commercially; and the Revolution spelled the death of the manorial system altogether. Finally, in 1782 the 10,000-acre tract was parceled out and the parcels sold at auction, filling the manor with the 200-acre (or so) farms that characterize it today. Prosperity came roaring in during the 1800–1840 period, when the manor's rich soils proved ideal not for tobacco but for wheat and corn, which could be ground in newly established mills (such as Monkton Mills, 1776) and shipped from Baltimore. Agriculture has remained the dominant force on the land-scape—although horses and hounds have largely replaced tobacco and wheat—and the manor, most of which lies in Baltimore County, remains a splendidly isolated bucolic community, easily distinguished from surrounding neighborhoods.

4-4. Edward Voss Studio
Pocock Road
c. 1930; Private   HA-58

Edward Voss and his brother Frank moved to My Lady's Manor from Long Island in the same wave of migrating New Yorkers that gave Maryland Harvey Ladew. And the motivation was the same for all three: fox hunting. The Voss brothers, nephews of Joseph Voss who served as secretary of the Elkridge Foxhunting Club in the 1880s, thrived in their new environment—Edward even won the distinction of being chosen MFH of the Elkridge-Harford Hunt. (In this he succeeded Ladew; Voss served off and on as MFH from 1939 until

1970, when he was succeeded by Cornelius Bliss.) Voss was also a watercolorist of note (brother Frank preferred to paint in oils) and built this thoroughly charming studio on the Elkridge-Harford grounds, possibly so he could escape the practical worries of running his farm (he owned the early nineteenth-century Atlanta Hall nearby) but possibly simply so he could be within earshot of his beloved horses and hounds.

4-5. Elkridge-Harford Hunt Club
Pocock Road
1938 (replacement); Private   HA-60

Thanks largely to the efforts of John Rush Streett, in the early years of the twentieth century the My Lady's Manor area of Harford and Baltimore counties became internationally famous for fox hunting. (This reputation has grown stronger as the century has waned, due in part to the natural beauty and charm of the countryside and, in part, to the conviviality and keen sportsmanship of the manor residents.) Streett lived in a c. 1771 Jarrett house called "Farmington" and he eventually leased the two-story, five-bay stuccoed structure to the Harford Hunt Club, with himself as manager. The club was founded in 1912, but not incorporated until 1915—no hurry about these legal trivialities when the air is crisp and the scent is fresh. In 1935 it merged with the older Elkridge Hounds, after the latter group decided that its location near Baltimore City had grown too suburban. In April 1938 fire ripped through the old Streett house; paintings and trophies were destroyed, but the club's spirit remained strong and members, led by Harvey Ladew and Edna Parlett, and assisted by Ladew's favorite architect, James O'Connor of New York, devised this splendid Georgian revival replacement. Indeed, many would agree with club historian J. Rieman McIntosh, who felt that the new building was a decided improvement on the old: "One real advantage resulted from the fire," wrote McIntosh, "because the building could now be designed to function much better as a club house."

4-6. Chrome Valley Mill
1532 West Jarrettsville Road
1857; Private   HA-309

In April of 1857 the trustees of Samuel and Rebecca Reed sold this tract to Samuel Wetherill, who then built the 3½-story stone and frame mill, crowning it with datestone (still visible

4-4

4-5

4-6

4-7

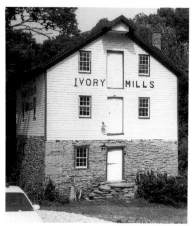

4-8

in the south wall) which reads "Wetherill's Mill 1857." Wetherill died that same year, but the 1858 county map still shows "Wetherell's Mill" on this site. (An ad in the May 8, 1858, *Southern Ægis* notes that Henry W. Archer was about to sell the "Real Estate of Samuel Wetherell . . . large new grain mill, 3 pair of burrs, 1 of country stones . . . sawmill.") The mill repeatedly changed hands during the next few decades but at least one of these many owners deserves comment—the Baltimore Chrome Mining Company, which held title between 1866 and 1869. The mining of chrome hereabouts not only gave the area several place names (such as Chrome Hill and Chrome Valley), it also made the Tysons of Baltimore very, very rich and a scion of the family, Jesse Tyson, used his chromium-derived profits to hire architect George Frederick to design the great house Cylburn in Baltimore City. Members of the prominent Streett clan owned the mill off and on from the 1870s through World War II. Samuel Streett, who acquired the property in 1919, had flour sacks that boasted "Chrome Valley Mills, Queen of the Pantry Flour." In 1922 Streett bought a new steel overshot wheel for the mill for $1,780, and the *Ægis* claimed that the wheel was the "largest of its kind in the country." The mill closed shortly thereafter and stood vacant until 1959 when Mr. and Mrs. James Campbell purchased it and remodeled it into a house.

4-7. Matthew Wiley House
5009 Norrisville Road
c. 1811; Private   HA-455

It would be difficult to find any family anywhere whose members have so thoroughly been identified with a single occupation as have the Wileys and their mills. Indeed, since the first Joseph Wiley came to America from Ireland in the early eighteenth century and settled in Chester County, Pennsylvania, seven generations of the clan have been grinding corn and wheat into flour. One of Joseph's grandsons, Matthew Wiley (1751–1840), left Chester County for Harford in 1778 where he gradually built up a self-sufficient empire. The 1798 tax list reveals that he owned 823 acres of land, more than adequate to produce large enough crops of grain to keep his three mills (now called Ivory, Amos, and Jolly Acres) profitably busy. In 1790 Wiley purchased an old frame mill here, which he replaced in 1818; he also built this three-bay coursed-stone

house for himself across the road from the mill. Variously dated (1819, according to C. Milton Wright; 1811, according to the datestone) it is clearly of the era of the mill. It also reveals that the architectural aesthetic the Wileys encountered in Chester County continued to dominate their thinking after they had moved to Maryland; this substantial south-facing structure, built into a hill with a high, exposed cellar, pent roof porch, and massive gable end chimneys, could easily have come from the banks of the Brandywine. (There are, of course, similar buildings in Harford and Baltimore counties but the origin of the species is undoubtedly southeastern Pennsylvania.) The utilitarian cellar, built to contain the kitchen, has been altered a bit, but the upstairs (with its center-hall plan) remains largely intact down to its simply molded window and door surrounds and beaded board trim.

4-8. Ivory Mill
Harford Creamery Road
1818; Private   HA-448

A mill has prominently occupied this site since the eighteenth century (period deeds in the neighborhood often refer to it, and in 1790 county officials used it as the starting point when they laid out a new road, now known as Harford Creamery Road, "from Matthew Wiley's lower mill . . . to the road leading to Belle Air"), but by 1818 that ancient structure had simply grown obsolete. So its owner, miller Matthew Wiley, tore it down and replaced it with a mill built of stone and planed lumber. When Wiley died in 1840 he bequeathed this building, which he called the "Lower Mill," and 251 acres to his son John, who on his death in 1868 left it to his son Richard, and either John or Richard named it "Ivory." According to the 1880 census R. N. Wiley's "custom mill" was worth $1,500, and, with its "9-foot fall" on Deer Creek it could turn out "400 bbl flour, 1.2 tons buckwheat, 72.5 tons meal, and 80 tons feed," altogether worth $5,780. (There was also a sawmill worth $700 with one employee.) Remodeled in 1890, the mill remained in operation—and under Wiley ownership—until well into the twentieth century. The grounds here contain a variety of interesting outbuildings, such as a nineteenth-century frame combination carriage house and granary, the ruins of a springhouse, and the abutments of a covered bridge that once spanned Deer Creek.

4-9. Ivory Mill House

Harford Creamery Road
c. 1842; Private   HA-449

When miller Matthew Wiley died in 1840, he left his "Lower Mill" to his son John, who is generally credited with building this five-bay, two-story frame house. (A frame, 1½-story rear wing is often said to be older.) The house is large yet straightforward, with regular massing and window placement and a center-hall plan. John Wiley almost certainly built it for himself (it is shown on the 1858 county map labeled "J. Wiley") and placed it facing the road near the structure that map calls simply "Mill."

4-10. Ayres Chapel

Route 23 (Norrisville Road)
1896; 1946; Regular services   HA-461

According to long-repeated tradition, the area's intrepid Methodists first met here in tents before they had funds to erect an actual church building. That building day arrived in 1870, and the congregation erected a simple frame church on land donated by Mr. and Mrs. Thomas Ayres. (Another Thomas Ayres died in 1886 and his tombstone, in the nearby cemetery, reads, in part, "How peaceful the grove its quiet how deep / Its zephyrs breathe calmly and soft in its sleep. . . . Here the traveler worn with life's pilgrimage dreary / Lays down his rude staff like one that is weary.") The congregation quickly grew too numerous for the old church and hatched plans for a new building in 1890; the result is the present clapboard structure, dedicated in August 1896 and extensively remodeled in 1946. The colored glass in the windows is simple and plain, in keeping with Methodist philosophy, while the whimsical steeple rises in elaborate contrast.

4-11. Wiley Upper Mill

Jolly Acres Road
c. 1800; remodeling; Private   HA-458

On September 7, 1781 ("and in the Fifth year of American Independence"), "Matthew Wiley, Yeoman" paid "Andrew and John McKemson, Yeomen," £16,000 "current money of Pennsylvania" for 115 acres here. The McKemson brothers had patented the tract a decade earlier and had built the mill referred to in the deed ("a mill about five yards from Deer Creek on the North side thereof"). According

to the 1798 federal tax assessors, Wiley owned 823 acres here (he continued to buy property) as well as a "gristmill 30 × 25," and he reportedly replaced the old mill with the present chinked-log structure around 1800. At his death this property passed to son Matthew Jr., thence in 1878 to George Wiley, whom the 1880 census-takers credited with a "custom mill worth $2,000" capable of producing "200 bbl flour, 10 bbl rye, 125 tons meal, 100 tons feed, and 25 tons buckwheat" all worth $6,235. The Black and Decker Company bought the property from Dora Wiley Treadway in 1927 and turned the grounds into Jolly Acres Park for company employees; in 1947 it became a Lutheran day camp. The mill has been extensively remodeled but the rustic setting remains largely unspoiled.

4-12. St. Mary's Roman Catholic Church

St. Mary's Road
1895 (dedication); Regular services   HA-470

They did things right in those days: when Cardinal Gibbons came out from Baltimore to dedicate this handsome granite church on September 15, 1895, the Baltimore *Sun* reported that "a special train . . . brought 350 passengers from Baltimore" for the ceremony. (They were joined by enough countians to make a crowd of 4,000, according to the *Ægis*.) The cardinal, who had come out the evening before to spend the night at the country house of Henry Jenkins, had been met by "a guard of honor" of sixty men "mounted on fine horses and wearing cardinal sashes." At the service "Hayden's Third Mass was sung by a choir augmented from the Cathedral" and His Eminence observed that the first church (1855 and still standing nearby) on this site was "the smallest" but that the present was "the most beautiful and perhaps the largest in the county." Architect Thomas C. Kennedy of Baltimore designed the idiosyncratic Gothic/Romanesque structure which is built of gray Deer Creek granite. In his dedication remarks, Cardinal Gibbons credited the new building to the parish priest, Fr. William J. Kane, a "young and energetic pastor" who had recently (1890) graduated from St. Mary's Seminary. (After the ceremony, the cardinal went to St. Ignatius Church, where he gave two sermons, one called "Agriculture" and one "On the Advantages of Country over City Life.")

4-9

4-10

4-11

4-12

4-13

4-14

4-15

4-16

4-13. Brick House Farm
Nelson Mill Road
Mid-eighteenth century (?); Private   HA-495

John Rutledge came to America from England in 1640, acquired large land-holdings in Baltimore County, and his descendants have held sway in the upper reaches of the Gunpowder Falls ever since. In 1785 John's great-grandson Joshua Rutledge bought a tract called "The Brick House Farm" (still owned by his descendants) which may have contained a portion of the extant house: the two-part dwelling certainly *is* of brick; the walls in the main section are four bricks thick while those in the rear or kitchen wing are three, which has led some to suggest that there have been two stages of growth. (Regrettably, those portions of the 1798 tax list pertinent to this important building have been lost.) Joshua Rutledge became one of the area's more notable farmers and, in addition, took an interest in education; he served as one of the original trustees of the Bel Air Academy, which first opened in 1815. He died in 1825 and left the 360-acre farm "I now live on" to his sons Thomas and Jacob (but daughters Ruth, Jane, and Penelope, who received a slave and a bed apiece, "could board" in the house until they were 16). Various Rutledges have remodeled the old house several times, a natural enough result of its having been continuously lived in for seven generations. Happily, the remodelings have all been carried out with care and sensitivity—doubtless also a result of the seven generations'–long tenure.

4-14. Salisbury Plains
Norrisville Road
Early nineteenth century; Private   HA-1010

Two for one: although now sheathed in asbestos siding, and with proportions, rooflines, and overall massing that suggest all-of-a-piece construction, it is easy to discern two distinct houses here. Both are log and, while they stand touching each other, each had—has—its own entrance. Until recently it was impossible to walk between the two: the units are now internally joined, thanks to modern doorways, but their individuality remains largely intact. The eastern, three-bay section seems to be older; built into a sheltering hillside it originally faced south and consisted of a one-room plan with a corner, closeted stair. This plan remains on the ground floor, whose single room is dominated by a large cooking fireplace on the western wall, complete with iron crane; wooden beams are exposed in the ceiling; walls are simply plastered. A large board-and-batten barn and a working windmill still stand on the property, adding to its interest and importance. Several generations of the Duncan family owned this roughly 100-acre tract from 1816 until the 1850s.

4-15. Industry
(Sweetbrier Farms)
3061 Church Lane
c. 1822; 1868; Private   HA-1019

That northwestern Harford County was settled well after the tidewater regions becomes clear here, where a 311-acre tract of land was patented to John McClure in 1796—a full century and a half after patents had been granted for bayfront acreage. McClure sold thirty-eight acres of the tract to Thomas Marshall on March 25, 1822, for $400 and Marshall probably then built the two-story, three-bay log (center) section of the present dwelling. Inside, this original house has a one-room plan on the main floor with two small rooms above; beaded board doors are found throughout; a corner winder stair is placed in a closet in the western wall; and a fireplace marks the center of the eastern wall. Pegged beams are visible in the attic as are traces of clapboard siding on a wall that was originally exterior but is now interior. That phenomenon is explained by the two-story, two-bay rubblestone section, built adjacent and to the west. (The western attic peak of addition contains a stone plaque encircled by brick headers; now blank, a former owner says the plaque was inscribed "1868.") The two-story, one-bay eastern addition is of uncertain date, as is the whimsical scalloped eaves' trim.

4-16. My Lady's Manor Farm
Old York Road
c. 1865; Private   HA-1078

Straddling the northeastern border of the My Lady's Manor tract this thriving dairy farm owes its general layout to the Patterson family, who owned it between 1865 and 1908, and its present prosperity to the Smith family, who have owned it since 1910. The two-story, L-plan frame house is, perhaps, another variation on the Greenwood scheme but the dignified main door, with seven-light transom and sidelights, gives it great individuality. The farm also boasts a remarkable collection of working outbuildings; the oldest of these include a clapboard blacksmith shop (at least three generations old and still with its original forge), a dairy, a board-and-batten meathouse, and a large barn that retains its original pegged framing system.

4-17. William Wilson House II

3004 Sharon Road
c. 1805; Private   HA-1232

The Reverend William Wilson began buying land in this neighborhood as early as 1790, when he acquired 178 acres of Pheasant Range from Aquila Massey. Wilson's first house, now numbered 1120 Rigdon Road (and gutted by fire in the 1980s), was a simple, one-story, rubblestone dwelling that was quickly superseded by this more substantial structure. The second house, notable for its dressed stone, is large in scale but simple in massing; it is shown as "Rev. W. Wilson" on the 1858 and 1878 county maps. Wilson, obviously a man of prominence, was an elder of the Old Brick Baptist Church near Jarrettsville from 1807 until the issue of temperance split the congregation in the 1830s. Then he and several members left to form the Rock Ridge Regular Baptist Society, which met in a church near Cherry Hill. According to C. Milton Wright the schism was healed in 1859, and Old Brick's minutes note that its doors "are open . . . to receive any or all of the members that may feel desirous to return to the bosom of this church."

4-18. Belle Grade

1500 McDermott Road
c. 1850; Private   HA-1234

One of the most interesting houses in this part of the county, this two-story brick structure is built on land Martin Low acquired in 1848. Little is known of Low but he was clearly a man of imagination, because he took a basically prosaic building form and made it his own; note particularly the whimsically arched windows. (Low obviously liked that arched shape, because he repeated it in every window lintel—even in the attic—and strung a series of them together as trim for the front porch.) Low died in 1889 and nothing in his rather meager estate inventory (total value $670.75) suggests any unusual aesthetic forces at work—although it *is* interesting that he was planting tobacco here at this late date: his "one half interest [in] two acres tobacco" was valued at $90 while "2,000 tobacco laths" were altogether appraised at $5.00.

4-19. Ladew Topiary Gardens

(Pleasant Valley Farm)
3535 Jarrettsville Pike
c. 1800; 1930s; Private (regularly open)
National Register   HA-1245

Few artistic creations in Harford County have an international following, but the house and garden created by Harvey Ladew have been studied, written about, and admired by cognoscenti from at least five continents. (In 1993 alone, the property drew 30,000 pilgrims from forty countries.) Harvey Ladew, born into the fluid yet nonetheless upper strata of New York society in 1887, knew at an early age that he required three things in his life: good fox hunting, a good house, and a good garden. When Ladew returned to his native Long Island after World War I, suburban sprawl was threatening and he began looking elsewhere for the perfect place. By chance he went hunting in Harford County; he left enchanted— "What a natural wonderful country I found in Harford," he later wrote. "There were many nice farmers, who for the most part sympathized with fox-hunting. . . . Cattle grazed contentedly in lush green pasture. . . . There was not a strand of wire anywhere." He bought 200 gently rolling acres of Pleasant Valley Farm in 1929; the farm, long the domain of the Scharf family, bordered the Harford Hunt Club, which he joined. That took care of one of his three requirements and he immediately set to work on the other two. With the help of decorator Billy Baldwin and architect James O'Connor he transformed the ancient two-part frame house on the property into the magical place present today by adding a large service wing off to the south (c. 1930) and a series of idiosyncratic rooms to the north (c. 1938). ("He never could resist a little bit of extra fantasy," commented Baldwin.) But it is in the twenty-two acres of gardens—highly personal and rich in private meaning—that Ladew outdid himself: he planned and planted a wildflower garden, a berry garden, and a waterlily garden; he devised gardens of single color (white, pink, and yellow); he dug in an apple orchard and a rose garden. There is also, of course, topiary. Horses and hounds in yew greet visitors; hemlock obelisks and garland-draped walls punctuate terraces off the house; a sea of billowing topiary yew waves with serenely swimming swans encloses the Great Bowl; and, as a climax, his Sculpture Garden is filled with a brace of seahorses, a unicorn, lyrebirds, two

4-17

4-18

4-19

4-19

4-20

4-21

4-22

4-23

homages to Churchill, and a bewildering array of other forms all sculpted in topiary, all in yew. This truly distinguished creation, with its combination of sweeping vistas and small enclosed spaces, all exuding self-confidence and clear vision, is more fully explored in chapter 10.

4-20. Eli Turner House
4325 Norrisville Road
c. 1855; Private   HA-1246

"A paradox, a paradox," run some lyrics in *Pirates of Penzance,* lyrics that, regarding this frame house, might be switched to "anomaly, anomaly." It is hard to believe, but this one house represents one-third the sum total of Harford County's Greek revival domestic architecture. (See chapter 6.) Luckily, the little house is a good example of the style; its temple-form shape is perfect and the no-nonsense porch posts, squared-off entrance details (transom, sidelights, and so on), and fluted window trim are appropriately chaste. (The attic's Palladian window and the cornice's scroll brackets lessen the Hellenistic impact a bit, but are nonetheless endearing.) The inside displays further stylish period touches, including wood graining on some doors, a center-hall plan, and, in the two main (front) rooms, pilaster-flanked mantels. Eli Turner, about whom unfortunately little is known, began buying land in the area in 1850 and continued his purchases throughout the decade; he is shown as living in a house on this site on both the 1858 and 1878 county maps. He died in 1894 and his estate inventory suggests that he derived most of his income—income that produced this locally unusual structure— from his crops of wheat.

4-21. Madonna General Store
Norrisville Road
Late nineteenth century; Private   HA-1308

Although altered, this two-story frame structure still bears what has been called "the distinguishing characteristics of the classic nineteenth century corner store in Harford County," that is to say, the massing and fenestration, particularly the plate glass display window and central entrance. An aluminum awning now spans the front where doubtless there was once a canvas awning and the cornice details have been changed, but the building is clearly recognizable for what it is—a hub of local commerce, *the* place to go for beef

jerky or for tomatoes in August or cider in November.

4-22. Colonel John Streett House
Holy Cross Road
c. 1805; Private
National Register   HA-1517

This wonderful house stands as one of the two or three best Harford County examples of the high federal-era style. Streett (1762–1837) was born on his father Thomas's tract, Streett's Hunting Ground, which sprawled across 1,500 acres in the then-unsettled northern reaches of Harford County. Entering politics, John was elected to the first of several terms in the Maryland legislature in 1799. Many feel that Streett's interest in architecture dates to his years in Annapolis; the argument runs that he saw and was inspired by that city's elegant houses (William Paca's, Edward Lloyd's, and so on). In any event, he bought this 300-acre farm in 1801 and by the time of the 1814 tax assessment he had constructed the present house for the assessors called it "brick, 2-story, 42' × 21'," which is certainly accurate. It is also mundane and does not begin to describe the house's great and impressive beauty. It does not convey, for instance, the house's high ceilings, which give a sense of spaciousness one would expect to find only in a much larger building; nor does it suggest the marbleized mantles and grained doors. Streett resigned his legislative seat to take up the sword (or, more strictly, the reins) when war broke out in 1812; he joined a cavalry regiment and earned praise from his commander for his "highly honorable" action during the Battle of North Point in the defense of Baltimore. After years of neglect, this important house is now enjoying a full-scale restoration.

4-23. Erwin-Lauck House
3315 Rocks-Chrome Hill Road
c. 1880; Private   HA-1526

At first the house may not look like much, but closer investigation reveals that this frame structure is fairly bursting with architectural ambition. It has balanced massing on the exterior (down to the carefully placed end chimneys) and, within, a dignified center-hall plan, beaded wainscotting, a paneled chimney breast in the eastern room, and mitered trim around most of the windows and doors. In August of 1879 Thomas Erwin paid $340 for a thirty-five-acre lot and probably built the house shortly thereafter; he sold the same acreage to John C. Ayres for $450 in 1899 and Ayres sold it back to Erwin in 1900, at which time the deed describes the tract as the land "whereon Thomas Erwin resided."

4-24. Rocks Steel Truss Bridge
Route 24 at Rocks State Park
1934; Public   HA-1576

Constructed by the Fort Pitt Bridge Works in Pittsburgh, this steel span carries Route 24 over Deer Creek. One of the older metal bridges in the State Highway Administration's network, at least in Harford County, it is also among the more interesting such spans in terms of construction. The bridge is basically a single skew three-panel Pratt through truss 123 feet in length; portal bracing consists of triangular trusses. Although they are the products of mass-production and industrialization, the county's metal bridges actually display a good deal of variety and individuality: simply compare this span to the double truss near Wilson's Mill or to the single trusses near Noble's Mill and Whitaker's Mill.

4-25. William Glenn House
1644 Jerrys Road
c. 1865; Private   HA-1700

This house, like its contemporary Belle Grade, is a splendid example of how some of the county's late nineteenth-century farmers chose to assert their individuality. William Glenn, shown living here on the 1878 county map, took what is basically a standard two-story, cross-gable frame house—one of hundreds of similar structures in the county—and made it his own: he added distinctive trim to the windows and doors (shallow-arched enframements with scroll appliqué), placed a Gothic-arched window in the attic, and enlivened the porch's turned posts with delicate brackets containing quatrefoil details. Glenn presumably chose all these motifs from one of the many period architectural pattern books; these books were popular nationwide but it says a good deal about Glenn that he chose to embellish his house with such stylish touches while so many of his neighbors chose not to.

4-26. Old Brick Baptist Church
Baldwin Mill Road
1754; 1787; Special services
Harford County Landmark   HA-66

Considered to be the mother church of many Baptist missions in Maryland, this foursquare brick building is, with Priest Neale's Mass House, the oldest religious structure in the county. (It is somewhat ironic that the Church of England was the established church hereabouts throughout the colonial period, yet the oldest houses of worship represent dissenting sects.) A group of Baptists established a church on Falls Road near Baltimore in 1742 (now called Slater Baptist Church) and a dozen years later missionaries, led by Elder John Davis, established this parish and erected the sturdy Flemish bond brick church whose clean lines have remained surprisingly unchanged through the years. It has been so little changed that the major alterations (made in 1787) are easily cataloged: the windows lost their arches and became squared (the original arches are still somewhat visible), the earthen floor was replaced by bricks, and the pulpit and sounding board were reworked. Otherwise, the church remains almost exactly as Elder Davis built it. (And as caught the eye of Henry Ford; the great industrialist wanted to buy the church and move it to his recreated "Deerfield Village" as an example of ye olde Americana but the congregation wouldn't sell.) Davis played an important role in the political issues of his day and was one of ten men elected to represent Bush River Upper Hundred on the Harford Revolutionary Committee. He stayed on at the church until his death in 1807 and is buried, with his wife, in the surrounding cemetery.

4-27. Mary E. W. Risteau House
Jarrettsville and Rigdon Roads
Mid-nineteenth century; Private   HA-1240

This fine federal-style brick house derives most its importance from its most famous owner, Mary Eliza Watters Risteau, who moved here in 1917 (with her widowed mother) and lived here until her death in 1978. Born in Towson in 1890 to William McG. and Mary Amoss Risteau, "Miss Mary," as she was generally known, was the first woman elected to the Maryland House of Delegates (in 1921, just a year after women were given the vote) and to the state Senate (1935), and as a delegate to a national convention (the Democrat, in

4-24

4-25

4-26

4-27

4-28

4-29

1936), *and* as a member of the state board of education (1922). Long before she earned her law degree from the University of Baltimore in 1938, she had decided to make her mark in politics and thus, in the words of the book *Notable Maryland Women,* "helped to pave the way for women in politics and public life in the Old Line State." She may well have been first bitten by the political bug in 1912 when she and her mother traveled downtown by streetcar to watch the Democratic National Convention in Baltimore nominate—on the 46th ballot—Woodrow Wilson for president. Both Risteau women then campaigned vigorously for Wilson. Like so many other capable women of her time, when few doors were open to them, "Miss Mary" began her professional life as a teacher; she started her first job in 1917 but quickly found lobbying for the Baltimore County Teachers' Association more interesting than holding forth in the classroom. That same year, on the death of her father, "Miss Mary" and her mother moved to an old Harford County brick house and 200-acre farm that her mother had recently inherited (this structure) and the women learned how to manage a large dairy operation. Women were enfranchised in 1920 and the next year Risteau ran for the House of Delegates; she took the improvement of public education as her main campaign theme and was honest enough to acknowledge that good schools cost money. She won, which prompted the Baltimore *Sun* to editorialize (and patronize), "we trust her presence will help to raise the standard of manners. . . . May she show herself . . . free from feminine freakishness"—whatever *that* meant. Risteau had been a friend of Harford's other great politician, Millard Tydings, since the days when the two taught school together; she also won the respect of Governor Ritchie, who had initially opposed women's suffrage. She more or less retired from politics in 1954. But she couldn't just sit quietly and twiddle her thumbs, and that year she found another cause to champion, the Baltimore Orioles, who had just arrived on the local scene. (Even in her eighth decade she took pride in attending nearly every home game.) Still, politics was her game and, as Flora Wiley wrote in the July 1992 *Villager,* "statistics and tributes do not . . . reflect the whole personality of the woman . . . [who] could confound her opponents with logic, berate them in language seldom used by ladies of her day, and coerce them into supporting her causes. . . . History will accord her a rightful place among Maryland's great leaders."

4-28. Del Mar
Baldwin Mill Road
c. 1880; Private   HA-1775

Built on land that belonged to the McComas family seemingly since the beginning of time, this handsome frame house probably dates to around 1880 when the tracts (bearing the unlikely names of Ogg King of Basham and Weatheral's Last Addition) were owned by Gabriel McComas. He had inherited the land, roughly 135 acres, in 1838 from Robert McComas who, in turn, had been willed it by his father, Aquila. Gabriel, an enterprising farmer of the first rank, hired "Oliver Parkey, contractor" to construct this splendid residence. It is hard to know just when all the construction took place, although since McComas died in 1882 and since it appears that Parkey hadn't yet been paid (McComas's heirs had to pay the artisan $3,550 "for building dwelling house on Farm"), one assumes the house was fairly new in 1882. It remains astonishingly intact and its dignified mansard roof, regular massing, sawn trim (note especially the brackets and the porch brackets) and, within, door and window hardware, imposing staircase, and molded woodwork make McComas's house a superlative example of "country Second Empire style," the logical, low-key successor to such flamboyant Second Empire dwellings as Clement Dietrich's Fair Meadows. After Gabriel's death (his $31,000 net worth came from hogs, horses, sheep, wheat, potatoes, "applebutter and pots," and "canned fruit"), his daughter, Amanda Scarff, sold the farm in 1892 to Jordan McComas, fondly remembered in the Fallston commemorative booklet "The Gateway" for his "team of beautiful black prancing horses" that "were known throughout the countryside."

4-29. Model Farm
Fallston Road
Upper Cross Roads
c. 1840; c. 1880; Private   HA-1847

With its air of unpretentious dignity and comfort, this fine, frame two-section dwelling exemplifies all the best features one associates with the phrase "Harford County farmhouse." Interestingly, it has been home to only two families in its 150-year history—or, perhaps, to 1½ families for the owners, the Diverses and the Amosses, are, in fact, distantly related to each other. The first owner of record is Ananias Divers; when he died in 1846 his two sons, John and Ananias Jr., inherited his farm of 100 acres and "the mansion house," which doubtless refers to the older portion of the extant structure. While the senior Ananias's estate inventory doesn't suggest the shape or size of the house, it is clear that the deceased lived well, with a "walnut dining table," "mahogany breakfast table," "bureau and bookcase," "silver mounted sword," "thirty-hour clock," and other items of refinement. The inventory also strongly suggests that diversified farming provided the basis for his affluence; it lists bumper crops of oats, wheat, corn, cabbages, potatoes, and hay, as well as a dozen cattle, a yoke of oxen, a few horses (doubtless for transportation), thirteen sheep, a "black boar hog," ten shoats, and "8 fat hogs." John Divers slowly bought out his brother's interest in the place (it took two deeds, one in 1853, the other in 1871) and John is shown living in a house on this spot on the 1858 and 1878 maps of the county. ("A. Divers" is shown living a bit south, far off Fallston Road, near the present Kidd Road.) Divers, who was also great-uncle to the present owner's mother (according to Alva Mary Amoss and Alice Harlan Remsburg's delightful booklet, "The Gateway"), undoubtedly gave the house its current form, for his estate inventory, made on his death in 1899, cites specific rooms (kitchen, dining room, sitting room, hall, parlor, five bedrooms, an "upper hall," and a finished garret) that match up nicely with those present today. (Someone in the family enjoyed music—the sitting room contained "1 organ, 1 stool, and notebooks" all worth $30; someone also was an unreconstructed Southerner—the parlor had "1 photo of Lee & 1 photo of Jackson.") John willed "the farm whereon I dwell," including 100 acres of land "and all buildings thereon," to his grandson, John Walton Divers Melvin, son of Alice Belle Melvin and the Reverend Adolphus D. Melvin. When John Melvin died in 1907, the 100-acre farm, with its "frame dwelling house in fairly good condition," "Barn and Straw House," "Wagon House and Granary," "Hay House," and "Dairy House" were appraised in toto at $5,000; Hamilton Amoss purchased the property the same year and sold it to *his* son, the present owner, Benjamin H. Amoss, in 1935. Continuity clearly reigns here and although the Amosses have changed the name of the place from its original Pearson's Outlet and Bond's Gift to Model Farm (and have added to the original acreage), that name change simply describes what the property has become under their caring ownership.

4-30. Hidden Valley Farm
2916 Green Road
c. 1854; Private
National Register   HA-1540

4-30

In 1854 Joshua R. Green paid $7,680 for part of a tract called "Hill's Camp." The land, straddling the banks of the Little Gunpowder in Harford and Baltimore counties, was fertile and Green gained some renown in his lifetime as an expert farmer, "raising upon it," according to an 1897 biography of him, "various cereals . . . and . . . Jersey cows. . . . [He achieved] success in the farming and dairy business and at the time of his death he was one of the richest farmers in the district." Using plow-derived profits, he built this superb three-story brick house, a structure that manages to combine a traditional L-shape massing and center-hall plan with exotic detailing. Among these stylish touches, the elaborate cornice brackets and porch columns (brackets and columns display some Italian inspiration), the attic windows of the main façade with their Chinese-Chippendale trellis pattern (in which they resemble those in the attic at Pleasant Valley Farm), and the gable-end attic windows, a *sui generis* hybrid of Palladian and Gothic revival motifs deserve special mention. Inside, Green lavished the finest period trim on his house—walnut main stair, paneled doors, elaborate window surrounds, white marble mantels. All these and other touches remain in place and suggest the owner's sense of style. Green also took advantage of the rolling site to create one of the area's earliest "natural" gardens; the driveway entered the property via granite gateposts and then meandered along to end in a teardrop-shaped loop in front of the house's main (south) façade. Green placed spruce trees, seemingly in random clumps, along the drive and must have reveled in their deep color. The drive has been somewhat simplified, but the trees remain, silent and scented reminders of Green's horticultural ambitions. Green died in 1892 and Dr. John S. Green, a son and executor, sold the farm out of the family in 1901.

4-31. Berry Farm Complex
Rock Ridge Road
Late nineteenth century; Private   HA-1585

4-31

Albert Berry Sr. purchased approximately twenty-five acres here in 1882 and the farm he established—now covering ninety-seven acres—has been continuously owned by his descendants ever since, perhaps most notably by the late Albert Berry Jr. and *his* wife, Edith. The oldest building on the property is an abandoned 2½-story log bank house. Built by Albert Sr. to house his aged father (both men were born slaves), the bank house faces south and contains a cellar kitchen; each upper story has a single room heated by a gable-end fireplace. Other buildings in the complex include the main farmhouse and a shop where Albert Jr., a celebrated woodworker, crafted handles for axes, hatchets, sledge hammers, and other hand tools from 1910 until the 1980s. As Katy Dallam observed in the December 6, 1979, *Ægis* ("At 87 Al Berry Still Makes the Best Ax Handles Around"), places such as this have an importance that is "awesome in retrospect. . . . [Albert Berry's] hands have been responsible for the tools which helped build a hydro-electric dam [Conowingo]; to quarry stone; to maintain roads; to chop firewood; and to erect houses."

DISTRICT 5
Darlington, Dublin, and Whiteford/Cardiff

5-1. Wilson's Mill House

702 Darlington Road
c. 1856; 1931; Private
National Register   HA-10

Thought to have been built shortly after a fire destroyed the original log house on the site, this two-story stone dwelling was the residence of the miller for Wilson's Mill. (The Wilsons themselves lived in a house across the road.) The three-bay structure is a fine example of country craftsmanship with large stone quoins and lintels (necessary for structural reasons), but few other visual refinements. Inside, the original plan probably consisted of two rooms per floor, each warmed by its own fireplace; that spatial arrangement is still present on the second story but the ground floor was altered in the 1930s into a single large space. (The first story's two simple mantels were, however, retained.) At the same time windows were rehung and a wing was added to the rear. These modifications date to the Francis J. Stokes era. Mr. and Mrs. Stokes, wealthy Philadelphians, bought the entire Wilson's Mill complex in 1931 and, with the help of the architectural firm Mellor & Meigs, spruced up the buildings for use as a country retreat. They added a large stone barn (using local stone) as well as a garage, chicken coop, storage shed, and corncrib, and tied the entire assemblage together through a sophisticated (though seemingly simple) system of courtyards and walls in a manner worthy of Lutyens in England. To be brief, the Stokes creation defines the word "charm." Mr. Stokes died in 1955; Mrs. Stokes died in 1973; to ensure the preservation of this beautiful, secluded spot, the Stokes heirs donated a perpetual easement on the property to the Maryland Historical Trust.

5-2. Wilson's Mill

702 Darlington Road
Mid-eighteenth century; c. 1931; Private
National Register   HA-11

So just how old *is* Wilson's Mill? No one seems to know, but it is significant that when Dr. W. Stump Forwood compiled his "Homes on Deer Creek" series for the *Ægis* in 1879–80, he reverently noted that this "Old Mill" had "supplied the 'staff of life' to several generations." It seems likely that the mill dates back at least as far as the life of Nathan Rigbie, who had inherited the property when his father, Nathaniel, died in 1752. When Nathan Rigbie died in 1783, he left all his assets to his daughters and his grandson, Nathan Rigbie Sheridan. It is not clear, but it could be inferred from his estate inventory that a mill existed, since his appraisers listed over 100 bushels of various grains (in addition to "250 Bushels Wheat at Farm") as well as several casks and barrels. In 1802 Daniel Sheridan, Rigbie's executor (and presumably his son-in-law) sold fifty acres here to Joseph Brinton for £1,000; the deed bristles with references such as "the mill dam," "the mills thereon," and "free ingress and egress from and to the mill as now used," making it clear that a mill was then standing. Brinton may have been the miller here a bit earlier, for the 1798 tax assessment lists one John Brinton as owning a stone gristmill on this site. In 1812 Susannah Brinton, widow, sold the mill and fifty acres to Reuben Stump for £1,427. In 1821 Stump sold "the mill lot" (fifty acres) to Rachel Price Wilson and it stayed in the Wilson family until Mr. and Mrs. Francis Stokes bought it in 1931 and re-outfitted it so it could supply hydroelectricity to the farm. In its industrial prime the mill was a busy place: for instance, the 1880 census cites David E. Wilson (and five employees) as producing "250 bbl. flour, 26 tons meal, 9.7 tons feed, and 1 ton hominy." The mill and associated outbuildings are now in their pastoral

5-1

5-2

5-3

5-4

5-5

prime and will be preserved as such forever, thanks to an easement granted by the Stokes children in 1976.

5-3. Wilson's Mill Bridge
Route 161 at Deer Creek
1935; Public
National Register   HA-1578

Products of the Industrial Revolution, mass-produced iron and steel truss bridges of the late nineteenth and early twentieth centuries were integral parts of rural landscapes throughout America. Quickly assembled and relatively cheap, they helped make road travel fast and easy and thus played an important role in tying together once-remote regions. Wooden bridges have spanned Deer Creek near this site since the middle of the last century; this structure replaced a covered bridge (fondly remembered by many) that had become structurally unsafe. (There have been at least two covered bridges on or near this site.) The present metal bridge is an interesting combination of two different truss types, a Parker through truss 180 feet long and a pony triangular truss 81 feet long. The bridge is only 20 feet wide, too narrow for the State Highway Administration's safety guidelines and as of 1994, a wider concrete span is being planned.

5-4. Stafford
Stafford Road
c. 1799; Private
National Register; Historic American
Buildings Survey   HA-200

Architect James Wollon wrote in 1983 that "Stafford's architectural importance is the sophistication and abundance of detailing incorporated into its original construction, as befitted the residence of one of the area's wealthiest men." Wollon was referring to John Stump III, known as John Stump of Stafford, who acquired this property in the 1790s. This substantial house does not appear in the 1798 tax rolls but is clearly present in the 1814 tax list: "John Stump, Dwelling House, Stone, 45′ by 28′." The house bears several similarities to the Stump-Holloway House, built by John Stump's first cousin, William Stump; David Hopkins was the mason for that latter dwelling and many assume that he did work here as well. The masonry is outstanding, well up to the standard one associates with Hopkins (see 3-8): just note the quality of the large,

regularly shaped ashlar stones on the main façade; the stones are laid with apex pointing, that is, mortar carefully brought to a point between stones, a locally rare refinement. The cantilevered hood sheltering the main door on the north façade is also rare, although it is seen at the Stump-Holloway House and at the main house at Rock Run (once owned by Stump of Stafford's daughter Ann Archer, further evidence of a possible connection). Within, Stafford abounds in original decorative features, but the woodwork in the hall and parlor may be the most outstanding, particularly the center hall's cornice, the staircase's newel post and distinctive shadow rail, and the rippling chairrail in the parlor. Stump furnished the house, which remained in family ownership until the 1940s, with an abundance of the finest material goods of the period. His estate inventory (made on his death in 1816) virtually bulges with 372 ounces of silver, seemingly tons of mahogany, and several complete sets of imported china; living was jolly, for there were "15 gallons French Brandy," "18 gallons madeira Wine," and "1 case champaigne." In Stump's time the name Stafford took in an entire Stump-owned village here, including houses, stores, and a post office, and the family made a tidy profit from the gristmills and sawmills, flint mills and iron furnaces they owned and operated all under the name of Stafford. But economic conditions changed and the various industrial enterprises at Stafford began to cease functioning, finally to be washed away altogether in the great Deer Creek Flood of 1904.

5-5. Stump-Holloway House
1247 Stafford Road
c. 1800; Private
National Register; Historic American
Buildings Survey   HA-176

W. Stump Forwood, preparing the December 19, 1879, episode of his "Homes on Deer Creek" Ægis series, nearly broke down: "The writer can scarcely trust himself," he wrote, "for it was here that his mother was born." Dr. Forwood's mother, née Rachel Cooper Stump, was a daughter of William Stump. William was a grandson of Johann Stumpf, who immigrated to America in the early eighteenth century. Johann had two sons, John II and Henry (1731–1814) the latter of whom moved to the Deer Creek Valley in 1747; William was his son. Dr. Forwood wrote that "the house, which is of stone, was built about the year

1800" and credits David Hopkins, "a celebrated stone mason of his day," with its construction. He accurately observes that Hopkins "took unusual pains. . . . He selected the corners and frontings with extreme care and arranged the stone in front so that each row, whether wide or narrow, was continued exactly the same width entirely across from corner to corner, giving it a very handsome appearance." William Stump died in 1831 and seven years later his widow sold the place to their bachelor son, Henry, "for his better maintenance," although Mrs. Stump lived on with Henry until her death in 1869. Henry Stump (clearly a learned man, for his library contained several volumes of Pope, Byron, and Locke) died in 1872 and left the farm to two of his nephews, Albert S. and William R. Holloway, whose descendants have owned and maintained this important structure to this day.

5-6. James Forwood House

1226 Stafford Road
c. 1871; Private
National Register   HA-179

Located on a large, wooded tract, this 2½-story stone dwelling is one of the newer structures Dr. W. S. Forwood covered in his thorough "Homes on Deer Creek" series of 1879–80. Herman Stump, a son and heir of the very rich John Stump of Stafford, owned hundreds of acres along the north bank of the creek, including the land on which this house is built. But Herman ran into financial trouble: he had to file for bankruptcy in 1842 and his property was then sold off in a leisurely manner; this particular 155-acre tract did not hit the block until 1853 when James Forwood and John McCausland bought it for $6,900. Forwood bought out his partner in 1871 for $3,750 and, wrote W. S. Forwood, "latterly erected a large, stone dwelling house, which is a great improvement to the property." The overall massing and the prominent stone sills and lintels might be read as a deferential nod to the superb Stump houses nearby (such as Stafford) but the wooden porch, with its scroll-sawn brackets and balustrade, is clearly a product of the Forwood era, just as the dormers on the main façade and the concrete block addition on the rear are products of ours.

5-7. Henry Harlan House

1145 Stafford Road
c. 1819; Private
National Register   HA-180

Two stories tall and two bays wide, with walls of massive granite blocks marked by even more massive quoins, this stone house may be the architectural "personification" of its best-known resident, Henry Harlan, a man W. S. Forwood described (and underlined) in 1879 as "one of our *solid men.*" Henry's father, Jeremiah Harlan, moved to Harford County from his native Chester County, Pennsylvania; in 1800 he married Esther Stump, a daughter of Henry and Rachel Stump, and in 1812 bought a 181-acre tract from his kinsman Reuben Stump for $4,000. This house is on that parcel. A stone bank barn on the property has a datestone inscribed "1819," which could well be when Jeremiah completed the entire complex of structures here. Near the house is a 1½-story stone shop, a small building of great importance; its upper story is traditionally said to have contained a schoolroom where Jeremiah's sons (Henry and David) and nephews (including future judge John H. Price) were taught by Dr. Samuel Guile, a Harvard man Jeremiah hired as a tutor. The little building's roof merits architectural attention: cantilevered to extend out to shelter the doorway, it resembles similar details on several area contemporary structures, including William Stump's house nearby, Rock Run, and, farther afield, the c. 1800 schoolhouse at Box Hill. Jeremiah died around 1848 (his gravestone in the Stump cemetery is undated). With brother David established in Churchville (he married a Herbert daughter and thereby acquired the Homelands property), Henry bought the farm out of his father's estate that year for $5,600. Henry's nephew, also named Henry Harlan and the solid man mentioned above, took over management of the farm around 1879. Born in 1848 and educated in Baltimore and Philadelphia, young Henry was, according to Dr. Forwood, known for his "mental capacity and pecuniary success." An 1897 biography of the man observes that his "sound judgment and well-known integrity have been the means of having him appointed administrator of many estates, including that of his uncle." He was a knowledgeable agriculturist as well; the "well-tilled fields and neat appearance of the place," runs the anonymous 1897 document, "indicate the progressive spirit of" Henry Harlan II. The younger Henry died in 1899. Neatness

5-6

5-7

5-8

indeed was important to him, at least in the garden; his estate inventory is filled with items such as "3 tree pruners," a "lawn mower," "garden line" (for laying out straight rows?), and a pair of "grape shears."

5-8. Tucker-Flannery House

Stafford Road
1858; with additions; Private
National Register   HA-183

Location, location, location runs the modern real estate cliché and a sense of location has been paramount here for 150 years. W. S. Forwood wrote in 1879 that Ellis J. Tucker built this "comfortable stone dwelling" in 1858, carefully placing it "exactly on the brow of the steep hill which overlooks the river and the lower end of Deer Creek. The view extends to Port Deposit and Havre de Grace, and away beyond, down the Bay, which, taken in connection with the Creek and canal, forms one of the finest water views of the many that are in the neighborhood." But Tucker was not the first to enjoy the view, since Forwood commented that the new house was built "on the site of the old one" Samuel C. Stump built in the 1830s. Stump bought the 137-acre farm here in 1835 and died on it in 1854; his widow, née Hannah Carter, left the farm to Tucker, her nephew, in 1872. (Tucker had apparently taken charge before he took title and built the house to suit his own needs as well as those of his aunt. The dwelling must have remained of interest to Mrs. Stump since her will twice refers to the "new house.") Tucker, who drew a biographer's praise in 1897 ("among the energetic and prosperous farmers of Harford County, none is more deserving of mention"), lived here until 1905. In the 1930s the noted painter Vaughn Flannery and his wife, attracted by the expansive views, bought the farm; they made substantial changes to the house—for example, they added a terrace, the front columns, and a studio—but they made certain that these changes adhered to the spirit of the place; in this they were doubtless helped by the sensitivity and understanding of their mason, Lloyd Weaver.

5-9

5-9

5-10

5-9. Stafford Flint Mill

Stafford Road
c. 1870; Public (restricted access)
National Register   HA-199

For well over 150 years, from the mid-eighteenth to the early twentieth centuries, the

Deer Creek Valley's citizens took the Ruhr Valley as their model and lined the now-bucolic banks with iron forges, gristmills, tanyards, and flint mills. The community of Stafford, under the Stumps, was the focus of much of this fiery industrial activity. This structure, however, postdates the Stump era, for it was built c. 1870 by Thomas Symington of Indian Spring Farm, who planned to use it to produce soapstone. After Symington died in 1875, the brothers Joshua C. and B. Gilpin Smith bought the property and adapted it to make flint for pottery. The 1880 census observes that the Smiths' "kaolin and ground earth [flint] works" was worth $12,000 and that their fifteen employees produced $8,400 worth of goods. Flint, a hard white rock, was commonly quarried throughout northern Harford; transported to mills by mule cart or barge, it was broken up, then tossed into stacks such as this where it was heated and then ground to a fine powder invaluable to the production of china. This stack, roughly 30 feet tall, has a square, rubblestone base, a cylindrical shaft, and a brick cap; solitary and sentinel-like, it is all that remains of the Stafford industrial complex. The Smiths decided to focus on paper production and sold the flint mill property to Horace Stokes in 1887; he continued operations under the name of the Staffordshire Flint and Feldspar Mill until work stopped altogether around 1920. It should be noted that nineteenth-century writers such as W. S. Forwood did not share our modern romantic fondness for Deer Creek's quiet charms: he, like most Victorians, wanted industry and lots of it, and in 1879 he reveled in the prospect that, thanks to the "active and skilled management" of the Smiths and others, Stafford "now bids fair to rejoice" as a booming "business mart" where "canal boats load and unload" and "several new buildings have recently been erected."

5-10. Price-Archer House

2239 Price Road
c. 1880; Private
National Register   HA-316

In his first installment of the *Ægis* "Homes on Deer Creek" series (December 19, 1879), W. S. Forwood praised this farm, then owned by Judge John H. Price and occupied by Price's son, David, for its "high state of cultivation" and for the "excellent quality of the land." John and Mary Price bought the farm, part of Parker's Chance and Mount Yeo, in 1847 from

Margaret Wilson Stump, widow of Reuben, for $2,500. The deed notes that this is "where Mrs. Stump now resides"; thirty years later, Forwood fussed that the Price farm ("formerly Reuben Stump's") was marred by a house "not in keeping with the fine quality of the soil," which lends credibility to the locally held belief that a ruin about 100 yards toward the creek from the house is the old Stump place. The senior Prices lived nearby and doubtless used this 225-acre farm for extra income. In 1880 they sold the farm to son David, who undoubtedly built the extant handsome frame dwelling shortly thereafter. He marked his new house with such fashionable touches as an elaborate main entrance, elongated ground-floor windows, and an attic gable. David became renowned for his Mount Yeo–brand corn, grown in the farm's rich soil and canned (with the help of artisan/laborer "Had" Harris) right on the place. Mount Yeo passed out of the family's ownership in 1937, only to return in 1970, when it was purchased by John P. Archer, a Stump descendant.

5-11. Corrigan-Murray House

1334 Stafford Road
c. 1865; Private
National Register   HA-174

In 1879 Dr. W. S. Forwood wrote that "this property has been greatly improved within the writer's recollection. A handsome new stone house and out building have been erected within the last few years and the land has been correspondingly improved." Much the same could be written today, for the house, which now could be considered venerable rather than new, has been restored after a period of neglect and the surrounding dairy farm seems prosperous indeed. In 1850 Bartholomew Corrigan bought the land from the heirs of Richard Coale; Corrigan died in 1866 and his estate inventory suggests that the "handsome . . . stone house" was then standing; appraisers cite such spaces as "Room No. 1" (obviously a dining room, because it contained a mahogany sideboard, dining table, and "12 old hair seat chairs") and "Room No. 2" (just as obviously a parlor for there is a "sofa," "2 tables," "lot of carpeting," and "2 old rocking chairs"). There were three beds (representing three bedrooms?), as well as a group of goods that could only have come from a kitchen (coffee pot, "kitchen table," and "1 lot crockery ware"). Corrigan left the house to his widow for her life and then to their son, James;

they, mother and James, sold it in 1871 for the somewhat high price of $8,627.

5-12. E. M. Allen House

725 Darlington Road
c. 1870; Private
National Register   HA-319

For several decades, this property was bound to the adjacent Wilson's Mill property by ties of blood, use, and ownership. These have disappeared over the years, but the two important sites have remained interconnected, if only visually. In the early nineteenth century Rachel Wilson, the dowager of the neighborhood, lived in a house on this site. She, born Rachel Smith, had married David Price in 1803. David Price died (date unknown) and his widow married William Wilson in 1822; Wilson died in 1840 but Rachel Smith Price Wilson went serenely on for decades; even after her own death, which occurred in 1873, she was recalled by W. S. Forwood as "the kindhearted . . . , excellent, widely known and well-beloved old lady." Mrs. Wilson was also known for her "delightful" daughters, one of whom, Sallie E. Wilson, married Bel Air attorney Edward M. Allen. In 1866 Mrs. Wilson sold the couple 128 acres here "for the sole and separate use of . . . Sallie Allen." (Mrs. Wilson may have been "kind-hearted," but she was nobody's fool and kept close tab on her accounts; when she died, her books revealed carefully monitored debts due her of $5,035 from John Price and $7,524 from the Allens.)

Dr. Forwood wrote that shortly thereafter the Wilson house burned and "on its ruins was built the present, handsome, modernized structure by Mr. Allen." Allen's house is a rambling, three-sectioned, coursed-stone structure whose romantic skyline befits its picturesque setting. (The stone is important; as far back as the 1840s deeds here mention that the Wilsons and Allens reserved the right "for obtaining stone" from a quarry across Deer Creek from Wilson's Mill; the Allens presumably used that stone to build this house and one wonders how many other structures in the area have their walls laid in this very local rock.) Allen read law under his brother-in-law Price, entered politics, and was elected to the state Senate pledging low taxes and lowered government salaries "which . . . brought him the enmity . . . of some politicians." His political career didn't last long. What has lasted, and which all countians are the better for, is his novel idea of hanging portraits of Harford's

5-11

5-12

5-13

5-14

5-15

5-16

distinguished men and women in the court-house in Bel Air; widely praised, the practice remains unique to Harford. In 1896 the Allens sold the property "with a stone dwelling there-on" to their sons Edward Jr. and J. A. Greme Allen, the former a local industrialist with mills all along Deer Creek and the latter a West Virginia financier. The rosy careers of the Allens ended in the Great Depression and creditors sold the farm out of the family in 1932.

5-13. Charles Y. Thomas House
3160 Deth's Ford Road
c. 1878; Private
National Register   HA-326

In a December 1879 installment of his "Homes on Deer Creek" series, W. S. For-wood observed that Joseph Edge "recently" di-vided his own farm, selling part "to his son-in-law, Mr. Charles Y. Thomas, formerly of Baltimore." Forwood added that Thomas "has erected, within the past year, a very pretty frame dwelling on a very high point, which can be seen from afar." Thomas was a dairy farmer who augmented his income with car-pentry and one may safely assume that, when new, his "very pretty frame dwelling" was fes-tooned in sawn trim. In its center-hall plan the house resembles others in the area and its basic massing is also not unknown (for exam-ple, the frame Price-Archer dwelling) but its location is second to none and Thomas, who obviously wished to take advantage of his val-ley views, added porches to the house's south and west façades.

5-14. Wilson-Edge-Hopkins House
1951 Trappe Church Road
c. 1851; c. 1870; Private
National Register   HA-328

The rolling acres of this farm were, like most of the land on the north bank of the lower Deer Creek, originally part of the Stump fam-ily's vast holdings. In 1869 Joseph Edge bought 324 of those acres when an equity case forced the sale of Herman Stump's land; Edge's deed notes that the farm was then "occupied by William W. Wilson," who may have begun the existing frame dwelling. Some sources sug-gest that Wilson's house forms the rear wing of the present house and that Edge built the front section. That three-bay front unit forms an interesting small-scale variation on the usu-al five-bay frame house typified by the Isaac C.

Wilson House nearby. W. S. Forwood noted in his "Homes on Deer Creek" series (1879–80) that Edge's "comfortable dwelling . . . is so situated in a valley as not to show to advantage at any distance," but, Forwood ad-mitted, this sheltered location made the owner "more comfortable in winter . . . than some of his neighbors." Jane P. Edge married Johns Hopkins, a nephew of Baltimore's great bene-factor, and their descendants have continued to live in and maintain the place.

5-15. Isaac C. Wilson House
3137 Deth's Ford Road
Mid-nineteenth century; Private
National Register   HA-327

In 1844 Isaac Wilson purchased 165 acres here out of the crumbling Stump family holdings and built this quintessential Harford County farmhouse, a dwelling with clear stylistic ties to, *inter alia,* the Finney family's Greenwood and the Wilson-Edge-Hopkins House. W. S. Forwood, in an 1879 installment of his "Homes on Deer Creek" *Ægis* series, com-ments that the land here "is decidedly hilly, but was worked by [the late] Mr. Wilson with great skill and success. A few years ago . . . [Wilson] erected a very handsome frame house, on a high and commanding position, showing to great advantage for many miles in different directions." Laura Wilson, a daugh-ter, sold the farm in 1913.

5-16. Samuel C. S. Holloway House
1161 Stafford Road
c. 1865; Private
National Register   HA-1076

In massing and general appearance this frame house has definite similarities to other struc-tures in the area. But God, as they say, is in the details and the details here clearly distinguish the building from its apparent mates. No oth-er house in the area boasts triple-hung sash windows as this one does (they facilitate walk-ing from within to without), no other house in the Deer Creek Valley has the projecting second-story room found here (a detail possi-bly derived from Swansbury, a c. 1800 house near Aberdeen), and the brick chimney stacks, with their concave profile, are, if not unique, then at least notable. Duckett Cooper Stump (daughter-in-law of Henry Stump) bought the unimproved 140-acre property, which bor-dered the Stump GHQ at Stafford, in 1813. It eventually passed to Mary Stump, wife of

Frederick Stump, whose 1865 will left it to Samuel Cooper Stump Holloway, noting that it is "now occupied by my grandmother, Mrs. Duckett Stump." It is, however, highly unlikely that this house was then standing and it seems far more likely that the old woman (she was born in 1775 and didn't die until 1869) lived in a different dwelling on the property and that S. C. S. Holloway built this frame house when he took title to the land. (Mary Stump's will seems more concerned with the distribution of various pieces of silver and jewelry than with real estate; she left W. S. Forwood "one cow and calf" and left his wife, "Mrs. Dr. Forwood," "one gold bracelet and two chairs.") The house has remained in the Holloway family ever since. The working farm also contains a large, three-part frame barn and a dairy; both of these important buildings seem to date to the time of the main house.

5-17. Wildfell

Conowingo Road
1854; Private
National Register   HA-2

In the 1950s the "in" things were hula hoops and 3-D movies; today it is jogging shoes. Back in homier mid-Victorian times the truly trendy went in for octagonal houses, or they did after 1848 when Orson Fowler published his best-selling book, *A Home for All*. Fowler, a phrenologist and part-time sex therapist, believed that nonsquare buildings were more economical to put up, were more efficient in their use of space, and were healthier to live in than conventional houses. Others agreed with him and hexagonal and octagonal buildings popped up throughout America: there are three in the Darlington area alone, the hexagonal Prospect School, the octagonal Sanctuary in the Darlington Cemetery, and this eight-sided dwelling. Mr. and Mrs. Joseph Jewett, Baltimoreans who wanted the house as an escape from the city's heat, proved themselves not only stylistically *au courant* but practical as well: they hired William Hensel, a retired ship's carpenter, to build their dream house and when they learned that an old War of 1812 clipper ship had been abandoned in the Baltimore harbor, they bought her, had her dismantled, and sent the wood to this site, where the short oaken timbers lent themselves perfectly to the short walls an octagonal house required. Wildfell's double front doors lead to twin double parlors with the dining room and kitchen to the rear; trim is simple and original.

(In addition to the house's fashionable shape its construction details, as architect James Wollon has recently pointed out, incorporate dicta espoused by such important building theorists A. J. Downing and William Ranlett.) The Jewetts sold the house in 1874 and moved to Virginia; it was then home to five generations of the prominent Scott family, who bred trotting horses on the farm.

5-18. Rigbie House

Castleton Road
c. 1752; Private
National Register; Harford County
Landmark; Historic American
Buildings Survey   HA-4

In the 1720s Nathaniel Rigbie inherited land called Phillip's Purchase, an event that proved to be of more than routine interest in Maryland's colonial history. The tract sprawled across 2,000 acres and bordered the Susquehanna from present-day Shure's Landing to Glen Cove. Using his twenty-two slaves, Rigbie then began farming. His acres yielded bumper crops of tobacco that he sent to London merchants in his own ships from his own docks at Lapidum. Lord Baltimore made him a colonel in the colonial militia and Lord High Sheriff of the county. When Rigbie died in 1752 his net worth of roughly £7,000 made him one of the richest men in Maryland in those rough-and-tumble times. He bequeathed Phillip's Purchase to his eldest son, James, who either built the present house or completely remodeled whatever house was then standing. The 1½-story frame dwelling has a massing typical of the larger dwellings of the time, but its exquisite pine paneling is truly extraordinary: the living room is particularly impressive, for every wall is covered in richly molded panels. The exposed stair is also notable: in the 1750s nearly every staircase in the county was small and twisty and enclosed in a closet; Rigbie's stair is grand and open and was obviously meant to serve as a visual feature, for it is embellished with carving on the step ends, molded panels on its underside, and a walnut railing. (It probably, in fact, represents a reworking of an earlier closeted stair; see chapter 3.) Forgotten for generations, this important building was discovered by Alexis Shriver of Olney in the 1930s, and he made its restoration one of his several pet projects.

5-17

5-18

5-19

5-20

5-21

5-19. Deer Creek Friends Meetinghouse

Route 161
1784; 1888; Regular services
National Register; Harford County
Landmark; Historic American Buildings
Survey   HA-12

The minutes of the Nottingham Meeting reveal that in September 1737 Nathaniel Rigbie sold a 3½-acre lot here "to the people called Quakers" for £28. (Rigbie probably didn't miss the land all that much, since his holdings covered over 2,000 acres.) The property already contained two buildings, one of which the Friends used for services until they began the present stone meetinghouse after the Revolution. Classic in its simplicity, the structure resembles dozens of period meetinghouses throughout northern Maryland and southeastern Pennsylvania; its interior still has its original wooden partition to divide the space in two (half for men, half for women) and simple benches. But this building also contains several features, such as a Victorian era Tudor-arched fireplace and intricate door hardware, which separate it from its peers. These touches were added in 1888 by railroad magnate Hugh Judge Jewett of Lansdowne. Jewett's parents, John and Susanna Judge Jewett, were, according to Walter Preston's 1901 county history, devout Friends "whose upright lives and good works have established lasting memorials." Preston particularly admired Mrs. Jewett, "a woman of strong mind and a powerful minister," who served as clerk of the Baltimore yearly meeting and, from 1813 until 1820, led services here at the Darlington meeting. To the north of the building is a small cemetery; the oldest marker is a slate stone inscribed "Sarah Ely 1775."

5-20. Dr. Kirk House

1034 Main Street
c. 1810; Private
National Register; Historic American
Buildings Survey   HA-21

Named for the father and son physicians who lived and practiced here from the 1890s until 1968, this two-story stone house is one of the oldest structures in this part of the county, and invites comparison with such buildings as Stafford and the Stump-Holloway House. Indeed, the Kirk House is a literally local building—the rocks were quarried from the huge beds of Wissahickon schist and Port Deposit

granite that underpin much of northeastern Harford County and the roof's slate came from quarries at nearby Cardiff. The house has an L-plan configuration; a recessed bay in the north wall of the rear ell provides an interesting second-story gallery and affords picturesque views of the courtyard formed by the house's two sections and the detached two-story stone meathouse. The largely intact interior is, like the exterior, in the words of architect James Wollon, "typical of the early nineteenth century traditional architecture, with only a suggestion of the style changes of the early Republic." Within, the building contains a stylish double parlor to the left (south) of the center stairhall and a much plainer room to the north. Deeds mentioning a "stone dwelling house" date as far back as 1810. Three early deeds, one in 1818 and two in 1830, involved the "free men of color" Moses Harrison and Cupid Paca (see 5-42), which suggests the easy-going racial attitudes and generally tolerant spirit that pervaded the Quaker village. (According to legend, the building may have contained Philip Silver's house and store; if so, it is likely that the storeroom was in the plain space mentioned above.) Walter Kirk, a native of Cecil County, came to Darlington in 1893, the year he was graduated from the University of Maryland's medical school. A writer in 1897 commented that the young doctor (he was born in 1868) had "gained the confidence of the people by his reliability . . . and his practice now extends through several districts." Dr. Kirk, known for "his breadth of culture," was "not unmindful of the benefits to be derived from fraternal organizations" and he was a stalwart Mason.

5-21. Darlington United Methodist Church

Shuresville Road
1852; Regular services
National Register   HA-24

Darlington's Methodists met in the old Darlington Academy building across the street until they were able to erect their own church in 1832. That structure, of log construction, eventually became too small for the popular sect and was replaced with the present handsome frame church. With its simple, classic lines, oak-shaded lot, and attractive cast-iron fence, the Methodist church has long figured prominently in village vignettes. Its very construction was a cooperative community effort: one person donated the lumber, someone else woodworking skills; in all probability black-smith Joshua Gorrell (who lived across the street at 2125 Shuresville Road) contributed the fence. (Gorrell is known to have made the handsome gates for the Darlington Cemetery.)

5-22. Joshua Husband House
Old Forge Hill Road
c. 1850; Private
National Register   HA-45

In 1866 Joshua Husband Sr. bought a 161-acre site on Deer Creek and established a flint mill. Both Husband and his son apparently lived in this two-story frame house, now deteriorated into ruin, for "J. Husband" is shown on both the 1858 and 1878 county maps. Joshua Sr. sold the mill to Joshua Jr. in 1883, and the son continued operations here. On his death in 1890 Joshua Jr. left $100 to his father (who died in 1896), $100 to his brother, William, and "all the rest of my property," including the mill, to his sister, Hannah P. Husband. (His estate inventory includes "25 tons of ground flint" worth $125, far less than his farm produce such as the "15 acres of corn" worth $300.) Samuel Mason's *Historical Sketches of Harford County* suggests that the mill in Hannah Husband's era was a not-altogether happy place: for instance the "eighteen to twenty mules used at the plant were housed in a barn of Miss Husband . . . but were unfortunately burnt to death" during a freak fire; similarly, one of her employees "had been bled . . . at a hospital . . . and, rather enjoying the sensation, made a habit of climbing the hills behind the kilns and bleeding himself" until one day he was discovered to have "bled himself to death." Hannah Husband defaulted on a mortgage and the property was sold in 1932, marking the end of the family's "prosperous and useful" milling dynasty.

5-23. Otto Monsees House
2129 Shuresville Road
c. 1855; Private
National Register   HA-75

The workshop, sales office, and residence of German-born shoemaker Otto Monsees, this frame structure typifies the multiple uses village buildings served in Darlington before the advent of strict zoning laws. Monsees paid $350 for the lot in 1857, but there may have already been a building here since the description in the deed begins "at the corner of the

house and on the edge of the road leading from Darlington to Stafford." (This also suggests that the lot was a good place for a commercial enterprise, convenient as it was to travelers on their way to and from Darlington and then-busy Stafford.) The building seems to show on the imprecise 1858 county map; it is clearly present and labeled "Shoe Shop" on the 1878 map. Harry Webb Farrington, in his classic 1930 book of reminiscences of nineteenth-century Darlington, *Kilts to Togs,* recalls Monsees as "the fattest man in Darlington. He put shoes on people and kept hogs. . . . His toes were turned in so much from holding the shoes between his knees that when he went out to slop his hogs, he waddled like a duck." After Monsees's death, his heirs sold the property to Charles P. Dern in 1896.

5-24. Christopher Wilson House
1011 Main Street
1866; Private
National Register   HA-77

Perhaps the most idyllic residence in a village of idyllic residences, this 2½-story, cross-gable frame house reposes in the center of a large lot embowered in ancient oaks and maples; it faces south, directly toward Westacre, which rises majestically in the distance across a rolling lawn and through a split-rail fence and hedgerow. Everything about the Wilson house suggests tranquility: the deep front porch that spans the main façade, the ground-story floor-length windows that, when flung open, enable one to saunter from parlor to porch and back again—everything. A. P. Silver's 1905 history of Harmony Church notes that the house was built by John F. McJilton, who was born in Darlington in 1805, a son of a village shop-keeper. (According to an oral history tape of George Scriven, the senior McJilton "operated a store with drygoods and groceries" he obtained on "bi-monthly [trips] to Baltimore.") John McJilton became Darlington's first post-master (1826) and then went off to test the political waters in Baltimore: they proved to his liking and he served as president of the city council under Mayor Thomas Swann (1856) and as surveyor of the Port of Baltimore under Lincoln. "In 1866 he retired to his native town and built" this house, where he remained until 1878; he died shortly thereafter and his widow sold the house and its surrounding twenty-one acres to Darlington merchant Christopher Wilson in 1880. Wilson, born near Darlington in 1827 (according to an 1897 bi-

5-22

5-23

5-24

5-25

5-26

5-27

ography), was educated at the Darlington Academy and then moved to Illinois; he "returned . . . in 1878" and married Susannah Lyon in 1880. The Wilsons "occupied a high social position," according to Harry Webb Farrington's *Kilts to Togs,* a book that contains many reverent references to the "beautiful drawing room" in this house.

5-25. Grace Memorial Episcopal Church
Main Street
1876; Regular services
National Register   HA-78

Darlington's only "published" building, this early English Gothic revival church was featured in the August 24, 1878, issue of *American Architect and Building News.* Merchant/philanthropist D. C. Wharton Smith of Winstone had the church built as a memorial to his father, Milton Smith, and hired Philadelphia architect Theophilus Parsons Chandler, FAIA, to design the structure. Chandler (1845–1928) was a Harvard-educated Bostonian who took advanced work in Paris at the Atelier Vaudremer. Well known for his church designs, Chandler also worked easily with America's monied elite, and designed a house in Philadelphia for John Wanamaker, one on Dupont Circle in Washington for L. Z. Leiter (Marshall Field's original partner in Chicago), and Winterthur for the duPonts. Chandler's design for Grace Church is fully within the accepted medievalism of the day and is (generally) executed in local materials: the building's buttressed stone walls are laid in carefully dressed greenish-gray Deer Creek soapstone; the steep gable roof is covered in slate from nearby Cardiff. Windows are single, tall, narrow lancets set directly into the stone without frames. All glass (except in the chancel) is original: some is softly stencilled, some is brightly stained, all is of English origin. Within, shafts of green marble, also from Cardiff, support tracery at the baptistery arch while overhead the arch-braced roof trusses supported by carved angel heads spring from the stone walls. The original oak pews survive, as does the chancel furniture (such as altar and pulpit), all rendered in locally felled black walnut. An account of the church in the *Harford Democrat* (February 11, 1910) notes that "the architect has always felt much pride in his work, especially after learning that the late Bishop Pinckney considered this church the most beautiful in his whole diocese." Who to-

day would argue with the bishop's verdict? Just northeast of the church is a handsome frame rectory designed by Smith's other favorite architect, Walter Cope, and built in 1885.

5-26. Massey-Ely Tavern and Store
2101 Shuresville Road
c. 1820 (?); c. 1900; Private
National Register   HA-22

Darlington's earliest extant structures, the stone and frame buildings near the intersection of Shuresville Road and Main Street (see also 5-20, 5-27), were all originally of mixed commercial and residential use as befits their site on the thoroughfares that connect the village to once-busy sites such as the Rock Run complex, Stafford, and the wharves at Lapidum. This two-story frame building, doubled in size around 1900, seems to date from the 1820s when deeds suggest that Aquila Massey ran a tavern here. Massey expanded his interests and subsequent deeds refer to the "Tavern, house, lot and stable" on this site. Massey sold "the Tavern stand" and a half acre to Isaac Ely in 1846 for $1,000 and Ely and his descendants prospered in the village. Trained as a wheelwright, Ely ran a general store here; his son Joseph (born 1832) clerked in the store. Joseph inherited the property on his father's death and in the 1850s "held the office of postmaster of Darlington," according to an 1897 biography. (The 1858 county map shows this building and labels it "P.O."; the 1878 map labels it "J. R. Ely.") In his prime Joseph was something of a bon vivant; an 1858 *Ægis* article describes "the most delightful pic nic of the season" held near Deer Creek ("whose banks are adorned . . . by specimens of the most tasty architecture") and arranged in part by "J.R. Ely . . . whose kindness and industry were amply repaid [by the faces of the guests] . . . who enjoyed themselves . . . until the clock told out the little hours of the new-born day." Ely ran into financial trouble in the 1890s and his creditors sold this property in 1892 for $2,060; but then Maryland's Governor Brown appointed him justice of the peace in 1892 and reappointed him in 1896.

5-27. Stump-Whitelock House and Store
2102 Shuresville Road
c. 1810; rebuilt; Private
National Register   HA-81

Interior framing and other construction techniques suggest both an early nineteenth-century origin and a later remodeling for this massive stone building. Hand-hewn material form a post-and-beam structure, which is the early part; the attic has vertical rafters and each truss is numbered, and that may be early; the numbers, however, run randomly and *that* suggests dismantling and reconstruction. In plan, the north section seems to have housed a shop, separate from the living quarters to the south. It had been the property and residence of Thomas Stump, a son of John Stump of Stafford and one of nine men to organize Harmony Church in 1837. His estate inventory (1859) suggests that he may have kept shop here. It contains an enormous stock of metalware and other dry goods; the appraisers describe his house in a room-by-room manner and cite "Dining Room," "Room Over Dining Room," "Middle Room," "Room Over Middle Room," "Parlor," "Parlor Chamber," "Garret," and "Porch Room." Stump's widow, Ann, sold the place in 1864. The Whitelock family acquired the property ("the same lot on which stands the old dwelling house") in 1877 and owned it until 1913. It was probably during their tenure that the building was remodeled; it is certainly when the store was at its zenith. The shop is shown here on the 1878 county map, and an 1897 biography of George Whitelock notes that "in 1876 he opened a general store in Darlington, where he carries a full and complete line of goods." George's brother Franklin spent his life "carrying on a mercantile business at Darlington" until he died in 1881. It was a general business; his estate inventory includes items ranging from "drugs and patent medicine" to "81 lbs. coffee" to "37 pairs mens shoes" to "111 pairs ladies shoes damaged by mice."

5-28. Darlington Cemetery and Sanctuary
Shuresville Road
1885; Regular hours
National Register   HA-82

In Dr. W. S. Forwood's "Report to the Secretary of Darlington Cemetery Company" (1886), he noted that "the most prominent object that adorns the Cemetery, and shows to the eye for miles around, is the Sanctuary, completed in the past autumn. It is a beautiful building: it is a work of art and an ornament to the grounds, which will stand as a monument to the good taste and skill of the Architect . . . Mr. William D. Shure, the president of the Board." The company, established in

November 1881, purchased this grassy hillside from the Holloway family. Since its inception the cemetery has been open to all, regardless of race, creed, or color. The company's folio-sized minute books, still used, reveal that the organizers gave great care to aesthetics and, in effect, created a large public garden. Their lengthy discussions focused on matters such as fencing (the iron gates were constructed by Joshua Gorrell, village blacksmith), placement of trees and shrubbery, layout of the flint and oyster-shell roads, and the sanctuary. Octagonal in shape, the highly decorative frame sanctuary is crowned by a steep conical roof topped by a terracotta chimney pot. Architect James Wollon has suggested that its builders used the octagonal Chapel of Baltimore's Greenmount Cemetery for inspiration, although this is by no means proven and area builders had long shown fondness for polygonal forms and a penchant for superb design in buildings of a spiritual nature.

5-28

5-29. Deer Park
Ady Road
c. 1741; altered; Private
National Register   HA-90

One of the more surprising houses in the county, Deer Park looks as if it belongs on a tobacco plantation overlooking the Potomac or the Rappahannock, not in corn country overlooking Deer Creek. And perhaps it does, for its builders, the Wheelers, came to Harford from southern Maryland. The first, Benjamin, arrived around 1715. In 1744 Ignatius Wheeler, Benjamin's grandson, was born, and according to some that event took place in this house. If true, using that date as a gauge the frame building would rank as one of the South's earliest wooden exemplars of full-blown Georgian design. That is *possible,* but it is far more likely that the present mansion (which is just what the house was in its day) dates to Ignatius Wheeler's era, although it probably incorporates some (or all) of the earlier structure. It has a center-hall plan with two rooms to each side, each with a corner fireplace; the stair rises elegantly along one wall in the hall and is magnificent in its boldly turned balusters, molded railing, and elaborate carving at the visible ends of its dignified, low-rising steps. Opening to the east of the hall, the parlor contains the house's most exuberant woodwork, including a modillioned cornice, an arched corner cupboard with pilasters and a keystone, and paneled wainscoting. The

5-29

5-30

5-31

Wheelers were Catholics and, according to tradition, celebrated mass in the Deer Park parlor since English law forbade Catholic services except in private chapels that were part of houses. (See Priest Neale's Mass House.) Ignatius Wheeler rose to the rank of colonel in the American forces during the Revolution; he later served in the state assembly. With American independence came religious freedom and Wheeler, among the first in the country to exercise this right and privilege, worked with the archdiocese in planning St. Ignatius Church near Hickory and in 1793 agreed to pay the wages of the church's mason. He died later that year. (He is buried the church cemetery.) In his will, Wheeler divided his lands among his sons, Ignatius, Bennett, and Joseph. (The colonel was immensely rich for the time: his personal property was worth nearly £5,000 and his heirs eventually received a whopping £6,900 in debts due the estate; yet Wheeler was illiterate and signed his will with an *X,* "his mark.") The 1798 tax rolls cite Henrietta Wheeler, Ignatius Sr.'s, widow, owning and living in a frame house (whose dimensions exactly match the extant dwelling), with 3,277 acres, seventeen slaves, and a huge complex of outbuildings. This great lady was so well known that when a new road was laid out from Bel Air to Peach Bottom in 1800, "the corner of Deer Park" and "Mrs. Wheeler's House" were used as landmarks for the surveyors. But that was about the end of the Wheeler era at Deer Park. Although the house was substantially remodeled in this century, much of the superb interior remains intact.

5-30. Snodgrass House
(Moore-Snodgrass House)
Prospect Road
c. 1852; Private   HA-91

Temple-form buildings of any sort are rare in Harford County and only three examples come to mind, the Presbyterian churches in Bel Air and Fallston and the Eli Turner House near Norrisville. At this partially stuccoed stone house near Mill Green it is easy to see the body of the temple—all that is lacking is the portico. Within and without the house superbly captures the essence, just not the flashiness, of the Greek revival: note the squared-off door and window openings (particularly the center one on the main façade's second story), overall proportions, and, within, fluted door trim with bull's-eye corner blocks. Leedom B. Moore bought 156 acres here in May 1852 and

probably built the house soon after, for such a date would place it at the beginning of countians' awareness of the Greek revival. (See also Rochelle.) L. B. Moore is shown living in a house on this site on the 1858 county map, but he evidently ran into financial trouble shortly thereafter: his $1,000 mortgage was foreclosed that June and the 156 acres "on Broad Creek" and "on the road to Mill Green" were sold for $3,640. In 1867 John I. Snodgrass acquired the property, then still known as the Moore Farm, and his descendants lived here until the 1960s.

5-31. Mill Green Miller's House
Mill Green Road
c. 1770; with additions; Private
National Register   HA-92

Mills, centers of industry and commerce, were among the most important features in the Harford landscape for 150 years. Firmly fixed spots in peoples' minds—*everyone* knew where X Mill was—they were often used as benchmarks for land surveys and as political meeting places. William Ashmore established a mill on Broad Creek at what is now Mill Green in the middle of the eighteenth century and, judging from courthouse records, it must have been the hub for all of northeastern Harford County: as long ago as the 1750s, deeds refer to "the road from Ashmore's Mill," and citizens used the building as a polling place in 1775. By all accounts, this two-story rubblestone dwelling, with one room per floor, was built with the mill and it has remained associated with it ever since. On Ashmore's death the property passed to his son, John, who was assessed in 1798 for the gristmill, 1,208 acres of land, several outbuildings, and this "2-story stone house." The Ashmores also built a sawmill and a store here, to ensure that their property remained at the center of things. In 1821 Ashmore and his wife, Margaret, sold the mill property to their daughter Susanna, wife of Nathaniel Bemis, with the proviso that the Bemises would provide life-long care for the Ashmores. (The Ashmores were guaranteed "Firewood left at the door" as well as a "sufficiency for three persons of wheat, corn, and rye flour, sugar, tea, and coffee, pork, beef, and fish, and also two cows and one horse" to be kept "the same as they [the Bemises] keep their own.") Mill and house changed hands several times during the ensuing generations, and each new owner added a bit to suit current needs and tastes; as a result the house has evolved into a rambling and thoroughly charming compendium of two centuries' of county building patterns, from the mantel, window trim, and paneled doors in the original section's parlor to the high-tech kitchen of the 1990s added by the present owner, a pioneer in computer technology.

5-32. Mill Green Mill
Mill Green Road
1827; Private
National Register   HA-93

The successor to the eighteenth-century Ashmore Mill, this rubblestone gristmill was built on the site of the older structure by Nathaniel Bemis in 1827. (Bemis had acquired the property through his marriage to the miller John Ashmore's daughter.) A man of some enterprise, Bemis must have felt it necessary to replace his in-laws' mill (by then a half-century old) with something contemporary; he also must have been pleased with the result for he placed a large medallion inscribed "N.S. Bemis Mills 1827" high in the Broad Creek–facing wall. Bemis sold the mill to Thomas H. Roberts in 1838 and Robert's Mill is clearly shown on the 1858 county map. Margaret Street, Roberts's daughter, bought the mill in 1866 and it remained in her family until 1915. In the U.S. census of 1880, Margaret Street's "custom mill" was valued at $4,000; the census taker further noted that, thanks to the fourteen-foot fall on Broad Creek, the mill's wheels were capable of turning out "200 bbl flour, 70 tons meal, 13.7 tons feed, and 1 ton buckwheat" all worth $3,100. While operations ceased here decades ago, the mill retains an astonishing amount of original (or, at least, period) machinery; even the millrace still flows, channeling the waters of Broad Creek through what is unquestionably one of the county's most important industrial sites.

5-33. Mill Green Hotel
Mill Green Road
c. 1858; Private
National Register   HA-96

By the time George Huff bought this land in 1858 (sixty-two acres for $1,350), Mill Green had been an economic, political, and industrial center for nearly 100 years. Owners of the mill itself had, over time, built a sawmill, a tannery, and other industrial structures and throughout the nineteenth century entrepreneurs erected stores, a tavern, a post office, and other income-producing buildings in the bustling community. This rambling frame structure, perched on a hill overlooking the community, was, according to tradition, a hotel.

5-34. Huff House
Mill Green Road
c. 1858; Private
National Register   HA-99

George Huff bought sixty-two acres in Mill Green in 1858 and his heirs continued to own that property until the 1920s; he or his descendants are said to have built a hotel on part of the tract while they lived here. (A building belonging to "G. Huff" is shown on this site on both the 1858 and 1878 county maps.) The two-part house, firmly a product of the mid-to late nineteenth century, still contributes to the village's overall character (note such period features as the steep attic gable and corbeled chimney caps) while the two-room, two-door plan links it to vernacular dwellings in nearby southcentral Pennsylvania.

5-35. Cooper's Pleasant Hill
Tabernacle Road
c. 1800; Private   HA-104

Many of the county's first settlers built themselves dwellings in what today's scholars call the "British Cabin" folk house form. These were simply one-room cottages with a large, end-wall fireplace; stairs, if present, were enclosed in a closet beside the hearth. Well-known documented examples in the lower and central reaches of Harford include the original Norris house (or Prospect) on what is now Olney and, on a larger scale, Woodview and Joshua's Meadows. This rubblestone structure is not well known and documentation is only sketchy; nevertheless it seems as if Thomas J. Cooper, cited in deeds as "of York, Pennsylvania," built the house after he began buying land here in the 1780s. (Many tracts in the area still go by names such as Cooper's Prospect and Cooper's Pleasant Hill, the title of this property.) Not much is known about Cooper, but he sensibly picked a prime location for his house, near what was then the main road to the Susquehanna ferry at Bald Friar. A bit conservative, in building this house he followed patterns that had been established in the county a half-century earlier.

5-32

5-33

5-34

5-35

5-36

5-37

He also followed the sensible folk practice, popular in his native Pennsylvania, of siting the place in a "bank-house" manner: he built the dwelling into a sheltering hillside, exposing it on two stories to the south but on only one to the north. He was also a man with some style, for he gave elegant beading to at least one window enframement and the structure's rubblestone walls are nicely set off by massive quoins. His heirs passed the land back and forth among themselves in the 1850s and '60s; one Stephen P. Cooper took title in 1869 and is shown living here on the 1878 county map.

5-36. N.T.'s Stone Cottage
140 Ridge Road
c. 1820; Private   HA-126

Located less than a mile from the huge quarries at Cardiff on land that once belonged to the Proctor Slate Manufacturing Company, this small-scale stone structure was in all probability built as a quarryman's cottage. It certainly is a colorful building, for despite its small size, it displays a remarkable range of hue and tone in the rock: even individual stones vary in color from green to yellow to pink; odd pieces of dark slate appear at random in the walls or, at times, as lintels. Pieces vary as much in size as they do in tone and the effect, while attractive, is somewhat bewildering. Perhaps most bewildering of all is the simple hunk of nearly square slate placed in the southwest gable; it is inscribed "N.T." (complete with periods) but the initials do not precisely coincide with any owner and there is no date. (Perhaps N.T. was the mason the slate company employed to erect the structure—if this is, in fact, a company-built house.) One James Hogstine bought 350 acres here in 1808 for the high price of £962. (See also Montgomery's Delight.) When Hogstine died in 1822, he left his sister, Margaret Thompson, "the house wherein I now live" and an income of $40 per year; title for this property eventually passed to her children, Jane and James Thompson. So perhaps—*perhaps*—the T refers to a Thompson; but the N. . . . It is maddening not to know more about Hogstine: he was clearly illiterate (he signed his will with an *X*) and he was just as clearly a small-scale farmer, for his estate inventory was only worth $578. (The most valuable items were "two beef steers" worth $40, 20 acres of "grain in ground" worth $45, and an "apple press and trough" worth $15.) Nevertheless, his house—

assuming this cottage was his house—boasts a most up-to-date plan with one room per floor and a full-length side stairhall. A modern addition to the northeast adds little aesthetically, which is a shame since the original structure is superbly sited on the south side of a hill with long vistas down the Deep Run Valley; abandoned yet still sound, it offers wonderful restoration possibilities.

5-37. Trap Church
(St. James Church)
Trap Church Road
c. 1874; Regular services
National Register   HA-166

By the middle of the eighteenth century, the valley of lower Deer Creek had become well settled and could more or less hold its own, economically, with the older bay-oriented regions of the county. The men and women who carved out farms and mills along the creek must have been a religious group, for they established places of worship at an early date: the Quaker meeting in Darlington was organized in the 1730s and Catholics, forbidden to have public churches, were privately ministered to by priests from the "Mass House" beginning in the 1740s. Episcopalians had their spiritual needs attended to as well and St. George's Parish (Spesutia) established St. James chapel of ease at this site ("called the 'Trapp,'" wrote Walter Preston in 1901) around 1760, the year St. George's also decided to tax bachelors. The rector from St. George's officiated at Trap at certain specified times. That old chapel, which was said to match the dimensions of St. George's, was replaced in 1800; the chapel became a full parish in 1851 and yet another new church—this building—was built around 1874, after a fire destroyed the 1800 structure. It is a one-story rubblestone church with a remarkably steep gable roof and wide eaves. The parish declined in numbers in this century since worshipers were drawn to Churchville and Darlington, and the building was eventually abandoned. But in 1957 the Trappe Missionary Baptist Church took out a ninety-nine-year lease on the church, restored it, and it flourishes today under their care. One of their first acts was to clean up the adjoining cemetery, an important spot containing, among other stones, the grave of Angus Grême, the Frenchman who served in Lafayette's army in the American Revolution and then, after Yorktown, returned to Harford County and built the house known as Maiden's Bower.

5-38. Swallowfields
Castleton Road
c. 1830; 1850; 1880; Private   HA-175

Built in at least three stages, this rambling frame farmhouse is important not only for what can be seen, but for what cannot. And it has always been thus, for Swallowfields was a station on the Underground Railroad, that secretive network of hiding places established by abolitionists to shelter and assist fugitive slaves fleeing to freedom in the North. Documenting such stations now is extremely difficult because secrecy was so important then: if discovered, the slaves would be returned to bondage and certain punishment and those who aided them (and thereby broke federal laws) would be fined and/or imprisoned. The Darlington area, settled by Quakers, became a center of abolitionist activity but only two sites—this property and the ruins of the William Worthington house nearer Conowingo—can be documented as such with any certainty. Historian Christine Tolbert, whose mother worked at Swallowfields in the early twentieth century, vividly recalls how the house's then owner, Bernard Gilpin Waring, would show her secret places "where they would hide slaves." The most poignant of these must be the icehouse, "a kind of eerie place," recalls Mrs. Tolbert. "I could not imagine people would go down there, let alone huddle and hide—it's just a dark, damp pit."

5-39. Columbia Mill Ruins
Deer Creek
c. 1775; Private
National Register   HA-178

Described as "old" as long ago as the 1830s, the Columbia Mill has been a ruin for at least a century. In the 1770s John Rodgers of Rodgers Tavern and Arthur McCann established a merchant mill on this site. Documents prove that their mill was in operation by 1778, but it did not last long: the partners quarreled and in 1780 Rodgers began advertising that he would "no longer be responsible for McCann's debts because there were no articles of agreement between" them. McCann continued to run the mill until he was sued by Baltimore merchant William Smith, who in 1792 wrote to Gen. Otho Williams of "an unfortunate connection I have formed" with McCann who

"robbed me of five or six hundred pounds." In 1797 Smith, to whom the court had awarded the mill, sold the property to John Stump of Stafford for the high price of 1,600 "pounds, current money." (The deed notes "on which a mill commonly called McCanns and Rodgers is erected" and refers to the cast as "William Smith of Baltimore City, Gentleman" and "John Stump, Miller.") As matters continued to deteriorate, so did the mill, until it simply became a ruin. By 1880 W. S. Forwood, a thorough Victorian with that era's love of the picturesque, was able to write of the "wild and romantic [mill ruins, a] . . . monumental object of interest . . . illustrative of the temporary character and the comparative futility of man's works when viewed in connection with the works of nature. . . . Time's ravages have destroyed the roof. . . . The grim walls, with their great openings for doors and windows, like the apertures for eyes and mouth in the head of a huge skeleton, alone stand in their deep and abandoned solitude." Nearby is one of the cuts made for the Deer Creek and Susquehanna Railroad, begun in 1889 and never completed, another example of "the comparative futility of man's works."

5-40. Red Gate
Castleton Road
c. 1885; Private   HA-208

One of the least-known Darlington-area houses attributed to Philadelphia architect Walter Cope, Red Gate deserves more recognition than it has so far received. The house was built for Bernard Gilpin Smith, industrialist and farmer. Smith owned the Susquehanna Power and Paper Company, the Conowingo Flint Mill, and other such establishments. Samuel Mason, in his *Historical Sketches,* recalls, "I . . . well remember . . . hearing in the dead of night the ceaseless grinding of the machinery at Conowingo," adding, "personally I prefer it to the noise of automobiles." Mason ascribed the paper company's "birth" to "the fertile brains of Joshua C. and B. Gilpin Smith," and added that the brothers "had, in 1880, a flint mill" but then became "interested in the manufacture of paper" and established that company, whose "first order for paper was from the 'New York American,' a pink journal at six cents a pound. This was a very high price and the company made a lot of money." Jean Ewing and Elizabeth Newlin Smith Ewing credit Cope with the design of Smith's house, Red Gate. Cruci-

5-38

5-38

5-40

5-41

5-42

5-43

form (but with additions), the 2½-story frame house sports prominent gables with ridgelines that meet at a central chimney; this assures picturesque massing. It also is a reminder of Cope's (and Smith's) awareness of modern technology; Red Gate was among the first houses in the county equipped with central heating, and the large chimney was centrally placed so it could efficiently serve a huge coal furnace.

5-41. Hosanna A.M.E. Church
Castleton Road
1880; Regular services   HA-211

Since its settlement by Quakers and other enlightened souls, the Darlington-Berkeley area has been one of the most tolerant neighborhoods in the county: all religions seem to have flourished here and the Darlington cemetery's original bylaws note that its trustees would not discriminate by race, creed, or color. Thus it is not surprising that the area boasted one of the earliest free black settlements in the county and land transactions involving "free persons of color" appear in deeds from the very early nineteenth century. This frame church has helped meet the spiritual needs of the black community since 1880, although it postdates the adjacent school and cemetery. The flourishing state of things here may be deduced from the many new structures on the site including the stuccoed parish house (1949) and annex (1961).

5-42. Hosanna School
Castleton Road
1868; Private
National Register   HA-210

Modest in appearance, the Hosanna church and school rank high among the county's historic structures. Here can be traced events as monumental as the birth of local black education and as personal as one family's struggle for economic success and personal dignity. It all began on March 4, 1822, when Cassandra Rigbie Corse (a daughter of James Rigbie) sold fifty acres of land for $700 to "Cupid Paca, freeman of color." No one knows Paca's origin although it is difficult not to assume some connection with the prominent Abingdon-area white Paca family. (Cupid Paca's surname was sometimes *Paca* and sometimes *Peaco,* before it eventually evolved into the name *Peaker* that is well known today.) Paca dabbled in area real estate until his death in

1847. In 1844 he began dividing some of his holdings among his children, many of whom then established their own farmsteads in the area in the 1840s and '50s. After the Civil War (and resulting federal legislation) guaranteed blacks their freedom, the issue of black education arose. The federal government established the Freedmen's Bureau to oversee the education of ex-slaves but many blacks took matters into their own hands, which is precisely what happened here. On January 8, 1868, Joseph Peaker, Cupid's son, sold one-quarter acre of his patrimony "for the purpose of a schoolhouse lot" and then he and a group of fellow residents incorporated themselves and built this frame school. (Actually, they built a two-story school; the second level was torn off by a hurricane in this century.) The county eventually took over operations in 1879, but a group of black trustees, including several members of the Presberry family, reassumed control in 1907. The last records of enrollment date to 1945. Cupid Paca would have been pleased by the school's work: he himself was illiterate and signed all his documents with an *X*, but his descendants, even though they faced discrimination on almost every other front, were at least able to write their own names. The saga of the Paca-Peaker family is more fully explored in chapter 5.

5-43. Grey Rock Farm
Castleton Road
c. 1830; with additions; Private   HA-261

Two stories tall and five long bays wide, this elegant—and largely unchanged—two-sectioned house bears clear visual and stylistic association with the earlier Carter house at Rock Run and Woodlawn on Deer Creek. One of the nation's main north-south roads crossed this property in the early nineteenth century; it led from Baltimore to the original Susquehanna bridge at Conowingo (chartered in 1808 and built considerably upstream from the present dam) and thence to Philadelphia. Generations of the Jones family earned a good living because of the road, bridge, and attendant activity, and the clan's progenitor, Hugh Jones, is generally credited with building this house. Jones also comanaged, with his brother, Charles, a hotel and bar that they built directly across the road from Grey Rock Farm. Catering to the needs of the fishermen and travelers made the Joneses wealthy and they conservatively invested their riches in Baltimore bank stock: when Hugh Jones died in

5-44

5-45

1864, the bulk of his estate (roughly $12,000 out of $14,000) was in such shares. That wealth is clearly evident in this house: note, for example, how Jones used granite as a counterpoint to the walls' rubblestone: he placed large granite blocks as lintels above every window and, as an extra bit of élan, laid large granite stones in a row near the roofline to form a cornice, an effect he then accentuated with three stepped rows of bricks to complete the transition between wall and roof. The main section is one room deep with a center-stairhall plan, and that layout seems to be original, as do most of the interior details, including the insulated plaster walls. The Joneses' stay here was closely entwined with the old bridge's: when cattle caused the wooden span to collapse in 1854, Jones cared for the uninjured bovines and ferried them across the river the next morning. Jones's grandson, Fred, ran a general store nearby. And Hugh A. Jones gained an immortality of sorts through his writings, for his histories of Darlington and Conowingo remain valid and useful. The bridge was virtually swept away by ice in 1904 and was burned in 1907; it was finally dynamited in 1928 and whatever remained was submerged in the lake that followed the Conowingo Dam.

5-44. Meadow Farm
Conowingo Road
c. 1830; 1877; Private
National Register   HA-280

Generations of historians and citizens have attributed part of this rambling, many-sectioned house to the Rigbie-Massey family and have dated it to the middle of the eighteenth century. Unfortunately nothing in either the 1798 or 1814 tax lists corroborates such a claim. Jean S. Ewing, who has thoroughly investigated this and other structures in the Darlington area, has written that "the largest wing . . . was built by Miss Hannah Evans of Philadelphia in 1877 for her summer home." On the other hand, Samuel Mason, who devotes several pages in his generally reliable *Historical Sketches* to the house, states that the center section was "standing during the Revolution" and that the larger section dates to "around 1830." Documentary evidence suggests that everyone is correct: Isaac Massey left the property to Aquila Massey who, in 1843, took out a $1,000 mortgage on the place; that was foreclosed in 1861 and Edward M. Allen and his wife, Sallie (née Wilson), bought the

216-acre farm in 1876 at the resulting sheriff's sale fifteen years later. The Allens sold the farm to Hannah B. Evans "of Philadelphia" in 1879 for $2,000, and it is clear that something was standing, for the Allens reserved the right "to enter and remove" all "personal property on said land"—presumably furniture in the house. Perhaps it would be safe to say that Miss Evans remodeled the old Massey house; by doing so in the 1870s, she earned herself an important niche in the county's architectural history, for after she showed them the way, other Philadelphians such as D. C. Wharton Smith and Francis Stokes filled the hills around Darlington with high-style country retreats. The large, clapboard section has a side-hall/double parlor plan; the two main rooms are virtually square with fireplaces centrally placed in each room's southern (exterior) wall; the staircase has a simple handrail and newel post and low treads. All of this—plan and details—suggests a simple late federal house and corroborates Mason's 1830 date. The two rooms in the center section may well antedate the larger unit, but remodelings have made any date difficult to prove. When Hannah Evans died in 1937, she left the farm to her niece Edith Silver and it is still owned by the Silver family. For Mason's delightful account of the farm, see his *Sketches,* pages 133–38.

5-45. Grey Gables
4528 Conowingo Road
Late 1880s; Private
National Register   HA-310

Philadelphia architect Walter Cope briefly flashed across the Harford scene, but his light—the buildings he designed—still gives a lovely glow. Cope, after completing his education and the then-obligatory tour of Europe, set up practice with John Stewardson in 1885; Stewardson's younger brother, Emlyn, joined them in 1887 and historians have attributed about a dozen buildings in the Darlington area to the firm Cope & Stewardson. Unfortunately it is only the rare house—Winstone—that has signed drawings; the rest of the buildings depend on oral traditions, visual similarities, and other evidence. Mrs. Emlyn Stewardson recalled that this house was built for Horace and Helen Stokes in 1886; Cope was a Stokes relative and Helen Stokes (described in deeds as "wife of Horace Stokes") bought two acres of land here in 1885. The widow and children of Samuel Mason sold Stokes the land and all parties were from Ger-

5-46

5-47

5-47

5-48

mantown, Pennsylvania, thus cementing the ties between Darlington and Philadelphia. (Prior to the 1880s, the unimproved land had been part of the Meadow Farm tract.) Stylistically, the house's steeply pitched multiple roofs, half-timbering, projecting bays and porches, and asymmetrical floor plan make it a superlative example of the Queen Anne manner of building, a style at its most fashionable in the 1880s and a style Cope used with great success in other area projects such as Westacre and Lansdowne. Interior details, surprisingly simple for a house so rambunctious on the exterior, remain essentially intact.

5-46. Trappe School
1400 Block Trappe Road
c. 1860; Private   HA-315

Abandoned for most of this century, the Trappe School is one of three known mid-nineteenth-century stone schoolhouses built in the county. (See also Emmorton and Prospect; by the way, the present spelling Trap*pe* is a corruption of the original—and simpler—Trap.) Maryland established a state system of public education in 1825 whereby each county would create its own board empowered to collect funds for books, buildings, and equipment. Operating under this system, Harford's board acquired land here in 1854 and this building followed shortly thereafter. It measures roughly 20 by 16 feet and originally contained one room beneath its gable roof. (It was later remodeled.) Brick arches over the windows and doors add interest to the gray of the stone façades. (There are also traces of stucco on the façades, which suggests that the building's rubblestone walls may have been covered in that material, doubtless for a more finished look.) The 1825 system was not without its critics; no less than the governor complained in 1856 that "education is in utter and hopeless prostration." Matters were sorry indeed locally, for the 1852 *Gazetteer of the State of Maryland* singled out Harford as "poorly supplied with means of education." So one might view the Trappe School as the last local structure built in the old—and unsatisfactory—regime. In 1864 and '67 the new state constitutions revolutionized Maryland's school system. The Trappe School building, no longer needed for education, was used as a tenant house in the late nineteenth and early twentieth centuries, and an 1899 deed for the property notes "that school building and lot formerly used . . . for school purposes." That

same year the county school board built a replacement frame school about a quarter-mile away but it was taken out of service around 1940.

5-47. McCann House
3247 Forge Hill Road
c. 1880; Private   HA-317

State highway maps still refer to the nearby intersection as McCann's Crossroads, doubtless a reference to the family who built this frame house and lived here until Albert McCann sold the property to Donald Symington of Indian Spring Farm in 1926. One wishes one knew more about Mr. McCann, for he clearly was a man who acted as his whims directed: contemporary photographs show that when he bought the house in 1890, it was a plain three-bay structure with a utilitarian porch and straightforward shingled roof; but then, perhaps prompted by the arts and crafts movement (then all the rage in international circles) or perhaps acting on his own, he relaid the roof slates in a decorative pattern and added an overscale entrance hood to the porch. He let his imagination run wild at the latter and gave it huge brackets—far larger than the mere laws of physics might dictate—enlivened with sawn ducks' heads.

5-48. Bayless-Hopkins House
837 Darlington Road
c. 1870; with additions; Private
National Register   HA-321

Much added to over the years, this two-story brick house stands on part of the Elberton (or El Britton) tract from which many of its neighboring farms were carved. In March 1868 Hannah Hopkins and James Worthington sold ninety-four acres of this tract to S. M. Bayless, and the 1878 county map shows a "Mrs. Bayless" living here. The price in the deed—$5,649—was high for 1868 and corroborates the current owner's belief that part of the house was then standing. But if so, Bayless must have completely remodeled what was here; the present dwelling, in massing, in proportion, and in detail certainly reads as a product of the 1870s. The house stayed in the Bayless family until 1906. Historian and activist Jean S. Ewing, who has studied most of the Darlington-area farms, noted that in this century residents here supplemented their income "by distilling very good whiskey," and added that the Mick family, who owned the place from 1926 till 1935, were "especially prosperous during Prohibition."

5-49. Westacre
2035 Trappe Church Road
c. 1887; Private
National Register   HA-322

By any standard, Westacre ranks as one of the outstanding works of art in northeastern Maryland. It is the product of two Philadelphians, financier D. C. Wharton Smith and architect Walter Cope. In 1885 Cope designed the estate Winstone for Smith; two years later, on May 26, 1887, Smith bought this ten-acre site across the road from his own house and commissioned Cope to design a suitable country seat for his son, Courtauld W. Smith. The result is Westacre, an "outstanding estate" when built, according to a University of Maryland publication (*350 Years of Art and Architecture in Maryland*), and still one of the area's show places. Cope placed the rambling Queen Anne–style house carefully so it gained sweeping views of the woods and fields, hills and valleys that roll down to Deer Creek two miles away. The building is equal to the site: its studied asymmetry, sweeping roofs, tall decorative chimneys, and varied wall coverings combine to create the very model of the picturesque. On the interior, the large principle rooms, designed for entertaining and with their spatial effects in mind, remain largely unchanged; the paneling, stairways, ceilings, chimney pieces, and so on, rendered in chestnut, pine, walnut, oak, and other native woods, are just as successful as the exterior. Original shingled outbuildings (undoubtedly also designed by Cope) include a stable (with tower and cupola), icehouse, and pump house.

5-50. Winstone
2100 Trappe Church Road
1885; Private
National Register   HA-323

A textbook example of Queen Anne architecture (only with more personality and less "bookishness" than that phrase sometimes implies) Winstone is one of architect Walter Cope's many gifts to northeast Harford County. Philadelphia physician and financier D. C. Wharton Smith bought an unimproved thirty-two-acre tract adjacent to the Grace Church lot in 1885 and hired Cope to design a group of buildings to which he might escape

on weekends, far from the concerns of Broad Street. The young Cope (age 25 and just beginning his first year of practice) gave Smith a stylistically cogent creation. The main house (stone and frame and bulging with porches and dormer windows), guest house (stone enlivened by a variety of window treatments), windmill (shingled), and stable (shingled and stone and turreted) all combine to make Winstone the quintessence of period theories and fashions. The interiors, in design and execution, are just as fine as the exteriors. Smith eventually moved to Darlington year-round and contributed to such projects as the town cemetery (where he is buried), Grace Church, the academy, and the Darlington Good Road League ("one of the first of its kind in America," according to local historian Fred Jones). He was also a prime investor in B. Gilpin Smith's Susquehanna Power and Paper Company, then the area's largest industry, but as Harry Webb Farrington points out in his 1930 *Kilts to Togs,* Philadelphia "is where he [Smith] made his money."

5-51. Hopkins-Hall House
1839 Trappe Church Road
c. 1730 (?); with additions; Private
National Register   HA-329

In scale, configuration, and roofline, this frame dwelling resembles the Rigbie House. These similarities have led some historians to suggest that the two structures are contemporaries. Unfortunately, while the Rigbie House enjoys thorough and convincing documentation, the "paperwork" for this house remains, and probably will remain, sketchy, making a firm date impossible. The building crowns a hill overlooking Deer Creek on part of the Bachelor's Good Luck tract, a huge patent of land on which various generations of the Husband-Jewett family built Lansdowne and Woodlawn. Does this house, on the north bank of Deer Creek, antedate the other two, which are on the south bank? The house's central (main) section has exposed beaded beams, a large fireplace, and other details that suggest age. The lower section to the east is thought to have contained the original kitchen; its large fireplace and hearth have been rebuilt, but the workmen carefully reused many of the original fieldstones and retained the old mantel beam. An 1873 deed to the property states that it was "the Home Farm upon which Joshua Hopkins resided at the time of his death"; Hopkins, who died in 1863, inherited the

5-49

5-50

5-51

5-52

5-53

5-54

place from his father, Samuel, who had died in 1839. Based on Samuel's estate inventory, it seems clear that his house contained a parlor, passage, and dining room on the ground floor ("parlour carpet," "passage carpet," and "dining room carpet"); there were eight beds, but it is impossible to tell if they were in bedrooms, or if there were two stories to the house, or where the kitchen was. It is clear that the place was elegantly furnished; appraisers noted several pieces of silver and other expensive touches. (Interestingly, Hopkins was one of the area's last farmers to raise tobacco: "1 lot leaf tobacco, $80.") He had established himself in the area at an early date; in 1816 the court had to appoint a special investigation into the "divers disputes and controversies [which] have arisen between Thomas Chew and Samuel Hopkins" over their boundaries in Bachelor's Good Luck; the resulting survey mentions Hollands Branch, a stream that still flows through the property.

Just how Gerrard Hopkins, a noted Baltimore cabinetmaker (he advertised his shop on Gay Street—where "he makes and sells in the newest fashions . . . tea chests, desks, book cases, scrutoires"—in area newspapers as early as 1767), fits into all this is unclear, particularly since a Gerrard Hopkins, according to the 1798 tax list, owned 259 acres on Deer Creek and a "17 × 34 1-story wood house." Several Hopkins properties are mentioned in those tax rolls, including the tantalizing entry for "Samuel Hopkins of Joseph" who was assessed for 200 acres of land and one "18 × 22 wood house, not finished," dimensions that closely match the size of the present center section. Samuel willed the "dwelling house" to his widow, Sarah, for her life; it all was to pass to their sons Joshua and William, if the boys provided "for the comfortable maintenance of my son Joseph," who was insane. As noted, Joshua died in 1863; his estate inventory suggests a larger house than his father's did ("suggests" is not conclusive): mention was made of a "long room" and a "square room" as well as a passage, parlor, and kitchen; "stair carpeting" certainly implies an upper story.

5-52. William Hopkins House
East Noble's Mill Road
c. 1865; Private
National Register   HA-332

The patent for the tract of land this structure is built on, Bachelor's Good Luck, dates to the seventeenth century; the Hopkins family, who

actually built this house, seem to have been established in the area for at least as long. While it is difficult to pin an exact date to the building that may be the original Hopkins house, assigning a year to this frame building is easy. A man named William Hopkins of Joseph built it shortly after he purchased seventy-eight acres here in May of 1865 from Henry C. Stump, who had purchased the property for $4,025 at a sheriff's sale in 1862 after Gerard Gover, owner of Noble's Mill (then called Gover's Mill) defaulted on a deal to buy the seventy-eight acres for $4,000 from Joshua Hopkins. (Joshua inherited the land in 1839 when his father, Samuel, who owned vast acreage on the north shore of Deer Creek, died.) The house left the Hopkins family in 1890. (See 5-51.)

5-53. Adams Blacksmith Shop
East Noble's Mill Road
Mid-nineteenth century; Private
National Register   HA-334

As invaluable to life a century ago as mechanics and gas stations are today, blacksmiths and their shops once formed the center of communities throughout rural America. Harford County boasted dozens of such establishments—it would not be going too far to say that virtually every crossroads had its own "village smithy," with or without the poetic chestnut tree. No more. Today only four shops— or, rather, traces of four shops—remain: a frame building once in Level, but now at the Steppingstone Museum, traces of a stone shop on the Woolsey farm near Churchville, the stone structure in the Jerusalem mill village, and this one-story rubblestone structure. Standing abandoned in a field near Noble's Mill, the building was indicated as a blacksmith shop on the 1878 county map when the surrounding farm was owned by William Hopkins of Joseph. But it may antedate the farmhouse, because a blacksmith would have been highly useful to milling operations (note Jerusalem Mill) and a cluster of unidentified buildings are shown clustered about the mill on the 1858 county map.

5-54. Noble's Mill
Noble's Mill Road
1854; Private
National Register   HA-335

The rich loamy soils hereabouts have lured grain farmers to the Deer Creek Valley since the mid-eighteenth century, and where wheat and corn grow millers cannot be far away. Members of the Husband, Jewett, and Hopkins families farmed these hills well before the Revolution and a gristmill has stood on this site nearly as long. The original structure was called Smith's Mill, and leases between various millers and the mill's owners, Thomas and Martha Smith, date to 1764. That mill eventually passed to the Gover family and Gerard Gover built the present massive frame structure in 1854. Gover's miller, Benjamin Noble, bought "Gover's Mills" and about 2¾ acres in 1869 for $9,000. Noble took advantage of the creek's power—C. Milton Wright has described the spot as "the best in the locality," estimating that the water generates "forty horsepower"—to create one of the county's most flourishing milling operations: the 1880 census valued the mill at $8,000 and stated that the undershot wheel drove a "5-foot turbine at 40 rpm" to produce "400 bbl flour, 240 tons meal, 23 tons feed, and 2.5 tons buckwheat." When Benjamin died in 1894 he left the mill to his son, William S. Noble, who kept things going until the 1940s. Abandoned for almost forty years, the mill is now (1994) being adapted into a residence and artist's studio.

5-55. Noble's Mill Bridge
Noble's Mill Road
1883; Public
National Register   HA-335

One of the longest metal bridges remaining in the county and certainly the span with the most idyllic setting, the Noble's Mill Bridge is a 152-foot through truss manufactured by the Wrought Iron Bridge Company of Canton, Ohio. (Until they were stolen in the 1980s, plaques placed above the two entrances proclaimed the manufacturer and date.) The importance of this delicate, picturesque structure to the "valleyscape" is self-evident and is equal to the importance of the manufacturer to the history of American bridge construction. The company was established by one John Laird around 1840; in 1871 David Hammond and Joe Abbott reorganized the foundry and reincorporated themselves as the Wrought Iron Bridge Company. The two men were inventors as well and had patented the "Hammond and Abbott Arched Bridge," which they featured in their publication, *Book of Designs.* (They sold thousands of spans through the mail thanks to that catalog, which is how the Harford County commissioners acquired the

Noble's Mill Bridge.) The company quickly grew into one of the leading bridge-building firms in the country, employing 270 workers in 1881. Examples of their work have been documented in twenty-five states. By 1900 Hammond and Abbott were taking out ads in trade journals for "iron and steel bridges, girders, turntables, buildings and structural work"; shortly thereafter their company was absorbed by U.S. Steel.

5-56. Noble's Mill Miller's House
Noble's Mill Road
c. 1870; earlier wing; Private
National Register   HA-337

During most of this two-section frame house's existence, its history was completely entwined with that of the nearby mill. Structural evidence suggests that the rear unit of the house is older than the front section and probably dates to the era of the Govers, who owned the mill prior to 1869. That year Gerard and Cassandra Gover sold the mill property to Benjamin Noble. Noble ran the mill and almost certainly added the 2½-story front wing to the house. Millers were, almost by definition, among the leading citizens of their community and Noble's house makes that status clear: he embellished his dwelling with highly fashionable carpenter Gothic trim (note particularly the sawn designs in the wood at the eaves and within the attic gables) that sets this house apart from its simpler contemporaries.

5-57. Indian Spring Farm
Priestford Road
c. 1810; 1862; c. 1925; Private
National Register   HA-342

Like most of the Deer Creek Valley, this farm was once part of the vast holdings of John Stump of Stafford. Stump's son William built a five-bay, center-hall stone house on the land—which his father still owned—and settled in here with his friend, Joseph Parker, according to the 1814 tax rolls. When the senior Stump died in 1816 he willed to William "the farm where he now lives," then amounting to a bit over 1,000 acres. (The will also makes clear that William was a bit of a wastrel, for Stump of Stafford spent many words fussing about his son's bills and "store accounts.") The farm, called Stump's Prospect, declined in quality and ruin seemed imminent—as early as 1821 Christopher Wilson of Darlington testified in court that the buildings here were "in

5-55

5-56

5-57

5-58

5-59

a very dilapidated condition." Thomas Symington of Baltimore bought the old house in 1862 and repaired it (and substantially added to it), built a new stone house closer to the road for his farmers, and brought the fields back to productivity. Symington died in 1875 and the farm was passed around among his many children; ruin again seemed imminent until another Symington appeared. This time it was Donald (a grandson of Thomas and a son of the dashing Civil War hero Maj. William) who with his wife (née Elsie Jenkins) brought the old place back to perhaps greater glory than it had ever known: they built new wings onto the already large house, added a highly picturesque group of cattle barns (for his internationally famous herds of Jersey cattle), and created superb, informal gardens to set it all off to perfection. Donald Symington died in 1944; his widow sold the farm shortly thereafter.

5-58. Belle Farm II
Graceton Road
1820; Private   HA-477

A fine example of late federal design, this solid stone house is equally important to both the county's religious and architectural histories. During the eighteenth century, the land was part of the vast Deer Park farm of the Wheeler family. Ignatius Wheeler died in 1793, and in 1805 his daughter Teresa acquired 366 acres of her late father's farm. (The land was described as being "on the Great Road.") She had married Henry Macatee in 1799, and in 1820 the couple built this house, as a semicircular datestone in the west gable end attests. (Where they lived in the intervening twenty years is unclear.) The Wheelers were among Harford's wealthiest citizens and one would expect their houses—and houses built by their in-laws—to reflect their economic success. (See 5-75.) Belle Farm II does not disappoint: its plan (a through center hall with one room to each side) is certainly representative of its era, and its details (chairrails, elaborate window surrounds, beaded door trim) are stylish and remain largely intact. Both the Wheeler and Macatee families, staunch Roman Catholics, were instrumental in founding churches: the Wheelers will forever remain associated with St. Ignatius just as the Macatees will with St. Mary's, Pylesville. In fact, before St. Mary's was built, mass was celebrated in parlor of this house and it is thought that the exceptionally wide opening between parlor and hall was de-

signed to hold an overflow congregation if the number of worshipers exceeded the capacity of the parlor. Henry Macatee died in 1852; in his will he left an acre of ground for a new church (St. Mary's) to be built "whenever the Arch Bishop of Baltimore shall determine." He also left one aged slave, Milly, who was free to live with "whichever of my children" she chose and the child was instructed to treat Milly "with kindness." Judging from his estate inventory, Macatee did not farm but invested his capital in mortgages and in area industries such as the "740 bbl of bar iron at La Grange Iron Works." One of Henry's sons, Sylvester Macatee, eventually sold the 368 acres of Belle Farm II out of the family in 1871 for $11,500.

5-59. Rigdon House
Grier Nursery Road
Mid-nineteenth century; Private   HA-484

Members of the Rigdon family acquired large tracts of land in this area during the late eighteenth century and a stone survey marker for the tract this house is on still exists; it is inscribed "TBR," which stands for Thomas Baker Rigdon. In October 1797 Rigdon sold 100 acres here to his son Stephen but nothing described in either the 1798 or 1814 tax lists suggests that this large stone house was then standing. Stephen Rigdon served in the county grand jury in 1796; during the Revolution, Joseph Rigdon (relationship to Stephen or to Thomas unknown) was a private in Company No. 10 of the Harford County militia while Alexander Rigdon (again, relationship unknown) captained Company No. 12. Stephen Rigdon almost certainly built this house and lived here all his life; when he died in 1865 he willed his land "and house" to his son, Benjamin. The structure seems to have been built in stages, judging from the quoins and placement of the chimney in the larger unit but both sections have been substantially remodeled and now function as two apartments. Stephen Rigdon's estate inventory suggests that he was a reasonably prosperous and diversified farmer: he raised cattle, sheep, and hogs (as well as workhorses and oxen); he kept a variety of files, knives, saws, and other useful tools (including "2 spinning wheels" valued together at $2.00); he cleared fields with "1 briar hook & garden rake" (together valued at $1.50) and planted the soil in clover, wheat, potatoes, timothy, rye, corn, and—surprisingly for this late date—tobacco. (He was also a man of religion and donated a lot of ground to the Rockridge Baptist Church in 1831.) The property left the Rigdon family in 1899.

5-60. Windfall
3624 Dublin Road
c. 1790; with additions; Private   HA-507

Known primarily as the nineteenth-century home of the talented Warner family, this many-sectioned house actually antedates Warner ownership. Elisha Daws bought 100 acres of land here in the late eighteenth century, and the 1798 tax list notes that "Elisha Daws (bricklayer)" owned 100 acres improved by a "15 × 28, 2-story part brick and part stone" house and a variety of outbuildings. Those dimensions line up nicely with the two-story stone section that now forms the center of the rear wing of the pleasantly rambling, much-enlarged dwelling. Daws sold the property to Silas Warner for $100 in 1800. (Daws, proud of his trade, is cited in the deed as "Elisha Daws of the City of Baltimore, Bricklayer.") Silas and his brothers, Aseph and Joseph, were partners in Aseph Warner and Company, manufacturers of clocks, woolen goods, and, most important, silver. C. Milton Wright states in no uncertain terms that "the most noted of all the county's silversmiths was Aseph Warner," who "specialized in beautifully engraved silver spoons" bearing the "punch mark A.W." Warner labored in his shop "between Mill Green and Dublin" "for fifty years beginning just after the Revolution," retiring in 1844 and then only because of blindness. Silas Warner died in 1822; his most valuable item of furniture, an "eight-day clock nailed fast to the wall," was appraised at $40. One of Silas's daughters married into the Hollingsworth family, another into the Harry clan. (In the 1920s and '30s Judge James Warner Harry of Baltimore used the farm as a summer retreat; the judge was interested in county folklore and his tale of "The Headless Ghost of Peddler's Run," published in the *Bel Air Times* of May 6, 1932, remains a classic in the genre.) Windfall stayed in Warner-Hollingsworth-Harry ownership until the time of the Second World War. Warner silver is proudly displayed at the Maryland Historical Society, the Baltimore Museum of Art, and the Historical Society of Harford County.

5-61. Forwood-Cummings House
3073 Sandy Hook Road
c. 1830; 1835; Private   HA-605

Built by physician Parker Forwood on land he inherited from his father, John Forwood, this two-part log and frame house tells tales both architectural and sociological. The smaller of the sections is a two-story, two-bay log building with a simple shed-roofed porch across the main (east) façade and a massive fireplace in the south wall. Thought to have been the first structure on the tract, it is a rare county survivor of pre-1850 log construction. When John Forwood of the Spittle Craft (3-4) died in 1835, he left Parker 300 acres on the north shore of Deer Creek "on which he [Parker] now lives" and it is all but certain that Parker was living in the log house. Upon inheriting the property Dr. Forwood, described in 1897 as "one of the leading physicians of his day [with] . . . a large and profitable practice," built the larger, more "finished," part of the house. Also two stories tall, it presents a totally different appearance from the wing: it has a four-bay, two-door façade common to folk architecture in southern Pennsylvania (the Forwoods came to Maryland from Pennsylvania) and a roofline suggestive of the South—or, at least, the Tidewater—for the slate roof sweeps out beyond the wall to allow for a two-story gallery. Parker Forwood, as a rural doctor, was almost *ipso facto* a man of prominence in the area. His house served as something of a landmark; deeds for other land in the vicinity from the 1830s through the 1850s refer to "the road to Dr. Forwood's." A noteworthy stone springhouse stands about forty feet southeast of the house: two stories tall and stone (with the cooler level below grade), the little hipped-roof building has a projecting, gable-roofed entrance to the north. According to local tradition, the lower, springhouse level was built first and the upper, exposed story added as slaves' quarters. The doctor died in 1866 and his estate inventory reveals that, in addition to practicing medicine (and curing tobacco!) he kept a busy and diverse farm, growing corn and wheat and tending a few cattle, a large flock of sheep (70 head), some hogs, and "7 ducks." The property passed to the doctor's daughter, Mary, and therein lies a classic American story. This aristocratic young lady, whose veins coursed with Stump and Forwood and Archer blood, chose to marry Andrew Dunnigan, an Irish immigrant; the Dunnigans sold the property in 1872 for $6,000.

5-60

5-61

5-62

5-63

5-64

5-62. McCoy-Jackson House
Robinson Mill Road
1804; Private   HA-650

Still owned by direct descendants of the builder, this two-story stone building has always served as something of a landmark in this part of the county; indeed, long-time residents often simply call it "the old stone mansion." On February 17, 1802, William McCoy paid Israel Cox (described in the deed as a "miller") "two silver dollars" for a little over an acre of land here on Broad Creek; two years later he completed this house and marked the event by placing a datestone in the parlor fireplace. (He bought an additional seven acres in 1814.) McCoy gave the house a straightforward three-bay shell with rubblestone walls relieved by stone quoins and by lintels over all windows and doors. He had some sense of classical design, because he made the windows on the main story taller than those above, and to this day ground-floor sashes are paned nine-over-six; those on the second floor are six-over-six. Within, however, the house has a distinctly nonclassical three-room plan: the main (east) room fills two-thirds of the ground floor; it has an enclosed winder stair to the west while a large fireplace fills the east wall. (The kitchen was in the basement, which has a huge cooking fireplace that was used until the 1930s.) Small twin rooms, with back-to-back corner fireplaces, fill the rest of the floor space. Plastered walls and beaded ceiling beams seem to be original. (But the roofline *has* been altered: the house's recent owner, Charles Jackson, a great-grandson of William McCoy, stated that around 1870 the pitch of the roof was lowered and received its present slate covering.) In June 1827 McCoy sold the house and 4¾ acres of land to David McCoy for $200. Most sources credit David with building a flour mill on the property, but something was there when he purchased it; the deed is full of references to landmarks such as "the factory race." Perhaps he rebuilt it; in any event, he ran the mill for about a decade, probably in conjunction with William, because the latter's estate inventory, made on his death in 1833, includes barrels of grain, grindstones, and similar entries. (But where did he get "I conk shell" worth "37c"?) The mill was later owned by the Robinson family, hence the name Robinson Mill Road. David kept the age-old association of milling and Quakerism alive; C. Milton Wright notes that "a group of Quakers, chief of whom was David McCoy, erected the Broad Creek Meeting House in 1828."

5-63. McCoy-Zamzow Log House
Robinson Mill Road
Early nineteenth century; Private   HA-652

Behind the nineteenth-century porch and beneath the twentieth-century asbestos siding sits a massive, two-story log building. Nearly square in shape, the structure has a two-room plan. The rooms were heated by back-to-back fireplaces whose massive chimney still dominates the roofline. (The chimney is actually fed by three flues, the two downstairs and one from an upstairs room.) Inside, the west room, probably the original parlor, has an enclosed winder stair to the second story; the east room probably served as the kitchen and the fireplace still has what appears to be its original iron crane in place. Both rooms have plastered walls and ceilings; pegged log beams are visible in the attic. This is pure folk construction and as such is crucial to an understanding of the county's architectural history; that it has been so well preserved (the later coverings are superficial) is a miracle. Fortunately, the building's new (1994) owners value it and its preservation seems guaranteed. For much of the nineteenth century this building and the nearby stone house were owned by the McCoy family; one might assume that the log house was built first, but because the more formal stone house is firmly dated to 1804, that usual sequence of events may be dismissed. It is more likely that the simple building served as the residence for the miller at the nearby mill on Broad Creek and ownership of the house (McCoy, then Mitchell, then Robinson) coincides with that of the mill until Ernest and Clayton Robinson finally ceased milling operations in the 1940s.

5-64. John Dunnigan House
1229 Boyd Road
c. 1870; Private
National Register   HA-331

Here is an example of what wonderful things can happen when a man of imagination and spirit meets the conservative, mid-nineteenth-century Harford County building pattern: the 2½-story frame dwelling began as a period farmhouse—there are hundreds of examples in the county. But that evidently was not enough for the builder, John Dunnigan, who customized the basic shell with an elaborate porch with chamfered posts and scroll brackets, paired windows, projecting polygonal bay windows enlivened by brackets and perforated trim, pedimented attic gable ends, and large attic dormers with round-arched windows. While Dunnigan doubtless found these motifs in one or more of the pattern books then popular with carpenters throughout the country, the center bay of the main façade—a squared-off projection three full stories tall and encompassing the front door—is harder to explain. Is it an interpretation of a medieval entrance-stair tower? or a latter-day version of the center bay at the federal-era masterpiece Swansbury near Aberdeen? It is all a bit unclear. Dunnigan's 1897 biography notes that he was born in Ireland and spent his youth "on the Emerald Isle, where he learned the stone mason's trade" before coming to America "with the hope of bettering his financial condition." He settled in Harford County around 1860, began buying land, and through four purchases over twenty years put together a 153-acre farm. This farm, "under a high state of cultivation," placed him "among the leading citizens and wide-awake business men of Harford County." Safe to assume, then, that in traditional fashion, Dunnigan marked his financial success with a house bursting with architectural enthusiasm. In 1890 Dunnigan sold the farm to his son James with the proviso that James provide free room and board for his father in "a room to be selected by the said John" as well as a horse and "shelter for a buggy." John died in 1904 and James eventually sold the farm out of the family in 1939. South of the house a frame wagon shed—doubtless the one mentioned in 1890—and a frame bank barn (also of the period) complete the still-functioning agricultural landscape and bear witness to the success won by a "promising young man of thrifty and industrious habits."

5-65. James Silver House
(Silvermount)
937 Priestford Road
1870; Private
National Register   HA-339

James Silver, wrote his brother Dr. Silas Silver, "in the year 1870 . . . built upon an elevated part of his farm, overlooking a beautiful situation, a very fine mansion. He began to build in June 1870," and moved in that December. His "mansion" is very fine indeed and stands as an excellent example of how Victorian-era

county builders borrowed freely from the period's fashionable styles: the general massing suggests several plates in Calvert Vaux's influential book, *Villas and Cottages* (which James's brother Benjamin owned) while the trim is a robust hodgepodge of Queen Anne, stick style (note especially the stick-shaped brackets), and Gothic revival elements. (Lively as the façades are now, a c. 1900 photograph shows that they were originally even more exciting. An elaborately bracketed porch, similar to one across the road at the farmhouse at Indian Spring spanned the entire north façade; the porch was removed in the 1930s, but some of the brackets are still stored in a barn on the property.) The interior shows similarly varied origins: Silver gave it a traditional center-hall plan, but embellished the spaces with stylish decorative plasterwork (including many ceiling medallions); the ballroom (!) is appropriately elaborate with plaster corbels and a black marble mantel. Was there an architect? That question remains unanswered. That the family loved to indulge in design is clear from their houses near Glenville and James may well have acted as his own architect, perhaps borrowing his brother's *Villas and Cottages*. On the other hand, the farm immediately adjacent this tract to the south was owned by the renowned Baltimore architect J. Crawford Neilson—in fact, Silver bought this property from Neilson. (The architect's wife was a Stump who had inherited the place.) It seems reasonable to suppose that Neilson offered some neighborly advice, particularly since his involvement with the nearby Trap Church and the neighboring Symington family are so well documented.

5-66. Ady-Laird House
3340 Ady Road
c. 1885; Private
National Register   HA-606

Resembling, and probably inspired by, the nearby John Dunnigan House, this 2½-story frame structure stands as a little-changed example of how at least a few countians braved the censure of their conservative neighbors and embellished their vernacular farmhouses with stylish trim. This house is not shown on the very reliable 1878 county map and is thus a bit later than the Dunnigan house but it is remarkable how similar the buildings are: not only is their massing virtually identical, but their details match as well, from the arched attic windows to the entrance tower to the front

5-65

5-66

5-67

5-68

5-69

5-70

doors. Presumably the same talented artisans built both houses. One wishes their names were known so they could be given their due.

5-67. John T. Carter House
101 Cherry Hill Road
c. 1902; Private   HA-783

For more than two centuries the fertile hills of the tracts hereabouts (Robert's Garden, Garden Fence, and Timber Ridge) were owned and farmed by generations of the Wheeler-Rutledge family. But this 2½-story frame house, which stands on Rutledge land, was not built until John Carter bought 375 acres of Robert's Garden in 1902. It is a good example of what might be called "early twentieth-century transitional" vernacular architecture. Some elements (such as the polygonal bay, L-shape plan, and deep porch) are clearly holdovers from traditional late nineteenth-century houses such as the James Silver House, while the compact and volumetric form, with punchcard-like fenestration and few if any frills, presages the efficient and economic manner of building that has come to characterize domestic building in the mid-twentieth century. A frame garage, about thirty yards east of the house and contemporary with it, furthers these thoughts: placed where a wagon shed would have been fifty years earlier, its structural timbers and frame siding are clearly machine-sawn.

5-68. Deer Creek Methodist Church
2729 Chestnut Hill Road
1885; Regular services   HA-874

Built to replace the original log church on this site, this simple frame structure serves the spiritual needs of one of the oldest established Methodist Protestant congregations in America. Its origins go back to the 1820s when worshipers met in John H. Barrow's house "for the first Methodist Protestant preaching in that section of the country," according to Barrow's obituary. Around 1826 Joseph Ward donated this site to the congregation and a log building was erected. Known as Ward's Chapel of the Christian Society, it operated under the aegis of the Bel Air Circuit until it was incorporated as the Deer Creek Methodist Protestant Church on March 16, 1869. (The various Methodist sects arose due to disputes over, among other issues, slavery and temperance.) The growing congregation eventually required a larger church and in 1885 the log building

was replaced by the existing church, with its clean lines and lancet-arched stained glass windows. (A neighboring farmer, Thomas J. Robinson, is said to have bought the old church, dismantled it, and used the timbers to build a barn.) The interior originally had two side aisles and the sexes customarily sat on separate sides of the room (men to the left, women to the right); coal stoves provided heat and oil lamps light. In 1942 the pews were rearranged to their present center-aisle pattern and electricity was installed.

5-69. Robinson's Store
900 Deer Creek Road
c. 1875; Private   HA-895

During the nineteenth century, before cars and malls and regional shopping centers, nearly every crossroads community required its own stores. Offering general merchandise and often housing the post office, these buildings spawned now-forgotten but once-busy hamlets throughout the county, from Prospect P.O. in the north to Boothby Hill P.O. near Swan Creek on what is now the Aberdeen Proving Ground. Chestnut Hill P.O., according to the 1878 county map, had two (or three) stores but this abandoned frame structure is all that is left. The raised basement contained cooling troughs for milk cans (the troughs were fed by a small stream routed through the cellar) and the single room on the main level, with its deteriorated plastered walls, doubtless once burst with counters and shelves filled with Lydia Pinkham's medicine and other staples. The store may have been built and run by members of the Robinson family, who owned the surrounding farm from the middle of the nineteenth century until the 1930s.

5-70. Famous-Jackson House
3213 Ady Road
c. 1880; Private
National Register   HA-903

On January 20, 1886, William Jackson paid William Pyle $279.35 for twenty-nine acres here; Jackson also assumed a $710 mortgage (due "in the gold coin of the United States") on the property, suggesting that the present house was then standing. Its stone walls and slate-covered gable roof are now just barely standing and the house was probably abandoned shortly after "William Jackson, widower" sold the property in 1930. But Jackson, a black man, was well known in his day as the valued mule-driver of the Husband Flint Mill. The mill was located on Deer Creek, about three miles to the southeast, and Jackson is said to have walked there every day until, wrote Samuel Mason in his *Historical Sketches,* the mill closed "about 1920." Mason was among the first in the county to credit the contribution of black men like Jackson; they "made Harford County what it is," he wrote. "They were the wheels that made our clock tick." Mason observed that few of these laborers "had horses and they walked from place to place along the dusty roads, and strange noises were heard along these old roads, and strange things were seen. Today we have reached that particular tension when these things are neither seen nor heard."

5-71. Slate Ridge Quarries
Quarry Road
Begun 1785; Private   HA-955

Historian and civic activist Jean S. Ewing has written that "Harford County architecture owes its greatest single debt, perhaps, to the excellent slate roofs that protect and enhance many if not most of the houses, churches, schools, barns, and even the minor farm buildings." It is an interesting proposition. A broad and deep vein of slate begins more or less at Pylesville and runs in a northeasterly direction for about a dozen miles, between present-day Route 165 and Slate Ridge Road, into Pennsylvania. Technically the deposit is called Peach Bottom slate, a material the U.S. Geological Survey polysyllabically describes as "blue-black hard graphitic slate approaching phyllite in crystallinity. Locally contains abundant chloritoid porphyroblasts. . . . Slate of commercial quality near center of outcrop belt." And it is that last phrase that is important: around 1725 two brothers, James and William Reese, arrived in the area from their native Wales and purchased a tract called York Barrens. While excavating for farm buildings the Reeses discovered the bed of slate, extracted some, and fashioned it into shingles, which they used to cover their barn. By 1785 commercial operations had begun in earnest and would grow and attract skilled immigrants well into the nineteenth century. These quarrymen were generally Welsh and people with surnames such as Jones and Davies filled the streets in the Harford County community of Cardiff. Workers blasted solid masses of slate out of the open pit mines; these were then broken into smaller pieces and ultimately split

with a chisel or knife. Ms. Ewing, who interviewed miners' descendants in the early 1970s, wrote that "the highly skilled . . . workers never disclosed to an outsider, even if he was the owner of the quarry, how they dressed the slate; when a strange carriage or auto came to the mill the operation would close down until everybody went away again." Perhaps the industry's finest hour came in 1850 when Peach Bottom slate won first prize at the London Crystal Palace Exposition. During the 1920s the industry entered a sharp decline (asphalt roofs are cheaper), and the quarries were closed by 1930. Some workers then found employment mining green marble, an operation that boomed from roughly 1910 to 1950. But that industry, too, has closed and the pits, 200 feet deep and several times that across, now sit water-filled, silent, and eerie.

5-71

5-72. Slate Ridge Presbyterian Church
Cardiff
1893; Regular services   HA-941

Built during the Cardiff quarries' heyday, this substantial brick church clearly suggests how permanent the community's prosperity must have seemed at the time. Ambitious in design and skillful in execution, the church building has an L-shaped plan with a three-story square tower topped by an octagonal pinnacle. The tower's Romanesque arches combine with the round-arched windows in the main body of the church to give a sense of earthbound solidity to the building, a highly appropriate sensation in quarrying-focused Cardiff. Before this church was built, some Presbyterian settlers in the region worshiped in private houses in the well-named community of Stonetown; others attended the "Log Church in the Barrens" near Muddy Creek, Pennsylvania. (Many of the Welsh immigrants were Congregationalists and they formed their own church around 1850.)

5-72

5-73. Slate Ridge School
Old Pylesville Road
1912; 1940; Private
National Register   HA-1741

The years between 1910 and World War I constituted the economic peak of the Slate Ridge community and the towns of Whiteford, Cardiff, and Delta reveled in their mineral-based prosperity. Slate, still being mined in impressive quantities, was joined in 1913 by

5-73

5-74

5-75

green marble to form an apparently permanent source of wealth; skilled Welsh workers guaranteed a steady supply of quarried rock; and the Maryland and Pennsylvania Railroad guaranteed efficient transportation to the port (and construction industry) in Baltimore. In December 1910 the community's two-room school burned to the ground, and Baltimore architect Otto G. Simonson was hired to design a replacement. Simonson, born in Germany in 1863, ranks among the leading Maryland architects of the time and his selection certainly suggests Slate Ridge's optimism. The architect, who had immigrated to this country in 1884, served as superintendent of public buildings for the federal government before he moved to Baltimore in 1902. He garnered scores of commissions after the great Baltimore fire of 1904, "so many," ran his *Evening Sun* obituary, "that the skyline of Baltimore might be said to be part of his own creation." His best-known works include the Tower Building (demolished), the Southern Hotel, and the Maryland Casualty Company Building (now the Rotunda Mall). Simonson gave the school a conservative shell (encouraged by the board of education's quest for economy) but was able to embellish the shell with locally quarried stone that added needed flourishes to the design and cemented the school's sense of place: note particularly the raised basement, window lintels, entrance steps, and—of course—the slate roof. In 1940, in the midst of a misplaced burst of optimism, the county hired Pennsylvania architect J. B. Hamme to design an extension for the school (he had designed the Bel Air Armory in 1914 and the Darlington Elementary School in 1936); but by then the Slate Ridge region was on the downslide economically and enrollment declined until the school finally closed in 1983.

5-74. Parry-Proctor-Robinson House
1619 Chestnut Street
c. 1880; Private   HA-1306

Although most people think of the Delta-Cardiff-Whiteford community as a one-industry town, this elaborate frame structure makes it clear that there was more going on here than slate-quarrying. On August 16, 1909, Howard Proctor bought this large house and lot from the South Delta Land Company. The house had been built a generation earlier by John Parry, who died in 1889. (Parry's estate inventory describes a two-story house with "Garret," at least two bedrooms, and "parlor,

sitting room, dining room, kitchen, summer kitchen," "cellar" and a smokehouse.) Parry was a large stockholder in the mines (he controlled, according to his testamentary papers, "one-fourth interest in the Welsh Slate Co."). Proctor, too, was a prosperous man; he was a canner and the putting-up of fresh vegetables remains, thanks to the Whiteford Packing Company, a source of income for many North Harford residents. (The importance of agriculture here was underscored when Proctor sold the house to Arthur Robinson, owner of a profitable seed store and, later, an International Harvester franchise.) The substantial house not only bespeaks its owners' economic success, it neatly sums up one era in architecture and anticipates another: the gables and bay windows certainly suggest themes that had been stated in the county's buildings since the Civil War (note especially the delicate brackets at the base of the main façade's attic dormer), while the porch, with its Doric and Ionic columns, looks forward to the clean lines of colonial revival houses such as Grandview Farm.

5-75. Jenkins Mansion / Belle Farm
4402 Jenkins Road
c. 1860; Private   HA-958

Recently restored, this large stone house is at once innovative and romantic. The romantic part first: When revolutionary war hero Col. Ignatius Wheeler died in 1793, his thousands of acres of land were generally divided in two parts, his home farm of Deer Park and "the fertile estate called Belle Farm . . . one of the finest . . . of the county, now as well as in early days," according to Walter Preston's 1901 county history. Belle Farm, totaling about 1,000 acres, was itself divided into sections when Wheeler's daughter Teresa and her husband, Henry Macatee, took possession of their 366-acre share and built the attractive stone house called Belle Farm II; the rest of the land remained vacant. Then on March 13, 1857, Ignatius W. Jenkins of Baltimore County paid Elizabeth Brown (née Wheeler) $10,000 for 342 acres ("Lot No. 1 of Belle Farm") and built this house, a revolutionary structure in that it was among the first in America built in the novel Second Empire style. Ten thousand dollars was a hefty price in the 1850s, but Jenkins could afford it. Moreover, it was all in the family—Jenkins's wife, Ann Maria, was Brown's daughter, and the purchase assured that Belle Farm might remain in Wheeler ownership for a few more generations. The Wheelers, Harford County's leading Catholic family, met their equal in the Jenkinses: Ignatius Jenkins's "great-great-grandfather, William Jenkins," wrote a biographer in 1897, "came to America in 1634 in company with the . . . proprietor of the colony and settled in St. Mary's County, where he became an extensive landowner." Later Jenkinses grew quite rich, thanks to Baltimore industries and railroads; the Wheelers helped found St. Ignatius Church while the Jenkinses built Corpus Christi Church (correctly Jenkins Memorial) on Baltimore's Mount Royal Avenue. Ignatius Jenkins was born in Baltimore County (near the community of Jenkins) but worked his Harford acres until he died in 1894; his son Henry Jenkins acquired the house and 220 acres from his siblings. Born in Baltimore County in 1850 Henry Jenkins, according to an 1890s biography, "was reared on the farm" here and "farming has been [his] life occupation. . . . Some of the land is devoted to cereals, and the remainder to pasturage for stock." Henry Jenkins served on the building committee for St. Mary's Church (along with Henry Macatee). He died in 1899 and his appraisers then noted a "stone dwelling house in good condition" with the following rooms: "parlor, library, dining room, kitchen, six finished bedrooms on the second floor," and a "finished third story." (They also recorded "frame barn 50 × 60 with straw shed 30 × 40, smoke house 12 × 12, carriage house 14 × 18, ice house 10 × 10, tenant house 14 × 16 at annual rent of $500.") In 1919 one of Henry's sons, Ignatius Walter Jenkins, bought out the other heirs and lived here until 1932 when he defaulted on a mortgage. The property was then sold, thus ending two centuries of Wheeler-Jenkins ownership. (See 5-58.)

5-76. Grandview Farm
2665 Conowingo Road
c. 1930; Private   HA-980

Three hundred and more years ago, these rolling hills formed a 1,000-acre tract called Wheeler's and Clark's Contrivance and served as the homestead of John Wheeler (1630–93). During the nineteenth century, much of that land was owned and farmed by Gustave Fritz and many of the outbuildings here date to the Fritz era. But the acreage's colonial past was never forgotten and, when the main house (built by Fritz) burned around 1930, the owners of the farm decided to build a new colonial

revival dwelling to evoke the perceived order and dignity of those distant times. That style's simplified massing, clean lines, and limited amount of decorative detail stood in contrast with the previous era's architectural excesses, and this house shows what it was all about. Note particularly the ground floor (perhaps more successful than the second) with its regularly placed and sized windows and tabernacle frame doorway (with blind fanlight and engaged Tuscan columns). The monochromatic stucco façade is a further simplifying element and was no doubt intended to separate the house—and its builders—from the polychromatic piles built by an earlier generation.

5-77. Clark-Grier House
3246 Grier Nursery Road
1859; Private   HA-1001

Barnet Clark Sr. and Jr. owned much of the land along this stretch of Deer Creek for most of the nineteenth century. (The Clarks earned a tidy living from farming and from their sawmill, shown on both the 1858 and 1878 county maps near "Clark's Bridge.") In 1859 Clark Sr., who had served a term as county commissioner and was living in a log house on the property, hired James Alexander Grier of Washington, D.C., to design and build a dwelling more commensurate with his high status in the community. (Grier, born in Pennsylvania in 1817, had worked in Philadelphia and Baltimore before he moved to Washington; he numbered among his many clients no less a figure than Robert E. Lee, who hired him to do construction work on the great Custis-Lee mansion, Arlington.) This elegant two-part brick house is the result. Clark's slaves fired the bricks from a bluish-colored clay found on the property, which the masons (Kellog Brothers of Rocks) then fashioned into crisply coursed walls; Clark himself served as carpenter. Inside, the soapstone hearths were cut from stone dug from a quarry on the property on the north bank of Deer Creek. In 1891 Clark Jr. sold the house and 135 acres to John P. Grier—son of the architect—for $5,500. It has remained in the Grier family ever since. The house is important as a rare example of brickmasonry in an area where frame and stone predominate. It gains further importance for its association with the Griers: besides the architectural prowess of the family's progenitor, later Griers founded an eponymous landscape business and nursery.

5-76

5-77

5-78

5-79

5-80

5-78. Wysong House

(Shirley)

3316 Sharon Road

c. 1850; Private   HA-1026

Probably built by James B. Preston, farmer, miller, and father of Judge Walter Preston, this two-story frame house is best known as the residence of the Reverend Thomas Turner Wysong. (The Preston and Wysong families have intermarried for generations.) Wysong bought this 106-acre farm from the Prestons in 1873 and, while living here, compiled his still-valid book *The Rocks of Deer Creek* (1880), a charming mix of history and legend that covers everything from the Mingo Indians to the King and Queen seats to the witches of Mine Old Fields. (He noted that "in the existence of witches and other malevolent beings . . . our ancestors had the most implicit faith. They saw spirits and to them devils appeared; strange sights were seen and strange sounds were heard. The jack-o-lantern was recognized as a personality whose very purpose was evil.") The house, too, is a charming mix, combining features of a straightforward farmhouse with fashionable period trim such as the original board-and-batten covering (now hidden beneath asbestos), the dentiled cornices on the porch's and the main roof's eaves, and the porch's elegant cusped trim.

5-79. Whiteford House

Whiteford Road

1792; with additions; Private   HA-1087

Although today one associates slate and marble with the Whiteford area, the region's first settlers were farmers (as they generally were elsewhere in the county), a point that this rubblestone house underscores. When William Whiteford died in 1789, he bequeathed a life estate in hundreds of acres here to his brother, Hugh, at whose death it was all to pass to Hugh's son, William. (This arrangement was confirmed in Hugh's will, probated in 1810, which left William 292 acres of the tract William's Inheritance, "where William now lives.") Either father or son built this two-story, four-bay house: a datestone in the west gable end is inscribed "1792," and the 1798 tax list shows William Whiteford owning 290 acres of William's Inheritance with a "22 × 30, 2-story stone house," dimensions virtually identical to those of the stone wing of the extant dwelling. ("Hugh Whiteford, Sr." owned 1,116 acres.) The house is a textbook example of what folk historians have identified as "the

farmhouses most usual in the Mid-Atlantic region," according to the subject's leading scholar, Henry Glassie; these buildings "combine Georgian with earlier folk features. . . . They are two rooms deep, have internal gable end chimneys, a placement of windows and doors which approximates symmetry, and a low pitched roof like the Georgian houses, but they lack most of the stylish trim." These features are self-evident in this house. Generations of Whitefords lived here, farming and playing active roles in the development of the county. In 1800 William Whiteford, a "collector of fines" for the county war committee during the Revolution, was appointed by the governor to help lay out public roads in the Deer Creek Valley. Hugh was an election judge in 1800; another son, Hugh Jr., was an original trustee of the Bel Air Academy. Later William Whitefords were elected to the House of Delegates (in 1821 and 1840), as was Samuel Whiteford (who owned the place from 1835 to 1887) in 1867. Samuel's son Morgan sold the farm out of the family in 1892.

5-80. Thomas Streett House

Holy Cross Road

c. 1870; Private   HA-1214

Somewhere in the depth of this substantial frame house are traces of the building that was the birthplace of Col. John Streett. Colonel Streett's father, Thomas, emigrated from England to Maryland in the early eighteenth century; in 1759 he obtained a patent for 700 acres here, which he called Streett's Hunting Ground, and built himself a frame dwelling. The 1798 tax rolls show him with a pair of "14 × 18 wood" houses. The western room of the present structure apparently was one of those houses; pegged beams are evident in the ceiling and the cellar contains traces of a large fireplace arch. Colonel Streett went off and built one of the county's great federal-era houses while this farm remained in the hands of less flamboyant kinsmen. The present house, a fine period piece in its own right, was probably built by the Thomas Streett who acquired the farm in the 1830s and died here in 1891. The appraisers of Streett's estate noted "one dwelling house with 10 rooms, with cellar and porch; house in fair condition"; they also observed "one tenant house, one Barn, Hay house, wagon house, straw house attached to barn, one smoke house" as well as "one orchard occupying two to three acres."

5-81. Montgomery's Delight
Ridge Road
c. 1800 (or earlier); Private   HA-1220

Of uncertain date, this stone folk house stands on land called Montgomery's Delight, which was patented by John Montgomery in the mid-eighteenth century. The 1798 tax rolls show Montgomery owning 126 acres of Patrick's Purchase and an "18 × 30, 1-story stone house" with a stone kitchen. (John and William Montgomery jointly owned 380 other acres of Montgomery's Delight, but that property was unimproved.) The extant house measures roughly 20 by 25 feet; its ground story was clearly the original kitchen and still contains traces of a massive cooking fireplace (since closed) with corner winder stairs to the main floor. In 1808 John Montgomery sold Patrick's Purchase and Montgomery's Delight to James Hogstine for the high price of £962, which suggests that some sort of house was standing. Hogstine died in 1822, and the property passed back and forth among his nieces and nephews until Mary Bennington (a niece) and her husband, Jeremiah, eventually acquired the parcel; they may have expanded the house into its present form for they owned the property until the 1880s. (Another niece, Jane Thompson, got another part of the farm; see N.T.'s Stone House.) Two stone outbuildings also deserve mention: a three-bay structure (located northeast of the house and now containing livestock stalls) and a root-cellar/well house that is built into the ground just east of the main dwelling.

5-82. Soapstone Quarries
Broad Creek
Prehistoric; Private
National Register   HA-1227

These extensive and well-preserved quarries are among the few documented sites in America where Native Americans went to obtain the boulders they used to fashion their vessels; this makes the quarries, according to the U.S. Department of the Interior, "vital to studies of . . . the Susquehanna Soapstone tradition, ca. B.C. 1700–1000." The quarries abounded in soapstone boulders of varying size; members of the Susquehannock tribe simply selected a rock that closely approximated the dimensions of the vessel needed—a large stone for a large bowl, a small one for a cup, and so forth. Researchers in Washington have determined that "quarrying activities at the site probably

represent periodic visits throughout this period [1700–1000 B.C.] to replenish the exhausted supply of previously obtained bowls."

5-83. George Whitelock House
1110 Main Street
1883; Private
National Register   HA-1256

In May of 1883 George Whitelock bought an unimproved one-acre lot in Darlington and proceeded to build this frame, cross-gable house. Whitelock, born near Swan Creek in 1845, had moved to the village in the centennial year of 1876 and opened a general store; in 1879 he married Annie Hopkins, a connection that certainly cemented his ties to the community, and both Mr. and Mrs. Whitelock became active in the Darlington Methodist Church. Whitelock's biography, written in 1897, observed that the store carried a "full and complete line of dry goods, groceries, etc.," and the shop is consistently mentioned in the state gazettes of the time. One must assume he did a brisk business because he built a distinctive house that, with its variety of shingle patterns, multipaned stained glass windows, and elaborate porch trim, is precisely what one might expect of a prosperous merchant in Victorian Darlington. The widowed Mrs. Whitelock and her daughters sold the property in 1943.

5-84. Broad Creek Bridge
Maryland Route 623
1927; Public   HA-1581

One of the oldest state-owned metal truss bridges remaining in the county, this 148-foot span actually consists of two Pratt trusses placed end to end. Structural members are surprisingly light, probably lighter than those of other steel bridges in the region. Plaques welded to the "open" ends of the bridge show that it is a product of the American Bridge Company, a division of U.S. Steel.

5-85. Gladden House
3881 Rocks Station Road
c. 1800; Private
National Register   HA-1600

Members of the Gladden family thrived in the Rocks area since the 1770s, when Jacob Gladden began buying and selling land from Thomas Streett. This stone structure is probably not that old, however, since nothing re-

5-81

5-83

5-84

5-85

5-87

motely resembling it shows up in the 1798 tax rolls. According to a late nineteenth-century family history, Gladden came to the area from York County, Pennsylvania, and "during the War of 1812 he served in the army and participated in a number of engagements with the enemy." He died in 1829; his son, also named Jacob, was born on this farm and "his life was actively spent in the cultivation of the land." (He was also something of an industrialist; an article in the April 26, 1838, issue of the Bel Air newspaper the *Madisonian* refers to the "Woolen Factory near the Rocks owned by Jacob Gladden.") It is not clear whether or not Jacob Jr. was born in this house, but when he died in 1868 his estate inventory strongly implies that the large house, with its center-hall plan, was standing, because it lists the following spaces: "Shed Room," "Kitchen," "Dining Room," "Parlor No. 1," "Passage," and "Parlor No. 2," as well as three bedrooms and an attic, which correspond with the existing rooms. There was a "stair with carpet and rigging" and the "window blinds" in both parlors and in "Bed Room No. 1" were deemed important enough to mention. (The elegant woodwork in the parlor was salvaged and installed when a high-style federal house in Baltimore was demolished.) Jacob Jr. left the property to his son, James, who, according to the 1897 *Portrait and Biographical Record of Cecil and Harford Counties,* was "born on the farm" in 1835. James "was reared to a knowledge of farm work . . . and in it has gained prosperity," but he also gained prominence as "founder of the post office and station at the Rocks." He built the post office and "from the rental of the property's pic-nic grounds, which he owned, he received considerable money." James had married a daughter of the Thomas Streett who built the Streett House on Holy Cross Road and their descendants continuously owned this property until 1945.

5-86. Husband Flint Mill Site
Deer Creek near Kalmia
c. 1866; Private
National Register   HA-1226

Deemed by the U.S. Department of the Interior as "the best preserved example of the extinct flint industry in Maryland," these ruins are all that remain of the flourishing flint mill run by Joshua Husband and his descendants. In 1866 Husband paid $4,000 for 161 acres here; this was probably the site of an old (and by then defunct) iron foundry established by

the Nottingham Company of Baltimore County. Husband took whatever buildings were standing and adapted them for the manufacture of ground flint. It was a good location for such an operation: Deer Creek provided water and power and the main road to Bel Air ran through the site, crossing the creek by means of a covered bridge. (Forge Hill Road has since been relocated.) It was also a good project for a man like Husband because, as a writer in 1897 observed, "members of the family have . . . been involved in the manufacture of iron and flint" since the mid-eighteenth century. Husband, his son, Joshua Jr., and his daughter, Hannah, kept the mill going until the 1920s; the Great Depression forced the family to sell the property in 1932. Very little remains above ground but if one tries one can discern the remains of the kiln and the quarry pit.

5-87. Judge John H. Price House
(El Britton)
3201 Deth's Ford Road
c. 1840; Private
National Register   HA-325

Something of a seminal work, this handsome stone house influenced the way two generations of Darlington-area residents thought about architecture. In 1837 John H. Price bought 121 acres of El Britton from Robert Parker Jr. for $1,000 and shortly thereafter began building his house. (An 1847 deed to a neighboring property refers to this farm as "where John H. Price now resides" and it is clearly shown on the 1858 county map.) That date means Price's center-hall house anticipates by a decade the heavy wooden cornice, solid porches, decorated attic gable window, French doors (later closed), and similar motifs used at more celebrated nearby stone structures such as Silverton and the E. M. Allen House. C. Milton Wright wrote that Price, a Stump descendant, was born in 1808 "near Stafford" and was educated at Dickinson College. Admitted to the Harford County bar in 1829, Price, "by devoting himself diligently to his profession," rose to become circuit court judge in 1855. Price and his wife bought several Deer Creek farms as investment property (for example, Mount Yeo, the 225-acre spread they eventually sold to their son David in 1880) while living here in what W. Stump Forwood described in 1879 as "one of the most beautiful homes" in the entire valley. When Judge Price died in 1892, he left the place to his widow,

Mary; she died a few years later and their children sold El Britton in 1918.

5-88. Whiteford-Silver House
Near Whiteford
Late nineteenth century; Private   HA-954

Although no architect's name has ever been associated with this splendid frame house, the building's evident sense of style, wonderfully architectonic massing, excellent details, and overall panache certainly imply ties to such important area dwellings as Rosecrea and Grey Gables, both designed by Walter Cope. The house's sweeping, open façades accurately suggest the open plan within, and at least one authority claims that the dwelling was among the first in the area to boast central heating, indoor plumbing, and gas lighting. Anna Silver purchased the property here in 1899 from the Whiteford family—her relatives—who are said to have built the house; it remained in Silver ownership (most famously with David Silver, who died in 1927) until the mid-twentieth century.

5-88

DISTRICT 6

Havre de Grace

6-1

6-2

6-1. Oakington
Oakington Road
c. 1816; c. 1905; c. 1915; Private   HA-9

One of the best known—certainly one of the most beautiful— estates in the Upper Chesapeake, Oakington, calm in its lapidary splendor, has watched congressmen, presidents, and chorus girls come and go. The history of the tract goes back to the seventeenth century but the history of the buildings begins with John Stump of Stafford, probably, in relative terms, the richest man who ever lived in Harford County. Stump owned the 700-acre tract and when he died in 1816 (worth an incredible $340,000—in 1816 dollars), he left instructions to divide his holdings equitably among his seven children. In his will, he bequeathed son John Wilson Stump "Oakington Farm, estimated at thirty thousand dollars," and young Stump and his Baltimore-born heiress wife then began building what is, in effect, the core of the present house (in the center of the photograph). They erected a highly elegant structure, a cube measuring roughly 40 by 40 by 40 feet and gave it an unusual five-room floor plan that marked a sharp departure from the standard sidehall or center-hall plans of the day. Herman Stump (whose name was an intentional corruption of the surname of his ancestor Augustine Herrman) was born here in 1837 and went on to become president of the Maryland Senate and a U.S. congressman. The Stumps tumultuously stayed on until 1865 and, after a relatively dull era, in 1905 the estate passed to James L. Breese, a New York financier and bon vivant of the first order. Breese hired architect Stanford White to build two flanking frame wings off the Stumps' house and to make over the old place generally so it might be suitable for gilded age duck-hunting parties and stag dinners. (Stag, that is, except for the occasional Ziegfeld Follies beauties who acted as hostesses and/or popped out of cakes.) In 1915 Commo. Leonard

Richards of the New York Yacht Club bought Oakington and added the present immense south wing (to the left in this c. 1920 photograph). Sen. Millard Tydings (1890–1961), one of the state's most influential politicians, purchased the 550-acre farm in 1935; his family still owns most of the surrounding acreage, but they sold the house to a drug and alcohol rehabilitation center in the 1980s.

6-2. Swan Harbor Farm
(Wilton)
401 Oakington Road
c. 1790; with additions; Private   HA-243

The French engineer and cartographer C. P. Hauducoeur published his famous map of Havre de Grace in 1799 and on it, way off to the south, he indicated the presence of a large rectangular house and some outbuildings on this site, which he labeled "J. Adlum." One year prior the tax assessors had listed John Adlum, who bought the tract in 1797, as owning 360 acres and a "61 × 20 2-story part brick and part wood" house, dimensions remarkably similar to the present house's 60′5″ by 20′5″. Adlum, a man of affluence, a protégé of Thomas Jefferson, and a pioneer in American winemaking, was also a prime mover and shaker in Havre de Grace's early history. His two-story brick dwelling is laid in English Bond (a row of stretchers alternating with a row of headers), a locally rare touch. Inside, a highly elaborate mantle, complete with foliated scrolls and bead-and-reel trim, suggests Adlum's ambition, perhaps even his sophistication, as do the outbuildings listed in 1798. In addition to the usual kitchens, quarters, barns, and overseer's house ("usual," that is, for an estate of this caliber) one finds a frame "house for the gardener," something not seen elsewhere in Harford at that time.

6-3. Susquehanna and Tidewater Canal Lockhouse and Lock

Erie Street
c. 1840; Public
National Register   HA-112–113

Chartered by Pennsylvania and Maryland in 1835 (but envisioned as far back as the 1780s), the canal, its backers hoped, might enable Havre de Grace to secure a monopoly on the trade with Pennsylvania's rich heartland. And, indeed, for a time the city's roustabouts were kept busy unloading the lumber and whiskey, slate and grain and coal, that had been floated down from deep within the Quaker State. Once in Havre de Grace, some of the goods were transferred to oceangoing ships or to cars on the newly completed Philadelphia, Wilmington & Baltimore Railroad; others stayed on the canal boats and bobbed on down the bay to Baltimore. Soon, however, the PW&B—and other railroads—rendered the canal obsolete; it lost money for decades and finally closed around 1900. Yet a few vestiges of it somehow remain, and nowhere more so than here, a site that contains the two-story, red-brick, hipped-roof Lock Master's House (now a museum filled with canal memorabilia), the foundations of a bulkhead wharf, and the rough-hewn granite walls of the canal's outlet lock which marks the spot where canal meets river.

6-4. Belle Vue Farm

Oakington Lane
Eighteenth century; Private   HA-242

How many farms in Maryland—or America—have remained in the same family since the Revolution? That, remarkably, is the case here, a Davis property since Dr. Elijah Davis moved here in the 1780s. Actually, the farm has been in the same family a good deal longer than that. Dr. Davis's wife, née Mary Garrettson, could trace her ancestry back to Garrett Rutton, grantee of 300 acres here in 1661. When George Garrettson, Mary's father, died, the Davises bought out Mary's siblings' interest in the property in 1794. (Mary's sister Elizabeth married Samuel Griffith of Swansbury.) The 1798 tax rolls show "Doctor Elijah Davis" owning 300 acres with a "40×20, 2-story brick house" as well as dependencies such as a kitchen, carriage house, two slaves' quarters (there were sixteen slaves), a stable, meathouse, and henhouse, and, here on the shores of the Chesapeake, a "fish house 11 ×

11." A year later Hauducoeur published his famous map of the Havre de Grace area and, neatly drawn on this spot, one finds buildings and grounds simply labeled "Dr. Davis." (Conditions hadn't changed when the 1814 tax roll was compiled, except that the doctor had increased his slave holdings to thirty-four.) Dr. Davis's house is laid in Flemish bond on its main façades; windows on the south side display interesting elliptical arches that suggest some reworking. Inside the center-hall structure remains much as it was in Dr. Davis's day, down to the rooms' paneling, mantles, closets, and chairrails. Dr. Davis, who studied medicine with Benjamin Rush at the University of Pennsylvania (his scholastic paraphernalia have been preserved at Belle Vue), went on to serve in both the House of Delegates and Maryland state Senate and eventually become president of that latter body; his descendants have continuously valued and maintained their patrimony.

6-5. Brown House

Oakington Road
1860; 1931; 1952; Private   HA-241

Now apartments, this fine old house wears its dates on its sleeve: a datestone on the wing is engraved

    A.F. Brown 1860
    C. Wheeler Brown 1931
    Ozalya Carlson 1952

6-6. Concord Point Lighthouse

Concord and Lafayette Streets
1827; Public
National Register   HA-251

After ship after ship met disaster in the treacherous Susquehanna flats, the Maryland General Assembly voted to build a lighthouse (and keeper's quarters) here at Concord Point. (Their decision came in 1826, which seems a bit belated—ships had run aground and crews had drowned since the early 1700s.) John Donohoo, responsible for many early Chesapeake lighthouses, received the contract to construct the simple, plastered, conical stone structure. Another John, named O'Neill and much better known locally, was named keeper as partial reward for his heroism in defense of Havre de Grace during the War of 1812. O'Neill kept the job until his death in 1838; remarkably, his descendants kept the job until the lighthouse was automated in the 1920s, causing office staff at the National Register of

6-3

6-4

6-5

6-6

6-7

6-8

6-9

6-10

Historic Places to comment that "this dedication on the part of the O'Neills is unrivaled in the history of Chesapeake lighthouses." What is also unrivaled in O'Neill's entry in the 1814 tax rolls; the assessors made a "List of property owned by the brave John O'Neal"—the only instance in the county when they were moved to respectful adjectives. (O'Neill owned "1 lot in Havre de Grace, ⅓ acre with 1 story wood house 22 × 18 valued at $250.") O'Neill's great-granddaughter, Mary, made an indirect mark on world events: her son, four-term U.S. senator Millard Tydings, became Harford's most influential politician—ever.

6-7. St. James A.M.E. Church of Gravel Hill and Graveyard
4139 Gravel Hill Road
c. 1864; 1970; 1985; Regular services HA-1591
Harford County Landmark

Throughout its 145-year history, St. James has served as the center of the religious, educational, and social life of its members. "Gravelly Hills" was established as a freedmen's community before the Civil War. (The oldest grave in the cemetery dates to 1834.) The church was founded by community residents who had been worshiping at St. James in Havre de Grace but who began to weary of the drive (or walk) to and from town. These men and women thus purchased a lot and built their new church in 1857; in 1864 they built an entirely new structure (the core of the existing church) and purchased additional land for an expanded cemetery. Of the estimated 300 graves at St. James, four, perhaps, give the site its transcendental importance: these are the graves of four Civil War veterans, Lewis Bowser (born a slave at John Mitchell's Mount Felix and died in 1913), Santa Bowser (?–1895), Peter Moses (1845–90), and Abraham Turner (dates illegible), all United States Colored Infantry volunteers. Although an estimated 179,000 black men served in the Union Army and Navy between 1861 and 1865, little information is known about their lives or their deaths; that four known graves are here, in a relatively unpopulated spot, seems remarkable.

6-8. St. John's Episcopal Church
Union and Congress Avenues
1809; 1833; Regular services
National Register HA-544

Surviving calamities both natural and man-made, this venerable brick church has served

the Rodgerses, Stokeses, Tydingses, Jameses, and other members of Havre de Grace's Episcopal community for nearly two centuries. William Stokes gave land for a chapel here in 1805. But an 1809 windstorm destroyed whatever Stokes built and shortly thereafter the state legislature authorized Samuel Hughes of Mount Pleasant and Mark Pringle of Bloomsbury to organize a lottery so that "a church, parsonage house, and market house [could] be erected" once the winnings totaled $5,000. That sum was quickly reached, lotteries being what they are, and work began on the building that still forms the core of the present church. It was burned by the British during the War of 1812 and rebuilt; it burned again after lightning struck it in 1833 but was rebuilt again. (Somehow many 1809 features have survived, notably the arched door and window openings and the panels in the exterior walls.) Despite this turbulent history, the church has a simple elegance inside and out that is as satisfying—and as enduring—as its sound proportions.

6-9. Old Bay Farm
Old Bay Lane
1937 (replacement); Private HA-1721

A 1961 Ægis story by Michael Chrismer notes that this waterfront "home has had three names but just one excellent location." The land was patented by Jacob Giles of Mount Pleasant as Brother's Lott; around 1803 Samuel Hughes, the then-owner of Mount Pleasant, acquired the property and called it, for obvious reasons, Bayside Farm. The present name dates to the 1840s and William Sappington's ownership. Old Bay Farm entered the James family in 1919 when the well-known building contractor and, later, canner, Roy James purchased the site, attracted, it is said, by a huge c. 1855 stock barn (which has since burned down). Mr. James, father of the late senator (and Maryland treasurer) William S. James, built the seventeen-room frame house entirely of wood scraps in 1937 and resplendently paneled the ground story in three native woods, white pine, black walnut, and cherry.

6-10. S. J. Seneca Mansion
200 North Union Avenue
c. 1896; Private
National Register HA-815

As the nineteenth century strutted to its optimistic conclusion, all across America merchant and industrialist families swaggered along, buoyed by a deep and seemingly eternal prosperity. Havre de Grace's merchants swaggered with the best of them. Yet of all the city's many rich canners, shippers, and wholesalers, various members of the Seneca family must be counted *primus inter pares,* at least in terms of the visual heritage left behind. The Senecas were hard-working Swiss—sometimes national stereotypes are valid—who had arrived in Havre de Grace by way of Pennsylvania. Stephen J. Seneca amassed a fortune canning tomatoes and fruit and used some of his wealth to create this superbly "plastic" mansion. It is said that Seneca built the very open house so he could enjoy the views down to the canning complex he and his brother Robert owned on St. Clair and Green streets. It is clear that Seneca threw himself into the house's design: the walls seem to scoff at right angles and explode in a frenzy of turrets, dormers, and porches, all roofed in copper and all combining to create a skyline worthy of a small village. Seneca, a fervent Methodist, had a new church built as a present to the congregation. He hired William Lewis Plack to design the Port Deposit granite structure (which still dominates the corner of Congress and Union avenues); Plack won international awards for some of his work, but his contributions, if any, to the design of the Seneca Mansion are unclear.

6-11. Sion Hill
Level Road
c. 1785; Private
National Register; Historic American
Buildings Survey; National Historic
Landmark   HA-525

Superlatives, often dangerous, are inescapable at Sion Hill, arguably the finest remaining house of its time in the county, certainly among the most important houses of its time in the state. One must look beyond conservative Harford County, perhaps way off to sophisticated urban areas such as Philadelphia or Georgetown, to find its architectural equal. The Reverend John Ireland began the three-part brick mansion partly as a residence and partly as a boys' school. Havre de Grace, then a thriving newly founded city with a limitless future, seemed in need of an academy where its sons could learn Latin, French, even, according to period documents, singing. New England merchant Gideon Denison bought Sion Hill in 1795 and is shown in the 1798 tax

rolls as owning a two-story "brick dwelling . . . 40 × 42." He died in 1799, leaving the mansion (no other word will do) and 1,800 acres to his daughter Minerva (1784–1877) and it is with Minerva's 1806 marriage to John Rodgers that Sion Hill begins its period of glory. Rodgers (1772–1839) was a son of the Col. John Rodgers who, with his wife, Elizabeth, operated Rodgers Tavern in Perryville, a counterpart in Havre de Grace, ran a ferry line across the Susquehanna, and, according to the *Dictionary of American Biography* founded "the most noted of American naval families." The Rodgerses' multigenerational seafaring career spanned the years from the Barbary Pirates to naval aviation; they and their house are more fully discussed in chapter 4.

6-12. Mount Felix
Level Road
c. 1850; with additions; Private   HA-526

It should be self-evident from looking at Mount Felix that its builder, canner and agriculturist John Mitchell, was financially successful. The house is, as architect James Wollon, AIA, has pointed out, "a true mansion, being of a thoughtful and regular design, its details symmetrical, its features evenly spaced." What is unexpected about Mount Felix is its date: it is either an extremely late example of Georgian design or an extremely early example of Georgian *revival* design; in either case it misses (either postdating or anticipating) the mainstream by a generation or two. The massing and façade treatment are right out of the 1780s, but the materials (pressed brick) and details (the way the wooden trim is carved) are firmly of the mid-nineteenth century. Mitchell's original structure forms the 2½-story central block and lower, west (kitchen) wing; their bricks are uniformly bonded and only the smaller scale of the wing suggests its inferior service status. Inside, the glorious staircase, which rises openly and majestically to the attic, deserves special mention. The entrance porches, the north façade's three-part window, and the entire east wing date to the twentieth century.

6-13. Havre de Grace Armory
333 Old Bay Road
1922; Public
National Register   HA-1574

A distinction of sorts: of the dozens of armories in Maryland, Havre de Grace's is the

6-11

6-12

6-13

6-14

6-15

only one not built by the state for the National Guard. Instead, it was built by the proprietors of the late, lamented Havre de Grace racetrack as a clubhouse/hotel. It still looks the part with its long resortish pillared portico, French doors, and pedimented and pilastered main entrance. The track, founded in 1912, added immensely to the Harford scene. It drew equine luminaries such as Seabiscuit and Man-O-War; Citation ran here three times, first in 1947 as a two-year-old and then twice in 1948, his Triple Crown year. The track drew equally colorful humans but their (to be polite) Damon Runyonesque behavior eventually proved too much for countians who, aided and abetted by some high-level shenanigans, contrived to bring about the track's closing in 1950.

6-14. Aveilhe-Goldsborough House
300 North Union Avenue
1801; Private
National Register   HA-788

In 1801 Jean Baptiste Aveilhe, cited in his deed as being "of Charleston, South Carolina," paid $400 for five lots between Green and Franklin streets and began this square, stuccoed brick house. In material, design, and plan the building, one of the most architecturally interesting structures in Havre de Grace (and one of the few to survive the 1813 fire), clearly reflects its builder's French background. It also suggests connections with the Caribbean, and while it is not known how Aveilhe got to Charleston, that city was a major center for refugees when the island of Santo Domingo exploded in slave rebellions in the 1790s. The slate-covered hipped roof is easily the house's most distinctive feature: its steep, concave curve rises to a peak which the large, stuccoed brick chimney marks as succinctly as an exclamation point. The graceful, scalloped frieze at the roofline (repeated in the gouged frieze in the front room's mantel) adds another distinctive and decorative touch to this Caribbean cottage. One can almost hear the steel band. In financial trouble, Aveilhe had to sell the house in 1803 (for $1,500); it passed to Howes Goldsborough in 1816. A merchant and shipowner, Goldsborough was responsible for civic improvements such as the city's wharf (1831) while his wife, Mary, was a sister of Commo. John Rodgers of Sion Hill.

6-15. Elizabeth Rodgers House
226 North Washington Street
c. 1780; Private
National Register   HA-798

This is precisely the sort of building that comes to mind when one thinks of federal-era townhouses: streets in cities such as Philadelphia, Georgetown, Alexandria—even Chestertown across the bay—all lined in 2½-story structures where keystoned lintels act as crisp counterpoints to Flemish bond brick walls. But the Rodgers house is the only such structure in Harford County. This says something about the essentially rural nature of the county in the 1780s, since one can't have townhouses without towns and at this time Bel Air, Abingdon, and Joppa were hardly worthy of the term. Only Havre de Grace seemed destined for urban greatness, so it is fitting that this house is here. The structure's stylishness also says something about the architectural aspirations of the Rodgers family. In 1788 Col. John Rodgers, tavernkeeper and ferryboat captain, had arranged to buy a "house and lott" that had belonged to a pair of men named Thomas McCleary and Abraham Huff; Rodgers already operated the busy tavern across the Susquehanna in Perryville and he may have wanted to establish an inn in Havre de Grace so he could monopolize trade and control traffic on both shores. Ferries and taverns loomed large in the lives of eighteenth-century American travelers, as the many memoirs of these sojourners reveal. George Washington's diaries, for example, frequently mention stops along the post road in Maryland. While in this neighborhood the general seems to have preferred to stay at Rodgers Tavern in Perryville, but in his entry for September 20, 1787, he notes, "crossed the Susquehanna and dined at Havre de Grace at the house of one Rodgers," which makes one suspect that Rodgers had been operating the "house and Lott" as an inn even before he actually purchased the property. Rodgers died before the deed could be executed, and the property passed to his widow, Elizabeth, who, "desirous of having the aforesaid House and Lott . . . duly and legally recorded" executed her own deed in 1802. Mrs. Rodgers died without a will and her eldest son, Commo. John Rodgers of Sion Hill, bought his mother's house—the only real estate her appraisers mentioned—from his siblings and co-heirs in 1822 for $2,500.

6-16. Spenser-Silver Mansion

200 South Union Avenue
c. 1896; Private
National Register   HA-549

Built by fishpacker John Spenser, this enthusiastic granite pile is the city's only stone example of full-blown High Victoriana and makes a fitting companion to the frame Seneca Mansion, also on Union Avenue. Spenser's 2½-story creation (the architect, if there was one, is unknown) is an eclectic mix of styles executed in rough-faced Port Deposit granite. These gruff walls stand in marked contrast to the almost delicate wooden trim of the half-timber gables, window frames, and the varied balusters and spindles that enliven the house's many porches and balconies. Although the interior has been remodeled into apartments, some rooms retain enough original detailing to allow one to imagine what the place once must have looked like in its prime. Note, for example, the fireplace in the ground-story northeast front room: its wooden mantel is embellished with egg-and-dart trim, Ionic columns, and a garland-draped frieze, while tiles (with an embossed floral design) cover the hearth. Spenser's stay here was brief, for in 1917 the place was sold at auction to canning magnate Charles B. Silver.

6-17. Abraham Jarrett Thomas House

(Lafayette Hotel; American Legion)
501 St. John Street
c. 1834; Private
National Register   HA-790

Built in what has been called "hangover Georgian style," this massive 2½-story building is one of the most memorable structures in Havre de Grace. It seems to loom particularly large in the memories of Amtrak riders, highly appropriate since the building, like the city, is a product of mass transportation. The early growth of the community once known as Susquehanna Lower Ferry was determined by its location at the spot where the Susquehanna broadens out to become the Chesapeake Bay. Ferryboat captains earned a nice living moving travelers across the waters, often working in conjunction with the community's many tavernkeepers, such as the Rodgers family. A. J. Thomas, a prominent banker, is thought to have built this Flemish bond brick building shortly after he bought the property (eleven lots) in 1834. It is, however, reasonable to as-

sume that he built the place on the site (possibly incorporating the foundations) of an earlier tavern since the Havre de Grace Ferry Company had once owned the property. The Philadelphia, Wilmington & Baltimore Railroad (now Amtrak) purchased the place in 1856 and ran it as the Lafayette Hotel until the 1940s. Now covered in stucco, the building is otherwise surprisingly intact, with its center-hall plan, six-panel doors, and window trim.

6-18. St. James A.M.E. Church

615 Green Street
1874; Regular services
National Register   HA-1590

The focus of one of the oldest black communities in Maryland, this simple church was begun when the energetic Joseph Robinson served as minister here. But oral history, and other sources of documentation, date the city's free black activity at least as far back as 1849 when a group met in the brick home of Mr. and Mrs. James Peaker and established the Mount Zion Meeting House; a school soon followed. (Peaker was a relative of Cupid Peaker, so instrumental in founding the Hosanna church and school.) In 1850 Bishop A. W. Wayman sent the Reverend W. M. Waters to Mount Zion to serve as the church's first minister.

The Civil War and the ending of slavery brought rapid change to the legal status of the county's black population. To oversee the education of former slaves, the federal government established the Freedmen's Bureau and in 1865 older parishioners of Mount Zion, including the Peakers, Presberrys, and Stansburys, helped the bureau set up the Anderson Institute on Linden Lane near Otsego Street in Havre de Grace. By the 1870s, membership in Mount Zion had grown, making a new church necessary; a steering committee selected a site on Green Street, hired the Havre de Grace firm of Mitchell Brothers to do construction, and began building in 1874. The church's official history notes that when it was time to consecrate the new structure, the church was named St. James to honor "the diligence of Mr. James Peaker." In 1928, under the ministry of the Reverend Robert Stansbury, St. James assumed its present form when the choir stalls were relocated, central heating was installed, stained glass windows were put in, and the exterior of the frame building was stuccoed.

6-16

6-17

6-18

6-19

6-20

6-21

6-19 Blenheim

Osborn Lane

Eighteenth century (ruins); c. 1875; Private

HA-107

The history of this tract is woven around a truly rich collection of characters and events—from a signer of the Declaration of Independence to an English duchess and from Thomas Jefferson to Victorian-era industrialists. The earliest record of the property goes back to the early eighteenth century and one William Smith, by tradition a nephew (or, depending on the source, ward) of Sarah Churchill, first duchess of Marlborough. Smith acquired land on the busy post road and named his estate Blenheim, after the Churchills' great estate, Blenheim, in Oxfordshire. Interestingly, the Churchills acquired their Blenheim at about the same time Smith acquired his. (To further cement their ties to the Churchills of Blenheim, for generations the Smiths of Blenheim gave their sons the resonant Churchillian name Winston.) Smith prospered here and he, his children, and grandchildren married into the colonial elite—the Pacas of Abingdon and Annapolis, the Gileses of Mount Pleasant, and the Dallams of just about every place. William Smith III died in 1795, willing "My Dwelling Plantation commonly called Blenheim" to his only son, Paca Smith (1779–1830). The property clearly shows on Hauducoeur's 1799 map of the upper bay (see page 57) labeled "Smith's Heirs" since Paca and his sister, Frances, were then minors. Unfortunately little physical evidence remains from the Smiths' era: just Paca's grave and the ruins of a sidehall-plan stone house. (Paca Smith's estate inventory refers to a "passage carpet.")

What *does* remain at Blenheim is canning magnate Henry Amos Osborn's sprawling frame mansion (now painted white but originally painted two contrasting colors, as the accompanying c. 1900 photograph indicates). A masterpiece and a true work of art, in that it so perfectly expresses its time and the aspirations of its creator, Blenheim was actually constructed by Jacob Bull, Harford's "master builder." Still owned by the Osborns, Blenheim faces an uncertain future since its sheer bulk renders it impractical for modern domestic residence. For more on this fascinating structure, see chapters 4 and 5.

6-20. Harry Mitchell House

Chapel Road

c. 1880; Private   HA-760

This house, banked high with holly, magnolia, laurel, and boxwood, offers a splendid view across the Chesapeake. Doubtless to capitalize on the setting, the builder of the 1½-story frame structure gave the dwelling an open, cross-shape plan, wide porches, and a porte-cochere to open the airy rooms to the outdoors. The elaborate sawn wooden trim—on the house and on the outbuildings—ranks among the finest in Harford County.

6-21. Mount Pleasant II

Chapel Road

1907 (replacement); Private   HA-763

Something called Mount Pleasant has stood as a Maryland landmark since Jacob Giles built the first mansion of that name on this site in the 1750s. Giles, an enterprising Quaker of the first order, was arguably Harford's leading citizen in the colonial era: he owned thousands of acres of farms; he established gristmills, sawmills, and iron forges; he ran ferry lines, founded towns, and laid out roads. And, as noted, he built Mount Pleasant, a grand center-hall mansion with brick walls two feet thick, elaborate plaster cornices, window seats, double doors with lion's head knockers, and a graceful Chinese Chippendale stair. Financier Samuel Hughes eventually acquired the estate from Giles's bankrupt heirs. In 1798 he was assessed for 3,354 acres of land and a "brick 2 story dwelling 45 × 33. . . . 4 rooms and a passage on each floor. Ceilings are 10 feet high. . . . 2 small houses in the garden." (The appraiser added "Hath been built near 40 year—the front and back walls are cracked.") The 1814 tax rolls show Hughes with a brick house measuring 47 by 33 feet, which seems close enough; they also show him owning more than 2,600 acres of farmland and "200 Town lots in Havre de Grace." Telephone company executive Charles Bryan and his wife purchased a ruinous Mount Pleasant in the early twentieth century (he famously said the bricks had become so soft the birds pecked holes in them). They saved what could be saved (most important, that gorgeous stair railing) and hired the Baltimore architectural firm Parker and Thomas to design, according to a story in the April 1907 *Ægis,* an "elegant new house" of "colonial design." Fallston's Dennis J. Shanahan was the general contractor.

Photo Credits

All of the photographs in the catalog section of this book came from the Harford County Department of Planning and Zoning. Images used in the "front" section came from many sources, and grateful acknowledgment is hereby given to the following individuals and institutions: Aberdeen Proving Ground (pages 17, 18, 220), the Baltimore Museum of Art (pages 34, 81), the Baltimore *Sun* (pages 33, 72, 228 [lower]), Julia D. S. Cameron (pages 183, 228 [upper]), Judge William O. Carr (pages 21, 133 [left]), Josephine Dallam (page 11), Eleanor Tydings Ditzen (pages 75 [upper], 158, 159, 167), the late H. Chandlee Forman (pages 24, 43, 92 [upper]), The John Work Garrett Collection of the Milton S. Eisenhower Library (pages 57, 87, 176), Jean Reed Graybeal (page 107), Jeremy Green (65, 70, 75 [lower], 76), The Historical Society of Harford County (pages 4, 15, 19, 36, 37 [left], 45, 50, 54, 77, 86, 88, 90, 126, 145, 146, 156, 174, 209, 226), Ladew Topiary Gardens (pages 177, 203, 229, 230), Albert and Emily Laisy (page 55), the Library of Congress / Historic American Buildings Survey (pages 22, 26, 27, 28 [lower], 38, 39, 41, 42, 53, 58, 64, 67, 168, 190), the Liriodendron Foundation (pages 143, 162, 214), the Maryland Historical Society, Baltimore (pages 3, 13, 14, 37 [right], 59, 68, 71, 93, 121 [left], 132 [left], 155 [lower], 157, 165, 172, 176, 207 [right]), Maryland State Archives (pages 7, 8, 62), the Old Line Museum (page 83), the Peale Museum (pages 129, 131), Pattie Symington Penniman (pages 150, 151, 152), the Virginia Museum of Fine Arts (page 208), *Woman's Home Companion* (pages 198, 199), Yale University (page 61).

INDEX

An Architectural History of Harford County, Maryland, by Christopher Weeks.

Designed by Glen Burris, set in Adobe Garamond by The Composing Room of Michigan, Inc., and printed on 80 lb. Frostbrite Matte by The Maple Press Company.

Library of Congress Cataloging-in-Publication Data

Weeks, Christopher, 1950–
  An architectural history of Harford County, Maryland / Christopher Weeks.
      p.   cm.
  Includes bibliographical references and index.
  ISBN 0-8018-4913-6 (acid-free paper)
      1. Architecture—Maryland—Harford County.   2. Harford County (Md.)—History.   I. Title.
NA730.M32H378   1996
720′.9752′74—dc20   95-5325